THE ROUTLEDGE COMPANION
IN THE ARTS

The Routledge Com... ...Research... York St ... major co... ... of new writings on
research in the crea... a... **Library and Information**... ... ... the world. It
provides theoretical and p... ... ... to identifying, structuring and resolving some
of the key issues in the debate about the nature of research in the arts which have surfaced
during the establishment of this subject over the last decade. It will provide a point of
reference for the further development of that debate in the years to come by making specific
assertions about what this phenomenon is (or is not) so that subsequent scholars will have
something definite to agree with or to criticize.

This critical anthology benefits from a wide range of contributors from all of the major
constituencies in arts-based research. The contributions are located in the contemporary
intellectual environment of research in the arts, and more widely in the universities, in the
strategic and political environment of national research funding, and in the international
environment of trans-national cooperation and communication. The book is divided into
three principal sections – Foundations, Voices and Contexts – each with an introduction
from the editors so as to orientate the reader with regard to the main issues, agreements
and debates.

The Routledge Companion to Research in the Arts addresses a wide variety of concepts and
issues, including:

- the diversity of views on what constitutes arts-based research and scholarship,
what it should be, and its potential contribution
- the trans-national communication difficulties arising from terminological and
ontological differences in arts-based research
- traditional and non-traditional concepts of knowledge, their relationship to
professional practice, and their outcomes and audiences
- a consideration of the role of written, spoken and artefact-based languages in the
formation and communication of understandings.

This comprehensive collection makes an original and significant contribution to the
field of arts-based research by setting down a framework for addressing these, and other,
topical issues. It will be essential reading for research managers and policy-makers in
research councils and universities, as well as individual researchers, research supervisors
and doctoral candidates.

Michael Biggs is Professor of Aesthetics and former Associate Dean Research at the
University of Hertfordshire, UK and Visiting Professor in Arts-based Research in
Architecture at the University of Lund, Sweden. He coordinates a network of excellence in
the field, and has published widely on research theory in the creative and performing arts.

Henrik Karlsson is Assistant Professor in musicology, former research secretary at the Royal
Swedish Academy of Music and consultant to Riksbankens Jubileumsfond. He headed the
assessment of the Swedish Research Council's grants to artistic research (Context-Quality-
Continuity, 2007) and has edited a great number of anthologies in music and cultural
sciences.

THE
ROUTLEDGE COMPANION
TO RESEARCH IN THE ARTS

Edited by

Michael Biggs and Henrik Karlsson

In collaboration with Stiftelsen Riksbankens Jubileumsfond, Stockholm

www.rj.se

 Riksbankens
Jubileumsfond

 Routledge
Taylor & Francis Group

LONDON AND NEW YORK

First published 2010 by Routledge
First published in paperback 2012 by Routledge
2 Park Square, Milton Park, Abingdon, Oxon OX14 4RN

Simultaneously published in the USA and Canada by Routledge
711 Third Avenue, New York, NY 10017

Routledge is an imprint of the Taylor & Francis Group, an informa business

British Library Cataloguing in Publication Data
A catalogue record for this book is available from the British Library

Library of Congress Cataloging in Publication Data
The Routledge companion to research in the arts / edited by
Michael Biggs and Henrik Karlsson in collaboration with Stiftelsen
Riksbankens Jubileumsfond, Stockholm, www.rj.se. 1st ed.
p. cm.
Includes bibliographical references and index.
1. Arts – Research. I. Biggs, Michael (Michael A. R.) II. Karlsson,
Henrik. III. Riksbankens jubileumsfond.
NX280.R68 2010
700.72–dc22   2010016552

ISBN: 978-0-415-58169-1 (hbk)
ISBN: 978-0-415-69794-1 (pbk)
ISBN: 978-0-203-84132-7 (ebk)

Typeset in Goudy OldStyle by
HWA Text and Data Managment, London

MIX
Paper from
responsible sources
FSC® C004839

Printed and bound in Great Britain by
CPI Antony Rowe, Chippenham, Wiltshire

CONTENTS

ILLUSTRATIONS

Figures

LIST OF CONTRIBUTORS

Annette Arlander is Professor of Performance Art and Theory at Theatre Academy, Helsinki. Her artwork is focused on performing landscape by means of video or recorded voice. Her research interests include artistic research, performance as research, performance studies, site specificity, landscape, and the environment.

Michael Biggs is Professor of Aesthetics and former Associate Dean Research at the University of Hertfordshire, UK and Visiting Professor in Arts-based Research in Architecture at the University of Lund, Sweden. He has extensive experience as a professional artist and academic, and has published widely on research theory in the creative and performing arts.

Henk Borgdorff is Professor of Research in the Arts at the University of the Arts, The Hague, The Netherlands and Visiting Professor in Aesthetics at the University of Gothenburg, Sweden. He is one of the founders of the Society and Journal for Artistic Research and has published widely on the political and theoretical rationale of research in the creative and performing arts.

Donna Lee Brien is Associate Professor, Creative Industries and Head of School of Creative and Performing Arts at Central Queensland University, Australia. Immediate Past President of the Australian Association of Writing Programs, her current research interests include food writers and their influence, and teaching and research in the creative arts.

Daniela Büchler is Senior Research Fellow and project leader at the School of Creative Arts at the University of Hertfordshire, UK; Visiting Research Fellow at Mackenzie University, Brazil; and Guest Scholar at Lund University, Sweden. She has degrees and experience as practitioner and researcher in architecture, urban planning and industrial design.

Linda Candy is an Honorary Research Fellow at the University of Technology, Sydney and is a co-founder of the Creativity and Cognition conference series. She conducts research into creativity using practice-based methodologies.

Halina Dunin-Woyseth is Professor of Architecture at the Oslo School of Architecture and Design, Norway where she was the founding head of the institution's doctoral programme. She is also Senior Professor in Research Design at Sint-Lucas School of Architecture in Brussels and Ghent, Belgium. She has published extensively on research related issues in architecture and design.

Catharina Dyrssen is Professor of Architecture at Chalmers University of Technology, Sweden where she specializes in architectural research methods connected to the fine arts as well as urban design. She is an architect and musicologist, and conducts art-based research on sound and urban space with the interdisciplinary group Urban Sound Institute.

Ernest Edmonds is Professor of Computation and Creative Media at the University of Technology, Sydney. He is Visiting Professor at University of Sussex and Visiting Research Fellow at Goldsmiths College, UK. He has more than 30 years experience of supervising practice-based PhDs and has served on both arts and science funding bodies.

Henrik Frisk is an active performer of improvised and contemporary music as well as a composer of chamber and computer music. His music has been performed by himself and others in many countries and since the late 1990s he has been affiliated to Malmö Academy of Music at Lund University, Sweden.

Morwenna Griffiths is Chair of Classroom Learning at Edinburgh University, UK. Her recent research includes philosophical theorizing and empirical investigation, related to epistemology, the nature of practice, feminization and creativity. Her books include *Action for Social Justice in Education*; *Educational Research for Social Justice,* and *Feminisms and the Self*, published by Routledge.

Lin Holdridge is the Visual Resources officer at the University of Plymouth, UK. She has spent many years researching in the disciplines of Art History and Fine Art and issues surrounding the PhD in Fine Art. She is currently researching and publishing in the field of visual arts and material culture in Native American Studies.

Mark Johnson is Knight Professor of Liberal Arts and Sciences, Department of Philosophy, University of Oregon. His research focuses on the role of the body and imagination in the experience and making of meaning. His work appropriates empirical research from the cognitive sciences as it bears on the nature of mind, thought, language, and aesthetics.

Henrik Karlsson is Assistant Professor in Musicology and a former research secretary at the Royal Swedish Academy of Music and consultant to Riksbankens Jubileumsfond. He headed the assessment of the Swedish Research Council's grants to artistic research, and has edited a great number of anthologies in music and cultural sciences.

Torsten Kälvemark retired in 2007 from his post as senior advisor at the Swedish National Agency for Higher Education. For a number of years he was head of a working group on practice-based artistic research within the Swedish Research Council. He is a frequent contributor to arts pages in newspapers and magazines in Sweden.

Søren Kjørup is currently Professor of Arts-based Research at the Bergen National Academy of the Arts, Norway, after many years as Professor of the History and Theory of the Humanities at Roskilde University, Denmark. He has published widely on arts-based research, history and theory of humanities, aesthetics, art history, film studies, literary studies, museology, philosophy, and semiotics.

Susan Kozel is Professor of New Media with the MEDEA Collaborative Media Institute at the University of Malmö, Sweden, and is Director of Mesh Performance Practices. Her performances and installations have toured internationally and she

has published widely. She is the author of *Closer: performance, technologies, philosophy*, published by MIT Press.

Katy Macleod is Reader in Fine Art, Kingston University, UK. She has extensive experience of teaching and examining in Fine Art. She has undertaken research into student and supervisor experience of doctoral study and doctoral submissions. Her publications include *Thinking Through Art*, published by Routledge.

Joan Mullin is Professor and Chair of English Studies at Illinois State University and focuses on intersections of writing in visual disciplines. 'Appropriation, Homage and Pastiche' in her co-edited book, *Who Owns This Text*, exemplifies her interest in comparing international and interdisciplinary uses of writing and visual-textual ownership.

Darren Newbury is Professor of Photography at Birmingham City University, UK. He has published widely on photography and research education in art and design. He has served on the postgraduate committee of the Arts and Humanities Research Council. His most recent book is *Defiant Images: Photography and Apartheid South Africa*, published by University of South Africa Press.

Helga Nowotny is Professor Emeritus of Social Studies of Science at ETH Zürich, and President of the European Research Council. She has extensively analysed recent developments in the science system, in particular at the interface of disciplines and in science-society relations (Mode 2 research).

Malcolm Quinn is Reader in Critical Practice at the University of the Arts, London. His writing deals with relations of aesthetics and politics, focusing on psychoanalytic models of the social bond. He is the co-author of *Knowing Nothing Staying Stupid: Elements of a Psychoanalytic Epistemology*, published by Routledge.

Hans-Peter Schwarz is Professor of Art and Media Theory and founding president of the University of the Arts, in Zürich. He was formerly Director of the Museum for Media-Art at the Centre of Art and Media (ZKM) in Karlsruhe, Germany and has published a great number of research studies on art, architecture and media.

Stephen Scrivener is Professor of Design and Director of Doctoral programmes at CCW Graduate School, University of the Arts, London. He has authored numerous publications on a range of art and design topics, including the relation between art and design processes, products and the conditions of research.

Henk Slager is Dean of the Utrecht Graduate School of Visual Art and Design (MaHKU), Professor of Artistic Research and General Editor of *MaHKUzine, Journal of Artistic Research*. He was one of the curators of the 2008 Shanghai Biennial and, among other curatorial and academic practices, has been a tutor at De Appel's Curatorial Program since 1994.

Joost Smiers has been Professor of Political Science of the Arts at the Utrecht School of the Arts. His *Arts under Pressure: Promoting Cultural Diversity in the Age of Globalisation* has been translated into ten languages. He is the co-author of *Imagine there's no copyright and no cultural conglomerates too*.

Graeme Sullivan is Director, Penn State School of Visual Arts, and Professor of Art Education, Penn State University. He researches the critical-reflexive thinking practices of artists and methods of inquiry in visual arts, and has published numerous chapters and articles in the USA, Europe and Australasia. The second edition of his text, *Art Practice as Research*, is published by Sage.

Jen Webb is Professor of Creative Practice and Associate Dean Research, at the University of Canberra, Australia where she also teaches creative writing and cultural theory. Her recent books include *Reading the Visual*, the story collection *Ways of Getting By*, and *Understanding Representation* published by Sage.

Siegfried Zielinski is Founding Director of the Academy of Arts and the Media, Cologne. He holds the chair for Theory, Archaeology and Variantology of Arts and Media at Berlin University of Arts, where he also directs the International Vilém Flusser-Archive. At the European Graduate School, Saas Fee he currently holds the Michel Foucault professorship for media archaeology and techno-aesthetics.

Advisory Board

Bruce Brown is Pro-Vice-Chancellor Research at the University of Brighton, UK and Professor of Design. He has led art and design research nationally through, for example, his chairing of the Main Panel for Arts and Humanities in the UK Research Assessment Exercise 2008 and through personal research in the field of graphic memory.

Halina Dunin-Woyseth (see author listing).

Michael Jubb is director of the Research Information Network and was formerly Director of Research at the Arts and Humanities Research Council in the UK. He has extensive experience in funding and leading research programmes in the arts, humanities and social sciences.

Torsten Kälvemark (see author listing).

Yudhishthir Raj Isar is Professor of Cultural Policy Studies at The American University of Paris and the co-editor of the Cultures and Globalization series. Earlier, at UNESCO, he was Executive Secretary of the World Commission on Culture and Development and Director of the International Fund for the Promotion of Culture.

Chris Wainwright is an artist, curator and the Head of Camberwell, Chelsea and Wimbledon Colleges, of the University of the Arts London. He is President of The European League of Institutes of the Arts, a member of the Tate Britain Council and a Trustee of Cape Farewell, a UK arts organization that promotes a cultural response to climate change.

Evelyn Welch is an art historian specializing in material and visual culture and Professor of Renaissance Studies, Queen Mary, University of London. She is the Programme Director of 'Beyond Text: Performances, Sounds, Images, Objects', a £5.5 million AHRC strategic project which interrogates communication that challenges traditional forms of textual documentation.

EDITORS' PREFACE

The idea of producing a new anthology in arts-based research arose in the context created by a donation that was made by the Swedish foundation 'Creative Man' (*Skapande Människa*) to Riksbankens Jubileumsfond. The resulting fund was used to award prizes and scholarships to artists working close to science in the period 1996–2006. Towards the end of that period, Riksbankens Jubileumsfond was looking for a sympathetic project in the arts to conclude the practical projects that had been undertaken. Henrik, as their adviser, recommended that they fund a project on arts-based research and Riksbankens Jubileumsfond invited us to submit a proposal that would address this on a fundamental level. We identified the need for a book that would ground the current debate on research in the arts. Riksbankens Jubileumsfond accepted our proposal, generously added a substantial budget to cover administrative costs and honoraria, and asked us both to develop the proposal and act as editors. In May 2007, we discussed the initial concept of the book at a lunchtime meeting we had at a restaurant in Lund, Sweden. At that time, Michael was being funded by the Swedish Research Council (*Vetenskapsrådet*) as Visiting Professor at the Department of Theoretical and Applied Aesthetics at Lund University. Henrik was still advising the research-funding agency Riksbankens Jubileumsfond on matters concerning arts-based research. Unfortunately the meal was a bit of a disappointment – among unforgivable blunders throughout, at one point we were even denied the proper 'sense of place' when our order for a bottle of Ramlösa, the famous mineral water from Skåne, was substituted for a carafe of carbonized tap water! One positive outcome of this traumatic experience was our resolve to not accept any further substitutes for what we knew we wanted.

Another outcome of the meeting was the establishment of an editorial stance. We agreed that it was more important to find similarities than differences in the landscape that we were exploring. Differences, for example in terminology, were all too apparent: practice-based research, practice-led research, art-based research, artistic research, etc. Nonetheless, these terminological differences indicated an underlying common view that there was a new and problematic activity emerging in the creative and performing arts. The activity was being led by art schools and universities with arts faculties, so it

seemed to us to be an academically-led issue. As a result of this activity being funded as research, it was impacting on other disciplines that were interested in new research approaches, and, since it was also producing creative outputs, the activity was also beginning to impact on the professional world of the creative industries. This was not news to either of us, but we both felt a certain frustration at the lack of progress on the fundamental nature of research in the arts following about 20 years of international discussion. To aid us in ensuring the international relevance of our work, we established an Advisory Board consisting of: Bruce Brown, Halina Dunin-Woyseth, Yudhishthir Raj Isar, Torsten Kälvemark, Michael Jubb, Chris Wainwright and Evelyn Welch.

We decided to compile a critical anthology of new writings that could provide a firmer platform for the further development of the debate in the years to come. In particular, we wanted to make a book that made specific assertions about what this phenomenon was, or was not, so that subsequent scholars would have something definite to agree with or to criticize. We were, ourselves, critical of earlier books that we felt had failed to take such a stance and that preferred to adopt an ambivalent attitude to the subject. As a result we felt that such books failed to provide students, supervisors and professional researchers with tools that could improve the rigour and quality of what they were trying to do. Inevitably, our quest required us to find a group of arts-researchers in this emergent field that shared our agenda; or at least agreed sufficiently that a stimulating but not contradictory anthology could emerge. Finding these contributors took some time.

The process of selection began with a literature review, which identified experienced authors who were leading authorities in the field of research in the creative and performing arts. Through the literature review it also became clear that, because this was an emerging field and there were therefore, as yet, few visible benchmarks, it was not obvious which were the key works or concepts. National agencies such as the research councils, the bodies controlling graduate education, and organizations conducting activities such as national research evaluations, had all published criteria and definitions. However, if one sought the genealogy of these arguments, one was often referred to case studies of pioneering PhDs and funded research that we felt, naturally enough, could not themselves provide an adequate account for the activity of knowledge-building or art-research production. We therefore thought it important that a section of the book be dedicated to a careful consideration of the foundations of arts research: a consideration of the conditions that any activity needs to meet in order for it to function meaningfully as research in a subject, duly acknowledging and modified by the considerations of what might characterize this activity in a culturally determined field such as the arts. We did not think that arts research would be primarily concerned with exploiting new materials or technologies, nor with sociological aspects of arts production or consumption, since these could already be accommodated by research in materials science or social sciences, etc. Instead we intended the foundational discussion to identify the particular conditions and needs that were not already met by existing research models, so that both the subject and the aims of arts research might be established from, as it were, first principles.

But in saying this, and in saying it in this way, we recognized that we were already adopting a somewhat deterministic voice that could be regarded as alien to the ways of understanding materials and ideas in the creative arts. We recognized that the scientific model, construed in its broadest sense as *Wissenschaften*, was only one possible voice

with which to describe fundamentals – if we could be permitted to continue to use that term for a moment – and that other voices would need to be included in the anthology. In particular we wanted to find ways of discussing the experiential aspects of the creative arts whilst maintaining a position on auto-ethnocentricity that would enable researchers from other disciplines to understand what was being claimed and make use of the discussion. By so doing, we intended to form a bridge between traditional research and these non-traditional concerns that would facilitate comparison and evaluation activities across academia. Aspects that emerged as non-traditional in our reading included an instrumental role for the individual creator/research, for their sense of self and embodiment, for their constructive perspective on the phenomena of experience, and how these are construed and communicated to others through artefacts and creative production. While these aspects were not necessarily unique to the creative arts, design, music, etc., since one can find autoethnographic approaches and *auteur* theory, for example, elsewhere, nonetheless the agency of the researcher/user seemed to call for some acknowledgement in our discussion. So too did the agency of the artefact, and the user's experience of it.

We also noted the apparent omnipresence of writing in research. Although the media of the creative and performing arts are essentially non-linguistic, research in these areas seemed to embrace and sometimes even exaggerate the use of text compared with other disciplines that are arguably equally non-linguistic, such as mathematics or medicine. As a result, we wanted to allocate some space in the book to a consideration of the role of written and spoken language in the formation and communication of understandings. Such understandings take shape in relation to specific problems and their solution for a particular interest group. From this we saw a need to consider the context in which all this research was being undertaken, for whom it was done and the perceived outcomes and benefits from both within the specific context and more widely. We were also aware that a common description of research is that it produces communicable knowledge. This implies that the means of communication – whether the PhD thesis, the research report, the creative artefact, or the medium of creative practices and art production – all needed unpacking if they were to tell us about the core nature of research as a practice in this field. And since we were both academics, we wanted all of this to remain situated not only in a relevant relation to professional creative production but also in relation to other academic disciplines. In accordance with our editorial stance, we were not and still are not, sympathetic to 'special pleading', i.e. that these creative disciplines require completely novel conditions and are therefore incomparable with other academic disciplines. History showed us that each of today's apparently traditional and unproblematic disciplines in the academy had at one time been the problematic newcomer, and that now-established methods and subjects – such as qualitative research and cultural studies – had difficulty in establishing themselves in the period immediately preceding ours.

Owing to our aim of identifying shared issues that were not unduly influenced by parochial national interests, we had assembled an international team. As a result we might have produced an even more fragmented book than the ones that we had been criticizing. We were able to avoid the risk of fragmentation and turn diversity into a benefit through the generosity of Riksbankens Jubileumsfond who, in April 2009, funded a workshop in which we had the opportunity to bring together our team of authors from

all over the world. This two-day workshop, which was held at the Royal Society of Arts in London, was an unusual opportunity in the production of such an anthology because it gave us the chance to share face-to-face our views on arts-based research, as well as our points of agreement and disagreement. We organized the event at a time when the authors had prepared and shared drafts, but before they committed to final versions of their chapters. All the authors were invited, and were flown over for the event. As a result, we were able to find some level of collective agreement about what we wanted and what could not be substituted. Group discussions also encouraged a greater synergy between the chapters in the book. The outcomes of this workshop helped both the individual authors as well as the editors. It helped the authors through their involvement in group discussion of emerging core themes. The editors benefited from the consensus that the book should be structured in three parts: foundations, voices and contexts. Of course, despite our best efforts of selection, we found that our authors did not agree on all points. However, it was notable that they did seem to agree in principle that arts-based research was not incomparable to other forms of research. Indeed, arts-based research would only have value – or its value would be enhanced – to the extent that it could be compared, its quality assessed and its contribution identified in the light of an understanding of research in other areas and of the social and cultural value of artistic production. This was facilitated by our authors' experience of several different national research evaluations and quality assessments in their own countries.

In this book it was never our intention to attempt to cover all art genres by dedicating chapters to individual media or art forms. Even at the stage of receiving the commissioned abstracts we could see that the majority of the authors more often referred to visual or fine arts when giving concrete examples rather than to other art genres. However, this tendency did not reflect the actual proportions of doctoral theses or research projects in the creative and performing arts as a whole. It could be regarded as a manifestation of what has been called the 'visual turn' (alluding to the linguistic turn in philosophy), which has resulted in subjects such as visual anthropology, concepts such as 'the Gaze', theories such as picture theory and methods such as Geometric Data Analysis. Such oculocentrism tends to diminish the creation and experience of culture and arts through other senses, such as the aural and the embodied mind. Instead, we have tried to balance the diversity of subjects by providing a kind of progressive order from theories to practices, and to find the meta-level commonality expressed in our three parts. It is at this level that we chose to make our editorial introductions, enabling us to exercise our editorial stance that similarities are more productive than differences in this debate. Towards the end of 2009, and thanks to very positive reviews that came from both academia and the professional arts world for the need for such a book, our publisher Routledge saw that this anthology had an impact to make in both the academic and the practice market, and to act as a focus for the next round of debate. For this reason, we commissioned two Forewords, one addressing the theme as an element of the European Research Area and the other as an element of the professional preparation of both researchers and practitioners. Furthermore, the platform that Routledge have given us in their Companion series strengthens our aim that the book should provide an authoritative grounding for further informed discussion and research on the theme of research in the arts.

FOREWORD

Helga Nowotny

The contributions in this volume bear testimony to the emergence of a new trend of practice-based research in and through the arts. In its wake, almost as many questions are raised as answers are given. Many of the questions are context-dependent, since they grow out of the experience gained in certain kinds of institutions, specific countries, and different creative environments. They result from the changing relationships between the arts and the wider society. No wonder then that many answers must remain tentative and will be unsatisfactory for some. As the institutionalization of research in the arts progresses, disagreements and controversies are likely to continue to dominate the scene in the years to come, but productive contestations are also the defining characteristic of any significant innovative enterprise. As the old saying goes: whoever wants to keep the world from changing, wants it to cease to exist.

The innovative impulse pushing for change is based on the imagination of a world different from what it is now. It necessarily involves a lot of speculative conjecture and leaves space for tacit wishes and desires. This is why imagination pushing for change, once it transcends the individual and enters the realm of the collectivity, provides powerful incentives to disagree. At the same time, if we are to move from imagining a different order of things to actually designing and shaping it, disagreement must be put to the side if a common goal is to be achieved. The project of institutionalizing research in the arts by putting it firmly into the established structures of institutions of higher education is one such ambitious undertaking. It brings to the fore inherent tensions, doubts, and disagreement, and yet comes at the right time. In the following I want to spell out these three components.

An ambitious undertaking

Art, like science, is a form of human creativity that has found an institutionalized space in modern societies. Curiosity and the desire to explore the unknown are its main driving forces. Curiosity aims to go beyond the familiar, to explore a space that opens up to the realm of possibilities. It actively strives to hone itself on reality and to gain

experience that gives reality a clearly perceptible form that can be interacted with. To gain this experience, curiosity uses all the senses and means available. It is insatiable in two ways: first, because the space of possibilities – and the human imaginative capacity to open them up – is vast, if not infinite; and second, because more and more means and instruments, mostly but not entirely scientific and technical, are at our disposal to expand the space of imagination (Nowotny 2008).

Today, the cultural-economic preference of contemporary societies for the new, be it new scientific knowledge, new technologies and technological gadgets, or the culturally expressed desire to let the familiar appear in an ever-changing, unfamiliar perspective, comes in a socially explosive mixture. The quest for innovation, which has long since assumed a global dimension, is celebrated by some, while leading to widespread feelings of unease in others. For how can society accept and affirm the unforeseeability that is inseparable from research? As François Jacob put it:

> What we can suspect today will not become reality. There will be changes in any case, but the future will be different from what we think. That is especially true for science. Research is an endless process about which one can never say how it will develop. Unforeseeability is part of the essence of the venture of science. If one encounters something really new, then by definition this is something that one could not have known in advance. It is impossible to say where a particular area of research will lead. [And he adds:] One must also accept the unexpected and the disquieting. (Jacob 1983: 94)

Between society's preference for the new and its attempts to gain or regain control over what is uncontrollable, since it is not known where curiosity and the 'play of possibilities' will lead or what consequences will result from it, a vast zone of uncertainty is emerging as the true breeding ground of creativity, be it scientific or artistic. The greater the desire for the unexpected and unforeseeable that research stimulates, the more the pressure of expectation grows to bring it under control and steer it in specific directions. The aim is to tame curiosity, and yet it must be given free rein. While the forms that the attempts to tame scientific curiosity take are different in the techno-sciences from the arts (which are long accustomed to pressure from censorship and other efforts at curtailment), the line to tread requires a fine balancing act. If human creativity is tamed too much, it can atrophy or be driven underground. If taken too far, the taming of scientific curiosity risks killing the goose that lays the golden eggs; while in the case of artistic imagination and curiosity, the sources that replenish cultural life and its renewal may simply cease to flow.

Science and the arts are therefore much closer to each other than their currently institutionalized forms might lead one to expect. They share the creative impulse and their main driving forces of motivation: curiosity and imagination. They thrive – and continuously struggle – in the zone of uncertainty where what is yet to be explored is at home. Uncertainty is therefore inherent in scientific research and in the artistic production of new knowledge alike. The ambition to explicitly anchor the process of research in the arts also aims to bring together the two kinds of practices that once were closely related, but became separated due to their different historical trajectories.

Research is the curiosity-driven production of new knowledge. It is the process oriented toward the realm of possibilities that is to be explored, manipulated, controlled, given shape and form, and transformed. Research is inherently beset by uncertainties, since the results or outcomes are by definition unknown. But this inherent uncertainty proves to be equally seductive: it promises new discoveries, the opening of new pathways, and new ways of problem-solving and coming up with novel ways of 'doing things', designing and transforming them. To put research (back) into the arts, to (again) make visible and explicit the function of research in the arts and in the act of 'creating knowledge' (Seggern *et al.* 2008) is a truly ambitious undertaking, because it takes up a vision and a project that originated in the Renaissance. After centuries of separation, it promises to close a loop.

How did this ambitious project come about? And what does it mean, what can it mean today in a globalizing world in which economic competitiveness is based on science and technology as the recognized engine that drives economic growth? Where is the place of artistic practices in a world in which economic forces seem to appropriate all forms of human creativity and make it subservient to their own ends?

Some of the driving forces are external, coming from outside academia and from the wider societal context. Others are internal, originating in the dynamics of artistic developments. Among the external forces, two stand out and receive ample, mostly critical comments in the contributions to this volume: the pull of the market and the role of the state. There is no doubt that the consumption of artistic production has significantly expanded over the last decades. This is partly related to the general increase in economic wealth in contemporary, especially Western, societies although the more recent emergence of an art market in countries like China and India underlines the global dimension of the phenomenon. But the expansion is not merely quantitative. There has also been an enormous differentiation as well as cross-fertilization between different genres and art forms, in addition to the emergence of ever-new designs and ways of performing. The pull of the market provides new opportunities. Needless to say, it also brings its pitfalls. One specific manifestation of the expansive and continuing pull of the market is the thriving of the creative industries.

Yet, there has also been another, less recognized market expansion, namely that of the labour market for graduates with a background in the arts and design (Menger 2006). They are employed and/or work under precarious conditions in a rapidly growing segment of the tertiary sector, the 'creative sector'. The artist as worker is becoming a familiar and more frequent figure at the beginning of the twenty-first century. While precarious working conditions are by no means limited to artists, there is nevertheless an interesting convergence with other forms of (self-) employment and work organized around temporarily limited projects that shows that the boundaries between the 'creative sector' and other forms of economic activities are becoming porous.

The role of the state manifests itself in the ongoing expansion of higher education, although outside Europe the market is strongly present. This expansion is a worldwide phenomenon, with parents increasingly expecting to give their children better chances to succeed in life through education. It also is in line with the efforts of governments, business, and industry to set up framework conditions for the emergence of a 'knowledge society' and thus prepare for the ongoing transformation of the economy by becoming more 'knowledge-based', especially through the widespread use and diffusion of modern information and communication technologies. Especially in Europe with its tradition of a state-dominated system of higher education, the state has been present by initiating and promoting the kind of changes in the universities that have been so aptly summarized by Torsten Kälvemark (Chapter 1). In the context of the emergence of a European Higher Education Area, the Bologna process – used, misused, and abused in its implementation – has brought about irreversible changes for and in universities in Europe. With it, perhaps inevitably, issues of quality control have arisen to which the arts are also subject if they claim space inside the university structure.

The changing relationship between the arts and society

These forces of change with a major impact coming from outside would, however, not have gone very far, had they not been accompanied or even preceded by dynamic forces from within the field of the arts themselves. These internal forces are by no means homogeneous or pushing in the same direction. They come in a colluding or rebelling mode; they are farsighted in their vision of the future or hostile to institutional innovations while nostalgically turning backward. Just as the role of the market and of the state are conditioned and constrained by the global context, the internal forces in the arts are not autonomous, either. At their core is the ongoing transformation of the relationship between society and the arts.

First comes the ongoing proliferation of sites and modes of artistic production. They are now widely distributed and spread throughout society. No longer confined to princely courts or to the ateliers of artists producing for the rising bourgeoisie, today's artistic production takes place in many, even unlikely places. They range from the familiar studios of architects, which may extend even into the field to study and support 'informal cities'; to the countless exhibitions and works in museums that mix their treasures with artistic ways of displaying them; to artists working in and with 'soundscapes' in built-up environments; to the ongoing innovativeness we have come to expect from the performing arts; but above all in the new media that have allowed the arts to infiltrate society in unprecedented ways and that have considerably enhanced the subversive, critical potential of artistic expression. With this comes a change in the self- and other-definition of the artist; no longer the 'genius', but a worker aiming to become a researcher.

Second, there are the ongoing attempts to find, and define, the place of the arts within the structure of universities and other institutions of higher education. Having escaped, or perhaps only delayed, the formalization of education and training within the disciplinary matrix that characterized the structure of the modern university in the second half of the nineteenth century may turn out to be a comparative advantage. It may be easier for the arts to cross disciplinary boundaries, research fields, and genres and to engage more fully and creatively in the kind of inter-, multi- or trans-disciplinarity that is currently so much in demand by policy-makers, university rectors, vice-chancellors, and researchers alike. If a world-leading university like Harvard sets up a commission to deal with the role and function of the arts within its own research-intensive premises, this sends a powerful signal to the rest of the academic world that cross-fertilization between the domains of the arts and the sciences is not only possible, but a most welcome and much desired way of enhancing creativity across presumed disciplinary borderlines (Harvard 2008).

Third, and perhaps most importantly, the observed changes in the relationship between the arts and society at large have been greatly facilitated, enhanced, and enabled by the fervent embrace of the new media by artists. Whether in the visual or auditory arts, in performances of all kinds, in architecture and design and far beyond, new modes of creating, producing, and expressing 'creative knowledge' and new links of communication between the various fields of arts have emerged, but diverse and partly new audiences have also been established, leading to new forms of unprecedented interactivity. What the sciences can only dream of, namely to establish better forms of communication with society, seems to come much more 'naturally' to the arts in their playful and often ironic way of reaching out to society.

In short, the ambition to give research a firm place in the arts through PhD training and as an ongoing, conscious effort consists in finding ways of translating these transformative forces, which have been unleashed on a global scale, into a coherent and meaningful assemblage. Individual creativity, but also collective forms of working together, must converge with material practices and institutional structures that enable them to cohere, thereby empowering research in the arts to unfold its dynamic. Obviously, the institutional forms needed must be sustainable and sufficiently flexible. They must include the prospects of sustained funding and research-adequate support. The way forward proposed in this volume is to institutionalize research in the arts by anchoring it in a solid, state-of-the-art PhD training and thus bringing the arts back into the fold of research. With exemplary clarity, Henk Borgdorff has spelt out how to go about this (Chapter 3). According to this vision, *artistic research* will take its place beside *scientific research* on equal footing. It is a vision with which I wholeheartedly concur. Artistic practices, just like scientific practices, will thereby widen the scope of research, with the enormous potential to enrich all fields of research.

Not surprisingly, such an ambitious undertaking reveals inherent tensions that accompany its implementation. Some of them point to real obstacles that must be overcome, while others can perhaps be dispelled, as the following section shows.

Tensions and disagreements

Disagreements and tensions arise around the concept of artistic research itself. What is it? What does it mean in relation to art and art-based practices? How does it differ from scientific research – if the two can be compared at all? My preference is to use the term 'artistic research' instead of arts-based research, since it emphasizes the analogy to scientific research. Just as there are 'science-based technologies' that are the result of scientific understanding and manipulation, there are also arts-based technologies. Borgdorff's often-quoted characterization of artistic research rightly emphasizes the purpose of expanding knowledge and understanding 'by conducting an original investigation in and through art objects and creative processes' (Borgdorff 2006). He emphasizes the role played by (leading) research questions and their pertinence to the art world. 'Researchers employ experimental and hermeneutical methods that reveal and articulate the tacit knowledge that is situated and embodied in specific artworks and artistic processes.' By explicitly including not only the research community, but also the wider public as the (interactive) recipients and partners in this kind of production of new knowledge, this concept of artistic research articulates an ideal that scientific research still struggles with: 'public engagement' and 'public awareness'.

This is not the place to compare the obvious and not-so-obvious differences between artistic and scientific research. Many of the seemingly insurmountable or insoluble issues and many of the alleged incompatibilities between them arise from definitions in the analytic philosophy of science, with its emphasis on propositional knowledge. Taking these definitions as a yardstick overlooks that research processes and practices that are based on the pursuit of propositional knowledge constitute only a minor part of the broad range and vast differences in the actual practices in the production of new scientific knowledge. Contesting this philosophical tradition and its narrow range, STS, as science and technology studies are called, have over the last few decades elucidated knowledge practices at work in the laboratory and far beyond. In its constructivist mode, STS, by conducting empirical studies designed to reveal the complexities, contingencies, and uncertainties of techno-scientific processes, have insisted on their heterogeneity.

To take but one example: far from what philosophers claimed, actual practices reveal that what counts as 'evidence' differs from field to field without losing its central importance for the practitioners. As shown in numerous empirical studies, not only does the historical context matter, but so does the present. The laboratory is merely a set of procedures and instruments that together form an 'experimental system' designed to bring forth what is not yet known, due to its essential unforeseeability, and the 'play of possibilities'. Certainly, a controlled interior has to be separated from an uncontrolled exterior. The unstable experimental object must be rendered stable to allow controlled variation. But scientific practices are not restricted to the laboratory or even to an experimental system. Far from it. STS has unravelled many heterogeneous networks that extend throughout society and among its actors and institutions. In these heterogeneous networks, 'humans' and 'things', i.e. artefacts, are linked in multiple and mutual relationships. By extending the concept of 'agency', ANT or actor-network theory claims that the production of new knowledge is taking place in numerous sites and through many transactions and transformations that extend throughout society and its institutions without losing sight of the 'objects' and their materiality. From an ANT perspective, humans and the artistic phenomena they produce and interact with, can also be seen as constituting continuously reconfigured assemblages. Researchers in the arts are therefore well advised – and invited – to delve into the burgeoning STS literature. There they will find much that appeals to them intuitively, but also much that allows them to 'make sense' of their own artistic practices.

While STS originally was keen to deconstruct the accounts offered by analytical philosophers of science and to demystify their and some scientists' narratives, it has since moved on to describing, analysing, and understanding processes of co-production and co-evolution between society and scientific-technological advances. Following such an approach, the social order and the scientific order condition each other. Cultural, economic, and political prerequisites have to be fulfilled before certain scientific achievements and their spread in society are possible. For this reason, the organization of research, its epistemological goals, and its funding structure also change.

Is there room for artistic research in this changing epistemological, institutional, and normative landscape in the bewildering zones of uncertainties? According to STS, the answer is a definitive 'yes'. This is not to deny the many differences between the arts and the sciences and their respective practices. Nor is it to deny 'the fact that the art system – the institution named Art – aggressively stabilizes its perpetuity through all kinds of destabilizing processes' (Brown 2009), since something similar can be said about the science system. It too stabilizes itself, albeit in a different way, through the destabilization processes caused by the enormous societal impact that results from the accelerated advances in the techno-sciences.

Other emerging tensions and disagreements that surface in the following contributions are not unique to artists, either. Together, they make up a long list partly, but not only, of complaints about what is seen as an audit society's growing bureaucratic interference with the autonomous space needed for any creative activity. Take the discussion about evaluation and quality control (Chapter 23). Which criteria are to be used when comparing texts and artefacts? What indeed constitutes a 'significant contribution' to the field of artistic research when evaluating a PhD thesis? What are the specific guiding norms and tests to be applied for artistic research (Chapter 5)? Similar discussions arise in the humanities, and partly in the social sciences, whenever the scientific community is called upon to set up its own standards of quality control and come up with its criteria of evaluation. It does not need to be emphasized that the resistance against the Bologna process, too, is far from unique to the arts. As Torsten Kälvemark rightly points out, there are marked national differences in the acceptance or rejection of Bologna, as well as of the way it has been implemented. One must therefore look to the still largely national university politics and the organization of higher education in particular countries in order to figure out the specific needs of artistic and practice-based research in the wider context of the European integration of higher education systems (Chapter 1).

Another set of issues concerns the tensions between the individual creative act and collaborative forms of work. The subjectivity of the artist as worker has definitely changed. Although not exclusively restricted to the arts, the risks for artists working as 'culture producers' under precarious conditions may be greater. The overall tendency in the sciences is to move increasingly toward collaborative practices, reinforced by the need to share expensive instrumentation and equipment. Forms of collaboration can be quite nuanced, however, and are never free of tension, since the attribution of credit to the individuals involved is always at stake, and mobility, while considered necessary for the flow of ideas, often carries a hidden personal cost (Chapter 22). Yet, in contemporary societies, an individual can hardly undertake anything without finding himself or herself caught in a complex network of interdependencies.

The 'network society' (Castells 1996) is no longer a mere vision, but has turned into a reality of increasing surveillance and data glut. But it also offers new opportunities to realize projects that no individual alone could aspire to achieve. Forms of collaboration do not negate the individual, quite the contrary. Arts practitioners, with their strong record in collective work, may also be more open and disposed to experiment with new forms of trans-disciplinarity. While the quote from Claude Bernard, 'l'art, c'est moi, la science, c'est nous', might have been an accurate description in the nineteenth century, the challenge today consists in how to merge these multiple collaborative forms into the shared culture of the emerging artistic research communities.

The discussion of methods appropriate for artistic research also occupies a good part of the centre stage in the ongoing discussion. Experimentation is frequently mentioned and is one of the oldest methods with which artists have always worked, as central for them as it is for scientists. Although the spaces in which experimentation is carried out differ (the laboratory is a strictly controlled space, separated from the outside for the purposes of controlled variation), the laboratory is not the only kind of 'experimental system'. Whether experiments are performed in exhibitions (Kräftner et al. 2007) and other 'creative sites' in society or have shifted from artistic practice as production to practise as a dynamic reference point for theory-driven experimentation, as diagnosed by Slager (Chapter 19), their alleged uniqueness and aesthetic singularity form part of a larger pattern that always includes the local and its unique aesthetics without confining it to one locality and one aesthetic.

In the arts, as in the sciences, there is an enormous heterogeneity of actual practices (Chapter 13). They range from verbal to visual and auditory; from creative writing to creative dance; from performing arts to the original production of arts; from time-dependent or real-time arts (Chapter 16) to the virtual and the corporeal (Chapter 12). Yet this heterogeneity and its explosive mixture of styles and genres, each of which has its own tradition and dynamic projections into the future, is the cauldron for creativity as it erupts and emerges in the experimental system set up for artistic research in all its manifold manifestations and configurations.

This creative heterogeneity may be bewildering, especially when practical and policy-relevant recommendations are to be made for what should go into PhD requirements (Chapter 7). Yet, this is at the core of the ambition of the overall project that now must be attended in greater detail. A good starting point is to ask what the students' needs are (Chapter 21) and how to design curricula to meet them. Some very mundane, but no less important considerations arise at this point: engagement with the faculty and the tedious process of negotiating the standards of evaluation and the criteria to use as an incipient research community. The role of artistic research in the overall setting and structure of the university is largely still to be defined. The Harvard University report, although currently on ice due to the financial crisis, offers a seductive vision of what might develop.

One last but important question is how to obtain funding for research from outside sources. It may be a somewhat symbolic, but nevertheless important signal that the European Research Council,[1] which was set up by the European Union in 2007 to fund 'frontier research' in all fields of science and scholarship, is principally open to funding artistic research as well. Since the ERC targets individual excellence, it supports 'Principal Investigators' and their 'individual teams'. However, one prerequisite is for the applicant to have a PhD as well as a track record of excellence that does not necessarily consist of publications only, but is appropriate to the specific field.

So the pathways forward are multiple and the 'principle of uncertainty' (Menger 2009) is inscribed in all of them. Undoubtedly, it will take time for some of the tensions to settle or to reconfigure. The ongoing debate thus offers powerful incentives to disagree. But all disagreement should be wisely accompanied by reflectiveness and reflexivity (Chapter 10). This means to take into account – and be accountable toward – the changing place of and relationship between the arts and society. Just as science is no longer considered to be solely the pursuit of some eternal 'truth' to be revealed to humanity, artistic practices can no longer be equated with the expression of some hidden, eternal 'beauty'. Important as such ideal visions may have been in the history of arts and of the sciences, at the beginning of the twenty-first century we have definitively entered the age of the co-production of science, art, and society. Human creativity in its manifold expressions has found a privileged home in the structure of universities and research institutions, although it is by no means confined to them. It continues to radiate outward, transforming – and being transformed – by the multiple sites in society where it is received, appropriated, contested, transformed, and subversively played back. In other words, the natural order with which scientists are mainly concerned, and the order of imagination and inventiveness of the arts, are co-produced with the social order (Nowotny *et al.* 2003).

Epilogue: Why now?

The last question concerns the timeliness of the project. Why now? In the context of globalization, it is increasingly difficult to escape marketization. A knowledge-based society recognizes that the production of new knowledge is an indispensable precondition, but this process is fraught with uncertainty, as we have seen. Paradoxically, although knowledge is a highly valued good, it is not a scarce good. It is abundant, but what is scarce is knowledge that will lead to innovation. Today, the entire spectrum of knowledge with its impressive technological, scientific, and creative capacities is oriented toward a future that does not promise so much a new beginning as a further intensification of what has already been achieved. Science and technology cross the threshold between the present and the future unhindered, for what appears possible in the laboratory today can already be in the market tomorrow or the day after. In this broad sweep for new ideas and discoveries, for new products, processes, and combinations of what is already available, the quest for innovation is an ongoing and urgent pursuit of what remains unforeseeable and yet promises to further expand the range of possibilities.

Art has always been finely tuned to a fragile future and sceptical toward promises made in the name of human betterment. It should keep its sceptical stance whenever innovation is evoked as the collective wager our scientific-technological civilization has made on the future. But at the same time, art cannot escape or exempt itself from the lure of uncertainty, which is an inherent component of the processes of research and of innovation alike. If innovation is contemporary society's way of coping with the vacuum that inhabits its present concept of the future, artistic research – and not just the production of art – may lead to forms of innovation that shape the elusive phenomena and events that only the individual and collective imagination can conjure.

The idea that the limits of seeing and knowing as laid down by Aristotle can be transcended first arose among the humanistic artists of the Renaissance. One of them, Leon Battista Alberti (1404–1472), articulated for the first time in his essay on perspective, *De pictura*, the idea that the human way of seeing could be extended and deepened by introducing mathematical knowledge into the material world. With his perspective grid (a geometric object that he imagined as a veil cutting through the visual pyramid), he developed techniques that would make it possible to bring 'mathematical things into view'. He insisted on a special ethos for humanistic painters in order to legitimate the active crossing of the boundaries between the natural and the artificial, which mastering the techniques of perspective enabled him and his contemporaries to do. Alberti was not the only one to tackle the problem of how to render the invisible visible. When Galileo Galilei problematized the presumed limits of the visible by directing his telescope toward objects in the sky that were believed to be invisible to the human eye, he was deeply rooted in and thoroughly knowledgeable about the material culture of contemporary artists and their practices (Feldhay 2009). The phenomena he observed in the sky were thus transformed into objects of a novel astronomical experience, just as Alberti succeeded in creating novel objects for the experience of space.

In the contemporary world, much more has been rendered visible that once was thought to be invisible. We can now reach back in time to the beginnings of the universe and observe molecules and their dynamic motion in real time. This has been achieved largely by continuing to cross the boundaries between the natural and the artificial and by the fruits of curiosity and the results from a process of research that began in the Renaissance. It has led to amazing discoveries and feats of bio- and other forms of engineering, resulting in new life forms and making entities that never existed before. The exploration of processes on the nano-scale have just begun and the limits of creating new knowledge are nowhere in sight.

But the techno-sciences, important as they are, are not alone in leading these explorations and pursuits. Artists have quickly realized the artistic challenges offered by hybrid forms and the vast domain of crossing the natural with the artificial. Most significantly, they extend their creativity beyond the range covered by the techno-sciences. True to the humanistic spirit of the Renaissance, they bring the human back into this world that continues to be transformed by the techno-sciences and their societal impact. It is this *humanistic impulse* that should continue to invigorate research in the arts. It has the potential to bring forth a new Renaissance.

Note

1 http://erc.europa.eu (accessed 25 February 2010).

FOREWORD

Hans-Peter Schwarz

Translated by Wolfgang Schnekenburger

More than a decade ago, a disagreement ignited as to the pros and cons of art-based research, a disagreement that continues to this day. The dispute focuses above all on the dilemma of how art-based research is to differentiate itself from fine art, music and theatre studies on the one hand, and the practical arts on the other. One question that has been discussed for an extensive period of time with considerable vehemence, and which is of great importance for the acceptance of art-based research, at least in the science community, is whether epistemological potential is inherent in the production and reception of art. Research conducted by the Berlin-based philosopher Simone Mahrenholz concerning the relationship between music and epistemology may be considered paradigmatic for this discourse and can with some justification be transferred to other fields of art (Mahrenholz 2000). Based on the system of symbols developed by Nelson Goodman in his book, *Languages of Art*, which refers mainly to the fine arts, she searches for the uniqueness, or at least the distinctive features, of an epistemological view of the world through pure music, or, to use one of Goodman's central terms, through musical 'worldmaking'. Admittedly, expressed in a simplified manner, Mahrenholz looks for a specific epistemology of the world which can be provided only by musical production or musical reception and by no other epistemological method. In doing so, she moves beyond Goodman by integrating into her philosophical aesthetics results provided by recent brain research. Undoubtedly, these findings are meaningful for a discourse in scientific theory concerning the validity of art-based research and its differentiation from other disciplines within the arts.

Although I by no means wish to underestimate the importance of a discourse for the dynamics of an epistemological gain overall, it does seem to be high time to stop doubting whether art-based research exists at all and accept that it has long ago become an everyday occurrence in most art universities, irrespective of whether they are organized as parts of universities, as is the case in most Anglo-Saxon and some Scandinavian countries, or whether they are the result of a horizontal merger of various institutions of higher art education to form a university of the arts, or, as is the rule in central, southern and western Europe, as mono-disciplinary universities along the lines of the Academia or Bauhaus.

The present volume, which contains outstanding and exceedingly well-written studies on different conceptions of art-based research, is proof of the fruitful existence, liveliness and viability of art-based research in all European countries and in the institutionalized art education systems developed along European traditions in America and Australia. It also becomes evident – and that is not a drawback, but rather an advantage – that art-based research does not exist as a monolithic instrument of epistemology, but as a multitude of equilateral approaches based on the different traditions in the various disciplines of the arts. The present condition of literature and music, the visual and fine arts, architecture and design, and let us not forget media art which came about as a result of the media revolution that emerged over the past few decades, was formed in a long process of development characterized by mutual attraction and rejection. This differentiation should not be covered up by a research model that is normative or defined too narrowly.

However, even if we assume that it does not makes sense to dispute the justification of integrating young art-based research into the circle of traditional systems of epistemology, it is very much justified, even necessary, to petition for specific art-based research. And there undeniably is a need. There is an internal need in terms of research that aims at developing the toolbox further, the instrumental resources of art production. Formerly, the aim was to continue developing the basic material conditions, which in terms of researching new colour pigments and binding agents resulted in the formation of entire industrial sectors. In the 1990s, demands coming mainly from the United Kingdom from so-called creative industries for exploitable results, including among others from the arts and art teaching institutions, stimulated the discourse concerning the necessity for an independent research infrastructure. Often however, under the veil of 'applied research', they served the economic interests of companies whose image as 'creative' entities stemmed from their market acumen. Understandably, this nourished the fear of most artists, regardless of whether they were researching or producing, that they were instruments of purely economic interests. In Central Europe, at least, economically driven controlling systems recommended by organizations promoting public art contributed significantly toward the discrimination of art-based research. The new relationship between the arts and technology, especially to digital media technology, which in the 1980s developed into the driving force of post-modern globalization cultures, finally ensured that the issue of art-based research was transported from the highs and lows of academic dispute to the to-do list of education policy. The digital toolbox of media technology faces instrumental art-based research with completely new tasks of undreamt of and unusual complexity. Not only do digital tools expand the possibilities of art production, but they also expand the horizon with regard to the meaning of art reception.

This has led to an oscillating process that questions all disciplines in the arts which formerly had been clearly separated. The parameters of these processes resulted in a hybridization that not only demanded new forms of knowledge production from traditional scientific forms, but also developed into those hybrid art forms which in cultivating the possibilities of the virtual space of digital interaction apparently provided some of the post-modern utopian promises made in the writings of the German philosopher Jürgen Habermas. This so-called interactive media art, especially, opened up art discourse to the ideas of art-based research which extended far beyond instrumental motivation. It is possible that the dynamics of the complex hybridization process of the practical arts and art reception is also due to the fruitful diversity of what we today call art-based research. Hybrid media art, which requires its own research to steer production and reception processes or even produce a work of art from them, took advantage of all the methods and parameters for its research that it found and considered useful. That is why, as Michael Schwab demanded somewhat apodictically, 'the definition of art-based research must be postponed for a good reason as its creation is a part of the transformation process of practical art' (Schwab [forthcoming]: 71).

Only a brief look at everyday research carried out at most universities of art shows that the focus on only one individual concept of art-based research could miss out on some of the facts, and the research published in this volume offers convincing examples and justification. Not only is a new research method tested, but so are several 'old' and disciplined and some new, still undisciplined, research methods with an antagonistic relationship toward one another, especially concerning competition for financial and personnel resources – an everyday occurrence at universities of the arts.

In addition to what has been said, the complexity resulting from the sheer number of research methods is an advantage as current research at universities of art is not, or not yet, carried out in accordance with fixed methodological guidelines. In its most interesting examples it is trans-disciplinary and therefore follows a line of development that now has to be arduously captured by traditional research cultures in the humanities and the sciences.

This trans-disciplinary basic understanding represents a considerable advantage over most mono-disciplinary approaches to research dealing with art at scientific universities if we assume – and this is my opinion – that art-based research is not only a self-sufficient theoretical structure but also the driving force of innovation for art production and art reception. A withdrawal from the discourse concerning the continued development of the arts represents a further reason underscoring the need for independent art-based research.

In order to guarantee innovation, innovative and therefore trans-disciplinary research infrastructure has to be developed at the universities of art. At the beginning, they may well be informal, individually oriented networks, but they must be given an adequate place in university curricula. Although this may sound like a platitude for the theory of science, it is absolutely essential considering the predominance of modest ideas of teaching at any universities of art. First, however, the myth of institutionalized education in the arts has to be deconstructed: the alleged self-renewal process of teaching at universities of art triggered by practical experience outside the academic sphere.

To a large extent, an agreement reached during the anti-academic period of secession in the heroic phase of modern times holds that innovation in teaching is guaranteed by the fact that teachers are simultaneously also practitioners and therefore practise their 'true' profession outside the university. Consequently, the real avant-garde was (and is) conceivable only outside government institutions. Except in a few reformed universities, this resulted in rather craft-oriented curricula characterized by taking the master craftsman as an example or by a culture of shaman-like laying of hands in the style of Joseph Beuys, which was analysed by Beat Wyss in a perceptive and sardonic publication (Wyss 1997: 64ff.).

As the working environment of the arts increasingly suffers under the constraints of the creative industries, space and time for avant-garde experiments will soon be completely sacrificed to the dictate of efficiency. It may take some time before it is understood that only universities can provide the space required for experiments. However, owing to the persistence of the traditional understanding of teachers at traditional universities as described earlier, it may also take a while before the innovation potential of art-based research projects is included in the teaching curricula in a targeted and organized manner. However, this may not be as easy as it sounds. Very little experience is available on just how this transfer of knowledge can take place. Usually, a transfer of knowledge is assumed by the teaching staff, who together frequently carry out the research as well. Nonetheless, should the transfer of knowledge be successful, to which some of the contributions to this volume provide optimistic proof, then universities of art could find a way out of the dilemma that the measure for valuing successful practical art is defined not within the university but outside it: in the opera house or on the art market, in the ballet company or at the state theatre.

A need for art-based research is therefore recognized in both the permanent development of university curricula and in the transfer of these 'autonomous' curricula into the socially integrated institutions of art production and art reception.

If we recognize that differentiated and differentiating art-based research is of fundamental importance for the development of both, art production and art reception, then the question concerning the position of the art-based researcher in society is superfluous: as is the case in every system of research, the genuine place is mainly the university itself, both for persons who consider themselves as 'full-time' art-based researchers and those who practise art-based research occasionally to advance their own artistic activity.

On the other hand, a publishing culture based on non-verbal forms of discourse should be developed or, rather, different discourses on art-based research should be released from their segregation and their results made comparable and made available to the necessary criticism by peer groups, thus providing them with a really animated research environment.

While I am not sure that in the future universities of art will actually be required to make this happen, merging the different disciplines of art into one institution facilitates the trans-disciplinary approach of the discourse on art-based research, and I am certain that the way that universities of art perceive themselves must change. The centre of our efforts concerning research at universities of art should not focus on the competition between research and teaching, on the apparent disagreement between theory and practice, or on the differences among research cultures, but on a creative and critical willingness to cooperate that can endure the conflicts that have always boosted the arts.

Part I

FOUNDATIONS

In the Preface we identified that research in the arts is principally an academic concern. We had in mind our observation that the whole activity arises as a consequence of the academicization of the arts. This could be viewed in a number of ways, for example as a historical trend or an intellectual trend. Viewed historically, one can identify certain key events including the incorporation of arts schools into universities at various specific dates in national histories. As an intellectual trend, one can see the progressive adoption – over decades and even centuries – of different fields of study by the academy, and the transformation of the values and concerns of those fields into ones that have an academic focus. What happens with either of these trends is that an activity that has a particular manifestation in one realm – such as the realm of professional arts practice – is transformed so that it manifests itself in an academic way. In this sense, academicization is not a passive process that simply adds to a community's knowledge about a particular activity, but instead, it is an active process that transforms the object of study.

When one approaches the subject of research in the arts and seeks to inquire into the foundations of this activity, one is already approaching it from an academic point of view. An inquiry into the foundations of research does not have as its focus the practical activities of artists or researchers, but rather it attempts to define the activity according to essential criteria that determine whether the activity is research, and of what kind. Such definitions are usually based on either a comparative study – in which criteria are identified in cognate fields and transferred to the one in question – or else they proceed, as it were, from first principles. Part I of this book presents elements of both approaches.

Apart from the historical genealogy of the subject, Part I looks in detail at the relationship between the existing field of professional arts practice and existing conceptions of academic research, what is shared between these two areas and what is particular and distinct to each. On the one hand, if one sees research in the arts as a combination of art with research, then one needs to account for the amount that is shared. Is it the case that there is just a small portion that is common and represents shared interests and concerns between professional arts practice and academic research, or is there a very large commonality between the two? It may even be that there is a complete convergence between arts practice and arts research if they are construed in a particular way. And if one's understanding of these concepts depends upon construing existing terms – such as 'research' – in particular and perhaps novel ways, then foundational inquiry will help to make explicit the understanding of these terms. On the other hand, one might think that this new field of research in the arts produces completely new outcomes and provides a new context for both study and practice. If arts research is something completely novel, then there will need to be new structures within which the professional practice of arts research can operate and within which individuals can be trained and find careers.

A potential benefit of arts-based research is that it might reveal new ways of researching and provide insights and understandings beyond the arts themselves. This would occur if arts-based research offered something new to the academy in terms of its methods and outcomes rather than simply its interest in art. The 'something new' that it might offer is a change to the dominant knowledge model. The academy has been dominated until very recent times by a largely scientific concept of knowledge building. This kind of knowledge is somewhat impersonal and does not reflect the subjective interest of any one individual; it is supposed to tell us something objective about the world and that is why it is contrasted to 'opinion'. If the term knowledge can be applied to the arts, then it seems unlikely that knowledge will be of this kind. Artistic knowledge seems to have more potential in relation to the human individual, their experience, their emotions and their embodied relationship with the world rather than something as abstract as the scientific concept of knowledge.

A further aspect that a foundational inquiry can clarify is whether it is significant that arts-based research generates artefacts such as musical compositions, performances, paintings, etc. Clearly this is a very striking difference of output compared to research in other subjects. Indeed, most universities have had to modify their regulations regarding what kind of submission doctoral candidates can make in order to accommodate this difference. Traditionally the expectation has been for an extensive written report (a thesis) that contains critical analysis and makes an explicit claim regarding the original contribution that the study makes to the field. Although in some subjects it may be the case that experiments have been undertaken, it is the critical reflection upon, and analysis of, the significance of these experiments and their results that forms the content of the doctoral submission. However, the newly incorporated arts faculties have often demanded that they be allowed to additionally or alternatively submit non-textual material in the form of artefacts and artistic productions.

Some artistic researchers claim that the artefacts themselves embody knowledge or in some way play an instrumental role in the research or its communication, and that is why they must be allowed as part of the submission. This claim is apparently reinforced at institutions in which the size of the textual document is reduced in proportion to the scale of the artefact-based submission thereby implying that one substitutes the other. The potential for artefacts to embody or communicate knowledge is a bold claim that should have impact far beyond the arts. This will be achieved when the nature of this embodied knowledge is clarified and when there is an agreement about its relationship to concepts such as skill, know-how and experience.

1
UNIVERSITY POLITICS AND PRACTICE-BASED RESEARCH

Torsten Kälvemark

The emergence of practice-based research in and through the arts is closely connected with politics of higher education and research, nationally and internationally. This connection is twofold. On the one hand the discussion around practice-based research as a special concept has in some countries been prompted or encouraged by politically motivated structural changes in the university landscape. On the other hand the development of practice-based research has led – and will certainly in the future lead to – significant changes in national research policies and institutional patterns.

The aim of this chapter is to describe and analyse this process. The perspective will partly be historical. The historical prism is due to my own academic background (although I have been a university administrator for most of my life) and the reason is simple: it is impossible to understand the present state of discussion without looking back at a process which has been going on for the last decades in the international academic world.

The description and discussion will be done under five different headings:

- Art schools and structural reforms of higher education systems
- European integration, the Bologna process and the third cycle
- Research and the 'creative industries'
- Quality assurance and research funding
- Practice-based research and degree-awarding powers

Writing from a Swedish perspective I may be excused for taking some of my examples from my own country. The reason is that I have been rather heavily involved in the national debate here. I have also to some extent taken part in the decision-making process, in particular with regard to funding artistic research. Since Sweden has a rather coherent system of higher education and research it is also easy to see the institutional structure and its relevance for the subject.

The second perspective is European. Although I will pay some attention to the debate in Australia, I will leave other continents aside. The first reason for this is of course a lack of knowledge. The second reason, however, is a feeling that the specific organizational pattern of higher education and research in a country like the United States gives the subject of 'university politics' quite a different meaning than in Europe. Despite the fact that European higher education and research is more and more deregulated it can still be perceived in terms of national systems where general policies for the sector of tertiary education affect art schools and their programmes for teaching and research.

Art schools and structural reforms of higher education systems

In many countries the issues related to research in the performing and fine arts have been prompted by changes in national policies in the higher education area. This was certainly the case for Sweden when, back in 1977, the whole tertiary education sector was subject to wide-ranging reforms.

One part of the structural changes was the integration of art schools into the wider national system of higher education. Some colleges of arts and music were integrated into universities. Others were left with an independent status but still subject to rules and regulations designed to fit mainstream universities or other research-based institutions.

In this context a natural question was raised. If research in the classical sense is the basis for teaching and training in universities, what then is the equivalence for the teaching and training in art schools? The answer was the creation of a new concept: 'artistic development'. A policy document written at the time defined this concept as a means of developing 'experiment with artistic forms of expression, as well as research'. It went on to say that some of these experiments could be regarded as research, even if the line of demarcation could not be clearly described.

Art schools were given additional funds for this new activity but there was great confusion about the content and validity of the new concept. The funds were happily received but it is obvious from the discussions going on in the 1980s that art schools were really not aware of what the government was expecting of them in terms of renewal, development or research. A review made in the early 1990s showed that the concept of research was emerging in the art schools, although it was obvious that many teachers in the schools were reluctant to describe anything in their field of activity as related to research.

In broad terms the situation could be described as a government intervention in the life of the art schools. They were encouraged to define their activities in terms of the historical and general academic distinction between teaching and research. Once this problem was put on their agenda the discussion about the foundations of the teaching led to an 'academic drift' in the search for a research equivalent. Further on in this chapter I will try to discuss the implications of this in a longer perspective.

A similar development could be seen in relation to a structural reform in the tertiary education sector that was initiated in Australia in 1987 (The Unified National System).

Again a number of art schools were integrated into the classical university structure and again the question was raised about the basis for academic teaching in this field. Added to that was the desire from the art schools to get access to the general funding streams for research (The Research Quantum) or the extra project funding from the Australian Research Council. The problem was described by Dennis Strand from the Canberra School of Art in a report to the Australian federal government in 1998:

> The question of what is research in the creative arts is one that has special significance in Australian universities today but little significance elsewhere. Its importance lies in the fact that there are scarce dollars attached to the definitions of research. This has led to the need to define research in the creative arts in ways that will give the creative arts in universities a foothold in the competition for research dollars. Attempts to force mainstream creative arts activities into the mould of scientific research has led to semantic arguments that often have not been particularly helpful. However, with only two funded categories – teaching and research – the opportunities for alternative arguments have been limited.
>
> (Strand 1998)

In his report he also wrote that a literature search on the topic of research in the creative arts yielded very little result: 'it is not the subject of popular or widespread discussion among researchers or artists, either in journals or other forms of publishing, the extent of the literature being quite limited'.

It is a bit surprising to note that this statement was made only a decade ago. One reason for the lack of results in his search was of course that the Internet had not yet been the prime source of information and discussion. But the most important reason is obviously that the concept of artistic research was only the subject of public discourse in a limited number of countries.

The fact that national university policies and the structure of the higher education and research systems triggered a special kind of debate was also underlined by Malcolm Gillies, professor of music at the University of Queensland. In 1997 he noted:

> Our problematic role within this research environment is made more difficult by the very definition of 'research'. While in the United States the move during the 1980s and 1990s has been more for establishment of *research equivalent* categories of professional work in the arts – largely driven by the university staff in the Arts for career progressions and recognition equal to those in other disciplines – the tendency within Australia has been more to agitate for the broadening of the definition of 'research'. The reason for this is simple: with only two funded categories, 'teaching' and 'research', the opportunities for 'research equivalent' arguments have been limited.
>
> (Strand 1998)

In 2000 I made a review commissioned by the National Swedish Board of Universities and Colleges with regard to the international debate on artistic and practice-based research (Kälvemark 2000). At the time it was obvious that three countries stood out

5

as examples of a lively national debate on these issues. Australia was of course one of them. The other two were Finland and the United Kingdom.

Compared to the situation in Australia and Sweden, it was difficult to find external factors for the emergence of a vibrant research community in the art schools in Finland. No major national reform could be mentioned as an explanation. Compared to the situation in Sweden it was easy to see a contrast between the uniform and strictly regulated Swedish scene on the one hand, and a more traditional university autonomy in Finland on the other. In combination with a historically strong position for the art schools in Finland this had apparently led to the call for artistic research from within the schools themselves.

As far as the United Kingdom was concerned it was easier to point to a number of commissions and reform strategies that had triggered debates about teaching and research in universities and colleges during the 1980s and 1990s. Looked at from the outside developments in Britain seemed exemplary. The Arts and Humanities Research Board had produced a booklet where basic problems seemed to have been sorted out. The guidelines with regard to the PhD process were eagerly studied in many other countries and provided a much-needed background for developments outside the UK.

A common feature for the countries engaged in the discussion around research in the arts was, however, the general academic and philosophical climate. They were all strongly influenced by an analytical philosophical tradition in which the performing and creative arts were some kind of strangers in the academic community. In countries on the European continent like France and Germany the debate was lacking. In their philosophical tradition and intellectual environment art schools were not primarily thought of as belonging to a system where the distinction between teaching and research was relevant.

In the decade since this review was made a number of changes have taken place in countries where arts-based research was not on the agenda at the end of the 1990s. Some of these developments are due to the changing face of the European higher education landscape, which will be described below. Others are resulting from continued structural changes of national higher education systems.

Austria could be mentioned as an example. Through changes in national legislation in 1998 and 2002 six higher education institutions in the arts (*Kunsthochschulen*) were formally recognized as having the same legal status as universities. In December 2008 the Austrian Research Council convened a conference on the theme of Arts and Research and this could be seen as a formal recognition of the need for the research establishment to take funding of artistic research into account. The subsequent institution of a funding programme for arts-based research in Austria (further described on the following pages) shows that the German-speaking area of Europe has entered the field of discussion.

The main reasons behind the developments in Europe are, however, to be found in the swift process of European integration in the field of higher education in the first decade of the twenty-first century.

European integration, the Bologna process and the third cycle

The 1990s saw some important developments on the higher education scene in Europe. The Erasmus programme, an important student and teacher exchange scheme within the European Union had been started in 1987 and expanded rapidly during the following decade. EFTA countries like Norway, Sweden and Switzerland joined the programme in 1992. Other nations in Eastern Europe followed suit even before becoming members of the enlarged European Union.

The Erasmus programme was important in the sense that it forced teachers and students from all types of higher education institutions in Europe to exchange views and compare notes about national policies and institutional curricula. The debate which was going on in some countries about artistic research, was spread through increased personal contacts and teacher exchange. A kind of pan-European discourse in the field was rapidly emerging.

This pan-European development was further enhanced with the so-called Bologna process that started in 1999. This process is surely well known to most readers of this book. Suffice it to say that the aim of this (still ongoing) project is to shape a European Higher Education Area by making academic degree requirements and quality assurance standards more comparable and compatible throughout Europe. Of particular significance in this context are two goals of the process:

* Easily readable and comparable degrees organized in a three-cycle structure (e.g. bachelor-master-doctorate).
* Quality assurance in accordance with the Standards and Guidelines for Quality Assurance in the European Higher Education Area (ESG).

Countries that are signatories to the Bologna process have proceeded at variable speeds. Some governments have seen the process as an opportunity to rationalize higher education by making programmes shorter and more vocationally oriented. The uniform pattern of the three cycles has (as could have been expected) created opposition in many quarters. Art schools in a number of countries have expressed their doubts about a reform that they have regarded as bureaucratic and as an affront to time-honoured academic ideals.

On the other hand it is obvious that the new movements on the European scene have contributed to lively national debates on higher education policy in the field of arts education. These debates have sometimes been linked to the theme of research in the arts but also more generally to the Bologna structures. The need to enhance educational quality in a European comparative perspective has led to mergers and reorganizations in a number of countries, changes that will inevitably also have a bearing on the future of research activities.

Switzerland can be mentioned in this connection. In parallel with the implementation of the Bologna process, a number of art schools have been merging from 2005 and onwards. In 2005 the Hochschule der Künste Bern was formed, in 2006 the Haute école d'art et de design in Geneva was launched, and in 2007 the Zürcher Hochschule der Künste was created as an integrated art school. One of the reasons for these merger activities is apparently the need to shape a broader base for Masters programmes and, at a later stage, research activities.

In contrast to the Swiss example, simultaneous mergers in England seem to be more linked to factors other than those connected with the Bologna process. The University of the Arts London and the University for the Creative Arts have been established over the last few years but the reasons for the merger of a number of institutions have apparently more to do with British quality assurance mechanisms and the policies of degree-awarding powers. One reason is that the Bologna process has never been such a revolutionary scheme in the UK as in other countries.

Still, Bologna is an important driving force in the development of arts education and research in Europe. Henk Borgdorff from the University of the Arts, The Hague underlines this fact in a recent interview:

> The current hype about 'artistic research' cannot be fully understood without taking into account the higher education reforms now occurring all over continental Europe. Consistent with the Bologna process and the establishment of three-cycle structure (bachelors, masters, doctorate), 'research' has been introduced into areas of higher education that used to focus mainly on professional training. 'Research' has now become a central task in former polytechnics, *Fachhochschulen* and universities of applied sciences, including (in most countries) institutes of higher arts education.
>
> Not everywhere in Europe do people feel comfortable with this, in some quarters – for instance in Germany – there is still strong opposition to 'Bologna'. The issue is whether Bologna, and the introduction of research, is a dictate and threat coming from outside art and arts education, or whether it is a chance and a challenge for art and arts education. My assessment is that introducing artistic research enables a free space to be created within arts education for what might be called 'material thinking'.
>
> (Borgdorff 2009b)

The general picture of European art school after the first years of the Bologna process has been described in a document published by the *'inter}artes' thematic network*:

> The overall picture of higher arts education in Europe shows that a large variety of universities and professional training institutions, as well as independent academies, delivers Higher Arts Education that leads to similar levels of qualifications, regardless of whether it is delivered in a professional or academic institution. Most institutions providing higher arts education have now implemented a 2- or 3-cycle structure, with a 3- or 4-year Bachelor's degree and a 1-, 1½- or 2-year Master's degree. This does not necessarily mean that the clarity and transparency has increased.
>
> In some countries as well as in some arts disciplines, such as Dance, Higher Arts Education is not (yet) entitled to deliver Masters' programmes and/or third cycle programmes, which will lead to persisting problems of mobility and comparability of qualifications. Some arts institutions, delivering similar qualifications as other institutes, have no higher education status and in some countries arts institutes are accountable to their Ministry of Culture, rather than to their Ministry of Education, which leads to very different

structures and regulations. Although arts institutions have taken significant steps, the full implementation of the 3-cycle system in arts institutions in the Bologna signatory countries has yet to be fully realised.

(ELIA 2008a)

Whether this system will be fully realized in the near future is an open question. The opposition to the Bologna process has been particularly strong in the art schools in Germany. The leaders of these institutions (*Kunsthochschulrektorenkonferenz*) issued a statement in 2005 in which they reiterated their previously expressed opposition. They underlined the fact that arts education is neither '*modulisierbar*' (possible to express in terms of modules) nor '*standardisierbar*' (possible to standardize). The opposition has led some German regional governments to exempt the art schools from the general Bologna degree pattern.

On the other hand it seems that some of this opposition has been muted over the last couple of years under the influence of the wider European debate. The *Universität der Künste* (University of the Arts) in Berlin is but one example of developments with a direct bearing on the third cycle of the Bologna Process. The recently started Graduate School for the Arts and Sciences within this university is devised with reference to the new structures. It is intended to serve as an interdisciplinary platform. The graduate school will be open to artists from all fields and to PhD students from the humanities (such as art history, musicology, cultural studies) as well as – in co-operation with other universities and research institutions – the natural, engineering and life sciences. It will therefore comprise both a research-oriented cluster and an arts-oriented cluster.

Still, the reluctance to introduce some kind of a special research degree in the arts is resisted in many quarters.

An important role in the process of European cooperation between art schools has been played by the European League of Institutes of the Arts (ELIA). It is an independent membership organization representing approximately 350 higher arts education institutions from over 45 countries and founded in 1990. ELIA represents all disciplines in the arts, including architecture, dance, design, fine art, media arts, music and theatre.

ELIA has been an important forum for discussion and support among art schools when it comes to implementing the Bologna process. It has also taken action together with the Association Européenne des Conservatoires, Académies de Musique et Musikhochschulen (AEC). In a joint position paper in 2005 these two organizations emphasized the importance for the European cultural sector that professional training in the arts is recognized at first, second and third cycle higher education levels in all countries. A problem in this context is that in some European countries arts institutions and disciplines have no higher education status. This creates obstacles to mobility, recognition of studies, qualifications and quality assurance procedures at European level, resulting in negative effects on the employability of arts graduates.

With regard to research in the arts ELIA has taken the initiative of reviewing the situation in a number of countries. Summing up the European scene in 2005 ELIA found that a significant number of institutions were in the process of establishing research teams and research centres within which larger projects are being developed, often with a combination of funding and support in the form of external assignments and contracts. In this process many institutions have also developed a research infrastructure, policy and strategy with identifiable and accessible outcomes enabling them to take advantage of their national contexts and identifiable areas for supporting research through funding bodies.

By underlining the important role of the funding bodies ELIA pointed at a crucial issue for the future of artistic research. From where will the necessary funds come? From government sources, research councils or from third party contract? Plus – an equally important question: what type of research is worth funding?

Research and the 'creative industries'

A Google search on the combination of the terms 'creative industries' and 'research' yields some 575,000 hits (January 2010). This is an indication of the fact that the creative industries are seen increasingly as important factors in the national and international economy.

In the United Kingdom the mapping of the creative industries started as a political initiative in the late 1990s. Other countries swiftly drew inspiration from this exercise and the subsequent discussion focussed on ways and means to enhance the competitiveness of arts and design through research and development activities. The growing economic impact of the creative industries was subsequently used as an argument for the funding of research in and through the arts.

A number of universities worldwide have created some form of research unit in this field, particularly in the UK, Australia and New Zealand. Some of these units are oriented towards the business sector; others are initiatives promoted by regional councils or local authorities with the aim of providing new job opportunities. Even so there is, in many cases, room for research and development projects involving the fine and performing arts.

Just to take one example: the Auckland University of Technology in New Zealand has established a Creative Industries Research Institute, a hub which weaves together the many creative strands running through the Faculty of Design and Creative Technologies. According to the university the aim is to create a focal point for collaborative research and practice between the varied areas of expertise, encourage excellence and promote the innovation that is core to many of the creative industries. The definition of 'creative industries' is a very wide one, as can be expected in a university of this kind with its particular focus on the interaction of technologies and design. However, a Centre for Performance Research is also part of the Institute which was set up in 2007.

Switzerland is another country in which practice-based research in the arts is partially linked to the creative industries. This was underlined by the Rector of the Zürcher Hochschule der Künste, Hans-Peter Schwarz, in a conference speech in 2008. He noted that the discourse on the creative industries has been mixed with the debate on arts-based research over the past few years. Representatives of the art schools have increasingly tended to make this connection as a way of legitimizing the developing research activities. He envisaged that this line of argument will be even stronger in the wake of the international financial crisis and particularly in Switzerland this utilitarian approach for education in the arts has been fundamental because of the fact that it has been by and large privately organized.

The 'utilitarian approach' towards education in the arts is very obvious in a recent report published by the European Commission (Directorate-General for Education and Culture) with the title 'The Impact of Culture on Creativity'. The report has this to say about art schools in the European Union and their contribution to the goals of a culture of creativity:

> Art schools exist in all EU Member States and provide programmes including music, dance, fine arts, design, theatre, film, crafts, new media, fashion and architecture. The key common point of all those disciplines is that they enable students to develop their creative potential by teaching them a wide range of artistic, technical, professional and personal skills … Creativity is a skill that features in all learning of arts disciplines provided by art schools. The reason why art schools particularly nurture creativity lies in the way art is learned and taught. The modes of teaching consist of promoting critical reflection, innovation, and the ability to question orthodoxies.
>
> (KEA 2009)

An important characteristic of arts education is that students are best able to connect with their education through practice-based learning and experimentation. Divergent thinking, improvisation and experiential learning are mainstays of all education that takes place in art schools. Fine arts graduates' work processes are akin to the notion of interpretive innovation, involving collaborators across sectors, industries and disciplines. Dance and theatre, for example, are usually taught as part of a multi-disciplinary environment (such as the ability to perform in public and present and control the body) that can become transferable skills (e.g. communication, the ability to work effectively as a member of a team, risk-taking). The study shows that such skill sets are valued in other working contexts such as the creative, managerial and entrepreneurial ones.

Oddly enough, the report has very little to say about the role of research if art schools are supposed to deliver these types of skills to society. This may be due to the peculiar fact that higher education and research are separated phenomena in the context of the European Commission. The EU research policy has after all historically been focussed on 'hard' scientific research related to technological development and industrial output.

It would, however, not be surprising if art schools throughout Europe were to take the main conclusions of this report as an argument for better funding of arts-based research in the future.

Quality assurance and research funding

Practice-based research in and through the arts may sometimes be easy to accept in theory by the wider academic community. More problems arise when it comes to quality assurance, peer-review procedures and research funding. These problems can be encountered on both the national and the institutional level.

A pioneering role with regard to quality assurance and the subsequent research funding has been played by the United Kingdom and the Research Assessment Exercises (RAE) instituted by the funding agencies. The RAE has had an enormous impact on the entire system of higher education in Britain. This comprehensive evaluation process was started already in 1987 and has been performed at regular intervals with the two latest exercises in 2001 and 2008.

A number of review panels look at the results of various subject areas. In 2008 there were 15 main panels and 67 sub-panels. As well as reviewing a great number of pieces of research work submitted for assessment, panel members assessed the research environment and esteem indicators in each submission. In the latest review one of the panels was in charge of the following subjects: Art and Design; History of Art, Architecture and Design; Drama, Dance and Performing Arts; Communication, Cultural and Media Studies; Music.

The outcomes of the evaluations expressed on a five-point scale, are the basis for subsequent research funding. The 2001 RAE resulted in the allocation of 3.6 per cent of all basic research funding to artistic institutions or departments.

It is obvious that the quality assurance mechanisms in place in the United Kingdom have been instrumental over the last decade in enhancing the quality of the research in the arts. They have also contributed to raising the awareness in a wider academic community about the existence of this particular field and its legitimacy in terms of generally accepted academic standards.

The quality assurance schemes in some European countries have been influenced by the UK example. At the same time the intra-European co-operation on quality assurance in general has been a driving force behind developments in other countries. An example of this is the Irish quality regime now managed by the Higher Education and Training Awards Council (HETAC). In 2005 the *National Guidelines of Good Practice in the Organisation of PhD Programmes in Irish Universities* was published (IUQB 2005) and a second version is now under review. This document is a good example of a systematic approach to questions of quality assurance in this field based on respect for the specific problems of assessment in the artistic field.

In the Irish document the core issues pertaining to the provision of arts practice-based research degree programmes are summarized under the following headings:

- understanding practice-based research in the arts and contextualizing it;
- qualifications and programme structures;
- the challenges of supervision;
- the research environment;
- the presentation of the research and assessment;
- towards a code of good practice;
- the economic dividend: current performance and future potential.

A Swedish group charged with the evaluation of a number of research projects took a thorough look at the usefulness of the British RAE approach in a report a few years ago but concluded that it was not applicable in this particular Swedish case. It stressed the problem of applying one national scheme in another country. According to the group

> evaluation methodology in this area may be said to be at the same tentative experimental stage as the development of the paradigm (if it may be described as such) of artistic research, or not even there.
>
> (Karlsson 2007: 163)

The thick manual entitled *RAE 2008. Panel criteria and working methods: Panel O* for the arts and cultural spheres that the British RAE (Research Assessment Exercise) issued in 2006 is a rigorous, detailed schedule that is impossible to apply, since our university systems are so dissimilar (RAE 2006). Other difficulties are that language and terminology for quality assessments in the artistic research category are lacking, and that the university colleges of fine arts, and practitioners themselves, only reluctantly commit such assessments to paper.

Although Sweden has quite a rigorous quality control regime in place, it has so far not covered the evaluation of research in institutions and departments on a regular basis. It has been up to the Swedish Research Council or other national bodies to assess the quality of research. In the case of externally funded research in the arts this was done in 2007 when the already mentioned international group of experts were commissioned with a review of the research projects in the creative and performing arts which had been funded by the Research Council since 2001.

I have personally had some experience of the debate on the national level in Sweden over the last few years and I may be excused for presenting in some detail the problems encountered in quality assessment and research funding in this country

The background is to be found in a research policy bill back in the year 2000 when the Swedish government decided to set aside special funds for research in and through the arts. The money was allocated to the Swedish Research Council with a mandate to distribute the support according to normal procedures for the funding of research projects. An annual budget of some 20 million Swedish crowns (approximately 2 million euros) was allocated. The Council set up a special expert panel to review and assess the projects submitted from the art schools.

This committee in turn reported to a wider body of researchers from the entire area of humanities and social sciences. As expected, conflicts arose rapidly with regard to the quality of the artistic projects. Professors and teachers from established academic disciplines looked with some suspicion at the funding of projects that they had problems in judging based on their conventional academic experience.

It is easy to understand the tensions that arose between the proponents of artistic research and the representatives of well-established subject areas. It must be admitted that some of the projects financed by the special committee for artistic research (and I was one of the members) were not always scrutinized in a way similar to that which people in the academic community were used to.

One of the most obvious problems was the question of peer review. Who are the peers in a research area that is just developing and where outside expertise is difficult to find? What criteria can be used for assessing projects in subjects as diverse as dance, painting and architecture? In order to avoid some of the problems the committee decided to allocate money to clusters of researchers from traditional academic subject areas and art schools (so-called *collegia*). The optimistic presumption was that these groupings would be natural meeting points for the development of methods and research strategies. If universities are the centres of dialogue and discussions, why wouldn't the intellectual discourse between artist and researchers yield exceptional results?

In the subsequent evaluation of this process the evaluators were critical with regard both to the construction and the outcome of this form of initial funding of the new research field. They noted that the primary strategy for support for and development of the area of artistic R&D had not been understood and complied with by the collegia, intentionally or for other reasons. They also suggested that the actual basic idea, as such, was conventional and fruitless:

> This is because as conceived by us it was based on the hope that organised *encounters* between Art and Science would bring about the creative environments that would result in a corpus of texts and other results. Several of the collegia have pointed out that the collegium model lacks solid support among the university colleges of fine arts, and that the 'encounters' between Art and Science are based on dichotomies that tend to lock the status quo instead of promoting the emergence of a new research field on its own terms.
>
> (Karlsson 2007: 164f.)

The judgement is probably true. But one of the reasons for the strategy to give grants for encounters between artistic researchers and the traditional academic community was to pre-empt the criticism coming from the representatives of established research areas. This in turn indicated that the idea to allocate funds for practice-based artistic research under the structure of a research council for humanities and social sciences was mistaken in the first place, at least as long as suspicion is palpable on both sides of this research divide.

The prevailing suspicion, which is closely linked to the assessment of quality in practice-based research, has been wisely commented upon by Henk Borgdorff:

> A pressing, but less widely debated, issue is the assessment of quality in artistic research. It is pressing because a sometimes understandable scepticism exists in both the art world and academia about the results of such research – either the art produced or the justification of the knowledge gained. More particularly, if the artistic outcomes of the research should fall short of what counts as worthwhile and meaningful in the art world, artistic research would lose its rationale; one would then be justified in asking what the point of the whole enterprise is. This scepticism is fuelled by experiences with artistic PhD research projects over the past 10 years or so, which have not always been convincing, to put it mildly. This threat to artistic research is even more critical than the scepticism from within academia, where one might expect some resistance anyway (as the emancipation process of other research domains in the history of science has shown us).
>
> (Borgdorff 2009b)

In their closing remarks the Swedish evaluators recommended the building of bridges between the colleges of fine arts and the closely related arts disciplines, the purpose being to eliminate once and for all the misunderstandings and distrust that prevail between them. This distrust seemed to have increased, rather than decreased, since support for artistic R&D was introduced:

> Progressive development of artistic research is possible only if there is collaboration with the closely related artistic disciplines, and both parties

have everything to gain from a mutual exchange. Unless artistic R&D can be accepted as a research field in its own right, with an earmarked annual budget and ... independent status ... our conclusion is that a different public agency or principal for artistic R&D support should be considered.

(Karlsson 2007: 166)

It is interesting to compare the experiences from Sweden with those of neighbouring Norway. In the latter country artistic research was brought to the university agenda at a later stage and another type of support scheme for the new research area was devised. This was a programme for research fellowships in the arts.

The objective of the Norwegian programme is that the chosen research fellow shall produce an independent work of art at a high international level and simultaneously study theory and method in depth in order to acquire greater knowledge in his/her own field. Through the three-year programme, the research fellow is supposed to receive training in communicating and teaching at a high level. The aim is not to imitate the research training programmes that lead to a doctoral degree.

The question of degrees, which is a hot issue in some other countries, has thus been left aside. On the other hand it is clearly stated that completion of the programme with a satisfactory result confers associate professor competence on the basis of the artistic qualifications for appointment to teaching and research positions at Norwegian universities and university colleges.

The Norwegian model has obvious advantages compared to the Swedish scheme in the sense that it is an independent programme separated from the normal research council structure in the country. The tensions between 'old' and 'new' research traditions have thus been relaxed. Also, by distinguishing the Norwegian fellowships from traditional doctoral training, the discussion around the artistic doctorates and regular PhDs has been avoided.

This does not mean that fellow Norwegians will escape a very rigorous scrutiny of their produced work when the three-year period is over. Apart from the artistic project, a critical reflection must be presented and documented. In this the candidate must justify:

- personal professional perspective/work in relation to chosen subject area nationally and internationally;
- how the project contributes to professional development of the subject area;
- critical reflection on process (artistic choices and turning points, theory applied, dialogue with various networks and the professional environment etc.);
- critical reflection on results (self-evaluation of the revised project description);
- the results of the critical reflection must be available to the public and durable in character. The researcher can, however, choose the appropriate medium and form.

The Norwegian model, in which the successful researcher will be granted eligibility for certain teaching posts is an interesting feature. There has been a debate in some countries about the relation between teaching posts in art schools and the formal research training. Will professors in art schools in the future be judged upon their artistic or their more academic skills? Will the emergence of a generation of artistic PhDs lead to an 'academic drift' that prevents the promotion of otherwise outstanding artists to become teachers of painting and music?

This is indeed a question that goes to the heart of the discussion around university policies and practice-based research. So far we have not seen the conflict arise in cases of the recruitment of professors or other teachers in the art schools. But it will probably not be long before this tension will be shown in some countries where the number of people who have undergone research training or been part of fellowship programmes is steadily growing.

There are some similarities between the Norwegian programme and the Fellowships in the Creative and Performing Arts scheme established by the Arts and Humanities Research Council in the UK. The aims of these fellowships are:

- To support artists who have not had the opportunity to carry out a significant programme of research at post-doctoral level within a research environment, and who would benefit from time to pursue a sustained programme of high quality practice-led research within the creative and performing arts. The artist's own creative/performance practice must be integral to that research.
- To enable artists to develop their research careers by working in a research environment, and by improving their research skills, including developing their knowledge and understanding of advanced research methods.
- To encourage and nurture the development of new or existing research environments and cultures within the host organization through supporting the work of individual artists.
- To maximize the value of the creative and performing arts by promoting their dissemination of research outcomes and where appropriate, to facilitate the knowledge transfer of those outcomes, both to the research community and to other contexts where they will make a difference.

In order to be eligible for funding under the fellowships scheme the research questions or problems, the outputs and – most importantly – the research methods, must involve a significant focus on the applicant's practice as distinct from history or theory. The proposed research should also be placed within an appropriate context of research.

According to the rules established by AHRC the proposed work must have a clear research focus which distinguishes it from work which is purely a development of an individual's professional practice. It should further aim to illuminate or bring about new knowledge and understanding in the discipline.

The applicant is supposed to demonstrate his or her postdoctoral standing. An important feature of the programme is, however, the clear distinction between a postdoctoral standing and the PhD. As explained in the funding guidelines:

> This does not mean that you must have a doctorate, as long as your CV demonstrates that you have equivalent experience that would prepare you for undertaking research at post-doctoral level. For example, if you are able to

demonstrate significant achievements in your area of work such as research/ critical enquiry resulting in performances or exhibitions at home or abroad. If you are already studying for a PhD (full-time or part-time), it is expected one year will have elapsed between completing your PhD (that is, submitted your thesis and passed your oral examination) and taking up appointment as a Fellow.

(AHRC 2009: 25)

The AHRC fellowship scheme is thus not intended to continue or extend research carried out in a PhD. Those who already have a PhD in a related area to the proposed Fellowship need to make clear in their proposal how the programme of research for which they are seeking funding is distinct from the PhD.

A further example from Europe is the newly establish Austrian programme, initiated by the FWF – Fonds zur Förderung der wissenschaftlichen Forschung – Austria's central agency for research funding. In the summer of 2009 it sent out its first call for applications to the 'Program for Arts-based Research (PEEK)', an initiative of the Austrian Federal Ministry of Science and Research (BMWF). The total sum for this first round of applications is 1.5 million euros. The target group is described as 'any person engaged in arts-based research who has the necessary qualifications'.

The programme document describes the background and aim of PEEK:

There is a variety of terms currently used in English to identify the kind of research that the Program for Arts-based Research (PEEK) seeks to support. By adopting the term 'arts-based research', the Program associates itself with those approaches to research known variously as 'artistic research', 'practice-based research' and 'practice-led research'. However, the use of terms of this kind varies between the arts disciplines that this Program intends to cover, as well as between countries in which some project partners may be based. While it is expected that investigation into art itself will be central to the projects that the Program funds, the term 'arts-based research' has been adopted in order to indicate that the relationship to artistic practice can be of various kinds.

(PEEK 2009: 3)

All artistic productions are based on the work and the creativity of artists who apply artistic methods and skills to particular forms of artistic expression. The focus of the PEEK is different: the production of artistic knowledge that is accompanied by reflection and so leads to an increase and advancement in society's knowledge. It is aimed at supporting arts-based research in this sense.

The following goals for this support scheme have been set:

- Support high quality and innovative arts-based research in which artistic practice is integral to the inquiry.
- Increase research capacity, quality and international standing of Austrian arts-based researchers.
- Increase both public awareness and awareness within the academic and the arts communities of arts-based research and its potential applications.

Projects funded by PEEK (for a maximum of 36 months) will take place at various institutions in Austria, primarily at arts universities. Because of their available infrastructure, university and some non-university institutions can offer artists the possibility of undertaking arts-based research in appropriately supportive environments. However, the lack of appropriate funding mechanisms has meant that these possibilities have been insufficiently exploited. To ensure the exceptional quality of the projects within the programme, close ties to high quality art institutions will be expected, whether applicants are associated with universities or non-university institutions.

Any person engaged in arts-based research who has the necessary qualifications is entitled to apply. The applicant must give proof of the project's infrastructure, (connection to an appropriate university or non-university institution in Austria, so that the necessary documentation, capacity support and quality of the results are ensured). No particular academic title is needed. Interestingly enough Austrian citizenship is not required, which makes this programme truly international in its scope.

The expert panel that will review the projects is also truly international with members from Denmark, Finland, France, Sweden and the United Kingdom. At the time of writing the application period is still open and final results of the quality assessment will be known some four months later.

The examples given above from countries like Austria, Sweden, Norway and the United Kingdom indicate some of the developments related to funding schemes, quality assessment and funding in a European context.

On the other side of the globe, in Australia, funding of arts-based projects seems to be a bit problematic. Jacqueline Martin describes the situation in an article published in the yearbook for artistic research 2009 from the Swedish Research Council. She notes that the higher education sector in the country has been subjected to numerous reviews over the past ten years or so, mostly to do with the allocation of Commonwealth funding to the country's 37 universities. These reviews have brought about major upheavals in the day-to-day balance between teaching and research. Artistic research has suffered more than research in other faculties, since it has struggled to be recognized as legitimate and thus entitled to the same funding support as other more scientific faculties:

> In Australia each individual university is subject to a 'research quota'. The Australian Research Council (ARC) has strict constraints on the number of points that may be allocated for monographs, book chapters etc. It has taken a long time for arts practice – or practice-led-research – to be acknowledged as worthy of 'research points'. These points are of monetary value, as well as giving researchers credit that enables them to obtain promotion at their respective universities.
>
> (Martin 2009)

Funding from the ARC is thus a problem. A second funding source is the Australia Council for the Arts, which supports projects of high artistic value. The problem, though, is that this council does not fund university research, except in some cases where the topic is in line with its own research priorities. The result of the policies of these two funding councils is thus a 'catch 22'-situation where the individual researcher has problems securing funding for projects that cross established boundaries between the research and arts communities.

Coming back to Europe, the general situation with regard to these problems was summed up in ELIA's strategy paper, published in May 2008:

> In common with all higher education in Europe, arts education is subject to increasingly complex internal and external assessment and has to meet stringent requirements. National and European funding councils use standards for quality and for transparency of artistic research that are not necessarily different from the sciences. In order to be successful, the level of credibility of artistic research is often required to be of similar significance as the sciences. The increasing importance of artistic research and development should also open possibilities for European funding of artistic research in a cross-national context. The European Research Area, which aims to create free circulation of researchers in Europe in all scientific fields, also has great relevance for artistic research.
>
> (ELIA 2008b: 1)

The last sentence may be more of a pious dream than reality. So far research policy makers on the European scene have shown very little interest in including the creative and performing arts in the concept of the European Research Area. The report from the European Commission on the creative industries only underlines this attitude when it totally neglects the research side. In a situation of recession where politicians eagerly grasp for solutions and funds for industrial and economic revival there is little hope for additional funding for any type of research that cannot be defined as 'useful' in a more narrow sense.

Degree-awarding powers

The problem of degree-awarding powers in relation to artistic research has two aspects. One is the actual right to award research degrees, the other is the question of what degree to award.

The ELIA 2004–2005 survey 'Research in and through the arts' (ELIA 2006b) showed that artistic research and third cycle degrees are defined differently within the Higher Arts Education and professional arts sectors across Europe. In a subsequent strategy paper from ELIA published in 2008, it was noted that the inclusion of the third cycle in the Bologna process has had a significant impact on Higher Arts Education and the conditions for developing research:

> In most countries – with some exceptions – Higher Arts Education Institutes are authorised to award third cycle degrees or develop third cycle programmes in collaboration with universities.
>
> (ELIA 2008b: 1)

In countries where art institutions do not have the right to award third cycle degrees the quest for such a right seem to have prompted a number of schemes for mergers of institutions. Arts colleges have merged with other colleges in order to gain the critical mass necessary. Other colleges have joined universities or signed co-operation agreements with regard to research training.

My own country, Sweden, may be one of these exceptions, at least when it comes to the right for art schools to award research degrees (Switzerland is apparently another example). A few paragraphs about the Swedish scene may be of interest since the problems raised in this country are of a general nature.

The problems of degree-awarding powers in Sweden have been related to the varied status of art schools in the country. The schools in Stockholm are generally old, regarding themselves as rather prestigious. Some of them are quite small but they all enjoy institutional autonomy. The schools in the two other major cities, Göteborg and Malmö, form parts of larger universities, the University of Göteborg and Lund University, respectively.

Universities have traditionally had the right to award doctoral degrees as a matter of course. This historical fact was confirmed in university reforms in the 1990s when the right to award research degrees became an option for university colleges throughout the country if they had a proven track record of research excellence in a given area of research. The condition to prove excellence in research before being given the right to award research degrees is of course difficult to achieve in an emerging research area.

The schools affiliated to universities have, on the other hand, been able to profit from the general licence to award research degrees given to universities and similar research institutions. Dynamic environments for research in the arts and formal research training have therefore been established in Göteborg and Malmö. A considerable number of doctorates have been awarded in these art schools whereas the schools in Stockholm have been left behind.

Recent legislation has, however, changed the landscape. The right to award research degrees could no longer be taken for granted even in universities. More stringent rules for quality assurance will be applied in the future. A university that fails to fulfil quality criteria in research assessments may be deprived of the right to award degrees in specific areas.

What will the consequences be for practice-based research in the arts in Sweden? It is yet too early to foresee what will happen. It may become easier for the schools in Stockholm to pass a quality test and be eligible to award doctorates and it may simultaneously become more difficult for the schools in Göteborg and Malmö to continue with business as usual.

An added circumstance is the fact that the government has introduced a special research degree for the creative and performing arts. The 'old' PhD will be reserved for research in traditional academic disciplines and it will be supplemented with the new doctoral degree, which will be defined in distinctive terms related to the practice-based research. This means, for example, that the statutes for the 'artistic doctorate' will avoid the word 'thesis' but rather talk about a 'documented artistic research project'.

According to the government, an important motive for the establishment of a special doctorate in the field of creative and performing arts is to allow research in this field to be based on purely artistic grounds.

Would this in the long run be seen as a wise decision? That remains to be seen. On the wider European scene there are voices who would argue that it is counterproductive to perpetuate and reinforce the divide between artistic research and research in other academic disciplines. Henk Borgdorff from the Netherlands is one of them (Chapter 3).

> Yes, I am a strong supporter of research in the arts and, yes, I think there are good reasons to maintain that artistic research differs in some respects from other academic research traditions. But with equal emphasis I argue that artistic research must have a place in academia, whether at universities or art schools (if there is still a distinction). That does not mean that no tension exists in the relationship between artistic research and academia. That tension could be a productive tension, however. I have written more about that elsewhere. The introduction of artistic research into academia might even modify our perception of what the university or the academy actually is.
>
> As for the PhD versus professional doctorate discussion, I am in favour of the 'inclusive' model. That is, to avoid an unnecessary proliferation of titles (PhD, DMA, DFA and other doctoral degrees), I argue for one single degree for the third cycle in Europe: the PhD. That degree would no longer be an indication of having successfully completed a specific kind of research training programme, but a manifestation of a level of competence, irrespective of its domain and with due regard for the specific nature of the research objects, claims and methods that are prevalent in the domain in question. The entire spectrum from theoretical research to design research, from the natural sciences to classical studies, from dentistry, food quality management and civil engineering to theology, fiscal law and creative arts, could all be encompassed in that PhD degree.
>
> (Borgdorff 2009b)

According to Borgdorff, institutions might be satisfied for the time being, and for strategic reasons, if they were to be given the right to award a professional doctorate, but in due time that would inevitably lead to undesirable inequality and to a reinforcement of the outdated divide between thinkers and doers. A professional doctorate might somehow seem right for researchers who are inclined to compare their research in the arts to endeavours such as technical, applied research or design research. On the other hand, those who would stress the relationship to critical theory or cultural studies research would feel more at home with a PhD.

Concluding remarks

As shown above, practice-based research in the arts is a field that has seen a rapid development over the last few decades. This is mostly due to the emancipation of art schools as full members of the academic community. In an environment where research is the base for education and training, the pursuit of new knowledge and understanding is of paramount importance in all academic fields.

Higher education policies, nationally and internationally, have played an important role in this context. In some cases comprehensive reforms have led to the integration of art schools in the system of higher education. Other developments have been triggered by reforms on the supranational level. The Bologna process with its three cycles have led to a minor revolution in the higher education landscape in Europe, affecting not least the schools of arts in participating countries.

Still, research in and through the arts is not universally accepted as a research field in its own right. Several reasons could be mentioned in order to explain this non-acceptance. One of them is the initial quality of practice-based research. Some of the earliest examples of doctoral work in the arts was simply not of an acceptable standard, a fact which has contributed to suspicion from the rest of the academic community.

This phase of trial and error should be over by now. The research field has entered a stage of maturity. Policy documents for good practice and more rigorous quality assurance regimes in many countries have helped to shape deeper respect for doctoral training and research activities in art schools. It is imperative that those who are responsible for research training and quality assessment continue to develop standards and methods in order to increase the respect for this field from other actors in the community of scholars and researchers.

In some countries practice-based research is obviously not high on the agenda in terms of university politics or research strategies. This may be due to a philosophical climate where art is detached from a scientific discourse or where art schools are seen as objects of cultural rather than educational policies. Intellectual reflections on art and practice in the arts are certainly very visible in these countries but not really defined in terms of research. The same is true for countries that lack the European tradition of national higher education systems dependent on political decisions.

In countries where artistic research is part of the university landscape some problems remain to be solved. One of them is funding. If this research is competing for scarce resources with other and more established fields, chances are that art schools will be the losers unless special earmarked funds are set aside. In the shaping of national policies lessons can be learnt from the different models employed in some European countries. The advantages or disadvantages of core funding, allocations through research councils or the establishment of fellowship programmes can be taken into account based on recent experiences in various national settings.

It is easy to agree with conclusions drawn by Hans-Peter Schwarz from the Zürcher Hochschule der Künste in a lecture in December 2008: The research funding in arts institutions can't be exclusively project-based. Long-term investments are necessary if art schools are to be transformed from a 'workshop culture' to being future-oriented 'arts research laboratories'.

This transformation does not entail a rejection of classical virtues in arts education. Traditional artistic skills must of course be preserved and developed but they should be placed in an environment of enhanced reflection and analysis.

The creation of a critical mass and the establishment of research environments and graduate schools are also things that need to be discussed based on experiences in a number of countries. The results of networking between art schools nationally and/or internationally can be demonstrated and evaluated. Lessons can be learnt from experiences of multidisciplinary environments involving traditional university departments and artistic institutions. The conditions for success or failure of institutional mergers should be studied.

Another issue to be discussed in this context is the combined problem of degree-awarding powers and quality control. Again, there are a number of national solutions that could be studied and evaluated in order to find a good way forward.

All this points to a need for a continued international dialogue. In Europe, ELIA and similar organizations is certainly a framework for such a dialogue on the institutional level. The challenge is to involve other partners as well: ministries, research councils, university organizations, rectors' conferences. The discourse on contents and methods of practice-based research in and through the arts must in coming years be complemented with a debate on political and administrative solutions to consolidate and further this new area of research.

2

PLEADING FOR PLURALITY: ARTISTIC AND OTHER KINDS OF RESEARCH

Søren Kjørup

One of the worst misfortunes that might hit the budding tradition of artistic research is if it should get squeezed into one single format.[1] Fortunately, the concrete activities that go on around the world under the umbrella of 'artistic research' and related terms like 'arts-based' or 'practice-led' do not show any signs in that direction. Whether they have the status of PhD-studies or not, they are as diverse as one might wish. If there is any common denominator at all, it seems to be that artistic research is any kind of research and development – any kind of production or original use and dissemination of knowledge – that artists make as part of or in connection with their artistic creativity.

As my title makes clear, my present contribution is a plea for plurality, and first of all plurality in concepts and understanding of what artistic research may be and how it should be conducted. Not only will this be the only way of doing justice to what is actually going on in the artistic world and not imposing restrictions for purely formalistic reasons, I also feel convinced that a pluralistic approach that leaves problems of quality and category to a discussion about each research achievement and not its formal setting, will secure the most interesting and diverse results of artistic research. Therefore I am, simply, pleading for a way of understanding artistic research that accepts the plurality and, if necessary, finds ways of defending it. What I am up against, then, is fellow theoreticians (and some practitioners) who want to define some specific kind of activity as the one and only *real* artistic research, and especially those whose reason for this position is their conviction that to be research at all, artistic research must meet the requirements of what they take to be the one and only *real* kind of *scientific* research.

Arguing my point, I plan to go the other way round. Instead of presenting a picture of scientific research to which artistic research might have to comply, I want to argue that 'scientific research' is not just one thing, but many different things – and therefore there is no reason to expect artistic research to be just one thing. And I want especially to introduce a few standard issues, views and concepts from philosophy and from the theory and history of science that suggest this plurality and discuss how they can contribute to a broader understanding of artistic research.

Science in a broad sense

But let us take one important point right away: as most of my readers probably know, not all languages that have such a narrow use of the word 'science' as English: 'Science is the effort to understand how the physical universe works, with observable evidence as the basis of that understanding,' as stated by Wikipedia on the English-language 'disambiguation' page for the concept.[2] In German, the Scandinavian languages and many others, corresponding words – like the German *Wissenschaft* – do not only refer to studies of 'the physical universe', not only to the natural sciences (like physics and biology), but also to formal sciences (like mathematics and formal logic), social sciences (like sociology and anthropology) and the humanities (like linguistics and art history). To avoid too many clumsy expressions like 'the sciences and the humanities', which do not cover the whole scope of *Wissenschaften* anyway, I shall mostly use the simple word 'science' in this broad sense (but I will do my best to indicate that this is the sense I am aiming at). And when I really mean only the natural sciences, I will write 'the natural sciences'.

The issues, views and concepts that I want to introduce are first, the varieties of 'scientific' disciplines and their relations, especially the position of the humanities within the general scientific field; second, the varieties of fundamental research activities, especially the difference between basic research, applied research and experimental development as defined by the OECD for statistical purposes; third, the character and use of definitions and the Wittgensteinian concept of 'family resemblance'; and fourth, the Kuhnian concept of 'paradigms'. After these discussions I will conclude with a flashback to the position of the visual and other arts and sciences in the Renaissance, hoping that this may also throw some light on the situation of artistic research today. But I want to start out here by just sketching four examples of artistic research projects with a few commentaries to suggest some different models that have actually been used (and not in any way trying to be exhaustive or systematic): three PhD-projects but also one example of a project that does not belong to any kind of PhD-program.

Artistic research as the study of creative processes

When I first got involved in the discussion of artistic research in Norway nearly 20 years ago, several of us theoreticians were looking for the special contribution that artists can make to the body of knowledge in the world, and our answer was that it would be natural for artists to study creative processes with their own work as the main example (Kjørup 1993). Our reasoning was that if artistic research is supposed to be different from all other kinds of research, it is natural to focus on the artist as the researcher, and what is specific for the artist is her or his privileged access to her or his own creative processes. You do not have to be an artist to do research *on* art (like art history) or *for* art (for instance developing techniques), but it seems sensible to think some kinds of research *in* art (or *through* creative work in the arts) can only be conducted by artists, to use Henk Borgdorff's later, but well-known twist on Christopher Frayling's even better known categorisation from the 1990s of the main types of artistic research, (Frayling 1993; Borgdorff 2006). And this way of conceiving of artistic research is still alive. You meet it for instance in the preface to the book *Artistic Research: Theories, Methods and Practices* (Hannula *et al.* 2005) where Hans Hedberg and Mika Hannula give this definition of our theme: 'artistic research means that the artist produces an art work and researches the creative process, thus adding to the accumulation of knowledge.' Artists' explorations of their own creative processes are probably pretty rare, however, as suggested by the fact that none of the four interesting examples of artistic research projects that Hedberg and Hannula present in their forth chapter ('Artistic Research in Practice') is of this kind.[3]

I am also still of the opinion that perceptive studies by artists themselves of their own creative processes may be of great both general and professional interest. Let me mention the analysis by Tone Saastad of her own creative work for an exhibition of her printed textiles as an example (Saastad 2007) – the non-doctoral project on my little list.[4] Yet there is good reason to notice a few reservations, not of the actual activity, but of the thinking behind it.

First of all it is an open question how weighty the argument about the privileged access of artists to their own creative processes really is. Somehow the artist has to become both a creative maker and an inquisitive analyst, and it is by no means obvious that whoever is a master in the creative field, is also a master in the analytical one. One natural procedure in that kind of research may be that the artist keeps some kind of log of her or his creative venture, and afterwards analyses the process as it appears from the notes (which is what Tone Saastad has done convincingly) – but should a social anthropologist or psychologist of adequate training and experience not be at least just as qualified as the artist for mastering this part of the task? The immediate answer is of course that the artist knows which experiences, sensations, emotions, etc. are hidden in the necessarily rudimentary notes, but some of that knowledge might just as well come out in interviews with the anthropologist or psychologist. And while the artist undoubtedly is closer when it comes to the tacit knowledge embedded in the process, the researcher may be able to ask questions and spot patterns that escape the artist.

These reservations do not mean that producing an artwork and researching the creative process is not a feasible format for artistic research. And the fact that the specific research part of such a project can be performed by a non-artist, does not make it obsolete either; the question is not who can or who may do the research part, but who actually does so. But this kind of artistic research is certainly not the only one.

Gathering, using and disseminating knowledge as part of the creative process

The Norwegian sound and visual artist Trond Lossius does not analyse his own creative process in his report *Sound, Space, Body: Reflections on Artistic Practice* (Lossius 2007), even though he does tell us about its main steps, drawing on the blog of reflections that he has been maintaining through his three year fellowship.[5] The aim of the project was to produce a series of multi-media installations, some in collaboration with other artists, but the final one, *Cubic Second* (2006), alone. One might describe Lossius' work behind the installations as research *for* art, since he has been experimenting with digital programs and equipment and gathering knowledge from various sources, but he insists (correctly in my opinion) that it is more than that, namely some version of research *in* the arts, in so far as his artistic practice has been 'an essential component of both the research process and the research results' (Lossius 2007: 6).

Trond Lossius has not been conducting research to create results about some theme that should be communicated through his artistic works, but the results of his research are both a prerequisite for his installations and expressed in or through them. In a certain sense, his works 'say' that 'This can be done in this way!' His colleague in the Norwegian fellowship programme, the embroiderer Hans Hamid Rasmussen, however, formulates the aim of his research project, *Homage to the Hybrid*, as 'to look into intercultural experiences and see how they can be expressed through visual art' (Rasmussen 2008: 1). One theme for his research, intercultural experiences, can thus be said to belong outside the specific artistic field, but this – for him very personal – theme is explored through the artistic work, and even though the results are sketched in the (very short) written report that accompanies his embroideries, it is first of all through the embroideries that they are conveyed. Another theme for his research, however, is 'visual art', and he experiments with means of expression within embroidery to develop this medium to convey his findings about intercultural life. One might say that his works not only claim that 'intercultural experiences are like this', but also that 'intercultural experiences may be expressed like this'.

These are both examples of artistic research where the artistic work is the main result and the one aimed at, not, for instance, what is written in the report. The written report is a prerequisite for achieving the degree, but the actual communication of the results of the research is done through the artwork.[6] Most other projects within the same programme, whether within visual arts, music, film, dance or whatever, have the same character (not least because the rules of the programme put up the artistic work as the aim, of course),[7] but I shall not refer to them because their results (or documentation of the results like concerts and exhibitions) are very difficult to get hold of, and most of the writings are not in English.[8]

Other artistic research projects have another weighting of (and connection between) artistic result and writing, and also another use of the verbal medium. Let me just mention what may be considered the main example in the James Elkins-edited issue of *Printed Project* with 'The New PhD in Studio Art' as its theme (Elkins 2005a), the photographer Jo-Anne Duggan's *Beyond the Surface: The Contemporary Experience of the Italian Renaissance*. Duggan does not use the word 'research' about her work in her dissertation with that title, but opens her abstract with the declaration: 'It is the intention of this Doctor of Creative Arts to convey the complexity of viewing art in museums' (Duggan 2003: viii). And she conveys this theme – concentrating, as her title suggests, on great palaces, collections and museums like Palazzo Vecchio, Galleria Doria Pamphili and Palazzo Pitti – through a combination of verbal text, older photographs of museum interiors, etc. and her own photographs. The pictures are joined to the printed text on a CD-ROM, to the PDF-document on the net as interposed pages – but her own photographs have also been exhibited in two exhibitions, 'Before the Museum' and 'Impossible Gaze', and two of the chapters in the dissertation contain her reflections on these exhibitions.

But behind the text and the photographs lies of course a research project where Duggan has not only used her theoretical knowledge of the history of viewing, but also her professional insights into the ways that museums have shown art from the Italian Renaissance, into ways of viewing and into photography (her bibliography covers around 250 entries). And first of all she uses her own photographs as part of her study of the contemporary museum of the art of the Italian High Renaissance (and the way it is seen), namely, she uses her creative work both as a tool in her research and as a tool for the dissemination of her findings.

A study in (one's own) creative processes; experimental development as a prerequisite for artistic results; creative work as a means to interpret own cultural experiences and finding ways of expressing the results; and creative work to study the experience of art in museums then and now: these four examples of artistic research are not easily put into one strictly defined category (and especially not into one that takes the natural sciences as its model) – but why should they be?

Humanities and natural sciences

If we want to understand the current situation of the fairly new artistic research within the broader field of science, it may be elucidating to look at the situation of the humanities in the middle of the 19th Century. A good place to start would be in 1843 when the English economist and positivist philosopher John Stuart Mill (1806–1873) launched his huge work *A System of Logic* and opened its sixth and final 'book' with the remark 'The backward stage of the moral sciences can only be remedied by applying to them the methods of physical science, duly extended and generalised' (Mill 1987 [1843]: 19) – 'the moral sciences' being what was right away translated into German as *die Geisteswissenschaften* ('the sciences of the spirit'), i.e. roughly the social sciences and the humanities. Many humanistic scholars and theoreticians protested against Mill's view of the backward stage of 'the moral sciences', but others followed Mill in claiming that the social sciences and the humanities should imitate the methods of the natural sciences to become real scientific disciplines, obviously on the premise that whatever wants to be recognized as research, has to proceed in the very same way, and that way could only be the one known from physics, first of all. Towards the end of the 19th Century, however, one can distinguish two types of defence of the specificity of the humanities, represented by the *hermeneutic* tradition (with Wilhelm Dilthey as the main spokesman) and the *neo-Kantian* tradition (Wilhelm Windelband), respectively, the first ontological, the second epistemological.

The hermeneutic philosopher Wilhelm Dilthey (1833–1911) claimed that what he and his fellow theoreticians called *die Geisteswissenschaften* simply had to use other methods than the natural sciences because the two types of research were concerned with ontologically different objects: while the natural sciences would conduct research into something that is alien to man, namely nature, the social sciences and the humanities are concerned with man himself (or herself, as we might want to add) and with her or his cultural products (works of art, history, institutions). Dilthey therefore argued that the natural sciences have been forced to design specific methods to investigate its 'dead' subject matter and to give some kind of 'external' *explanations* of what goes on in the world of nature, while 'the sciences of the spirit' might use the researchers' 'empathy' (*Einfühlung*) in human actions and cultural phenomena as a basis for creating some kind of 'inward' *understanding* of them (cf. Dilthey 1991 [1883]).

The neo-Kantian philosopher and historian of philosophy Wilhelm Windelband (1848–1915), however, did not look for the difference between disciplines in the ontology of the *subjects* for research, but for the difference between the *aims* different kinds of sciences (obviously in a broad sense) actually have. The important distinction here was between what Windelband would call (with his own newly invented terms) 'nomothetic' and 'idiographic' sciences, respectively. *Nomothetic* sciences are the ones that search for *general laws* (or at least general knowledge) as most of the natural sciences, and Windelband makes the remark that even a humanistic discipline like history might have an aim like that, so there is no intrinsic differences between disciplines. It is, however, a fact, he maintains, that when we study history (or art, it is tempting to add), we are normally not interested in general laws, e.g. for historical development, but in single events, single periods, single personalities, and the *idiographic* disciplines are the ones that study these subjects in their specificity (Windelbrand 1915).[9]

Several aspects of this historic discussion should be interesting for artistic research today. The most obvious one, of course, is that the humanities, just like artistic research quite often, were met by the idea that there is only one kind of research, and that the only acceptable methods for research are the ones known from the natural sciences. Seeing the historical parallel may encourage us to shrug off the claim and wait for the recognition of the special character of artistic research, just like the humanities have achieved recognition (at least in most circles). But it is also worth at least considering the two different rejoinders, the ontological one and the epistemological one – even though a conclusion may be that none of them will be completely satisfying for our theme, first of all because both take artistic research to be one and only one thing, which of course is unsatisfying for the pluralist.

If we want to claim that artistic research should be left alone to develop its own methods, should the reason be that the *object* of artistic research is something special, or should it be that the *kind of knowledge* artistic researchers want to produce, is different from the knowledge produced in traditional disciplines and not least in the natural sciences? It is indeed tempting to argue that artistic research is research into art, and that art has a special ontological status, different from the physical world studied by the natural sciences – but as we have seen, e.g. in Hans Hamid Rasmussen's project, not all artistic research takes art and the creation of art as it object. And it may be just as tempting to argue that the knowledge produced through artistic research has an idiographic and maybe even special subjective character, alien to the natural sciences. Yet even though the study by Tone Saastad of her own creative process behind one specific work of art (or rather group of works) may indeed be idiographic, we may also be interested in the knowledge produced for nomothetic reasons, i.e. for the insight it gives into creative processes in general – and the 'subjective' point of departure for studies like this should hopefully not make the results unreliable, hence less 'objective'.

So let us not get caught up in the exact criteria discussed by Dilthey and Windelband for maintaining that not all 'sciences' should follow the example of the natural ones. At any rate it should be noticed that Windelband did not claim that all humanistic disciplines are idiographic; he only pointed to historical studies (and could have added at least most of the aesthetic disciplines), but maybe he just remembered that a core humanistic discipline like linguistics looks for general grammatical patterns (not just the way you or I happen to talk), and is therefore nomothetic, not idiographic, breaking up the nice and much too clear distinction between supposedly nomothetic natural sciences and idiographic humanistic ones.

The whole discussion about the status of the humanities should first of all be taken as a reminder that there are many kinds of research with different objects and intentions, and that goes not only for the relationship between artistic other kinds of research, but also between different kinds of artistic research.

Three different interests

In the 1960s the German philosopher Jürgen Habermas tried to escape the then still vigorous positivistic, monolithic understanding of science and scientific methods by formulating a modern version of how one might differentiate between scholarly disciplines, more inspired by Windelband's epistemological trend than Dilthey's ontological one (but also with a hermeneutic element). He distinguished not two, but three types of research according to what he (or rather his translator) called the 'knowledge-constitutive interests' (*Erkenntnisinteressen*) they would try to satisfy, and therefore also the different methods they would have to develop to satisfy these interests (Habermas 1972).

One type of disciplines would satisfy *a technical interest* by producing knowledge that might be used for prediction and control (and the creation or prevention of events); these 'empirical-analytical' sciences, first of all the natural sciences, would therefore typically develop *experimental methods*. Another type, however, would rather satisfy *a practical interest* by creating an understanding of cultural phenomena through studies of texts, that is through *hermeneutic methods*, and these 'historical-hermeneutic' disciplines are obviously first of all the humanities. And finally we have what Habermas calls 'the systematic sciences of action' as economy, sociology and political science. Some of these try to formulate general laws like the natural sciences, but they also have 'critical' varieties with an *emancipatory interest* that through *self-reflective methods* try to find out which laws describe real constituents of social action, and which of them are only expressions of hardened ideological convictions.

Habermas' insistence on the interests behind research procedures can be seen as a blow to a positivistic insistence on impartial objectivity of research: we choose scientific methods out of interests! And of course we do. Research is not just following certain rules, but trying to find answers to questions that we find pressing or interesting, solving urgent problems, creating things we want or need – or just satisfying curiosity. And hopefully we find the relevant methods for solving those problems. But Habermas' insistence on the interests behind research may remind us of the one thing that we more often than not must search for in vain in general and abstract discussions of artistic research, namely statements about the *aim* of these kinds of research. What do we want to know that artistic research will be able to tell us? What do we want to achieve through artistic research?

Looking at the three kinds of knowledge interests that Habermas mentions, it is obvious that much artistic research is guided by a technical interest, while studies in creativity are guided by what Habermas calls a 'practical' interest and uses hermeneutic methods. That art and artistic research can articulate a critical view on man and society, and work for emancipation through self-reflective methods is obvious (here Hans Hamid Rasmussen's project may be a case in point), but my feeling is that Habermas' specific involvement with various kinds of nomothetic social sciences alienates his thinking from the artistic one.

Basic research, applied research and experimental development

One thing is the discussion between philosophers and theoreticians of science (and often also the practitioners themselves) about the character of research. Quite another are the official standards used by huge international organisations when it comes to statistics of a nation's research and related activities. The best known organisation in this field is of course the 'club' of 30 democratic nations with an open market economy (cooperating with another 100 nations that more or less fulfil the criteria), the Organisation for Economic Co-operation and Development, better known as the OECD. To be able to gauge the nations' expenditure on what is here called R&D ('research and experimental development'), the organisation needs some working definitions of what they are looking for, and the latest version of these you can find in the no-less-than-256-pages-long 2002-edition of the so-called *Frascati Manual* (OECD 2002), that carries that name because the first version was sprung from a meeting in Frascati in Italy in 1963.[10]

Fortunately, while the many pages contain lots of technicalities that are of no concern for us, the definitions of R&D are rather concise. The overall definition goes like this:

> Research and experimental development (R&D) comprise creative work undertaken on a systematic basis in order to increase the stock of knowledge, including knowledge of man, culture and society, and the use of this stock of knowledge to devise new applications.
>
> (OECD 2002: 30)

It is worth noticing that for the OECD both the production of new knowledge, and the use of existing knowledge to devise new 'applications' are drawn into consideration. The OECD does not make a fundamental distinction between 'fine' research proper and 'inferior' use of knowledge to solve practical problems.

Research, however, is divided into two categories by the OECD, *basic research* and *applied research*, as we see in this slightly broader account, which also gives a much more comprehensive description of what *experimental development* may comprise:

> Basic research is experimental or theoretical work undertaken primarily to acquire new knowledge of the underlying foundation of phenomena and observable facts, without any particular application or use in view. Applied research is also original investigation undertaken in order to acquire new knowledge. It is, however, directed primarily towards a specific practical aim or objective. Experimental development is systematic work, drawing on existing

knowledge gained from research and/or practical experience, which is directed to producing new materials, products or devices, to installing new processes, systems and services, or to improving substantially those already produced or installed. R&D covers both formal R&D in R&D units and informal or occasional R&D in other units.

(OECD 2002: 30)

Maybe the wording of these definitions is not as clear as one might wish,[11] but that is not the issue here – and the *Manual* actually uses 15 pages to discuss the distinctions between the three activities in detail, admitting that 'Breakdown by type … is usually more easily applied to R&D in the natural sciences and engineering (NSE) than in the social sciences and humanities (SSH)' (OECD 2002: 77), plus no less than 20 pages to discuss borderline cases. What is important, however, is that even the OECD is not caught up in the false view of research that it is just one thing, with just one aim, method, etc. Or maybe one should not say 'even the OECD', but rather suggest that once you are forced to take a bottom-up approach, looking at what is actually going on out there where people do research (so that you – as the case is here – can get it into your statistics), you have to realise the plurality of the field, for instance in such a way that the simple statement about experimental development that it is 'the use of this stock of knowledge to devise new applications' grows to several lines as we just saw above.

It should not be hard to make different kinds of artistic research find their places amongst the three categories (with subcategories), at least if we stretch the formulations a bit in the way the *Frascati* authors have done themselves with the ones for 'experimental development'. Quite a few artistic research projects are examples of development (if not necessarily *experimental* development) in the sense that they use already existing knowledge to devise 'new applications' in the form of works of art (to a large extent like the one by Trond Lossius), while others are a kind of basic research, at least in the sense that they are not intended to solve any practical problems, at least not right away – like the one by Jo-Anne Duggan, although she does also formulate an objective:

> Through examining these museums with their multiple histories and contents I hope to argue for a slower, more considered engagement with art, that encourages the viewer to experience the sensual as well as the intellectual aspects that this opulent environment offers.

(Duggan 2003: viii)

Artistic research, however, is not mentioned in the *Frascati Manual*. Or, to be precise, it is mentioned, but at one place only, and a rather strange place at that, namely as an insertion, looking like an afterthought, in a passage in Table 3.2. 'Fields of science and technology' as part of the enumeration of the humanities (after history and linguistics with subcategories):

> Other humanities [philosophy (including the history of science and technology), arts, history of art, art criticism, painting, sculpture, musicology, dramatic art

excluding artistic 'research' of any kind, religion, theology, other fields and subjects pertaining to the humanities, methodological, historical and other S&T[12] activities relating to the subjects in this group].

(OECD 2002: 67)

It is, indeed, surprising to find artistic research – with 'research' in warning quotes – excluded from dramatic art, of all things, as if that is where it would belong. So let us neglect that. The important thing is that also at a place like the OECD we meet a pluralistic view on what science is, and that the categories of the OECD may invite us to think more deeply also about artistic research.

Definitions

It is a natural thought that not only if we need categories for statistics, but also if we just want to discuss things like research, art and science unambiguously, we need clear definitions of these various items. On the other hand, it should not take too much reflection to realize that it must be impossible to give satisfying *descriptive* definitions of cultural terms like these, i.e. definitions that simply draw the lines in such a way that everything that may correctly be called research, art or science falls within the boundaries of the definitions and everything else is kept outside. You can of course give *stipulative* definitions, stating which way you intend to use the terms for a specific purpose (as the OECD has to do). Or even *persuasive* definitions, that rather common type of stipulative definition where you purport to indicate the 'true' or 'commonly accepted' meaning of a term, while in reality you promote an altered use, perhaps as a justification of some specific view of yours.

Cultural phenomena like research, art and science are simply too diverse to fit into standard descriptive definitions enumerating necessary and sufficient conditions (and some philosophers would even claim that this goes for all phenomena that we talk about in natural languages). That does not mean, however, that it is impossible to formulate sensible elucidations of what research, art or science are all about. The problem is only that we cannot mention one single rule or condition that would not have exceptions.

An example of an element in a definition may be the statement that one criterion for research is that it is the production of *new* knowledge, and new, not just to the researcher, but also to all of her or his peers (or in principle to all of humanity). A very sensible criterion, indeed, that we need to know to be able to grasp the point of research, and that seems to fit in nicely in some more elaborate descriptive definition – yet a criterion that will have absurd consequences in certain extraordinary, yet not unrealistic cases. If you go though all the normal research motions to solve some problem and come up with your own solution that you get published in a peer reviewed journal, and then, a couple of years later, you find out that some hitherto unknown Brazilian colleague of yours had published the solution to the problem already in the 1930s, would you then have to reconsider the genre of your work? Does the emergence of the Brazilian article mean that you had not been doing research after all? (And if not, what had you been doing?)

One more example might be that we cannot understand what art is, if we do not grasp that works of art are products of human creativity, not of natural coincidences.

However, if we put that up as an absolute criterion, what about driftwood as sculpture? (And the answer is that you have to invent stopgap solutions like 'Picking up a stick at the shoreline and taking it to the exhibition, is also a creative act' – which may of course also be true, but is not exactly what was originally intended by the formulation 'products of human creativity'). Or we could use the example that it is normally completely all right to make a distinction between science and religion by claiming that science is based on observation, religion on speculation – but we should not forget what I will here let the Austrian-English philosopher Karl Popper (1902–1994) formulate (and Sir Karl was absolutely not an anarchist in matters of science and philosophy): 'the modern theories of physics, especially Einstein's theory… were highly speculative and abstract, and very far removed from what might be called their "observational basis"' (Popper 1963: 255).

Family resemblance

The fact that we cannot squeeze cultural and many other phenomena into standard descriptive definitions, has been forcefully pointed out by another Austrian-English philosopher, Ludwig Wittgenstein (1889–1951), in §§ 65–78 of his *Philosophical Investigations* (Wittgenstein 1953). His examples are things as supposedly exact as numbers (cardinal numbers, rational numbers, etc.) or as loosely conceived as what Wittgenstein calls 'language games' (various ways of using language in various situations), but his main example of a concept that cannot be pinned down in a descriptive definition, is 'game' (in his original German as *Spiel*, which is somewhat broader than 'game', also covering 'play' – and here I quote most of his §66):

> Consider for example the proceedings that we call "games". I mean board-games, card-games, ball-games, Olympic games, and so on. What is common to them all? – Don't say: 'There *must* be something common, or they would not be called 'games'' – but look and see whether there is anything common to all. – For if you look at them you will not see something that is common to *all*, but similarities, relationships, and a whole series of them at that. To repeat: don't think, but look! – Look for example at board-games, with their multifarious relationships. Now pass to card-games; here you find many correspondences with the first group, but many common features drop out, and others appear. When we pass next to ball-games, much that is common is retained, but much is lost. – Are they all 'amusing'? Compare chess with noughts and crosses. Or is there always winning and losing, or competition between players? Think of patience. In ball-games there is winning and losing; but when a child throws his ball at the wall and catches it again, this feature has disappeared. Look at the parts played by skill and luck; and at the difference between skill in chess and skill in tennis. Think now of games like ring-a-ring-a-roses; here is the element of amusement, but how many other characteristic features have disappeared? And we can go through the many, many other groups of games in the same way; can see how similarities crop up and disappear.
>
> (Wittgenstein 1953: §66)

It is easy to 'translate' this passage into a text about 'research': I mean making chemical experiments, sending out questionnaires, bird watching, interpreting poems, digging for archaeological remains, solving problems in formal logic, gathering astronomical data by way of radio telescopes, and so on. What is common to them all? Don't say: 'There must be something common, or these actions would not be called "research"' – but look and see whether there is anything common to all.

Let us now look at art:[13] I mean sonnets, ready-mades, operas, novels, paintings, films, pantomimes, and so on. What is common to them all? Don't say: 'There must be something common, or these products would not be called "art"' – but look and see whether there is anything common to all.

Now, let us turn to science: I mean statistics, history, philosophy, neurology, semiotics, agricultural science, dramaturgy, political science, glaciology, and so on. What is common to them all? Don't say: 'There must be something common, or these academic fields would not be called "sciences"' – but look and see whether there is anything common to all…

But how do we give the same name to various groups of phenomena, counting them in the same category, if they do not have anything in common? Wittgenstein seeks a solution to this problem by taking his point of departure in the last phrase of my quotation: 'similarities crop up and disappear'; the quote continues 'We see a complicated network of similarities overlapping and criss-crossing: sometimes overall similarities, sometimes similarities of detail.' And in the next paragraph Wittgenstein gives this pattern a name:

> I can think of no better expression to characterize these similarities than 'family resemblances'; for the various resemblances between members of a family: build, features, colour of eyes, gait, temperament, etc. etc. overlap and criss-cross in the same way. – And I shall say: 'games' form a family.
>
> (Wittgenstein 1953: §67)

We might add that this is the same for various kinds of research and research methods, the different arts and the different sciences.

Wittgenstein has been much criticised for his use of the catchy term 'family resemblance', because it does not seem evident that his observation about the criss-cross of physical and psychological traits among members of a family is at all true, not even among the genetically related. But the point is not how much members of families are alike, but whether his point about our use of words and concepts is both correct and illuminating. And that he is not dependent on the specific metaphor of the family, can be gathered from his just as metaphorical remark about how the concept of number develops:

> And we extend our concept of number as in spinning a thread we twist fibre on fibre. And the strength of the thread does not reside in the fact that some one fibre runs through its whole length, but in the overlapping of many fibres.
>
> (Wittgenstein 1953: §67)

Again this is a reflection that we easily recognise from histories of art and aesthetics, and which is just as pertinent when it comes to research and science: cultural phenomena like research, art and science develop through time, not only by adding new features, but also in such a way that old features may get obsolete and may even be contradicted by new ones, yet we can still talk about common traditions.

Prototypes

But if concepts like games and numbers cannot be circumscribed by single descriptive definitions, how can we both learn them and use them and explain them to one another in a reasonably consistent way? Wittgenstein's solution (shared by many others) is that we see something as for instance a game by seeing the similarities between it and some standard example or prototype of a game:[14]

> How should we explain to someone what a game is? If we don't have a common thread running through everything we call a 'game' it seems very chaotic! How on earth do we teach people to use this term 'game'? I imagine that we should describe games to him, and we might add: 'This and similar things are called "games"'.
>
> (Wittgenstein 1953: §69)

And again it is easy to see the parallel to concepts like research, art and science. Explaining what art is, consists in mentioning various artists from different art forms, genres, epochs, etc. and examples of their work, maybe adding 'This and similar things are called "works of art"'. And obviously the same should go for concepts like 'research' and 'science'. But as suggested above, many formulations in theoretical texts that are called 'definitions' are strictly not definitions at all, but exactly these kinds of elucidations, often mixed up with sketches of how the concept has developed and explanations of what the item in case may be used for.

But even such elucidations that avoid the definition trap of trying to do the impossible, may be what we should rather call 'stipulative elucidations' or even 'persuasive elucidations', – elucidations with the aim of narrowing down what sensible artistic research may be, often owing to an overly narrow concept of what is scientific research.

Paradigms

In the theoretical discussion of what artistic research might be, a distinction is often brought forth between what is called 'the scientific paradigm' and artistic research, maybe even 'the artistic research paradigm'. But even though the concept of 'paradigm' may be useful in the discussion, starting out with the premise that there is only one scientific and only one artistic research paradigm, sets the whole discussion on a false track.

Unfortunately, there is no general consensus about what a paradigm is. In this context of epistemology, the concept stems from the American physicist and historian of science Thomas S. Kuhn (1922–1996) and his book on *The Structure of Scientific*

Revolutions, now best known in the enlarged edition with a new postscript from 1970 (Kuhn 1970 [1962]), yet not even within the covers of that book does the concept stand out with just one clear content. As the English Wittgenstein-disciple and computer linguist Margaret Masterman (1910–1986) made clear in her essay on 'The Nature of a Paradigm', Kuhn uses the term in at least 21 different ways (Masterman 1970: 61). The first meaning that Kuhn gives the term in his book, is the etymologically most obvious one (since *paradigma* in Greek means 'example'), namely 'that some accepted examples of actual scientific practice … provide models from which spring particular coherent traditions of scientific research' (Kuhn 1970 [1962]: 10).

In present-day science Kuhn thinks of the large, basic textbooks, but before that genre broke through in the natural sciences in the middle of the nineteenth century, big 'classic' works played this role: 'Aristotle's *Physics*, Ptolemy's *Almagest*, Newton's *Principia* and *Opticks*, Franklin's *Electricity*, Lavoisier's *Chemistry*, and Lyell's *Geology*'. It is already tempting here to make the reflection that each of the natural sciences have and have had several different paradigms – and also that artistic research is still far from having standard textbooks, not to mention classics.

Better known than 'paradigm as example' is a derived meaning of the term, namely the scientific ways of thinking that these standard works exemplify, the traditions they have created and keep alive: 'Ptolemaic astronomy' (or 'Copernican'), 'Aristotelian dynamics' (or 'Newtonian'), corpuscular optics (or 'wave optics'), and so on. Once again it is a presupposition for the concept that there is not only one paradigm of natural science, but many. And this grows to very many if one looks at some of those places where Kuhn writes about the size of the groups that are adherents to or work within a certain paradigm. While the examples so far suggest something like all researchers within a certain field in a certain period (which may stretch through many decades or even centuries), other examples of the original text point in the opposite direction, and the 'Postscript' of 1970 makes it clear that it is not only possible to talk about groups as large as 'all natural scientists', but also of subgroups like all organic chemists or all radio astronomers, down to 'communities of perhaps 100 members, occasionally significantly fewer' – each group gathered around its specific paradigm.

It is therefore safe to conclude that even if we only conceive of science as natural science, we do not have just one, but many different paradigms. And the picture gets even more motley if we do not only consider the natural sciences, but also the social sciences and the humanities, not only physics, chemistry or astronomy, but also anthropology, sociology and economics, and the studies of art and culture, language and history – plus non-empirical disciplines like mathematics and philosophy. One type of science, one paradigm that an eventual specific artistic research paradigm might resemble or differ from, does not exist.

The pre-paradigmatic stage

In his book on scientific revolutions Thomas Kuhn does not only discuss the 'revolutionary' transition from one paradigm to another, but also the situation of a given scholarly discipline before one broadly accepted paradigm imposes itself at all (Kuhn 1970 [1962]: 10–22). In his first treatment of this theme he clearly uses the concept of a paradigm in the sense of a prototype or standard work like the ones mentioned above by Aristotle, Newton, Lavoisier, etc., and his point is that what such works have to offer, is on the one hand 'sufficiently unprecedented to attract an enduring group of adherents away from competing modes of scientific activity,' and on the other 'sufficiently open-ended to leave all sorts of problems for the redefined group of practitioners to resolve' (Kuhn 1970 [1962]: 10). And as I have just clarified, standard works like that do not exist in our artistic field. Artistic research is still a pre-paradigmatic activity.

In his postscript to the second, enlarged edition of his book, however, Kuhn more precisely enumerates four main characteristics of what he now prefers to call 'a disciplinary matrix' (Kuhn 1970 [1962]: 182–7), but what in the tradition after Kuhn is still called a 'paradigm', now nearly always in the sense of a broader disciplinary way of thinking. In this version of Kuhn's theory such a paradigm is determined by a set of first, symbolic generalisations, second ontological commitments, third, values, and fourth examples.

In our connection we can nearly ignore the symbolic generalisations because they are almost only known from Kuhn's own main discipline, physics, namely formulae like $f=ma$ (force equals mass times acceleration) (Kuhn 1970 [1962]: 183). The point in these formulae is that they do not only show the mutual relationship between certain concepts, but also make it possible to treat measurements mathematically. Things like that are obviously completely unknown in artistic research, but the reason why we can only 'nearly' ignore the symbolic generalisations, is their ontological element (for instance the explanation of what 'force' is), which is carried on to the next common element of paradigms, and which is not without importance for artistic research.

Kuhn's examples of the ontological element (which he himself calls 'metaphysical') is inevitably also from physics, namely conceiving heat as kinetic energy or of molecules of gas as tiny elastic balls (Kuhn 1970 [1962]: 184). And obviously, different concepts of what artistic research is – different artistic research paradigms – may be rooted in different assumptions of what kind of reality is explored by the artistic research project in question, and how this reality is constituted (a version of a thought that we met already in Dilthey's defence of the special character of the humanities).

The third element of the paradigm is values, and here Kuhn again first mentions examples from physics, for instance about predictions: 'they should be accurate; quantitative predictions are preferable to qualitative ones; whatever the margin of permissible error, it should be consistently satisfied in a given field; and so on' (Kuhn 1970 [1962]: 185). But he also mentions more general values like 'science should (or need not) be socially useful' – and once again it is easy to find equivalents for artistic research in formulations like that: while some artistic researchers and theoreticians of the field would argue that artistic research should melt into artistic work, others would claim that artistic research should use artistic work or take its point of departure there, but should stand alongside the work (for instance as a written dissertation) and satisfy 'normal research criteria'.

To Kuhn, the most important, nay principal, element of the paradigm is the shared examples, because it is first of all through them that researchers acquire (often only tacit) knowledge about and allegiance to the other elements and come to understand which role they play. And once more: since we do not yet have any generally accepted examples or prototypes of artistic research, the whole field of artistic research is still in a pre-paradigmatic stage. One sign of such a stage, he suggests, is that the contributions to the field most often have the format of 'major works', 'starting from first principles and justifying the use of each concept involved' (Kuhn 1970 [1962]: 19f.). If you look at the more formal contributions to our field, the final writings of PhD students, you can find this observation corroborated, for they nearly always have these introductory chapters on how their authors conceive of artistic research.[15]

The question is, however, whether we should hope and strive for the constitution of just one or, a more probable situation, a few common paradigms within artistic research, or rather be satisfied with the actual pre-paradigmatic stage – or, if the situation turns out to be permanent, should be satisfied with what should maybe rather be called a *non*-paradigmatic stage (which would not mean that artistic research projects could not be described within an adapted version of Kuhn's disciplinary matrix, the way I suggested above).

In the original edition of his book, Kuhn makes the remark that 'it remains an open question what parts of social science have yet acquired [their first universally received] paradigms at all' (1962: 15). One might however argue that Kuhn's picture of periods of 'normal science' with 'puzzle solving' based on a certain paradigm and interrupted by scientific revolutions that introduce new paradigms, needs meticulous adaptation when used outside the natural sciences. In my own book on the humanities I have for instance argued that it is characteristic of humanistic disciplines that partly competing, partly supplementary paradigms can exist side by side within the very same fields in periods of 'normal science', and that this does not mean that the humanities are simply pre-paradigmatic in the sense of immature (Kjørup 2001: 90–5). It might therefore also be natural to expect that artistic research will never live up to Kuhn's picture, but find its own mature format.

For the sake both of the development of artistic research as such and of the theory of this kind of research we must hope that the whole field as soon as possible will reach a stage where we will all settle on a set of standard examples – for imitation, variation, opposition and theoretical analysis and discussion. Compared with other disciplines it is rather surprising that after 10, 20 and at certain places even nearly 30 years of institutional commitment artistic research has not developed any generally known classics and no stars (while the names of a small group of theoreticians have become quite run-of-the-mill).

Rhetoric and academic prestige

Allow me to approach the conclusion of this chapter by posing a few questions:

- Why do we talk about 'pictorial composition'?
- Why did history painting range on top in the classic hierarchy of genres – and why was it called 'history painting'?
- What is the name of the well-known bodily posture that we for instance know from Apollo in classical Greek statuary (one leg stretched, the other bent, shoulders bent etc.) – and why?

Obviously, my questions are rhetorical in the sense that my readers are not really expected to answer them; they are just supposed to make a point. But the point might be said to be rhetorical in another sense, because their common answer is 'rhetoric'.

To answer the questions we have to go back to the early renaissance and to the (successful) attempt by theoreticians of painting to move the visual arts out of the sphere of craft and into a more prestigious sphere, namely the scholarly or academic (Blunt 1940; Baxandall 1971). One of the most important disciplines in the university world at this point was rhetoric, the most important of 'the seven liberal arts'[16] which constituted the official nucleus of university teaching up to the level of bachelor, and as performative practice and pedagogical basis rhetoric was the foundation of any kind of academic activity.

Music already belonged there, since one of the liberal arts was a kind of mathematical harmonics. And poetry joined in by simply being part of the rhetorical field. So if it could be demonstrated that the making of paintings rested on the same theoretical basis as the use of verbal language, painting could be considered as a learned discipline, equivalent to the academic ones.

One of the important academic projects of the early Renaissance was to resurrect classical Latin after the many years through which the antique Roman language had developed into what we now know as the Romance languages (Italian, French, Spanish, etc.), while it was used in more and more simplified versions within the Church and the universities. Cicero's elegant and elaborate way of putting words together, i.e. of *composing* (from the Latin *componere*) words to phrases, phrases to sentences, sentences to paragraphs, etc., was admired and imitated – and Leon Battista Alberti (1404–1472) argued in his book on painting from 1435 that the very same thing happens in painting where elements are assembled into larger wholes (Alberti 1966 [1435]: 68–72). Hence *pictorial composition*.

But according to Alberti, composition is just a means to what he points out as the most important element of the art of painting, namely what he in the Latin version of his book calls *historia*, in the Italian *istoria*, hence *history painting*: 'The greatest work of the painter is the *istoria*' (Alberti 1966 [1435]: 70). And in the tradition this became what rhetorically educated orators would draw on in their speeches making rhetorical allusions and comparisons, i.e. figures and tales from classical antiquity and the Christian tradition.

Finally, the classical posture is of course the *contrapposto*, 'the opposition', conceived as a visual reminder of the base form of rhetoric, the discussion of some topic highlighting the *pro* and the *contra*, the arguments for and against – once again giving visuality a chance of connecting to the rhetorical tradition and in that way giving painting a chance of coming across as a learned discipline.

Learning from history

My reason for taking up this episode from the history of painting is that the early renaissance situation is not unlike the one we have today, and that we may learn from it. Also today artistic disciplines – and now not only painting and music, but also for instance film and various forms of performing arts – try to be accepted as on a par with academic disciplines, such as being part of the Bologna process. And since particularly the educations within the third cycle of the Bologna process, the doctorate level, are research educations, the concept of research has been called up and applied to artistically creative disciplines.

I am not blind to the fact that this way of putting the background for the contemporary discussion about artistic research may sound somewhat ironic, but it is certainly not meant in that way. On the contrary, I am heading for the point that one of the things we may learn from history in this connection is that the renaissance rapprochement from the artistic side to the academic (to such an extent that the new institutions for education in the visual arts that were erected in Europe during the first couple of centuries after Alberti, were called 'academies') did not ruin the artistic field or create institutions alongside it, but on the contrary strengthened it, even on its own premises.

Alberti and his peers did not create completely new artistic activities. They created a specific perspective on already existing activities and promoted some at the expense of others, but they did not promote anything radically new and different. Yet it is obvious that the new perspective in the longer run did have consequences for the direction of the development of art, for instance through the focus on history painting and the founding of institutions that insisted on these perspectives. In this way it also became influential concerning what was expected of those who would get jobs to teach in these institutions.

It is the same pattern we observe today. The focus on the research dimension of creative activities reminds us of the fact that artistic creativity has always presupposed a certain amount of creation or at least retrieval and use of knowledge. One cannot write a history painting without having acquainted oneself in depth with the story one wants to tell and the figures one wants to discuss; one cannot compose a symphony without mastering the symphonic conventions that are handed down and deciding how one wants to make use of them or maybe rather transcend them; and one cannot rehearse a Shakespearean role without analysing the text that one is going to perform. This is certainly not 'Research' with a capital R, but always at least more or less 'systematic work, drawing on existing knowledge gained from research and/or practical experience, which is directed to producing' – in our case – new works of art and design (to partly quote, partly rephrase an excerpt from the *Frascati* definition of 'experimental development').

Questioning quality and craving a canon

I started out by expressing my satisfaction at observing the huge variability in what goes on under the heading 'artistic research', i.e. in the production, use and dissemination of knowledge and insights connected to creative work in art and design. And I hope to have made it clear that any attempt at squeezing artistic research into one single format with reference to 'the scientific method' (in the definite form of the singular) or to one single concept of research, will be a misunderstanding: there are many different kinds of sciences using many different methods to solve many different kinds of research problems.

Pleading for plurality in artistic research when it comes to problems and methods is not the same, however, as neglecting the question of quality. On the contrary, once you let go of the ideal of a small set of formal criteria for what may count as 'real research', you open the doors for a serious and much more interesting discussion about what should be considered *good* research, research that gives us interesting, eye-opening, inspiring, enlightening, fascinating, edifying, uplifting contributions to knowledge and insights that are also well-founded, justified, persuasive.

That discussion, however, is best conducted not in the abstract, but in connection with concrete research contributions. One thing of which my presentation here of a few standard issues, views and concepts from the philosophy of science has reminded us, is the blatant need for some kind of 'canon' of artistic research projects, a stock of commonly known examples of remarkable contributions to this still fairly new tradition, some prototypes to imitate, analyse, criticise or make one's mind up about and use and discuss in other ways. Another deficiency on which I have not had any opportunity to comment, is the absence of a kind of public sphere with means of communication (journals, blogs or the like) for reviews of results of artistic research. May the next wave of contributions to the understanding of the potentials and promises of artistic research not be purely theoretical – like mine here – but take its point of departure from various outstanding examples of arts-based research.

Notes

1 In this chapter I use 'artistic' as short for what belongs to both art and design.
2 1 April 2009. Nearly four months later, on 26 July, the first part of the sentence has been changed to the just as narrow phrase 'Science is the effort to understand how the universe works through the scientific method'.
3 The four projects are: a study of artists' books by the editors of the Swedish art review *OEI*, the Icelandic-Danish Olafur Eliasson's explorations of basic elements of daily life like sun, light, water, soil and wind in his work, British Jacqueline Donachie's inquiry into the illness myotonic dystrophy as basis for her artistic work, and Finnish-American photographer Lisa Roberts' work.
4 I played a supervisory role regarding Tone Saastad's project.
5 The report is the written part of a project within the National Norwegian Artistic Research Fellowships Programme. The outcome of going through the programme is not a PhD, but it is equivalent to a PhD.
6 But especially the 119-page report by Trond Lossius does contain lots of material on sound, installations, computers and computer programs, etc., that must be of interest to other artists and practitioners in the field.
7 See http://www.kunststipendiat.no/en/regulations.
8 Of the first seven candidates from the programme, only the writings by Lossius, Hamid Rasmussen and the composer Øyvind Brandtsegg are in English. Brandtsegg's project was called 'New creative possibilities through improvisational use of compositional techniques: a new computer instrument for the performing musician' – and he actually developed and demonstrated such an instrument as part of his research. His reflections, divided into several digital-only documents, can be reached through http://oeyvind.teks.no/results/ (accessed 4 December 2009).
9 Please note that Windelband's term is 'idiographic', not 'ideographic'; 'idiographic' means literally 'what describes the specific', whereas 'ideographic' means 'what describes ideas' and is the term for a specific kind of written signs that do not mirror the pronunciation of words but 'directly' signify the actual concepts (like numbers or signs for chemical compounds). 'Nomothetic' is derived from the Greek 'nomos' that means 'law'.
10 My inspiration to look at the Frascati Manual in this connection comes from a keynote speech by Henk Borgdorff – 'Artistic Research within the Fields of Science' – at the fourth 'Sensuous Knowledge' conference, arranged by the Bergen National Academy of the Arts at Solstrand, Norway, in November 2007, now published as Borgdorff (2009a).
11 To mention just one problem: How can statisticians – or more or less centrally placed respondents to questionnaires – be sure whether investigations are undertaken with or without practical

aims? Who is supposed to be conscious about the aims? How long down the line of participants in the research projects?

12　'S&T' is an abbreviation for 'Science and Technology'.

13　The American philosopher Morris Weitz (1916–1981) has famously made the same kind of argument for 'art' only a couple of years after the publication of Wittgenstein's book (Weitz 1956), but I am not quoting him directly here.

14　Wittgenstein himself does not use the term 'prototype', nor do his translators.

15　A typical example might be the discussion in Mike Bode and Staffan Schmidt's dissertation Off the Grid (Bode and Schmidt 2008).

16　The seven liberal arts were the three 'verbal' ones (the trivium): rhetoric, grammar and logic, and the four 'mathematical' ones (the quadrivium): arithmetic, geometry, music and astronomy.

3

THE PRODUCTION OF KNOWLEDGE IN ARTISTIC RESEARCH

Henk Borgdorff

Introduction

This chapter examines artistic research as a form of knowledge production. It will conclude, however, by saying that artistic research seeks not so much to make explicit the knowledge that art is said to produce, but rather to provide a specific articulation of the pre-reflective, non-conceptual content of art. It thereby invites 'unfinished thinking'. Hence, it is not formal knowledge that is the subject matter of artistic research, but thinking in, through and with art.

The expression *artistic research* connects two domains: art and academia. Obviously the term can also be used in a general sense. Every artist does research as she works, as she tries to find the right material, the right subject, as she looks for information and techniques to use in her studio or atelier, or when she encounters something, changes something or begins anew in the course of her work. Artistic research in the emphatic sense – and as used in this chapter – unites the artistic and the academic in an enterprise that impacts on both domains. Art thereby transcends its former limits, aiming through the research to contribute to thinking and understanding; academia, for its part, opens up its boundaries to forms of thinking and understanding that are interwoven with artistic practices. These specific 'border violations' can spark a good deal of tension. The relationship between art and academia is uneasy, but challenging. That is one reason why the issue of demarcation between the artistic and the academic has been one of the most widely discussed topics in the debate on artistic research in the past fifteen years.[1]

In some quarters, one prefers to speak not of artistic research, but of 'artistic development'.[2] The word 'research' stays reserved for activities in traditional universities or industrial research centres. Indeed there is something to be said for preferring the term 'artistic development'. Artistic research certainly contributes to the development of the arts, just as all other research tries to contribute to the discipline in question. Research and development are intimately entwined, and it may sometimes make sense to highlight the developmental aspect, especially when one is inclined to question the importance of research for art practice. One issue that continually resurfaces in the debate involves where, precisely, the distinction lies between *art practice in itself* and *art practice as research*. Although I will not address this question explicitly here, it will be present in the background. The entanglement of artistic research with art practice and with artistic development is so close that a conceptual distinction often appears contrived.[3]

In discussing artistic research as a form of knowledge production, I begin by tentatively describing this type of research – in terms of subject, method, context and outcome – as *research in and through art practice*. Embedded in artistic and academic contexts, artistic research seeks to convey and communicate content that is enclosed in aesthetic experiences, enacted in creative practices and embodied in artistic products.

In the second section, I explore similarities and differences between artistic research and other spheres of academic research, in the domains of humanities, aesthetics and social sciences and in fields of natural science and technology. Artistic research, so I will claim, distinguishes itself in specific respects from each of these research traditions, whereby neither the natural science model, the humanities model nor the social science model can serve as a benchmark for artistic research.

The third section addresses the issue of whether artistic research can be considered academic research. By virtue of its distinctive context, its studio-based research practice, the specific types of knowledge and understanding it deals with, and its unconventional forms of documentation and dissemination, artistic research occupies its own place in the realm of academic research.

I conclude the chapter with a series of observations on the epistemology and metaphysics of artistic research. The current programme of phenomenologically inspired cognitive science offers tools for examining the issue of the non-conceptual content[4] enclosed in artworks and art practices. Clearly research in and through artistic practices is partly concerned with our perception, our understanding, our relationship to the world and to other people. Art thereby invites reflection, yet it eludes any defining thought regarding its content. Artistic research is the acceptance of that paradoxical invitation. It furthermore enhances our awareness of the pre-reflective nearness of things as well as our epistemological distance from them. This makes artistic research an open undertaking, seeking the deliberate articulation of unfinished thinking in and through art.

A preliminary account of artistic research as research in and through art practice – subject, method, context, outcome

Despite all the differences of opinion that exist within the ascendant programme of artistic research, there seems to be general agreement about one thing: the *practice* of the arts is central to artistic research. On the surface, such an assumption seems commonplace. After all, doesn't all research that engages with the arts concentrate on 'the practice of the arts'? Even disciplines like historical or sociological research on the arts focus on that.

In the case of artistic research, however, art practice plays a different role – and in terms of science theory a more fundamental one. Characteristic of artistic research is that art practice (the works of art, the artistic actions, the creative processes) is not just the motivating factor and the subject matter of research, but that this artistic practice – the practice of creating and performing in the atelier or studio[5] – is central to the research process itself. Methodologically speaking, the creative process forms the pathway (or part of it) through which new insights, understandings and products come into being.

Another distinguishing feature is that contemporary art practice constitutes the relevant context for the research, alongside the academic forum. The research derives its significance not only from the new insights it contributes to the discourse on art, but also from the outcomes in the form of new products and experiences which are meaningful in the world of art. In part, then, the outcomes of artistic research are artworks, installations, performances and other artistic practices, and this is another quality that differentiates it from humanities or social science research – where art practice may be the object of the research, but not the outcome. This means that art practice is paramount as the subject matter, the method, the context and the outcome of artistic research. That is what is meant by expressions like 'practice-based' or 'studio-based' research.

In the literature on artistic research, we regularly see a distinction made between research *on* the arts, research *for* the arts and research *in* the arts. This differentiation, which derives from, but also deviates from, categories proposed by Frayling (1993: cf. Borgdorff 2006), expresses different perspectives on the status of art practice. The interpretative perspective ('research on the arts') is common to the research traditions of the humanities and social sciences, which observe a certain theoretical distance when they make art practice their object of study. The instrumental perspective ('research for the arts') is characteristic of the more applied, often technical research done in the service of art practice; this research delivers, as it were, the tools and the material knowledge that can then be applied in practice, in the artistic process and in the artistic product itself. In this case, art practice is not the object of study, but its objective. And as we see, the place of artistic practice becomes more central to the research here.

We can justifiably speak of artistic research ('research in the arts') when that artistic practice is not only the result of the research, but also its methodological vehicle, when the research unfolds *in and through* the acts of creating and performing. This is a distinguishing feature of this research type within the whole of academic research.

This is not to say that viewpoints in art criticism, social and political theory or technology play no part in artistic research. As a rule they do play a part. The discourses about art, social context and the materiality of the medium are in fact partially constitutive of artistic practices and products. The distinctiveness of artistic research, nevertheless, derives from the paramount place that artistic practice occupies as the subject, method, context and outcome of the research. Methodological pluralism – the view that various approaches deriving from the humanities, social sciences, or science and technology may play a part in artistic research – should be regarded as complementary to the principle that the research takes place in and through the creation of art.

Behind the four specified dimensions of artistic research – subject, method, context and outcome – are a range of problems that require more detailed analysis.

First, the content of what artistic research investigates seems to elude direct access. It has an experiential component that cannot be efficiently expressed linguistically.[6] The subject of the research is partly the *je ne sais quoi* of artistic, aesthetic experience;[7] as a matter of principle, it refuses every explanatory gaze. What ontological status does this research object have? What sort of content lies enclosed in artistic experience? And how can one articulate that content?

Second, the focus, in the research process, on the practice of creating and performing is in line with what has been called the 'practice turn in contemporary theory' (Schatzki *et al.* 2001). Knowledge and experiences are constituted only in and through practices, actions and interactions. In the context of discovery, pre-reflective artistic actions embody knowledge in a form that is not directly accessible for justification. What is the methodological import of this 'enacted approach' in artistic research? Is the researcher trying to reveal something of the secrets of the creative process, of artistic practice, or is the methodological deployment of the artistic creative process best suited because it takes an unmediated route to investigate from inside what is at work in art?

Third, works of art and artistic practices are not self-contained; they are situated and embedded. The meaning of art is generated in interactions with relevant surroundings. As noted above, the context in which artistic research takes place is formed both by the art world and by academic discourse; the relevance of the subjects and the validity of the outcomes are weighed in the light of both those contexts. Yet the situatedness of artworks and art practices also raises the question of the situatedness of practice-based research done within them. Does that research always aim to shed light on the way that artworks and practices affect our relationship to the world and to other people? Or can that research also confine itself to articulations that do not go beyond the domain of the artistic and the aesthetic?

Fourth, the experiences and insights that artistic research delivers are embodied in the resulting art practices and products. In part, these material outcomes are non-conceptual and non-discursive, and their persuasive quality lies in the performative power through which they broaden our aesthetic experience, invite us to fundamentally unfinished thinking, and prompt us towards a critical perspective on what there is. What is the epistemological status of these embodied forms of experience, knowledge and criticism? And what relation does the material-performative have to the rational-discursive and the engaged-critical in the research?

In the debate on artistic research, these ontological, methodological, contextual and epistemological issues are still the subject of extensive discussion. In anticipation of a more elaborate account, the following preliminary characterization can already be given: artistic research – embedded in artistic and academic contexts – is the articulation of the unreflective, non-conceptual content enclosed in aesthetic experiences, enacted in creative practices and embodied in artistic products.

Affinities and differences to other academic research traditions

Artistic research has both historical and systematic affinities to a range of philosophical and scientific research traditions. A historiography of artistic research (which remains to be undertaken) might show that, from the Renaissance to the Bauhaus, there has always been research conducted in and through artistic practices. The fact that such research in retrospect often does not qualify as 'academic research' may say less about the research itself than about what we currently understand by 'academic'.[8]

The domain of art has long been interlaced with that of academia, from the practice of the *artes* in the late medieval monastery schools right up to today's postmodern farewell to the separation between the life domains of art, knowledge and morality that has characterized modernity since the eighteenth century. In the current discourse on art, the realm of the aesthetic has reconnected with the epistemic and the ethical. The emergence of artistic research is consistent with this movement to no longer subordinate the faculties of the human mind to one another, either theoretically or institutionally.

On the contemporary research agenda at the interface of phenomenology, cognitive sciences and philosophy of the mind, we now encounter a theme that is also central to artistic research: non-conceptual knowledge and experience as embodied in practices and products. I will come back to this in my final section. I shall now make a series of comparisons between artistic research and research in the humanities (cultural and arts studies in particular), philosophical aesthetics, qualitative social science research, and technology and natural science research.

Humanities

There is a self-evident kinship between artistic research and the research in musicology, art history, theatre and dance studies, comparative literature, architectural theory, and moving image and new media studies, as well as the research in cultural studies or sociology of the arts. In all such academic disciplines or programmes, art (the art world, art practice, artworks) is the subject of systematic or historical research. A wide array of conceptual frameworks, theoretical perspectives and research strategies are employed, which one might summarize with the umbrella term 'grand theories of our culture', among them hermeneutics, structuralism, semiotics, deconstruction, pragmatism, critical theory, cultural analysis. To study its research objects, each such approach has its own specific instruments available – iconography, musical analysis, source studies, ethnomethodology, actor-network theory.

Important for a comparison with artistic research is that those frameworks, perspectives and strategies generally approach the arts with a certain theoretical distance. That is even true of fields like hermeneutics, which acknowledge that the horizons of the interpreter and the interpreted may temporarily merge, or cultural analysis, where theory may be seen as a discourse 'that can be brought to bear on the object at the same time as the object can be brought to bear on *it*' (Bal 2002: 61; italics in original). Obviously the dividing lines cannot always be clearly drawn, and any delimitations will always be partly artificial. In the research agendas just mentioned, however, the interpretive, verbally discursive approach appears to prevail above research strategies that are more practice-imbued. And precisely here lies a characteristic feature of artistic research: the experimental practice of creating and performing pervades the research at every turn. In this respect, artistic research has more in common with technical design research or with participatory action research than with research in the humanities.

The kinship with the humanities is often reflected in institutional proximity. Research centres, research groups and individual researchers that engage in practice-based research in the arts are often accommodated in arts and humanities faculties and departments. Funding for their research often also comes from humanities research councils and funding agencies (and this partly explains the impassioned nature of the demarcation debate between art scholars and artist-researchers). Outside the traditional universities, at professional schools of the arts, artistic research can develop more freely, although here, too, it may be accommodated in a separate department for art theory and/or cultural studies. The importance of interpretation, theory and reflection in artists' training cannot be emphasized too strongly, just as technical knowledge of artistry is also a *sine qua non*. But the prime focus in artistic research is on concrete creative practice. The research aims to make a substantial, preferably cutting-edge contribution to the development of that practice – a practice that is just as much saturated with histories, beliefs and theories as it is based on skilful expert action and tacit understanding.

Aesthetics

A rich source for the artistic research programme is philosophical aesthetics, which has studied the non-conceptual knowledge embodied in art since the eighteenth century. I will highlight three examples from this tradition: the liberation of sensory knowledge in Baumgarten, the cultural value of the aesthetic idea in Kant, and the epistemic character of art in Adorno.[9] The purpose of my brief review here is to show that the issue of the non-conceptual content in art has not appeared out of the blue, but has been thought through in many ways in centuries past.

Alexander Baumgarten called it *analogon rationis*: the ability of the human mind, analogous to reason, to obtain clear, but purely sensory, knowledge about reality. Great art is pre-eminently capable of manifesting that perfect sensory knowledge. In our context, the significance of Baumgarten's views lies in his accentuation of the sensory, experiential knowledge component in artistic research (cf. Kjørup 2006). In post-Baumgarten art research and aesthetics, the links to epistemology and perception became less prominent. The theme of sensory, non-discursive knowledge has regained currency in our times in research taking an embedded, enacted and embodied approach to mind and perception.[10]

Immanuel Kant's critical investigation of what today is called the non-conceptual content of aesthetic experience culminated in his legendary articulation of the aesthetic idea as a 'representation of the imagination which induces much thought, yet without the possibility of any definite thought whatever, namely concept, being adequate to it, and which language, consequently, can never get quite on level terms with or render completely intelligible' (Kant 1978 [1790/93]: §49). Kant assigned greater cultural significance to this non-conceptual realm of the artistic, which in Baumgarten had remained limited to sensory knowledge. Characteristic of artistic products, processes and experiences is that – in and through the materiality of the medium – something is presented which transcends materiality. (Kant identifies here one of the links connecting the worlds of imagination and pure reason to the 'intelligible world' – a transcendence later elevated by Hegel into the 'sensory manifestation of the Idea'. After the linguistic and pragmatic turns in philosophy, what now matters is a naturalized understanding of this transcendence; it all depends, of course, on what we mean by 'naturalized'.) Artistic research focuses both on the materiality of art – to the extent that this makes the immaterial possible – and on the immateriality of the art – to the extent that this is embedded in the art world, enacted in creative processes and embodied in the artistic material.

The significance of Kant's analysis lies in part in the distinction he drew in his *Critique of Judgment* between judgment of art and judgment of taste. Taste judgment (as analysed in 'Analytic of the Beautiful') focuses on the formal aspects of beauty, including disinterestedness and purposiveness without purpose. Art judgment surpasses taste or aesthetic judgment, because it focuses on the cultural value of artworks as well as on their beauty. That cultural value lies in their capacity to 'leave [something] over for reflection' and to 'dispose ... the spirit to Ideas' (Kant 1978 [1790/93]: §§53and2). This is the quality through which art gives food for thought and distinguishes itself from a mere aesthetic gratification of the senses. The content of the aesthetic experience is identified more specifically here as that which brings thinking into motion, as it were, or as that which invites to reflection. Artistic practices are therefore performative practices, in the sense that artworks and creative processes do something to us, set us in motion, alter our understanding and view of the world, also in a moral sense. We encounter this performative aspect of art in artistic research to the extent that it involves the concrete articulation of what moves and engages us.

The ability of art, as articulated in artistic research, to speak to us is compellingly present in the work of Theodor W. Adorno. Here, the cultural value of art lies in its 'epistemic character' *(Erkenntnischarakter)*, through which art reveals the concealed truth about the dark reality of society. Whereas in Baumgarten the non-conceptual content of art liberates itself from explicit rational knowledge, and whereas in Kant the non-conceptual aesthetic content invites us to reflection, Adorno assigns this content an even more potent and critical valence as the only thing that is capable – because it is antithetical to societal reality – of keeping alive the utopian perspective of a better world, and of recalling the original (albeit broken) promise of happiness. As no one after him, Adorno thought through art's engagement with the world and with our lives. Even if we distance ourselves from his dialectics and his philosophy of history, all engagement that lies enclosed in contemporary art and art criticism must take account of his legacy.

Art's epistemic character resides in its ability to offer the very reflection on who we are, on where we stand, that is obscured from sight by the discursive and conceptual procedures of scientific rationality. Noteworthy in Adorno is that thoughts and concepts are still always needed – thoughts and concepts which, as it were, assemble themselves around a work of art, in such a way that the art object itself begins to speak under the lingering gaze of the thought. Herein may lie a key to exploring the relationship between the discursive and the artistic in artistic research.[11]

Social science

In the discourse about knowledge in artistic research, some observers emphasize the types of knowledge acquisition and production that derive from models of natural science explanation, quantitative analysis and empirical logical deduction, which are encountered in the exact sciences, as well as in types of social science that follow natural science methods. Contrasting with this tradition of explanation and deduction is the academic tradition which, especially since the rise of interpretive (*verstehende*) sociology, seeks to 'understand' social and cultural phenomena. In the past hundred years, a qualitative research paradigm, inspired by hermeneutics, has developed which in many ways gives direction to social science research being done at present. It regards *verstehende* interpretation and practical participation as more relevant than logical explanation and theoretical distance.

Artistic research shows a certain kinship to some of these research traditions. In ethnographic and action research in particular, strategies have been developed that can be useful to artists in their practice-based research; these include participant observation, performance ethnography, field study, autobiographical narrative, thick description, reflection in action and collaborative inquiry. The often critical and engaged ethnographic research strategy acknowledges the mutual interpenetration of the subjects and objects of field research. It might serve as a model for some types of research in the arts, given that the artist's own practice is the 'field' of investigation.

Action research aims at transforming and enhancing practice, and as such it also has affinities with artistic research, as the latter seeks not only to increase knowledge and understanding, but also to further develop artistic practice and enrich the artistic universe with new products and practices. Artistic research is inseparably linked to artistic development. In the intimacy of experimental studio practice, we can recognize the cycle of learning in action research, where research findings give immediate cause for changes and improvements. This is also recognizable in the engaged outreach and impact of the research – artistic research delivers new experiences and insights that bear on the art world and on how we understand and relate to the world and ourselves. Artistic research is therefore not just embedded in artistic and academic contexts, and it focuses not just on what is enacted in creative processes and embodied in art products, but it also engages with who we are and where we stand.

The 'practice turn' in the humanities and social sciences not only sheds light on the constitutive role of practices, actions and interactions. Sometimes it even represents a shift from text-centred research to performance-centred research, whereby practices and products themselves become the material-symbolic forms of expression, as opposed to the numerical and verbal forms used by quantitative and qualitative research. Artistic research also fits into this framework, since artistic practices form the core of the research in the methodological sense, as well as part of the material outcome of the research. This broadening of qualitative social science research to include research in and through art practice has led some observers to argue for a new distinguishing paradigm (Haseman 2006a).[12]

The methodological and epistemological issues of artistic research are also addressed in the key writings relating to arts-based research in the tradition of the Eisner school (Eisner 1981; Knowles and Coles 2008). In studying the role of art in educational practice and human development, these social scientists use insights from cognitive psychology to argue the importance of artistic-cognitive development of the self, in particular in primary and secondary education.

Science and technology

Art practices are technically mediated practices. Whether this involves the acoustical characteristics of musical instruments, the physical properties of art materials, the structure of a building or the digital architecture of a virtual installation, art practices and artworks are materially anchored. Artistic practices are technically mediated at a more abstract level of materiality as well. Consider the knowledge of counterpoint in music, of colour in painting, of editing in filmmaking, or of bodily techniques in dance. Technical and material knowledge are therefore indispensable components in the professional training and practice of artists.

Research that focuses on this technical and material side of art in order to improve applications, develop innovative procedures or explore new artistic possibilities can rightly be called applied research. The knowledge obtained in exploratory technological and scientific research is put into practice in artistic procedures and products. This is research done in the service of artistic practice.

In artistic research, by comparison, art practice is not only the test of the research, but it also plays a critical role methodologically. In other words, as well as generating new or innovative art, the research is conducted in and through the making of art. The boundary between applied research in the arts and artistic research is thin and rather artificial, just as the dividing line between artistic research and performance studies or ethnography may also seem contrived. In the practice of artists, or even in their training, such a distinction is not always useful; the reality is more like a continuum that provides leeway for a variety of research strategies. But as argued above, methodological pluralism is merely complementary to the principle that artistic research takes place in and through the creation of art. For conceptual clarity, I would argue in this case that what sometimes does not hold true in practice may still be useful in theory.

Especially in the world of design and architecture, the methodological framework of applied research seems suitable. Many of the training programmes in these fields have strong ties to technical universities, or are even part of them. At first sight, it would seem that one must choose: either an orientation to art or to science, engineering or technology. In practice, though, most design academies and architecture schools aspire to a fruitful combination. 'Research by design' is the peer of artistic research; there, too, the debate is still underway about the methodological and epistemological foundations of the research.[13]

An artistic experiment in a studio or atelier cannot simply be equated with a controlled experiment in a laboratory. Nonetheless, in many artistic research studies we can discern an affinity with fields like engineering and technology that use methods and techniques with origins in scientific research. In that case, the empirical cycle of observation, theory and hypothesis development, prediction and testing, and the model of the controlled experiment serve as an ideal type in the often haphazard context of artistic discovery (just as such principles are often applied in empirical social science research as well). Values inherent in scientific justification – including reliability, validity, replicability and falsifiability – are also relevant in artistic research when it is inspired by the science model.

When artistic research has technological or scientific attributes, collaboration between artists and scientists seems only natural, since artists, as a rule, have not been trained to do those types of research. Bringing together expertise from these two worlds can lead to innovative findings and inspiring insights. Collaboration between artists and other researchers does not, however, confine itself to areas like technology, engineering and product design. Research in other fields may also serve art practice or form productive ties with art. Consider the cooperation between artists and philosophers, anthropologists or psychologists, as well as economists and legal theorists; projects involving artists are also conducted in areas such as the life sciences, artificial intelligence and information technology.[14]

Roughly speaking, multidisciplinary cooperation between artists and scientists can take two different forms: either the scientific research serves or illuminates the art; or the art serves or illuminates what is going on in the science. Currently there is great interest in the latter mode in particular. The assumption is that the arts will be able to elucidate, in their own unique ways, the procedures, results and implications of scientific research. BioArt can exemplify this; this art form, whereby artists make use of biotechnological procedures like tissue and genetic engineering, leans heavily on scientific research, while often training a critical light on the ethical and social implications of research in the life sciences.

In the debate on research in the arts, these and other kinds of art-and-science collaboration are often wrongly classed together with artistic research as explored in this chapter. Although the term 'art-and-science' may imply convergence at first glance, if anything it represents a reinstatement of the partition between the domain of art and the domain of science, between the artistic and the academic, between what artists do and what scientists do. There is nothing wrong with that, of course; it can only be applauded that these oft-segregated spheres and cultures are now meeting each other in projects where people learn from one another and where critical confrontations can take place. Yet multidisciplinary research projects like these must still be understood as collaboration between different disciplines around a particular topic, whereby the theoretical premises and working methods of the separate disciplines remain intact. The scientist does her thing, and the artist does hers. Even if the artist borrows right and left from the scientist, the aesthetic evaluation of the material, the artistic decisions made in creating the artwork, and the manner in which the results are presented and documented are still, as a rule, discipline-specific. Only very rarely does such multidisciplinary research result in any real hybridization of domains.

Whilst artistic research is not entirely at odds with these types of art-science collaboration, it should still be regarded as an academic research form of its own. The science model cannot be a benchmark here, any more than artistic research could conform to the standards of the humanities.

Artistic research as academic research

Even if one accepts that artworks somehow embody forms of knowledge or criticism, and that such knowledge and criticism is enacted in artistic practices and creative processes, and also that the knowledge and criticism is embedded in the wider context of the art world and academia, then that still does not mean that what artists do may be construed as 'research' in the emphatic sense. 'Research' is 'owned' by science; it is performed by people who have mastered 'the scientific method', in institutions dedicated to the systematic accumulation of knowledge and its application, such as universities, industrial and governmental research centres.

It is indeed the case that 'what artists do' cannot automatically be called research. In the debate about artistic research, the discussions often turn on the distinction between art practice in itself and art practice as research (cf. Borgdorff 2006; 2009a). Few would contend that each work of art or every artistic practice is an outcome of research in the emphatic sense of the word. I shall confine myself here to the question of which criteria must be satisfied if artistic research is to qualify as academic research. I will show that artistic research incorporates both the interests of practice and those of academia.[15]

In the world of academia, there is broad agreement as to what should be understood by research. Briefly it amounts to the following. Research takes place when a person intends to carry out an original study to enhance knowledge and understanding. It begins with questions or issues that are relevant in the research context, and it employs methods that are appropriate to the research and which ensure the validity and reliability of the research findings. An additional requirement is that the research process and the research findings be documented and disseminated in appropriate ways.

This description of academic research leaves room for a great diversity of research programmes and strategies, whether deriving from technology and natural science, social sciences or the humanities, and whether aiming at a basic understanding of what is studied or a more practical application of the knowledge obtained. Artistic research also falls within this characterization of academic research. Let us focus more closely on the various components of this description.[16]

Intent

The research is undertaken *for the purpose of* broadening and deepening our knowledge and understanding of the discipline or disciplines in question. Artistic practices contribute first of all to the art world, the artistic universe. The production of images, installations, compositions and performances as such is not intended primarily for enhancing our knowledge (although forms of reflection are always entwined with art). This points to an important distinction between art practice in itself and artistic research. Artistic research seeks in and through the production of art to contribute not just to the artistic universe, but to what we 'know' and 'understand'. In so doing, it goes beyond the artistic universe in two ways. First, the results of the research extend further than the personal artistic development of the artist in question. In cases where the impact of research remains confined to the artist's own oeuvre and has no significance for the wider research context, one can justifiably ask whether this qualifies as research in the true sense of the word. Second, the research is expressly intended to shift the frontiers of the discipline. Just as the contribution made by other academic research consists in uncovering new facts or relationships, or shedding new light on existing facts or relationships, artistic research likewise helps expand the frontiers of the discipline by developing cutting-edge artistic practices, products and insights. In a material sense, then, the research impacts on the development of art practice, and in a cognitive sense on our understanding of what that art practice is.

Originality

Artistic research entails *original* contributions – that is, the work should not have previously been carried out by others, and it should add new knowledge or understandings to the existing corpus. Here, too, we must distinguish between an original contribution to art practice and an original contribution to what we know and understand – between artistic and academic originality.[17] Yet artistic and academic originality are closely related. As a rule, an original contribution in artistic research will result in an original work of art, as the relevance of the artistic outcome is one test of the adequacy of the research. The reverse is not true, however; an original artwork is not necessarily an outcome of research in the emphatic sense. In the concrete practice of artistic research, one must determine case by case in what way and in what measure the research has resulted in original artistic and academic outcomes.[18]

In any research study that pretends to make a difference, it is important to realize that it is hard to determine at the outset whether it will ultimately result in an original contribution. It is an inherent quality of research that 'one does not know exactly what one does not know'. Consequently, guiding intuitions and chance inspirations are just as important for the motivation and dynamism of research as methodological prescriptions and discursive justifications. Contributing new knowledge to what already exists is characteristic of the open-ended nature of every research study.[19]

Knowledge and understanding

If artistic research is an 'original investigation undertaken in order to gain knowledge and understanding',[20] then the question arises as to what kinds of knowledge and understanding this involves. Traditionally, the central focus of epistemology is on *propositional* knowledge – knowledge of facts, knowledge about the world, knowing that such and such is the case. This can be distinguished from knowledge as *skill* – knowing how to make, how to act, how to perform. A third form of knowledge may be described as *acquaintance*: familiarity and receptiveness with respect to persons, conditions or situations – 'I know this person', 'I know that situation'. In the history of epistemology, these types of knowledge have been thematized in a variety of ways, ranging from Aristotle's distinction between theoretical knowledge, practical knowledge and wisdom to Polanyi's (1958) contrast between focal and tacit knowledge. Different notions exist as to the relationships between the three types of knowledge – notions which are also identifiable in the debate about artistic research. Sometimes the emphasis lies on propositional knowledge, sometimes on knowledge as skill, and sometimes on 'understanding' as a form of knowledge in which theoretical knowledge, practical knowledge and acquaintance may intersect.

In the case of artistic research, we can add to the knowledge and understanding duo the synonyms 'insight' and 'comprehension', in order to emphasize that a perceptive, receptive and *verstehende* engagement with the subject matter is often more important to the research than getting an 'explanatory grip'. Such an investigation also seeks to enhance our experience, in the rich sense of the word 'experience': the knowledge and skills accumulated through action and practice, plus apprehension through the senses. In the debate on the status of the experiential component of artistic research, disagreement exists as to whether this component is non-conceptual, and therefore non-discursive, or whether it is a cognitive component that definitely resides in the 'space of reasons'.[21] The dispute between epistemological foundationalism and coherentism, which mainly concerns propositional knowledge, does not figure at all in the debate about artistic research. Many observers, though, do not view knowledge primarily as 'justified true belief' or 'warranted assertibility', but as a form of world disclosure (a hermeneutic perspective) or world constitution (a constructivist perspective). I shall return to these epistemological questions in the final section below.

Questions, issues, problems

The requirement that a research study should set out with well-defined questions, topics or problems is often at odds with the actual course of events in artistic research. Formulating a question implies delimiting the space in which a possible answer may be found. Yet research (and not only artistic research) often resembles an uncertain quest in which the questions or topics only materialize during the journey, and may often change as well. Besides not knowing exactly what one does not know, one also does not know how to delimit the space where potential answers are located. As a rule, artistic research is not hypothesis-led, but discovery-led (Rubidge 2005: 8), whereby the artist undertakes a search on the basis of intuition, guesses and hunches, and possibly stumbles across some unexpected issues or surprising questions on the way.

In the light of the actual dynamics of current academic research, the prevailing format for research design (such as that required in funding applications) is basically inadequate. Especially in artistic research – and entirely in line with the creative process – the artist's tacit understandings and her accumulated experience, expertise and sensitivity in exploring uncharted territory are more crucial in identifying challenges and solutions than an ability to delimit the study and put research questions into words at an early stage. The latter can be more a burden than a boon.

As we have seen, research studies done in and through art may be oriented to science and technology or more to interpretation and social criticism, and they may avail themselves of a diversity of methodological instruments. By the same token, the topics and questions addressed by the research can vary from those focusing purely on the artistic material or the creative process to those that touch on other life domains or even have their *locus* and their *telos* there. The subject matter of the research is enclosed, as it were, in the artistic material, or in the creative process, or in the transdisciplinary space that connects the artistic practices to meaningful contexts. The research, then, seeks to explore the often non-conceptual content that is embodied in art, enacted in the creative process or embedded in the transdisciplinary context.

Context

Contexts are constitutive factors in both art practice and artistic research. Artistic practices do not stand on their own; they are always situated and embedded. Artworks and artistic actions acquire their meaning in interchange with relevant environments. Research in the arts will remain naive unless it acknowledges and confronts this embeddedness and situatedness in history, in culture (society, economy, everyday life) as well as in the discourse on art; herein lies the merit of relational aesthetics and of all constructivist approaches in artistic research.

Contexts figure in artistic research in another way too. The relevance and urgency of the research questions and topics is determined in part *within* the research context, where the intersubjective forum of peers defines the state of the art. This formally invested, or abstractly internalized, normative forum assesses what potential contribution the research will make to the current body of knowledge and understanding, and in what relationship the research stands to other research in the area. Every artistic research study must justify its own importance to the academic forum, which, like the artistic forum, looks over the researcher's shoulder, as it were.

Methods

I have commented above on the distinctive nature of artistic research in terms of methodology. This is characterized by the use, within the research process, of art practice, artistic actions, creation and performance. Experimental art practice is integral to the research, just as the active involvement of the artist is an essential component of the research strategy. Here lies the similarity of artistic research to both laboratory-based technical research and ethnographic field study. The erratic nature of creative discovery – of which unsystematic drifting, serendipity, chance inspirations and clues form an integral part – is such that a methodological justification is not easy to codify. Just as in many other academic research studies, it involves doing unpredictable things, and this implies intuition and some measure of randomness. Research is more like exploration than like following a firm path.[22]

Much artistic research does not limit itself to an investigation into material aspects of art or an exploration of the creative process, but pretends to reach further in the transdisciplinary context. Experimental and interpretive research strategies thus transect one another here in an undertaking whose purpose is to articulate the connectedness of art to who we are and where we stand. Much of today's visual and performing art is critically engaged with other life domains, such as gender, globalization, identity, environment or activism; philosophical or psychological issues might be addressed in artistic research projects as well. The difference between artistic research and social or political science, critical theory or cultural analysis lies in the central place which *art practice* occupies in both the research process and the research outcome. This makes research in the arts distinct from that in other academic disciplines engaging with the same issues. In assessing the research, it is important to keep in mind that the specific contribution it makes to our knowledge, understanding, insight and experience lies in the ways these issues are articulated, expressed and communicated *through art*.

Documentation, dissemination

The academic requirement that the research process and the research findings be documented and disseminated in appropriate ways raises a number of questions when it comes to artistic research. What does 'appropriate' mean here? What kinds of documentation would do justice to research that is guided by an intuitive creative process and by tacit understandings? What value does a rational reconstruction have if it is far removed from the actual, often erratic course taken by the research? What are the best ways to report non-conceptual artistic findings? And what is the relationship between the artistic and the discursive, between what is presented and displayed and what is described? What audience does the research want to target, and what impact does it hope to achieve? And which communication channels are best suited for putting the research results into the limelight? Questions like these have been the subject of ongoing discussion for the past 15 years in the debate on practice-based research in the creative and performing arts and design – not least in the context of academic degree programmes and funding schemes, which demand clear answers in their admission and assessment procedures.

Because artistic research addresses itself both to the academic forum and to the forum of the arts, the research documentation, as well as the presentation and dissemination of the findings, needs to conform to the prevailing standards in both forums. Usually, though, a double-blind reviewed academic journal will not be the most appropriate publication medium; the material and discursive outcomes of the research will be directed first of all to the art world and the art discourse, one that extends beyond academia. But a discursive justification of the research will be necessary with the academic discourse in mind, while the artistic findings will have to convince the art world as well. Even so, the discursive space of reasons need not remain confined to that of traditional scholarly writings. The artist can also use other, perhaps innovative forms of discursivity that stand closer to the artistic work than a written text, such as an artistic portfolio that maps the line of artistic reasoning, or argumentations coded in scores, scripts, videos or diagrams. What matters most is the cogency of the documentation with respect to both intersubjective forums. For all that, language does remain a highly functional complementary medium to help get across to others what is at issue in the research – provided one keeps in mind that there will always be a gap between what is displayed and what is put into words. Or more precisely: given that the meaning of words often remains limited to their use in the language, a certain modesty is due here in view of the performative power of the material outcomes.[23]

The written, verbal or discursive component that accompanies the material research outcome may go in three directions.[24] Many people place emphasis on a rational reconstruction of the research process, clarifying how the results were achieved. Others use language to provide interpretive access to the findings, the material products and the practices generated by the research. A third possibility is to express something in and with language which can be understood as a 'verbalization' or 'conceptual mimesis' of the artistic outcome. The concepts, thoughts and utterances 'assemble themselves' around the artwork, so that the artwork begins to speak.[25] In contrast to an interpretation of the artistic work or a reconstruction of the artistic process, the latter option involves an emulation or imitation of, or an allusion to, the non-conceptual content embodied in the art.

Some remarks on the epistemology and metaphysics of artistic research – non-conceptualism, realism, contingency

Non-conceptualism

To begin this final section of the chapter, I return to the provisional description of artistic research I proposed at the beginning. Artistic research – as embedded in artistic and academic contexts – is the articulation of the unreflective, non-conceptual content enclosed in aesthetic experiences, enacted in creative practices and embodied in artistic products. The theme of unreflective action, non-conceptual content and embodied knowledge is explored in phenomenology, which, starting with Husserl and continuing via Heidegger and Merleau-Ponty, has focused attention on the nature of perception and the constitution of intentionality and normativity, beyond an ontology in which the world was thought to be independent of our situatedness.

In the work of Maurice Merleau-Ponty, embodied knowledge is also concretely 'bodily knowledge'. The *a priori* of the body assumes the place of the *a priori* of intellectual knowledge, making the pre-reflective bodily intimacy with the world around us into the foundation of our thinking and acting. By virtue of our bodily constitution and our bodily situatedness in the world, we are capable of 'getting a grip on reality' as we observe, learn and act, and of 'acting in flow' prior to any reflection and without following rules.[26] Conversely, pre-reflective knowledge and understanding already lie enclosed in how we understand and engage with reality.[27] That is why the world is familiar to us, even before we gain access to it via concepts and language.

Part of the significance and singularity of artistic research seems to lie in its appraisal and articulation of this pre-reflective knowledge as embodied in art practices and products. Some argue that artistic research targets these non-conceptual forms of knowledge and understanding, which emerge in and through the creation of art, without wanting or being able to explicate them further. Others feel that it seeks to give explicit discursive (that is, verbal) expression to the knowledge that is embodied and enacted in works and practices of art.

If the artistic research programme were to confine itself solely to explicating this non-propositional knowledge, it would, as a consequence of its epistemological gaze, risk losing the research object along the way. It would risk shrinking the programme into a sort of decoding exercise, rendering it doubtful whether the research would even be useful at all to art practice and our understanding of it. After all, the dynamic of art practice seems to be inseparably bound to its categorical *je ne sais quoi*; secrets have a constitutive function both in the creative process and in the artistic outcome. For this reason, many observers argue for not making these secrets explicit at all, but for articulating and communicating them solely in and through the production of art. Clearly the standpoint we adopt here will partly determine which demands we put on the content and form of the documentation in contexts such as doctoral research in the arts.

The implicit, pre-reflective knowledge and understanding embodied and enacted in art practice is also at issue in that particular strand of post-Heideggerian cognitive science that distances itself from the predominant physicalism. A recent dialogue between Hubert Dreyfus (2005; 2007a; 2007b) and John McDowell (2007a; 2007b) has compellingly highlighted the core issue here: does the phenomenological account of our embodied coping skills and our immediate expert intuitive understanding (which are also pre-eminent issues in art practice) point to an essentially non-conceptual, and hence non-discursive, content in research? Or is a smooth transition conceivable between pre-reflective forms of knowledge and experience and their linguistic-conceptual translation or conversion within the space of reasons?[28]

The same question re-emerges here which has been pivotal to the debate on artistic research from the very outset. Is it possible to achieve a linguistic-conceptual articulation of the embedded, enacted and embodied content of artistic research? The significance of the current discussion at the intersection of phenomenology, cognitive sciences and philosophy of mind lies in the prospects it may open for liberating the content of research in and through artistic practices from the explicit, explanatory, descriptive or interpretive approaches that are so common in other research in the arts. Artistic research might just prove to be an ideal sphere for testing the scope and fecundity of this contemporary phenomenological research agenda. And conversely, artistic research might benefit from the insights that the phenomenological agenda has to offer.

Realism

A distinctive characteristic of artistic research is that it articulates both our familiarity with the world and our distance from it. It owes this ability to a special quality of art practice, which at once elicits and evades our epistemic stance. This Kantian theme links the programme of artistic research to the current broader interest in theories of knowledge and strategies of research which leave room for our implicit, tacit, non-conceptual, non-discursive relations with the world and with ourselves. Artistic research articulates the fact that our natural relationship with things we encounter is more intimate than what we can know. At the same time, it also familiarizes us with the fact that those things are in some way foreign to us. In art, we sense something of our pre-reflective intimacy with the world, while realizing simultaneously that we will never explicitly understand what lies there in such plain view. When we listen to music, look at images or identify with body movements, we are brought into touch with a reality that precedes any re-presentation in the space of the conceptual. That is the abstractness of all art, even after the long farewell to the aesthetics of early Romanticism. In a certain sense, this reality is more real, and nearer to us, than the reality we try to approach with our epistemological projects. This is the concreteness of all art, even in its most abstract forms and contents. In the critical and aesthetic distance to the world of representations that arises in the unfinished process of material thinking in and through art, art invites us to think, 'without the possibility of any definite thought whatever, i.e. concept, being adequate to it'.

Artistic research is the acceptance of that paradoxical invitation. The artistic, pre-reflective, non-conceptual content enclosed in aesthetic experiences, embodied in art works and enacted in artistic practices is articulated, amplified, contextualized and thought through in the research. That content encompasses more than just the tacit knowledge embodied in the skilfulness of artistic work. This 'more' is the ability of art – deliberately articulated in artistic research – to impart and evoke fundamental ideas and perspectives that disclose the world for us and, at the same time, render that world into what it is or can be. If some form of mimesis does exist in art, it is here: in the force – at once perspectivist and performative – by which art offers us new experiences, outlooks and insights that bear on our relationship to the world and to ourselves. Artistic research concerns and affects the foundations of our perception, our understanding, our relationship to the world and to other people, as well as our perspective on what is or should be. This articulation of the world we live in is what we may call the realism of artistic research.

Contingency

The non-conceptual content that is addressed in artistic research is by nature undefined. Although it is materially anchored (in a broad sense of the word 'material'), it simultaneously transcends the materiality of the medium. Here lies not only the *je ne sais quoi* of the aesthetic experience, but also a call to reflection. Artistic research provides room for a multidimensional unfolding of this undefined content – in and through creating and performing, in and through discursive approaches, revelations or paraphrasings, in and through criticism encountered in the artistic and academic research environment.

At least two perspectives can be adopted on what artistic research has to offer: a constructivist and a hermeneutic perspective. The constructivist perspective holds that objects and events actually become constituted in and through artworks and artistic actions. Only in and through art do we see what landscapes, soundworlds, histories, emotions, relations, interests or movements really are or could be. Here lies the performative and critical power of art. It does not represent things; it presents them, thereby making the world into what it is or could be. The hermeneutic perspective assumes that artistic practices and artworks disclose the world to us. The world-revealing power of art lies in its ability to offer us those new vistas, experiences and insights that affect our relationship with the world and with ourselves. Artistic research addresses this world-constituting and world-revealing power of art – the ways in which we constitute and understand the world in and through art.

The fundamentally non-conceptual nature of this act of constitution and revelation – which comes before any theoretical reflection about the world – is what enables art to set our thinking into motion, inviting us to unfinished reflection. Artistic research is the deliberate articulation of such unfinished thinking. It reinforces the contingent perspectives and world disclosures which art imparts. Artistic research therefore does not really involve theory building or knowledge production in the usual sense of those terms. Its primary importance lies not in explicating the implicit or non-implicit knowledge enclosed in art. It is more directed at a not-knowing, or a not-yet-knowing. It creates room for that which is unthought, that which is unexpected – the idea that all things could be different. Especially pertinent to artistic research is the realization that we do not yet know what we don't know. Art invites us and allows us to linger at the frontier of what there is, and it gives us an outlook on what might be. Artistic research is the deliberate articulation of these contingent perspectives.

Notes

1 The demarcations and dichotomies employed in this chapter should not be interpreted too absolutely, but rather taken as imperfect dialectical tools to put the subject matter into perspective. See Borgdorff (2006) for a discussion of this problem of demarcation, and Candlin (2000) and Borgdorff (2008) for insights into the uneasy relationship between art and academia. The relationship between the seemingly undisciplined artistic and the ultimately disciplinary academic makes the project of artistic research into an endeavour in which that relationship is a constant focus. Is this state of uneasiness and reflexivity something to be overcome, or is it intrinsic to the place of artistic research in academia?

2 In the Netherlands, a government advisory committee has advised using the term ontwerp en ontwikkeling (design and development) to denote research activities in non-university professional schools. Norway uses the term kunstnerisk utviklingsarbeid (artistic development work), Austria uses Entwicklung und Erschließung der Künste (development and promotion of the arts), and some people in Denmark and Germany also tend to avoid words for 'research' such as forskning or Forschung.

3 Such distinctions are usually made by people who first create a caricature of the one activity, believing they are protecting the other activity by doing so.

4 The reflexivity of art – its quality of both questioning itself and giving food for thought, and of thus also showing a 'conceptual' dimension – must not be construed in opposition to the (in a philosophical sense) non-conceptual and pre- or unreflective content that lies enclosed in it. For an anthology on this subject, see Gunther (2003).

5 I use an expanded notion of 'studio', referring to artistic experimental practice in which the studio or atelier might be an element, but does not always need to be. Many contemporary artists are not physically located in the studio, or even oppose such an isolated, non-situated position and condition.

6 Cf. Biggs (2004).

7 No distinction is made in this context between the artistic, aesthetic experience of the artist during the production process and the experience the audience has in receiving the artwork. Both the production and the reception of art have an experiential component that evades the conceptual grip.

8 Historiography needs to show modesty in two directions. The normative structure of today's academia should be neither a measure for evaluating the past nor a predictor to judge how intellectual and artistic efforts will be valued in the future. Current developments within academia, such as those involving commercialization of academic research or the advent of hybrid transdisciplinary research programmes, show that the edifice of science is under constant reconstruction.

9 A more extensive reconstruction of philosophical aesthetics in its relation to artistic research would draw on topics from Hegel, Heidegger, Lyotard and others.

10 For an overview of this cognitive science agenda, see Kiverstein and Clark (2009) in a special edition of Topoi dedicated to the subject.

11 Adorno (1966: 36), and cf. Borgdorff (1998: 300ff.). The debate on the relationship between the discursive and the artistic, between the verbal and the demonstrable, often centres on whether the research process should be documented in writing and whether a verbal interpretation can be given of the research results. A third option is perhaps more interesting: a discursive approach to the research which does not take the place of the artistic 'reasoning', but instead 'imitates', suggests or alludes to what is being ventured in the artistic research. See also the subsection 'Documentation, Dissemination' in the third section of this chapter.

12 Whether artistic research constitutes a new paradigm is not something that can be decided here and now. Biggs and Büchler rightly point out that the 'criteria that define academic research per se' must be met whether research is conducted under a new or an existing paradigm (Biggs et al. 2008b: 12). I concur with Kjørup (Chapter 2) that the characteristic of artistic research is 'a specific perspective on already existing activities' – a 'new perspective [which] in the longer run [will] have consequences for the direction of the development of art.' And of academia, I would like to add.

13 See, for example, the discussions about research by design on the PhD-Design mailing list, http://www.jiscmail.ac.uk/lists/phd-design.html (accessed 22 February 2010).

14 For a detailed review, see Wilson (2002).

15 See Chapter 5. Biggs and Büchler argue for a balance between academic values and artistic values. To strongly simplify the matter, I would suggest that academic values have dominated in the British discourse thus far, whilst on the European continent the emphasis has lain more on artistic values. In their analysis of values – demonstrated through actions that are meaningful and potentially significant – in relation to the two communities – practice and academia – Biggs and Büchler appear to hold 'artistic practice' and 'academic research' constant, whereas in fact our notions of what both artistic practice and academic research are become enriched under the emerging 'paradigm' of artistic research.

16 An ontological, epistemological and methodological exploration of artistic research in Borgdorff (2006) culminated in the following definition: 'Art practice qualifies as research if its purpose is to expand our knowledge and understanding by conducting an original investigation in and through art objects and creative processes. Art research begins by addressing questions that are pertinent in the research context and in the art world. Researchers employ experimental and hermeneutic methods that reveal and articulate the tacit knowledge that is situated and embodied in specific artworks and artistic processes. Research processes and outcomes are documented and disseminated in an appropriate manner to the research community and the wider public.'

17 This is mainly a theoretical distinction to help clarify the principle of originality. As with other demarcations and dichotomies, it needs to be interpreted freely in the light of the diversity of practice. It is important to avoid any overly close association with the early Romantic originality principle as held by the eighteenth-century aesthetics of genius, which still haunts in the minds of many as a sort of implicit paradigm.

18 See Pakes (2003) for a more detailed critical analysis of the originality principle in artistic research.

19 (Rheinberger 2007). The full quote is: 'Das Grundproblem besteht darin, dass man nicht genau weiss, was man nicht weiss. Damit ist das Wesen der Forschung kurz, aber bündig ausgesprochen.' (The basic problem is that one does not know exactly what one does not know. Put succinctly, that is the essence of research [my translation]). Cf. also Dallow (2003: 49, 56).

20 This is the wording used by the Research Assessment Exercise in the UK; for the full RAE definition of research, see (RAE 2006: 80).

21 Cf. Biggs (2004).

22 Theoretical physicist Robbert Dijkgraaf in an interview (Balkema et al. 2007: 31).

23 Language-based creative practice (poetry, prose) is a challenge in this respect. Here the performative power of the art is intermingled with and indissolubly connected to the play with the meaning of the words.

24 I decline to discuss here any numerical ratio of the verbal to the material. Any general prescription of the number of words to be required for an artistic PhD does no justice to the subject. An adequate and suitable relationship between the two needs to be determined separately for each artistic research project.

25 Cf. note 6.

26 In the current debate, key Merleau-Pontian notions as 'maximum grip', 'intentional arc' or 'motor intentionality' play an important part. Merleau-Ponty's insights have had strong influence in theatre studies, particularly dance studies; see e.g. Parviainen (2002). But the voices of post-structuralist and neo-Marxist critiques of phenomenology can also be heard in the debate on artistic research. The pre-reflective engagement with the world is a theme often encountered in the writings of philosophers influenced by Wittgenstein's 'rule-following considerations'.

27 Charles Taylor (2005: 34), in discussing the importance of the phenomenological heritage for contemporary philosophy of mind, speaks in this connection of 'pre-understanding'.

28 See Rietveld (2008); cf. also the debate between Luntley (2003) and Säätelä (2005) on aesthetic experiences and non-conceptual content.

4
SOME NOTES ON MODE 1 AND MODE 2: ADVERSARIES OR DIALOGUE PARTNERS?

Halina Dunin-Woyseth

Briefly on Mode 1 and Mode 2

Numerous publications on research and knowledge production have reported in the last twenty or more years that there was a radical, irreversible, world-wide transformation in the way that science is organized, managed and performed (Ziman 2000: 67). Profound changes can be traced in epistemic institutions like universities, research institutes and industrial laboratories.

In their canonical book *The New Production of Knowledge. The Dynamics of Science and Research in Contemporary Societies*, six international scholars under the academic co-ordination of Michael Gibbons maintained that these changes concerned not only science, but also technology, social sciences and the humanities (Gibbons *et al.* 1994: 1). Changes in the practices of knowledge production bear certain attributes which encouraged the authors of the book to call them a new mode of knowledge production. While the traditional academic mode of knowledge production was given the name of Mode 1, the new emerging mode was called Mode 2.

The authors begin the book by delineating the differences between Mode 1 and Mode 2:

> In Mode 1 problems are set and solved in a context governed by the largely academic interests of a specific community. By contrast, Mode 2 knowledge is carried out in a context of application. Mode 1 is disciplinary while Mode 2 is transdisciplinary; Mode 1 is characterized by homogeneity, Mode 2 by heterogeneity. Organizationally, Mode 1 is hierarchical and tends to preserve its form, while Mode 2 is more heterarchical and transient. Each employs a different type of quality control. In comparison with Mode 1, Mode 2 is more socially accountable and reflexive. It includes a wider, more temporary and

heterogeneous set of practitioners, collaborating on a problem defined in a specific and localized context.

(Gibbons *et al.* 1994: 3)

Transdisciplinarity constitutes the major concept of Mode 2. Since the book appeared in 1994, an extensive discourse on transdisciplinarity has evolved. Transdisciplinarity epitomizes a critical perspective on discipline-bound knowledge; on its insufficiency with regard to the contemporary needs for socially critical knowledge. In order to better comprehend the concept of transdisciplinarity, it is necessary to understand what is being criticized. What we today call academic disciplines is a relatively new construct and is associated with the development of modern universities, commencing with the Humboldt reforms of the German universities at the beginning of the nineteenth century (Nyseth 2007: 19). The notion of 'discipline' is related to an area of instruction of students. The establishment and maintenance of academic disciplines is connected with both a specific kind of knowledge and with power (Moran 2002: 2). Disciplines are organized and work within special communication and control networks. They represent a kind of knowledge production monopoly (Harris 2002: 488).

Many attempts to tear down, or only weaken, these disciplinary walls have been made. There are several ways of doing so. The most well known are: multidisciplinarity, interdisciplinarity and transdisciplinarity. While evaluating Swedish architectural research 1995–2005, an international panel agreed to use the following descriptions of the differences between these three notions:

Interdisciplinary research can be considered as a means to share disciplinary knowledge in order to create new concepts and theories, create a product, or solve specific problems. In contrast, transdisciplinary contributions involve a fusion of disciplinary knowledge with the know-how of lay-people that creates a new hybrid that is different from any specific constituent part. Trandisciplinarity is not a process that follows automatically from the bringing together of people from different disciplines or professions, but requires an ingredient that some have called 'transcendence'. It also implies the giving up of sovereignty over knowledge, the generation of new insight and knowledge by collaboration, and the capacity to consider the know-how of professionals and lay-people on equal terms. Collectively, transdisciplinary contributions enable the cross-fertilization of ideas and knowledge from different contributors, they can lead to an enlarged vision of a subject as well as new explanatory theories.

(Forty *et al.* 2006: 42)

Multidisciplinarity ... refers to the connecting of contributions from several disciplines, directed towards elucidating a common meta-level problem complex. Various disciplines work, one could say, in parallell with regard to each other, and each of them contribute to elucidating the potential of one's discipline. Multidisciplinary co-operation does not demand integration, but the various contributions can inspire and develop the individual contributions.[1]

While the interest for Mode 1 and Mode 2 has been strong in established academia and in various public spheres, it is a rather recent phenomenon in creative fields like the arts, design and architecture. The examples addressed in the chapter and the literature referred to have mainly been drawn from architecture and design related literature, but their more general relevance could probably also apply to a broader spectrum of the arts. The chapter relies to a strong degree on the author's own practice as a teacher at doctoral level within research education in several European countries, and consists of three main parts.

The first of them introduces Mode 1 and Mode 2 with reference to relevant literature on the issues. The next part includes two cases, of which one could be called a 'Mode 1 project' and the other one a 'Mode 2 project'. The first case, '"Diagramming" Mode 1 and Mode 2', presents how these two modes were introduced to four cohorts of practitioners (2006–2009) who considered undertaking their doctoral studies at the Sint-Lucas School of Architecture in Brussels. The participants did not have any previous scholarly background, so the 'meeting with the diagram' was one of the first encounters between them and architectural academia (Dunin-Woyseth 2009).

The second case, 'On Securing Housing Safety. A Transdisciplinary Project', reports on a co-operation between a policeman and an architect (Klarqvist and Rydberg 2004). Both of them, while working on this project, were unacquainted with the concepts of Mode 1 and Mode 2. Yet they recognized their project as transdisciplinary *a posteriori*. An abbreviated version of the 'project story' makes up the second case. This case was introduced to the PhD students as an example of Mode 2-related research, supplementing the 'diagram lecture'.

In the concluding part these projects have been examined through a 'matrix of comparison between Mode 1 and Mode 2, elucidating the differences in their character, both with regard to the contexts within which the projects were executed and to the different features these projects had. The closing part of this section reflects on what opportunities for developing field-specific design research can be offered by each of the modes.

'Diagramming' Mode 1 and Mode 2

Introduction

This section of the chapter will present and discuss a specific case of using diagrams as a core of a lecture series presented by the author to several groups of architecture and design practitioners at the Sint-Lucas School of Architecture, Brussels, in the years 2006–2009 (Dunin-Woyseth 2009). These lectures have focused on some complex issues concerning various existing 'knowledge landscapes' (within Mode 1), with emphasis on the emerging new mode of knowledge production (Mode 2). The aim of these lectures has been to help the prospective PhD students to position better their own research in these 'knowledge landscapes'. One specific diagram will be studied in depth. The students have over the years given a positive response to the pedagogical potential of this diagram as an adequate tool for sharing complex information, transferring new knowledge, clarifying complex issues and offering a transparent mode for the lecturer's arguments. The use of the diagram also opened discussions with the prospective PhD students who were able (not only 'physically') to draw their own comments on the lectures and to argue with the messages of the lecturer's diagram.

> The diagram is an icon. Being an icon the diagram is characterized by its similarity to its object – but while the image represents its object through simple qualities and the metaphor represents it through a similarity found in something else, the diagram represents it through a skeleton-like sketch of relations... The diagram is the only sign by the contemplation of which more can be learnt than lies in the directions for its construction.
>
> (Stjernfelt 2007: 90)

The usefulness of diagrams in studies of literature and the other arts, leading to the establishment of an approach called diagrammatology, was first discussed in 1981 (Mitchell 1981). Yet, the diagram has not earned the name of a form until it has been interpreted or explained in some verbal or propositional expression (Mitchell 1981: 628). After having conducted the diagramming of Wordsworth's poem 'The Prelude', some of Mitchell's conclusions were:

> The form of the poem is the structural image *plus* the interpretive rules or principles, which make it apply to the text. Take away the principles and you have the mute image, declaring its own importance but unable to spell out what it is. Take away the image and you have a lot of talk about the poem but no concrete sense of its form.
>
> (Mitchell 1981: 631)

The diagram which will be studied in this part of the chapter consists of three diachronic parts. The first part of the diagram illustrates how doctoral dissertations by practitioners have developed in the Scandinavian countries since the early 1970s and until approximately the beginning of the 1990s. The middle part of the diagram, concerning the period from the early 1990s and until around the first five years of this century, presents the development of 'doctoral scholarship' in the same geographical region. The third part of the diagram is devoted to the recent international developments in new modes of knowledge production and suggests several possible ways for how design-related knowledge can become an important contributor to the new 'knowledge landscapes'.[2]

The whole diagram 'Introduction to knowledge forms and knowledge production' consists of four figures which appear diachronically. For each figure, illustrating the relationship between doctoral scholarship in architecture and design, and other forms of knowledge, three kinds of utterances are given place. First, comments on situations observed in the Scandinavian context are provided. Then the graphic part of the diagram follows, with a brief argumentation for its specific shape, thus complying with Mitchell's plea for the interdependence between the visual and the verbal parts of the diagram. Finally, references to various authors are given to support the logic behind the construction of the diagram. While the first part is a report, written in an 'impersonal' form, the two following parts are written as the author's personal narrative, which describes and argues for her own graphic and textual steps in constructing the diagram.

After this sequence, no summary is proposed, as the diagrams are not regarded as complete 'products'. They serve to open up a dialogue with prospective doctoral students and can be changed in the future when good arguments for doing so come up.

Constructing the diagram 'introduction to knowledge forms and knowledge production'

Doctoral scholarship in architecture and design until the mid-1970s

During the 'initial phase', until the mid-1970s, PhD students derived their subject of research from their professional or pedagogical practice. The motivation to take a doctoral degree was most often to conclude a professional career by reflecting on one's professional interests. The doctoral students carried out their research in the framework of an individual arrangement with their supervisors, most of whom were not scholars, but highly esteemed practitioners. It was not unusual that a doctoral candidate spent 15–20 years on preparing his or, far more rarely, her scholarly 'opus'. Very few doctoral degrees were conferred on practitioners. The doctoral theses represented a kind of professional internal discussion with the subject matter. Attempts to engage in an academic dialogue with the traditional knowledge disciplines were few and far between. The language of these theses is most often that of informed professionals, not that of scholars seeking broader academic communication.

I began to sketch the diagram by drawing a horizontal line, representing time, but also a traditional split between the everyday world, including the matters connected with architecture and its practice, and the world of academic knowledge production as expressed by academic disciplines. I marked the first time period, the middle of the 1970s, by a vertical line. This period is characterized by a series of university laws in the Scandinavian countries, which made a strong impact on doctoral scholarship in these countries. I drew under the horizontal line a hatched circular figure, thus signifying the practice field of architecture. Above the line I drew several oblong, contour-marked figures to represent academic disciplines, like sociology, psychology, anthropology, etc. They remain unfilled to denote their 'non-material' character as opposed to the 'material' character of architecture and its everyday practice. Both kinds of figures were clearly drawn to indicate that they in a way represented autonomous entities. Two crossed arrows between the circular figure and the oblong ones are meant to illustrate that there was not much dialogue between the world of architectural scholars and that of academia. The 'products' of the architectural research seem to remain in the realm of practice.

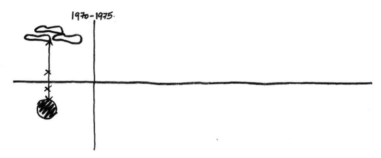

Figure 4.1 Doctoral scholarship until the mid-1970s.

For the pedagogical purpose of simplification, I identified architecture and its practice with the architecture profession which made it possible to regard them as an autonomous field. 'Studies of professionalism, ... identify certain characteristics that differentiate the professions from specialized vocations in general; the most important being the professionals' claim of autonomy within a field' (Burns 2000: 262). 'most professionals are consumed by establishing boundaries around themselves that determine who can legitimately engage in a particular craft' (Sutton 2000: 205). As such I denoted graphically architecture and its practice/the architecture profession, as a hatched circular figure. Similarly, academic disciplines are here regarded as autonomous fields and marked as oblong, closed figures. '...disciplines are defined by groups of objects, methods, their corpus of propositions considered to be true, the interplay of rules and definitions, of techniques and tools' (Foucault 1972 [1969]: 222).

> a discipline participates in the *alignment* of ideas and knowledge, and various combinations of alignments form the separate disciplines. What determines and maintains any alignment, what gives it its singularity and delimits its boundaries, what assists in adjudicating its decisions, is its *theory*'.
>
> (Johnson 1994: 2, emphasis in the original)

Thus I have denoted the relations between architectural doctoral scholarship and the world of academic disciplines for the first period of consideration. These relations deserve the well-known metaphor of 'a badly made patchwork quilt', even if a more well known metaphor for such relations is 'knowledge landscapes' (Becher and Trowler 2001: 29).

Doctoral scholarship from the mid-1970s to the beginning of the 1990s

The 'second phase', from the mid-1970s to the beginning of the 1990s, coincides with the period when the schools of architecture were pressured by their national authorities to develop a more academic profile, i.e. a more research-oriented one.[3] For architectural vocational studies, such a demand was a serious challenge, as no strong tradition for this aspect of the field existed. The schools and faculties of architecture began to look for more strategic and institutionalized ways in which to build up such an academically oriented profile. Some theoretical disciplines, especially the social sciences, offered models to follow and they were taken up. Architectural and design practice was regarded as a sort of 'applied science'. As a consequence of this, PhD students were expected to 'renounce' their professional backgrounds as designers and architects. In the doctoral theses of this period it is difficult to trace any awareness of a scholarly stance among the authors. Consequently, the 'dialogue' between architectural research and various academic disciplines, addressed in order to discuss architectural matters, lacked on the part of architecture any awareness of its own intellectual identity. There were few examples of the newly acquired doctoral knowledge and insight being applied in professional practice. Most often, doctoral research in architecture and design could be regarded as rather humble imitations of humanistic, social and technological research. That model of doctoral work does not seem to have addressed these important questions: What is unique about design knowledge? Does the concept of design

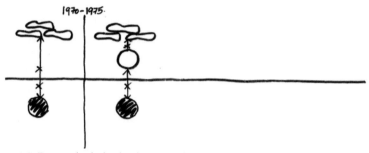

Figure 4.2 Doctoral scholarship between the mid-1970s and the 1990s.

knowledge as 'an applied science' allow for adequate theoretical and epistemological foundations for design thinking? Do such questions also concern other professional disciplines?

I have indicated by a new vertical line another period for the doctoral scholarship; that between the mid-1970s and the 1990s. This period saw the implementation of a series of new university laws in the Scandinavian countries, which made a strong impact on doctoral scholarship in these countries. I have drawn similar figures to those above for this period as well; a hatched circular figure for architecture and its practice, and oblong figures for several academic disciplines. The arrows are still crossed, and this illustrates that there was not much dialogue between the architectural scholars and the practice of architecture. The contributions of the former did not reach back to the practice, and they did not seem to have gained acknowledgement in academia. The empty circular figure signifies the undefined position of architectural scholarship during this period. This figure has been placed over the horizontal line to signify that the architectural scholarship of this period was often a rather humble imitation of scholarly work in the disciplines it attempted to emulate.

Criticism of adopting methodologies by architectural scholars 'from the outside', first from the social sciences and then from the humanities, was clearly expressed by some informed practitioners at the end of the 1990s (Burns 2000: 266). Social sciences can describe what 'is', necessarily presented as 'seen as'. It can contribute with certain knowledge, but it is never complete with regard to what is addressed by architecture and its practice (Mo 2001: 93). 'Our job is to give the client, on time and on cost, not what he wants, but what he never dreamed he wanted; and when he gets it, he recognizes it as something he wanted all the time' (Skjønsberg 1996: 49). 'What humanistic studies have in common is an interest in history, in the reading of texts, in interpretation, which is seen as tradition, philosophy, form of scholarship, and research method all in one' (Mo 2001: 97). People in various disciplines think that architecture is 'just' an application of the kind of academic study that they themselves are doing. But 'architecture cannot be seen as a trivialized art form, an aestheticized engineering practice, or a dressed-up sociology. Other disciplines can give perspectives on it, but never capture the entirety' (Mo 2001: 131).

Doctoral scholarship in architecture and design in the 1990s

A discussion about the desirability of a more architecturally pronounced epistemological stance began at several Scandinavian schools of architecture early in the 1990s. The new university laws in Scandinavia, which demanded a more academically professional model of scholarship (including doctoral programmes with organized research education) from all institutions of higher education with university status, provided a direct incentive for this discussion.[4]

In March 1992 a Nordic network for co-operation in research education for design professionals was established.[5] Their members represented several Scandinavian schools of architecture offering professional training within design, architecture and spatial planning, which were called the *making* professions in this milieu. These schools were in the process of establishing their doctoral programmes based on mandatory research education.[6] There was a strong need to discuss issues at a broader level than national contexts, possible contents, and methods of research education in the fields of *making* knowledge. The Network continued to co-operate and organized a series of Nordic courses in research education, sponsored by the Nordic Academy of Advanced Study (Nordisk Forskerakademi). These courses contributed to the 'third phase' in the development of doctoral studies, where the focus lay on establishing the identity of design thinking. During the 'third phase' several attempts were made to answer questions like these: Is it possible to find unity in the diversity of our approaches to design and design research? How do artefacts come into existence? What are these artefacts and what are their properties? What are the outcomes of artefacts in the individual and collective lives of human beings?

Another vertical line denotes the third period in architectural scholarship, that between 1990 and 2000. The circular figure still marks architecture and its practice, and the oblong figures represent several academic disciplines. The contributions of architectural doctoral scholarship are illustrated as a circular figure, partly filled (under the horizontal line) and partly empty (over that line). This placement of the circular 'result-figure' indicates that the research was derived from and targeted towards architecture and its practice, but it was also informed by academic disciplines, and, hopefully, contributed to them. The arrows are not crossed, to signify that there has been dialogue between the two worlds, that of architectural scholarship and that of more traditional academia.

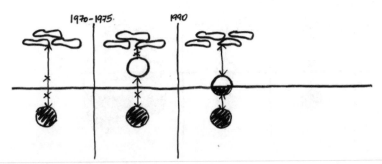

Figure 4.3 Doctoral scholarship 1990–2000.

The challenge of developing architectural and design scholarship has been to comply with the demands of two worlds: in addition to the world of its own profession, to abide by the rules of the academic world. While the main criterion of viability in the former world is its relevance to the practice of the professions; in the latter it is its ability to fulfil the criteria of scholarship. In the USA a debate in the 1990s about architecture as a discipline was presented in the publication The Discipline of Architecture (Piotrowski and Robinson 2000). One of the contributors, Stanford Anderson, there recognized both the profession and the discipline of architecture. They are two realms of activity which 'intersect' each other; they are partially but not wholly coincident. The author means by the 'discipline of architecture' a collective body of knowledge that is unique to architecture and, though it grows over time, is not limited in time or space (Anderson 2000: 292–4). The Scandinavian concept of the creative disciplines has been an attempt to formulate a kind of quality supportive framework for *making* discourse rather than of traditional discipline in a strict sense (Dunin-Woyseth and Michl 2001). It has been an attempt to respond to both the criteria of professional relevance and, not least, of a qualified dialogue with academia.

Mode 1 and Mode 2 of knowledge production with regard to architectural and design scholarship

The network for co-operation in research education, joining several schools of architecture and design in the Nordic countries, has held the professionalism of research education as its aim. Between 1999 and 2001 the network organized a Scandinavian research education programme, called the Millennium Programme, in which more than 50 Nordic PhD students participated (Dunin-Woyseth 2002: 7–18). At the conclusion of the courses, the network's teachers agreed that the current status of research education offered adequate training opportunities for the growing Nordic community of architectural and design researchers. However, this seemed to apply mainly to traditional disciplinary and interdisciplinary, academically initiated research. The network teachers decided that the next phase of co-operation should be committed to the preparation of young researchers to meet the demands for new types of a broader research competence in problem and solution-oriented research. A new Nordic pilot study course, sponsored by the Nordic Academy of Advanced Study, was arranged in

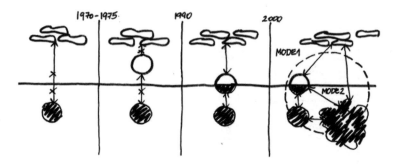

Figure 4.4 Mode 1 and Mode 2 of knowledge production with regard to architectural and design scholarship.

2003. Its intention was to introduce the Nordic doctoral students to the international discussion on new modes of knowledge production.

Since the Nordic course on Mode 1 and Mode 2 in 2003, the issues of new modes of knowledge production have been addressed both in the research education at the Oslo School of Architecture and Design, and through the individual doctoral projects of the PhD students.

This part of the diagram includes the previously used figures; that of architecture and its practice, and those of academic disciplines. In addition, an amorphous figure, placed under the horizontal line, suggests everyday problems being solved through transdisciplinarity / Mode 2 of knowledge production. 'Arrows of dialogue' stay uncrossed between the various 'stakeholders' in the research process as communication between them makes the basis for this form of research. Both architectural expertise and architectural scholarship can contribute to solving everyday problems, as can the academic disciplines. Architecture and other design fields can achieve a strong position within Mode 2 of knowledge production, as they can both act as fields of practice and fields of inquiry. The contributions of the design fields within Mode 2 stay solidly in the sphere of everyday life on the diagram, but they can also be acknowledged within Mode 1, as illustrated for the previous period (1990–2000).

In 'The New Production of Knowledge', the authors describe two parallel and competitive modes of knowledge production:

> Mode 1: The complex of ideas, methods, values and norms that has grown up to control the diffusion of the Newtonian model of science to more and more fields of inquiry and ensure its compliance with what is considered sound scientific practice. Mode 2: Knowledge production carried out in the context of application and marked by its: transdisciplinarity; heterogeneity; organizational hierarchy and transience; social accountability and reflexivity; and quality control, which emphasizes context- and use-dependence. It results from the parallel expansion of knowledge producers and users in society.
>
> (Gibbons et al. 1994: 167)

The definition of Mode 2 introduces the notion of transdisciplinarity, described in the following way:

> Transdisciplinarity is a new form of learning and problem-solving involving cooperation among different parts of society and academia in order to meet complex challenges of society. Transdisciplinary research starts from tangible, real-world problems. Solutions are devised in collaboration with multiple stakeholders. A practice-oriented approach, transdisciplinarity is not confined to a closed circle of scientific experts, professional journals and academic departments where knowledge is produced. Through mutual learning, the knowledge of all participants is enhanced, including local knowledge, scientific knowledge and the knowledge of concerned industries, businesses, and non-governmental organizations. The sum of this knowledge will be greater than the knowledge of any single partner. In the process, the bias of each perspective will also be minimized.
>
> (Klein et al. 2001: 7)

Mode 2 has appealed to the design scholars as a new 'in practice model' (Lawson 2002: 114). This mode opens various ways in which the design professions could contribute to knowledge production. The question was even posed whether designers were not '...just ahead of the game rather than behind it after all' (Lawson 2002: 114). Some examples of transdisciplinary research by architects and designers have been discussed in the milieu of several Scandinavian schools of architecture (Dunin-Woyseth and Nielsen 2004).

The protagonists of transdisciplinary research maintain that, in spite of its growing importance and extent, it does not replace the traditional forms of research, such as disciplinary research. Even if competing, it is still an additional form of research that involves partners from outside academia (Häberli *et al.* 2001: 8). The founders of the Mode 1/Mode 2 movement maintain that in order to master the tasks of Mode 2, one has to get through an apprenticeship in Mode 1. One first has to develop a kind of intellectual identity of Mode 1 in order to be able to acquire multiple cognitive and social identities for practising research in Mode 2 (Gibbons *et al.* 1994: 149).

Mode 1 and Mode 2 'diagrammed'

Figure 4.4 has served as the backbone for the introductory lectures on Mode 1 and Mode 2. It seems to have had the two features of a generic diagram, as formulated by Stjernfelt: (i) being an icon, the diagram is characterized by its similarity to its object, but it represents this similarity through a skeleton-like sketch of relations, and, (ii) the diagram is the only sign by the contemplation of which more can be learnt than lies in the directions for its construction.

In order to introduce the first period of doctoral scholarship in architecture in Scandinavia, one of the well-known systems of knowledge classification was presented (Kaiser 2000). The basic norms of the scientific ethos, the so-called CUDOS, as formulated by Robert Merton, were then briefly elaborated on for scientific knowledge purposes (Ziman 2000: 28–55). While covering the second period, the role of the world outside academia, in this case in the form of certain university laws, was discussed and its direct impact on doctoral scholarship in architecture and design was pointed out. Elucidating the third period in the diagram, the three aims for organized doctoral education, as applied in the UK and Norway, were presented. These were: (i) to introduce the PhD students to the 'landscapes of knowledge' in order to position their own field; (ii) to strengthen the PhD students' intellectual identity with regard to this knowledge; and (iii) to prepare the PhD students to cooperate in research with other knowledge fields. Subsequently, it was mentioned how the Nordic network for research education has developed ideas about the 'making disciplines' as a possible response to the 'second' aim of the research education (Dunin-Woyseth and Michl 2001). The diagram's first three figures created a skeleton-like sketch for a discussion on disciplinarity, interdisciplinarity and multidisciplinarity. This discussion was essential as an introduction to new modes of knowledge production, where transdisciplinarity constitutes the cornerstone. The diagram thus facilitates the consideration of design research as monodisciplinary, multi- and interdisciplinary (i.e. Mode 1-based), as well as transdisciplinary (i.e. Mode 2- based).

On securing housing safety: a transdisciplinary project

Introduction

In this section of the chapter a collaborative research project will be presented and discussed. When a pilot Nordic research course on transdisciplinarity was carried out in autumn 2003, the participators suggested several improvements for the forthcoming courses on this issue. Among them there was the suggestion that at least one of the presented transdisciplinary projects should include a recognizable contribution from some of the creative professions such as architects, landscape architects, planners, designers or artists. The challenge for future courses on Mode 2 was thus not so much the finding of such a project, but rather making the researchers of that project aware of the transdisciplinary character of their work.

In Sweden, as in other western countries, there is a long tradition of architectural research being done in collaboration with stakeholders such as national authorities, municipalities, the construction sector; all more or less involved in housing, building and planning. There is a wide range of subjects in this field which cross traditional and professional boundaries (Forty *et al.* 2006: 42–3). But the great majority of the Swedish architectural research community is not aware of, and consequently does not recognize, their own work as transdisciplinary. This is probably not only the case in Sweden. If so, a strengthened awareness in this regard could support the position of the creative professions in Mode 2 development.

An architect and professor in Urban Planning, Björn Klarqvist, collaborated with a policeman, Anders Rydberg and his colleagues, on a project on securing housing safety in the city in which they lived. The scholar promised to examine their project in the terms of Mode 2 and transdisciplinarity. In the following account, the present author has made an attempt to abbreviate and retell the story told by the architect and the policeman. In the closing of this section the architect-scholar then discusses transdisciplinarity with regard to their own project and in more general terms.

The fairy tale recounted

There was a Swedish policeman who always tried to do his best. He looked for order, protected lawful citizens and apprehended offenders in his district. He was well-liked by his colleagues and his superiors considered advancing his career. Statistics revealed that crime had been increasing in his district for a long time. It worried the boss of the policeman, especially because his own boss expected him to provide an explanation for this development. The mid-level boss remarked to him that one of his policemen was particularly good at his field work. Thus, a promotion was proposed to him, with a new position in the administration. That was not what the policeman looked forward to, as he mostly enjoyed doing field work. So he asked for some time to consider the offer before accepting the promotion.

When the policeman got a few days off as a compensation for his overtime, he left for his summer house to think about why crime seemed to grow in volume and why the policeman's job resembled a Sisyphean task. The perspective of another 30 years of such a job suddenly seemed less than tempting; a burn-out prospect not too far removed from the present moment. So the policeman saw the proposal of a more stable job in administration in a new light. After his return to work, the policeman accepted the new position under the condition that he would be given a four-month period to investigate how burglaries in his district occurred. He intended to begin humbly, by observing how cellar and attic burglaries happened in the housing areas. In spite of initial objections on the part of his boss, the policeman was allowed to begin his investigations. He was even supported by a few other policemen.

The policeman read all the reports and court files about burglaries in cellars and attics during the last two years. It seemed that certain buildings were more frequently 'visited' than others. The policeman made several inspections of those buildings and he tried to understand how the crimes had been executed. What made the policeman pay special attention was the lack of reporting information on when the burglaries took place and why it was possible to execute them. Some caretakers and tenants mentioned that not all burglaries were reported to the police as the value of the stolen goods was not that high and the percentage of solved burglaries was not so impressive. The policeman and one of his colleagues resolved to sit on folding chairs in an empty cellar storage area and wait for the thieves. During the school lunch break two children arrived and pulled at the lock. They left, but returned after school hours and broke into the cellar. During only three days, the two policemen reported fifty children aged between eight and twelve, all of them caught red-handed. The policemen interviewed the children to find out the reasons for these petty crimes. The results were surprising. Through the burglaries, the children said they experienced excitement, discovered new spaces for play and looked for what could be vandalized. Economic gain was the reason for only a few burglaries.

The colleagues of the policemen began to pay more and more attention to the project. They went on guard for a few nights, and this was rewarded with new insights. Around one o'clock in the morning another group of burglars arrived. These ones were more professional and goal-oriented. They looked in the cellars and attics for more valuable objects to be stolen and sold. While the child burglars were those living in the district, the adult burglars arrived from other districts or even other counties. Money from the thefts was to be used mostly on drugs. It was not difficult to break into the cellars or attics. Around 100 burglars were captured over the space of two months.

Whereas in the past, the police mainly responded to alarms and reports, they now began to investigate crime patterns in order to recognize mechanisms, which in turn led them back to the crimes at a better rate. The policeman who initiated these investigations and proposed preventive measures was invited by the national Police Administration to act as an expert on crime prevention. He became the head of a new development unit based on three components: IT, context and future analysis, as well as CPTED – Crime Prevention through Environmental Design.

The policeman and his team examined urban plans and housing projects in order to guide people on how to prevent crime. They developed a serious expertise on what mistakes architects, builders, planners and landlords used to make in their projects. The policeman decided to write a manual, based on many investigations from crime scenes as well as results of his unit's own tests of different technical solutions. The people in the unit were aware of their unique expertise and of the value of it being shared with housing owners and others. The county authority and its board supported the unit in providing such a manual. The alliances included the major housing and building companies in the county, the town planning office and the School of Architecture. A few weeks later, a reference group was created and the work on the manual was launched.

The team began to write down all their best recommendations on locks, doors, windows, entrances, lighting, etc. The members of the team that were recruited from the School of Architecture attempted to discuss those practical issues in light of theories of a general character or from the perspectives of urban planning principles. The builders and managers expected to get checklists for their daily practice. Practitioners supplied examples and comments. The new manual, 'Bo tryggt 01' (Live Safely 01), appeared at the Housing Exhibition. The manual design was deliberately a loose-leaf binder, which provided space for future additions of information. The manual's text was also published on the police website and was thus accessible for downloading (Rydberg 2001). The police team offered the manual to every company involved in housing projects. It was used by the police authorities, by urban planning offices, architects' offices, local crime prevention boards, as well as housing and building companies all over Sweden. The manual has become a kind of nationwide standards guideline, even if its origins were local. National authorities in the field applauded the success of the manual. The policeman was offered new positions, but he stayed at the regional level, where he believes it is still possible to have an overview and remain what the Swedes call 'earthbound'.

Comments on a fairy tale

Klarqvist (2004) reports that while he, the architectural scholar, cooperated with Anders Rydberg – the policeman in the 'fairy tale' – they were not aware of the discussions on Mode 1 and Mode 2 knowledge production. But when invited to report on their work process, after having read Gibbons' book, they recognized 'a posteriori' various components of their own work process as the constitutive elements of Mode 2 knowledge production. When their manual for crime prevention was published, they continued their Mode 2-like research activities. He describes them in the following way:

> We invited construction and housing companies to choose one of their projects as a test bench. Around each project the scholars organized three workshops together with the employees of different positions and professional backgrounds. In the workshops a) we tested how the existing crime prevention manual and checklist were understood and applicable to the project, b) we developed, introduced, tested and discussed new theories and methods, c) we designed a second version of the manual to be discussed and tested amongst the participants. This bi-directional knowledge mediation and production will certainly a) make the manual better adapted to real world processes within the companies, b) introduce the staff to new aspects of crime prevention in what is a rather tradition bound sector of society, and c) develop new theories, methods and processes going beyond its prime intention.
>
> (Klarqvist 2004)

77

Mode 1 and Mode 2: What can they offer to field-specific design research?

This chapter has been built on the two cases, both taking place in a context of research education for professionals from creative fields like architecture, urban planning, industrial design and the arts. The objective for presenting and discussing these cases has been to examine what the opportunities are with regard to the development of design research within frameworks inherent in each of the two modes of knowledge production. While the major part of the chapter was devoted to introducing these two modes and to presenting them further through the two cases, this part will briefly examine the cases in terms of a comparison between Mode 1 and Mode 2 and will conclude with what each of the modes can offer to field specific design research.

The 'diagram case' builds on the statement of Helga Nowotny, one of the key figures of the Mode 2 movement. Nowotny maintains that in order to qualify as a Mode 2 researcher, one has first to be competent as a Mode 1 researcher. The diagram illustrates how doctoral scholarship has developed from the middle of the 1970s and until the present in the Scandinavian academic milieux of creative professions, mainly architecture and design. The diagram helped to show that while this scholarship previously seemed to emulate disciplinary fields, the discussions on Mode 1 and Mode 2 that started around 1996 facilitated more field-specific concepts of design scholarship. The most recent part of the diagram argues that the two modes of knowledge production can be adequately addressed by design professionals in their field-specific scholarship.

The 'diagram case' was devised in a traditional academic context, i.e. that of Mode 1 knowledge production. The components of the diagram have been defined as (a) the result of a free *search for knowledge* which has traditionally been an obligation and a privilege of university staff, to which the author belongs. The diagram expresses (b) a *search for basic causal relationships* between doctoral scholarship in design fields and various premises. The internal premises have been based on design research itself, while the external premises were the national, and later on, European university laws. The causal relationships and the logic of their construction, pointed out in the diagram, had to be discussed by a community of peers. To do so they had to be presented in a way which exposed (c) *the ideas, methods, values and norms* considered as sound research practice. In this presentation the author of the diagram made (d) an *emphasis on her individual creativity*. Although the diagram was developed in recent years, it was only possible to construct it over time as (e) a *continuous process*. The (f) *quality control* of the diagram construction process was executed by a peer-review commission of the scientific committee of an international research conference. The scientific committee that had the authority to accept or refuse the diagrammatic reasoning of the author consisted of a group of international experts, which is a typical (g) *hierarchical organization form and decision-making system directed top-down*. The (h) *distribution of the knowledge* developed through the diagram's construction happened through a Mode 1 medium in the form of conference proceedings (Dunin-Woyseth 2009).

The 'fairy tale case' of the transdisciplinary project on securing housing safety, presents and discusses a project on crime prevention by an architect and a policeman. The project built on a long process of various activities by multiple stakeholders, a process initiated from the need for practical solutions for housing safety. In the postscript after the project presentation, the architect-scholar looked at the work

Mode 1	Mode 2
(a) Free search for knowledge	(a) Politically defined research objectives, ecological considerations, holistic approach, economy, etc.
(b) Search for basic causal relationships	(b) Interest in methods in order to develop complex systems or processes
(c) Ideas, methods, values and norms	(c) Knowledge production carried out in the context of application and decided upon by academic community marked by its heterogeneity and transience. Social accountability regarding what is considered sound research practice
(d) Emphasis on individual creativity	(d) Emphasis on team-work, co-ordination
(e) Continuous process	(e) Time-limited projects
(f) Quality control through internal criteria	(f) Quality control with emphasis on context and user-dependence of academic community ('peer-review')
(g) Hierarchical organisation forms and decision-making systems directed top-down	(g) Networks operating through information and communication technology in heterarchical relationships
(h) Distribution of knowledge through the media: books, academic papers, journals, conferences etc.	(h) Social distribution of knowledge: the diffusion of knowledge production and different contexts of application or use over a wide range of potential sites

Figure 4.5 'Matrix of comparison between Mode 1 and Mode 2' (Dunin-Woyseth 2001: 93, based on Gibbons *et al.* 1994)

process and examined it with regard to establishing whether it met the criteria of transdisciplinarity. Even though many research projects over the years have been in their essence transdisciplinary, there has not been a great collective awareness around them. By strengthening such awareness, practice-based research could get stronger legitimacy and economic support while competing for research funds within the milieux of academic disciplines. The architect-researcher in the project has given a good picture of how he operated between the two modes of knowledge production. While in action, using his professional expertise, and as a coach/mentor for the project as a whole, he was clearly a Mode 2 researcher. When reporting to the research community, he followed the usual Mode 1 criteria of scholarship. This transdisciplinary project illustrates a situation when both modes of knowledge production have been in a synergetic dialogue.

The 'fairy-tale case' is based on many activities which happened in the context of Mode 2 knowledge production, even if this context was not, at the time, recognized as such. Recognized – *a posteriori* – as a transdisciplinary research project, the (a) *objective* of this project, i.e. housing safety, was *political*. The numerous participants of the project showed (b) an *interest in different methods in order to develop complex processes* and developed new, appropriate methods to first of all diagnose the problems more clearly and, later on, to propose adequate measures to solve them. The (c) *knowledge production* was, thus, *carried out in the context of application.* It was *heterogeneous,* as it originated from negotiating the various knowledge positions of the participants (policemen, users, architects, etc.). It was *transient,* as the solutions it proposed were adopted for specific places at specific times. The people who co-operated on the project dispersed after it was concluded. The knowledge which was developed step-by-step, had to be *socially accountable.* Each step in the process needed economic sources from various sponsors; therefore each was appropriately argued for. From the very beginning the project was truly (d) *team-work,* needing effective *coordination.* Each step was (e) *time-limited* and (f) *quality control* was inherent *in the context and use-dependency* of the project. Each successive step depended on whether the previous one was successful. The (g) *networks* of various groups of participants operated both through face-to-face contact and *through information and communication technology in heterarchical relationships.* The (h) *social distribution of the new knowledge* happened *through the diffusion of knowledge production and different contexts of application or use over a wide range of potential sites.* New guidelines for safer housing were distributed through user organizations, police circulars and via various channels of information and communication technology.

These two cases, examined through the author's 'matrix of comparison between Mode 1 and Mode 2', elucidate the different character of various research aspects within the framework of each of these two modes. The key differences relate to various practice contexts in which they have been carried out. The examination of the two cases attempts to clarify the differences between the premises and the consequences of operating within each of the two frameworks. It also highlights the potential for a dialogue between what may initially seem as irreconcilable positions.

Mode 1-related academic systems do not tend to view Mode 2 as a serious knowledge producer, while the discipline-bound knowledge of Mode 1 is perceived by the protagonists of Mode 2 as legitimate, but as having a restricted sphere of applicability (Nicolescu 2002: 44). It can be argued that there is not only a potential for bringing these two modes together, but that this might be beneficial for both perspectives.

Mode 2 offers a broad, inclusive framework for field-specific research in the design fields. It welcomes the traditional disciplinary design research, but it also opens for explorative initiatives where professionals can contribute in innovative ways, both as practitioners and scholars in their fields. The awareness of these opportunities should be built into research education for prospective design researchers, as well as among mature practice-based researchers who have produced Mode 2-related, transdisciplinary research, without being cognizant of the fact. Both research educational strategies could strengthen the intellectual identity of both junior and senior design researchers and make them more successful while competing for research funds with knowledge producers from other, academically more established fields.

Notes

1 'De ulike fagene legger seg så å si ved siden av hverandre og bidrar med hva de kan til det temaet som drøftes. Flerfaglig samarbeid krever ingen faglig integrasjon, men ulike faglige bidrag kan inspirere og utvikle de enkelte faglige bidragene' (Nyseth 2007: 22).

2 The first part of the diagram is based on the author's experience as an academic evaluator. Over the past 15 years she has often served as a member of Scandinavian evaluation committees for

assessing the competence of applicants for associate professorships and full professorships. Part of this job involved becoming familiar with the scholarly output of the applicants for which a doctoral thesis often represents the cornerstone. Over the same period of time the author has been an external examiner for a substantial number of doctoral dissertations. Her notes from studying more than 50 doctoral dissertations have made it possible for her to notice some tendencies concerning how academically professional scholarship is developing through the doctorates in the Nordic countries. The middle part of the diagram concerns the period since the author began her work as the founding director of the Doctoral Programme at the Oslo School of Architecture in 1990. This long period has provided her with a broad experience as an academic manager at various levels of such responsibility, from a micro level to a macro level. The third part of the diagram addresses the period of her extensive activity as an academic teacher at the doctoral level, with a special interest in matters concerning knowledge in design fields.

3 Around the middle of the 1970s, new reforms and university laws made a significant impact on the higher education in Scandinavia. In Denmark the University Law of 1973 modernized the existing university system first time after 1858 (KU 2010). In Norway the doctoral degree became the standard qualification for the 'middle group' of the academic staff to be granted a tenured position (UiO 2009: 9). In Sweden, the Reform 1977 (*Högskolereformen* 1977), included professional and artistic education into a unified university system and it introduced a two-tier educational system, based on basic education and research education (KMH 2007: 3). Higher education in professions should be from then on based on research.

4 In 1993, new university laws were adopted in the three Scandinavian countries. In Norway the new law (Kongelig resolusjon) decreed a merger of 98 regional colleges into 26 so-called state colleges. Only the four universities and the six autonomous university colleges then had the right to confer a doctoral degree, but it was opened for the new state colleges to build up their scholarly competence and apply for this right (NOU 2008). The Danish University Law, concerning all institutions of higher education, opened up a stronger academic and economic autonomy for them (Børing and Maassen *et al.* 2003). It established a new, formalized position for doctoral degrees in the national system of higher education. The Swedish decree regarding higher education (Högskoleförordningen) also granted stronger academic and economic autonomy, but in return demanded higher and more explicit results.

5 The members of the Nordic network for research education for architects, designers and artists, were professors: Niels Albertsen, Aarhus School of Architecture, Denmark; Halina Dunin-Woyseth, Oslo School of Architecture, Norway; Jerker Lundeqvist, Royal Institute of Technology, Stockholm, Sweden, and, Anna-Maija Ylimaula, Faculty of Architecture, Oulu University, Finland.

6 After several years of preparation, the ministers in charge of higher education in all the countries taking part in the Bologna Process decided to adopt the future of doctoral programmes as a specific Bologna objective at the September 2003 meeting in Berlin. Doctoral education has been recognized as the third and highest cycle of education, after Bachelors' and Masters' degrees. 'They emphasize the importance of research and research training and the promotion of interdisciplinarity in maintaining and improving the quality of higher education and in enhancing the competitiveness of European higher education more generally. ... Ministers ask higher education institutions to increase the role of relevance of research to technological, social and cultural evolutions and to the needs' of society' (quote source: Berlin 2003).

5

COMMUNITIES, VALUES, CONVENTIONS AND ACTIONS

Michael Biggs and Daniela Büchler

Chapter overview

This chapter sets out a theoretical framework that addresses dissatisfaction in research in the arts. This dissatisfaction is related to the emergence of something called 'practice-based research'. There are different names for this kind of research, and some communities are very sensitive about the different nuances that these names connote. Finding a good name to describe the field has proven to be difficult, and the list of names used by others is very long. For example, terms like 'artistic research' are rejected by the design community; 'creative research' suggests that other research is not creative; 'practice-based' does not clarify what kind of practice, e.g. arts, education, healthcare, nor does the term clarify how practices leading to research outcomes differ from practices leading to professional outcomes. We intend our use of the term 'practice-based' to include the visual and performing arts, music, and those aspects of architecture and design that emphasize aesthetic rather than technical values. Broadly speaking they all present the same problem and that is: what it is to undertake research in a practice-based area. In particular, there is an interest in research that is not historically led or to do with technology, but instead is to do with the actual production of the stuff itself. We think that the problem arises when these professional activities are pushed into the academic context.

We began writing this chapter from the simple observation that many well-informed people in the creative and performing arts in academia have disagreed for a long time about the concept of research in their field. The various communities have plenty of experience of both the professional and academic worlds, the needs of doctoral students and research funding agencies, etc. So how is it that there are so many different, yet strongly advocated, models of what constitutes valid research in the arts? It seemed to us unlikely that it was simply the case that one side was right and one side was wrong. But we were also reluctant to conclude that the matter was just discretionary, or a matter of personal opinion, because that would not help to develop general policy or guide research councils and others in the allocation of funds and the evaluation of research. Asking what model would constitute valid research in the arts presumes that there is a model that would satisfy both the creative practice and the academic communities. Given the long running debate, we concluded that perhaps there is not a single research model that would satisfy both communities, and instead we should ask what is the source and nature of the dissatisfaction with the existing models of research that are available to practitioners, in order that new approaches to the problem might emerge.

Changing the question means that we have shifted from focusing on what model would satisfy the communities, to focusing on what it is about the existing models that dissatisfies these communities. Our hunch was that this long-running disagreement was grounded in different notions of what was required in research, owing to different values. As a result, we asked 'how coherent are these actions as a form of advancement, given the culture of knowledge and values held by this community?' The advantage of this question was that it substituted a 'right or wrong' judgement by a 'satisfied or dissatisfied' judgement. It seemed to us that dissatisfaction could be observed, whereas the 'correctness or incorrectness' of a model could only be determined if one had a standard to which it could be compared. The long-running debate is evidence that, as yet, no such standard exists in research in the creative and performing arts.

We observe two different communities presenting conflicting claims: the community of academic researchers working in contexts such as university departments, and the community of professional practitioners working in contexts such as the concert hall or the art gallery. We also observe these communities being thrown together by external forces, and a new community of so-called practitioner-researchers becoming visible (Chapter 1). In a nutshell, the practitioner-researcher archetype refers to individuals who hold practitioner values but produce research in an academic context.

In the parent communities, we see dissatisfaction. On the one hand, we hear the academic community at large – understood as academic researchers in any academic area and discipline – express the dissatisfaction that what creative practitioners produce is not academic research. On the other hand, we hear the dissatisfaction of the creative practitioner community that their values are not reflected in traditional academic research models and, as a result, when they use these models the outcomes are not relevant to them. Hence, there is dissatisfaction in both camps. In this chapter we identify the source and diagnose the nature of dissatisfaction that we observe in both the academic and creative practice communities, and discuss some of the actions that are employed in response to the problem.

Concept of community

In the fields of cultural studies and activity theory, a community is defined as a group of individuals who share common values. A community has a shared set of values that define them and to which the members broadly subscribe and thereby identify themselves as part of that community. Values include cultural beliefs and also ontological and epistemological beliefs about the nature of the world and how one can interact with it (Kroeber and Kluckhohn. 1952; Hofstede 1991). When communities evolve naturally, these values reflect the community's practices and these practices reflect those values. Such a community thus possesses an internal coherence between its values and the actions it performs and as a result it is apparent why each community does what it does given what it believes and values (Engeström *et al.* 1999).

The actions that a community performs emanate from the values that it holds (Rokeach 1973; Schein 1991). Members of a community perform a variety of actions, some arbitrary and some more purposeful, and some will make their way into the norms for that community's behaviour. Conformity to the community's norms is usually the way one determines whether a person is a member of that community. This involves judging an explicit behaviour rather than trying to judge a person's implicit values. Aiming to act in accordance with a community's norms is a way of gaining admission to a community. Membership of a professional community often involves the adoption of certain characteristic behaviours (Bourdieu 1992) and, as a consequence, these become constituting behaviours.

A community formalizes its values as norms and codes of conduct through the establishment of conventions. These conventions form a kind of shorthand for how to act in ways that will satisfy the other members. However, over time these conventions can become disconnected from their original rationale. As the community evolves, certain actions that were once purposeful and undertaken mindfully may start to be performed mindlessly. Members of the community may not notice this and the purposelessness of obsolete conventions may not be visible to individuals who have been members of a community for a long time. Purposelessness is often exposed when new members join or when the boundaries of communities change and conventions fail to adapt.

The values that are held by a community determine what are meaningful actions and significant activities. Conventions represent and formalize what is valued and define what is meaningful – likely to produce relevant outcomes; and what is significant – likely to make a contribution that is of consequence to others. Ensuring that actions are meaningful is a professional competence that consists of critical reflection on practices, and is facilitated by professional training. Education and enculturation reinforce the shared values, and as a result they are not discretionary (Weisner 2000). This explanation is a social-psychological theory of knowledge rather than a correspondence theory of what it is to know. The disadvantage of the correspondence theory is that it encourages one to seek corresponding facts. The advantage of the social-psychological theory is that it focuses attention on the users of research and the way in which certain activities reinforce the aims and values of the community. One of our interests in this chapter is why different communities find different value in the same activities.

Certain actions that are performed by a community are simply meaningless or arbitrary owing to a lack of content. But others that are meaningful, when networked together, form significant activities that have impact. Therefore, actions are meaningful when they have a coherent relationship with the values of a community. This coherent relationship characterizes that community and even non-members can appreciate its internal coherence. Significant activities are composed of a network of meaningful actions. The community that performs the actions determines which are the meaningful ones, with the aim of constructing a 'value-reflecting' set of actions, i.e. an activity that is significant to the community. However, it is not the actions that characterize a community because actions on their own do not have meaning. It is only through their inter-connectedness to other meaningful actions that they become significant. Writing a report or making a painting is not significant *per se* but only as part of a network of other valued actions (Hirsch 1984).

Satisfaction through coherence

There is a relationship between a community's value system, the activities that they deem relevant, and the actions that comprise these activities. When this relationship is coherent the community is satisfied because their values have conditioned the actions and are therefore reflected in them. This is the case within the communities of creative practice and of academic research when they are addressing their respective aims and interests. These activities have evolved in each community over a long period of time, hence their internal coherence with the community's values. In traditional academic research, the connection between actions is of a particular kind that reinforces and responds to the academic concept of knowledge production. Similarly, in the areas of creative practice we find communities producing culturally significant outcomes in the context of the concert hall or the art gallery, that respond to the changing nature of the cultural environment. These activities reflect the creative practitioner's concept of creative production. In each case, satisfaction results from coherence between what is needed and what the activities supply.

Our definition of academic conventions is that they are a cipher for the network of actions that constitute meaningful research, and establish membership of the community by determining its professional codes and standards. In the same way, the world of professional creative practice has its codes which determine success and by which membership can be judged. We claim this even for contemporary creative practice, which appears to thrive on breaking rules and changing standards. However, in our view the professional practice of any activity is never a case of 'anything goes', despite occasional appearances to the contrary.

Academic aims and interests are embodied in the conventions of academic research, manifested in such things as the regulations for doctoral study, the requirements of research councils and academic journals, etc. From observing these academic conventions one can begin to see what the concepts are of academic research *per se*, prior to a consideration of how these might be applied in ways that satisfy particular communities. We believe that academic conventions provide a kind of shorthand for what activities the academic community needs and wants. If these academic conventions are unpacked, it will be possible to identify what are the specific requirements of each academic community. If these conventions are considered as a meta-level system, it will be possible to identify the actions that constitute research activity that is significant to the academic community in general, and that thus reflect the values of the academy. These values include elements such as rationalism – meaning the ability to explain the logical connection between one concept and another; and communication – meaning that ideas are shared and the academic community grows in its knowledge by this process (Searle 1993). The aspect that we focused on was not whether this element or that element was important, but the observation that these elements described actions: the action of rationally connecting ideas, the action of disseminating outcomes, etc. These actions were undertaken because they reflected what the academic community valued, in this case for example, the values of connecting, building and sharing.

These academic values inform the actions that are performed by the academic community. Meaningful actions are the ones that, given the value system of the academic community, will compose the significant research activity. The concepts and actions that are mobilized in a research project or thesis are joined together in a particular way that forges the research activity, and which is done through an argument. Connection through argumentation refers to a structure that produces an argument rather than any one particular argument – meaning that it refers to the rational connection of ideas rather than the advocacy of a particular position. This is a special kind of narrative that networks concepts and authorities in a way that is particular to the academy.

Elsewhere we have claimed that there are four issues that are persistently indicative of the research activity that is meaningful to the academic community: the possession of a question and an answer, the presence of something corresponding to the term 'knowledge', a method that connected the answers in a meaningful way to the questions that were asked, and an audience for whom all this would have significance (Biggs and Büchler 2009). The network within which these elements exist is what makes them significant as academic research to the academic community. Academic argumentation refers to the building of a network in which a case is made for the instrumentality of these elements. The academic community has spent a long time refining these meaningful actions into requirements, to the point of conventionalizing them. However, these requirements only have meaning as research in the context of the academy, i.e. they do not have intrinsic context-independent value.

One value held in the academic community is that research is a cumulative process (Biggs and Büchler 2008b). This helps to differentiate two common and non-interchangeable uses of the term 'research': in academic research and in personal research. In the latter, one is concerned to find out about something that one does not already know, but which may already be known by others. As such it is personal development. In the former, one is concerned to find out about something that nobody knows, and will result in a contribution to knowledge and understanding (Biggs and Büchler 2007). If research is defined as being cumulative then it is clear that one is concerned with academic research. Therefore the methods need to include inquiry into what has been done already, and making the outcomes public so that other researchers do not duplicate the work. It also clarifies that research is something done by communities resulting in collective benefit rather than by the isolated genius who does not share their work and whose potential contribution remains unknown.

As a consequence of the value of accumulation, there are criteria by which research can be identified and to which it should conform. Such criteria are complex to identify because they both constitute, and are constituted by, the works themselves. However, this is not an intractable circular problem as we have described elsewhere (Biggs and Büchler 2008b). To avoid the circularity problem, we took an axiomatic approach and developed a logical system that describes how actions can be taken in line with academic values. The axiom we adopted was that research is cumulative. This enabled us to propose a set of four generic requirements that must be met by academic research in all disciplines. The generic requirements consist of 'question and answer', 'method', 'knowledge' and 'audience'. These can be construed as a network of interdependent concepts. Assuming that research is cumulative, one needs a question in order to provide an answer. The answer will add to our knowledge and to what is understood. The question will arise in a context for which there is an audience. This audience will judge whether the outcome is a satisfactory or relevant response to the question, and therefore whether they are any the wiser as a result of the research. The appropriateness of the answer to the question for the audience will be reflected in the use of methods that appropriately connect one to the other, and are used by the community who form the audience for the outcome. Thus we see that for a community, certain questions are relevant, certain actions are appropriate, and certain outcomes are of interest to their concerns. These communities constitute disciplines, but also share beliefs about what they are doing and therefore inhabit the same larger academic community. Discipline boundaries are defined by identifying communities of practice that share certain interests and concerns, and expressing it in this way brings to the fore the relationship of the community to its research and knowledge base (Wenger 1999). It identifies that certain questions are meaningful, that certain methods are preferred, certain solutions are regarded as satisfying, and others are not.

The academic community is satisfied with the coherent relationship between its values and its actions. There is satisfaction that its value of accumulation is manifested in the academic conventions that require the archiving and dissemination of outcomes from the research activity. It is also satisfied that the actions that compose the research activity are the ones that are meaningful towards the accumulation and dissemination of knowledge, i.e. through publishing and reviewing of compiled literature. Thus the research activity that is significant to the academic community is one that performs actions such as publishing because it is a meaningful action towards the community value of accumulation.

The creative practice community is similarly satisfied with the coherent relationship between its values and its actions. The creative practice community values the notion of 'the singularity of the event'. There is satisfaction that this value is manifested through the convention of using non-linguistic communication. In this context, the significant creative activity is the promotion of the direct encounter with the artefact. To this end, the creative community is satisfied by actions such as exhibiting or performing. Thus the creative activity is composed of actions such as exhibiting or performing because these are meaningful actions towards the community value of 'the event'.

Our social-psychological knowledge model means that any community will find satisfaction if there is coherence between what it does and what it values. In mature communities, one can find these values formalized as conventions and sometimes as regulations, norms and expectations. Alteration in either the community values for which that activity is significant or in the actions that make the activity meaningful for that set of values will disrupt this coherent relationship. In our view, the hasty academicization of the creative practice community has pushed the creative practice and the academic communities together. This has caused a disruption of the internal coherence of values and actions, leading to community dissatisfaction.

Conflict and disruption

At a theoretical level, academicization involves the adoption of the dominant academic conventions and the values that support it. However, academicization is not just a theoretical concept: there is tangible evidence of this process. At a practical level we can find indicators of these changes such as the incorporation of arts schools into universities, the funding made available through research councils which also broaden their remit into practice, availability of doctorates, etc. For example, in the UK the majority of art schools were located in polytechnics as part of the vocational education sector. In 1992 the polytechnics were legally incorporated as universities, which had the immediate effect of increasing both the opportunity and the competitive necessity to compare the creative and performing arts with all other university-based subjects. The new breed of practitioner-researcher had to compete for resources, and were also now in an academic environment in which new levels of study were available. Since the highest level of qualification in universities is the PhD, this, rather than the MA, became the target terminal award. But the PhD is a research degree and therefore somewhat different in its aims and objectives from the more professional oriented degrees such as the BA or MA (Chapter 1).

There are some disciplines that have conducted academic research for longer than others, and have therefore helped to shape the notion of what constitutes academic research. When we look back at the period of academicization, for example through the discipline of chemical engineering, it may seem that there was always a harmonious relationship between academics' values and their research activities. The natural evolutionary situation is that the values of an academic community determine the research activity that the community adopts and that, therefore, they develop coherently. This is not, however, the case of disciplines such as the creative and performing arts, which are being hastily academicized owing to having been pushed into the academy. In response to the immediate call for an infrastructure for knowledge production, we have claimed that these disciplines remedially built a collage from the resources in other areas. Academic resources were only superficially modified in order to accommodate the production of the creative practice community (Biggs and Büchler 2011). To some extent this is understandable because they did not already have research models that were both coherent with their values and met their newfound academic needs.

If we look for how professional values are transmitted, we find that the atelier model has been a persistent teaching model in the creative and performing arts. In this model the lecturers in advanced studies in the institutions are also active professional practitioners, and as a result the student is exposed to the values of the professional community. Until recent times it has proven to be a very successful educational model, but one which was not primarily focused on academic values. However, the contemporary environment is changing substantially in response to the academicization of these formerly vocational subjects. At a practical level, practitioner-researchers now find themselves having been professionally trained for one type of activity but asked to perform another. The type of training that they have hitherto received regarding research has been pragmatically driven, and has consisted in their ability to find out what they need to know about a subject to enable them to operate within that subject as 'guest workers'. However this type of research is not academic research. As we have already said, this type of research is finding out something that one does not know, whereas academic research is finding out what nobody knows. The former type of research has an important place in the creative practice community as part of a cultural network of the production and consumption of experiences. The latter kind of research is quite different, and traditionally consists of the production of journal articles, books, theories, etc., as part of an academic network of the production and consumption of knowledge.

In the UK, one can observe that, under pressure for productivity in the new regime of post-1992 academia, universities, funding councils and others, hastily adopted apparently productive models from traditional subjects. Concepts from the creative and performing arts were mapped on to these models, but this mapping failed to take account of the difference in community values between these traditional academic subjects and creative practice. The values of the creative practice community include many significant activities for its members, but amongst these are not, for example, prediction and control. This is perhaps more clearly exposed if one looks at the broadly scientific model from which many concepts were adopted by practitioner-researchers (Chapter 2).

The hasty academicization of the creative practice community has had a disruptive effect. The phenomenon has caused the coherence between values and actions to be broken and each community finds itself judging activities that did not emerge from their own values. In response to the demands of this hasty academicization, the practice community has adopted some of the conventions and actions of the academic community in order to try to produce research of the academic kind. Although these actions conform to the conventions of academic research, they do not result in a significant research activity. As we have said, actions are not meaningful in isolation. The performance of isolated actions results in a loss of coherence and in dissatisfaction.

We observe that, as a result of academicization, there is dissatisfaction from the academic community that what practitioners do is not research; and from the practice community that their values are not represented or reflected in academic research. We have focused on these as the interests of distinct communities, who do not feel they have a stake in the outcomes, and so the outcomes of one lack meaning for the other (Biggs and Büchler 2008a). Dissatisfaction with explanations comes not from the inadequacies of language, but from a misunderstanding about where satisfaction is to be found. The reason one is satisfied with an answer to a question is because one sees some connection between the two. The satisfaction comes from the user perceiving in the answer something that adequately responds to the question. This means that answers, *per se*, do not satisfy questions owing to anything external, but rather it is the perceived connection between the question and the answer that is satisfying.

A social-psychological knowledge model builds on the understanding of knowledge as a perceptual and consensual act. It is perceptual because it relies upon members of a community finding knowledge potential in the same phenomena. It is consensual for two reasons: individuals elect to belong to a given community, and they consent to the new knowledge that is added by their peers. A social-psychological knowledge model reveals the internal coherence that exists in a community between values and actions. The coherence between values and actions is a factor that might be problematic for the integration of the communities of creative practice and academic research. This is owing to the stereotype of academic knowledge being, in many ways, a scientific one. For example, academic research assumes that knowledge is communicable and impersonal, whereas creative practice often emphasizes the personal and subjective experience. It is stereotypical even in the creative areas, where one can find the common title of 'scientific committee' for selection and review panels of conferences and journals.

The ongoing debate around what would be academic research in areas of creative practice is a symptom of these being two distinct communities holding different values. Each is dissatisfied when it does not find in research what it thinks is significant. We have already shown that the academic community conventionalizes its actions and expectations, and that doing something that is recognized as academic research means producing something that satisfies those expectations. Rather than being logically determined, conventions are socially determined. It becomes meaningless for the practice community to say that the academic community is wrong about what is significant in academic research. Similarly, it is meaningless for academics to say that the professional community is wrong about what is significant in creative practice. The individual communities are the ones who are responsible for identifying what is of value and therefore what will be significant to them. As a consequence of the hasty academicization of the creative practice community, we have identified dissatisfaction in both communities. The coherence between values and actions that had satisfied each community prior to academicization has been broken. With the consequent lack of coherence between values and actions comes dissatisfaction.

Sources of dissatisfaction

Dissatisfaction emerges from the lack of meaning of a given action. The same action or concept may exist in core activities that are undertaken in both the academic and the creative practice communities; however, they will be meaningful in different ways. For example, the role of personal or subjective experience in practice is not exclusive to the creative practice community, as any researcher in any area would also have 'lived experiences'. However, the role of subjective experience in creative practice is different from its role in the sciences, for example. In the latter case, the subjectivity that accompanies experience is usually seen as an undesired variable that is to be controlled rather than enhanced. This is owing to the value that the scientific community places on the 'objectivity of facts'. All research actions that are performed in response to an activity that a community undertakes are networked according to what that community values. However, this network need not be explicit, conscious, systematic, transferable, etc., which are all properties of how the academic community would interconnect the concepts that are meaningful to them towards forming an argument.

The differences between the academic community and the practice community emerge at the fundamental level of values. This difference, when these two communities are pushed together, leads to each being dissatisfied. There are aspects of the research model that satisfy the academic community but that do not satisfy the practice community. The research model described above is composed of the question and answer, method, knowledge and audience; is coherent with the value of accumulation but leaves aspects of the creative practice values dissatisfied. On the other hand, the actions that satisfy the creative practice community because they are coherent with their values, when seen by the academic community, are meaningless towards the construction of a significant research activity.

One very apparent point of tension between these two communities is the non-linguistic output. Given that one academic convention is that a written document of a determined length and in a determined format is expected as a thesis, the practice community will be at a disadvantage given that their outputs are mainly non-linguistic. Indeed, one of the conventions that the practice community encounters as an obstacle is that research, and particularly any outcome, is normally expressed linguistically. This becomes problematic if we infer that expressing outcomes non-linguistically reflects some fundamental values of the creative practice community.

Another point of tension comes from the academic convention that research must have explicit questions. The reason for this convention is that it is essential that the researcher come up with an answer or some kind of response in order to make a contribution to the accumulation of knowledge. 'Question and answer' is a pillar of academic research activities in other disciplines. However, this can present a stumbling block in areas of creative practice because the creative practice community values 'the event' which promotes the direct encounter with the artefact. The direct encounter, in turn precipitates a plurality of experiences and, because these experiences are all different, a single unified answer does not emerge. As a result, where the academic research model attempts to home in on a single answer to a question, the creative practice community remains open to the plurality of experiences. The creative practice community tends to be dissatisfied with having to ask a question and pursue an answer because these sound somewhat final and relate to the idealized world of facts, of cause and effect, of mechanical relationships. In areas of creative practice, both questions and answers, both issues and how they are addressed, are more volatile. They are 'culturally determined': as the culture changes certain issues become pressing and certain other issues fall away from the field of view or interest.

Another stumbling block relates to the role of question and answer in research for each community. In academic research, knowledge must be transferable and therefore the questions and answers are presented as being broadly generalizable. This is contrary to the value that the creative practice community places on the individual event. Events are singular and there is no motivation to connect the experience of one event to the experience of another. Therefore, we begin to see why this type of question and answer would be dissatisfying to the creative practice community; for example, that the answer is not as significant as the journey.

According to the social-psychological theory of knowledge, the nature of questions and answers are community-dependent. In other words, what a question and an answer would look like is a result of a community's understanding of knowledge. Knowledge can be of different kinds, and depending on the nature that is attributed to it, there are different expectations as to the contribution that it will make. Knowledge can contribute in an explicit and/or theoretical way, a practical way that can pertain to skills, an embodied way as part of personal experience and know-how, and so on. Furthermore, the understanding of knowledge and the expectation of how and what that knowledge will contribute is in turn conditioned by the interests of different audiences.

Academic research takes place in a context of relevance that is supplied by the academic audience, i.e. the audience sees meaning in the research actions. For example, if astronomers were asked 'What is the moon?', they might reach for tables of measurements and satellite photographs in order to answer the question. However, if creative practitioners were asked, they might reach for some paint and a canvas, or write a poem. There are different ways of responding to a single question that are relevant and meaningful to different audiences. As a result, questions, answers and methods cannot be transferred freely from one discipline to another because they may lose their context-dependent meaning. Give a poem to astronomers and they would be deeply dissatisfied with it as an answer, and the same can be said for the creative practice community who would be deeply dissatisfied with an answer involving rocks and orbits. Beyond the interests of particular disciplines, the answer to a question is also dependent on the general nature of questions: what it is to ask something and, particularly, what it would be like to answer this question, i.e. what would satisfy us (Wittgenstein 1958).

In a community, the understanding of what is the general nature of questions is perceptually determined, which means that it is connected to the understandings of the audience. Because there is a difference in audience for the production of academic research and for the production of creative practice, the notion of what is a relevant question and answer varies as well. The audience for academic research consists of a group who share a belief that the argument-based answer to a question is significant. They expect to receive the outcomes of the research in a particular form, usually linguistic, and the form is designed so that the audience will all find in it the same content and thereby accumulate the same knowledge. On the other hand, the audience for the creative practice outcome shares an interest in having experiences based on exposure to a singular event, i.e. the particular type of work presented at the concert hall or in the exhibition. They will have different personal experiences resulting in different perceptions of content, and consequently they will each take away something different from the encounter. There is a whole field of inquiry called 'interpretation' that investigates whether there is fixed content in a particular work. We do not have to come down on one side or the other of this discussion because what is relevant here is to note the difference in activity between the two communities regarding content. Owing to the academic interest in accumulation, their activities have as an objective a singular shared interpretation of content. This is aided by a preference for textual communication owing to its explicitness and generalizability. On the other hand, creative practices, through preferring non-linguistic communication, select forms that tend to promote plurality of interpretation and therefore diversity of content.

In the academic model, method relates to the concept of question and answer. There is initially an overlap between question and answer, because a well-formulated question implies its answer within an audience-led context: a philosophical question begs a philosophical answer, a causal question begs a causal answer, and so on (Biggs and Büchler 2007). Different disciplines have discipline-specific interests for which discipline-specific answers are required and for which discipline-specific methods must be used. There is a linkage that is represented by the overlap between question and answer, and method provides a further connection, i.e. if one is interested in this particular question, then only certain routes would be acceptable in order to find out something or develop the interpretation of this issue and precipitate a significant outcome.

This way of describing the connection between the expectations for academic research reveals that method is judged to be appropriate according to the established convention in that discipline. This expectation does not arise in such a prescriptive way in the creative practice community. Nor does the creative community follow a single specific or dominant model of enquiry, as happens in other subjects. In chemical engineering, for example, the 'leaching test' is currently administered as a means of verifying the stabilization/solidification of hazardous waste in pollution prevention and control. The technique and analysis involved in the leaching test is therefore part of the professional training that should be adopted by all researchers in the area. This does not happen in areas of creative practice. In order to meet this academic expectation, it would therefore be necessary to find a pragmatic way of evaluating the appropriateness of a method for a person and their work. The academic response for determining the appropriateness of method is based on how the answer is a consequence of, and relevant to, the question, in the context of the expectations of the audience. For the creative practice community, the option for a method is not as formulaic. This may be because the creative community is less answer-driven and more process-driven. If the creative practice community is not interested in formulating an answerable question, then method does not arise as a meaningful link between these two for that community.

Non-linguistic communication is a convention of creative practice, however, when adopting existing research models, practitioner-researchers find themselves having to justify the use of the non-linguistic part of their practice in their academic research. If the academic discourse of argument-building is used, one needs to find an essential role for every element in that argument. However, images are not always essential and may fall into different categories depending on their role. For example, an illustration may accompany a text such as *Alice in Wonderland*, but it is also possible to read an un-illustrated version and not be worse off. Indeed, some people might prefer to do so in order to create their own mental images. For the appreciation of the work, images are optional. On the other hand, there are successful examples of the use of imagery instead of words for communication. For example, the international furniture store IKEA could use multi-lingual written instructions for how to assemble their furniture, but instead have developed an effective system of visual communication using images alone.

The non-linguistic is not only a product equivalent and substitutable for text. For the creative practice community, practices more commonly enable discovery through non-linguistic means, through sound or through imagery, in which something is discovered that could not have been discovered by any other means. For example, when designing the Parque Güell in Barcelona, Gaudí hung chains from the ceiling, photographed them, then turned these images upside-down and copied the arches that were formed, thus determining the catenary curves that would be used in the construction. As a practitioner, Gaudí had an embodied sense of the aesthetic 'rightness' of these curves. In this example, non-linguistic forms were used to create knowledge that was relevant to the practice community. This knowledge, of the 'rightness' of the curves, was created directly using visual means. On the other hand, it is possible to use non-linguistic methods to create knowledge that can be replicated through text-based media. In graphical statics, non-linguistic forms are used as an alternative method for calculating forces in structures. Graphical statics is a method that does not function numerically but is a diagrammatic technique for making calculations in which one draws lines and measures angles and lengths. It is a visual method for gaining non-visual knowledge about structures. Although this may be a fruitful paradigm within which images contribute to knowledge, the first book ever published about graphical statics by Carl Culmann in 1865 contained text as well as images for the validation of this as an alternative method.

Both Gaudí and Culmann exemplify the use of non-linguistic forms for the creation of new knowledge. However, in Gaudí's case, the non-linguistic form was essential to the creation of knowledge whereas in the case of Culmann's graphical statics, this knowledge could have been reached through alternative forms of notation. Nevertheless, these are both very interesting examples of a practice – whether it is drawing something or doing something or making something – that results in a solution to a particular problem without the intervention of text-based language. These examples also serve to reveal a fundamental difference between practice and academic research: the latter seeks to make explicit its claims and rationale, often through text because text allows a meta-commentary on *why* the technique works and not just a demonstration *that* it works, as occurs in practice. Regardless, most creative practices are not undertaken in order to have concrete outcomes and contribute to knowledge. Rather, the majority of creative practices are undertaken to produce experiences.

Creative practitioners often consider experience as the most important contribution of the artefact and that it therefore has an essential role in the outcome of the practice. However, experience is a problematic component in academic research because of its philosophical subjectivity, by which we mean that it relates to the individual's personal experience. What is experiential is first-person, and therefore cannot be shared with other people. Because experience is something personal, its transferability is problematic and thus goes against the value of accumulation and the idea that there is something that can be shared in order to build a body of knowledge and interpretation. According to the practice community values, what is shared is the event rather than the experience that each one has of it. The event is the form and the experience is the content; this is why the performance or the exhibition is a meaningful activity to that community. The academic choice for the argument-driven thesis reinforces the value that the community places on the transferability of impersonal knowledge, i.e. the aim is that everyone receives the same content from the same academic text. The academic community is dissatisfied with a performance or exhibition because these result in a diversity of experiences rather than in the unambiguous communication of the intended content.

Towards the production of the experience, the encounter with the artefact is central to the creative practice community. However, academic research must be contextualized so that it is clear where the contribution to knowledge is going to be made. This contextualization requires a level of transferability and that the researcher step beyond the particularity of the artefact. Although the linguistic medium is an efficient way of addressing that requirement, it is perhaps not the only form. The practitioner-researcher could contextualize an exhibition with another one, or take the viewer through a process prior to being presented with the work in question. One of the advantages of linguistic form is the ability to abstract from the particular and discuss the matter in more general terms. For example, when one is confronted with a piece of classical music, it is hard to take that as a representative of the genre of classical music. Its structures and particular performance constantly remind one of just 'this' piece rather than facilitating thinking about classical music more generally. On the other hand, the linguistic expression 'classical music' facilitates discussion of the genre without reference to any particular performance.

Certain kinds of form are more effective for the communication of certain kinds of content. In order to understand the relationship between form and content it is necessary to step away from any prescribed form and revisit what is trying to be achieved in the process of research before assuming that *this* particular form is the best way of achieving *that*. The inclusion of creative practice in the academic research model requires a justification of whether the non-linguistic form is the most effective way of dealing with the issues at hand in the research. Similarly, the academic researcher who habitually writes a research report should reconsider whether this form has the capacity to communicate the content of the research. When the content is reconsidered, it is possible to move away from conventions, particularly ones that are led by stereotypes or preconceptions about form. The form of traditional academic research both facilitates and prioritizes transferable outcomes and these are opposite to the creative practice value of the singularity of the event. In any area, the choice of form already invites and precludes certain types of content. The distinction between form and content reveals that in form there is content.

The ability or desire to articulate the content of form is also a matter of rhetoric, by which we mean 'constituting things through language', rather than 'persuasive oration'. As such, rhetoric refers to the impact that language has on what one can and cannot think. How something is said, and indeed saying anything at all, begins to direct thoughts in a particular way (Chapter 9). This seems to be an objection that many practitioner-researchers have regarding the academic model, as they feel that speaking may compromize the potential for description, argumentation and outcome – or their non-linguistically determined alternatives – in the creative realm. This may be because these aspects of creation do not share the linear structure of language. In order to discuss the issue of rhetoric that arises when the creative practice community produces academic research, it is important to identify and break down stereotypes that are often hidden and deeply rooted in conventions that communities have adopted. This helps to steer away from preconceived notions of what research should look like, which is a consequence of the problem of rhetoric (Biggs 2002).

We can summarize by observing that, when creative practice is academicized, the originally coherent structure of each community – comprised of values, conventions, meaningful actions and significant activities – is disrupted and each finds itself dissatisfied. In particular, the academic community is dissatisfied that its value of accumulation is not supported by the creative practice conventions of using non-linguistic communication to encourage the subjective experiences resulting from direct encounter with the artefact. As a result, the academic research community is dissatisfied that certain actions, such as performing or exhibiting, are not the ones that are meaningful towards their value of the accumulation of knowledge. On the other hand, the creative practice community is dissatisfied that its value of 'the singularity of the event' is not addressed in the academic convention of argument-building because the latter emphasizes the general rather than the particular. The creative community is also dissatisfied with actions such as publishing and archiving because these create problems for the direct encounter with the artefact. Ultimately, the academic community's interest in producing single transferable outcomes is contrary to the creation of diverse personal experiences.

Consequences of compromise

Because dissatisfaction is a function of the disjunction between values and research models, it often seems to stem from academic conventions. However, this is misleading, because it is not the actual academic conventions that stifle the evolution of the practitioner-researcher community but rather the nature of conventions *per se*. The conventions that communities adopt are shorthand for what actions and activities are coherent with their values. As such, they act as facilitators for maintaining the original intra-community coherence. Any newcomer to that community need only act in accordance with those conventions in order to be seen as belonging to that community. Once established, conventions tend not to change but act as gatekeepers for the community. However, when circumstances change, conventions get disconnected from the values that they served. When this happens, conventions inhibit the natural evolution of the community and, consequently the internal coherence is disrupted. Rather than setting out how members of a community should behave, when the coherence is disrupted, conventions ultimately reify the actions, thus potentially causing them to get out of step with the values that they were originally intended to sustain.

This may explain why, when we consider the academic community, one of the complaints we hear is that research in areas of creative practice does not meet their conventions. On the other hand, practitioners feel that meeting those conventions produces research that lacks coherence with their values. However, we claim that, rather than being dissatisfied with the actual research models that are available to them, the practitioner-researchers are dissatisfied with the fact that adopting those models and meeting those conventions is not coherent with their practitioner values. It is important to draw attention to a subtle distinction in the practitioner-researcher community dissatisfaction: between the dissatisfaction with the existing research models and the dissatisfaction with the lack of a research model that is coherent with the practitioner values.

Coherence between values and actions defines a satisfied community. Any disruption to that coherence leads to dissatisfaction. In the case of the newly emerging practitioner-researcher community, the disruption of this coherence in both the parent communities has led to each being dissatisfied with reciprocal aspects of the production of academic research in areas of creative practice. The creative practice community is dissatisfied that it has to perform academic actions that do not reflect their values. These actions are meaningless to them and the resulting research activity is not significant to their community. They are also dissatisfied that the actions that are meaningful to them, lack meaning to the academic community. In turn, the academic community is equally dissatisfied because the actions that the creative practice community want to include in their research activity are not meaningful to the academic community. Hence, when these creative practice actions are included in the research, they do not reflect the academic community values and are therefore not significant as a research activity.

Of course, it is not the case that every practitioner-researcher feels dissatisfied with the research that is produced, and its reception. When attempting to produce academic research, practitioner-researchers often meet the academic conventions and produce research that is regarded as being of the academic kind. It is therefore possible that both the academic and the creative practice community may find the research that is produced is satisfactory because the conventions have been met. However, owing to their different value systems, compromises have had to be made along the way. This is often done by adopting strategies that aim to bridge the two community values, either by producing actions that are significant to the academic community, or by attributing creative practice values to those academic actions.

When adopting community-bridging strategies, practitioner-researchers will, for example, borrow traditional elements of academic research and apply them to value-reflecting questions, or take their value-reflecting methods and attempt to modify them so as to make them more acceptable to the academic community. So traditional research elements are borrowed or new and modified elements are proposed. However these are somewhat isolated strategies that compensate for what practitioner-researchers perceive as the limitations of the existing models of research. The academic community generally recognizes research produced by these practitioner-researchers but the issues inherent to the creative practice community values will be more or less compromised. We observe the practitioner-researcher adopting a variety of research strategies in order to try to compensate for perceived shortcomings. A characteristic of these strategies is that, while the research is accepted as being academically valid, practice and research are kept separate.

The community bridging strategies all originate from the position that the communities of practice and of academia are distinct and separate. Many of the previous attempts at conducting academic research in areas of creative practice did not resolve the sense of dissatisfaction that we identify, hence the continuing debate. This is because, although practitioner-researchers might produce academic research and although they do consider the values of the creative practice community, they do so through compromise. Practitioner-researchers transit between the creative practice community values and the academically valid models of research. The ongoing debate about the nature of research in areas of creative practice continues because both the community representing the interests of academic research, and the community representing the interests of creative practice, see themselves as distinct, separate and opposed. As a result, both communities are dissatisfied with the outcomes of academic research in areas of creative practice because they fail, to some degree, to embody the values of the parent communities. Dissatisfaction arises from a feeling of compromise on both sides.

In a coherent relationship between research model and community values, no strategies are necessary for ensuring that the values are reflected and represented in the research that is produced. When research models emerge from the community values, in what we have described as a natural evolution, there is coherence between the values and the research model. The research model that emerges in a natural evolution is authentic, in the sense that it faithfully embodies the community values and leads directly to appropriate actions. However, owing to the hasty academicization of the creative practice community, the conditions have not facilitated the emergence of an authentic research model and, as a result, the practitioner-researchers have had to adopt various strategies for ensuring that their value-reflecting actions are present in the research.

It may appear that discussions on the emergence of the practitioner-researcher community were already undertaken in the 1990s when art schools merged with universities. At that moment, the academic and practitioner communities combined their interests in order to create adequate syllabi and curricula. However, this was done by employing strategies, i.e. through negotiation and compromise rather than through a re-evaluation of what were the fundamental values of each community. There is on-going debate about academic research in areas of creative practice, and debate is symptomatic of negotiation, the result of which is always compromise and, we claim, some degree of dissatisfaction for all involved. Had a fundamental re-evaluation of values occurred, dissatisfaction would not still be visible.

In the chapter overview we suggest that there cannot be a single research model that satisfies both communities. We have shown this is because any collaboration between the two communities would involve negotiation and compromise and this would lead to dissatisfaction. As an alternative, we propose that there is a third and distinct community that is the offspring of the two parent communities. In line with the concept of authenticity, there should be a distinct research model that emerges from this community's own distinct values. This is not a third research model that can be hybridized from the values of the parent community, but instead should be faithfully linked to the values of this new distinct community of practitioner-researchers. The practitioner-research community needs to take responsibility for identifying its practice-academic values and to be critical of any values and conventions they feel they have inherited from their genealogical roots. Once the fundamental values of the community are visible, then meaningful actions can be identified and the significant activities conventionalized. In this way it will be clear why the practitioner-research community does what it does given what it believes and values.[1]

Note

1   The authors would like to acknowledge the financial support of the Arts and Humanities Research Council (UK) for funding their research into non-traditional knowledge and communication.

6
ARTISTIC COGNITION AND CREATIVITY

Graeme Sullivan

Introduction

For as long as I can remember I have 'pictured' the problems solved, the concepts understood, or the histories read, because for me 'to see is to think.' Information received, situations encountered, or systems experienced, are always being felt as much as framed because there is always another way to look at something. Reflecting on these curiosities and capacities raises important questions about what we do as individuals in the various roles we take on as researchers, academics, teachers, and artists. What guides these motives and actions are seamless connections that link these roles and responsibilities, perceptions and representations. What glues them together is an unwavering belief in the pervasive power of creative and critical insight. Yet there is a general misunderstanding about what it means to 'see' as a way of thinking, acting and making, and how artistic cognition can give rise to powerful forms of human understanding. After all, the thoughtful practice of making art and the thought-provoking process of encountering art makes an impact on individuals and communities through the insights offered and perspectives opened up. This intensive activity is imaginative, sometimes troubling, but it is hard to ignore because it adds to the store of human understanding in profound ways.

In this chapter I align a theory of artistic cognition within the context of creativity and suggest that research into these constructs remains limited within the existing conceptual boundaries of disciplines. The argument presented is that it is within a notion of art practice as research that the full potential of cognition and creativity as informing human capacities can be realized. Artistic cognition can be described as seeing and thinking that is partially shaped by the cultural contexts that inform 'what' it is we see, and partially governed by the biological processes that connect 'how' we see. Collectively, these dynamic interactions activate cognitive processes that are distributed throughout the various media, languages, and settings that shape the way images are made and what they might mean. Further, 'doing art' in a research setting requires the use of the imagination and intellect to respond to the incessant need to know, and to do so in a way that meets the rigorous demands of inquiry undertaken within scholarly communities. Within this academic environment conventional research in general proceeds from the known to the unknown, yet it is important to acknowledge the benefit of inquiry that moves in the other direction – from the unknown to the known – for fresh perspectives as much as prior knowledge are determinants in creating and constructing new knowledge. This is the trajectory of inquiry that characterizes practice-based research (Sullivan 2005; Mäkelä and Routarinne 2006). Henk Slager described it this way:

> Artistic research seems to continuously thwart academically defined disciplines. In fact, art knows the hermeneutic questions of the humanities; art is engaged in an empirically scientific method; and art is aware of the commitment and social involvement of the social sciences. It seems, therefore, that the most intrinsic characteristic of artistic research is based on the continuous transgression of boundaries in order to generate novel, reflexive zones.
>
> (Slager 2009a: 51)

Purpose of the chapter

In exploring artistic cognition and creativity, two related themes are described in this chapter that provide the argument and rationale for proposing a theoretical alignment of the two. The initial section, *The Cognitive Turn to the Visual*, suggests that our understanding of cognition remains limited by the continued tendency to study how we think and act within existing paradigms of theory and practice. The second section, *Creativity in Context*, profiles how different conceptions of creativity have framed our knowledge of this critically important human and cultural construct. In drawing the cognitive and creativity arguments together, a theory of visual cognition is presented. I describe visual cognition this way:

> Visual cognition is both a biological and cultural construct where mindful practices are structured, framed, and embodied. These cognitive practices take place within, across, between, and around the artists, artwork, viewer and setting. Visual cognition creates ideas and insights that connect 'within' and 'across' individual dispositions and experiences, and produces cultural capital that questions existing knowledge systems and structures 'between' and 'around' discipline boundaries and cultural contexts.

The evidence to support this explanatory thesis is drawn from the way artist-researchers make use of private processes and public practices that exemplify what visual cognition and creativity might achieve when seen as integrated modalities within the practices of research.

The cognitive turn to the visual

The theme of cognition forms the core of this chapter, while the theme of creativity provides the context. The purpose of this section is to bring several perspectives into focus and to arrive at an explanation of artistic cognition that may be useful in considering how art practice yields new knowledge within the context of practice-led research. The cognitive arguments draw on several sources that describe the current theoretical issues being debated concerning cognition and the significance of visual processes in how we come to know things. Early arguments that saw a need to consider perception and conception as interrelated mindful processes are briefly surveyed, along with the initial enthusiasm for cognitive symbolization perspectives (Arnheim 1969; Gardner 1985). Theorists that identify the significance of the cultural basis of cognition bring to the debate important long-term assumptions about the interrelated evolution of cognition and culture (Donald 1991; Dissanayake 1992; Solso 2003), while recent trends towards linking artistic and scientific conceptions of the mind (Stafford 2007; Edwards 2008) are challenging many ideas about discipline-specific traditions of the function and meaning of visual images. Finally, an account is given of recent developments in our understanding of visualization and the role played by the embodied mind and the brain, and the rise of provocative discussions about universal modes of visualizing that engages feeling states, the unconscious, and in some instances, broader philosophical areas such as 'neuroaesthetics' (Zeki 1999; 2009).

Perceptual forms and cognitive structures

Rudolf Arnheim's (1969) transdisciplinary argument that thinking and seeing were inextricably linked as mindful processes was a radical jolt that challenged the dominant view at the time that *thoughts* were the essence of cognition, and 'feelings' were the province of affective, emotional states. Arnheim's attempt to figure out how we make meaning from what we saw was, of course, a longstanding quest that tracked back to Plato's claims about 'immaculate perception' and the shady reputation of perception as a source of truth. But Arnheim was part of a growing cognitive coalition who rejected the idea that perception was mindless sensation. Although it may be immediate and intense, it was argued that perception did not merely provide data picked up by the senses; it also played an active role in concept formation.

In taking cognition beyond the limits of binary thinking that had kept it tied to experimental needs for operationalizing concepts suitable for clinical intervention, deeper questions were asked of cognition. Consensus suggested that cognition involved thinking and acting whereby a range of mental processes were used to make sense of knowledge and how best to use it to make decisions about our interactions with the world around us. This meant that not only was the challenge to understand one's immediate world of experience, but also the necessity to be able to infer from past knowledge and to anticipate what to do next. In other words, the kind of thinking processes we use every day involved more than rationality and reasoning and invoked messy constructs such as memory, intuition and feeling, and these capacities were found in abundance in the arts.

Explanations about how human cognition undertook this task of 'coming to know' varied at the time Arnheim and others were opening up the debate. One popular conception was that information processing was best explained by the distinctively human proclivity to understand that things could be represented by symbols. Arnheim's Harvard colleagues, Nelson Goodman (1978) and Howard Gardner (1973), for instance, took the argument in a structuralist direction and described the cognitive processes used in coming to know things to be a condition of symbolic functioning. Other cognitivists used metaphors such as the computer and modularity to illustrate the workings of the mind (Sternberg 1990), but most agreed that the separation of human knowing into dichotomies of cognition and affect was unnecessarily reductive. Gardner found his metaphor and means in arts practices where thoughts and feelings were inextricably linked and given form in images and objects. Gardner's cognitive model identified three systems – making, feeling and perceiving – and the process of symbolic functioning as the process that guides understanding through these thinking and doing processes. The symbolic processing approach gained popular support, especially among arts educators, because it presented a notion that 'art knowing' was a blend of intuitive and intellectual functioning that took place within a cognitive framework. At its most basic, the symbol systems approach proposed by Gardner placed the cognitive structures in the mind, which did its business in the head, and involved symbolic functioning whereby forms and media were encoded and decoded for meaning.

In his later critique of the symbolic processing model of cognition, Efland (2002) raised several concerns. First, he questioned the computer analogy, explaining that the reduction of information to modular bits and to operations carried out on symbols meant that the necessary mix between the 'hardware' of the mind and the 'software' of content was difficult to reconcile. A second concern for Efland was the apparent context free aspect of symbolic functioning. He argued that Gardner created an artificial barrier between the individual and the environment whereby actions in the real world were transformed into symbolic representations that disembodied them from the individual and cultural context. But it was less a consequence of conceptual tinkering within the discipline structures of arts and education that ultimately rendered Gardner's theory of symbolic functioning moot. Rather it was partly a result of his search for a more comprehensive, systems approach to human intelligences that could account for the variability of biological and culturally valued mental dispositions – which he found in his theory of Multiple Intelligences (Gardner 1983).

The other threat to the idea that the mind mostly serves a symbol encoding and decoding function is more recent and comes from neurobiology where many of the capacities that early cognitive scientists felt unable to study scientifically, such as felt emotions, subjective experiences, and the like, are now understood to be very much involved in human knowing. But before looking at that area it is necessary to examine the other expanding canvas of cognition that has unfurled in recent decades that highlights the powerful cultural influences on artistic cognition.

Cultural cues and thinking in practice

Studying individual ways of thinking and culturally based forms of knowing has long been seen to be two quite different tasks with each based on different theories and methodologies. On the one hand, the psychological study of individuals is undertaken within the methodological controls of clinical settings in search of universal explanations of cognitive thought processes. Field-based researchers, on the other hand, are interested in human cultures and social processes and investigate real-world contexts to understand how culture impacts on cognition. In recent decades these paradigmatic positions are becoming tentatively integrated under the broad rubric of cognition and culture (Schleifer *et al.* 1992; Cerulo 2002; Ross 2004).

Researchers interested in diverse modes of knowing that are evident within and across cultural divides not only consider how immediate situational factors might impact on thoughts and actions, but also the influence of broader social contexts. The argument is that cultural experience plays an important role in helping individuals make sense of themselves as thinking, feeling, beings who live in complex socio-cultural settings and this enculturation process allows for shared values and beliefs (Chapter 5). There are twin elements to this process. The first is the socially constructed nature of theories of practice that describe the relationships among individuals, others, and the communities in which they live. Second, there are the systems of knowledge upon which communities and cultures are built. These areas of focus are now seen to be in a more dynamic relationship whereby 'culture is an emerging phenomenon evolving out of shared cognitions that themselves arise out of individual interactions with both social and physical environments' (Ross 2004: 8). The pervasive impact of cultural processes and practices on the way we think and act individually and collectively has long been of interest to artists and part of the challenge is to consider how artist-researchers might participate in these inquiries in ways that open up new conceptions that go beyond the limits of discipline-based views and practices.

The content of culture is negotiated much in the way of theories of social practice (Bourdieu 1977; Giddens 1979) whereby a cognitive orientation acknowledges the interactive nature of human agency and the 'relational interdependency of agent and world, activity, meaning, cognition, learning, and knowing' (Lave and Wenger 1991: 50). As Lave and Wenger also note, 'learning, thinking, and knowing are relations among people in activity in, with, and arising from the socially and culturally structured world' (1991: 51). The focus on cognitive processes that have individual and communal relevance has been of more interest to culture-based researchers who are critical of past perspectives than essentialized cultures. The need was to look more closely at similarities and differences among individuals and groups within cultural contexts. One intriguing development has been the need to fashion new forms of inquiry that are critically reflexive and more appropriate in studying cultural and cognitive practices as processes that exist when individuals make things.

The interest in the research setting as an interactive site was seen in the 'visual turn' evident in anthropology and some areas of sociology with a new methodological interest in visual research methods (Pink 2001; 2006; Stanczak 2007). Although visual forms of documentation in a range of media have long been part of the armoury of field researchers, it is only relatively recently that the assumed objectivity of these forms has been challenged. The quip that 'cameras don't take photographs, people do', has taken a long time to filter into the methodological consciousness of some disciplines. Furthermore, it is not so much a visual account of phenomena that is revealing, but the manner by which individuals and cultures make sense of their reality through the production and understanding of visual forms of representation and communication. Hence, there is tentative acceptance emerging in these areas of social science research that visual data cannot only be collected but also 'produced' that has the capacity to yield important information (Rose 2007).

When the concepts, mental structures, schema, and forms of representation that had at one time mostly been of interest as universal cognitive traits were re-positioned as constituents of cultural practice, new tensions arose around explanatory models of human cognitive variability. The most dominant metaphor, the computational model, has proved to be more robust in some modalities than others, such as Noam Chomsky's hard-wired theory of language development. Less sustainable has been the model of the mind as merely a symbol encoding and decoding structure because there is no stable filing cabinet of pre-set codes we draw on and apply in new learning situations – the cognitive scripts and schemas that frame the way we see are ever-changing and help us interpret a situation, rather than read it, or decode it. Even the digital revolution and the networking features of internet space have been unable to support the common analogy that the mind is the software and the brain is the hardware.

The other competing image of cognitive processing is the connectionist view of parallel processing (Bechtel and Abrahamson1991) that is gaining momentum. Here the argument is that the architecture of the mind consists of an enormous array of parallel neural networks that enable learning to take place as a process of 'connecting.' In this model, information happens 'in' the process of making connections, rather than the neural network merely being a delivery system that loads up knowledge and shunts inputs and outputs back and forth as the individual interacts with the world. In this sense, the meaning is in the making and content connections can come from anywhere within the labyrinth of the mind. Based on an associationist model, the neural architecture is seen to be a system of interconnected hubs and units that can be activated simultaneously in many areas of the brain as information is accessed (Linden 2007). This is a parallel, rather than a serial process, for connectionism is not governed by any executive function or central processor. Rather cognition activates links strengthened by prior knowledge, but new learning is also open to intuitive and opportunistic connections (Hoffman 1998).

Arts practitioners will have little difficulty appreciating the explanatory power of the connectionist view. There is something attractive about the notion that knowledge creation and construction is partially a process of integrating prior experience with the possibilities of new connections within and around the ideas, media, and settings usually encountered in the studio, classroom, street or the Internet, or wherever art making takes place. One example is the argument that this distributed view of art knowing means that the binary-bound idea that art is a 'process' or 'product' needs to be abandoned. Conceiving art inquiry as a practice that is distributed throughout the various media, languages, situations, and cultural texts offers the possibility of a more convincing cognitive account.

The visual brain and embodied minds

The psychologically grounded description of cognition and the socio-cultural situated view have both been shaken up by the emerging neuropsychological insights into the pervasive role visualization plays in our cognitive constructions. Although David Linden describes the design of the brain as 'inefficient, inelegant, and unfathomable,' he acknowledges that it 'works' (2007: 6). His point is that the evolution of the brain has given us an entity that is part 'kludge' (he describes this as a poorly assembled bunch of ill-fitting parts), and part strategic design. What is clear from recent research in neuroscience is that the assumed linear link between what is perceived and what is known is far too simplistic an equation. A common theme is that while our understanding of brain functioning initially emerged from a perceptual paradigm that was grounded in the psychology of stimulus and response, the way we actually make sense of the world we see is far more non-linear. However, the use of new methods in brain imaging using functional brain scanners are giving tantalizing accounts of what can be inferred about how the mind works by observing what the brain does. By tracking changes of blood flow throughout the neural network of the brain as an individual undergoes tasks under the watchful eye of brain scanning it is conceivable to be able to map patterns of thinking as impulses activate various areas of the brain (Frith 2007; Stafford 2007; Zeki 2009).

The active mind that is inferred from the kinetics of the brain 'lighting up' give some sense of the transformations that take place in response to sensory input. Perception is therefore far from passive – a lot happens after light patterns hit the retina and we proceed to make sense of it. Sensory perception begins by taking in incomplete information from our surroundings and these visual bits and pieces are tracked to an array of places in the brain that process it so that conjectures are able to be made about the possible meanings of what we see (Hoffman 1998; Solso 2003; Frith 2007). The French impressionists and post-impressionists more or less did the same thing and showed the pathways of visual thought and action by sculpting forms from patterns of light and movement and thereby leaving much of the detail to the imagination. What we see is not what flows in through the eyes, but rather how the brain makes sense of the electrical impulses activated by what is sampled from the environment. Ann Barry describes it this way:

> What we 'see,' then, is a combination of the processing of external stimulus by the visual system, of the simultaneous firing of particular neurons in patterns, which make us conscious of what we see, of learning appropriate perceptual skills at the right time, and of prior learning, which is brought to bear on present perception. Perception is a process, which utilizes not only the retinal image, but also the whole of a person's being as well.
>
> (Barry 1997: 65)

The balance between what is hard-wired into our brains and what is adapted from our encounters with the environment has moved from broad debates about nature versus nurture, to more focused accounts of human capacities previously thought to be the province of the heart rather than the head. For instance, Semir Zeki's (2009) text on the brain and art, is sub-titled *Love, Creativity and the Quest for Human Happiness*. Building on his decades of studies in neuroscience and the psychology of art, Zeki is adamant that the most profound of human abstract experiences are matters of the mind and can be investigated and understood using brain imaging technologies. He asserts the main function of the brain, and for that matter, art is to acquire knowledge and it takes place through concept formation and some concepts are 'inherited' and some 'acquired'. Zeki distinguishes these nature-nurture constructs this way:

The inherited concepts organize the signals coming into the brain so as to instil meaning into them and thus make sense of them. The acquired concepts are generated throughout life by the brain, and make it significantly independent of the continual change in the information reaching the brain; they make it easier for us to perceive and recognize and thus obtain knowledge of things and situations.

(Zeki 2009: 21)

For Zeki, creativity emanates from a sense of dissatisfaction and ambiguity that is resolved by making aesthetic responses and creative products, which open up multiple ways of satisfying this sense of disquiet. Furthermore, there is a neurobiological basis to how aesthetic concepts are perceived and processed in this knowledge-seeking and knowledge-creating task because it is not possible to separate seeing from understanding, perception from conception. Zeki defines his approach as 'laying the foundations of a neurology of aesthetics, or *neuro-esthetics*, and thus for an understanding of the biological basis of aesthetic experience' (Zeki 1999: 2, emphasis in the original).

For Ann Barry it is not so much the neural networks that hold the conceptual clues for melding of artistic and scientific interests, but the way research suggests a radical change in our understanding of the role of emotions in visual processing. It seems that the non-linear relationship between sensory experience of the world and the neural networks puts in place a sequence where emotional responses precede more rational reasoning. In other words, 'we begin to respond emotionally to situations *before* we think them through' (Barry 1997: 18, emphasis in the original). For those in the arts, this crucial observation confirms what many have intuitively known and gives new emphasis to the significance of feeling states in cognition. The pre-emptive role of emotions in cognitive functioning challenges the common belief that we think logically in response to external situations as a basis upon which to act, and 'then' we think about how we feel about it. Stephen Rose explains it this way:

Brains are not primarily cognitive devices designed to solve chess problems, but evolved organs adapted to enhance the survival chances of the organisms they inhabit. Their primary role is to respond to the challenges the environment presents by providing the cellular apparatus enabling the brain's owner to assess current situations, compare them with past experience, and generate the appropriate *emotions and hence actions*.

(Rose 2008: 8, emphasis added)

There are two critically important notions that emerge from these explanations of the visualization process. The first is the re-assessment of the role that emotions and feelings play in coming to know our world, not as some lower level form of precognitive processing, but as leading elements in the cycle of understanding. With the continual interplay of sensory perception, individual consciousness, prior experience, and rational reasoning, what we come to know will be greatly influenced by memory and emotions. This is a far cry from the image of the mind as first and foremost the source and site of rationality. A second important outcome of neurobiological studies is the ultimate rejection of the mind-body duality, as the embodied nature of feeling, acting, and thinking becomes better understood. If the means of processing information is through feeling states, mental imagery, and diverse forms of representation, then this implies a new significance for the imagination and metaphor as agencies of visual cognition (Lakoff and Johnson 1980; Damasio 1999).

These two conditions give new importance to the construct of embodied cognition. Katherine Hales explains that although embodied experiences 'are culturally constructed, they are not entirely so, for they emerge from the complex interactions between conscious mind and the physiological structures that have emerged from millennia of biological evolution' (2004: 229). She adds, 'the flexibility of the human neural system enables new synaptic connections to form in response to embodied interactions' (2004: 231). Examples of changes in the extent of embodied experiences is very much part of her argument about how we became 'post human' (Hales 1999) and can be seen, for instance, in digital environments that are inhabited as embodied spaces on our behalf by avatars and cyborgs. The premise is that we live in a dynamic, interconnected, relational world whereby the element of 'self' that was more or less denied by the cognitive scientists, takes centre stage.

Summary: beyond the disciplinary limits of cognition

Previous attempts to isolate artistic cognition, as a discrete, observable human capacity did not yield the insights expected. Visual knowing proved resistant to efforts to explain it within the causal regimes of clinical study and experimental design where language and behaviour were the units of analysis. Although recent efforts at tracking the biological basis of visualization within neuroscience are yielding more probable explanations of the inextricable relationships between the mental and physical processes of how we make meaning with images, what we are coming to know remains dwarfed by what we don't. The identification of neurobiological determinants of visual cognition may, in the future, explain more of the variance in how we process what we see. However, as argued in this chapter, there is little doubt that as a human condition, visual knowing is also influenced by broader, informing contexts as we creatively negotiate our way in the world.

Creativity in context

Creativity is not only a habit of mind but also a form of socio-cultural practice that helps us understand issues of our time. Two themes are explored in this section that chart conceptions of creativity. The dominant direction has been the psychological study of creativity, which has, in part, been revived by investigations in neuroscience and constructs such as intuition and emotional states. Once the socially constructed nature of creativity was accepted, more systemic models evolved that loosened the disciplinary ownership that had variously been claimed by the arts and the sciences. Parallel to these socially mediated approaches are culturally specific insights that emerge from the shifting social diaspora that led to new ways of theorizing culture (Braziel and Mannur 2003). These themes are taken up as creativity is positioned as the contextual factor that mediates between the creative insights that emerge from visual cognitive processing, and the critical processes that occur when these insights are interpreted within discipline frameworks and other socio-cultural parameters.

Creativity as a bio-psychological construct

A common approach in coming to understanding the conceptual basis of creativity research was to construct binary or categorical concepts that characterize its distinguishing features, methods, and uses. This in itself was a telling strategy for it reflected the predominance of a scientific mindset in analysing and synthesizing creativity as an individual and social construct. For instance, in his review of creativity research, Richard Mayer frames his analysis around several questions and asks whether creativity is a 'property of people, products, or processes? … is creativity a personal or social phenomenon? … common or rare? … domain-general or domain-specific? … quantitative or qualitative?' (1999: 450–1). In answering these questions Mayer identified the dominant psychological perspective and the tendency to see creative behaviour as a valued human capacity that existed in varying degrees. Even for those interested in broader analyses of creativity that moved beyond the focus on individual capacities to broader social and cultural contexts, the convenience of dualism remained. For instance, Todd Lubart's review of the study of creativity across cultures cut neatly down a Western and Eastern divide.

> The analysis of creativity in diverse cultures shows that creativity is context dependent. Culture is involved in defining the nature of creativity and the creative process. The Western definition of creativity as a product-oriented, originality-based phenomenon can be compared with the Eastern view of creativity as a phenomenon expressing an inner truth in a new way or of self-growth.
>
> (Lubart 1999: 347)

A curious feature of the psychological and psychometric approach to creativity research was the way that reductive or convergent methods were used to investigate a capacity prized for its divergence (Edwards 2008). The tendency to reduce complex artistic practices to a performance that was assessed to be creative because of the fluidity, frequency, and flexibility of ideas and how rare or original they might be (Lubart 1999), offered a limited perspective at best. Similarly, the assumption that creativity was a problem-finding and problem-solving human drive that was brought into sharp relief by a reflective practitioner (Schön 1991) and can be rendered in equally sharp profile by a cognitive psychologist, underestimated the cogency of creativity.

Perhaps it is in investigations that are less constrained by discipline conventions where a more profound understanding of the human attributes and capacities surrounding the psychology of creativity might be found. Not only are assumed definitions rendered moot, but also the methodologies necessary to match the complexity of the construct need to be re-invented. Some of these conditions are being explored in emerging fields such as neuroscience and visualization. For instance, although we know that the brain is limited in the periods when growth and development is sparked by experiences, such as the capacity for enhanced visual and aural knowledge in the early years of life, we also know that the brain is amazingly adaptable. Even if certain potentials are lost if they are not exercised, we know from brain research that some functional capacities move from one hemispherical region to another if an area is impaired. Furthermore, this can occur at all ages. It may be that the divergence and connectedness so typical of creativity is a human capacity that is not temporally limited but exceedingly resilient if actively utilized in non-habitual ways.

For Ann Barry it is 'in the visual artist we see the perceptual logic of interconnectedness and gestalt formation kept open and alive to new influence' (1997: 64). Artists combine specialist knowledge in a medium or field with a broad repertoire of approaches to thinking and doing that is characterized by cognitive flexibility and neural plasticity. A study of aging artists wonderfully titled, *Above Ground*,[1] shows clearly that artists never give up creating – they never really 'retire.' Rather, as Robert Butler explains in the preface of the report, this 'sheds new light by the unique solutions artists embrace in living – for retirement (they don't), for social networking, for communication … and as productive members of society, working in their studios on a daily basis' (Jeffri 2007: n.p.).

Although the creative practice of artists of all ages continues to reveal the cognitive richness of sustained critical engagement, it is the study of images themselves as they are created and perceived visually, figuratively, and mentally, that is moving debate along after being bogged down by discipline intransigence for several decades. It may be that other less constrained views about creative processes, practices, and products, can be revealed in looking with a new perspective. One intriguing example identified by Ann Barry (1997) is the application of aspects of non-linear systems to the study of perceptual processes at the heart of creativity. A key feature of complex dynamical systems is that they reveal how constraints can trigger changes and self-organizing behaviours that create connectionist networks that appear to exist at the cellular level and all the way up to observable human activity. Conceiving of consciousness in this way is, according to Barry, understandably controversial. Especially enticing, however, is the idea that experience may provoke cellular change that creates turbulent neural activity and opens up new possibilities for awareness before settling into a stable, self-organizing pattern that is given form in a creative product. Furthermore, this description captures new ways of considering the thinking practices associated with creativity, such as intuition, imagination, memory, and subjectivity.

Creativity as a socio-cultural construct

The realization that creativity was more than a series of discreet human capacities, a greater range of methods of inquiry was used to look more closely at the socio-cultural contexts that influenced creativity. For some, this involved examining the outcomes of creative behaviour by investigating what creative people did. The argument was that there was merit in looking at the profiles of people seen to be creative, to get a better sense of how they work within particular settings, contexts, and times. Constructing case studies of artists, writers, composers and, scientists has a long history and continues with more comprehensive use being made of qualitative methods such as biographical accounts (Smith and Watson 2002; Knowles and Coles 2008), auto/ethnography (Reed-Danahay 1997; Rolling 2004) and A/r/tography (Springgay *et al.* 2008).

Others looked at the environmental impact on creativity and identified a range of social cultural, political and, personal factors that influenced creativity (Lubart 1999). Mihaly Csikszentmihalyi (1996) was convinced that creativity was not something that was contained within the head and heart of an individual, but was an outcome that was given meaning by what others had to say about it. Although psychological investigations offered valuable insight into human creative proclivities, whether something was considered to be creative or not was ultimately determined by the impact it made across the public domain (Feldman *et al.* 1994). In some cases judgment was arbitrated through constituencies such as the art world and associated peer processes. At other times, taking art 'to the streets' is a conscious community act where the political purpose overrode most other concerns.

The understanding that creativity is a highly valued human capacity that has a personal and public face shapes the socio-cultural research tradition surrounding creativity. An example of how creativity is framed as a set of relationships that encircle individual, situational and, global forms is seen in the conceptual strategies used by Robert Storr in his selection of artworks for the 2007 Venice Biennale.[2] In his essay he said that the characteristics of contemporary art:

> adumbrate a set of coordinates that may be extended far beyond the confines of this exhibition but will reliably gauge such qualities wherever they are found. Instead of naming tendencies or establishing stylistic lineages and hierarchies, this exhibition proposes such a matrix as a useful but provisional measure of contemporary art. And, instead of reaching backward to align its content with historical precedent, it suggests that the art conjugated to the present plural is sufficient for getting and maintaining our bearings.
>
> (Storr 2007: n.p.)

Storr asserted that past practices that categorized art and artists according to historical styles, groups, hierarchies, or ideologies was no longer viable. The tendency to divide art into binary genres of old-new, objects-ideas, forms-contexts, or insider-outsider, had limited utility as a way to capture what artists do and how we might benefit. In effect, Storr theorized how creativity in contemporary art could be explained as an individual, cultural and community practice.

The 'set of coordinates' Storr used to select work for the 2007 Biennale dealt with form and content that displayed a variety of visual qualities, expressed different ways of making meaning, represented complex thinking capacities, reflected personal and public interests, and displayed the need to communicate with others. He suggested that these characteristics of contemporary art were categories or scales that could be organized within matrices or conceptual frameworks. For instance, he described the art of the Cuban-American artist Felix Gonzalez-Torres, in terms of 'contextual aptness' and 'economy of means,' which could be seen as two different ways artists communicate meaning through their art. The former required an understanding of surrounding contexts to appreciate the full impact of what was being presented, whereas the latter adopted the position that the meaning of an artwork was contained fully within the form itself. Storr's reference to the necessary balance between the private realities of the artist and public participation helped address the educational consequences of art because creative and critical acts involved audiences as opportunities for learning were opened up. Here, his description of the visual qualities of Gonzalez-Torres' art reflecting 'intellectual courage' and 'toughness wrapped in

Figure 6.1 Frank Shifreen. *Mask: Portrait of Chief Pontiac* (2008). Steel and aluminium. Exhibited in Souped-up Pontiac exhibition, Pontiac, Michigan, May 10–June 7, 2008.

gentleness' allude to the cognitive dissonance offered by artists who encourage us to see things differently.

Another example not connected to the Venice Biennale but dealing with similar conceptual and contextual issues may be found in the art of Frank Shifreen. Frank has been an artist in New York for a long time, working along the fringes of the art world in those 'in-between' community spaces where artists' collectives thrive, and where the art is passionate, prolific, and public. Frank is also a doctoral student. His research interests involve theorizing notions of non-institutional art through practice. He is continually looking to involve artists in projects that have community interest and invest in social and cultural capital. Often personal, and always political, the art he creates and curates is of the moment. Many projects are often site-based community events and Frank has been initiating these projects since the early 1970s.

Figure 6.2 Frank Shifreen and Barnaby Ruhe. *Souped-Up Pontiac, Pontiac*, Michigan, May 10–June 7, 2008. Painting event, May 10. Photograph by Gila Paris.

For Frank, the intense personal focus of his art is best understood by his commitment to public interests. The art he created for the *Souped-Up Pontiac* project is a critique that takes place between the 'coordinates' that are of significance: between notions of 'us and them,' and beyond the centre and the periphery. The 'economy of means' depicted in the bruised metal mask of Chief Pontiac is part mythical distortion and part fender-bender. The distinctions that Storr identifies and Shifreen creates are important because what art 'means' and how it is expressed and communicated influences our understanding of the roles art plays in human development, community belonging, and cultural identity.

> Frank Shifreen: The show – which seems ever more prescient with the economic crisis, was about lasting values in a world where a name on a car or city indicates a genesis or patrimony. Yet nothing could be further than the truth – if so we have lost out way. I was looking for the soul beyond the material as if Chief Pontiac could come through the steel. Pontiac is an empty (really empty) city. I knew nothing of Chief Pontiac when I started. The face is a monster as when humans live through technology and become cyborgs.
>
> (Shifreen 2009)

The 'contextual aptness,' 'intellectual courage' and 'toughness wrapped in gentleness' Storr identifies as conceptual cues is evident in the performance painting event involving Frank and his colleague, Barnaby Ruhe, and takes its references from the situated meanings invoked by the local indigenous community surrounding Pontiac,

Michigan. As participants with a history of experience and awareness from previous collaborations with indigenous communities, both Shifreen and Ruhe embody their creative spirit and the power of conversation as a ritual encounter that strikes against uncomfortable realities. This aligns with Storr's conceptual structures for they serve not only a means for making decisions in selecting and presenting artwork, but also an approach for organizing and educating the public about contemporary art and culture that is thoughtful, provocative, and inclusive. What remains open is space between these conceptual frames to encourage other interpretive practices to take shape. The central premise to emerge is that creativity is both a personal process and a public practice that is a primary source for creating and critiquing knowledge structures and values that has the capacity to influence and change individuals and communities.

> I invited Barnaby Ruhe to participate in the Pontiac show. He is very serious as a shaman practitioner and as an artist. He was one of the founders of an artist organized exhibition called the Whitney Counterweight, which included artists who felt the Whitney Biennial survey was narrow and not representative of current art practice. We have worked together over the years. He paints portraits that are quick studies in serial sittings he calls portrait marathons. Barnaby and I have painted publicly over the years and both felt comfortable doing that. We chose a 900 sq ft room on the floor. We put up sheets of plywood, painted them the traditional sacred colours red, white and black. We each had an 8 × 8-foot panel and shared the panel in the middle and we each had two panels on one of the other walls. On the opening day we initiated a shamanic ceremony with the assistance of Native American Indians from local communities. Barnaby painted with an unconscious expressionism. I was looking for some connection with the material. My pieces turned out to be a young man who I thought of as young Pontiac and the other was a transubstantiation of the city of Pontiac. We started to paint.
>
> (Shifreen 2009)

An integrated theory of artistic cognition and creativity

The two important content areas of visual cognition and creativity discussed here are central to conceptions of artistry, and crucial in mounting arguments about the impact of art within academic settings and community and cultural contexts. Each has its own history as a contestable construct and bears the mark of particular methods of investigation believed to best reveal information about the roles served in human and socio-cultural transactions. However, to fully grasp the individual and cultural significance of these twin constructs it is proposed that they are best amplified and explained within the orbit of research in general, and within arguments that present art practice as research in particular.

When art practice is situated within the discourse of the research community the distinctive theories and practices of the relevant arts need to be defended. Therefore a goal is to reconcile what we know about cognition and creativity and to identify a conceptual structure that explains the elements of visual cognition and features of creativity, as they are currently understood within the literature. Also, a condition is that this approach is presented as a means to conceptualize visual cognition within the context of practice-based research, i.e. artist-researchers working within the constraints and potentials offered within degree-granting institutional settings of higher education. Here, theories of discourse and practices of research are some of the framing conditions of the academic art world that impact on how artists' cognitive dispositions and creative capacities are interpreted. The expectation of the artist-researcher is that he/she is creatively using practice-based research to produce new knowledge by creating artworks of critical acclaim that serve multiple ends related to theory and discovery.

Towards a theory of visual cognition

Elsewhere I have presented the argument that the construct of 'transcognition' can adequately explain the cognitive processes related to artistic practice (Sullivan 2002; 2005). The description of transcognition identifies three kinds of artistic practices that are involved that I describe as 'thinking in a medium,' 'thinking in a language,' and 'thinking in a context' (2005: 125–8). Thinking in a medium describes artistic cognition as primarily being the consequence of thought and action that is given form in a creative product. Thinking in a language acknowledges that cognition is a socially mediated process and visual artists and viewers make use of a range of languages of expression and communication to construct narratives and discourse through art and about art. The importance of context as an informing agency in learning and understanding is central to arguments about mediated cognition and this distributed structure captures the multiplicity of practices that characterize how artists work. The key role of visualization in these thinking processes is being taken up with renewed fervour in the burgeoning field of neuroscience and related interdisciplinary fields and this is giving new meaning to the significance of experience as a cognitive capacity.

Figure 6.3 describes cognitive practices observed in visual arts research activity and explains the relationships among visualization and creative and critical outcomes as they are conceptualized within institutional constraints and broader socio-cultural conditions. The cognitive and creative connections are forged over two phases that move from micro settings that surround individual creative behaviours and macro contexts that are socially situated.

Phase 1: cognitive dispositions and experiences

When transcognition is adapted to the information emerging from the literature of cognition reviewed earlier in this chapter, key biological processes are identified. These show cognition to be an individual disposition that operates 'within' and 'across' the neural architecture and explains how emotions, thoughts, ideas and, actions are enacted and embodied. This begins with the conceptual and perceptual processes that involve the mind, matter, and medium that privilege visualization processes.

Phase 2: creativity in post-discipline settings

Creativity lies within the reach of what we actually know, yet outside accepted understanding. Consequently it finds its place within the borders of possibility that

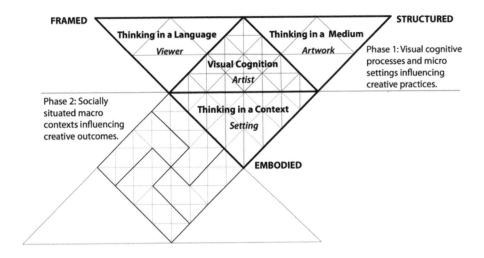

Figure 6.3 Theoretical structure of visual cognition and creativity. Visual cognition is both a biological and cultural construct where mindful practices are structured, framed and embodied. These cognitive practices take place within, across, between, and around the artists, artwork, viewer, and setting. Visual cognition creates ideas and insights that connect 'within' and 'across' individual dispositions and experiences, and produces cultural capital that questions existing knowledge systems and structures 'between' and 'around' discipline boundaries and cultural contexts.

bridge what we know and what we don't know. In many cases creative insight will emerge from within a relatively isolated pocket of unknown knowledge space that will spark a new way of 'looking back' at existing knowledge.

As the imaginative production of artworks proceeds a second phase of creative and critical processes is embraced. Here external conditions are brought into play in relation to other confounding factors. This is an interactive and mediating process that moves 'between' and 'around' the institutional and discipline demands that help determine areas of impact that might be expected. As knowledge or original insight that results from the cognitive process of visual knowing is assessed, the extent of the original contribution, or the related level of inventiveness achieved, becomes part of the discussion. Although the interpretive frameworks of existing knowledge are by no means finite, there will be appropriate terms of reference to consider in assessing outcomes. Just as likely, however, the interpretive lens may be open-ended and indicate directions for new questions and possibilities. As George Kubler noted back in 1962, 'the technique of invention thus has two distinct phases: the discovery of new positions followed by their amalgamation with the existing body of knowledge' (2008 [1962]: 58). Kubler further distinguishes between 'useful' inventions and 'artistic' inventions and his distinction is pertinent within the current discussion of visual cognition and research outcomes. He explains:

> Artistic inventions alter the sensibility of mankind. They all emerge from and return to human perception, unlike useful inventions, which are keyed to the physical and biological environment. Useful inventions alter mankind only

indirectly by altering his environment; aesthetic inventions enlarge human awareness directly with new ways of experiencing the universe, rather than with new objective interpretations.

(Kubler 2008 [1962]: 59)

It is the artistic inventions that Kubler describes that are relevant here and these are described in Figure 6.3.

The research environment needed to capitalize on cognitive and creative practices being explored within institutional research settings tends to cut across discipline boundaries. New post-discipline alliances are clearly seen in connections being forged among artists, sociologists, scientists, and technologists. For instance, Stephen Wilson's text, *Information Arts* (2002), is a comprehensive account of artists, designers, technologists, and scientists collaborating on topics of wide interest where methodologies are not constrained by discipline boundaries. The caricatures of the eccentric scientist, the reclusive artist, or the computer nerd have little basis in the reality of the post-disciplinary environment of today. Although critical theorists and visual culture commentators raise pertinent questions about problematic relationships among art, culture, science, and technology, there is a need to move beyond an analysis that still sees domains of knowledge cloaked in paradigmatic terms.

An emphasis on moving over and beyond the geography of conceptual and discipline boundaries is taken up by Irit Rogoff (2000) in her analysis of contemporary art practices and notions of space, movement, location, and difference. In the many situations where artists and scientists are collaborating, there is little talk that sees science as merely a rationalistic endeavour or art as only an expressive activity. Questions, issues, and abstractions guide those imaginative investigators working outside the edges of disciplines where new knowledge is seen as a function of creating and critiquing human experience. By necessity, this complex practice has to bridge disciplines and in doing so not only opens up new possibilities but also renders mute old arguments that bind inquiry to prescribed methods.

Conclusion: outside the limits of cognition and creativity

Social scientists may argue that progress leads to change because it builds upon accumulated knowledge; however, artists would argue that change leads to progress as imaginative leaps are made into what we don't know, and this challenges what we do know. Consequently, discovery may reside within the cracks and erasures of the structures in place, but it can also be found outside these normative systems. Artists create within these unlikely liminal spaces and offer new ways to connect to existing and possible perspectives. In the past artists have relied on others to translate these insights into cultural capital. However, new notions of cognitions and new sites of creative inquiry being opened up in institutional settings is giving rise to a new discourse of artistic research and artists are very active participants (Macleod and Holdridge. 2006; Barrett and Bolt. 2007). Mika Hannula provides sound guidelines in asserting that artists are well placed to take more public responsibility in communicating the theoretical richness that informs art practice. In thinking about the flexibility needed, he believes that it is a commitment to a principle that methods of inquiry remain flexible rather than fixed, for artistic research is partly a 'methodological map of reflection' (2004: 71–2). What he means is that when studio inquiry is undertaken, the artist-researcher has a 'desire to say something about something to someone' (2004: 71) and therefore the research can be read by others as a landscape of purposes, premises, and practices. A key point Hannula makes is that artistic research continually remains open to the critical possibilities of what visual arts can achieve:

> The basic idea here is to see artistic research as a practice. An engaged practice, which in each context is imbued with the necessary qualities and substance to make it what it is, and also to apply its own internal logic to deciding between what makes sense and what is invalid. A practice with a defined direction, but with an open-ended, undetermined procedural trajectory. A practice that is particular, content-driven, self-critical, self-reflective and contextualized.
>
> (Hannula 2008: 112)

Theorizing artistic cognition and creativity as a distinctive form of human knowing involves examining the way creative and critical insights are explored and enacted, as mind and matter converge in the many individual and cultural contexts within which art practice takes place. Theorizing is an approach to understanding that occurs at all levels of human inquiry and involves conceptual reasoning, creative action, and critical reflection. Artists, curators, and researchers all engage in theorizing in order to make sense of the complexities revealed in the inquiries and investigations undertaken. For many artists, theorizing is a reflexive process that can occur during the 'think-time' that happens when making art, or may be the consequence of reflective processes that take place afterwards. For instance, David Hockney explains that although he has an interest in theory he asks 'such questions and make(s) the theories only afterwards, not before – only after I have done something' (1993: 130–1). For curators such as Robert Storr theorizing is a crucial element in searching out interpretive systems that help us to understand what it is that artists do.

Researchers, on the other hand, have been debating the relationship between theory and practice for some time and the emergence of practice-based research in the arts has extended the boundaries considerably in conceptualizing how artists might contribute to this arena of human inquiry. Within the context of this chapter, a guiding assumption is that through their extensive training, sustained art practice, and immersion in complex cultural contexts, artist-researchers are important sources of information, expertise, and insight. In addition, their artworks and the contexts in which they are created and displayed, and the discussion and debates that arise, are sites of knowledge creation.

There are several conclusions that can be drawn from the arguments made in this chapter that cluster around conceptions of cognition and creativity. Let me deal with the implications related to artistic cognition.

- First, it is acknowledged that the thinking artist is a practitioner-researcher who uses many visual cognitive strategies that dislodge discipline boundaries, override media conventions, and disrupt political interests as they take on roles as creators, critics, and theorists.

- Second, seeing, experiencing, and thinking in artistic contexts activates cognitive processes that are both mental and physical. Whether artists are 'thinking' in media, languages or contexts, the modes of creative and critical actions are distributed and connected throughout the neural architecture of the visual brain, and the various situations and settings that shape the way images are made and what they might mean. As such, artistic cognition is a form of human knowing that is embodied within artistic practice and incorporates creative and critical processes as mind and matter converge in the many contexts within which art practice takes place.
- Third, the image instinct that gives rise to a creative impulse is a continuously changing, dynamic process that makes use of the connective capacity of concepts, forms, and contexts, and stimulates a mindful search that takes place within and beyond the parameters of existing knowledge systems and structures. In this sense, artistic research is a 'post-discipline' practice.

The information presented in this chapter also draws on sources that offer 'micro' and 'macro' perspectives that advance theories and practices about creativity as a significant human and cultural impulse that warrants a central role in contemporary research. The purpose was to position creativity as a cultural practice whereby the creative and critical processes, interpretive structures, and contextual factors that extend artistic cognition can be broadly situated within practice-led research. Creativity, it is argued, is more than a distinctive individual capacity that is best understood if seen through a psychological lens or as a bio-behavioural construct. Rather, the position taken sees creativity as being mediated by various socio-cultural factors, and although tentative, there is little doubt that neurobiological constraints are involved as well. Still, there are several conclusions that can be claimed.

- First, creativity can be described as the capacity to see things in new ways as a result of creative and critical inquiry that constructs knowledge that has implications others can identify with and value. Creativity, however is not merely a distinctive habit of mind, rather it becomes manifest through individual agency and creative social action.
- Second, creativity is the conceptual vehicle that translates visual cognition into forms, frames, and actions that transcend the self and positions imaginative outcomes within broader socio-cultural contexts.
- Third, creativity can be described as a distributed cultural practice that involves creative and critical processes that are enacted, embodied, and transacted across institutional, communal, and cultural domains.

When considered in relation to the theory of visual cognition described earlier, the issues raised in this chapter define a theoretical structure for conceptualizing how visual cognition is enacted and embodied within the distinctive nature of practice-led research.

Notes

1 When asked the question, 'How are you doing today?' a 97-year-old artist responded, 'Well, I'm above ground.' Retrieved from http://arts.tc.columbia.edu/rcac/Aging_artists (accessed on 20 March 2009).

2 The Venice Biennale is an international art exposition first held in 1897 and features a survey of contemporary art as well as national exhibitions shown in the various pavilions at the Giardini and Arsenale locations, and throughout Venice. Under Robert Storr's curatorship the survey show included 98 artists from five continents (Storr 2007).

7
THE ROLE OF THE ARTEFACT AND FRAMEWORKS FOR PRACTICE-BASED RESEARCH

Linda Candy and Ernest Edmonds

Introduction

This chapter is concerned with the role of the artefact in practice-based research and the frameworks necessary to the success of practitioner research in the creative arts. We begin with the artefact and its role in research and knowledge creation and go on to place it within the context of practitioner and organizational frameworks. We describe the way in which conceptual frameworks play a central role in the practice-based research process, illustrated by specific examples from recent PhD programmes in the digital arts.

Two types of frameworks underpin and facilitate the practice-based research process: one is practitioner-determined and research-led whilst the other is organizational, comprising funded research and doctoral programmes. The organizational frameworks are important and essential vehicles for giving the artefact a legitimate role in research. These developments have required changes to existing organizational rules and are relatively recent in the history of knowledge production. The opportunities for including artefacts in formal research remain limited on a world wide scale, and those that exist can only be seen as the beginning of a longer transformational process, the consequences of which we are still working through.

There has been a growing awareness in some research communities that the outcomes of creative practice, as presented by practitioners themselves, can make a significant contribution to generating new knowledge. Gradually, for example, practitioner knowledge, with its own unique value, is becoming accessible through the increasing numbers of practice-based doctoral awards. The distinguishing feature of practitioner research in the arts, design and digital media is the importance given to artefact generation as an integral part of the research process and the generation of new knowledge. New knowledge generated by research, whether practice-based or not, is expected to have two characteristics: first that it is shared and second that it can be verified or challenged.

Certain key issues concerning practice-based knowledge generation are at the heart of the argument to be made here. These are the relationship between research, knowledge and the artefact, the nature of practitioner knowledge and frameworks for practitioner research in relation to the artefact. In order to explore these issues we draw upon knowledge and experience gained from relevant funded research and PhD programmes in the arts, design and digital media.

In the English-speaking world, the UK, Australia and New Zealand are leading the way in the development of structures for formalizing research that explores knowledge in and from practice, particularly in the art, design and digital media domains where the creative artefact assumes a central role. In other countries, including Sweden and the USA, there are new initiatives in practitioner-led research programmes, which have similar characteristics, although the organizational frameworks are less well established at the time of writing. An important influential factor shaping the way these initiatives take root and grow is a country's university system and its regulatory standards, which affect the take-up and expansion of such initiatives.

A number of funded research initiatives have been taken in which collaboration between, for example, science and art have been facilitated. Two examples are the SciArt programme[1] in the UK and Synapse[2] in Australia. In such cases, although the normal outcomes including learned papers are expected, artefacts that are exhibited in some way are also seen as legitimate and valued contributions from the research.

From the point of view of the role of the artefacts in practice-based research, the PhD is particularly interesting because the research process is necessarily of high significance and receives considerable attention by practitioners and supervisors. PhD processes represent models of research processes more comprehensively. In the general research context, it is the outcomes that receive most attention but, by considering PhD programmes, we are able to address issues of research process. For that reason we focus on PhD programmes in practice-based arts research where an artefact plays a significant role. We also consider the organizational contexts that constrain and direct such research and we consider the artefact in relation to the actual research processes.

Awarding PhDs for practice-based research is not often justified solely by the making of works. Research includes the production of some kind of description of what is new, or what has been discovered or created. Practice-based art research can be about the creation of new apprehensions but any art object made as part of that research does not, by itself, embody knowledge. However, the text that accompanies the work may indeed illuminate new apprehensions or a new way of creating apprehensions that we can claim as the new knowledge produced.

It is important to recognize that following the pursuit of a PhD award, and learning how to do research in that sense, is not a necessary requirement for an artist or for any other kind of practitioner. Practice may well be enhanced by research but it need not depend on research skills. Most probably we go to dentists, doctors and solicitors who do not have PhDs. We enjoy poems, music and paintings without needing to check for PhD qualifications. For the artist, research can enhance practice or illuminate it but it is far from obvious that all creative practitioners can benefit equally. We need to be aware of how the nature of an artist's practice influences the likelihood of doctoral-style research having value.

From the wide spectrum of possibilities consider two kinds of artist: the first systematically explores and reflects upon alternative paths, processes, structures and materials as an integral part of his or her practice; the second develops an outstanding facility with a chosen medium and spends a lifetime applying it. For the first case, it is a relatively small step to work in a way that incorporates formalized research by defining problems, methods and outcomes and, at the same time, produce artefacts that embody the ideas and processes. In any case, the requirement to write text is most often a key issue for a doctorate by research or for the outcome of funded research and that, in itself, may be a natural barrier for some people.

Artefacts in practitioner research: domain context

Research as part of practice is not a new idea, but formal research by creative practitioners has become a part of university life and of doctoral programmes in a small number of countries and in fields where it has proven to be particularly appropriate. The practitioners, whose research provides the grounding for the concepts presented in this chapter, are working primarily within the field of interactive digital art. These artists are at the forefront of an inter-disciplinary movement in which visual and sound artworks, installations and performances are enabling audiences to participate in interactive experiences. The research was undertaken at the Creativity and Cognition Studios[3] associated with a public exhibition space in a major museum where interactive art works are exhibited to the public and audience experience is evaluated.[4] Exhibitions of interactive artworks are mounted, where the works are technically finished but still in need of development in the light of audience experience. In interactive art, the artist is interested in seeing how the interactive elements work. Interactive works invite the audience to explicitly engage with them and, in so doing, participate in the realization of the work itself. Experiencing art is driven by perception, where perception is an active and constructive process. Experiencing interactive artworks involves the same condition in addition to active engagement with the work, which involves being in the space of the work, interacting with it and constructing an experience through this interaction. The domain of interactive digital art faces the particular problem for the practitioner of understanding how audiences engage with specific works. This implies that practice has research problems associated with it and so the domain is especially appropriate in our context.

Bolt (2006) points out that theorizing out of practice is very different from applying theory to practice. Both can form part of a practice-based research project but it is important to be clear how each (theory and practice) can lead to developments in the other. Sullivan (2005) discusses art practice as research and identifies one context that frames the concerns of this chapter. He calls it 'making in systems', which he defines in terms of moving 'beyond discipline boundaries and into areas of inquiry that interact and intersect and require new ways to conceptualize forms and structures'. Having closely observed creative practitioners, who might be said to be 'making in systems', undertaking PhD studies over many years, we believe that it is now possible to describe some general features of the way practitioners undertake their research and, in particular, how they develop conceptual frameworks that inform and guide the making and evaluation of artefacts.

Amongst the practitioner-based researchers referred to in this chapter, the designing, developing and making of artefacts was the central activity in the research process. Through making artefacts, practitioners were able to generate questions and also to explore the answers to those questions through further making. The role of practice in relation to the research began with the generating of questions carried out in two distinct ways: in one, the starting point was to explore the literature of the field and, in parallel, to generate questions relating to practice; in the other, the questions came directly out of the basics of practice without reference to theoretical knowledge, at least in the first instance. The type of artefact includes interactive and tactile art and installations as well as software instruments and performances: For example:

- interactive art systems that explore the role of the system as an agent in facilitating patterns of emergent behaviour;
- interactive virtual musical instruments and a series of concerts which featured music composed specifically for these virtual instruments;
- two processes of creation and exhibition that resulted in two successful artworks, illustrating aspects of collaboration between artist and curator as mediator;
- interactive art installations exemplifying the concept of play using sensors to capture participant movement.

The artefacts that practitioners create are an integral part of practice whether or not there is a formal research process. However, within research, the making process provides opportunities for reflection and evaluation. It is also an opportunity to generate research questions from the exploration that is a normal part of practice.

The artefact, research and knowledge

For a creative practitioner, the object that is made, be it a painting or a novel or a symphony, is normally the main point of the exercise. That artefact is the art, we might say. As we will see, it is a little more complicated than that. For our purpose, a broad view of the meaning of 'artefact' can be taken. It might be an object, such as a table, painting or building. It might exist over time, such as a piece of music or a film. On the other hand, it might be less persistent in time, such as an exhibition or performance. An interactive artwork would also count even though, in some sense, it only exists in relation to the presence and behaviour of its audience. Going further, Goodman, drew an important distinction between what he called notional and non-notional works of art (Goodman 1978). In a novel, for example, he argued that any sequence of letters that corresponds with the original text is a genuine instance of the work. One might say that the essence of the novel is not the book object at all. It is in the 'notional object' that we access through the book. Our use of the word 'artefact' is intended to cover all of these cases.

Research and the artefact

Research may be a purely theoretical activity or it may use artefacts as the object of study or as experimental apparatus. Our concern, however, is with cases where the production or design of an artefact is central to the research process. *Research* is a systematic process that results in new knowledge or new understanding. Certain basic characteristics must apply to research as, for example, identified by Biggs and Büchler (Biggs and Büchler 2008a); as they put it, research must be *disseminated, original* and *contextualized.* Thus the new knowledge or understanding must be in a form that can be shared. It must be shown to be new (in the world rather than to the researcher) and the intellectual context within which it sits must be identified. For brevity we will take understanding to be a form of knowledge. The implications are that we expect new knowledge to be disseminated in a form that enables it to be verified or challenged within its context. For research to be considered worthy of a doctoral thesis or publication in a learned journal, for example, it must contain knowledge that is new, in the world, that can be shared with others and that can be challenged, tested or evaluated in some way. Accepting that much of what we know is known tentatively rather than absolutely, the properties of shared knowledge that can be challenged are more important in research than the absolute certain truth of the new knowledge.

Beyond knowing what is and knowing what causes what (*knowing that*), there is knowledge about action (*knowing how*), for example about how best to make a cake. Through research we are clearly able to find new knowledge about how to better achieve some end. 'Knowledge how' may not, however, provide the degree of explanation that 'knowledge that' does. The action researcher might generate new knowledge about how to do something but leave it open to others to discover why it works. A phenomenologist might argue that this kind of 'knowing how' must precede the related 'knowing that'. From that point of view, action research[5] should come before experimental research.[6] Until the action research is complete, it could be argued, we do not know what to study experimentally. If we were starting from a clean sheet of zero knowledge, perhaps that would be true, but reality is more complex. However, the concerns of this chapter are with forms of research that involve or are based on practice and so contain a non-trivial element of 'knowing how'. In such cases, the production of an *artefact* is often central to the investigation and is a key distinguishing feature.

Knowledge and the artefact

Scrivener's paper 'The art object does not embody a form of knowledge' argues against the notion of art research, for example towards a PhD, in the conventional model. He is against a course of research that includes the generation of new knowledge in the traditional sense because, he contends, art is not concerned with communicating knowledge based on a justification of that knowledge. Artworks offer perspectives or ways of seeing: art is made in order to create what he terms 'apprehensions' (Scrivener 2002). Scrivener has suggested a way forward that resolves this problem. He proposes that, in effect, 'new knowledge' can be understood within the context of any particular discipline by reference to the norms and tests employed in that discipline. Even between traditional disciplines, such as experimental physics and historiography, different norms and tests are used. He argues that arts-based research inevitably has its own standards and that they must be used in understanding the nature of the research being conducted (Scrivener 2009a). From this point of view, we can see that 'verification', for example, applies in all research but the ways in which it is conducted might vary widely according to the domain specific norms. This raises the need to ensure that, when research results are communicated, the relevant norms and tests are made explicit. Thus, the use and presumed context of the word 'knowledge', for example in the sense of 'knowledge how' or 'knowledge that', needs to be carefully articulated in any report on practice-based research.

As Biggs argues, the artwork, and hence, the apprehensions, only exist within a context (Biggs 2003). The artwork alone, without text, cannot be seen as a research outcome. As a minimum, a commentary is needed which frames the context in which the artwork is to be understood, including the research norms and tests. The context is seen to be physical, social or cultural but there is also another aspect to consider. In research, the context of a work needs to include the framing of its perception. We need to know how to look or listen in a very direct sense. We need to know more than which cultural glasses to wear. We need to know what to look at. Then we can see whatever it is that is significant. In other words we need to know how to look so as to experience the apprehensions.

The way that existing artefacts can reveal the development of practitioner knowledge can be illustrated from retrospective studies. In a study of the design of the Lotus bicycle ridden by Chris Boardman at the 1992 Olympic games, the history of the transformation of the bicycle artefact in relation to its predecessors provided insight into how new ideas arise from existing models and how conventions are used, changed and reformulated until a truly innovative concept arises. The artefacts studied provided evidence about the evolution of the designer's knowledge from the initial learning of craft skills to expert knowledge leading to ground-breaking design (Candy and Edmonds 1994). This kind of study is indicative of how artefacts can play a significant part in generating and embodying new knowledge and hence, can be justifiably included in research. This is the approach, sometimes known as *material culture*[7] that can inform our understanding of the nature of practitioner knowledge retrospectively (Tilley *et al.* 2006).

It is our position that the role of artefacts in material culture studies is entirely different from what happens with practitioner research where making the artefact is a significant part of the research methodology itself. The most common artefacts that form part of arts-based research projects are objects and artworks, designed within the research context, in all kinds of media, from musical performances to paintings and novels. These artefacts may well represent the core of the 'new knowledge' generated by the research, but the clarity with which that knowledge is communicated directly through the artefact is questionable. Given that one accepts that the artefact can, in some sense, represent new knowledge, the problem of sharing it leads to the perceived need for text describing the context, as discussed above, before the related work is normally described as 'research'.

Practitioner knowledge

Practitioner knowledge differs from other forms of knowledge such as that arising from scientific experimentation. The process of generating practitioner knowledge arises from sources that are often unique to the individual and are embedded in tacit understandings that require externalization and these understandings evolve over time as part of the practitioner's everyday creative process. Nevertheless, in research, the highly individualized nature of practitioner knowledge has to be made evident to others and it is in the methods of the practice-based research process that such sharable outcomes become possible. In order to achieve such advances in knowledge, the everyday research process common to professional practice has to be defined and executed in a manner that is commonly agreed. The research component of the practice-based research is, in most respects, similar to any definition of research, a key element of which is the transferability of the understandings reached as a result of the research process.

The type of practice that an artist undertakes is an important consideration in judging whether or not it lends itself to research. Some artists' practice is naturally close to research whilst others work in ways quite distant from research enquiry and sharing. Perhaps the key characteristic required is that the practice is fundamentally exploratory, involving innovation and risk in ways that are familiar to researchers in the broader community.

Practitioner frameworks for practice-based research

All research is conducted within a context of convention and tradition. Within a well established and focused field, such as Number Theory in mathematics, that context is so well understood that it is common to treat an understanding of it as tacitly understood by all involved. In such cases, there is no perceived need to describe the framework within which the work is conducted except in texts aimed at the lay public. In the case of practice-based research, however, there is significant variation between practitioners and, in general, the maturity of the field is such that a shared understanding of context may not be assumed even amongst experts. The existence of practitioner frameworks for practice-based research is, therefore, an important issue to discuss and be explicit about.

Frameworks for the research process

A framework for practice-based research comprises a conceptual structure that is used to influence practice, inform theory and, in particular, shape validation or evaluation (Edmonds and Candy 2010). Such frameworks may be tacit, in the sense that they are implicit but nevertheless implied by the cultural context or personal tradition, or they may be explicit and part of a practitioner's chosen approach.

In the context of research, we can expect the framework to be, or to become, explicit. The sharing of the framework would be one of the normal research activities. A framework may consist of many different things according to the individual practitioner's goals and intentions. Amongst the practitioners referred to here, common descriptors exist: for example, types, modes, qualities, categories, indices, etc., which may refer to similar concepts. At the same time, the methodologies that are developed have an impact on the way the framework is applied and how it is altered in the light of experience.

Some examples of framework types are:

- classifications for assessing the ways in which audiences respond to particular works;
- criteria for guiding the design of a new artefact or installation;
- questions, expressed as working hypotheses, to be explored using theoretical knowledge.

When practitioners carry out research in parallel with making works, they engage in a process of developing frameworks that guide their practice and the evaluation of the outcomes of that practice: i.e. artefacts that are submitted along with a written text. This is an essential part of the generation of insights and understandings that contribute to the final outcomes and, where a PhD submission is involved, comprise part of the new knowledge.

Practitioner frameworks are defined by whoever invents them (e.g. an artist) and the purpose they serve (e.g. to shape the developing artwork). The practitioners whose work is provided by way of example in this chapter, are working primarily within the field of interactive art systems using forms of digital technology to create experiences for direct audience participation in the creation of visual and sound artworks. These practitioners are engaged in doctoral research that involves a cyclical process of putting theoretical knowledge into practice and revising theory as a result of the outcomes. Theory and practice are intertwined in the development of their art. Research questions and issues come naturally from the practice and it is often a small step to articulate the context and methods associated with practice. There is, in this context, a reflexive relationship between practice and theory as well as evaluation that plays an important role in the practice-based research process. This provides a particular viewpoint from which the works are considered during the process of making and evaluating them.

Practitioner frameworks

We have studied a number of practitioners undertaking doctoral programmes and identified characteristics of their research processes including the development of individual conceptual frameworks. The authors have described examples of different trajectories followed by practitioners and the way in which the frameworks played a central role (Edmonds and Candy 2010).

In the example cases below, practice forms an integral part of the research process. In each case the practitioner has devised a unique framework that is used to guide the making of works and shape evaluation studies of audience experience and engagement with works. The understanding of the use of research frameworks has advanced significantly over the last quarter of a century.

A framework for interactive emergent experience

Jennifer Seevinck is a visual artist who is exploring how her artworks can stimulate emergent experience in audiences. By emergence is meant the appearance (to the viewer) of new forms not explicit in the source work. As an artist, Jen is continually making artefacts and for her, as with other practitioners, no research process begins without the prior existence of such works that may or may not be included in the ongoing research process.

An analysis of Jen's research process indicated that as she creates artworks she addresses questions as to whether or not they fulfil her expectations with regard to the audience or viewer. Underlying this is a stream of enquiry about emergence and how audience response is influenced by interaction with artworks. Separately, from an analysis of the theoretical literature of emergence, she derived a set of categories of properties for describing the compositions and shapes observed in audience interaction. Having derived this first framework, she then evaluated her existing artworks. These works had been designed to stimulate emergent responses in audiences according to a working hypothesis. The qualities of emergence were structured according to origin (e.g. perceptual and physical) and intrinsic and extrinsic structures (e.g. the emergent part changes or does not change the source). The results of the evaluation studies and the refined framework were used to inform and guide the making of the next work. Here the framework both informs the art making process and also provides a means of interpreting the results of observing audience response and behaviour through evaluation (Seevinck and Edmonds 2008).

A framework for interaction with virtual musical instruments

Andrew Johnston is a musician and programmer investigating the design and use of software to support an exploratory approach to live music-making. The resulting audio-visual performance work for trombone and 'virtual musical instruments', Partial Reflections, co-created with Ben Marks, was premièred at the Sydney Opera House Studio in 2006.

An analysis of Andrew's research process indicates that making works is the main driver of the research. He designed and implemented software (virtual instruments) that allows musicians to 'play' using the sound of their familiar acoustic instruments. The criteria generated from a documented reflective practice were used to guide the next iteration of the design of new works and were intended to achieve qualities in the instruments that would have particular effects: for example, the instruments would have attributes that were natural, consistent, interesting and motivating from a player's point of view. Once the virtual instruments were at a stage when they could be confidently handed over to other musicians, it was then possible to carry out a user experience study in which the instruments were evaluated against the initial criteria. The study examined what happened when the instruments were played in real practice and whether the criteria were satisfied. Based on results from the study, the criteria were refined and extended. Finally, a new conceptual framework for interpreting user interaction was derived. The framework and details of the studies that were undertaken can be found in Johnston, Candy and Edmonds (Johnston et al. 2008).

A framework for collaborative curatorial practice

Lizzie Muller is a curator, writer and researcher specializing in interaction, audience experience and interdisciplinary collaboration. Lizzie has developed an 'experiential' approach to her role as a curator of interactive art and in her PhD research sought to develop this as part of collaborative practice with selected artists.

An analysis of her practice and research processes showed that, although theory driven in many respects, it is distinguished by a strong reflexive relationship between theory and practice. This example provides insight into a practitioner researcher's approach that combines theory with practice in curatorial experience in a dynamic reflexive relationship. Theoretical knowledge drawn from the field of Human Computer Interaction was adapted for use in an artistic context and used to derive a framework consisting of tools and methods for understanding audience experience. The framework was then applied to two case studies of artists' developing and exhibiting their work in a public space and the results analysed. From the results of applying the tools and methods to the case studies of the collaboration between the curator practitioner and two artists, the practitioner was able to refine her understanding and generate a refined critical framework consisting of a set of qualities of audience experience. The revised framework was used by the practitioner for further curatorial activities and was found effective for interpreting the nature of the interactive artworks including the artist's response to the audience experience (Muller 2008).

A framework for interactive play experience

The fourth example combines art practice and qualitative research methods in a cyclical process of artefact creation and evaluation. Brigid Costello is a practising multimedia artist with expertise in interaction design, programming and visual design. Brigid has developed ways to enable playful experiences for audiences when interacting with her artworks.

The practice and research process identified here involved several stages of creation and evaluation, from formulating the main research question and generating design strategies that were tested with existing artefacts, to the creation of new works using the tested (and modified) strategies. It began with the creation of a number of interactive works that enabled her to explore audience experience using criteria for design to shape her works so that they engendered or encouraged play. From an exploration of theoretical literature about play and related phenomena, she developed a framework of play based on thirteen pleasure categories. The artworks created using the modified criteria were studied using the framework to support the evaluation of observational data gathered from audience experience studies. From the results of the audience studies, new understandings about the capability of interactive works for play experience were derived and the framework was refined. A relationship between the refined criteria and the final version of the framework was established. The 'play framework' of thirteen pleasure categories provides a structure both for creation and evaluation of works (Costello 2007; Costello and Edmonds 2007).

Trajectories of practice and research

In the examples described above, each practitioner devised an individual framework that was used to guide the making of works and shape the evaluation studies of audience experience. Practitioner frameworks of these kinds are constructs that evolve through their role in guiding creation, evaluation and reflection on practice. The processes whereby practice, theory and evaluation contribute to the development of the frameworks extend over significant time frames, and in relation to extended series of artworks. Those processes occupy a space of possible pathways in which the practitioner activities move between pure practice and pure research. The paths taken in this space of possibilities are here termed 'trajectories'.

In a *trajectory of practice and research,* there are three elements: practice, theory and evaluation. Each element involves activities undertaken by the practitioner in the process of making physical works, developing conceptual frameworks and performing evaluation studies. Trajectories of practice and research can work in a number of different ways. Where the primary driver is theory, a framework is developed that draws on theoretical knowledge and is used to shape the evaluation process and the creation of works. A second type of trajectory is one where the practice drives the development of theory. In this case, research questions and design criteria are derived through the creation of works and this leads to the development of a theoretical framework which is used in the evaluation of the results of practice. In both cases, the process is cyclical and there is often a tighter iterative sub-process in which the framework and practice develop together.

The trajectory of practice and research, whilst a time-ordered path, is far from a linear, step-wise set of activities that moves inexorably towards an intended goal. In reality, even under the time constraints of a research programme, the practice is interwoven with the other two elements: theory and evaluation. Sometimes the theory comes first but often, the need for it emerges as the practice process continues. The role of theory and practice in creative arts research is relatively familiar but that of evaluation, as we characterize it, is perhaps less well known and can be seen as representing a novel approach in this field. The nature and role of evaluation and the associated theory and practice is presented in full in a recent article (Edmonds and Candy 2010).

Practice is a primary element in the trajectory providing as it does motivation for conducting research as well as generating the activities for creating and exhibiting tangible outcomes such as artworks, exhibitions, installations, musical compositions and creative software systems. In the nature of practice-based research, experiencing these works is usually necessary for a full understanding of the contribution to new understanding (knowledge) that the practitioner is making. For that reason, the role the works play in evaluation is vital.

Theory, as it is understood in the context of practice-based research, is likely to consist of different ways of examining, critiquing and applying areas of knowledge that are considered relevant to the individual's practice. If, for example, the practitioner seeks to create a software artefact that can be used in ways analogous with a conventional musical instrument, then being able to select and adapt relevant theoretical knowledge of the physical modelling of sound is a necessary role for such 'theory'. On the other hand, practitioner theory may consist of an untested opinion ('hypothesis') that the artwork can elicit certain emotions or qualities of experience in an audience or 'user'; this will remain a personal 'theory-in-action' until it is subject to a more rigorous form of study that involves investigation as to whether or not the opinion has any truth beyond an individual viewpoint. Amongst practitioners, this is often referred to as design criteria or strategies operating as working theories in the creative process. Within the formal constraints of the doctoral research process, these working theories are developed into more rigorous forms through the exploration of theoretical knowledge and the examples of other practitioners.

Evaluation that informs practice has a particular role that is defined by practitioners themselves in order to facilitate reflections on practice and a broader understanding of audience experience of artworks, for example. It usually involves direct observation, monitoring, recording, analysing and reflection as part of a semi-formal approach to generating understandings that go further than informal reflections on personal practice. Whilst the methodology is less prescriptive than that of traditional experimental science, such studies are usually carried out using a variety of tested methods drawn from different disciplines. In the interactive digital arts, the fields of Human-Computer Interaction (HCI), Action Research and Ethnography, for example, are rich sources of inspiration, methods and techniques.

The position presented here with respect to the role of the artefact in the practitioner research process is one that can be related to existing research paradigms such as HCI. It falls, therefore, within what Biggs and Büchler (2008b) refer to as the Situated Position. In the examples described above, the making of the artefact is common to all and its role is critical but there are individual variations within this particular practice-based paradigm. Whilst all the practitioners create their own conceptual frameworks involving creation and evaluation of an artefact, some are more concerned to explore broader theoretical concerns focusing on the framework itself whilst others use the frameworks to obtain evidence that supports the artistic intentions for the artefact itself. Whatever the variations in the approaches are, they are all grounded in existing research methodologies that are developed and modified to address the particular requirements of interactive digital arts. Methodological steps are, therefore, quite often, significant outcomes of such doctoral research.

Organizational frameworks for practice-based research

Research processes, such as those discussed in the previous section, always take place within some intellectual, social or organizational context and those contexts inevitably influence both the details of the research and the practitioner frameworks that are employed. It is important, therefore, to give consideration to relevant organizational frameworks for practice-based research and the central place of the artefact in much of that work.

The artefact and funded research

When research is funded, the funding rules often place constraints on both the process and its outcomes. In some countries various funding programmes have been developed that support practice-based arts research. Often they involve collaboration between creative practitioners and other types of researchers, such as scientists. Whilst research papers often arise from these programmes, artefacts as significant outcomes are also common. Examples include the Wellcome Trust's SciArt programme in the UK, which concentrated on art practice that is informed by bio-medical research and the Australian Synapse programme, in which the Australia Council for the Arts and the Australian Research Council jointly fund artist and scientist collaborations. The Norwegian Artistic Fellowship programme (Chapter 2), is another example of funding for research involving practice.

In the UK, the Arts and Humanities Research Council (AHRC) has provided a careful definition of what it regards as research and has given particular attention to what it terms 'practice-led' research. For the purposes of this article we continue to use the term 'practice-based'. In general, the AHRC defines research in relation to process and does so in terms of what a description of research must contain. Three key elements are listed: questions or issues, context and methods (AHRC 2009: 66). They specifically state that creative outputs or practice can be included but are careful to delineate the cases that would count as research as against pure practice and require documentation of the research process and a textual analysis or explanation that demonstrates critical reflection. This last point is probably important to AHRC so as to distinguish its funding from those of the various arts funding bodies in the UK, such as the Arts Council of England. The need for such distinctions is not uncommon.

In the UK's Research Assessment Exercise (RAE), on the other hand, the definition of research includes 'the invention and generation of … images, performances, artefacts … where these lead to new insights' (RAE 2006). This definition would seem to briefly describe the view taken by the AHRC. A difference between the AHRC and RAE is that the latter will not accept teaching materials as evidence of research excellence whereas the AHRC allows curriculum development as an outcome of research. Perhaps the key point is that evidence of new knowledge, or new insight, must be demonstrated at the very least by a textual commentary on any artefact that is claimed to embody that knowledge.

The importance of sharing research is almost always stressed by funding bodies, such as the AHRC. It is assumed that research is cumulative and that the results must therefore be accessible. The AHRC's requirement that researchers identify their research question and that they are explicit in the end about their answer helps to facilitate the cumulative process and makes the development of personal experience and private understanding, for example, fall outside the realm of research, cf. the discussion by Biggs and Büchler (2008b).

The Wellcome Trust has published an evaluation of the SciArt programme which includes reports on its impact on the research funded (Glinowski and Bamford 2009). It shows, for example, that the collaborative research acted as a catalyst for change in artists' practice in a very high percentage of cases. Often, the programme introduced artists to the idea of research as an element of practice. Hence it is interesting to know that the practice was changed as a result. It was primarily the artists who were making artefacts within the programmes and it was the incorporation of that making into research that initiated the changes. The following quotations from artists indicates the range of those changes: it 'provided me with new insights into my work' (Glinowski and Bamford 2009: 60), 'it has influenced the way that I can articulate to myself what it is that I have been working on' (Glinowski and Bamford 2009: 61) and 'I was interested in the clarity and integrity of the scientific method can give to an artistic outcome' (Glinowski and Bamford 2009: 64).

Beyond direct funding, another form of support for artist researchers is the provision of specific facilities and a dedicated research environment. One such case is Beta_space, which is an experimental exhibiting space within the Powerhouse Museum Sydney and is a collaborative venture with the Creativity and Cognition Studios at the University of Technology, Sydney (Beta_space 2009). It is a working environment – a laboratory yielding research outcomes – that benefits both artists and interaction design researchers. It gives participants the opportunity to be creatively involved in the development of new forms of artistic expression, and it gives the general public an insight into the creative process of artists and technologists and the experience of audiences (Muller *et al.* 2006). A key aspect of this working environment is evaluation of the interactive artefacts shown, and every artwork exhibiting in Beta_space goes through an evaluation process. As in the SciArt case, practice is significantly influenced by this process (Edmonds *et al.* 2009).

The artefact and the PhD

As with funded research, where a PhD is undertaken, university rules have a significant impact on the research process. The examination frameworks developed under the Council for National Academic Awards (CNAA) in the UK, were to prove vital avenues to stimulate and foster a small but strong demand (CNAA, 1988). The criteria set down that allowed for the inclusion of an artefact in a PhD submission have migrated and evolved into the current AHRC guidelines for research. When university regulatory bodies for the award of doctoral qualifications began to allow creative artefacts to be included with a written thesis, the door opened to a new breed of PhDs in which the artefact is a research outcome that forms an essential component of the material presented for examination.

> The PhD is awarded to a candidate who, having critically investigated and evaluated an approved topic resulting in an independent and original contribution to knowledge and demonstrated an understanding of research methods appropriate to the chosen field, has presented and defended a thesis, by oral examination, to the satisfaction of the examiners.
>
> (University of Huddersfield 2009: F1.8)

Clearly, the submission of an artefact or a collection of artefacts as part of a PhD has to be treated differently in different cases. In fact, for the most part, it may not be possible to lodge the artefact itself in the University Library as is normally required. The submission is often of sufficiently good documentation of the artefact for the work to be understood in whatever sense is required to meet the PhD requirements. So, recordings of music, films, photographs of paintings, video recordings of performances and so on are likely to be submitted along with the written thesis in a practice-based PhD. The extent of documentation and the degree to which textual descriptions are needed will vary from case to case. Sometimes, examiners are shown the actual artefacts as well as the documentation. Thus an exhibition of paintings, for example, is sometimes staged for the examination. This does not remove the need for adequate documentation, however, because the PhD must be available for others to study and learn from after the examination is over.

One attempt to classify practice-based PhDs is by Elkins (2005b). He sees the dissertation as something that can inform art practice, be equal to the artwork or even be the artwork. In terms of formal rules along these lines, Glasgow School of Art allows a number of different forms of PhD submission. Of these, 'portfolio with written commentary' and 'joint portfolio and dissertation' seem to be the two core categories. The former is basically an innovative creative work with an explanation of what is innovative about it and why it is new in the world. The second is partly a conventional thesis but includes, as an essential element, a creative work (GSA 2007). There are two further categories. 'Portfolio with documentation' which allows the body of work to be submitted for the PhD in the form of, or together with, documentation. The candidate is not required to explain or discuss any new knowledge in a textual form. A candidate is also allowed to submit a 'thesis' on its own in the completely conventional sense. Figure 7.1 shows one way of viewing the Elkins and Glasgow models.

In summary, we identify four models of the PhD outcome:

- a work (artefact)
- a work with commentary
- a work with dissertation
- a thesis

In line with the earlier discussion of the requirements of research, we suggest that only the second and third correctly count as suitable for a practice-based PhD award. It should be noted, however, that this position is not agreed by all universities. For

	Thesis	*Dissertation plus portfolio*	*Portfolio plus commentary*	*Portfolio plus documentation*
History or theory	Practice-led			
Theory complementing practice		Two elements jointly representing research (complementary)		
Art as research		Two elements jointly representing research (unified)		
Dissertation as art				
Practice and exhibition			With a commentary necessary for understanding	Documented artwork

Figure 7.1 A table drawn from Elkins' models and the Glasgow categories

example, York University's highly regarded Department of Music has awarded PhDs purely on the basis of submitted artefacts (music) for a long time; compare their PhD by composition (York 2009).

In practice, particularly in recent times, text normally plays a part even under the York rules:

> while the option to not include text is a possibility, and might be recommended to candidates whose work clearly shows invention, innovation and originality, in recent times this has rarely been advised in the interests of definitive explanations for external examiners or simply because some aspects of, perhaps, less-well-realised-but-still-adequate folios, are not clearly expressed in the work.
>
> (Myatt 2009)

Biggs and Büchler (2008b) have contrasted what they call the *Situated* and the *Isolationist* position. By the former they mean the case where PhD regulations, for example, apply across a university so that a practice-based art or design PhD is situated in a broader academic context. By the latter they mean the case where creative practice has its own rules and so operates outside the standard academic tradition. They see the isolationist position as being unhelpful, resulting in poor scholarship. On this basis, the case for having university rules that allow an artefact alone to be submitted for a PhD is opposed. As has been clear from the earlier arguments, we agree with this position and as our examples suggest, a written text is an important aspect of the approaches described and, indeed, performs a vital function in presenting the practitioner frameworks and studies.

We have primarily drawn upon examples of funded research and PhD programmes conducted in the UK and Australia in order to illuminate our discussion. Similar considerations apply in other countries, such as Brazil and Sweden, for example (Büchler *et al.* 2009a; Büchler *et al.* 2009b). In the USA the practice-based PhD is rarely available, although one notable exception is at Washington University, where the Center for Digital Arts and Experimental Media offers a structured PhD programme that includes a significant practice-based component that follows the UK tradition (DXARTS 2009).

It is interesting to consider the actual situation in terms of the shape and nature of submitted and awarded arts practice-based PhDs. Clements and Scrivener conducted a revealing survey in which it appeared that a majority of UK arts practice-based PhDs did not conform to the requirements of research prescribed by the UK's Arts and Humanities Research Council (Clements and Scrivener 2008). Notwithstanding the fact that rules and recommendations are not always followed to the full, the organizational context defines the landscape within which research processes are developed and implemented.

Concluding remarks

Research in the arts is frequently about the nature of artefacts or the processes used in their generation. Designing, making or employing artefacts form natural parts of the research process and sharing the results of the research may be impossible to do without reference to the relevant artefacts. We have seen that some universities and research funding bodies have facilitated this kind of research that includes the artefact in explicit ways. Nevertheless, in large swathes of university regulations, there is no accommodation of the place of the artefact and where it is explicitly ruled out as part of a PhD submission, this can have a significant effect on the way the research is conducted. There is, however, a need for more finessed rules as to what practice-based research is, rather than definitions that are 'isolationist' and hence do not bear comparison with other forms of research.

When considering the artefact within the practice of arts based research programmes, we see the need to consider frameworks that identify the flow of actions and ideas between different aspects of the research process. Different projects will traverse different trajectories and the researcher needs to be clear about their particular path. For this and other reasons discussed above, the outcomes from a practice-based arts research programme are most likely, if not certain, to include both artefact and text that illuminates the context and trajectory of the research, and can, hence, frame our perceptions of the artefact.

The practitioner frameworks that have been described here represent different outcomes from PhD research by creative practitioners. The associated trajectories represent different kinds of relationships between theory, practice and evaluation as exemplified in the four cases. Whilst it is helpful to distil the main elements of the practice-based research process in this way in order to compare and contrast them, it should nevertheless, be pointed out that there are considerable variations in the way the frameworks were developed and applied. In each case, the interplay between practice, theory and evaluation involved many iterations and interaction between the elements as the creative process drove a continuous process of change. The fact that such variation can occur within a highly structured approach to practice-based research that the particular PhD environment demands, is indicative of the way individuality, so important to creative people, can nevertheless be accommodated in appropriately structured formal research. Each practitioner developed a unique appreciative system that was used to guide both research and practice. Because each system arises directly from the process of creating, evaluating and reflecting upon artefacts already inherent in the practitioners' normal practice, there is a strong propensity for carrying it forward into ongoing creative work. Most practitioners expected this to be a long-term outcome of engaging in practice-based research: in this sense, it can be expected to have benefit to practice that extends well beyond formal research.

Notes

1 Originally set up by the Wellcome Trust in 1996, the SciArt programme was run by a consortium of funders between 1999 and 2002 involving: the Arts Council; the British Council; the Calouste-Gulbenkian Foundation; the National Endowment for Science, Technology and the Arts (NESTA); and the Wellcome Trust. From 2002, the programme was run independently by the Wellcome Trust, at which point it broadened its remit to all art forms (Wellcome 2009).
2 The Australia Council for the Arts' Synapse initiative provides opportunities for artists and scientists to work together, and seeks to promote the benefits of such collaborations to the wider

community. By developing awareness and understanding of arts/science practice, Synapse aims to advance the role the arts plays in Australia's innovation system (Synapse 2009).

3 http://www.creativityandcognition.com (accessed on 6 September 2009).

4 http://www.creativityandcognition.com/betaspace/ (accessed on 18 March 2009).

5 Action research is essentially a theory-based approach grounded in real life that, in simplified form, consists of a cyclical process of conducting an investigation, taking action based on the results of that enquiry, followed by evaluation of the improvements in the situation under consideration. Action research requires intervention in order to study impact of change on a given situation and thereby understand the situation under consideration (Hughes 2009).

6 Experimental research is a collection of research designs which use manipulation and controlled testing to understand causal processes. Generally one or more variables are manipulated to determine their effect on a dependent variable. The experimental method is a systematic and scientific approach to research in which the researcher manipulates one or more variables, and controls and measures any change in other variables.

7 The term 'material culture' is often used by archaeologists as a non-specific way to refer to the artefacts or other concrete things left by past cultures. The study of material culture is concerned with the relationship between persons and things in the past and in the present. It can be contrasted with other cultural forms such as ideas, images, practices, beliefs and language that can be treated as independent from any specific material substance.

Part II

VOICES

As we observed in the Preface, considering the problem of research in the arts from a foundational point of view is only one possible approach. Examining foundations from a historical or intellectual point of view brings other issues to the fore whilst making some fade into the background or disappear completely. This has something to do with the relationship of the researcher to what is being researched. In adopting a certain historical or intellectual position in relation to a subject, one is also forced to adopt a conceptual vocabulary resulting in the use of a particular voice. We have a number of things in mind when we use the term 'voice'.

At its simplest level, there is a grammatical issue. It is noticeable that scientific writing tends to be undertaken in the third person. This is expressed as 'he' or 'she' did or thought such and such (which has the tendency to dissociate the author from any responsibility for what is being reported) or it is expressed in the passive voice: 'it was done' (tending to suggest that no one has responsibility for the interpretation). This is not an accidental feature of scientific reporting. The scientific method tends to emphasize impersonal properties that can be replicated, and hence it diminishes the voice of the researcher themselves in favour of more generalized outcomes. The use of the third person emphasizes their ideal 'disinterestedness' of the relationship between the researcher and the researched.

The ideal relationship in the arts is quite different. One is usually well aware of the author of an artistic production. Composers, performers, artists are known by name and part of the value that is attributed to their outcomes is that they were personally responsible for them and they actively mediate the audience's relationship with the topic in question. For example, it devalued the Tate Britain collection of sketches by John Constable when it was discovered that some of these sketches were actually by his son Lionel. The images themselves were unchanged but the value of the authorship had changed. The example shows that the audience was more interested in it being 'a John Constable' than in it being 'a representation of such and such'. Indeed one often refers to an artwork as being 'a Constable', 'a Rembrandt', etc. emphasizing the principle interest in the artist as the mediator of what is represented. As a consequence, one might expect that the grammar of arts research is different from the grammar of research in other subjects.

Voice also connotes the vocabulary being employed and, by implication, the critical location of the researcher. Thus a Feminist voice or a Marxist voice will deploy certain terms and will not deploy others. One of the cues to a critical position is the vocabulary being deployed to describe it. Of course the voice of arts research speaks through artefacts and not only through verbal language or written texts and it is common to hear the expression 'the language of art'. It may be that the content that art expresses through the language of art is different from the content of thought (as addressed in the philosophy of language) and instead expresses, for example, what can be experienced.

It is perhaps no accident that the outcomes of artistic research are not in verbal or written language. Researchers in other subjects have developed quite specialized forms of linguistic expression in order to be as clear and unambiguous as possible regarding the outcomes of their research. This belongs to the idealized aim of traditional research to discover or contribute something quite specific to the current body of knowledge in order to increase it in an identifiable way. But the generally constructivist tendency of arts research has an entirely different idealized aim. Owing to the interest of, and value placed in, the individual's interpretation of experience and the world, arts research engages with pluralistic interpretation. In our view, the multiplicity of interpretations arising from activities in the arts is an asset and not a drawback. This is because both arts and humanities subjects are able to sustain numerous diverse interpretations simultaneously, without feeling the need to prioritize one over another. Accordingly, non-linguistic outputs – that facilitate an even greater plurality of interpretation of their meaning and significance than textual ones – are appropriate in such a context. However, there is perhaps a need to clarify the relationship of the infinite pluralism within the arts to the seemingly singular determinism of scientific and academic research.

In Part II of this book we hear both the discussion of which voice to use, as well as the expression of issues using particular voices. Nevertheless, Part II as a whole shows an interest in the potential available to artistic researchers through their choice of artistic, instead of linguistic, media. The prospect that artistic research may address content that is inexpressible through other media is a radical one. There are, however, a number of indicators that this might indeed be the case. For example, art historical or art critical accounts of what the arts are doing often reveal great insight on the part of the artist, but only fractionally account for the impact of an artwork. Knowing what an artwork means, namely its meaning for a particular, usually specialist audience, is only part of the account. Artworks normally have aesthetic merit as well as meaning; they have social and economic functions, etc. What these partial accounts may be showing is that single-focus accounts fail to capture the pluralism of artistic outcomes, and that pluralism has something to say about the artistic concept of the world. As we have seen, the arts encourage pluralism but academic research traditionally does not. This may indicate something about the weakness of non-pluralistic conceptual frameworks rather than a weakness of artistic research, resulting in a role for artistic research to contribute to a revision of the academic concept of knowledge.

8

EMBODIED KNOWING
THROUGH ART

Mark Johnson

The problem with the notion of 'arts research'

Before the last American presidential election, my wife, who is a fibre artist, and I were listening to a candidate praising all the dedicated hardworking men and women who have contributed so much to our society, but who are now suffering the ill effects of our current economic crisis. Among those hardworking contributors to our communal well-being, the candidate included occupations such as plumbers, construction workers, doctors, teachers, military personnel, parents, janitors, and cab drivers. My wife turned to me and quipped, 'He forgot to mention artists!'

The general public almost never thinks about artists, and when it does, it almost never thinks of them as great contributors to the growth of human understanding and knowledge. I suppose that nearly everybody has heard of Picasso, and a lot of people even like his work, but ask them what contribution Picasso has made to knowledge and they are likely to be left speechless. Even worse, ask them what Picasso's art research consisted in, and they probably won't have a clue what you are talking about. Evidence of this relegation of art to an inferior cognitive status can be found in the now worn-out fact that the arts are always the first thing to be cut when schools face financial hardship. I'll wager that you've never encountered anyone exiting an exhibit of the work of artists like Pablo Picasso, Elizabeth Murray, Magdalena Abakanowicz, Mark Rothko, or Henri Matisse and heard them exclaim, 'Wow, I learned so much from that.' For the most part, we do not think of the arts as vehicles of important knowledge. Some people might say of some artist that she is insightful, but that remark does not translate into a belief that the artist's works give us profound knowledge. If you asked someone what profound truth they gleaned from Picasso's *Guernica*, I suppose they might say something on the order of 'war is absolute hell,' or 'what happened at Guernica was abominable', but that would be the lamest possible summary of the transformative power of Picasso's great work.

What I'm suggesting is that, because most people don't think of the arts as giving rise to knowledge, they find the idea of 'art research' confusing, at best, and meaningless, at worst. The reasons for this are simple: first, most people never think about the nature of knowledge, but when they do, they tend to associate it with the progressive accumulation of scientific knowledge – the building up of true descriptions and rational explanations, mostly in propositional form, for how things work in our physical, social, and cultural worlds. Second, by contrast, people typically think of art in terms of imaginative works that express and communicate emotions. Consequently, the public is not inclined to regard art as a source of knowledge. Third, the term 'research' calls to mind methods of theoretical inquiry, forms of experimentation, empirical testing, and confirmation or disconfirmation of hypotheses in pursuit of progressively increasing bodies of objective knowledge. Fourth, but the arts –especially the visual arts – don't seem to be in the proposition-stating business. People don't recognize any counterpart in the arts to research methods in scientific inquiry. Therefore, the whole idea of *arts research* may seem oddly misconceived.

Scholars in the humanities often experience a similar dismissal of their work as not rising to the level of serious research. After all, in what sense is it 'research' to read what others have written on a subject? Humanists often feel this same sense of oddness when they are asked on grant application forms to describe their *methods of inquiry* and *types of evidence* for their project. They hardly know what to say about their 'method', unless it is some dismissive humorous quip like 'I think really hard about the nature of Being, and then I wait for insight to come to me in a flash.' Just as with the arts, the whole question of method can seem a little bit out of place, and without methods of inquiry, what sense can you make of *knowledge* and *research*? I suspect that some philosophers often manage to get away with claiming to do research and to produce knowledge mostly because they boldly claim to be addressing certain perennial human problems that have no easy answers, and they then call their research 'abstract', 'philosophical', and 'deep' – not easily clarified and summarized.

Humanities scholars have at least one slight advantage over artists because it is part of their job description to write long complicated articles and books that appear to consist of propositional knowledge, even if most of it can seem incomprehensible to ordinary folks. Artists have no such crutch of quasi-propositional truth-claims, and so they feel stumped about how to measure up to alleged rigorous standards of inquiry and research.

I want to suggest that, in spite of these obstacles to the acknowledgment of a significant role for art in the evocation of deep understanding, there are, nevertheless, perfectly good notions of arts research and quite reasonable notions of inquiry in art. However, to articulate these notions, we have to overcome a very deeply rooted traditional conception of knowledge as a body of true propositions that capture the nature of some particular aspect of our world. The key is to stop thinking of knowledge as an abstract quasi-entity or a fixed body of propositional claims. Instead, knowledge should be a term of praise for success in a process for intelligently transforming experience, just as the American philosopher John Dewey argued some eighty years ago.

The prejudice against the visual arts as modes of research

So far I've been claiming that the chief reason the arts are not seen as research is that they are not granted the status of knowledge producers, especially when knowledge is defined very narrowly as consisting of propositional truths about the world. As is well known, the denial to art of the status of knowledge is deeply rooted in western philosophical treatments of art, and it has carried down to the present day as a cultural commonplace. In dialogues such as *Republic, Symposium, Phaedrus,* and especially *Ion,* Plato notoriously argued for a suspicion of the arts as pretenders to knowledge, on two grounds: first, the arts are not direct presentations of the real, but only distant copies (based on images) that offer no knowledge, but only imitations of imitations of what is real. Second, art 'feeds and waters the passions', thereby undermining the proper functioning of our rational faculties of knowledge.

Aristotle recognized a more positive role for artistic imitations, claiming that poetry can 'present the kind of thing that might be', thereby suggesting that the arts can reveal the possibilities of experience. However, Aristotle thought that the arts show what is possible via *mimesis* of human actions, whereas the sciences give causal accounts of how things come to be as they are and why they behave as they do.

Our contemporary tendency to deny to art the status of knowledge can be traced back at least as far as Immanuel Kant's taxonomy of types of judgment – theoretical, technical, moral, aesthetic, and so on. Kant inherited an Enlightenment faculty psychology that posited separate and distinct powers of mind, such as perception, imagination, understanding, reason, feeling, and will. The central idea was to explain the different types of judgments as the result of different relations of these faculties. Since Kant perpetuated the dominant Enlightenment conception of aesthetics as the science of feelings, he denied any cognitive content (hence, any knowledge potential) to aesthetic judgments concerning beauty in nature and art.

It would be difficult to overestimate Kant's profound influence on subsequent thinking about the relation of art and aesthetic experience to knowledge. Indeed, the very notion of an 'aesthetic experience' is an artefact of seventeenth- and eighteenth-century theories of mind and knowledge. In what is known as his 'Critical Philosophy', Kant asked how several types of mental judgment, each with its own distinctive character, were possible. His answer was that each distinct type involves a unique blend of operations of one or more mental faculties. Thus, for example, in his *Critique of Pure Reason* (1781) he asks how certain theoretical scientific judgments of nature are possible, judgments that articulate universal causal laws and produce objective knowledge of our physical world. In the *Critique of Practical Reason* (1787) he asks how moral judgments involving universally binding ethical imperatives can issue from pure practical reason, without any reliance on emotion. And finally, he concludes what he called his Critical Philosophy with the *Critique of Judgment* (1790), which tries to explain judgments of beauty in nature and art, as well as teleological judgments of purposiveness in nature, as resting on distinct operations of various mental faculties.

In Kant's classic formulation, knowledge is a *product of conceptual synthesis* that takes the form of *propositional judgments* descriptive of the world. Consequently, aesthetic experience, which he regarded as subjective and based on feelings, lies wholly outside the realm of knowledge. Simply put, aesthetic judgments of beauty in nature and art are not cognitive (and hence not conceptual), and so they issue in *no* knowledge whatsoever. Kant saw the value of aesthetic judgments as lying in the 'free play of imagination and understanding' evoked by artworks and beautiful natural objects, which is felt (*not known*) as a sense of harmony and right order. Kant's legacy was to set much subsequent aesthetic theory on a path where art was valued for the feelings it evokes and the ways it stirs our imaginative musings, but most definitely *not* for any theoretical knowledge of man or nature. Neither the beautiful nor the sublime could rise to the status of modes of knowledge.

Kant's view is not just an abstruse theory intended only for philosophers and art theorists. At its heart, it represents the common view of art as not primarily a vehicle for human knowledge. If, as the commonsense view goes, knowledge is about acquiring certain true beliefs (expressible as propositions) that correspond to certain states of affairs in the world, then the arts don't seem to have this as their central function. Knowledge, on this view, is an accumulation of true propositions or statements about how things are and how they work, which can be verified by past, present or future experience. Within this framework, research can ultimately be evaluated by how much knowledge its methods generate.

The problem, of course, is that the arts always seem to come up short when it comes to providing knowledge, as defined by this traditional set of criteria. Therefore, in order to articulate a realistic notion of art research, it is necessary to rethink our received conception of knowledge and research.

What can arts research consist in?

Stephen Scrivener (2009b) has offered three reasonable conceptions of art research, based on his fairly traditional definition of *research* as '1) a systematic investigation, 2) conducted intentionally, 3) to acquire new knowledge, understanding, insights, etc. that is 4) justified and 5) communicated 6) about a subject'. Scrivener recognizes three principal relations between art and the conditions of research: .

> The first, *research into*, identifies art as the *subject* of inquiry treating it as an object in the world to be examined, understood and explained. *Research through* art treats art as a *method* for understanding the world, which might be art itself. *Research for art*, ... like research into art, treats art as the *subject* of inquiry, but with the *goal* of producing art that transforms art.
>
> (Scrivener 2009b)

I assume, with Scrivener, that one important sense of arts research is the idea that good artists are engaged in an ongoing inquiry into the nature of their medium, into how to produce certain effects through it, and into how to expand the capacities of that medium. There can be no doubt, for anyone who has ever tried it, that this is an intensely rigorous mode of artistic inquiry into how to do certain things through art. It requires an arduous ongoing dialogue with your medium (or media), extending over the lifetime of an artist who remains open to discovering new things about the possibilities of her art.

Scrivener appears to recognize two forms of this art-centred research. The first, more mundane, process is what I have just called an investigation into how to make art and into the potentialities of your medium. The second process is what he calls 'research for' (and perhaps also, one type of 'research through art'), where the goal is to reconfigure arts practice itself: 'transformational practice produces new art by virtue of new understanding of the limits and potentialities of art'. Research *for* art 'claims material interventions that transform what is apprehended as art, together with a claim to knowledge of the manner in which art has thereby been transformed' (Scrivener 2009b). By these criteria, a painting that gives us new knowledge of some aspect of our world might *also* be innovative enough to shape our very understanding of art and open up novel possibilities for future art.

Although I appreciate the importance of this art-centred conception of research, I want, instead, to explore more deeply Scrivener's less well-developed idea of *research through art and design*, that is, of the enhancement of knowing through art. In the present book, Scrivener (Chapter 15) introduces this idea by noting how certain memorable paintings can actually give us some knowledge of their subject. He cites as an example Stubbs's paintings of horses giving us knowledge of equine anatomy and Constable's landscapes exploring various meteorological phenomena. Knowledge of this sort is clearly something we sometimes get from a painting, although I doubt that we care about painting mostly for this reason. I shall have a bit more to say about this later, in the context of Dewey's account of the working of art, but I am more interested in the idea that art might give us an understanding of our world that goes beyond particular subject matters like horses and clouds.

So, I want to explore an additional sense of 'research through art,' the articulation of which requires us to rethink our received understanding of knowledge. The basic idea is that we must emphasize the *process* of *knowing*, as contrasted with *knowledge* as a body of true statements. It is this process-oriented conception that I want to explore and defend.

Embodied knowing

As I see it, the best way to make sense of any notion of 'arts research' that is not limited only to explorations of the nature of artistic processes is to call into question our received views of knowledge as propositional. Fortunately, this turns out to be an important part of recent cognitive science, particularly in those approaches that study the bodily basis of meaning, conceptualization, and reasoning. There are two key aspects of this new 'embodied cognition' view of knowledge: First, we must release the stranglehold exerted by views of knowledge as a fixed and eternal state or mental relation, in order to focus, instead, on knowing as a process of inquiry rather than a final product. Second, we must recognize the role of the body, especially our sensory-motor processes and our emotions and feelings, in our capacity for understanding and knowing.

John Dewey (1984 [1929]) long ago observed the pan-human tendency to flee uncertainty in search of something allegedly fixed and eternal that never changes and that stands over against or behind the ongoing flow of our daily experience. This perennial 'quest for certainty', Dewey argued, has been the source of great mischief, not just in philosophy and theology, but also in the beliefs and actions of ordinary people. Such an ideal of absolute knowledge is predicated, in turn, on the existence of eternal essences and a metaphysical view of reality as ultimately changeless.

Dewey observed, to the contrary, that life is about change and growth. Clinging to imagined absolutes is one way people try to deny change, impermanence, and transformation. As we observed earlier, the propositional view of knowledge fits nicely with absolutist thinking, giving rise to the ideal of universal truths as eternal quasi-objects (propositions) standing in determinate relations with other quasi-objects (states of affairs in the world). Dewey famously showed how our fear of change, and our correlative anxious grasping for absolute knowledge, is based on a dramatically mistaken view of human mind and experience and is also ultimately counterproductive in our ongoing quest to deal with the real problems humans encounter in their lives.

The crux of Dewey's view is that the locus of human being is a series of continually developing organism-environment transactions which, although always changing, nevertheless manifest certain stable patterns that we can become aware of and guide our actions by (Dewey 1981 [1925]). According to this view, knowing is a process of intelligent inquiry into and transformation of experience, in light of our values and purposes. Our values are not absolute givens; rather, circumstances may arise that call us to subject our values to scrutiny and possible re-evaluation. Therefore, intelligent inquiry can be both about means *and* ends. Thus Dewey proposes knowing as an activity of thought in the service of constructive change in the quality and character of our experience:

> If things undergo change without thereby ceasing to be real, there can be no *formal* bar to knowing being one specific kind of change in things, nor to its test being found in the successful carrying into effect of the kind of change intended.
>
> (Dewey 1973 [1931]: 211)

The locus of knowledge, according to Dewey, is experience, interpreted in the broadest sense to include both physical objects and states of affairs, but also everything that is thought, felt, hoped for, willed, desired, encountered, and done. The basis for Dewey's idea of experience is an account of an organism continually interacting with its surroundings. In the context of trying to preserve itself and to flourish, each advanced organism engages in recurring structured interactions (or transactions) with aspects of its environment. In the case of higher animals and humans, those recurring interactional patterns can be thought of as habits of experiencing, thinking, feeling, and doing. Much of the time we drift along through life in routine channels of thought and action that result from a combination of both our past experience and our culturally inherited habitual modes of engagement with our world.

However, since experience is not static, there are frequent occasions where our sedimented habits cease to be adequate for the structuring of our experience and the pursuit of our goals. Sometimes our habits are not adequate for realizing a desirable state of affairs. Sometimes we have incompatible goals or conflicting values that cannot all be realized at the same time. In either case, we fall out of harmony with our surroundings, and we feel this falling out as frustration, blockage, indeterminacy, and inability to move forward fluidly. The problematic situation we find ourselves in can then be an occasion for inquiry, in which we must reconfigure our habitual patterns of behaviour, in search of more constructive, expansive, and harmonious modes of action. In other words, we need to engage in forms of inquiry geared to the reduction of indeterminacy in our situation and geared to the achievement of a more constructive relation to our physical, social, and cultural surroundings (Dewey 1991 [1938]).

To put it briefly, for Dewey *knowing* is a matter of cultivating appropriate habits of intelligent inquiry that allow us to more or less satisfactorily reconfigure our experience in the face of problematic situations. The goal is not some illusory fixed and eternal *knowledge*. Instead, to call something 'knowledge' is simply a way to valorize certain *ways of knowing – ways of transforming experience –* that tend to actually enrich our sense of the possibilities for action, that deepen and broaden our grasp of the meaning of a situation, and that help us lead more humane, constructive, and creative lives. So Dewey urges us to turn our focus away from the substantive term *knowledge* (as a noun) and to focus, instead, on *knowing* (as a verb). In this way we emphasize the character of the *process* of inquiry instead of some final *product* construed as a body of knowledge.

Dewey recognized different forms of inquiry as basic to human living. *Scientific inquiry* operates principally through selective abstractions, in search of generalizations over a circumscribed set of phenomena. Typically, those generalizations are thought to take the form of causal laws of nature, which serve the values of prediction and control of experience. *Artistic inquiry* is less abstractive and generalizing than science, focusing more on grasping the qualitative unity of a situation. Art, in Dewey's view, does not so much *describe* or *explain*; rather, it *presents* or *enacts* the qualities, meanings, and values of a situation.

Dewey saw that his account of inquiry and knowing reveals a deep parallel between acts of knowing and the processes of experiencing, making, and judging art. The parallel rests on Dewey's idea that the starting point of any experience is the sense of a unifying quality that pervades the entire situation and gives it its distinctive character and direction.

> By the term situation in this connection is signified the fact that the subject-matter ultimately referred to in existential propositions is a complex existence that is held together in spite of its internal complexity by the fact that it is dominated and characterized throughout by a single quality.
>
> (Dewey 1988 [1930]: 246)

This pervasive unifying quality is what binds the various components of any given situation together into a unified complex whole that has meaning for us. Not surprisingly, Dewey often used artworks to illustrate his claims about the role of pervasive unifying qualities. Say, for example, that you enter a gallery of a museum and behold a Vermeer on the far wall. You know it is a Vermeer, even before you can confirm the artist by the label next to the painting, and you can see that it is a Vermeer through a certain quality of the whole work. There is no unique set of properties that makes some painting a Vermeer, but rather 'the quality of the whole [that] permeates, affects, and controls every detail' (Dewey 1988 [1930]: 247). Moreover, the pervasive quality is not just its Vermeer-ness; rather, it is the unique particular unifying quality of *this* particular Vermeer that draws you in.

Dewey regarded art as the skilful enactment of the qualitative dimensions of some actual or possible situation. Art presents (enacts) the meaning of a situation, rather than abstractly conceptualizing it. So, to return to Scrivener's example, one might say that one of Stubbs's paintings of a horse might realize, through felt qualities, something about our experience of horses that is missed by the more abstractive and selective scientific accounts of horses set forth in a treatise on equine anatomy, health, and behaviour. There is something you come to understand through the painting that you could not fully grasp through the conceptual account of the scientific treatise.

The key point here is that only within this background qualitative unity are we able to select out the specific objects and structures that shape our experience, understanding, and response to the situation. In other words, it is the pervasive quality of any given situation that determines the meaning it offers us and the possible courses of action it elicits. This applies not just to artworks, but also to any meaningful experience. For example, I might be sitting across a table from you, vigorously arguing some philosophical point, when I become increasingly aware of a certain pervasive tension and disease characterizing our shared situation. Something isn't quite right, even though I cannot at this moment put my finger on what it is. Yet that felt sense of the situation can be the spur to further inquiry – that is, to my trying to figure out what seems to be wrong, and how I might possibly resolve some of the tension that pervades our situation. Perhaps you find the view I'm articulating offensive, or maybe my way of presenting it or holding myself puts you off. It is the quality of our shared situation, and not just my subjective response, that stimulates my wonder about what is amiss here.

Embodied meaning

Dewey's view of knowing requires us to give up any rigid dichotomy between what has traditionally been thought of as modes of conceiving and knowing versus modes of perceiving and doing. The rejection of this form of dualism has recently been supported by research in the cognitive sciences that challenges any such rigid distinction between the conceptual and the perceptual, and even between the perceptual and the motor dimensions of cognition. Cognitive neuroscientist Don Tucker summarizes the current view that our so-called acts of 'higher' cognition (such as conceptualization and reasoning) are based on structures of our sensory-motor processing:

> Complex psychological functions must be understood to arise from bodily control networks. There is no other source for them. This is an exquisite parsimony of facts.
>
> There are no brain parts for abstract faculties of the mind – faculties like volition or insight or even conceptualization – that are separate from the brain parts that evolved to mediate between visceral and somatic processes …
>
> If we assume that there is a nested structure of concepts that must take form across the – exactly isomorphic – nested structure of the neural networks of the corticolimbic hierarchy, we can then specify the structure of abstract conceptualization. This is a structure of mind based on bodily forms.
>
> (Tucker 2007: 202–3)

In short, there is no special set of faculties for 'knowing' that are entirely separate and independent from faculties for sensory (perceptual) and motor processing. Even before the advent of cognitive neuroscience, the renowned psychologist of art, Rudolf Arnheim, wrote extensively and brilliantly on the intimate connection between perception and conception:

The cognitive operations called thinking are not the privilege of mental processes above and beyond perception but the essential ingredients of perception itself. I am referring to such operations as active exploration, selection, grasping of essentials, simplification, abstraction, analysis and synthesis, completion, correction, comparison, problem solving, as well as combining, separating, putting in context. These operations are not the prerogative of any one mental function; they are the manner in which the minds of both man and animal treat cognitive material at any level. There is no basic difference in this respect between what happens when a person looks at the world directly and when he sits with his eyes closed and 'thinks'.

(Arnheim 1969: 13)

The relevant point here for thinking in art is that the visual arts operate according to principles and structures of cognitive processing that hold at all levels from the most concrete images and visual experiences all the way up to abstract thought using symbols, such as words. Though this is not my central focus, and I cannot argue this here, there is a great deal of evidence from the cognitive sciences that structures of meaning-making and understanding in art are the same ones that underlie our use and understanding of language and other forms of symbolic interaction. Our thinking is visceral and incarnate, whether that thinking is primarily artistic or primarily linguistic.

Art and the transformation of experience

One of Dewey's greatest insights was that art involves an imaginative, expressive transformation of the materials of existence in ways that enhance and deepen the meaning of our experience.

In short, art, in its form, unites the very same relation of doing and undergoing, outgoing and incoming energy, that makes an experience to be an experience. Because of elimination of all that does not contribute to mutual organization of the factors of both action and reception into one another, and because of selection of just the aspects and traits that contribute to their interpenetration of each other, the product is a work of esthetic art ... The doing or making is artistic when the perceived result is of such a nature that *its* qualities *as perceived* have controlled the question of production.

(Dewey 1987 [1934]: 48)

In other words, the value of a work of art is not objective facts it might reveal, not merely its expression of an artist's emotional state, and not that it captures some ideal, eternal formal rightness. Rather, the value of an artwork lies in the ways it shows the meaning of experience and imaginatively explores how the world is and might be – primarily in a qualitative fashion. Therefore, art can be just as much a form of inquiry as is mathematics or the empirical sciences. The principal difference is that art focuses more intently on the qualitative dimensions of experience that we tend to overlook in our other intellectual activities, which, by the way, are characterized as the activities they are by their distinctive pervasive unifying qualities. The sciences seek to formulate generalizations over groups of phenomena and often need to abstract somewhat from the particular unifying quality of a situation, in order to focus on selected characteristics of a situation that seem salient and explanatorily robust. What distinguishes art proper, on Dewey's view, is the way it presents the qualitative dimensions of an experience, instead of only abstract features, such as causal relations.

The making of artworks is thus an ongoing exercise – an apprenticeship – in how to remake experience to enhance meaning. It shows us how things might be developed in the service of consummatory experience, more than it gives us a particular body of knowledge. It is not just enough to say that artistic making is more a *knowing how* than it is a *knowing that*. The reason this is not enough is that, as Dewey argued, *all* knowing is a form of *knowing how*, insofar as it is a matter of reconfiguring experience for the deepening of meaning. So, the key point here is not that art is a form of *knowing how*, which is to be distinguished from science's acts of *knowing that*. Both art and science are about the transformation of experience to enrich meaning, open up new connections, and help us harmonize our experiences. Art may focus more intently on the qualitative unity of the experience (the work), while science focuses more on causal relations and connections, but both of them are transformative modes of inquiry. They both give us important ways to go on, to go forward, in life.

As an example, consider van Gogh's famous *Starry Night*. If we were to follow Scrivener's tripartite classification of types of arts research, we might suggest that van Gogh's painting could be a form of *research through art*, because it presents a certain vision of astronomical phenomena. But, although perhaps true, this cannot be a very enlightening thing to say about *Starry Night!* What seems more significant is the way the painting powerfully enacts van Gogh's organic vision of the universe as a whole. *Starry Night* presents us with a living, pulsing, growing world. It invites us to *feel, qualitatively,* this vitality of the cosmos. It *represents* a village under a starry sky, but it *presents* a way of being in and inhabiting a world. And that way of inhabiting a world is a legitimate form of knowing how to get on in the world. It gives us a vision – an understanding – of the nature of our cosmos, our world, our situation.

Should we balk at calling this an experience of transformative insight and understanding? I don't think so. And should we balk at seeing van Gogh's explorations in painting as 'research'? I don't think so, even though van Gogh himself might never have described his paintings in that way. The artworks exist as enacted in and through us. That enactment is a way of organizing experience. That particular way of engaging a world can be a form of knowing, and it can be more or less successful in helping us carry forward our experience.

Arts research

It is only within such a framework that I can make good sense of the phrase 'arts research,' in a way that does not subordinate art to other activities of thought taken to be superior modes of knowing. The *research* here would not be geared toward the accumulation of empirical facts or propositional knowledge, although that might be part of the story. Instead, *arts research* would be inquiry into how to experience and transform the unifying quality of a given experience in search of deepened meaning, enhanced freedom, and increase of connections and relations. Students of art are learning how things are and how they can be reconfigured to change the underlying quality of a certain experience. It is not too grandiose to say that, in their more successful moments, artists help us explore the possibilities of our world, our human relations, and our values and goals. And they do this, for the most part, through their grasp of emerging pervasive unifying qualities.

If, in our assessment of artistic activity, we would stop using models of knowledge and research traditionally applied to the sciences, we would be better off. The reasons we would be better off are, first, that what most people believe about the accumulation of scientific knowledge, about scientific method(s), and about how research actually works in the sciences is mostly inaccurate, if not downright false. Second, making strong contrasts between scientific methods and arts practices ignores the central role of the qualitative aspects of any inquiry, whether in the arts or sciences. Third, both the sciences and the arts are about modes of knowing, as opposed to bodies of facts and knowledge.

The idea of research as the progressive accumulation of objective knowledge is too impoverished a model to account for the full range of modes of human inquiry. It is overly narrow because it ignores the nature and varieties of human exploration and transformation of experience. It is a bad model because it ignores the reality of change in our lives and seeks fixity and eternal truth.

A more adequate conception of research would define it as ongoing inquiry aiming at the transformation of a problematic situation into one that is more harmonious, fluid, expansive, and rich in meaning. This view of research applies equally to science, mathematics, logic, and the arts. No matter what discipline we are in, we have to learn to rely on the cultivated judgment of accomplished practitioners in determining what counts as good work. If we were more honest and self-critical, we might acknowledge that, in fact, this holds true nearly as much for mathematics and the sciences as it does for the arts. True, there is no precise counterpart in art to what is called 'empirical testing' in the sciences, but sophisticated, experienced practitioners can very well distinguish between failed and successful artistic experiments.

Whenever I have served on MFA committees in Art or Landscape Architecture, I have always felt somewhat unprepared for the task. This is because I haven't developed the perceptual sensitivity, the sense of historical traditions, the 'language' of the arts, and sophisticated critical judgment appropriate to the art practices within a certain field. But the same could be said of any artist invited to sit on a PhD committee in Physics or Mathematics or Philosophy. In either case, one simply has to learn, through doing, the bodily and intellectual skills, forms of judgment, keenness of discrimination, and so forth that are at play in those disciplines.

Artists do 'research' via their continuing, laboured, persistent attempts to resolve problematic situations through the transformation of the materials of experience as a way of trying to realize certain satisfying pervasive unifying qualities of experience. Sometimes, indeed most of the time, their advances are very modest, consisting of subtle minor re-workings of a process. But occasionally something truly imaginative and transformative happens, and then we can experience new dimensions – new depths – of meaning, new possibilities for significant engagement with our world. It is consummations of this sort at which art research most spectacularly aims.

9

RHETORIC: WRITING, READING AND PRODUCING THE VISUAL

Joan Mullin

Rhetoric, lodged in the ancient art of oral presentation, is commonly described as the study or implementation of a process of invention, arrangement, and production of words to create a planned effect on a particular audience. For art practitioners, rhetoric's study of human discourse with this presumed focus on words might most closely align it with research in art history. However, studying art historically is not the only use of rhetoric; in its study of how communication takes place and is received, rhetoric is relevant as a useful tool for research in all arts practices since, in addition to the medium of language, the original components of ancient rhetorical practice included the purposeful use of voice, tone, performance and visual effect. Therefore, rhetoric already has for art practitioners a vocabulary for examining and naming their multimodal or single medium processes as well as a set of strategies that can be employed to create effective 'communication.' Together these provide two supports for defining and engaging in the production of art scholarship that would measure up to academic standards for postdoctoral production. Scholarship in art practice can include studies and examples of 'invention'; it may examine but also articulate creative ideas as rhetorical, that is, as communicative practices. However, the use of such rhetorical approaches in artists' scholarly activity can also help make a case that postdoctoral research can be just as rigorous when the 'texts' are multimodal or largely non-alphabetical.[1]

When art practitioners engage in research in their respective areas, they can use rhetorical analysis as a bridge between the academic expectation that defines 'scholarship' in terms of word-based documents and the visual, aural and kinaesthetic reality of art practitioners' knowledge production that occurs in forms other than alphabetic language. By drawing on the word-based 'canons of rhetoric' (e.g. invention and arrangement) for their own creative (knowledge) production, arts practitioners can employ language devices to argue for the efficacy of knowledge that is not alphabetical, but still communicative. Already some rhetoricians have challenged the very idea that rhetoric need be word-based and they use its methodology to examine any 'languages' whether physical (dance), auditory (music) and/or visual (e.g. sculpture, painting, landscape) or multimodal. By applying rhetorical analysis to movement, visual and aural productions, the arts practitioner can underscore that their scholarship involves studying and publishing in the language specific to their field; one with a grammar that is equivalent to print-only research.

Perhaps the corollary can be more easily seen by considering mathematical or computer science research. While words in these areas are interlaced with equations, codes and formulae, it is these, not the alphabetic communication that predominates and stands as knowledge. I am drawing here a parallel: that movement, sound, visual and spatial manipulation and production stand as knowledge in their respective fields, and that the use of rhetoric, because it is always about expression and effect, can play a crucial role in establishing what stands for research in the creative arts. Thus rhetoric becomes a useful research tool for artists who seek to produce and 'publish' – write, perform, exhibit and record – new knowledge that results from investigating and furthering their own and others' artistic performances and productions. The practice of doing so is as old as the very performative, public and evaluative space of the Greek forum.

Within the field of writing studies, informed by rhetoric, research about communication comprises theory and praxis: one theorizes practices which in turn challenge theories as conditions or subjects change. For writing as well as arts practice, this means developing and questioning theories about how someone writes (or dances), about what is or how an effective piece of writing (music) is composed, about giving language to what is observed (in design) and sensed (in landscape architecture). New theories produce new practices and new observations about communities, discourses and practices produce new theories about communication whether that is in writing or through media specific to the arts. Parallels between this circular process of knowledge-making in writing studies and the practices that result from art researchers/performers/creators drive this chapter and thus form the basis for arguing for rhetoric's usefulness as a tool to produce scholarship in the arts, and for considering it as a means of reflecting on and evaluating that scholarship. The same questions that have guided rhetorical research can be used as a starting point for scholarship in the arts: what the nature of the discourse[2] at hand is: what the elements used to declaim, persuade, unmask, affect, shift or praise are. By answering these questions in the medium in which art practitioners work, arts research can lead to doctoral quality scholarship, illuminating as well as demonstrating how performances/exhibitions/objects/spaces construct and communicate what we see and believe.

This chapter will further explore how the application of rhetoric to artistic practice is not necessarily cemented to alphabetical 'logic', but can cross all media, serving as a method of discovery and analysis of communicative processes and production. It will include an examination of how rhetorical research applied to art practice can produce multiple kinds of scholarship recognized today in higher education: scholarship of teaching and learning; analyses of practice that involve using alphabetical language alone and analyses of practices that combine the art medium under consideration with alphabetical language. In these three forms, artist practitioners can employ rhetorical tools to examine not only their practices (a useful and common default when one thinks of art scholarship), but also to inquire about the relationship between viewer and artist, artist and self, artist and medium. The final section of this chapter, will demonstrate how rhetoric that combines with art scholarship becomes itself visual, aural and kinaesthetic. Finally, art practitioners might not only use rhetoric to create new ways in which academic scholarship is defined, 'counted' and communicated, but contribute to how the ancient art of rhetoric continues to adapt itself to the media in which communication takes place.

Must it always be alphabetical?

Most would think that rhetoric would be most closely aligned with art history since they envision rhetorical/art examinations occurring within a historical period, identifying a series of marks that were applied to produce a building, painting, music, landscape, dance or other objects. Both art historians and rhetoricians often produce an argument as research whether they focus on traditional uses of marks and medium, or on multimodal productions. They may examine the interplay of print, image, sound, movement on a page, website or film to persuade someone how the context in which these occur contributes to their impact, whether it be an exhibition hall, a stage, or a natural or community-built space. Such examinations require attention and observation skills, as well as a vocabulary from a rhetorician/art historian's toolkit, and stand as professional productions: printed critiques, analyses, interpretations.

Admittedly the practices of art history shadow centuries of commentary that have explicated and dissected the long history of rhetoric, defining and debating who said what in Greece, how the Romans reinterpreted Greek rhetorical principles, and how each successive historical period changed or rediscovered rhetorical practices. However, rhetoric does not have to be tied to print or alphabetic language, and in fact has relied on the performative and visual since its inception. The focus of rhetoric has always been on communication, and it is here that there is a function for rhetoric within scholarship by arts practitioners. Whether communicating a movement, state, or emotion in dance, music or clay, or making a political point in graphics or architecture to an audience, rhetorical techniques are used to shape, measure, understand or influence a desired effect.

While art practitioners either intuitively or logically find results and effects, rhetoricians choose the medium of words to determine what oral and alphabetical (written) texts mean, what effect they produce, how their communication is shaped by a particular (kairotic) moment. They do this not merely to study other communicative acts, but to more succinctly effect the impact they themselves seek to produce. While over time, the medium used by rhetoricians to perform and paint has been words, rhetoric has recently turned to its origins in the performative and visual. Now a rhetorician might study how the use of yellow on a website can cause an audience to stop, click, and navigate in a direction. A rhetorician might well examine how a pathway through a Gehry building, mimics the expected architectural corridor, but how anyone who walks the path is moved to stop because of the irregular ceiling lines, or how another might not move quickly down the hall, despite its straightness, but explore and meander because of the planes of the walls. A designer might intuit or think rhetorically to more quickly understand that while yellow is the colour she wants, lemon yellow does not create the effect desired. An architect might realize that the building being designed becomes more useful and more playful when he changes wall or ceiling lines, slowing the pace of its occupants and creating collaborations among them. While these analyses may appear too cerebral, it is only because they are being explained here in words rather than in the media of artists who would employ rhetorical reflection by joining the vocabulary of their practice with that of rhetoric. As this chapter will later show, even the predominance of words has changed in some rhetorical research.

Pertinent to this initial discussion are recent acknowledgements of ancient rhetorical practices that included all aspects of the communicating body, for in the ancient forum the rhetorician was physically present. Therefore, effective communication included the ability to see that which 'is' before one (what one gazes upon), to hear words (sounds), to witness movement or images in order to respond to the entire performance. Such 'seeing' points to the emphasis on *deiktikos* – 'exhibit' – or, as others claim, on the sophistic use of epideictic rhetoric (ceremony, commemoration, display). In each instance, narrative pictures conveyed through the performance of oratory displayed in the forum were visual and performative necessities, created as part of the whole effect of a speech. Such thoughtful use of rhetorical strategies parallel not only the movement of body, sound, line or image in an artistic performance, but also is mindful of placement: where the body stands, how it gestures, when it moves, where it projects a sound, how loudly and in what space all this occurs.

Where and how artistic productions are exhibited or performed are just as essential within our own culture, and whether an artist analyses others in order to inform her own work, or whether she observes her own work in order to move it elsewhere, her use of the principles of *deiktikos* or her understanding of how to infuse her imagistic language with concepts of ceremony, commemoration and display may help her push her work further towards an effect of which she wasn't previously aware. Observation and reflection of the effect of a communication (with oneself or others) is key to rhetorical/creative production and itself demands some kind of articulation in some kind of medium: words might cross with paint or sound, but from the ancients onwards, the intricate play of word and image [articulation and result] were not only recognized, but required and essential to a construction of a world view (Fleckenstein 2007: 1–7). I am suggesting here that rhetoric brings to art practice another lens with which to examine work produced and that the work produced becomes in itself scholarly production because of the application, movement, refraction and implementation of knowledge that then produces new knowledge – new art.

That alphabetical language has a role in this is maintained throughout recorded history for there is a continual ebb and flow between word and image. The medieval absorption of the visual and iconic emerged again in the Renaissance, where the close tie between the painting of verbal pictures produced through written descriptive narratives for moral good, and the visual art produced at the time, is most evident in references to Horace's 'ut pictura poesis' (as is painting, so is poetry). Both the speaking picture (the poet's *pictura*, or verbal exemplary narrative) and the silent poetry (the painter's *istoria*, or visual narrative) are conceived in terms of making visible idealized images or patterns audiences could 'gaze upon' to communicate moral, philosophical or ethical lessons.

'Renaissance humanists presumed that all aesthetic displays are rhetorical performances before audiences capable of appraising the virtuosity of their execution'

(Prelli 2006: 5). But how does an artist who might care about his art being accessible, decide whether it is the audience which is not capable or whether his art isn't capable of communicating with an audience? I am suggesting here that art researchers employing rhetorical tools can produce scholarship which contributes to how we see the world and how we construct the world with what we see. On the one hand, art practitioners push the boundaries of communication in media other than words. On the other hand, the world could benefit from knowledge about how to see the ideas through other media. Rhetoric's methodology can form the bridge between and among media which represent knowledge in various forms.

Even in ancient Greece, Aristotle recognized that:

> All men by nature desire to know. An indication of this is the delight we take in our senses; for even apart from their usefulness they are loved for themselves; and above all others the sense of sight … The reason is that this, most of all the senses, makes us know and brings to light many differences between things.
>
> (Aristotle 1984: Metaphysics 980a)

Stafford (1997), Kress (2007) and others note that since that time a logocentrism increasingly forced out other forms of expression to the point of having 'dampened the full development of all kinds of human potential' (Kress 2007: 157). While the balance may have tipped towards the alphabetic, current scholars who have applied rhetoric to the visual, demonstrate that the power relationship between word and image at any given moment shapes a cultural reality and therefore the ability to produce a particular kind of artefact (word or image). Art practitioner research can contribute to this examination of how word and image, language as expression, works. They can join their understanding of their medium with rhetorical analyses to communicate what they see and how they see it. This cannot only push their own art to a new level, and push the understanding of their art to a new level, but also push a culture's understanding of itself to a new level. So arts-rhetoricians, because they can work with a dual perspective, might study how the application of logos to image or performance affects communication of that object(ive); the insider perspective provides a unique position for producing new knowledge – and new alphabetical and non-alphabetical vocabularies.

According to Martin Jay (1988), the West holds to a Cartesian perspective that separates the observer from the observed, giving to the detached researcher the ability to analyse from a privileged position. That distancing stance presumes a panoptic vision while, in reality, the position limits what is experienced, and what might be produced. To either view or to produce a written document about a visual or aural object is therefore to see from a position that limits engagement with that object. However, Schachtel describes an alternative 'allocentric perception'; one 'characterized by "profound interest in the object, and complete openness and receptivity toward it, a full turning toward the object which makes possible a direct encounter with it"' (Fleckenstein 2007: 14). This more Eastern perspective produces a very different relationship and product, one more familiar to the artist: descriptive rather than analytical, one situated in meditation and oneness rather than on the gaze and separation. Nobel laureate, Barbara McClintok claims her discoveries in plant cytology are due to her ability to acquire 'a feeling for the organism' in which she opens herself up to 'what the material has to say' (Fleckenstein 2007: 14). The close identification provided *her* the insights, rather than she laying over her observations an explanation already grounded in traditions of science. Her new vision produced new knowledge. This is often the creative flow in which a performer or artist finds herself in the moment of production; it can also be the space in which an observer or viewer finds himself. By adopting both stances an art practitioner can provide insight with/in two vocabularies. Knowledge of which rhetorical stance one takes at any moment can be used to perform an analysis of an artefact as well as to purposefully create an edginess, dissonance or cohesion in a creative work, upsetting assumptions and expectations of viewers known to be lodged within a Cartesian perspective. Conversely, a Western rhetorical researcher or artist might examine their positioning in order to ask how an 'allopathic,' deep engagement with an object or an analytical study, produces new results, questions or objectives, freeing them from their contained perspective (or not).

Perhaps a simple parallel can now be drawn: concerned with human sign-making as communication, rhetoric can be considered a method by which one defines and presents a perspective (point of view), describing it (picturing) by articulating (creating) a narrative (composition) that, through the medium of marks (paint, movement, stone, sound), causes an audience (viewer) to respond (react) to the declamation (artefact). It is with this in mind that rhetorical research, with its historical pedigree lodged in the interplay of oral presentation, the visual and the performative (Goldhill 1996) is now quite commonly applied to the practices and products of multimodal work. Among rhetoricians who study the visual, there is more and more consensus that lines between the visual and verbal have blurred, not only for the rhetorician, but between rhetorician, museum patron and art practitioner; between also the rhetorician and artisan, and even between the rhetorician and denizens of Facebook – between those who look at and those who create. For many rhetoricians the key concern is now one in which art practitioners can engage: developing a common vocabulary for examining images which would foster 'a collaborative venture, in essence for the disciplining of the study of visual phenomena … [that] would bring together a wide variety of disciplines' (Hill and Helmers 2004: 19), visual, aural and performative. The call for rhetoric to join other disciplinary perspectives that make up composing/designing/art research would also contribute to, or be, the subject of artistic production, raising questions from the physical (what role does the eye movement play in the production of multimodal or multi-movement communication?) to the abstract (what affective response do viewers exhibit and how do they describe it in relation to what they see?).

Words about art: rhetorical processing and creative production

Besides the development of concepts and vocabulary through rhetorical-art-practitioner perspectives, another result of research using rhetorical strategies in the arts is educational. The scholarship of teaching and learning would examine how art is produced so an artist herself as well as others can communicate more explicitly what they do and why and how they do it (e.g. International Society of the Scholarship of Teaching and Learning).[3] PhDs in creative writing, in the same relationship to research as art practitioners, provide a good example of creative pedagogical scholarship. Such scholarship draws on writing and rhetoric for terminology and strategies that foster research. For example, the 'canons of rhetoric' – invention, arrangement, style, memory and delivery – are a basis for examining written and art productions, and articulate persuasive appeals that a communicator uses: logos (arrangement, placement of marks on a background), ethos (the believability of the 'author') and pathos (the emotional impact and response to the marks because of their believability). Rhetorical analysis of musical, written, performative and visual texts using these appeals form the cornerstones of some US textbooks that teach writing modules to first year students in university with the objective of widening definitions of communication. In the attempt to create audiences *capable* of reading visuals, movement and sound, and of unpacking their component parts, US-modelled universities also offer modules in visual rhetoric or rhetorics of display. This latter module includes not just studying and producing alphabetic texts, but also visual and multimodal 'artefacts' (Fortune 2002). In such a class, students might begin by looking at how advertisers manipulate viewer responses by building texts on the basis of:

- ethos (celebrity driver)
- logos (a fast car = a celebrated life) and
- pathos (cute dog barking in the front seat).

The objective of these modules is to create a knowledgeable rhetorical reading within the author-audience-object context (Roberts-Miller 2009) at a particular kairotic moment.

Compiled by writing-scholars who seek to teach the multiple forms of communication in our culture (not only alphabetic but aural, performative and visual) what is missing from these is the voice of actual artists themselves (even if those who teach writing do call themselves 'compositionists'). These authors seek to explain facets of art practice but are often researching from a Cartesian (observer) viewpoint. However, an arts practitioner's allopathic perspective joined to rhetorical vocabularies would enrich these examinations, producing pedagogical knowledge about teaching students in and out of the arts communication practices beyond the alphabetical. These same processes could be used by students and art practitioners to examine the effectiveness of any visual, aural or performative work, in particular their own.

For example, a reader/student artist is often asked to talk about her own work, explaining the context. Such a requirement includes not only artist's cultural perspectives (e.g. Cartesian) but her ability to *find* a narrative, and the resultant and contributive emotions, beliefs and expectations that shape that narrative. As it is important for art practitioners to know what they know and what they don't, rhetorical readings of visuals can illuminate for viewers/artists their own narrative. If they care to think about audience, it can also illuminate others' experience of an artefact. Marguerite Helmers exemplifies a rhetorical unpacking of the painting *An Experiment on a Bird in the Air Pump* (1768) by Joseph Wright of Derby. She focuses on the reception by viewers whose reading of the picture is determined not only by the success of the rhetorical appeals (logos, ethos, pathos), but also by what these 'readers' bring to the piece.

In the case of *An Experiment* … focusing our sight on the bird in the air pump may lead us to read the painting as an allegory of life and death, that is, unless the bird is mistakenly identified as a dove. In the latter case, the painting will become a Christian allegory, referring directly to the place of God and redemption in a secular society.

(Hill and Helmers 2004: 84)

However, instead of studying this as art history, through reading, lectures and slides, and then writing the above typical response, such arts-directed rhetorical scholarship might result in students creating visual, performative or aural responses that represent an articulation of others' works. This can be a way for students to become as articulate and used to thinking about how their art further contributes to the long tradition of production in their area – how it produces more knowledge, more thought, more understanding about all of us who create the world by interpreting and explaining it.

While Helmers' examination of *An Experiment* is similar to an art historian's analysis, her use of rhetorical appeal and location of context within, as well as outside, an audience has much to teach an artist about how a work might – or might not – be understood, received, valued. For many art students, instruction, feedback and studying art history is seen as playing little part in nurturing their own talent. Much to the frustration of their instructors, these novices hold instead to the myth of the single genius in the *atelier* whose talent runs out of their arm into a work of art. In interviews conducted between 2001 and 2004, art and design instructors in the US and UK noted their students' reluctance to examine how others have created works of art is too often validated by other instructors who may have learned to support that same myth.[4] In a recent essay addressing the same problem in creative writing modules, Kimberly Andrews notes that tutors often comfort:

creative writers who are intimidated by the enormous body of literature and criticism that encircles them; it is much easier to speak of the genius of creative writing, to say, like a bad infomercial: 'you, too, can cultivate this genius in yourself!'

(Andrews 2009: 247)

They encourage the genius myth instead of providing research opportunities from which students should draw. Among art practitioner-instructors, that means asking students to do more than walk into a museum and look at the work or perhaps, more than only sketching what one sees.[5] Using rhetoric to examine the relationship between student attitudes towards art and their communicative productions would contribute to new knowledge in arts practice.

That students need tools to develop skills in visuality is supported by research such as that of DeSousa and Medhurst. They gave 130 communications students a two-part survey designed to test their abilities as visual interpreters. Results indicate that student respondents were surprisingly inaccurate in determining the correct meaning and elements of political cartoons, perhaps because of 'visual illiteracy,' 'cultural lag' or 'low socio-political awareness' (DeSousa and Medhurst 1982: 50). Rhetorical research such as this could be performed by art practitioners in order to find such gaps in their own and students' abilities. The reverse is also true: there is much work needed in adopting visual metaphors to explain logocentric processes which no longer speak to a wired generation. In 'Alternative Pedagogy: Visualizing Theories of Composition' (Mullin 1998), students in a writing module were too imitative of others, adopted visual vocabulary to assist with inventing, arranging, recalling, shaping and delivering their writing. More rhetorical analysis that focuses on the visual students' engagement with image and word would illuminate art practitioners' work and provide useful scholarship to their and to others' disciplines. A US architect provides a good example. Unlike a teacher in the humanities or in writing, when he notes students are too imitative of an architect (having not yet developed their individual voices) he encourages them to research the architect they have emulated; the more they study, the more they learn what moves them, what vocabulary they might take from that architect and how to express their own ideas (Mullin 2009). Rhetorical research of visual styles can encourage artistic visioning and appeals to the young self-focused artist-who-needs-to-be-researcher. Such scholarship at university level can start with what one knows, expects, sees and feels in response to what one likes, and then provide tools and language[6] to articulate what draws them, and in turn, how they might 'draw', how their terministic screen is shaping what they vision. This approach can develop into richer, deeper scholarship at postgraduate levels.

Applying rhetorical analyses to the words of artists provides another method for understanding and shaping visual practices and the processes of those who create and teach art practices. The interviews of art practitioners opened up for them the need for linking current issues of intellectual property to the tradition and practices of building on, and borrowing, in art (Mullin 2009). By asking what they own or borrow in their art and their obligation to acknowledge collaboration, and by examining the language of acknowledgement in art, practitioners found alternative ways to address these issues for their students as well as themselves. Likewise, colleagues and I interviewed students about their creative and compositional practices in their art, and then asked the same questions about their alphabetic writing practices. Analyses provided a window to the personal, constructed ground on which students position themselves in each medium and their practices, in rhetorical terms, for successful 'invention', use of 'memory' and final 'delivery' (Orr et al. 2005). Researching their visual and rhetorical practices, and the commonalities and gaps between them, leads to a greater understanding of how to support and foster each. However, it also illuminates for art practitioners the value of conducting rhetorical research for the purposes of creative production and knowledge making.

Cheryl Jorgensen-Earp examines how oral and print rhetoric surrounding the legal issues of the salvaging of the Titanic, affected public reaction to and, eventually, public memory of the site itself – that is, she studied the rhetorical effect of all elements leading to an exhibition. Instead of becoming an untouched, sacred graveyard in the ocean, proponents of salvaging and exhibiting 'countered with a cluster of secularizing metaphors that delegitimized the presumptive view of the Titanic as gravesite and substituted an alternative set of thoughts and actions' that became crucial to determining the way in which materials from the ship were displayed. 'By co-opting the sacralizing metaphors, the [Titanic] exhibitors resisted characterization as defilers of sacred ground and sought *post hoc* legitimacy for the secular interests underlying the exhibit' (Jorgensen-Earp 2006: 42). Such rhetorically examined cases underscore the role of exhibition in public reception as well as public memory, demonstrating how these processes leading to exhibition affect both production, placement and reception of art and are of value to art practitioners in all areas, especially those who like walking a line between public outrage and public engagement.

Finally, rhetorical analyses can be used pedagogically to foster creative work by providing another point of view. Graphic designers and illustrators produce pamphlets, brochures or posters that rely on words. Typography becomes part of the visual marking that determines how something is communicated and a rhetorical analysis of placement can open up new methods of design. Fashion designers might just 'know' what lines, hem, or shape will work to accomplish their design goals, but at the point of being stuck, when a choice is needed, another vocabulary can provide the necessary push to accomplish a breakthrough. Applying a rhetorical lens can help to determine what might be shifted to create or enhance a desired effect; it allows the designer to:

> optimize design in a very practical sense. The system of rhetorical figures reveals which design solutions are available to the designer, and organises those solutions according to their function, e.g., ellipsis, apposition, inversion, contrast or conjunction. So the designer can create a systematic overview of the available methods and test which of them prove to be appropriate for the design task in question'.
>
> (Gesche and Scheuermann 2007: 8)

Research in these areas by art practitioners would not only serve students who need to consider critically their work, but also add to a growing bank of knowledge about how art constructs viewers and viewers construct art.

Looking at rhetorical research and seeing art

One of the advantages of using rhetorical strategies for arts practice research is that it contributes to a vocabulary with which artists produce and examine their own art. Principles of rhetoric laid down by the Greeks and developed over time to suit the context already parallel how visual texts are composed: the arrangements, the colour, the line, the references, the argument, statement, historical and perspectival positioning at a particular kairotic moment. But before this seems like we are reading an arts practice textbook with some specialized words thrown in, researchers in the visual arts should look to the 'rhetorical figures' listed in the on-line compendium *Silva Rhetoricæ* (Burton 2009). Here, vocabulary such as 'coenotes' becomes the means by which visual production and viewer or artist response might be articulated: 'Repetition of two different phrases: one at the beginning and the other at the end of successive paragraphs'. Substitute some visual vocabulary and one might consider coenotes the 'repetition of two different brushstrokes: one at the beginning and the other at the end of successive sections' or 'repetition of two different themes: one at the beginning and the other at the end of successive parts of a composition'.

Rhetoric offers a trove of potential images resulting from this traditional terminology, and while the terms may not be familiar, they encapsulate visual forms and practices, extending the existing vocabulary. Drawing on rhetorical vocabulary which provides or names concrete images can help bridge the articulation between visual and alphabetical that can contribute to artistic invention, but art research can also expand our understanding of the visual and alphabetical intersections.

Visual and performance instructors have their vocabularies which, in turn might be adapted by those working alphabetically, helping them more closely examine the performative values of their productions. Art practice research might therefore seek to explore the communicative barriers that exist as a person switches code from one world view to another, both within art practice and without. Rhetorical vocabulary combined with visual and performance production or reflection might find useful such terms as *diasyrmus*. In alphabetic language this refers to

> rejecting an argument through ridiculous comparison. Examples: Arguing that we can clean up government by better regulating elections is like asking a dog to quit marking his territory by lifting his hind leg.
>
> (Burton 2009)

However, visually *diasyrmus* is the stuff of posters and political cartoons – another visual subject of rhetorical analysis. By researching creative communicative moves through traditional rhetorical terms, an art practitioner can expand the knowledge and understanding of their own work. What this might accomplish in terms of art practitioner scholars is a series of examples for how others think about various media, their use and effects, creating a vocabulary that doesn't contain another practitioner but gives additional tools for intuitive creative practices. Such scholarship would still use the medium of words, though visuals would be primary in the production of a print/ on-line final product.

Using rhetorical approaches and alphabetical text to investigate how an affect is created and received is also useful when examining the intersection of artistic and natural worlds. Performance art and landscape design through the eyes of a rhetorician-art practitioner might illuminate how they practise/might practise. This would also be primarily word-based, but has the potential for becoming more visual and performative as arts research comes into its own. Michael Halloran and Gregory Clark 'explore the rhetorical functioning of landscape in general, suggesting that the public landscapes constituted by the US national park movement display symbols that enable citizens to participate in a civic religion' (Halloran and Clark 2006: 141). This 'religion' valorizes a particular national image by examining the terrain, replacement of original buildings and design of historical artefacts within such spaces: a door of the Nielson farm house (c. 1777) left open, but entry not permitted; a tape of the original owner who sacrificed land and self during the American Revolution plays in the background.

> The image of an idealized, pastoral America alternates with the image of John and Lydia Nielson's sacrifice in pursuit of that ideal ... depicting the Jeffersonian ideal of the United States made up of self-sufficient farmers living on land won by sacrifice, determination and labor.
>
> (Halloran and Clark 2006: 153)

While this research is presented in a print text, arts research-practitioners might well choose to create an exhibition in which they use rhetorical strategies to illuminate the act of 'writing' on land. Through sign, symbol and physical form they could change, tame, leave, comment on the landscape, symbolizing through form, sound and movement, what Halloran and Clark write in alphabetical text. Such research, communicated through the visual and alphabetical articulate powerfully the rhetorical effect of placement, and artists who use that knowledge to effect, such as Anthony Gormley in his 2007 installation in London and its Hayward Gallery, are performing rhetorical acts through their art (Kidron 2007).

There are many such examples that demonstrate the application of rhetoric to a variety of art productions in order to examine how they communicate, what they communicate, and in some cases, why. At its simplest, rhetoricians assume that every element of a visual, musical or dance is purposefully chosen to effect a response in a viewer. Cara Finnegan exemplifies this sorting out of 'three moments in the life of an image for which a critic must account: production, reproduction and circulation' (Finnegan 2004: 199). She performs a rhetorical analysis of the influence of the picture magazine *LOOK* on public opinion by unpacking images in its 1937 publication that were chosen purposefully from a free 'bank' of photos contributed to by various photographers of the time. Finnegan compares the use of the photos by *LOOK* with the use of the same pictures by other publications in the late 1930s, providing evidence of two competing arguments that emerge from different editors' arrangements; shaping particular cultural attitudes towards race, class and children. She is, of course, performing rhetoric as she produces it. That is, while the act of examining the history of a production may be termed 'art history' an artist may find such a rhetorical approach to photography a fitting subject for a collage that juxtaposes original with historical images. For example, a dancer or musical composer might examine her own interpretation in light of the influences others see in the performance, placing each reception in context and then in dialogue with her own reading. This form of scholarship would open to the artist further paths for self-production and to other artists, knowledge about art practice. The form this scholarship would take should be a combination of words, image, sound and video (movement) in order to acknowledge the rhetorical power of each area's grammar and vocabulary (i.e. brush stroke or line; movement or gesture; tempo or arpeggio). Right now a computer might be the most easily available form for this scholarship, though a performance that is narrated, discussed or involves audience reaction, also stands as scholarship in the arts.

Perhaps the key to the idea of the 'rhetorical' as applied to art is that it is a public communication with an audience, one about which the artist/performer wants to effect. That might indeed limit the use of rhetoric as a means of producing art research to those who choose to speak to, and study, dialogues that art production and viewing enacts. However, just as art practitioners make use of materials as they become available, rhetorical theorists working with visuals have begun to change their own productions. Researchers examining digital and multimodal rhetorics have been producing print that may be in the form of a comic book (McCloud 1994), and research about web sites, digital art, and other visual productions are appearing on the web and beginning to look more like the art they examine.

Mash-up: rhetoric becomes physically performative anew

'Mash-up', the mixing of the already made to create something new, follows the tradition we call art – the building upon, the mixing of elements, materials and tools to create a new visioning. Mash-up also signifies the multimodal, a widening of the alphabetically formed picture with additions of tactility, sound and movement (and their absence), all made possible by technology. As 'art' has expanded beyond bricks, canvas and ink, so too have applications of rhetorical methods expanded to include the same elements that comprise art: the visual, tactile, aural or kinaesthetic. Robert Miltner takes up the rhetorical term *ekphrasis*, the act of vividly describing a work of art so a reader/listener can see it. Starting with early Modernist writers' responses to, and collaborations with, artists Miltner traces the practice of exchange of writer-visual-artist up to the contemporary poet Robert Creeley, who 'uses this dialogue as a means of collaboration in which his writing extends the art rather than merely responding' (Miltner 2001: 1). Citing his own 'ekphrastic collaboration' Miltner examines how his dialogues with printmaker Wendy Collin Sorin has stimulated his rhetorical readings of image and word, expanding his own visioning ability.

Carol Wiest applies rhetorical methodology to a tactile alphabet book, exploring the ways in which tactile pictures represent objects in the world and the strategies the pictures use to enact interactive-represented participant relations. In this sample of her rhetorical reading of a tactile children's book, Wiest demonstrates the interactivity of text, the reader and author, to tease out the affective-cultural response produced by arrangement.

> Objects represented at a 45 degree angle, such as the Lollipop and Key, seem most within reach while objects at an upright angle, such as the House and Rabbit, seem less so. I suspect that the physical position of a reader's hands has a great deal to do with this sense of 'within reach.' The angle of the reader's

Figure 9.1 Delagrange. *Wunderkammer* (2009)

arms and hands is not straight, but acute (less than 90 degrees relative to the centre of the torso). Picture elements that have a 45 degree angle of rotation, then, are more congruent with the physical position of the reader, creating the sense that they are more 'within reach.' In the alphabet book, objects over which the viewer is most likely to have the power of manipulation or use, tools and food, appear at 45 degree angles. Objects which are likely to be outside the reader's influence appear at an upright angle: House, Queen, Clown, Ears, Nose. The interactive participant is thus constructed in a social relation of power over tools and food and a relation of equality or of inferiority to people and certain objects such as houses.

(Wiest 2001: 6)

By interpreting these positional codes, Wiest opens space for the development of a tactile rhetoric, a potential methodology for art practitioner research that would benefit both the observer/viewer of art production and the artist (especially, for example, the sculptor, potter, fashion designer, collage artist) who could employ the vocabulary to examine, create, and push his or her own vision.

In Susan Delagrange's examination of the *Wunderkammer* (Delagrange 2009: see Figure 9.1), rhetorical analyses of the visual become an artistic expression of that which it analyzses; it becomes a piece of interactive art. Embarking on Delagrange's examination of one rhetorical canon, 'arrangement', the viewer clicks on the link to the article listed in the content page of that issue of the journal *Kairos*. The first sight that meets the viewer is of what appears to be the top of an elaborate carved wooden box or a massive door. If on-line instinct doesn't take over and cause one to click on the top of the box, the word 'open' in script appears in the bottom right hand corner as a clue. Clicking on the word 'open' however, does nothing; the visual has displaced the alphabetical as the key to enter this 'text'. Once clicked, the panels of the box top (doors?) slide back and there revealed is the *Wunderkammer*, a shadow box of thirty-six squares, each offering a colourful invitation to 'pick up' what is only glimpsed by the contained contents.

Clicking, one can open any individual square and the viewer/participant quickly finds that, not only does each square hold a myriad of objects – visual, alphabetical, filmic, auditory – but that reading this text does not have to occur from left to right, or in any order. As with any visual, the viewer participates in creating the perspective by wandering around, changing angle, focusing, stepping back: the point of careful arrangement on the part of the artist and an interactive engagement in the act of arrangement on the part of the observer.

At one point in the box of possibilities, Delagrange compares her work and her examination of the rhetorical concept of arrangement to the artist Joseph Cornell's shadow boxes:

Many of Cornell's constructions made use of the evocativeness of the partly-seen, using screens with holes, frosted glass, layered paper and wood, sand, bottled objects, and mirrors to provide multiple perspectives while never revealing all, insisting that the viewer both accept the ambiguity and continue striving to construct meaning in the gaps.

(Delagrange 2009)

The reader/viewer's engagement with Delangrage's text likewise deepens with discovery, is orchestrated through choice of mouse click and eye, and results in an individualistic encounter with and simultaneous experience of, arrangement. The author of this visual/rhetorical text notes that the:

> making of knowledge through arrangement and visual analogy in a *Wunderkammer* is a process of analogical manipulation that is deeply rhetorical. Each arrangement of objects creates new taxonomies – based on materials, or seasons, or humors, or the four elements, or even size – that carry with them unique ways of seeing and understanding the world. Designing these arrangements calls for visual tropes that connect in a material way habits of mind required to engage with the verbal rhetorical devices of metaphor, metonymy, synecdoche, hyperbole, anti-stasis, and catachresis.
>
> (Delagrange 2009)

Text and visual interact, movement draws the eye away from the words and vice versa, the hand participates in a tactile performance of rhetoric in the making.

The application of rhetorical vocabulary and theory for art practitioners and visual researchers, has become at times interchangeable, the same, and complementary. If, as Kevin DeLucca defines it, rhetoric is 'the mobilization of signs for the articulation of identities, ideologies, consciousnesses, communities, publics, and cultures' (DeLuca 1999: 17) the material nature of those marks – by letter, image or a combination of sensory stimulations – becomes both subordinate to, as well as the substance of, the vision of the artist-rhetorician. There is much more research for arts practitioners to explore, and scholarship to create, that would meet the current criteria for original and rigorous knowledge-making for postgraduate production.

Notes

1 The term 'text' has evolved to include any material artefact that can be read (a landscape, social group, painting, etc.). In this chapter, 'alphabetical' or 'written' text will refer to words, sentences or paragraphs in print or digital formats.
2 'Discourse' indicates here a communication that can be written, performed, heard or viewed by others or by the self.
3 http://www.issotl.org/index.html (accessed 12 January 2010).
4 While assessment of the interviews is still in process, many of the results appear in Mullin (2009).
5 This is not to ignore the necessity of any of these, especially since the act of sketching can be instrumental in producing an allopathic perspective. Within the West especially, the analytic perspective can complement the allopathic and vice versa; vocabulary of both provide artists a larger palette.
6 'Language' here may be alphabetical, visual, or what is suggested here as even more productive, multimodal.

10
RESEARCH AND THE SELF

Morwenna Griffiths

Introduction

This chapter considers the role of the self in research. It argues that arts-based, practice-based research needs to address the issue of the self of the researcher. It shows the significance of self within the processes and in its outcomes, whether these are propositions, descriptions, explanations, theories, artefacts, changed practices or changed understandings. In the first section, I present a brief overview of the theory of the self which informs the argument of the chapter. In the second section, I outline the logic of research processes from the initial conception of a research project through to its end. Section 3 contains three examples of different kinds of ongoing, arts-based, practice-based research which are used to ground the subsequent discussion of how the self enters into arts-based research, and the implications of this for researchers. The fourth section draws on the examples from the third in order to provide an overview of the intersections of self and research. The fifth section addresses criticisms sometimes levelled at arts-based, practice-based research focused on its partiality. The final section concludes with some remarks about the significance of acknowledging the place of the self in research.

What is it to be a self?

This chapter draws on a range of theories of the self which are only very briefly mentioned in this section. The purpose of the section is only to set the arguments of the rest of the chapter into context. It is not intended as a full account.

Why are there so many theories? Part of the reason is the mysterious nature of the self. In some ways it is utterly familiar, part of what it is to be a person, as impossible to be rid of as a shadow. We know ourselves – or do we? We deceive ourselves – how does that work? And we surprise ourselves saying, 'That wasn't like me!' Sometimes other people know us better than we know ourselves. And then again, just as we think we have caught what it is to 'be me', we get older, gain and lose family members, move countries, move jobs, discover new ideas and, generally, change for one reason or another. Even articulating who we are seems to change us: as we grasp at the self, it dissolves in our hand-reassembling itself somewhere else.

In trying to make sense of the mystery, I turn first to the connection of self with time and place. One popular view is that there is an essential self which remains unchanging through life; though external contours to the self may be formed by circumstance, they could be sloughed off if they are too uncomfortable. Opposing this is the so-called blank slate (or *tabula rasa*) attributed to Locke (1964 [1690]: Bk.II Ch.2). This is the theory that the self is a blank to be written on by its experience. Against both these views is the existential self, which proclaims the freedom to choose who he or she becomes. Indeed, choice is always already inevitable with the result that at all times a self can say, 'I am what I am not yet'.

Second, there is the relationship of the self to other people, to the social groups in which it is embedded. One powerful strand of thinking in Western societies is the idea of the individual as a social atom. The group, then, is an aggregate of such individuals each of whom is able to decide its own future, rationally and autonomously, and is responsible for the outcome. There is another powerful strand which takes the opposing view. This is the idea of an individual as determined by society. Determined by their class position, their gender, their race and ethnicity, individuals play out their roles in ways that economists and policymakers can predict. In a similar vein, there is an influential view, associated with deconstruction and poststructuralism, that, roughly, we do not speak our language, but that it speaks us. This postmodern self need not be a unity; rather it may be a collection of fragments, the nature of the fragments depending on the particular discourse in which a self is located at any given time.

The model of self used in this chapter can be positioned in relation to these latter ideas. It is one in which the self continually creates itself, but not in the circumstances of its own choosing, and, further, those circumstances contribute to its creation. (1) Each self is *unique* and its response to circumstance *is not determined*. Further, (2) the process is continuing: we are always in a state of *becoming*, always unfinished. (3) We make ourselves in *relation to others*. As I have argued elsewhere (Griffiths 1995: 16): 'I' is a fragment rather than an atom. That is, an 'I' is always part of a 'we', indeed of several different 'we's, which overlap with each other. For example, consider: 'we ballet dancers', 'we inhabitants of Rio favelas', 'we teenagers'. These groups sound very different, but a self that belongs to all of them (as in Beadie Finzie's film, *Only When I Dance*) is self-constructed in relation to all of them. (4) The circumstances that influence – and are influenced by – a self include *specificities of time and place*.

This model is strongly influenced by Arendt's concept of 'the human condition of natality' (Arendt 1958: 191). Her model of the realm of human affairs is one that is open to change, and indeed does change as new unique human beings are born, come into the world and use their voices to act in it, in concert with others. Arendt draws a useful distinction between who and what a human being is. The 'who', she says, is a unique personal identity which discloses itself when somebody acts and speaks. It is 'in contradistinction to "what" somebody is – his qualities, gifts, talents, and shortcomings' (Arendt 1958: 179). It is also in contradistinction to his self as a social or political being (an American or German, Jew or Negro, woman or man) (Arendt 1966). She argues that the attempt to reduce the self to either the 'who' or to the 'what' diminishes it.

Further, (5) *embodiment* is crucial. The world is understood through the body and also perceptions of our bodies constrain our relationships with others and ourselves (Merleau-Ponty 1962; Battersby 1998). This observation is at the heart of much theory of Otherness, in a wide range of theories. Think of the *Black Skin, White Masks* of Fanon (1986); or of the imaginary in Irigaray (1985); or of queer theory; or disability theory. More recently, overviews by Brand and Devereux (2003) and Leibowitz (2003) relate female and black bodies to self and to aesthetics. Carrie Sandahl (2003) discusses queer and crip (disability) solo autobiographical performance. To mention feminist, Black, queer and disability theorists is to introduce issues of socio-political structures of power. These are closely linked to the self and identity. So (6), a self constructs itself in response to the *social and political power structures* it inhabits. Power relations are present in all aspects of the self: who and what it can be and which relationships are ones of belonging.

These six different elements of a self are not like discrete building blocks. Rather they should be seen as fluid with semi-permeable walls, each one leaking into the others. For instance: the process of becoming is closely linked to changes in time or place; and relationships are partly made through, with and against the social and political power structures where they occur.

The research process

In this section, I outline an account of what it is to do arts-based, practice-based research in order to consider the relation of self and research in the rest of the chapter. In this chapter, the term 'arts-based, practice-based research' signifies research which depends methodologically on practice in the arts. I make no attempt to cover the full range of possible research methodologies and methods, concentrating rather on those research methodologies which have so far proved particularly relevant to arts-based, practice-based research. These include reflective practice, action research and self-study. They also include ethnography, autoethnography, performance ethnography and documentary research. All of these methods may be inflected as feminist, postcolonial, socially just, queer or antiracist, etc. For simplicity, I have not addressed research which takes it that the practice of art is itself research (Chapter 6) or research specifically about design though neither are necessarily excluded from the argument.

All of these research methodologies can be described as a series of stages. To do this is to describe the research in retrospect, as an analytical history. That is, the stages are analytical constructs, demonstrating a logic; they are not a description of what happened in real time. Viewed analytically, the research journey can be seen to start with one stage and move on to another. A more descriptive story would show that the stages are not experienced as being so discreet. They evolve, often mutually affecting each other, and, indeed, do not become finally stable until the research is completed. Moreover, they need not be reported linearly as stages. The stages are iterative and cyclical in much reflective practice or action research. In some arts-based, practice-based research, the focus only becomes clear towards the end of the process (Chapter 19).

In brief, the stages of the research process usually include, explicitly or implicitly, the following: (1) *Focus*: there may be an overall focus, or the focus may radically change as a result of the initial outcomes. Some studio-based or arts-based research is essentially exploratory and so the focus may change continually and this change may itself become a new focus of enquiry. Similarly the method by which data is collected or argument is constructed may become a major focus of the research. Collaborative methods for instance, or new techniques, may contribute as much to the outcomes as do the initial reasons for using them; (2) *Rationale*; (3) *Method or intervention*, including artistic processes or productions; (4) *Data collection or collation*; purely theoretical research will omit this stage; (5) *Analysis, Theorizing and argument*; (6) *Outcomes*: these may be in the form of conclusions and/or insights and/or questions; (7) *Presentation and dissemination*: the form of presentation and dissemination varies with the purpose of the research and with the intended audience. For instance, it may be published, presented, performed or exhibited.

Examples of arts-based, practice-based research

Having outlined models of the self and of the research process, I now move on to giving an explanation of how the self is significant in research, and the implications of this for the researcher. In order to ground this explanation I begin by presenting three examples of arts-based, practice-based research, all of which were ongoing at the time of writing. These examples have been written by the researchers themselves and then edited by me. The distinctive voices and actions of the researchers disclose something of their selves.

I myself have not personally carried out projects in arts-based research. However much of my work has involved working closely with those who have. I am a philosopher and researcher based in a university faculty of education. For the past four years I have been at the University of Edinburgh, in Scotland, where I have worked closely with Tony Gemmell, the researcher in the first of the examples. He is a lecturer in art and design within teacher education. Before moving to Scotland, I worked in England, at Nottingham Trent University, where I was involved in a number of capacities with artists and performers at Creative Partnerships Nottingham. The second and third of the examples are written by researchers I came to know professionally at that time. Nettie Scriven and Peter Rumney, are co-founders of Dragon Breath Theatre company, and direct a performance and education research programme. The account is also co-authored by the researcher on the project, Iryna Kuksa. Sara Giddens and Simon Jones are co-directors of Bodies in Flight performance company, where they are, respectively, choreographer and writer.

The examples have been chosen to demonstrate three different methodologies and approaches to research. They are, of course, just three among the very many different kinds of arts-based, practice-based research. The first can be described as reflective self-study focused on professional practice (Loughran *et al.* 2004; Tidwell *et al.* 2009). Gemmell, gives an account of a researcher feeling a way into arts-based, practice-based research through the use of video. This study focuses on his self-understanding as a researcher, in tracing his own movement from visually-based research to arts-based research, while also offering a research-based contribution to the improvement of his own and his colleagues' professional practice. The second example is reflective action research (Schön 1991; McArdle and Reason. 2006; Noffke and Somekh. 2009).

Scriven, *et al.* (2009) describe one cycle in a longer project of action research focused on and drawing on their own practice within Theatre in Education in order to develop their approach to theatre for young children. The third is a kind of reflective artistic research, what Borgdorff (2009a) describes as 'use-inspired, basic research' since 'it seeks to both to broaden our understanding of the world and of ourselves as well as to enrich that world by experimentally developing new artefacts, compositions, designs, choreographies, images and art installations.' Giddens and Jones (2010) provide a reflective commentary on their own artistic practice, tracing its evolution and the new understandings it provides within performance theatre.

Distant placements in teacher education: researching myself, researching my students

Tony Gemmell

As an art and design lecturer in teacher education, substantial time is spent in visiting student teachers in placement schools for the purpose of assessment and support. Recent changes in education policy encourage universities to send students to all parts of Scotland. This practice breaks with the tradition of placing students in relatively close proximity to the university.

I became excited about the prospect of undertaking research into what was different and stimulating about these new and unfamiliar locations. I decided to provide a video investigation of students' perceptions of being so placed. I was interested in using a school situation to say something about its environment, its time and place, but also in using my existing visual interest in Scotland. In my own art works, I use a range of ways of gathering information and ideas for paintings and ceramics. These typically involve using digital stills and video; making quick linear sketches in pen and pencil; and writing words or poems about my ideas and feelings about spaces and times, particularly in the Scottish landscape. Each method has its distinctive strengths but when pulled together back in the studio, they help to contribute a deeper and holistic recall of ideas, events and places. Filming and editing is therefore a natural part of my creative artistic process.

The video showed an interview from a student on placement in the Shetland Isles. The interview footage was preceded by images, commentary and music about the environment outside the school. Images included the architecture of the school; footage of a giant Norwegian barque under full sail, clearly visible from the steps of the school; marine traffic entering and leaving the local harbour; the narrow streets of the capital, Lerwick; the people going about their daily business; and even close-ups of puffins emerging from their burrows on the cliffs around the school.

The video was presented to educational researchers at Edinburgh, and also at an international educational research conference. It provoked puzzled expressions and interesting discussions. It seemed that the interview section of the film was accepted as a legitimate tool for gathering information from respondents but my reference in the video to a sense of time and place in the wider environment provoked surprise and controversy.

At this point I reflected on the meaning and direction of the research. I am used to working with video as an expressive visual medium. All art is created in one person's situated interpretation of events in time and place – as is all data gathering in qualitative research. Any researcher visiting the same interview location would undoubtedly produce alternative interpretations of the interview, and of the world around the interview. I too would do so if I visited it again. I and the student would have changed, the Norwegian barque would be gone and the puffins would be out to sea. The weather might be dark and forbidding instead of bright and inviting.

In making plans for filming subsequent students in distant placements, I reflected not just about the reactions of previous audiences but about my own changing, self-critical reactions. As an artist, I felt a sense of self-belief and justification in using video to record the environment around the subject. I expected comments from audiences about including 'peripheral' detail. I was also confident that an audience of art students would not share or display similar puzzlement. I was not consciously trying to provoke an audience reaction but found myself in a situation that artists commonly face; art provokes an audience response. Art can annoy, excite, disturb or please. The viewer is given an insight into the thinking of the artist whether willingly or not. It was also clear to me that I was becoming very much a part of the research. Audiences were invited to share my personal selections of time and space. The researcher, the audience, the environment and the respondent were becoming inextricably linked to the research. With this in mind, I began to become intrigued about my changing perceptions of the research. Whilst continuing with the original distant placement focus, the use of video was developing status as a parallel research focus.

Intrigued by my reflections on the use of video, place, time and audience reaction, I set out to experiment with subsequent video locations, respondents and settings.

Another two contrasting placements were filmed. They were in the small coastal village of Carnoustie and in the busy oil city of Aberdeen. In the Carnoustie video, students were filmed with art works done by pupils visible in the background, clearly locating the respondents in an art and design classroom. In stark contrast, in the Aberdeen location, the student was deliberately placed against a matt black curtain. I could see connections with art processes. Artists consider positive and negative spaces in a painting or the spaces around a sculpture. At what stage does the video image become superfluous to the research? At the micro stage with the subject against a black curtain? At the macro stage with the subject and their art room as a background? Or in the edited video in which the respondent in the art room is prefixed by images of the front of the school, harbours and cliffs?

The second edited video was presented to some student teachers. They could clearly associate with the respondent placed in the familiar art room setting of a placement school. Furthermore they made comments about the distinctions between their own urban placements in or close to Edinburgh and the environment around the respondent in the Carnoustie video. The responses showed that the meaning behind the framing and editing of the image was as significant to the research as would be more traditional aspects such as the transcribed words of the interviewee and an account of the policy context of teacher education placements in Scotland. It is clear that the material is not reducible to standard modes of representation, and that further presentation and dissemination will need to take account of this. Insights are to be found both in the words of the student and in my artistic response to a particular time and place. For instance the research produces an insight to the way that 'distant' is itself an expressive term for a place that is distinctly homely to the students concerned. And most significantly, it is an insight gained from the research presentation itself, which loses force and meaning if it is reduced to simple text.

As I continue to reflect on my practice, the study is continuing. There will be no obvious endpoint. I am reminded of a large canvas hanging in my lounge. At the time of painting I was confident that the painting was finished. Over the years I have developed the urge to make changes deterred only by the glass covering. I have changed since creating the artwork. Nothing is static. We are all stardust. This process of reflection interrogates the whole self of the researcher not just the part focused on the technicalities of teacher education.

The Cosmos Project: using performance, narrative and new media technologies to support young children's understanding of complex scientific topics[1]

Nettie Scriven, Peter Rumney and Iryna Kuksa

The Cosmos Project aims to explore the use of narrative and performative languages as well as new media technologies in relation to delivering complex scientific topics to school children aged three to six. The fulcrum of the project is found in the theatre performances. They are preceded by a series of creative collaborations with a wide range of partners and followed by a lengthy evaluation. At the time of writing the performances have taken place (March and May 2009) and the evaluation is ongoing.

The roots of our work can be found in the Theatre in Education movement (Jackson 1993) in which performers see themselves as 'actor-teachers', rather than simply as 'actors'. Currently we see ourselves as within the broad movement known as Theatre for Young People. We are a research and learning company. Each show is developed through reflective practice in smaller Research and Development laboratories, over a two year period. We work with a wide range of partners across the disciplines. As a Learning Company, we protect time to reflect upon our practice as part of creating the performances, and the education programmes that support them. We take the time to incubate ideas. We take risks in a practice-based research culture of reflection.

The Cosmos Project has developed from our previous work (Dragon Breath 2003–4 and Icarus 2005–7), examining how theatre in its most interactive forms can enable young people to connect with complex scientific ideas and explore ethical and moral issues. We are currently developing our practice working with scientists. The project explores Solomon's (1999) view that learners can develop their understanding of science through creative narratives instead of through an emphasis on memorizing precise scientific definitions. The project also examines the nature of didacticism in the performative context. Our aim is to maximize the engagement of our very young audiences through kinaesthetic activities during the performance, connecting with their emotional development which is in the early stages of 'looking beyond themselves'. We explore the potential for breaking the boundaries of audience participation by young children: how far they can be both spectator and 'spect-actor', interacting with the performers and with the staging of the performance.

We use the multi-layered and multiple languages of theatre to communicate with young people, making something visceral and very present to stimulate engagement on different levels and in different ways. We also engage with young people through our visual aesthetic. Different visual narratives unfold alongside adventurous and challenging texts. We fuse traditional technologies (e.g. puppetry and object theatre) with new technologies, such as digital media. The work is on both an intimate and on an epic scale. We explore the poetic and the vernacular together.

The goal here is to make a highly layered performance which includes 'awe and wonderment' and also enables the young people to form opinions through their emotions (ultimately developing their emotional intelligence), and to access complex scientific ideas through the use of different learning styles (see Gardner 1983) supported by multiple performative forms such as: (i) the interactivity of (abstract) dance narrative with (linear) verbal narrative text; (ii) the fusion of English (poetic) narrative and traditional South Asian rhythmical structures (Konokol); (iii) the congruency between Contemporary Dance with traditional Baratnathyam Indian Dance; and (iv) the relationship between the digital space and the crafted world of the object.

Our research investigates how successful we have been in our aims. It is both reflection *in* action and reflection *on* action (Schön 1991). We use reflection *in* action as we involve our partners, who include children, teachers, scientists, other professional artists and also university students and lecturers in theatre design and performance. The children are especially significant in the process of developing the work. We work with them to discover what is of interest to them, what is of value in their world experience. We do this through sustained relationships with particular groups over many months. For example, the themes, characters, issues and imagery of the plays come directly from the interdisciplinary arts workshops we run with children in school, whatever their age and whatever the subject matter. In addition to our own perceptions as artists, we are keen to understand the audiences' heads and hearts through the creative work we do with them.

We use reflection *on* action by systematically evaluating our work, focusing especially on the arts components that were specifically designed in. Our research question is: How far does the fusion of performance languages, and the active participation of the children within the performance, enable scientific understanding of the cosmos?

To answer the question, we focus on the following aspects of our work:

- the *active participation* of children within the performance, maximizing their *engagement with scientific questions and understanding*;
- the creation of *spectacle* to engender *awe and wonderment*, and to produce *memorable experiences* thus motivating learning;
- the fusion of performance languages, enabling greater access to ideas through engagement with *different learning styles*;
- the opportunity for *empathy* with human experience, thus supporting children to develop their *emotional intelligence*.

We evaluate these different aspects in a range of ways. We assess their participation as demonstrated by the children's sitting and watching, responding to questions and asking questions. We gauge their scientific understanding by exploring changes in children's concepts of many (planets), distance (planets, stars), inquiry, etc. We try to find out what fascinated them: what moments they remember. We consider how best to characterize these moments as, for example, spectacle, participation or human story. In relation to empathy, we try to find out which of the characters and planets the children remembered and what they remembered about them. We ask the teachers about their perceptions of all of these and also about learning styles. The techniques we use include: staff observation during the show; staff questionnaires; children using video diaries, video booths and the chatter-sphere; group discussions; and both before and after the show the use of an interactive set of concentric circles mapping space from home to planet with the children.

The impact of digital technology on our sense of our selves[2]

Sara Giddens and Simon Jones

Since 1997, through a series of intermedial collaborations with musicians, video and sonic artists, Bodies in Flight have progressively interrogated the impact of digital technologies on our sense of our selves and our inter-relationships with others, and how those technologies can be used in performance to expose this intimate process of incorporation into the human psyche – what Bodies in Flight call 'second-naturing'. This series of works has produced a sustained contemplation on contemporary human experience as *interstices in-between* various discursive fields and their related technologies. The following dialogue reflects on the series to date.

SARA GIDDENS: I remember being somewhat fearful of working with technology. Understanding technology as that industrial, then analogue now digital, beast resulting ultimately in all that heavy metal cluttering up the rehearsal rooms exacerbated by the need to hump it about and then wait for it to start up, break down and then start up again! Reassuringly, I could perceive that the body was indeed a technology in amongst all those others, in fact I could see the body itself as an assemblage of very practical, and multifarious and wondrous technologies. I could hear the production of language itself as a technology, as an example of *the cleft cleaving* as we called it. The *natural* and the learnt technology, of the tongue and the co-ordination of its sixteen muscles all having to work consensually and very hard, particularly in any Bodies in Flight show! Over time the rehearsal studio became a place to explore the different capacities of each technology, each element, and each separate line of flight and of course inevitably the gaps in between them.

SIMON JONES: In order to begin to unpack the density of the basic event-ness of performance, so that audience-spectators could disentangle themselves from its enveloping, white-hot interstices, we turned to Brecht. He had proposed in the 1920s a set of estrangements whereby the audience-spectators would be able to put themselves *as if* at a distance from the events unfolding on stage. By opening up the actual gaps both between and within media inherent in the theatrical experience itself, Brecht intended to open up the possibilities of engagement. This separation of the elements of performance was the basic aesthetic strategy we used in *Do the Wild Thing!* We later discovered that it had opened up the Pandora's Box of media in general, and the technologies that facilitated them, as a means of accessing the discontinuities of experience in general *as the basis for a performance of self in particular*.

SARA GIDDENS: As we reflected on all of our work (Giddens and Jones. 2001) we came to understand more fully that what had been drawing our attention, fuelling our desire, was this re-combining of choreography and text to create opportunities for articulations 'when words move and flesh utters'. Being at once fully and wholly in and in-between these technologies allowed an opening up of space-time that revealed those rich and fascinating blind spots. I was where I wanted to be: here with these real, fleshy, sweaty, wondrous bodies amidst the sound of [t]his poetry: the image and the sound, seeing and hearing, a making visible and being heard – a duet.

SIMON JONES: This separation *hear-see* became the fundamental principle of Bodies in Flight's work: from it flowed not only a working method, but a series of philosophical enquiries into what it means to be human amidst the technological.

SARA GIDDENS: In *Constants* (1998) two different performers were up close and very visible. This time the audience-spectators were seated individually in a broad sweep spiralling inwards, with *She*[ila] Gilbert and Patricia Breatnach moving in between them. *She* finally reaches the spiral's dead centre as Patricia exits with a final magnificent rush of youthful energy out of the furthest door. *Constants* was a show about memory and love, and, of course, that inevitable coupling – a loss of love.

The palpable presence of Sheila (then in her seventies) is my own overarching memory of this show: as I close my eyes I can still sense her. The frailty of a body, now more present than ever, a body beginning to fail, to fail to behave how its owner wanted it to behave, technically anyway. *She* used the walls and backs of chairs for support and her own physical 'capacities' became one structuring principle for the work itself. The other was the creation of the material through duets.

Emerging out of a later work – *Who By Fire* (2004) – we made *The Triptych: Who by Fire* to try to understand, to find out more about how I make live work. Ironically it brimmed over with the most personal, most human, most emotive material I had ever worked with – the movements and sounds of my daughter in and alongside these big emotive scenes full of power and movement and immense beauty (in its deepest often difficult form). It became a space-time for a gathering of memories of my own and others. It felt like we were finally dancing in time.

SIMON JONES: With *Who by Fire* we began to understand that this double work of separating and then bundling back together was a rich and powerful means of accessing or disclosing a generalized mood of together-aloneness in contemporary experience of self, enabled by the ubiquity of media technologies, of apparently increased intimacy and exposure and exacerbated feelings of disassociation and isolation. We combined our various concerns – the dissolving of the body's integrity, the opening up of the senses' aporia, face-to-face with our auditor-spectators. Our primary principling became a *de-second-naturing* – in effect a deconstruction of our commonsense of the everyday, an extension of Brechtian estrangement into the very interiority of the self, so that everything we thought we knew so intimately we did not even have to think about it, we simply did and felt it, is de-naturalized and once more made strange to us, even the very way we each walk or talk.

The self in the research

It is easy to see some ways in which the selves of the researchers in the examples above have influenced and been influenced by their research. Gemmell writes about his identity *as* an art and design teacher educator and *as* an artist, explaining how that complex identity influences the direction of the research. Scriven, Rumney and Kuksa talk of the themes, characters, issues and imagery being developed in sustained relationships with particular groups of children, and that these combine with 'our own perceptions as artists'. Giddens and Jones describe their whole project as revolving round an exploration of their selves and identities. But it is not just that the researchers acknowledge the role of the self. We, their readers, can see something of the way that their relationships with others (student teachers, child audiences, friends, family) have influenced those selves in ways that make a difference to their research processes. We are aware of their embodied selves through their specific visual and visceral responses. We can see something of how their selves have become what they were not and, as the research develops further, will become what they are not yet. The selves of the different researchers disclose themselves (to use Arendt's terminology) in how they give accounts of their research.

The model given in this chapter proposed six elements of self. Each of the elements of the researchers' selves can be seen in their different research projects. The model of research proposed that there are different analytical stages in a research process, though one of them, 'data collection' may be missing in some cases. While some of the more obvious connections between the selves and the research are easily visible, it would be impossible in the space of a short chapter to show how far each element of the self is implicated in all the various stages of research for each of the examples. Instead a few indicative connections are drawn from each example. I begin by looking at the connections from the point of view of the elements of the self.

'Each self is unique and its response to circumstance is not determined.' The different selves of the researchers can be seen in the actions described in each of the examples, and in the explanations given for them. This unique selfhood is very obvious in the case of Giddens and Jones, who share the same set of circumstances, but who have very distinct voices and different responses, each one contributing to the development of the performances. The uniqueness of selfhood is least obvious in the piece by Scriven, Rumney and Kuksa, probably because it was written in a joint voice in the academic genre. This genre tends to obscure individuality, especially in joint writing, where what is said necessarily expresses only those parts of their academic selves which overlap and agree.

'We are always in a state of becoming, always unfinished.' Gemmell and Giddens specifically refer to this. Gemmell comments that there is no obvious endpoint to the research as both he and his context change. As he puts it, 'We are all stardust'. Giddens reports that she began the project 'somewhat fearful of working with technology'. By the final stages of the project, she talks in very confident tones about using technology in the video, *The Triptych: Who by Fire*: 'It became a space-time for a gathering of memories of my own and others. It felt like we were finally dancing in time.'

'We make ourselves in relation to others.' All three accounts are full of references to others. Sometimes the relationships are more personal than structural. The relationship between Giddens and Jones is like this. They are choreographer and writer, respectively, but the account shows that the connection is created through the individual responses to each other's perspectives, rather than through formal delineation of roles. In contrast, Gemmell gives an account in which structural relationships influence the direction of the research. Both sets of his professional relationships, as a tutor and as an educational researcher, have a powerful influence on the starting point for the research and on its subsequent development.

'The circumstances that influence – and are influenced by – a self include specificities of time and place.' All three of these accounts are embedded in their specific time (the early twenty-first century) and place (Scotland or Nottingham, in the UK). Scriven, Rumney and Kuksa, in particular, take care to show the historical and location specificity of the research. They show how its rationale and methods derive from particular events and movements within theatre in the UK in the second half of the twentieth century.

'The world is understood through the body and also perceptions of our bodies constrain our relationships with others.' The accounts presented in the examples demonstrate some ways in which the world is understood through the body and how that impinges on the research. Gemmell's account depends on his visual appreciation of, and response to, his surroundings. The accounts are less reflective about how the bodies of the researchers are perceived by others. However it is possible to see how some such constraints exist. For Scriven, Rumney and Kuksa, the young children they work with, whether as partners or subjects, will inevitably react strongly to their initial perceptions of the adults as performers, observers or teachers; as friendly or frightening; as boring or interesting. All such perceptions will be structured by the bodies the adults present.

'A self constructs itself in response to the social and political power structures it inhabits.' None of the researchers comment specifically on their gender, race, social class or other socio-political influence. So any judgements about this must remain speculative in relation to these examples and their reporting.

Having looked at each element of the self, I now go on to give a few similar illustrations for how each stage of research is affected by elements of the self. This is to approach the same argument but from a different perspective. To emphasize this convergence, in each case one of the illustrations is the same as one given earlier.

Focus: The examples show how the focus of the research is influenced by the unique and undetermined responses of the individual researchers. Gemmell's focus is influenced by his visual responses. Jones's response to the developing inquiry, unlike Giddens', is strongly philosophical and theoretical. He describes the development of the inquiry in these terms. The longer piece of which this account is an excerpt, draws on Böhm, Foucault, Heidegger, Levinas and Merleau-Ponty. Giddens, on the other hand, draws only on Adorno.

Rationale: The rationale given for the pieces of research shows the significance of professional relationships and roles. Gemmell describes how his role as a teacher educator drove the reasons for embarking on the research. Scriven, Rumney and Kuksa explain the background to their research in terms of how they see their professional relationships positioned within the Theatre in Education movement.

Method: Scriven, Rumney and Kuksa emphasize the significance of theatricality, (awe and wonder) in their work. It is possible to imagine that the use of theatre in science education need not be so theatrical but still be effective. But to downplay the significance of theatricality would be to deny their self-identities within *Theatre in Education*. Giddens and Jones's method of working is clearly dependent on the relationship between them, as noted earlier.

Data collection: Gemmell shows that the method of data collection was influenced by his own personal responses, and how those responses have been shaped by time and place. Fifty years ago he would possibly have been using a camera, and a hundred and fifty years ago, a sketch book. Giddens' memory work draws on her embodiment: her visceral reactions are part of the evidence and she uses her body to help her remember clearly. She says, 'As I close my eyes I can still sense her.'

Analysis: In all three examples the research is presented and discussed within the context of change, of the researchers' changing identities through reflection and artistic interventions.

Presentation, dissemination: All the examples are ongoing, and, as yet, presentation and dissemination has been largely through academic conferences and seminars. The last example, from Giddens and Jones, is the most complete, and will shortly be published as a chapter in an edited collection (Giddens and Jones, 2010).

Troubling issues for arts-based, practice-based researchers

Some researchers, especially those who model themselves on scientists such as experimental physicists or chemists, often criticize personal involvement in research. This is because they believe that such research is inevitably partial. As detailed in Borgdorff (2009a and Chapter 3), this has become something to which arts-based, practice-based researchers need to pay attention. Partial is an interesting word, with three distinct, though related, meanings in the *Merriam-Webster Online Dictionary*, all of which are used in criticism of the involvement of self in arts-based, practice-based research:

- of or relating to a part rather than the whole : not general or total (a partial solution);
- inclined to favour one party more than the other: biased;
- markedly fond of someone or something – used with to (partial to pizza).

As I shall argue in this section, these criticisms derive from too narrow a view of knowledge and of ways in which it relates to research.

The first definition of 'partial' is used to criticize the context specificity of much arts-based, context-based research. Research which is focused on arts practices must be context-specific, because the context is dependent on specific arts and practices carried out by researchers whose selves are involved in creating and maintaining that context. This is sometimes cast as an issue of 'generalizability and transferability', as discussed below.

The close involvement of the self is also criticized when research presents judgements about a human situation. It may be argued that participation in the research context means that judgement cannot be dispassionate so the research cannot be trusted to be other than one person's idiosyncratic view, coloured by one's preconceptions and self interests. Inevitably, or so the critique goes, it will be biased, as in the second definition of 'partial'. At the very least, as in the third definition, the researchers will be personally fond of the participants or have a personal preference for the ideas and artefacts produced in the research – and so, as the word 'fond' implies, cannot be impersonal. This critique relies on a mistaken conflation of dispassionate, impersonal research with the production of unbiased, rigorous knowledge in which others can have confidence, can trust, and can then find useful and relevant in their own contexts. The issue of trustworthy knowledge is discussed below.

The critique may appear to be common sense, but these are complex epistemological and ethical issues and, as I shall show, the critique is misplaced. The ways in which the self is involved in arts-based, practice-based research does not take away from its rigour or relevance. In the rest of this section I take each definition in turn.

Generalizability and transferability

The models of physical and biological sciences have been hugely influential on other areas of human knowledge, to the extent that in some quarters, only research which could apply to anybody, anywhere is thought to be valid and valuable. However this is a mistake. There are two serious problems with it which are related to (1) the issue of the scope of knowledge and (2) the issue of how far generalizability is significant in any particular research project.

The first problem arises because models influenced by the physical and biological sciences tend to confuse the generalizability of knowledge with its scope. To put this another way, there is a tendency to ignore the question, 'How general is generalizable?' For knowledge to be generalizable it needs to be universally applicable but only across a defined field, as Onora O'Neill convincingly shows (1996). This field must be delineated in terms of its scope in place and time. To put this another way, it is always necessary to address the question, 'across what field is the knowledge applicable?' There is knowledge that might be universally applicable globally, but there is also knowledge that is universally applicable not globally but locally, nationally or across a continent or throughout a culture. It may be applicable this year, or this century, or for all human time. Clearly there are differences between the sciences such as physics and chemistry, and the humanities (including arts-based research) and social sciences (including practice-based research) with regard to the scope of knowledge. Within the humanities and social sciences very little worthwhile knowledge would have the scope of the sciences.

The second problem with generalizability arises because these models assume a view of what it is for knowledge to be relevant beyond the context in which it was first articulated. It assumes that knowledge must be generalizable before it can be widely relevant or useful. This is mistaken. When the purposes of knowledge are considered, the nature of the mistake becomes clear. In the sciences the goal is to discover facts, propositions and laws and explanations for them. But much knowledge is not of this kind or for this purpose. The humanities and social sciences have a much wider set of possible purposes. Beyond facts and theories, they are also interested in practices and skills. They want to provide ways of understanding current contexts and to provide insights, fresh ways of perceiving and acting in the world and to foster wisdom.

Arts-based, practice-based researchers are able to develop knowledge and ways of disseminating it which informs the development of practices and skills of people in similar but not identical contexts. Similarly they are able to provide new understandings and creative insights. Indeed these kinds of knowledge (often termed wisdom, sometimes professional wisdom) need not address themselves to generalities at all. Smith (2008) argues persuasively that poetry and fiction can be valuable forms of knowledge for educators. For much arts-based, practice-based researchers, it is not a case of finding contexts which are identical. Rather, it is being able to explain the context of the research so that the audience can judge how it relates to their own. For instance, Gemmell's work may appear to apply narrowly to a very specific situation in teacher education in one country. However, it would also be relevant in some respects to another country's teacher educators, in which it is necessary to visit schools at a great distance from universities in centres of population. This is not a matter of general similarities. The research would be irrelevant in much of the United Kingdom but it might be relevant in apparently very different countries, for example Botswana or Australia. How far Scriven, Rumney and Kuksa's work would be relevant to Botswana with its very different cultural history is difficult to say. However it would almost certainly be relevant to Australia. Giddens and Jones's work appears to be very much embedded in a specific technological, cultural and theoretical context. However it may be that their concept of 'de-second-naturing' as it presents itself through the creative deployment of technology might travel just as well as has technology. In all three cases the selves of the researchers would inevitably present themselves to the audience and would affect how the audience perceived the relevance of the projects to themselves, and so how far they could gain knowledge from the research.

Participant research, value positions and trustworthy knowledge

This section begins with a consideration of participant research as a source of knowledge. The view that participant research is not trustworthy tends to be linked with an argument that being a participant in something entails being unable to view it dispassionately and neutrally. Therefore, so the argument continues, it is impossible to make a reasoned assessment of the evidence, with the result that the conclusions are unreliable and there can be little confidence placed in them. But this view makes two contestable assumptions. It assumes first that an outside observer would be neutral, and that such neutrality is desirable. It assumes second that being part of a human relationship interferes with judgements connected to the relationship. Neither assumption stands up to scrutiny. The view also ignores some crucial ethical issues underlying participant research: the significant differences between researching *on*, *for* or *as* a subject of the research.

With respect to the first assumption, the call for neutrality can refer to either or both political or moral standpoints. It can also refer to a researcher having a personal and/or professional stake in the outcomes of the research. So critics who are looking for value neutrality address themselves to research which takes a clear political or moral stance. There is a suspicion that researchers inevitably find only what their initial position would lead them to expect, that, for instance, feminists expect and then discover knowledge about gender oppression, while postcolonialists expect and then discover knowledge about the baleful effects of globalized injustice. Artists who hold the position that they should develop their practice by learning, for example, from young children or from communities they are working with, expect and then discover that this is what happens. A similar effect can be seen in performers researching performances in which they have invested enthusiasm, time and resources.

I argue to the contrary. The call for value neutrality begs the question whether it is possible to be a value-neutral observer. Like many others, I take the position that it is impossible to research any human context disinterestedly (Griffiths 1998). There is no 'God's eye view' (Haraway 1991) or 'view from nowhere' (Nagel 1989). Researchers not only take political and ethical stances, but, being human beings, they also inhabit them and are not fully aware of them. Only when political and moral positions are acknowledged or exhibited can strategies be found to enable the outcomes to be judged rigorous or otherwise. Such strategies do not entail that it is better to be an outsider than a participant researcher.

The second assumption, 'personal human relations interfere with judgements', is as unwarranted as the first. We all learn to make judgements, including academic ones, within human relationships. Indeed, only if we understand the meanings and nuances of a human situation, can we be in a position to assess it at all. It is not necessary to be a participant, but in some cases being a participant is the only way to understand some of the subtleties of a research context. Working as a participant in research can help in other ways too. Bridges says:

> Simply, some social conditions and relationships are more likely than others to enable people to be open and honest about their experience, their perceptions and their feelings – and hence to enable them to contribute to a fuller and more truthful understanding of that situation. Hence, if researchers allow their work to be governed by principles which support those sort of social conditions and relationships, they will be able to produce better research.
>
> (Bridges 2003)

Further, when the researcher is part of the context, or a focus of the research, as in autoethnography or some reflective practices, he or she is the only one with access to some of the knowledge required.

Participant research is not only an epistemological issue. It is also an ethical one because it is about human relationships and how one person involves another person in their projects. Outsider research may be research 'on' or research 'for' others. This is something done to a person by another person, though in the latter case it is intended altruistically. In both cases there is a human relationship created, whether or not this is recognized by the researcher. Subjects of outsider research notice their position and its relative powerlessness. They may accept this. Or they may resent it and find ways to sabotage or subvert the research. Participant research may be research 'for' but it may also be research 'with' the subjects of the research and it may be research 'as' the subject of the research. In the last of these, the relationship is one of a self to his or her own self and immediate personal circle.

Scrivens, Rumney and Kuksa are plainly researching 'with'. They are 'developing our practice working *with* scientists.' They say, 'We work *with* [the children] to discover what is of interest to them.' Giddens and Jones are researching 'as', unsurprisingly in what can be seen as autoethnographic research project. They describe their personal reactions and theoretical journey: 'I remember being somewhat fearful of working with technology'; 'We turned to Brecht'. They invite us, the readers, as they invited the audience for the performances, to respond with personal reactions and understandings. Gemmell is, in a sense, researching both 'for' and 'as', since he is interested in what it is like to be a student in a placement that is homely to them but distant to the tutor. In a way he can become an advocate *for* them. But he is also interested in his own response *as* a lecturer doing distance placements.

Scrivens, Rumney and Kuksa are clearly participants in many ways in their research. They work collaboratively with others 'to understand their heads and hearts'. It is likely that the people they work with are able to express their perceptions in a way that is different and that is probably more accurate and sincere than if they were outsiders dropping in only for the purpose of research. Similarly, Gemmell has ease of access to the schools where his interviews take place, partly due to long established relationships. This access would not be available to outsiders. Similarly he has a pre-existing relationship to the students which will, of course, affect what they say, but which will also enable them to communicate easily to somebody who thoroughly understands the context. Moreover, while he is not the sole arbiter of the meanings of the videos of landscape, he has a particular knowledge of some of the reasons for his choice of frame and subject. Giddens and Jones are even more closely identified with what they research. Without their own understanding of the history of the project any assessment of the project and its meaning would be impoverished.

Bias

I have been arguing that arts-based, practice-based research can be trustworthy and transferable. But not all such research is good. Some of it is biased, something that all researchers condemn. Avoiding bias is best understood in ethical terms as academic virtue. This concept, which originates with Aristotle, has been widely taken up, most recently as Bridges usefully summarizes it. He presents the following list as examples of academic virtue which might be widely agreed:

> Careful attention to argument and evidence; thoroughness; honesty; humility with regard to one's own knowledge and respectfulness with regard to the knowledge claims of others; responsiveness to criticism; perseverance.
>
> (Bridges 2003)

Exercising these virtues counts as academic rigour and guards against bias, and the audience for the research has a right to expect that a researcher has exercised academic virtue and guarded against bias. That is, the audience needs the tools to assess how far to trust that a researcher has not skewed the evidence for self-interested reasons, and has been thorough in carrying out procedures of collection, analysis and presentation of the material. Recently, there has been a flurry of work in virtue epistemology, some of it focusing on skills as well as beliefs (Brady and Pritchard 2006; Greco 2006).

Since all research is affected by the selves (relationships, circumstances, perspectives and reactions) of the researcher, making these as clear as possible to the audience is one way of exercising academic virtue and removing bias. It may not be obvious how this is to be done. Nobody can be transparent to themselves, especially with regard to their basic assumptions and perspectives on the world. We have our being in relation to an indeterminate number of social groups. Moreover we are caught in social and political contexts that we cannot fully understand. We are embodied which means, as Merleau-Ponty (1962) pointed out, seeing the world while being unable to see ourselves. Arendt argues that it is to others that we reveal our identities when we act.

Reflective practice and reflexivity are two of the ways in which the audience can be given a means by which to evaluate the influence of a researcher's values and perspectives. Roughly, 'reflective practice' attaches more to the relational self embedded in time and place, and as becoming what it is not yet. 'Reflexivity' attaches more to the relational, embodied self in a specific social and political context: to his or her individual perspectives and positionality.

Reflective practice is associated with a set of research practices, including Reflective Practice, Action Research, Action Inquiry and Self-Study. Autoethnography may also be a reflective practice as in the case of Giddens and Jones. Reflective practice is carried out by the self or selves who are found in the thick of it. It is a passionate inquiry (Dadds 1995) which uses a range of means of symbolizing personal and inexplicit understandings, attitudes and reactions. For instance, Cancienne and Snowber (2003) discuss how this occurs through dance as well as through writing. Doloughan (2002) discusses how reflection on a range of multi-modal projects in art and design required multi-modal expression. Furthermore, reflective practice is a means of tracking the changing self as it becomes what it was not. The elements of time and space are crucial. The specific and changing context is explored, as reflections in one place connect with thinking in another, over time, with all the changes in the self and its practice acknowledged.

Reflexivity is linked to the social/political, relational self becoming what it is not yet. Exercising reflexivity involves paying explicit attention to the specific perspectives of the researcher. Perspective refers to the context which influences what a person can see and how they interpret it. It may indicate theoretical positions especially those which indicate political value systems (e.g. feminist, socialist, Marxist, anti-racist, post-colonial and queer research), and it may indicate positionality which refers, more narrowly, to the social and political landscape inhabited by a researcher (e.g. gender, nationality, race, religion, sexuality, [dis]abilities, social class and social status). It also involves making explicit those personal and professional relationships which may have influenced the research.

Reflexivity requires an attempt by the researcher to be self conscious about his or her own (or the research team's, and/or the research funder's) social, political and value position and positionality, in relation to how these might have influenced the design, execution and interpretation of the theory, data and conclusions (Marcus 1994; Griffiths 1998; Greenbank 2003). Such self-consciousness needs to acknowledge that the self is not fully transparent to itself, so enough description of the researcher needs to be given for the audience to make judgements about his or her social and political positionality. This is especially relevant for personal narrative (in whatever medium). In particular, it is this attempt at self consciousness about value positions, positionality and personal relationships – while all the time acknowledging the inevitable incompleteness of the attempt – which distinguishes autoethnography and reflective action research from autobiography or the writing of a journal.

Conclusions

My argument in this chapter has been that an understanding of the self and its place in research is crucial in the carrying out and presentation of arts-based, practice-based research. In arts-based, practice-based research the self is inescapable, because the person creating, responding to, working on, developing or evaluating performances, artefacts and practices is central to those activities. Sometimes, as in autoethnography, the self is the main focus of the research. I have shown that the model of self is crucial in that researchers need to be aware of the interaction between self and research at all stages, just to do unbiased, trustworthy and transferable research. But they also need to be able to deflect criticisms from other researchers working within the experimental and data driven paradigms of the physical sciences.

The self is best understood, I have suggested, as being embodied and embedded in both physical and socio-political time and place. The chapter also shows that arts-based, practice-based research has a crucial role to play in the world. It is not just another attempt to get knowledge or understanding, important as that is. It is this kind of research that stands against the tendency in our post-modern society to valorize the impersonal, the byte of information, the technical fix, the obsession with measurement and the elimination of risk, luck and chance. Arts-based, practice-based research upholds the personal, the creative, the imaginative and the passionate, the human. In short, it provides an essential reminder of the humanity at the core of society and its well-being.[3]

Notes

1 Part of this account is excerpted from Scriven *et al.* (2009). Cosmos is a partnership project between Dragon Breath Theatre, Narrative and Interactive Arts, NTU and CELS, NTU Alumni Fund, Leicester Theatre Trust and Dance 4 National Dance Agency in the East Midlands.
2 This account is excerpted from Giddens and Jones (2010).
3 The author would like to acknowledge the contribution of Tony Gemmell, Nettie Scriven, Peter Rumney, Iryna Kuksa, Sara Giddens and Simon Jones to the writing of this chapter.

11

ADDRESSING THE 'ANCIENT QUARREL': CREATIVE WRITING AS RESEARCH

Jen Webb and Donna Lee Brien

Introduction

Creative writing as a university-based discipline is simultaneously an art form and a part of the humanities. Its focus is the production of works of high literary quality across many forms and genres, including poetry, fiction, creative non-fiction, life writing, ficto-criticism, scripts for film, television, radio and theatre, digital texts, and genres that cross into professional writing and journalism such as travel, food and historical writing. The study of creative writing as a tertiary level discipline may include close reading of published texts, but the discipline's focus on the *production* of texts and, indeed, the types of texts themselves, distinguishes it from other disciplines.

Despite the discipline's focus on creative production, it is rare for creative writing to be housed within an art school, alongside other art forms such as the visual arts, craft, design, performing arts, film, television and electronic media production. Although its practice, traditions, orientations and trajectories lack a good fit with the logic of most faculties of the humanities, this is where it is more commonly housed, alongside the disciplines of communication, literature, cultural and media studies. The problem with this arrangement is that the research orientations of creative writing and the humanities disciplines have little in common. As Paul Carter points out, what the makers of artworks do is productively reflect on the creative thinking that created their works, integrating this usually unarticulated knowledge with the craft 'wisdom' of the artist to retrieve the 'intellectual work that usually goes missing in translation' during the process of making works of art (Carter 2004: xi–xiii). Researchers in the humanities, in contrast, offer exposition, critique or analysis of the finished artefact, and cannot usefully rationalize the creative process. Nonetheless, writing is often collapsed into the humanities, probably because the medium used in writing is the same as that used in humanities' disciplines – words, sentences and linguistic construction.

Perhaps as a result of these institutional arrangements, and because the medium of writing results in outputs that can seem to comply with traditional research products in traditional forms (written language), the particular ways in which creative writing is mobilized for research outcomes has received rather less attention than its cousins in the disciplines of visual and performing arts or in the humanities (and especially in literary and cultural studies). However, the problem of whether – and, if so, what – creative writing can deliver in the knowledge domain, and how this can be achieved, has a very ancient lineage. Famously, the problem begins with Plato, and what in the *Republic* he termed 'the ancient quarrel of poetry and philosophy' (Plato 1924: Republic 607b). His answer was to expel the art form from his ideal city on the grounds that it was unreliable, and based on intuition and mimesis rather than on actuality and philosophical reason.[1] A generation later, Aristotle articulated the opposite point of view: that poetry – or, more generally, mimetic creative works – do offer clarity and have the potential to generate knowledge, because (as he wrote) an audience's pleasure in mimesis is bound up with the opportunities it offers for learning (Aristotle 1984: Poetics 1448b–9b). This division has continued down through the millennia, and to a large extent continues to inform the positioning of writer-academics in contemporary universities.

In this chapter, we trace the ancient quarrel between poetry and philosophy in the contemporary context of practice-led research in order to: assess which offers the best account of being (and, therefore, knowledge); outline the context in which writing operates as both knowledge and aesthetic discipline; and discuss the issues, opportunities and problems associated with contemporary creative writing in the knowledge environment.

The ancient quarrel in the present context: research imperatives for writers in universities

For creative writers based in universities, the problem of knowledge has taken on great significance because of governmental and institutional imperatives for all parts of the academic community to contribute research outcomes and outputs. In most industrialized countries, how to measure and evaluate the level and quality of research produced by universities has emerged as a key higher education policy issue over the past years (OECD 1998). At the same time as public funding has decreased or otherwise been constrained, the higher education sector has expanded and demands on this funding have escalated. In response, governments have implemented increasingly complex and, seemingly, ever-shifting mechanisms to allocate funding in relation to measurable university research output and/or performance. These mechanisms include the Research Assessment Exercises (RAE) in the UK and Hong Kong, the Excellence in Research for Australia programme (ERA), and the Performance Based Research Funding programme (PBRF) in New Zealand. As these and other higher education quality assurance mechanisms are developed and refined, they are increasing in scope, level of organization and powers, and are consequently permeating all aspects of activity in the higher education sector. These powers include not only auditing, evaluation and recommending 'more rigorous criteria ... based around strengthening the link between teaching and research as a defining characteristic of university accreditation and reaccreditation' (Bradley *et al.* 2008: xxi), but also applying sanctions, including reduced funding and de-accreditation, against higher education providers that do not measure up against these standards (see, for example, Gillard 2009). University research rankings are now not only publicly available, but leagues tables of institutional and subject results are widely published and discussed in the press and low achieving departments are under threat (notably, despite an international campaign to save it, the Centre for Contemporary Cultural Studies at the University of Birmingham was closed in 2002 after it received a 3a result in the RAE).

The contemporary environment is thus one that, under the 'carrot and stick' approach to research management, demands a measurable level of institutionally recognized research outputs from all academics, regardless of the discipline in which they practise. The stick is, of course, the risk of sanctions; the carrot includes those benefits that attend academics and disciplines engaged in research. These take the form of institutional, cultural, symbolic and intellectual capital: that is, the resources that 'define the chances of profit in a given field' (Bourdieu 1991: 230–1). A discipline that can boast a body of substantial research projects and research outcomes acquires institutional capital in the form of recognition as a research body. Research-active members of that discipline acquire cultural capital in the form of expertise; symbolic capital in the form of, say, the prestige inherent in publications in high impact journals; and intellectual capital in the form of the knowledge that is then available to other members of that discipline. There is also, of course, economic capital – gaining the financial resources to conduct research, and any economic rewards that flow from that. Research, when strategically organized, can become a self-perpetuating system too, because the more research that is undertaken, the more likely it is that researchers will be able to identify further areas that need attention.

We note this because a result of the initiatives in this area is that academics have recognized not only that measurable research outcomes are part of university core business, but also that appointment, tenure and advancement depend on successes in this area. This has been a particularly significant shift for academics in the creative arts who in many cases were initially appointed to their university positions because of their art form expertise rather than their academic background. In creative writing, many of the early appointments to *academic* positions thus went to novelists, poets, scriptwriters or non-fiction authors of some professional standing. In the past decade, though, as a result of the institutional changes noted above, professional esteem has dipped in importance; prestige and credibility now more commonly rest on achieving a combination of scholarly *and* creative publication, research *and* art grant income, and postgraduate research student supervision/completion. What was previously largely a debate about the identity and value of the creative arts in universities has, therefore, taken on new impetus, and writer-academics have, as others have in the creative disciplines, begun to investigate their practice and analyse the ways in which their art form can also constitute a research methodology and generate reportable outputs.

There is a risk, in this move, that writer-academics might be captured by what is called *skholē*, a term whose original meaning refers to a place of leisure: the leisure involved in having time to learn and time for knowledge. Of course writers (like other artists) need a version of *skholē*, time to learn, make and reflect. But central to *skholē* is what Pierre Bourdieu terms the scholastic point of view (Bourdieu 1998: 127): the objectifying and universalizing perspective associated with the academy that, for Bourdieu, undermines practice because it turns it into an object for scholarly dissection rather than for creation. We may insist that our options are not only the false dichotomy of either compliance with the scholastic point of view, or a refusal to play the game of knowledge, but to take a different position: to make our work in a way that satisfies both aesthetic and scholarly imperatives. The research paradigm associated with creative practice is likely to offer this way through, and allow academic creative practitioners to marry their research and creative practice, or *skholē* and, say, *technē?*, in the interests of producing knowledge in a different but demonstrably valid way. Yet, for many within the system, and despite the increasing formal recognition of practice-based research, the fit between arts practice and research output is still uncomfortable; and, for many, a site of some anxiety. The ancient quarrel continues, then, to inform and inflect practice in the academy.

The ancient quarrel: origins and genealogy

It is of course Plato who is usually invoked as the father of the problem of the relationship between poetic and knowledge discourses. He wrote about this relationship, and more generally about the role of poetry in society, across a number of his works. For 'poetry' here we read 'creative writing' more generally – writing committed to the turn of phrase, the breath and pulse of a line, the imaginative presentation of an idea of actuality: writing that, in Plato's terms, is designed to enchant the mind and the senses rather than only delivering clear and reasoned communication.[2] But commentators often paint Plato in too negative a guise: in a number of places he wrote of the pleasures of poetry – and of art more generally – and of the contributions the arts can make to society. The *Phaedrus*, for instance, is not only a literary work in itself, but one that values the extra-rational. Socrates' Third Speech in that work is a paean to 'madness' – that is, a higher mode of thinking informed by desire, the effect on the poet of the divine, which generates a greater capacity to show and to know in the one so touched.[3] For Socrates (channelled by Plato), creative and non-rational practices enable a contribution to knowledge because the 'possession and madness from the Muses ... adorns ten thousand works of the ancients and so educates posterity' (Plato 1924: Phaedrus 244e–5a).

Thus, though many readers tend to recall only Plato's rejection of poetry as expressed in the *Republic*, on the grounds of its capacity to lure citizens away from rational thought, he clearly maintains a soft spot for creative practices and an awareness that the erotic drive associated with the extra-rational may allow doors to be opened and knowledges gained. Even in the *Republic*, where he has Socrates explicitly exclude poetry on the grounds that 'all poetical imitations are ruinous to the understanding of the hearers' (Plato 1924: Republic 595b), he does so with a certain regret, writing:

> let us assure our sweet friend and the sister arts of imitation that if she will only prove her title to exist in a well-ordered State we shall be delighted to receive her – we are very conscious of her charms; but we may not on that account betray the truth.
>
> (Plato 1924: Republic 607d)

That 'sweet friend', mimesis, could not of course prove her title; the divine madness of poetry's origin means that creative practice cannot finally be admitted to the ideal city; emotions and mimesis confound right thinking, and reason must, finally, in this argument, take the premier place.

Plato may have sparked this line of thought and laid out the grounds for the 'ancient quarrel', but his was not the last word on the subject. His work has generated a mass of volumes on the question of whether, and what, art can contribute to knowledge, and this discussion has established the context in which artists in the academy now work, one where creative practitioners seem obliged to take sides, and to commit to either the madness of art or the cool clear thinking of philosophy. In some important cases, assertions have been made that poetry has claims on both sides of the argument. In the sixteenth century, for example, Philip Sidney stated that poetry was 'the first light-giver to ignorance, and first nurse, whose milk by little and little enabled them to feed afterwards of tougher knowledges' (Sidney 1922 [c.1583]: 2): a view of poetry that combines inspiration and knowledge. In the final years of the eighteenth century, the early Romantics discussed philosophy as an incomplete form, and Friedrich Schlegel imagined a brave new world of collaboration between the arts and sciences (Schlegel 1971: 34). Ralph Waldo Emerson, a continent away and a century later, engaged not so much with Plato's 'ancient quarrel' as with his own conception of the 'old divorce' between poetry and nature – which he phrased as 'Nature and the mind' (Emerson 2009 [1876]: 52) – the harmony of which would support his imperative to achieve Intuitive Reason. In the twentieth century, C.P. Snow (who was himself both scientist and novelist) in his famed 1959 Rede Lecture argued passionately – and in a way reminiscent of Schlegel's point – that the lack of communication between the two spheres (the sciences and the humanities, which he called the 'two cultures' of modern society in his subsequent publication *The Two Cultures and the Scientific Revolution*), was significantly hindering the solving of the world's major problems. Australian poet Les Murray went even further in his lecture, 'The suspect captivity of the Fisher King', where he asserted that 'Any true poem is greater than the whole Enlightenment, more important and more sustaining of human life' (Murray 1997: 187).

Poets, then, insist that poetry is a knowledge discourse, though they rarely explain or provide evidence for this assertion. They do perform a useful function in pointing out the limits on philosophy and the need to infuse cold reason with intuition and passion. Typically, however, their view of knowledge is one that at best trembles on the edge of transcendentalism and is more closely affiliated with Romantic naïveté than with Enlightenment logic. Wallace Stevens, that superbly philosophical poet, took a critical view of this tendency, writing that 'After one has abandoned a belief in God, poetry is the essence that takes its place as life's redemption' (1990: 185). Certainly, the exchange of one form of magical thinking (religion) for another (art) can be seen in much of the writing about poetry and/as knowledge.

However, in the writings that result from this practice – that is, in the creative artefacts themselves – it is often possible to identify an approach to knowledge that does not rely on magical thinking, 'mere' intuition or affect. Poetry is, as the etymology of the word 'stanza' implies, associated with a 'standing place' or 'stopping point',[4] and thus affords a sort of viewing platform, a perspective from which to view what lies ahead before plunging down into it. In poem after poem it is possible to identify this pause in the flow of life, a perspective from which to view the world, and a position offered on that view. An example of this can be seen in the poem 'The eternity knot':

A twist of soft thread
gathers tangles
at the back
of the dusty kitchen drawer.
A figure-eight of string;
from *streng*, its root;
like *strength*. You know:
the tie that binds,
the safety line,
the knotty problem.
It's the simplest sign.
It's your baby curls
clipped, and twined,
and gently laid in mama's dresser drawer.
Soft hemp; or is it coir?
It's all the same to me
but see the care
that braids those blonde threads into time.
Now what twists in your gut?
What hangman's rope from Dickens
sways though disturbed-sleep nights?
– some twisted symbol, *da capo*;
the fugue starts
again / and again / and again.
It was Plato, or a Sanskrit scholar,
said a figure-eight means forever.
You can survive it once, twice,
even seven times;
and then you're done.

(Webb 2004: 32)

This poem was one of several products of a research project focused on the properties of being. Generated by questions associated with the nature of time and substance, it is an attempt to perceive and describe both the thing itself (the string) and ideas about the thing (in this case, being and time). Research methods employed include observation and reflection, archival investigation into related works of literature and philosophy, and practice-led work on imagery, lineation and expression. It is not an argument, but a way of seeing; still, it does incorporate a hypothesis about experiential reality – in this instance, the materiality of the experienced world and the problem of time and memory.

The non-transparent nature of the knowledge work that was involved in the making of a piece of creative writing may render it difficult to establish to what extent it can be said to contribute to knowledge, as opposed to it being simply a creative work. This is an ongoing concern and point of debate among writers in the academy, and also among the administrators and bureaucrats who determine what counts as research: in this way, the ancient quarrel retains its power and its capacity to influence both discourse and practice. A way through this may be offered by the cultural historian Nicholas Zurbrugg (2004), who in what again seems to echo and then develop Schlegel's notion of incomplete philosophy, suggests that in creative works we can see the presence of what Roland Barthes called 'prophetic technocreativity' (Barthes 1977: 67). That is to say, knowledge innovations emerge first in art works, and only subsequently emerge in philosophy. Paul Magee suggests something similar, raising:

> the possibility that a modern poem is not a knowledge-report, nor even a mode of self-expression, so much as a device for generating creative desire – the desire for meaning, for resolution, for further aesthetic experience, for an infinite number of things – in others.

> (Magee 2009)

This seems to invoke Plato and his conception of the link between divine madness, desire and knowledge; it also limits the knowledge contribution of a single creative work to a generative moment, one that does not offer knowledge in itself, but directs attention to questions that need to be asked, and understandings that need to be formulated.

Practice-led research and writing

A considerable body of work has been produced in the past decade or so to explore these issues and tease out the relationship between poetry (art) and philosophy (research). The so-called 'Strand Report' (Strand 1998) was a seminal Australian publication on the presence and impact of creative practice within universities. Since 1998, serious consideration of creative practice as research has increasingly marked academic publishing in the creative disciplines, and practice-led research has received an increasing level of formal attention both within the academic institution and from the publishing industry. This attention has been, in particular, in relation to the development of discourses and practices in writing schools in the UK, Australia, USA, Europe and more recently, South East Asia. In this, the understanding of the discipline of creative writing has moved from that of a practical craft that could be taught as such, to a tertiary level discipline framed by theory and methodology as well as a developing scholarly literature. This includes demonstrating that, as a discipline, creative writing is capable of combining conventional academic rigour with creative thought, or producing research with utility as well as art (and artefacts) of aesthetic value. While institutional, disciplinary and national policy and process contexts have had an impact on both the practices of writing, and writing as research, in tertiary institutions, creative writing academics have, in turn, contributed to discussions about, and definitions of, practice-led research.

While this also applies to other areas in the creative arts, there are specific epistemological and methodological issues associated with practice-led research in writing that do not apply, or not to the same extent, in the other creative fields. Because the creative medium is written language, creative writing does not readily permit the exploitation of performative or gestural research methods (such as those mostly associated with dance and music; see Haseman 2006a). Nor is the focus on tactility and materiality (mostly associated with the visual arts; see Carter 2004) particularly relevant to the more ephemeral, less tangible mode of creative practice that is writing. Thus, while creative writers do draw on the main body of literature on practice-led research, we have had to adapt and adopt other methods and modes of approach. Embodied and material thinking must be 'translated' if it is to be useful within the more silent, less tangibly gestural practice of writing. This means that much of the recent discourse around practice-led research lacks a comfortable fit with the methods and approaches that suit writing. Conceptualizations of research that are based on non-linguistic 'seeing' and 'perceiving', for instance, do not fully take into account the actualities of practice for writers. Nor do the conceptualizations of research in the humanities, with their focus on the critical, and often *a posteriori*, investigation and interpretation of textual content, provide a sufficient research methodology for creative writers.

However, despite the differences in specific modes of research, creative writers share with other creative practitioners, and with most humanities scholars, a rejection of the position that the world is finally knowable, that data is fully testable, that 'truth' can be uncovered, and that there is a stable source of knowledge. Roland Barthes identifies that (presumed) source as the 'Author-God', and points out the dangers involved in relying on an approach that anticipates the discovery of a 'single "theological" meaning', and fails to pay attention to the actual messy, multiple space of research (Barthes 1977: 147). Barthes is not, of course, writing here about practice as research; his point is one that is applied to critical research more generally. However, in writing, as in other creative fields, the approach tends to be Barthes-ian: less systematic, less easily reduced to an interpretive framework, less likely to offer its findings in a transparent mode and less susceptible to rational argument than is conventionally accepted as a research methodology.

One of the more convincing expressions of this comes from a letter written by poet John Keats to his brothers, where he outlines (in frustrating brevity) his concept of 'Negative Capability', or (as he writes) that condition 'when a man is capable of being in uncertainties, Mysteries, doubts, without any irritable reaching after fact and reason' (Keats 1817). Any research paradigm involves processes marked by ambiguities and uncertainties rather than precision, or confidence – this is the basis of experimentation. But, in creative work this uncertainty is particularly evident because – touched as we are by divine madness – creative artists are not afraid of what Bate calls 'an imaginative openness of mind and heightened receptivity to reality in its full and diverse concreteness' (1963: 18). Due to this, we are less likely, perhaps, than a humanities researcher might be, to become irritated when facts and reason are not immediately evident, and are instead likely to be willing to drift for a while, making work, feeling our way into a question or an idea that may lead to an original contribution to knowledge. We know that we do not yet know; we know too that knowledge can never be full or final; and so we are perhaps more willing than other researchers to linger at the point of analysis, and to accept gestures and notions rather than facts.

This is not a position held by creative writing researchers alone; as John Dewey wrote over a century ago:

> Pretty much all students [of philosophy] are convinced that we can reduce knowledge neither to a set of associated sensations, nor yet to a purely rational system of relations of thought.
>
> (Dewey 1972 [1897]: 4)

But then, showing his Platonic inflection, he continues:

> Knowledge is judgment, and judgment requires both a material of sense perception and an ordering, regulating principle, reason; so much seems certain, but we do not get any further. Sensation and thought themselves seem to stand out more rigidly opposed to each other in their own natures than ever. Why both are necessary, and how two such opposed forces co-operate in bringing about the unified result of knowledge, becomes more and more of a mystery.
>
> (Dewey 1972 [1897]: 5)

Still, he does not reject the sensate, as Plato/Socrates did; he merely admits to some confusion about how the affectual domain that is art can ally with the rational domain that is science to produce what constitutes knowledge.

We can not only follow Dewey's lead, but also extend his thinking, pointing out that the insights generated by the sensate domain have their own validity in knowledge terms, though we may not yet be entirely clear about how the two domains intersect. Musician Brian Eno suggests a way forward in this respect, one that affords space for sensate and rational encounters with both the material and the ephemeral worlds:

> As soon as you externalize an idea you see facets of it that weren't clear when it was just floating around in your head … In organising a thought in any way an unsuspected dimension is added to it. It's exactly the same way with music. You work on a piece of music, you put in certain ingredients, and suddenly they react in a way you hadn't predicted. If you're alert to that reaction, that's what you work from.
>
> (Eno and Grant 1982)

In this insight, Eno comes close to the position held by the poet, Wallace Stevens: that what is needed is close observation in order to achieve:

> the imaginative transfiguration of the real through poetic saying, a language that does not take flight from the real, but which both adheres to the real most closely and resists it in the supreme fictions that it writes.
>
> (Critchley 2004: 119)

By making work that is based on observation and attention, whether in poetry, prose or the plastic arts, we are able to examine and 'imaginatively transfigure the real', and to shift beyond either emotion or reason, to achieve a state that provides room for both: in effect, to mobilize a practice that might resolve the ancient quarrel.

One way to confront the challenge of this quarrel then, is to explore the questions opened up by both the process of making the work and the content of the work. Practice-led research in writing, as in other creative forms, begins at the point of practice; and practice begins with an idea, a context, a set of questions and a body of knowledge. It does not begin in a vacuum, or merely at a moment of inspiration: creative writers make work by relying on a set of creative writing and/as research skills. These include imagination, technical training, and a certain knowledge of the field – the rules or conventions of form, what the content is likely to be, and what are the main discourses, including the history and current trajectory of the field – that will necessarily inform the creative work. It is imperative that these be considered before plunging into the project because, in the absence of a relatively clear idea of the question and the context, any creative writing research project risks becoming what Jupp terms 'disastrous research' (2006: 73). It may be, for instance, that the necessary data cannot be collected; that the topic is too dangerous or fails to pass ethical clearance measures; that confidentiality issues prevent the work from being fully realized for publication; or simply that flaws in the epistemological preliminaries result in a flawed project overall, so that whether or not the creative work has professional value, the research findings lack validity or originality.

This embrace of the possibility of failure is, however, one of the hallmarks of blue-sky experimental research in any academic field, and a forerunner of real innovation and, therefore, should be valorized rather than guarded against. It is certainly one of the hallmarks of creative writing research, with failed drafts and deleted passages being the norm rather than the exception in the writing process. This is because although writing as research is committed both to the delivery of a creative work and to the delivery of knowledge, it has its own imperatives, as author Milan Kundera points out:

> the history of science has the nature of progress. Applied to art, the notion of history has nothing to do with progress; it does not imply improvement, amelioration, an ascent; it resembles a journey undertaken to explore new lands and chart them. The novelist's ambition is not to do something better than his predecessors but to see what they did not see, say what they did not say.
>
> (Kundera 2006: 15)

Research in creative writing does not, then, have a teleological orientation as its aim; creative writers cannot 'advance', as science can advance; we can rarely 'prove' or demonstrate that our findings are correct. But we can interrogate our own field, offer new ways of seeing and, in doing so, contribute some interesting and perhaps provocative facts to the knowledge community. By defining, reflecting, intuiting, paying attention, and experimenting, as Kundera suggests in the same chapter, it is possible to make an original contribution to knowledge. This contribution is about writing, surely, but it is also about observing and analysing context and, perhaps, about human society.

The OECD describes 'research and experimental development' as comprising:

creative work undertaken on a systematic basis in order to increase the stock of knowledge, including knowledge of man, culture and society, and the use of this stock of knowledge to devise new applications.

It goes onto clarify that:

> Any activity classified as research and experimental development is characterized by originality; it should have investigation as a primary objective and should have the potential to produce results that are sufficiently general for humanity's stock of knowledge (theoretically and/or practical) to be recognisably increased. Most higher education research work would qualify as research and experimental development.
>
> (OECD 2009)

In order for creative works to be understood as these 'stocks of knowledge' in themselves, creative writers must understand themselves as researchers and the work they engage in as experimental development. Once the research starting point has been clarified – both the epistemological issues and the ethical questions – it is possible to begin making the creative work and then, using the lines of thought that it generates, to tease out and analyse the contextual, theoretical or formal questions that are likely to deliver the required 'stocks of knowledge'. The initial work of thinking and structuring allows the subsequent creative research practice to develop experimentally in its own unique way: to move between order and improvisation; to make intuitive leaps or guesses; and to go off in unexpected and tangential directions. That is to say, good preparation allows flexibility in practice.

One example of how this has worked in practice is the case of creative non-fiction, a form with a genealogy almost as long as that of poetry, but that has, until fairly recently, been somewhat overlooked in literary circles. Yet, it is particularly in this form that the mechanisms, techniques and methodological imperatives of research become visible. Those writing creative non-fiction (in any of its many modes) work in a 'between space', one that is committed to both professional and imaginative writing, to both invention and documentation and, to recall Plato, to both the 'true/rational' and the mimetic/intuitive. The writing of creative non-fiction requires a complex range of authorial tools and positions, what Shawn Gillen identifies as 'the diligence of a reporter, the shifting voices and viewpoints of a novelist, the refined wordplay of a poet and the analytical modes of the essayist' (Gillen 2007). It is thus a form in which both sides of the ancient quarrel are brought face to face, and in which practitioners have made a contribution both to knowledge and to form, in generating a new way of writing, perceiving, thinking and knowing.

A striking example of how it provokes questions about truth, imagination and meaning is the novel *The Fog Garden*, by Australian author Marion Halligan (2001). This opens with a personal essay about the then recent death of her own much-loved husband, one that had been previously published as creative non-fiction (an autobiographical memoir) titled 'The Cathedral of Love' (1999b) and again in an essay collection as 'Lapping' (1999a). The protagonist of the novel is a recently widowed writer named Clare, but the inclusion of Halligan's essay, together with the book's marketing campaign which made much of the author's own sadness, encourages readers to read the work as a disclosure of the author's personal experience. This is despite Halligan's stated attempt to keep the two separate: 'Clare isn't me. She's like me. Some of her experience, terrors, have been mine. Some haven't' (2001: 9). The work undertaken to produce both novel and essay/memoir follows similar lines: investigation, observation, reflection. But its juxtapositioning of memoir and fiction both explores and draws attention to contemporary debates about whether literature can represent the complexities of life with any accuracy, and what it means to 'tell the truth' in a period when the idea of any absolute truth is outmoded and discarded.

Practice-led research that involves creative non-fiction to some extent replicates the work of a traditional humanities or social sciences researcher, as Lee Gutkind points out, writing that 'Creative non-fiction differs from fiction because it is necessarily and scrupulously accurate and the presentation of information ... is paramount' (Gutkind 1997: 15). Writers deal with this imperative by employing research techniques such as interviews, surveys, archival research and participant observation. However, they also employ the techniques of the creative researcher: thinking through writing, and analysing the data through the filter of creative practice. To a far greater extent than writers of poetry or fiction, they are bound by the data they have gathered; and, as a corollary, the ethical aspects of their practice are more focused. Readers tend to believe something that is labelled 'non-fiction' in a way they will not necessarily believe fiction – and creative non-fiction, drawing as it does on the seductive poetics of literature (as Plato warned us) is particularly good at convincing its readers about its truth, whether or not this truth can be substantiated. Theodore Rees-Cheney has noted that cognitive scientists suggest that:

> even the most conscientious and intelligent reader may soon forget the factual content of a piece if material [has] entered the brain with little emotion wrapped around it [and] humans remember best what enters the brain in an envelope of emotion.
>
> (Rees-Cheney 2005: 36–7)

This does place on producers of creative non-fiction a responsibility to ensure the quality of the communication of facts and evidences, and not simply to use the form to win over the minds of readers. In addressing this issue, researchers in creative non-fiction have also contributed knowledge about the limits and the shape of ethical responsibility in textual practice.

Daphne Patai sums up the question for writers:

> A person telling her life story is, in a sense, offering up her self for her own and her listener's scrutiny ... Whether we should appropriate another's life in this way becomes a legitimate question.
>
> (Patai 1987: 24–5)

This question seems particularly apparent in relation to a research assessment of how audience expectations and prior knowledge of actual events can shape perceptions and interpretations of the resulting work, even when those events and characters are changed and the work is declared to be one of fiction (Brien 2009). The reception of such work can often show how difficult it is to dissociate creative product from its source material once the public and media has made this connection, no matter how distant that finished product may be from the original facts. This has, of course, been challenged, as in Peter Ackroyd's statement:

> I don't find any real sacrosanct quality about so-called facts and so-called truths … as far as I am concerned, everything is available for recreation or manipulation.
>
> (Onega 1996: 214)

In this, he seems to be echoing Jacques Derrida's point that 'there is no testimony that does not at least structurally imply in itself the possibility of fiction, simulacra, dissimulation, lie, and perjury – that is to say, the possibility of literature' (Derrida 2000: 29). Certainly the fact that someone offers a memory, a set of facts or an account does not constitute proof of the verity of that material, but only a perspective, a point of view based on that individual's experience and context. This demands of writers the capacity to understand the limits of what they observe, are told or found in the archives, as Michael Hicks observes:

> Facts cannot lie, but they can be interpreted differently […] our facts do not come to us unvarnished, but are loaded, slanted, and embedded in narratives […] Almost every so-called fact comes with its accompanying bias.
>
> (Hicks 1991: 69–70)

Finding a way to minimize bias while interpreting and presenting facts in a manner that draws on modes from across the human sciences, while still committed to the logic of creative practice and its knowledge capacities, is a significant and ongoing aspect of creative writing research, in all writing genres.

Of course, works of the imagination are far less reliant, than are works of non-fiction, on conventional or factual investigation; however, in any mode or genre of creative writing, the research element must be experimentally developmental in its own terms; intentional, deliberate and systematic at heart; and committed to producing an outcome that is accessible both as knowledge and as artefact. When it achieves this, it is research, despite the fact that as creative writing it often appears to be an intuitive process while it is being carried out. The methodological frameworks cannot, though, usually be set in advance. Creative practice as experimentally developmental research is likely to rely on eclectic and diverse methods, determined by the needs of the project under consideration. Consequently, the researcher in writing is likely to function as Tess Brady describes it below:

> … a little like a bowerbird that picks out the blue things and leaves all the other colours. … This bowerbird researching requires its own skill. The skill to locate quickly, sort through, and accurately select all the blue pieces. It is also the skill of knowing where to look, where to find the blue pieces in the first place. … the writer needs to be able to work quickly, to know the questions to ask and to be able to isolate the essence.
>
> (Brady 2000)

A bowerbird, in other words, is a researcher capable of drawing data and ideas together from across fields and disciplines to find harmonies and synergies, and to combine them in a manner that produces not only a satisfying and resolved creative artefact, but a fresh way of understanding those points of connection and their wider implications and applications.

Another way to describe this 'eclectic and often wild' (Brady 2000) approach to research comes from the work of the anthropologist Claude Levi-Strauss, who introduced the term 'bricoleur' into the literature. A bricoleur is literally a handyman, or odd jobs man; in Levi-Strauss' terms, 'a Jack of all trades or a kind of professional do-it-yourself person' (1966 [1962]: 17) – someone who does not necessarily possess a wide range of specializations or specialized knowledge, but is able to make do with what is available. The principal skill at work here is the creativity that is necessary in order to be able to make what available functional for the necessary purpose. This 'making do' is what allows the intuitive leaps and creative shifts designed both to heighten the artistic quality of the work and develop its knowledge potential. The bricoleur's working methods also provide space for the multiple methodologies that allow the artist researcher to draw from an established 'toolkit' of research practice; because in this mode of practice, what matters is the making, and the making – built on a solid foundation of thought and understanding – is what will deliver the outcomes. The creative writing researcher may, for example, borrow the techniques of conducting quantitative surveys and qualitative interviews from sociological research, careful observation and recording from the natural sciences, close reading and textual analysis from the humanities, cognitive examination from psychology, audience and reception research from communication, and/or the processes of studying organizations from business research. They may use all or any of these in combination and at different times in the research process. Writers take what they need, from wherever they can find it. And though such a process may sound slapdash and too casual to be taken seriously, it is, in fact, grounded on very careful and sophisticated investigation into research methodologies and how they function. Sociologist Pierre Bourdieu is himself the model of a successful researcher who never simply obeyed a paradigm's logic, or straightforwardly went through the methodological motions. Rather, he insisted, 'You get what you can where you can' (Bourdieu 1990: 29). The point behind this is that methodology does not direct creative writing research (or art) practice; rather, the practice directs the bricoleur-as-bowerbird's selection of method.

The utility of creative writing research

Utilizing these processes, we argue, creative writing research is not only able to make contributions to improved practice and formal innovation in creative writing, but is also able to contribute to the generation of new knowledge about discourses on creativity as well as other areas such as social formation and historical narrative. Michel Foucault would not concur with this view. He resists the assumption that creative writing has either the capacity or the responsibility to deliver knowledge, pointing out that literature has, since the nineteenth century, distanced itself from knowledge discourses and has, he insists, a different role to play in society than that of generating knowledge:

at the beginning of the nineteenth century, at a time when language was burying itself within its own density as an object and allowing itself to be traversed, through and through, by knowledge, it was also reconstituting itself elsewhere, in an independent form, difficult of access, folded back upon the enigma of its own origin and existing wholly in reference to the pure act of writing. ... At the moment when language, as spoken and scattered words, becomes an object of knowledge, we see it reappearing in a strictly opposite modality: a silent, cautious deposition of the word upon the whiteness of a piece of paper, where it can possess neither sound nor interlocutor, where it has nothing to say but itself, nothing to do but shine in the brightness of its being.

(Foucault 2002 [1966]: 326–7)

For Foucault, then, poetry and philosophy (or, in his case, philology) must not be forced into a single frame. Creative writing, for Foucault, is not 'about' knowledge but must be permitted to exist of, and for, itself, and not to be forced into the domain of applied research. While we are sympathetic to this idea, and in many ways agree that the point of creative writing is first to deliver creative products and knowledges, we note that Foucault first published this work in 1966, and that his reference point was the shift, for language/literature, from the Classical through the Romantic to the Mallarméan periods and their related practices. Close to half a century later, it might be argued that the field has changed radically. Literature has moved past that late nineteenth-century struggle for identity to become part of the current episteme, one predicated on utility, public service and value for input. In addition, it might be said, those nineteenth-century battles have been fought and won; now it is time to turn our attention to what is important in the twenty-first century. That, we suggest, is the production of knowledge that will be of use in the creation of a more ethical, more democratically organized and more sustainable society.

An example of this approach comes from a recent work by Australian novelist Kate Grenville, *The Secret River* (2005a), which explores and exposes both frontier violence in Australia, and the dispossession of the indigenous people during the settlement of Australia. As a part of the debate which is known locally as 'the history wars', Grenville's work makes a significant contribution by offering readers a glimpse into how she imagined early nineteenth-century Australia. About this, Grenville writes:

I did an enormous amount of research. This book isn't history, but it's solidly based on history. Most of the events in the book 'really happened' and much of the dialogue is what people really said or wrote.

The point of this work, she continues, is that:

I hoped to create an experience for a reader in which they could understand what that moment of our past was really like. The great power of fiction is that it's not an argument: it's a world.

(Grenville 2005b)

We will return to this below but want to stress the point that this, like so many other practice-led research projects, is committed to gathering data from a range of places and through a range of methods – the *bricoleur*-bowerbird approach – and using the material to create 'a world', a way of feeling as well as rationally considering how people live together.

More pragmatically (and, more measurably), creative writing research has also, and continues to, contribute to national research priorities, and especially those that address creativity. It is increasingly being recognized that creativity is not only fundamental to human experience and personal satisfaction, but is central to the development of science, business and governmental actions, as well as a tool for promoting a nation and its economic interests. In this, to be creative is not just the ability to make beautiful or engaging works or to express a personal and/or 'artistic' vision. Many contemporary creative writing researchers, for instance, concentrate on how creative ideas can be generated and developed, and trace the processes of thought that led to innovation. This often includes such practical outcomes as knowledge about how to foster creativity, how to teach creativity, and how to rationalize the relationship between creative output and the institutions associated with it.

Finally, creative writing research is frequently directed towards the better delivery of ways of reading as well as ways of writing. Both are valued practices, as is evidenced in formal programs of compulsory literacy and education in many nations. Reading fiction remains a surprisingly popular pursuit, and there is evidence that even those who rarely open a book value the fact that their country has a body of national literature. Better knowledge about the professional aspects of writing, including audiences, genres, processes of dissemination, review culture and writing experiments, will contribute valuable knowledge about a field of practice that has economic, personal, national and pleasurable outcomes.

Concluding remarks: limits and possibilities

Practice-led research is galvanizing schools and departments in universities around the world, and reshaping practitioners' understandings of their own identity and of the meaning and value of their practice. Increasingly, creative writers understand their work as part of the knowledge domain, and not part of the autonomous world of art. There is a certain loss here – Plato's 'sweet friend' is being displaced in its pure form, and replaced by a two-headed creature that bears within its being both poetry and philosophy. However, there is considerable gain in this shift: not only in the personal and institutional capital associated with the move into the knowledge domain, but also in a heightened focus on ethics, meaning, rigour and value that is likely to result in more thoughtful and resolved literary works in the years to come.

Despite this, there is a need to continue observing and analysing what is meant by 'practice-led research' in creative writing, and what sort of contributions can be made utilizing this form of research. Tess Brady's model of the bowerbird researcher has great resonance for many practitioners, who know that their own practice involves ranging widely across fields and disciplines. But not all such practice is necessarily 'research'. It can be, rather, a matter of writers informing themselves about well established areas of knowledge that they will draw on to make their creative work. To paraphrase an example that has been used in a number of discussions about practice-led research in creative writing: if a playwright is writing a play about the Suffragettes, he or she might be reading about the Suffragettes, but that is an act of accessing already the existing knowledge that he or she needs to know in order to create the work. Any original contribution to knowledge will be embedded in how this information is presented to the audience in the form of the play.

This mode of practice is not research, but a gathering of the already existing 'blue bits', to use Brady's term, in order to make a new nest. The problem arises when the bowerbird researcher claims to have contributed new knowledge in an area that is already mined and known. Kate Grenville's experience in the making of her novel *The Secret River* is an example of precisely this problem. She claims, as we note above, to have completed a research process and contributed knowledge about Australia's history, but she is not an historian, and historians closed ranks against her and her work, criticizing her method and any claims for authenticity she has made in relation to the work. Gay Lynch, indeed, refers to Grenville's narrative as an 'apocryphal story' (Lynch 2009), though one that makes a contribution to the discipline of writing, if not to history. Similarly, it is possible to read Zbigniew Herbert's poem 'Pebble' (Herbert 2007: 197) as the outcome of research. This work explores ways of perceiving a stone, and demonstrates the use of a research question, context and methods: the observation of the natural world through a phenomenological encounter and observation. But the knowledge presented in 'Pebble' does not contribute to the field of geology – it presents ways of looking, sensing and otherwise experiencing a stone that may illuminate the work of a geologist, but tells us nothing, really, about geology. It does, however, force both poet and reader to reconsider not only the properties of stone, but also human encounters with stones and, by extension, the natural world.

Our point, then, is that practice-led research in creative writing affords researchers the opportunity to build knowledge in their field. While they may cross disciplinary borders in the process of gathering information for their work, their knowledge generation is typically confined to the domain of creative practice – to narrative, to poetics ... to the field in which they operate. In any discussion of the knowledge content of a work of literary production, it is important that the writer interrogate not only the work, but also the methods and epistemological frameworks used to produce that work, in order to determine what contribution it makes, and to which stocks of knowledge. In short, it is important that writer-researchers identify precisely what aspects of their work constitute original contributions to knowledge within the field, or in another field, and limit their claims to what can be substantiated by process and content.

In a period of significant and rapid change in higher education internationally, academic staff working in the creative arts in universities have transformed a series of individual art forms into a range of coherent academic disciplines, and developed those disciplines into viable components of the academy. In this process, it has been possible to demonstrate that creative writers, by creatively embracing and working with the dialectic of the ancient quarrel, have been able to craft a functional response to Plato, and to substantiate the extent to which poetry and philosophy can co-exist and co-produce knowledge and experiences. This practice, and the work produced, are important not just for writers, but for the social context more generally. A decade and a half ago, media theorist Tom O'Regan wrote, 'Conferring and creating meaning … is necessarily caught between individual enunciation and its social frame' (1994: 337). Our discussion of practice-led research in creative writing has been sited within a contemporary intellectual and policy environment that is beginning to value creativity for the contributions it can make to national economic as well as personal wellbeing, and striving to find ways to describe, measure and evaluate the research outcomes from creative practice-led research. Within such a context, creative writing's most concrete contribution to knowledge outside the boundaries of its own disciplinary practice has been, arguably, in defamiliarizing the familiar (Morley 2007), and thus inviting a reflective engagement with what is – a move that has the potential to recast social and global relationships, and contribute to changing attitudes, practices and policies.

Notes

1 Of course this is too simple and reductive an assessment of Plato's position; we develop some nuances of his argument later in this essay.
2 Socrates refers to rhetoric as 'a sort of art of leading souls by means of speeches' (Plato 1924: Phaedrus 261b).
3 'the poetry by the man of sound mind is obliterated by that of the madman' (Plato 1924: Phaedrus 245a).
4 From the Vulgar Latin, *stantia*, 'a stanza of verse', identified by the stop at the end of a set of lines (from L. *stans* (gen. *stantis*), prp. of *stare* 'to stand').

12

THE VIRTUAL AND THE PHYSICAL: A PHENOMENOLOGICAL APPROACH TO PERFORMANCE RESEARCH

Susan Kozel

Artistic research is a convergence of materialities; sometimes a clash, other times a smooth flow, occasionally it is as if different rhythms play in counterpoint pulling the researcher in different directions. Vision is material, as is the tactile engagement with objects; concepts have their own materiality, and movement provokes a dance of materiality and meaning. In contrast to many of the contributions to this book this chapter takes a kinaesthetic rather than a visual approach, addressing the convergence between the virtual and the physical in research in dance and movement improvisation. When working across bodies and digital technologies not only is the concept of knowledge restructured but, of necessity, our modes of perception and notions of materiality also shift. Further, the methodologies used need to be chosen in a way that is faithful to the research, and the voice and output may defy convention. This area of artistic research offers distinct challenges but is increasingly compelling as digital technologies become ever more ubiquitous, from tiny chips inserted in common objects to vast and interconnected networked applications impacting how we communicate, create and socialize. Perhaps the most contentious claim in this chapter is that research is a form of performance, but this is a by-product of the primary focus which is an application of phenomenological method to performance with technologies revealing an alternate construction of knowledge. What emerges is a reciprocity between models of knowledge and research practices: the practices point to different models of knowledge, and the models offer up refinements of the practice.

This chapter begins by revisiting basic tensions between practice and theory, revealing a deep entanglement between the two. Instead of stitching these domains together in a unifying gesture that still preserves a fundamental antinomy, a shift of perspective is enacted: by viewing both theoretical and practical pursuits in terms of motion and materiality it is possible to avoid reinforcing such an unhelpful distinction. Following this, the argument that research is reversible and performative leads to the heart of this chapter on methodology and constructions of knowledge. The methodology offered is a version of phenomenology drawn from Merleau-Ponty's late writings and refined over years of creating performances and installations with responsive computer systems. Basic instructions for doing a phenomenology will not be provided but a phenomenological description of improvising with a computer-based sensing system is inserted to support the argument for refiguring knowledge into four modes. This may satisfy readers who want to know what a phenomenology might look like and how it can be integrated into an academic discussion.[1] The modes of knowledge to emerge from the phenomenological account of improvising with a computer sensing system are deeply entwined, and together they allow a researcher to appreciate the complexity and richness of performative approaches to digital technologies. They are *concepts*, *affects*, *percepts* and *kinepts*.[2] As the chapter progresses, the discussion turns to a deeper consideration of Merleau-Ponty to suggest that it is almost impossible to avoid ontological questions, questions of being, when working with bodies and technologies, and that a material ontology is a viable and even pragmatic construction for the researcher.

The constraints and urgencies of practice

A pair of questions lie at the heart of artistic research. What can a studio provide that the simple act of reflection cannot? What does an academic environment provide that the exclusive act of making cannot? I'll let Pierre Bourdieu (1992: 27) answer the first question: 'the constraints and urgencies of practice' are provided by the studio. Many dancers who practise improvisation know that it is very hard to move in a complete void, but given something to work with (an idea, an object, music, a word) the movement gains focus and momentum. I always feel as if I can push against the structure (metaphorical or literal) and this enhances creative expression. This is called structured improvisation and is frequently the movement idiom used by dancers when they work within computer-mediated systems such as camera-based sensing systems or with intelligent devices such as wearable computers. The system provides a structure, or a set of constraints, and once a body improvises within that system a topology of meaning and movement is found that may not have been evident at the start. The second question, what the academy provides for artists, performers and musicians, can be answered in many ways but I prefer a simple response: the academy provides the opportunity to develop methodological rigour, conceptual depth, a refinement of practice, and community. A corpus of knowledge and a corps of colleagues.

Just by posing those questions it will seem as if I have fallen already into a theory-practice divide. I neither want to entrench a tension between concepts and practice, between the verbal and the non-verbal, or between the digital and the organic, nor do I want to imply these dualities simply do not exist, are not relevant, or should be side-stepped. This would be disingenuous. They need instead to be understood differently, with attention to the implications for knowledge, expression, and bias. Choreographers I have worked with expressed frustration with the conventions of academic research for imposing upon them the imperative to justify their work through the words of others

(Kozel 2008). Some philosophers I have known operate from an implicit assumption that the attention to explicit lived experience dilutes the richness of the extended web of ideas and the complexity of abstract thought. A digital artist pursuing her PhD whom I once supervised, exasperated by having to articulate herself in words, dismissed me as 'just a philosopher'. Value judgements abound. Bourdieu writes that our analyses of the 'logic of practice', what can be called the logic of handling, of moving, and of making, would 'no doubt have advanced further if the academic tradition had not always posed the question of the relations between theory and practice in terms of value' (Bourdieu 1992: 27).

I propose to mediate the problems of antagonism between theory and practice and bias based on perceived value by taking a phenomenological turn and focusing on materialities. Instead of digital versus physical, or ideas versus performance, I deal with materialities and motion. At first glance practice seems so heavy, and the theories so ephemeral. Yet in reality, ideas are felt, touched, lived, and breathed; practice is ephemeral, changeable, invisible, and disappearing. Writing and thinking are practices, just as moving and making are highly conceptually driven. By diluting the strong duality, changing the terms of the debate and making them fluid, it is possible to escape old value judgements and to appreciate the new terrain that opens. How do I propose to do this? By turning to Merleau-Ponty and by listening to the body in practice.

Research as reversible and performative

Reversibility is one of the key dynamic concepts of the late writing of Maurice Merleau-Ponty. Initially, it seems to be the same as the 'double articulation' sketched by Barbara Bolt in her consideration of studio practice 'whereby theory emerges from a reflexive practice at the same time that practice is informed by theory' (Bolt 2007: 29). The reversible, or 'chiasmic' (Merleau-Ponty 1968), structure that defines the perceptual structure of our engagement with the world can be seen as two positions reflecting upon one another. Yes, these positions might be 'I make and I write' coinciding with the academic paradigm of artistic practice but, more subtly, they can be 'I see and I am seen', 'I am both object and subject', and 'I observe myself as I create, I even observe myself observing'. A closer examination reveals how a Merleau-Pontian approach requires that we go deeper than simply a double articulation which still implies fundamental differences between the two positions. Practice making theory richer while theory challenges and deepens practice is, of course, the desired outcome but I want to move further than Bolt's well-articulated argument based on handling and material practices. The act of performing with responsive digital media in real time while reflecting on Merleau-Ponty has compelled me toward ontological and ethical dimensions. Subject and object do not just reflect upon each other. They are deeply entwined, as are practice and theory. It is impossible to pull them apart. Merleau-Ponty elaborates reversibility initially with respect to seeing, but immediately introduces the tactile: I touch and the world touches me, I touch my own act of touching and am subject and object both within myself. Things become appropriately sticky: I touch the world, certainly I do when I handle materials in the creative process, and these materials touch me back, challenging my autonomous role as creator of knowledge and bestower of meaning. I am quite literally caught up in the flesh of the world.

A kinetic dimension, too, can be elaborated: 'I dance and the forces I set in motion dance through me'.[3] When Merleau-Ponty writes, 'my body moves itself; my movement deploys itself' (Merleau-Ponty 1964: 162) a small hiatus is created between the body and the movement, this is a small lapse of control that is crucial for the reversible relation to work. There is a small interruption, never a collapsing of the elements of a reversible relation onto one another, never a moment when they come to rest. A link can be made with Joan Mullin's chapter on rhetoric included in this volume. She calls into question the commonly held 'story' people know of rhetoric: that it entails a focus on argument, reason and truth primarily in written language. Her repositioning of the practice of rhetoric begins by calling attention to something akin to what I have just called the small hiatus. 'Effective communication included the ability to see that which 'is' before one (what one gazes upon)'; she goes on to say that one forms words or images 'as a result of that activity' (Chapter 9). There is a small moment of reflection upon sensory experience, almost like a breath, prior to articulation in words or images. She calls this an important visual step in rhetoric. Graeme Sullivan also captures a similar moment when he begins his chapter with an effective phenomenological snippet, positing that for him 'to see is to think' (Chapter 6). Mullin is concerned with the application of rhetoric to visual domains and Sullivan argues for a visual turn in cognition, if these are read alongside my account of live performance and embodied methodologies and Frisk and Karlsson's on aural modes of perception (Chapter 16) it is possible to construct a multi-sensory approach to artistic research based on the contributions in this book. Yet it is important to realize that in none of these chapters is there an argument for sensory exclusivity. The senses bleed across one another, in artistic research as in life. For example, near the end of Mullin's text, where her discussion addresses the analogue manipulation of visual elements such as the *Wunderkammer*, she provides an opening for her ideas to be taken into a more corporeal direction: 'Text and visual interact, movement draws the eye away from the words and vice versa, the hand participates in a tactile performance of rhetoric in the making' (Chapter 9). I choose to read in Mullin's instance of tactile rhetoric, and in Sullivan's recognition of the importance of the embodied mind, the existence of a bodily state that exists either as precursor to words or as a disruption in the flow of words with the potential for changing the direction of thought and action. This disruption, according to a Merleau-Pontian approach, exists in the hiatus of reversibility between the seeing and the seen, between the touching and the touched, between moving and being moved.

Reversibility is more about instability than stasis, and never comes to a point of rest or closure. It is an exhausting process. In an earlier, shorter reflection on artistic research I suggested that this small hiatus, between performing a task and attending to this performance, is where research takes root and the rest is an articulation based on this moment of perception. 'The first task of a scientist is to learn to perceive, as it is with a child, or an artist. Once research is located in perception, with the scope for conceptualization and knowledge-building to follow, fears over the compatibility between artistic research and scientific research can be released' (Kozel 2008: 111). Returning to this, I realize that I only grazed the surface. Reversibility is a dynamic ontological state, by which I simply mean that it characterizes our being in the world. If we choose to do a phenomenology inspired by Merleau-Ponty, we choose to notice the constant, minute foldings of one thing onto the other, or of one state onto another (within oneself, across oneself and another, oneself and the world, immanently between one's vision and movement). There is infinite scope for sliding across the objective and subjective positions, for disrupting oneself in micro-movements of perception. This instability is profoundly creative, but profoundly unsettling. It is for this reason that some regard phenomenology as 'necessarily a transformative practice' (Maitland 1995: 229).

Research is not just reversible; research is a form of performance. This takes the Merleau-Pontian argument concerning reversibility one stage further and provides an additional anchor in performance as an art form, but not to the exclusion of other arts, for research in any domain can be viewed as performative. This is not to say that we are actors as we research, or to make the self-evident statement that all actions are performed, but to make a more subtle point that innate to performance is the ability to reflect on what we are doing while we are doing it. I practise, and I reflect upon practice in infinitesimal loops. This is the nature of my perception and my embeddedness in the world. It is not that the doing is the practice, and the mode of reflection is the theory. Both are reflective practice and, taken together, both make up research.

This means that writing and conceptualizing are also performative. Rosalyn Diprose's clear articulation of the argument that identity is performative can be used to put this into perspective. She writes, 'identity is actualized as it is performed, rather than being caused by an inner essence identity is open to disruption', as such identity becomes 'parody or imitation without an authentic original' (Diprose 2002: 67). When research is truly innovative, when new ground is opened, we are performing without reference to an original. One's actions and thought create the template of the new. This is not to diminish the community of people working on a growing body of knowledge; it is to say that we do so in relation to one another but from our own embodied, embedded contexts: hence the emphasis on original research or emerging knowledge in academia. The world is constructed on a moment-by-moment basis by multiple embodied selves.

Elsewhere I have written at greater length on performance and phenomenology (Kozel 2007a); for now it may be enough to extract from this argument symmetrical lines of thought: performance entails a reflective intentionality on the part of the performer to see/hear/feel herself or others *as* performing. Further, the performative moment is initiated by the intention to enact a reflective chiasmic loop (Kozel 2007a: 69). This is how one can see research *as* performance. The 'as' is important to this formulation. Performance theorist Richard Schechner indicates that from the perspective of performance theory, everything is a performance, but from the perspective of cultural practice some actions are performances and others not. His distinction relies on the pivot between *is* and *as*: there are limits to what is performance but anything can be studied, or framed, as performance (Schechner 2002). This is the same pivot that occurs when any action is taken *as* the basis of research – we decide to reflect upon what we have done as research, we decide to initiate the dynamic of reversibility and in doing so there is a witnessing of ourselves and others performing actions, in the most genuine and authentic way. When we perform, we mediate inner and outer. We translate, we regulate, we discover, we are surprised. Performance is attention, perception, and thought set in motion in such a way as to kindle, or ignite, the space for change (Kozel 2007a: 70–1). So too is research. This argument invites the question whether all performance is research, more explicitly stated, whether there is a difference between professional practice and research. The same phenomenological logic applies: if we intentionally choose to regard our performance as research then this is the first step toward it being research. The reflexive moment is key. As a dancer I have performed in pieces that have not been the basis of research, not because they were not rich with potential for academic reflection but because I was simply performing them as part of my professional practice. Once the intention and desire are there to frame an element of practice (such as the process, the choreography, or the audience response) as research then a whole new level of engagement is required. The intention to approach practice as research is the initial moment, the reflexive turn; it then needs to be elaborated with sufficient depth, intellectual rigour, appropriate methodologies, an awareness of context and related work.

Articulate listening

Two additional perspectives on the performative can be drawn into this discussion, both from visual artists who are also highly skilled with words: Matt Mullican (2008) and Barbara Bolt (2004). The performative is enactive, which is not to say that it is free from contemplation, in fact drawing is an excellent example of multi-sensory contemplative engagement with the world. Mullican writes, 'you can't answer the question, you can only demonstrate it. You demonstrate that issue through the work itself. I was just trying to figure out what the reality was that I was drawing' (Mullican 2008: 7). The act of demonstrating is like the act of describing, which is the basis of phenomenology: we are embedded in the world and when we encounter the unknown (from the spectacular to the mundane) the first move is to describe it rather than attempt to contain it within an existing conceptual framework. First comes description from subjective, multi-sensory experience, then comes the transformation of this information into shared meaning and knowledge.

Research begins with a question or an ill-defined inkling that there is something potentially interesting or troublesome in a certain domain. A motion capture performance I devised with collaborators Inka Juslin and Greg Corness can be used as an example. *Other Stories* (2007) began with the sense that when I improvised with digital data, represented as an array of points captured from my body's movement in real time, I was somehow, bizarrely yet intuitively, dancing with another being: with an 'other'. I received a sort of material information from the points of the animated figure or, to be more explicit, I received a kinaesthetic push, a force almost, from the spaces between the points. How could this be? And could I base a performance on this phenomenological moment? This was my starting point, not the attempt to prove substantially that I was, in fact, improvising with another being or to measure the material force, but an attempt to bring to life the question itself. Performing before an audience was the same as Mullican's act of demonstrating. His words regarding his own practice of drawing bear tremendous resonance for more than one reason: 'I believe,' he writes, 'that drawing is more involved with the 'how' question than the 'what' (Mullican 2008: 6–7). The motivating question for research can sometimes be crystal clear, but in my experience it is an affectively tinged pull or push, only traces of a question, invisible strings that propel me into motion. I refer explicitly to affect here because the refiguring of knowledge I offer in the second half of this chapter has affect as one of the elements (along with percepts, concepts, and kinepts) but it is important to make clear that affect permeates the research process; it is not just an end result. Research is not affectively neutral. The affective state that drives us to research can be euphoria, desire, repulsion, outrage or a sort of discomfort similar to an itch. It can be akin to the creepy compulsion to turn over a rock, the stubborn drive to 'misuse' a piece of software,[4] or the patient intent to experience kinaesthetically a cloud formation as it dissolves and reforms.

Methodologies are an essential part of research, for these are structures of or orientations towards knowledge indicating a disciplinary preference for the mode of knowledge to ensue. Is what comes out clear and irrefutable? Is it representative of a statistically reliable sector of the population? Is it enigmatic, suggestive and somehow more profound for leaving much unsaid? A different way of regarding the accumulation of knowledge is as an accumulation of questions, or the development of modes of questioning. Appreciating the reversible nature of our embodiment also implies an appreciation of the reversible nature of research, reminding us that modes of *questioning* also involve modes of *listening*. As researchers we need to become articulate listeners.

Implicit in this assertion is an ethical and philosophical world view that comes from the existential phenomenologists. Barbara Bolt (2004) also takes inspiration from this current of continental philosophy when she turns to Martin Heidegger in order to craft a new paradigm in visual aesthetics that challenges the dominance of representation. My Merleau-Pontian take on the performativity of research is consistent with her Heideggerian argument for the performativity of visual art inasmuch as both are grounded in concrete engagement with things and people in the world, escaping the subject-object divide that implies a dominant subject controlling objects. There is an implicit ethical and ontological foundation to both arguments according to which the performative is viewed in terms of artists, materials, and processes bringing something into being, imbued with a profound responsibility or even responsivity to the world and all that dwells in it. The primary difference between her argument and the one presented here is that the embodied practice animating hers is the handling or 'handlability' associated with visual art while my argument is based on dance improvisation. Further, her goal is to dismantle representationalism in aesthetics, which is 'a system of thought that fixes the world as an object and resource for human subjects' (Bolt 2004: 12) while mine is to offer a version of phenomenology based on Merleau-Ponty's dynamic of reversibility that is meaningful for corporeal exchanges with technologies. Bolt's embrace of performativity is, in some ways, born from the intensity of her antipathy to the dominant view of art as representational and her desire to introduce an alternate visual aesthetic. 'Movement,' she writes, 'is the key for overcoming the fixity of representationalism' (Bolt 2004: 14). Both Mullican and Bolt, coming from visual arts, present arguments that resonate strongly with the corporeal arts of dance and theatre improvisation. An obvious point to be noted is that for dance and theatre performance is the product as well as the process. While I acknowledge this, I will not emphasize it unduly for two reasons. First, because as a phenomenologist my construction of research as performative is concerned with the embodied dynamic of reversibility, whether this animates the creative process or the live performance resulting at the end of the research is not significant. Second, because definitions based simply on categorizing output risk collapsing in the face of increasing hybridity and interdisciplinarity of practice.

Before moving onto a specific consideration of knowledge as emerging from phenomenological reflections on the convergence between the digital and the physical, another seemingly simple but far-reaching observation from Mullican's discussion of drawing needs to be taken into account. In an interview he was asked to comment on the suggestion that it was possible to have 'an empathic response to something that isn't true or isn't real' (Mullican 2008: 7). He responded by describing his manipulation of the states of physicality in his drawings as a way of the metaphorical reference. This is another way of questioning the nature of knowledge which echoes Bolt's objection to representationalism as art reflecting the truth of reality. Artists know that our cultural fabric and the defining characteristics of people can be based on, and revealed by, reactions to the fictional. Artistic research lives across process, product, and reception; the research is received, evaluated or digested by those who encounter it, and responses are real. Once again, there is the necessity for articulate listening. We listen to the work but we also listen to those who listen. There can be a cacophony of reception or it can be quite still. The artists, the collaborators, the audience for the public showing, the PhD viva committee, friends, colleagues, family, those who access it in its documented and archived state, all will respond to the research either as real or as fiction. But how can we argue, in an academic context, that knowledge can be based on fiction?

Concepts, affects, percepts, kinepts

The phenomenological perspective on the convergence between the corporeal and the digital offered in this chapter provides a way to address the question of the fictional or real basis of knowledge. Becoming acquainted with a responsive computer system requires inserting oneself bodily into the environment; by spending time moving, breathing, and, indeed, listening to a system it is possible to create a relationship with both its interface and its outputs. This relationship is based on lived experience – it does not matter whether the digital data is real or false. The experience is material and the knowledge, instead of being deemed false or true, can be construed in terms faithful to experience. The expression 'material witness' is not entirely inappropriate, as it evokes a capacity for observing and being surprised by the process of creating an artwork. In some respects I witness the work as it emerges, responsive and receptive to it. Malcolm Quinn approaches the valuable notion of an altered position of the subject in his contribution to this book by proposing a psychoanalytic orientation to research that permits the emergence of unconscious knowledge. He objects to most applied psychoanalysis in art and design because 'it leaves the existing relations of subject, object and practice intact' (Chapter 14). Despite the tensions, and some might say incompatibilities between phenomenology and psychoanalysis, Quinn and I share the belief that disrupting subjectivity opens a space for creativity important to artistic research. He achieves this by exploiting the tension between identity and utterance and, to use his words, by 'putting the subject beyond his comfort zone' to clear some psychic space for artistic research. Quinn's psychoanalytic orientation seeks to achieve this by encouraging the eruption of the unconscious as a mechanism for interrupting the flow of self narrative. My own Merleau-Pontian approach plays at the edge of subjectivity by working the relation of reversibility according to which I am both subject and object, and am able to be disrupted by attending closely to my embodied experience and impact that others (including digital others) have on me.[5]

Some approaches to phenomenology strengthen and reinforce a transcendental subjective position (Edmund Husserl) but other renditions of phenomenology (Merleau-Ponty's late writings, Francisso Varela *et al.*, Natalie Depraz) lead to a decentralized or fluid subject constantly disintegrating and being reformed by virtue of a reciprocal relation to the world and other beings in it. A specific example will be elaborated below, both to demonstrate a version of phenomenological method in action and to reveal how what emerged from this particular application of the method was an understanding of the knowledge produced by artistic research. A deep entwinement between methodology and knowledge is made clear. Instead of the pernicious divide between verbal and non-verbal knowledge forms, this performance experiment produced knowledge that could be expressed best as a combination of concepts, percepts, affects, and kinepts. Functional definitions are provided in Table 12.1 below. They will be elaborated and made more complex as the discussion progresses.

The philosopher Gilles Deleuze spoke of three kinds of knowledge. Affects are the first kind of knowledge, concepts the second, and percepts are the third (Deleuze 1995: 165). He does not elaborate the reason for this ordering, but the motivation could be to prevent the prioritizing of concepts as some sort of primary and ideal form of knowledge. Concepts, he writes, do not just engage with other concepts, they 'move among things and within us: they bring us new percepts and affects that amount to philosophy's own non-philosophical understanding' (Deleuze 1995: 164). That concepts move within us is enormously significant. They become visceral. Further, the reference to the non-philosophical can also be seen as an implicit reference to practice. Philosophy, he says, requires the non-philosophical. And practice, in my experience, flourishes with the depth and exhilaration provided by philosophy.

In almost all collaborative research for performances and installations that draw together bodies and computers there is a stage of software development where the dancers and software engineers (both groups legitimately can be called artists) work together to create the responsive system. Deleuze indicates that affects, percepts, and concepts 'strain' against one another in a way that I find akin to the relational straining of different skills, languages, and value systems that occurs in interdisciplinary collaborations. An example of software development for 'Contours' (1999), quite an old performance by now, provides an enduring illustration of the relevance of Deleuze's concepts, percepts, affects pattern, and for the addition of kinepts. Here is some contextual information: I was an invited guest in artist Jeanne van Heeswijk's installation 'Hotel New York' at PS 1 in New York in 1999 where I laid the groundwork for Contours (van Heeswijk 2000). Collaborating with digital artist Kirk Woolford, the

Concept	pertaining to a philosophical or poetic construction that can exist across degrees of abstraction (matter, language, symbols, etc)
Affect	pertaining to bodily state encompassing emotion, spirit, vitality, imagination, and memory
Percept	pertaining to multi-sensory perception with an emphasis on the five senses (vision, touch, smell, hearing, and taste) but the scope for embracing more than five.[6]
Kinept	pertaining to corporeal movement, kinaesthesia, and proprioception

Figure 12.1 Functional definitions

devising process began with the creation of a piece of software. Woolford speaks with both precision and poetry about the computer code he writes:

> The software breaks the incoming image into X and Y lines and looks for changes in the image across these lines. It calculates compound change, or movement, for each line, determines the 5 greatest regions of change on X and Y lines. If the changes are greater than the threshold set by the performer at the computer, the computer calculates a direction vector based on previous and current movement region, and projects a line between past and current movements. This allows a more fluid tracking, opening, closing, and drifting. The threshold sensitivity is continually changed to allow movements to be caught, followed, and released.
>
> (van Heeswijk 2000: 26, footnote 2)

As I worked through a series of curls, extensions and inversions suspended in a harness, cameras observed my motion and conveyed this information to the computer; the computer then analysed the rates of change in bodily position and velocity and generated a visual response in real time. In this case, the imagery projected onto my body was a series of rapidly drawn lines that made a grid and tried to lock onto the part of my body that moved most quickly through space. The software tried to anticipate the movement by directing itself with the dominant flow (so if my arm rapidly travelled from left to right, the software would assume that the motion would continue along this linear path). This camera-based sensing system was not 'intelligent,' in that it neither made decisions nor adapted itself as would agents or bots in artificial intelligence, but it was sufficiently responsive and had enough 'fuzziness' in its system for me to feel as if I were engaging with a quasi-autonomous, and at times aggressive, being.

Despite not working with full or literal insertion into virtual space, the experience of entering into a responsive system of cameras, computers, and projected imagery was no less immersive, and was played out across physical, cognitive, and perceptual dimensions. Bourdieu, in his defence of practice, laments that Plato associated practice or action with an inability to contemplate and that this attitude has persisted (Bourdieu 1992: 28); yet in stark contrast to Plato, and possibly of comfort to Bourdieu, the focused mode of sensing and, above all, listening that comes from being inserted corporeally in a computer-mediated system is a powerful and creative form of contemplation. Phenomenological reflection is a form of contemplation; like a moving meditation it requires deep levels of focus and the ability to pursue a train of thought or physical impulse as it unfolds and transforms. Contemplation is a form of immersion, of dwelling in a system. Several stages of this immersive process are sketched below. It is also clear that there is a sort of learning curve[7] at play in obtaining a level of ease and pre-reflective exchange with the software.

The first stage of exploration within a system like this is very visually dependent and involves standing in front of the camera with a clear sightline to the computer monitor or projection to determine how the basics of movement are translated. It becomes a return to the building blocks of most dance techniques: orientation in space, speed, rhythm, weight and absolute stillness are offered for the computer to respond. This stage of movement is physically limited but it is by no-means purely visual. Instead of the dancer needing to do great leaps, the movement is more effective when it is subtle: a qualitative 'touching' of the space and a witnessing of degrees of response works better than quantitative or formal explorations. The eyes act as a gateway for the knowledge to be embodied, and an understanding of the responsivity of the system filters through. Without visual reference at this stage the dance risks being an improvisation disconnected from the system. (Of course if the system was only producing haptic or audio outputs the sensory pattern would shift.) Once a basic visual patterning is established the sightlines can be relinquished in short bursts. The effect is one of severing a metaphorical umbilical cord to the computer; the effect is also to open the performance perimeter outward into the round; if the dancer's gaze is directed throughout the space the computer is no longer seen to be the 'front', the ultimate audience or viewing subject. The perceptual relationship with the space is never narrowly visual, for the procedure is not simply one of information travelling in the eyes, followed by a decision to move, followed by a movement. Although vision is undeniably crucial, the perception is mediated across all the senses and as such it happens simultaneously with the physical response so that the receipt of information and the acting upon it converge.[8]

The process of learning by using visual perception and bodily motion just described supports the assertion that human cognition arises through embodied action. Varela *et al* (1999) draw upon experiments in cognitive sciences and the philosophy of Merleau-Ponty to present a compelling argument that perception and action are inseparably linked in lived cognition. They explain how there is no world outside to be recovered by the senses for cognition, nor is the world outside a projection of our internal cognitive processes; fundamental to their work is the refutation of both the realist and idealist philosophical stances. What they refer to as 'the enactive approach' has two tenets: '1. perception consists in perceptually guided action and 2. cognitive structures emerge from the recurrent sensorimotor patterns that enable action to be perceptually guided' (Varela *et al.* 1999: 173). The scientific experiments undertaken to explore these hypotheses often include animals (e.g. Held and Hein) or children (e.g. Piaget).[9] Since most of us do not engage in controlled laboratory experiments on a regular basis, it is rare to find an occasion to witness the link between perception, activity, and cognition once we are adults and our patterns of knowledge are well entrenched. The experience of navigating my body through space facilitated by computer systems generates a relatively fresh or 'naïve' context, affording me new insight into my perceptual and cognitive functions. Despite the validity of the argument that our use of mobile phones is an example of our navigating constantly through digital media, the ubiquity and embeddedness of the systems used in the collaborative performances I have worked on are of a different order, and the insight into perception and knowledge was at once more intense and less encumbered. The passage above describing the first stage, revealed the operation of percepts and, because the variation of perception was mediated by motion, kinepts. The second stage of the learning curve exemplified by the research process with the Contours software revealed the presence of affects by means of an inter-corporeal or social dynamic which is manifest through power relations of control, but also through intimacy and receptivity. Varela's notion of embodiment is based on the lived experience of 'a body with various sensorimotor capacities', but they also stress that 'these individual sensorimotor capacities are themselves embedded in a more encompassing biological, psychological, and cultural context' (Varela *et al.* 1999: 173). In other words, I am who I am because you exist. This is the implication of

Merleau-Ponty's notion of reversibility at its most basic but most profound level. When working in responsive systems, the I and the you can be digital as well as corporeal.[10]

The inter-corporeal dimension of performing with a responsive piece of software emerges with deeper levels of habituation within the system. This can be called the second stage of the learning curve and it is distinguished from the first by being more affective. Once I understood the basic responsivity of the grid produced by the software, the dynamic became one of control. The imagery, when projected onto my body, seemed so aggressive at first that I immediately felt as if the software was controlling me: it was active and I was forced into a position of reacting. In Merleau-Pontian terms, it was the subject and I was the object and the relation was not one of reversibility. Once I was suspended in the harness, a device integral to the choreography and dramaturgy of the performance, my sensorimotor patterns were altered. Some movement was facilitated such as weightlessness, rapid dives, sustained inversions; but other movement was thwarted, such as prolonged immobility – there was always a slight sway to the rope – and travelling through space. The harness added the factor of effort: much harness work looks effortless but is physically very strenuous and the quality of weightlessness it can produce requires considerable exertion. The grid seemed to control my movement by carving me up; it responded so well to my slightest movement that I could not escape it. In an extreme sense, it was the aggressor and I was the victim, with my agency curtailed by being 'trapped' in the harness. This imbalanced dynamic, with its associated sense of vulnerability, was a by-product of an early stage of software/movement development. As Woolford adjusted the sensitivity of the system and I grew more accustomed to the behaviour of the imagery, the movement dialogue become more of an exchange, interspersed with moments where I felt as if I could control or outwit the computer. As rehearsals progressed I could play with the software, it felt much more like a duet where occasionally it would lead and occasionally I would make it run to catch up with me. The affective texture of my relationship with the software changed as we refined the system. Like any intimate relationship, this took time.

A spill across concepts, percepts, and affects, mutually tinged, became clear across the stages of the phenomenological research process. The necessity for recognizing that each domain is influenced by the others has been stressed by many (Merleau-Ponty 1968; Deleuze 1995; Varela *et al.* 1999; Diprose 2002; Palasmaa 2005). Deleuze is concise on the topic:

> Percepts aren't perceptions, they're packets of sensations and relations that live on independently of whoever experiences them. Affects aren't feelings, they are becomings that spill over beyond whoever lives through them (thereby becoming someone else) … Affects, percepts, and concepts are three inseparable forces, running from art into philosophy and from philosophy into art.
>
> (Deleuze 1995: 137)

To this trio I would like to add *kinepts*, which allow for a physical and dynamic dimension to conceptual thought that maintains a resonance across individuals based on the fact that we negotiate our lives bodily through space.

A sense of play ensued. This is the third stage of the learning process, and this is where the dance really comes into being. It also coincides with a greater degree of balance across concepts, percepts, affects, and kinepts. I could attain a degree of immobility sufficient to make the grid disappear, then tease it into response with my fingers or toes; I could draw it down my arm and shake it off, only for it to return somewhere else. I tried to throw it from a hand to a foot. Yet these moments of feeling like I was an orchestra conductor were always pierced by the grid evading my control and playing me: projecting on me, carving me, and flattening me from 3D into something slightly more than 2D. Yet for all its flattening, I was able to bend the projected grid around my body and sometimes cause it to pool in unexpected circles at my joints, this way I made it something more than 2D. Like any game, the exchange was rife with unanticipated frustrations and satisfactions. These affective qualities from the early stages of research, mediated by percepts and expanded conceptually, were integrated into the improvised choreography of the final piece.

It is clear that despite having distinct qualitative domains (emotion, perception, thought, and motion) no clear boundaries exist between affect, percept, concept, and kinept – they overflow into each other in a pattern of merging and disengaging that, in itself, is a sort of choreography. We speak of ubiquity and embeddedness when we describe computer systems but, corporeally, the real ubiquity is human motion. It underpins perception, action, and knowledge; it lends quality to human intimacy and play; it distinguishes the quick from the dead.

Expanding the kinept

An illustration of kinepts at work with concepts, percepts, and affects can be drawn from my time in van 'Heeswijk's Hotel New York' installation at PS1, the place where the Contours residency occurred. A group of students from France visited the room which we used as a studio. My attempts to explain what was happening between the physical space and the computers were failing due to inadequate shared vocabulary and the shuffling inattention which characterizes bored teenagers the world over. Noticing that they were standing within camera range, I instructed them all to stop. Then all to move. The computer screen went completely black, then with their synchronized movement the outlines of a crowd – themselves – became evident. The software running at the time was not the grid, but a different piece which registered the outlines of moving body parts. After a beat or two of silent comprehension, a murmur of delight was released from the crowd followed by sprays of random movement. A crossing was enacted: from a state of incomprehension, passively waiting to receive information aurally or visually, to the full impact of understanding based on embodied experience.

'Perception, when it's working, is an action'. Bonnie Bainbridge Cohen is eloquent on the topic of human motion and perception (Bainbridge Cohen 1993: 65). Her discussion of the various systems of the body (skeleton, eye, muscles, organs, glands, brain, blood, cerebrospinal fluid, etc.) through which information is always flowing can be used to refine further the understanding of kinepts in the research process just described. The insights and techniques of Bainbridge Cohen's experiential anatomy of Body-Mind Centring are extensive, but my goal here is simply to introduce her distinction between sensing and feeling. There is a corporeal specificity behind her use of the two terms, as well as particular definitions of the terms. Sensing and feeling mean something quite different in philosophical terms, or in other schools of physical practice. I tend to avoid the word 'feeling' entirely because it skews reflections upon affect, but Bainbridge Cohen associates feeling quite precisely with fluid bodily systems and particular movement qualities. 'Sensing is related to the nervous system through the perceptions. Feeling and flow are related to the fluid system including the circulatory, lymphatic and cerebral-spinal fluids' (Bainbridge Cohen 1993: 64). She describes how a lot of dancers doing contact improvisation rely on sensing, rather than feeling/flow: this means that they initiate activity by shifting their location in space, by transferring weight both within and across bodies, and by moving limbs. An approach to bodily fluids, feeling rather than sensing, is different, 'The fluids,' she explains, 'are a counterbalance to the perceptions or the nervous system'. If the movement is initiated by the perceptual system, the fluids will act in the role of support. But there may come a time when you want to 'reverse that balance' when you want the perceptions 'to go quiet', to become the support, so that the fluids become the mover. The fluids have a different movement quality and temporality, they are more subtle, less dramatic; because these anatomical systems are more deeply internal, or parasympathetic, they manifest a different rhythm and can be accessed by pausing, meditating, and moving slowly. The more overt senses of the nervous system go quiet when the fluids take over. 'When I say forgetting them [the senses], I mean letting them go unconscious and letting the fluids become the control' (Bainbridge Cohen 1993: 64). Once again, the use of the word 'unconscious' can bring up a cluster of philosophical and psychological connotations that we may not want to visit just now, but listening to her point and accepting her terms I found myself better understanding my own phenomenology of the learning curve within a new responsive computer system. At first I worked across sensing (weight shifts, limb movement, travelling in space) but once I became more at ease in the system, once I understood on a tacit and corporeal level the way it behaved, I let the fluids take the initiative. Bainbridge Cohen makes it quite clear that moving from the fluids does not imply only moving slowly; when we move quickly with fluidity we move more efficiently and sense our surroundings more effectively. Her example is of moving quickly and fluidly in a crowd of people: if we let the fluid systems of the body lead we are less likely to bump into people. Sensitivity to the ebbs and flows of our environment is greater. Translated directly into a computer-sensing environment, activating fluid anatomical systems enhances my sensitivity to an environment that is designed to be sensitive to me. Kinepts contain both the overt sensing of the nervous system and the tacit sensing of the fluid systems.

Material ontology

It is almost impossible to avoid ontological questions when working with bodies and technologies. This has something to do with the material tension fundamental to the research experimentation: bodies can feel very organic when juxtaposed with ephemeral software and inorganic machinery. Ontological questions are questions into the being of something: a person or a digital creature. What is it? How does it exist? The initial confrontation between the digital and the corporeal subsides quickly; with time, breath, and motion in the responsive system the confrontation dissolves into a form of convergence between the two. Once again, a reversible relationship between digital and physical becomes clear: the dynamics of initiating and responding, folding and permeating, and a relinquishing of choreographic control shape the improvisation. Merleau-Ponty's words can be used to provide a perspective on this convergence,

'My body as a visible thing is contained within the full spectacle. But my seeing body subtends this visible body, and all the visibles with it. There is reciprocal insertion and intertwining of one in the other' (Merleau-Ponty 1968: 138). Following Merleau-Ponty's logic of the reversible, if the digital body is a visible thing then my body exists as visible along with it, but my act of seeing also shapes what is seen, both the digital body and my own. The result is a reciprocal intertwining; a motion that never ends. This is the ontology of the visible that takes shape in Merleau-Ponty's notion of flesh, this 'ultimate notion, that is not the union or compound of two substances,' it is a 'coiling over of the visible upon the visible' which can 'traverse and animate other bodies as well as my own' (Merleau-Ponty 1968: 140). 'Visible' in this context could be replaced with 'sonic' or 'tactile', also prevalent responsive modes in sensing systems.[11] This seemingly dense presentation of ideas is not intended to be anything but a pragmatic demonstration of two points pertaining to arts-based research:

- ontology is something we experience on a practical level in performance experimentation, meaning that questions of being are not the exclusive domain of abstract philosophy;
- ontology is contingent upon movement in the world made up of a plurality of beings, and these others can exist across a range of materialities along a continuum from corporeal to digital.

So where do we go from here, at the threshold of a discussion that could expand to fill the skies? Reflections upon materiality can take as many directions as art-based research chooses to offer, for artists are no strangers to materials. Materiality as I encounter it, is shaped by an embodied ontology appropriate to my fields of research, which are performance and philosophy. It is worth turning to two other contributions to the debate around practice-based research to see how materiality figures for them: Paul Carter (2004) reflects on material thinking, and Barbara Bolt (2007) upon material productivity. For Carter, material thinking occurs in the making, in a zone of plasticity and transformation imbued with affect but uneasy with accepted academic conventions of language. The materials selected for research display 'gifts of amalgamation and self-transformation analogous to the emotional environment characteristic of the human exchange,' while the act of theorizing in the present educational context is a 'vain, and often humiliating exercise'. He asserts that artists 'have little alternative but to master the rhetorical game of theorizing what they do', while critics and theorists who are not directly involved in producing the art are 'outsiders, interpreters on the sidelines' incapable of making sense of a creative process. It is the artist who can address the material of thought, because material thinking occurs 'in the making of the work of art' (Carter 2004: xi–xiii), but the scope for this actually happening seems fraught with failure because of the apparent gulf between thought and practice, which is belied by his own nuanced yet philosophically rigorous written text.

Bolt takes a more corporeal approach than Carter, distinguishing herself from him by asserting, with a satisfying corporeal metaphor suggestive of painting, sculpting or even knitting, that research in art occurs through 'handling' materials and ideas and not by theorizing what we do. 'It is art as a mode of revealing and as a material productivity, not just the artwork that constitutes creative arts research' (Bolt 2007: 34). She calls this 'praxical knowledge', and sees it as coming directly from the ideas tools and materials of practice. It is a fine distinction, the one she makes between practice and praxical knowledge, but it is a more generous assessment of the position of the artist in the academy than the one offered by Carter. Materials and processes are not to be used instrumentally in the service of an idea, but are to be respected as an emergent form of knowledge in their own right (Bolt 2007: 33).

Both Bolt's defence of material productivity and Carter's rigorous defence of material thinking, inspiring in its provocative way, fall short of the understanding of materiality necessitated by performative explorations across bodies and digital technologies. Bolt objects to a 'Cultural Studies agenda' that emphasizes social production and reception over material production (Bolt 2007: 34). I would say, from a phenomenological perspective, that social production and reception are materially grounded in the embodied experience of the bodies who make and those who encounter; I would not elevate the handling of artistic materials over corporeal engagement at all stages from creation to dissemination. Carter, however, operates with a different set of boundaries and distinctions. He describes collaboration as desire to 'integrate text-based knowledge with the plastic wisdom of the craftsperson' and while this may be an accurate description of some interdisciplinary artistic collaborations, the ones I have participated in cannot be described with such a rigid distinction between forms of knowledge. Text-based simply means ideas – but ideas are corporeal, they resonate and reverberate through our embodied existence. Plastic wisdom simply means intuitive corporeal handling, but such manipulation is conceptual as well as tactile and affective. In collaborations involving computer programming there is also the question of where to locate the computer code: according to Carter's dichotomy, would creative software production be text-based, or plastic and material? Felix Guattari writes that, 'with art, the finitude of the sensible material becomes a support for the production of affects and percepts' (Guattari 1995: 100–1). And this explicit reference to materiality in conjunction with percepts and affects returns us to the focus of this chapter: a description of phenomenological method applied to performance with technologies that reveals knowledge structured as affects, percepts, kinepts, and concepts. What this embodied knowledge then points to is a matter for the specific research project. If we are going to ask 'What matters?' it is best to do so without preconceptions about the incompatibility of sorts of knowledge, as Carter does when he distinguishes text-based from plastic knowledge, and implies that an outside critic cannot make sense of an artwork. Once the Merleau-Pontian turn is introduced it is impossible to separate corporeality from knowledge, and we might see that the critic also reads a material experience through her reversible corporeal exchange with it.

And with this, we come to the question that has been skirted throughout this chapter thus far: what is the virtual? In every creative project there is an invisible, and the writing of this chapter is no exception. The virtual is the invisible of this writing, despite being the first word of the title. The virtual, when it is freed from an overly reductive association with immersive digital technologies, and that now anachronistic term 'cyberspace', refers to something that has not yet happened but exists as a raw potentiality (Kozel 2007b). This formulation is in contrast with the one provided by Frisk and Karlsson, because they associate the virtual and the aural with 'non-space' (Chapter 16). My phenomenological approach to virtuality will never coincide with a construction of it as a non-space: the corporeal experience of spatiality is multiple and subtle, but it is experientially valid and spatially exists. It invites re-figuration but not negation. The spaces of memory, imagination and, with a nod to Malcolm Quinn's chapter, the unconscious are dimensionally and durationally different from standard constructions of spatial existence but they are not free from spatiality. The same is true of aurality – indicating that music occurs in non-space runs the risk of suggesting that it is disembodied. I have always sensed that the invisible in Merleau-Ponty has its own spatiality as well as materiality. It operates in Merleau-Ponty as the glue, or underpinning to the visible, and functions in the material ontology I offer here as a something perpetually unknown but excruciatingly intimate; it is that which spurs us onward, that which exists in the hiatus between breaths that meditation techniques seek to call to our attention. It is, in some ways, dark to us but is what motivates us as beings who crave to create, both something anew and ourselves once again. The invisible of this world 'sustains it and renders it visible,' it is 'a certain hollow, a certain interior, a certain absence, a negativity that is not nothing' (Merleau-Ponty 1968: 151). The invisible is an absence with materiality. It is dynamic; it is palpable but cannot be held. The virtual inhabits the invisible. It is not technological as such, but its intensity is felt particularly strongly when bodies converge with technologies.

Jean Luc Nancy writes: 'a body's material. It's dense', 'a body's immaterial. It's a drawing, a contour, an idea', and 'the void itself is a subtle kind of body' (2008: 150). I suggest that the virtual permeates this void, and that it is not a void in the standard conception of nothingness or emptiness. We have an uncanny ability to relate, physically, emotionally, and conceptually, to something that is not there, to something that is situated just beyond our present abilities to know or touch. From visual artists sketching the space between objects or between the limbs of a model's body, to a dancer's ability to improvise around notions of negative space or dark matter (Kozel 2008: 108–9), we are creatively disposed to respond to a void without necessarily filling it. This is why the virtual is so seductive, not because we can download a virtual body to our mobile device and carry it around with us as portable media, but because it contains within it the immense power of not-yet-materialized-materiality, and because this not-yet-materialized-materiality, this underdetermined materiality that is also invisibility, is with us at all times. It is incredibly intimate, because we pour into its spaces our hopes, fears, and desires. And it is incredibly familiar, because our own bodies are not fully known to us either. We are made up of shadows and blind spots, the invisible is in our very fabric, 'since evidently there is in the body only "shadows stuffed with organs"' (Merleau-Ponty 1968: 138).

Returning this discussion of ontology to the matter at hand, reflections on artistic research; it is helpful to step back a little to consider one more manifestation of the presence of the invisible: uncertainty or liminality. It is helpful to recall that perception 'includes our doubts, our confusions, our illusions, and our hallucinations. Perception is not a sheer normative positionality of the object but covers quite different experiences, from very common ones to more liminal ones' (Varela and Depraz 2003: 209–10). All research begins in multi-sensory perception, of being in the world and wondering about it. Methods, knowledge, output, and innovation follow from this corporeal encounter: I touch the world with doubt, hope, and desire and it touches me.

Notes

1 Two frequently asked questions regarding phenomenology are how it is done and what a phenomenology looks like. Both can be found in Kozel (2007a: 48–55), and a glimpse of what phenomenological writing can look like is provided in this chapter.

2 I have coined the term 'kinepts' but in no way say it is mine for I am certain others have come to see its relevance too. Many dancers working in interdisciplinary ways have had to extrapolate terms explicitly from human movement. In a similar vein my colleague Gretchen Schiller has written extensively about the kinesfield (Schiller 2003).

3 The dancing-danced was the basis of my PhD (Kozel 1994) whereas the recognition of forces operating through the dancer featured quite differently by Maxine Sheets-Johnstone in Phenomenology of Dance (Sheets-Johnstone 1966).

4 Other Stories was a research project in motion capture and ethics performed in the Interactivity Laboratory at Simon Fraser University (Canada) in 2007. We used a Vicon motion capture system in real time and wanted to drive an animation other than the preset wireframe humanoid. Both of these were deemed inappropriate use of the system by its designers and we had to struggle to get access to the source code that let us bypass the wireframe so we could generate more abstract imagery. This was our 'misuse' of the system.

5 Contrary to assumptions regarding their incompatibility, Merleau-Ponty sketched a mutual encounter for phenomenology and psychoanalysis. Together, phenomenology and psychoanalysis can acknowledge the lived reality of psychic activity in an intersubjective world shaped by history and culture. Phenomenology assists psychoanalysis by recognizing the embodied reality of psychic activity and fantasies. Psychoanalysis assists phenomenology by confirming that the psychic representations that make up consciousness are not merely a play of images or concepts, but are investments of desires and actions (Merleau-Ponty 1993).

6 Rudolf Steiner's system proposes 12 senses: touch; life sense; self-movement sense; balance; smell; taste; vision; temperature sense; hearing; language sense; conceptual sense; and ego sense (Palasmaa 2005: 77).

7 This reference to learning curve brings to mind Hubert Dreyfus's description of the stages of learning relevant both to distance learning and to driving a car. These are: novice, advanced beginner, competence, proficiency, expertise. His analysis is quite different but there is some resonance when he suggests that action becomes less stressful once we no longer use a calculative procedure to select alternatives (Dreyfus 2001: 40).

8 I italicize three passages and distinguish these words from the flow of the text because they are phenomenological passages taken from the moment of the performance experiment.

9 Varela and Depraz (1999) describe Held and Hein's 1958 experiment. 'In a classic study, Held and Hein raised kittens in the dark and exposed them to light only under controlled conditions. A first group of animals was allowed to move around normally, but each of them was harnessed to a simple carriage and basket that contained a member of the second group of animals. The two groups therefore shared the same visual experience, but the second group was entirely passive. When the animals were released after a few weeks of this treatment, the first group of kittens behaved normally, but those who had been carried around behaved as if they were blind: they bumped into objects and fell over edges' (1999: 175). They describe Piaget's discoveries: 'Within Piaget's system, the newborn infant is neither an objectivist nor an idealist; she has only her own activity, and even the simplest act of recognition of an object can be understood only in terms of her own activity. Out of this, she must construct the entire edifice of the phenomenal world with its laws and logic' (1999: 176). Held and Hein's experiment seems particularly relevant to immersion in computer-mediated spaces, situating the crucial question concerning whether the 'audience' can benefit from watching an interactive performance or whether they need to individually, or as a group, experience the interactivity themselves in the same manner as the performers. Is it true that experience is shared and translatable, or do we ultimately need to get into the system and 'enact' to establish our own sensorimotor patterns for personal cognitive impact? This is a crucial factor motivating the shift on the part of dance and performance practitioners from performance in conventional theatres to installation. The connection between perception, enaction, and cognitive structures is, I suggest, also at play in the state of dwelling.

10 The discussion of the digital other, or digital alterity, is made at greater length in Chapter 4 of (Kozel 2007a).

11 Merleau-Ponty's ideas are conveyed mainly through the visible, possibly because his artistic references were paintings by Cézanne and Klee and he was able to extrapolate their painterly visions into his own viewing of landscape, but touch is prominent in his thought and music makes a limited appearance.

13

NAVIGATING IN HETEROGENEITY: ARCHITECTURAL THINKING AND ART-BASED RESEARCH

Catharina Dyrssen

Introduction

The research landscape becomes increasingly multifaceted and heterogeneous. Traditional disciplines are constantly undermined by crossover problems and networking structures, and stable, coherent areas of knowledge production are rare. Approaches and strategies become more diverse and combinatory. We also see a growing interest from both technical research and the humanities to incorporate strategies such as innovation, elements of fiction, or associative rethinking of problems, using several tools for representation and communication apart from verbal text. Recognizing this sometimes contradictory diversity as a fundamental condition for most research today opens new possibilities for art-based research (AbR).[1]

Through art we can accept that most research problems are not 'pure', but often contradictory and vague, impossible to regulate, open for interaction, and where logical thinking is naturally intertwined with associative and intuitive conceptualization. The usual non-linear structure of AbR processes allows researchers to cope with complexities without controlling them. As AbR becomes more academically established, it faces increasing demands to be not merely creative on a personal level, or promote art as such, but to also generate effective contributions to knowledge production in a wider sense. If AbR is to reach out to a larger research community, it implies that more developed strategic tools are needed for enquiry, and for making AbR research methods explicit so that they may open up communication with other modes of research.

This chapter discusses how research can be approached through active construction and composition, oscillating interaction between experiments, critical re-modelling, and multimodal conceptualization and communication. It is an attempt to systematize

AbR knowledge production, not as a fixed scheme but as a series of approaches that can be combined. My perspective is architecture but, hopefully, the framework can also be used in other contexts of art, design or practice-based knowledge production and reach out to, for example, technical and social sciences, and the humanities.

Six themes stand at the centre of interest: *architectural thinking* as a mode to construct, perceive and conceptualize complex situations; *performance* and *performativity* as a mode of action, making and communication; *staging explorative experiments* as a way of setting up and examining specific situations; *modelling* and *simulation* as central interactive methods of enquiry and tools for addressing heterogeneity; *critical construction and reflection* as a strategy to maintain research integrity and navigate in heterogenic knowledge production; and *assemblages* as a gradual creation of configurations and flexible navigation charts for research situations. Together these six entries form a basis of thinking-acting-composing, and I will use a spiralling narrative through them to suggest a methodological framework for AbR.

Theme 1: architectural thinking

Architecture is a field that revolves around a creative practice on space and matter/materiality. It is rooted at the crossing point between art, technology and socio-cultural aspects of space. In terms of research methods it is *architectural thinking* that stands at the centre, i.e. to basically think in three dimensions regardless of scale, and to actively deal with complex spatial situations that are constantly changing over time.

Architectural thinking relates to design in the sense that both are activities that explore the possible and the future through invention and intervention. Design thinking, or designerly thinking, is a broad term discussed a generation ago by, e.g. Bryan Lawson (1980), and developed further by researchers such as Nigel Cross (2006), Thomas Fisher (2000), Halina Dunin-Woyseth (2004), John Rajchman (1998) and Graeme Sullivan (2005). Generally these research paradigms stress the research problem as 'fuzzy' or 'wicked' in terms of being impossible to define beforehand, specifically embedded in a situation and requiring combinations of creative and analytical strategies. But while design is often oriented towards a specific user, with the requirements attached to that, architecture generally works in broader contexts and more open complexities involving artefacts, spaces, processes and systems and ranging from the detailed to an interregional and global scale.

To a large extent architecture is also an intersubjective activity where communicative aspects are important and where knowledge production opens up for collective action or teamwork. A large part of my own practice-based research, especially within the Urban Sound Institute,[2] concerns crossovers between architecture and music/sound, art/sound design. The transitional character of sound challenges traditional understandings of architecture as something stable and, instead, emphasizes a concept of space as something constantly changing, relational, diverse and heterogeneous but still bodily and multisensorially experienced. Similar expanded and transient understandings of architecture are today embraced by many professionals and scholars, and it places architectural thinking, rather than the architectural object, in the foreground.

Although architecture as such may not be defined purely as art, I would argue that architectural thinking-making-composing is largely a complex, artistic activity, a mode of finding hidden connections between seemingly disparate elements to construct new coherencies. It investigates situations through spatial understanding in a wide sense, design actions, tentative proposals and explorative experiments. Thinking through sketching as a tentative activity has had an almost emblematic status among architects, described by Donald Schön (1991: 134) as a creative knowledge process heading towards new solutions to problems. One may, however, question why knowledge today is still so strongly glued to producing answers and solutions. Answers are only one part of generating knowledge. They are seductive in the sense that they deliver seemingly final conclusions, and may thereby contain lots of normative traps – prescriptions on how things *should* be, sometimes on quite loose grounds. If knowledge is understood as a networking, continuous and collective field of action, it must be equally important to produce alternative perspectives, ideas, strategies and new questions, including the innovation of models and products, not as final statements but as part of a shared action space extended over time. Because art-based research does not provide 'proof' in a traditional sense, one should beware of, and recognize, its prominence to serve the 'archive' of collective knowledge (as discussed by Michel Foucault, 1972) with fuel of diverse kinds where questions, alternative perspectives and new possibilities have the same dignity as underpinned verifications, especially in the process of providing gateways for communication and dialogue across paradigm borders. In the other direction, practice-based methods can incorporate, e.g. accuracy from technical measurements, critical perspectives from social sciences, and theoretical argumentation from the humanities.

The Japanese literary scholar Kojin Karatani argues that the 'will for architecture' – that is, to create constructions – is the starting point for all of Western thought. On the basis of Wittgenstein, Karatani sees architecture as an open, communicative event conditioned by the circumstances of the situation. He breaks down structuralistic attempts to bypass or exclude the subject, but at the same time he criticizes phenomenology's individual subjects with universal significance – subjects that 'hear themselves speak' – and emphasizes instead 'the multiplicity of subjects' and 'the relative other'. He says that because architecture is an event, it is always contingent; it is 'a communication with the other, who, by definition, does not follow the same set of rules' (Karatani 1995: 133–47).

Architectural thinking always involves the relationship body-space and often uses an active decoding of its surroundings that integrate all our senses and anchor them in bodily experience. In heterogeneity, the body is drawn into practice as an actively constructing, discursive agent. It emphasizes 'the multiplicity of subjects' and 'the relative other' (de Certeau 1986: 201ff; Karatani 1995: 93, 120, 33–38), challenging ostensibly neutral relationships between body, perception, representation and space, instead raising questions such as: whose body, whose space, which sight, how, when, why?

Thus, architectural thinking can be understood as a kind of *embodied realism*, discussed by George Lakoff and Mark Johnson (Lakoff and Johnson 1999: 17–22, 37ff., 77f., 102; see also Johnson 2007). As linguists and a philosopher involved in cognitive science, they hold that our understanding of the world is situation-based and corporeally anchored through our sensomotory system which acknowledges constructing as the most essential force in the understanding of our surroundings. Cognitive science supports a view that knowledge is promoted through an intimate criss-crossing between construction/making, perception/observing and conceptualization/understanding. In these processes we map both structures/patterns and specific focal points, or 'zones of convergence'.[3]

But 'bodies' may not only refer to human beings. Drawing from Actor-Network Theory (Latour 2005), physical objects and even immaterial artefacts like electronic signals or sounds, have an impact as actors involved in *agencies* in socio-cultural interactions and formations. As *agents* they take an active part in social processes and spatial situations, affect the scheme of things, bring about interference and change, or influence spatial conditions.

As architectural thinking moves between scales (detail–global) and aspects (artefacts, spaces, processes, user perspectives, systems), with a constant awareness of the physical/material, of agencies, environmental considerations, spatial relations and relational space, it continually produces temporary mappings and projective models as part of an innovative-analytical activity. The architect is trained to handle a large, multifaceted material in complex spatial situations and to create meaning, through the use of mappings-modelmakings, by identifying structures, key points (locations of special interest or with a certain potential), qualities, connections and relationships between agents and agencies in these situations. In this sense, the architect constructs semi-open systems for each situation. The architect is also trained to combine several types of tools to promote thinking; to rapidly shift between physical models, computer simulations, conceptual images and words, a multi-modal way of working that unites deductive thinking with intuitive precision, to see new relationships and to develop a sense of timing for action.

In the research process this constitutes a powerful toolbox with which architectural thinking can contextualize heterotopic conditions. It breaks up the traditional linear narrative of the research process, as starting with a problem, moving through analysis and theory, applying theory back to empirical studies, and finally arriving at concluding solutions. Instead, it promotes constant, quick shifts between innovation and analysis. Associative, lateral thinking is combined with logic/deductive reasoning and theoretical reflection. Creative experiments can be interspersed with series of systematic investigations and conceptual development. Starting off by a precise action, or a question, or an observation (or a given situation which one senses can be viewed in an alternative way), the architect-researcher gradually constructs – or composes – the *assemblage*, the open system which forms the research set-up with its relevant components and their internal/external connections. This assemblage, discussed as the sixth theme in this chapter, is also the material that the researcher models/re-models into the creation of new meaning and understanding.

Theme 2: performance and performativity

As the research situation is accepted to be in constant change and construction, performance means to actively interfere with it, through the making, interacting, simulating and communicating. Performance is both *to act in* a situation and *to make something act*, that is, to investigate by making-action as well as composing the set-up for it.

For instance, in a research by design course for our master students a few years ago we worked with the broad theme of space, sound and movement. Traditional recording techniques were questioned here, and different strategies explored. As a first experiment, one group put small microphones on their shoes. These close-up recordings were then confronted with images of what had caught their eye when moving in the space and presented as a series of sound-vision collages. Through this 'split' between sonic and visual the students could start asking questions on how different spatial sequences were present, how sound related to materiality, how visual and sonic details interacted, how border zones were constructed in a continuous public space, etc. They could remodel the material and present the theme from another, specific but different, approach. The active, explorative (re-)making generated a spiralling process of new questions-actions and the emerging contextualization of the problem.

Performance continuously produces examples that can reveal new aspects, meaning and questions. Analysis is accomplished through action, by staging, provoking or changing the situation. The process is continuously challenged by reflection and interrogation that aims to clarify choices and steps to be taken, with essential research questions like *why*, *what*, *how*, *where*, etc., activated in the making-composing and critical examination of the problem set-up. These questions are not ruling the process but can trigger further action and clarify where the knowledge process is heading.

Performance, and the making, also inverts the hierarchy between theory, method and action. In the humanities and social sciences, theory often forms a developed and coherent system of thought which is then applied to a material, or channelled through established methods with which to approach empirical studies, e.g. as in the scientific convention of case studies (Stake 1995; 2006). In technical science, theory is rather a hypothesis to be proved or falsified by experiments. Art-based research uses much more flexible interactions between practice and theory as it places the making at the centre, not as an object for theoretical processing or verification, but as an investigative, creative and compositional practice that may be put at interplay with several theoretical frameworks, specific concepts and experimenting activity.

Performance is seldom a singular act. Its impact in knowledge production often lies in the series of actions through which something can be discovered and understood. A situation can be remodelled with the change of components; different approaches may be tried out from a range of perspectives; a theme can be remodelled in extended variations of one material or detail; simulations of alternatives can be made. To tackle the complex or 'fuzzy' problem through performance is thus a compositional task that includes innovative, associative, analytical, deductive and inductive/analogical stages, in no particular order.

The possibilities in art for multimodal communication and representation in the situation – with the material, with oneself, within the research team, toward the outside world and others, etc – break the hegemony of verbal language and construct bridges of relationships between components in the heterogeneous process. This gradually forms the constructed 'context' that can be communicated and fed back (in text, image, models or sound), changing but also condensing into assertions about discoveries, conclusions, new questions and meaning. Thus, the boundaries between representation, conceptualization, and modelling tools are fluid. They are all parts of performance, and the shifts between different modes can be utilized to explore situations. The choice of communicative form early in the process becomes as important as choosing perspectives, since it is an integrated part of the making and since we thereby also choose which actors/actants will contribute, which relationships we construct, which points and links to articulate, and how we can communicate with ourselves and with others. These articulations can be switched, altered and set in motion along with the other research parameters, in a process largely conducted by a developed sense of intuitive accuracy and timing.

But, in turn, as the hegemony of written text is challenged by other modes of communication, language also has a performance capacity that can be expanded far beyond scientific conventions, and take on more diverse roles in the modelling process by interacting rather than describing. Text can engage graphically with images, constitute designations, factual descriptions, poetry and fictions (Hughes 2007: 99f.). Text can become both material and image. It can work rhythmically, poetically, or spatially as a score that emphasizes lines of tension, points of special interest, conceptions of movement, etc. It can also function both as mindmap, rhetorical convention and operative model for how to go on with an investigation.

Performance and AbR can have a tremendous impact on contemporary culture by producing examples that may affect individual choices and shared values, and spread rapidly as processes of change. While performance is a matter of singular actions or a limited series of interventions, *performativity* implies a stabilizing process made up by series of performances. As the political is often acted out through art, and with the increase of pluralistic research outside academia: what John Ziman discusses as post-academic research (Ziman 2000), practice-based methods and attractive examples may become fashionable objects that can instantly live a short medialized life. But they can also form dominant features with long-term impact on processes and larger collectives, providing ideas for others to take up, discuss, change and develop. When Judith Butler speaks of performativity, she especially investigates how the acts of performance, as well as of defining and categorizing them, are fixed by matter and materialization, thus creating self-generative mechanisms that influence the construction of boundaries and areas. These mechanisms, Butler contends, must constantly be exposed to critical scrutiny to avoid getting caught up in the hegemonic social *status quo* (Butler 2000: 136–81). Similarly, Sara Mills demonstrates how a field of research can become ensnared in power games as a result of various perspectives, approaches and proclamations (Mills 1999: 21 and 49f.). It can be marginalized or become a dominant part of the set of rules that constitute, activate and develop the game. This is of course particularly sensitive when it comes to AbR, which has been relegated until recently to the margins of academia, but is now assuming an important place. As artistic strategies are now largely being appropriated, the autonomy of academic 'truths' are exposed to, and interact with, other constructions of meaning, knowledge and socio-political processes in society, changing the legitimization process of research. This will be further discussed below, as theme 5.

Theme 3: staging explorative experiments

Staging explorative experiments is often the first part of performance. The operations are often interventions in a situation, fictional or real. According to Donald Schön there are three types of practice-based experiments: explorative, move-testing and hypothesis-testing (1991: 68f, 144ff.). Explorative experiments are set into scenarios through active, playful actions that can never be checked, while move-testing experiments assess a solution, and hypothesis-testing experiments are used to determine whether a hypothesis is true or false. For Schön all these categories are fundamentally solution-oriented. But the artistic approach also has the power to cut through conventional sets of meaning and challenge the hegemony between question and answer in knowledge production. This means that both move-testing and hypothesis-testing strategies can be drawn into creatively constructing artistic explorations, not to confirm 'a correct answer' but to formulate (alternative) game rules of performance. Art can simply be a very efficient way to see hidden connections in a problem situation, to switch perspectives, formulate complexities and reach new understanding.

Explorative experiments should subvert conventional strategies; shake up ingrained patterns of thought; provide quick feedback, increased curiosity, and discoveries of hidden possibilities; reveal possible links and points that need to be mapped; and get the creative process moving forward. The driving forces in the explorative process are invention and discovery. Added to this are sensitivity to improvisational possibilities and systematic contributions that, through links and key points, successively connect to other research and follow up on operations. Choosing the game rules becomes particularly important, therefore, in the initial phase of explorative experiments. This includes choices of representation or other modes of communication. The multimodal possibilities to communicate in art help the research process to work *with* heterogeneity, not against it.

Explorative experiments run the risk of, on the one hand starting from a totally open approach with too vague questions or, on the other hand, diving into the already well-known. The difficulty lies not in the creative, explorative activities themselves, but rather to expand the 'moment of discovery' through a series of sufficiently drastic interventions and surprises, with precision in actions and perspectives. The researcher-artist-designer should train the patience to linger – with joy and confidence – in the complex and 'fuzzy' state of exploration and uncertainty, but at the same time to make a situation respond and drive discovery forward as strongly as possible. This is game playing and dance, a choreography involving researcher, material and situation. It is meant to ward off both leading and overly general questions, and instead strive for precise yet opening inquiries that can expose something qualitatively new about the situation, develop alternative links, generate other approaches, give additional unanticipated insights, test and discuss relevance, confront with critical perspectives, and avoid the pitfalls of prematurely seeking final answers.

Explorative experiments could start anywhere in the symbiosis between conceptualization, perception and the making. The process may begin by questioning the meaning of, let us say, the bedroom as a concept of private space; asking oneself how it could be conceptualized differently. Or, it could begin with an observation of how people behave in a shopping mall and question the conventions of these collective spatial interactions. Or, one may investigate how two materials are combined, trying out a series of alternative ways of putting them together or tearing them apart. All these quite simple and precise starting points would probably generate many alternatives for further action. Choices have to be made: what is at stake here, how to play with this, what questions emerge, how to go on, what possible actions come into view, why is this important? The process of modelling and simulation has already begun.

Theme 4: modelling and simulation

In architecture a model generally represents how something *is* or *could be*. It may be *descriptive* (to demonstrate what something is like), *conceptualizing* (to investigate how something could be understood), or *prescriptive* (to suggest how something should be). But AbR, as often in technical and natural sciences, requires more operative modelling strategies – active tools that *do something*: 'what would happen if …?'

Modelling as an active tool closely relates to simulation as an investigating-constructing pursuit. As it is largely based on spatial and lateral thinking instead of a linear structure of thought, it helps in composing and re-arranging the enquiry and contributes to performance processes. Modelling involves materials, representations and technical working devices and is engaged in communication on several levels: models can act as machines in scenarios; they influence the situation but are, in their own turn, changed by it; and they can function in the critical (re-)examination of conditions, parameters and relationships in the research set-up. Thus they take part in the formation of the operational framework, in different kinds of dialogues, and in developing research as a collective practice.

Apart from investigating materialities, spatial thinking in modelling and experimentation can also stage *locations, heterotopias* and *liminal states.* Michel Foucault defines locations as the 'internal relationships between points and elements … mutually irreducible and entirely unable to overlap each other'. In the architectural or AbR situation this may identify key points or strategic set-ups of special interest. Correspondingly, heterotopias are locations that carry a complexity by connection (direct, referential or conceptual) to other places (Foucault 1999 [1984]: 176ff.). Such complexities may be difficult to grasp through logical thinking, but they may be investigated through the artistic modelling activity and, possibly, revealed in their richness of information and connections.

Through simulation/simulation the situation, or parts of it, can also be placed in temporary seclusions, *liminal states* (Turner 1982: 26; Dyrssen 1995: 136ff.) namely temporary 'as if' circumstances, out of ordinary space-time, in a marginal position or between one context and another. To situate a problem in a liminal state, possibly under extreme conditions, allows for other performances or games to be set up, and from which it can come to interplay with a 'real' situation. But a liminal state is also without time, which can imply that the research situation can be allowed to 'float' in a transitional state and intermediate zone, comparable to the concept of *terrains vagues* in a city, vague landscapes that allow for different programs or actions to take place and shape further change (Solà-Morales Rubió 1995). It gives the researcher a space for contemplation and deeper investigation. Certain components can be distinguished and placed in different relationship to their surroundings. Thus, the simulation/simulation can work as an abstraction, in the sense of pulling conditions or aspects out of their initial contexts. This may be used in experimental stagings or as part of a critical activity further discussed below.

For instance, in the research group Urban Sound Institute we made a one-year exhibition including a large sound labyrinth in a Swedish regional museum.[4] In one of the labyrinthine spaces we placed examples of old tales and stories from the sound archive in the museum. Some sound fragments were taken out of the narratives and spread throughout the space by forty small loudspeakers. A few of these were remodelled into 'musical' sounds. Other sounds were added, and thus we could investigate both the narrative, spatial and musical qualities embedded in the stories. In a way, this space in the labyrinth was in itself a liminal state of storytelling, floating in a vague terrain between the explicit meaning of words and sentences, speech sounds, musical sound, and a musical-sonic space. It emphasized shifting levels of focus, and it underscored an understanding of sounds and narratives from both constructional and perceptual approaches.

So, the work of modelling broadly spans representational models, idea diagrams, operative models, and modelling activities in a more general sense. The researcher becomes both navigator and co-player who reads the situation and the forces at play, enters a dialogue game with the set-up, follows the inherent movements between places, bridges the gaps between them, communicates with actors/actants, initiates boundaries and resistive forces that shift the assembled picture, extracts certain parameters and places them in liminal states in order to work with them, and so forth. The researcher takes a stand selectively on what the model is intended *to do* rather than what it shall be; i.e. the focus is set on what the model shall relate to, what secrets it can possibly reveal, what communicative reach it should have, and what representational forms would be most effective – but not what results it is intended to generate. The traditional research questions – what, where, when, for whom, by whom, why and how (in what way, with what tools) – thus relate not only to the initial formulation of a research project but also critically and creatively to what the modelling activity itself may perform.

In this way modelling and performance consciously operates with fiction to produce knowledge. To be workable, writes de Certeau, science (and any research) must abandon both totality and reality and incorporate 'fuzzy logic' and 'fuzzy relationships'. Science must accept the heterology – the discursive formations and doubled languages – that emerge between science and language, like 'science fiction' (de Certeau 1986: 210–22). Such acceptance will clarify its internal and dominant relationships to power. In de Certeau's interpretation, 'stories of diverse voices' are accompanied by a spectrum of different actions. This diversity of voices would also open up interesting possibilities for communication between scientific and artistic modes of making-thinking, e.g. by critically recontextualizing scientific data, or creatively expand a logic argument into artistic, associative experimenting.

In parallel with de Certeau, Thomas R. Fisher discusses how architects in general have pursued 'public fiction', 'imaginative acts and symbolic gestures that embody the collective values and ideas of community in a particular place and time'. Such fictions, says Fisher, are 'as diverse as the communities they speak to and the architects that work with them', and they involve

acting 'as if' something is true even when we know full well that it is not … .
A hypothesis is an idea that we hope to prove true. A fiction, in contrast, we

know to be untrue, but, like a tool, it proves useful to us at the moment to clarify something or to help us see it in a new way.

(Fisher 2000: 52f.)

Fiction in AbR – or artistic activity more generally – is not primarily a story about something, but rather a design tool for modelling. Fiction does not have to be literary or narrative, but can create an imagery that transgresses borders between different media, and goes in and models space, including the various agents' propositions, place-specific narratives, etc. By being aware of the fictions one creates, one can also recognize facts and conditions more critically. Fiction allows for complexity which, in turn, promotes surprise as total overview or control is impossible to maintain. Modelling is spatial and material fiction. Thus, modelling and fiction are strategic tools in the staging of explorative experiments and, as important parts in AbR, they are actions of active investigation, of knowledge production-interaction in the making, operating in the situation directly, changing the obvious to create or evoke new meanings. Part of this is to create tentative, fictive situations that can present alternative set-ups for the research framework. To consciously operate through fiction can provide possibilities of discovering a new context, a relevant system or configuration in which different components are engaged.

In the researching/modelling process, we can work *contrapuntally*, composing a contrasting interplay in which we, for instance, may: actively utilize tensions in the material that attract or repel different components; alternate materials; create conscious contrasts, contradictions, reinforcements and transformations; test extreme conditions; change perspectives; allow subject and object to change place; recast power relationships; construct new tension relationships, etc. Or, we can make small *variations and modifications* that, if they continue long enough, can give rise to what is known in physics as *phase transitions*, sudden changes of entire systems where new qualities appear. Experiments can allow questions in the material and its hidden possibilities, to temporarily occupy the context and appear in liminal or transitional states.

Through the simulation/simulation work, using floating or liminal conditions, finding temporary key locations and heterotopias, using contrapuntal techniques to search for tensions and contrasts, etc., in the research material, we find ourselves in a process oscillating between *disruptive* and *converging* mechanisms. The disruptive mechanisms dismantle, break up, provoke conditions, vary the material, shift positions and priorities and change perspectives in the research situation. In contrast, the converging mechanisms may use discursive and modifying processes to gradually focus the situation; they compose and shape it into a coherent construction of argumentation, in whatever form of representation.

In essence, these two main types of modelling actions compete and interact throughout the research process. They enable the work to emerge from the initial investigative activity to the composed 'product' of a thesis, a journal article, an exhibition or whatever form of representation this research activity is aiming at. Through architectural thinking and experimenting, this gradual compositional work can be understood as configurations – or choreographies – rather than a narrative rooted in deductive, verbal thinking. These configurations create meaning as the theme of research is gradually modelled, remodelled, simulated, constructed and composed. Architectural thinking gives a freedom here to use various kinds of logic, more related to art than the traditionally scientific, linear logic of cause and effect, theory and application, etc. It makes it possible to identify key points and construct lines of tension or qualities of relationships that can be investigated through modelling and simulation.

Again, essential research questions like why, what, where, how, etc., are important as instruments in the research work, serving as discursive and contrapuntal tools. By using the abstract as one of several operative models in a heterogeneous system, we can deconstruct the rhetorical line, create collages, set various forms of 'what' and 'why' in different configurations or spatial contexts. This makes it possible to keep thinking in terms of space, to zoom in and out between individual details and overall perspectives, and quickly alternate between opening and defining, disruptive and converging parts at different stages of a research project.

Theme 5: critical construction and reflection

Critical construction involves both reflection and remodelling, to actively explore a situation with an awareness of its positionings, ethical standpoints, performance, and power relations. Critical trials, experiments, variations and simulations/simulations may be used to sharpen the interplay between various types of convergences (observations, mappings, facts, conclusions, solution related proposals and questions, decisions, etc.) and disruptions (provocations, confrontations, drastic changes, modifications, explorative questions, etc.). Hierarchies can be revealed and shifted – between questions and answers, between what is taken for granted and the hidden possibilities, between different actants in power relations.

Critical construction and reflection may imply taking on a position, as when Jonathan Hill speaks of 'the illegal architect', to re-examine conventional roles of producing expected solutions to a problem and use the architectural project as 'criticism by design' that reveals other understandings and envisages alternatives for the future (Hill 1998; 2007). A critical perspective can help the researcher take a stand in the initial approach to a research subject or in the staging of explorative experiments. It may generate artistic-architectural action that challenges given hierarchies, political dominance, etc. When Doina Petrescu and Constantin Petcou of the French architectural studio *aaa* (atelier d'architecture autogérée) work in the city, they try to 'imagine other spaces to invest: grooves, cracks, breaches, loop-holes', they must 'multiply the modalities to act on the edge, the margins, the borders'. If Foucault speaks of heterotopias, aaa speaks of *Alterotopias*, spaces 'built and shared with others ... who are different from you'. But, they say, if 'we limit ourselves to a criticism of the institutions, that of the state and of Capitalism, there is little hope for change', as they are constantly in the threat of being either marginalized or absorbed by dominant forces. Instead they aim to 'reinvest urban space collectively, ecologically and politically' (aaa 2007: 321ff.).

Design and architectural thinking has a double capacity for critical positioning: as the architectural project not only appears in built form but also as models, simulations, series of action and theoretical argumentation, it may use the designerly capacity to both *project an alternative vision* for the future and to *direct this projection* to present repressed conditions from a critical perspective. In accordance, there is also a challenge to find the critical positions for performance activity and art in the processes of performativity (processes of dominance, subjugation and marginalization). Correspondingly, a critical re-positioning can be turned towards the research process itself, to challenge one's own operations. From initial explorative experiments, for instance, you may try out a change of game rules: a subversive perspective, inverted hierarchies, placing yourself in a subordinate or marginalized role, or switching the material, as indicated in the section on modelling and simulation.

What you do then, is actually to bring an architectural, design or AbR situation into discourse theory – or the reverse, to bring discourse theory into the designerly configurations, staging it in space and time, materiality and positioning of actants. Going back to Michel Foucault and *The Archaeology of Knowledge* (L'archéologie du savoir), one finds a terminology that is conspicuously spatial and therefore applicable in architectural modelling situations. Foucault speaks of systems of formation; discursive formations; points of diffraction; statements as acts of formulation from certain positions; and context-consequence as networks of relationships between different statements. The statement, says Foucault, is

> a function of existence that properly belongs to signs and on the basis of which one may then decide, through analysis or intuition, whether or not they 'make sense' […] a function that cuts across a domain of structures and possible unities, and which reveals them, with concrete contents, in time and space.
> (Foucault 1972 [1969]: 86–7)

In accordance with his many references to geography, one may stretch his concepts and apply them to AbR and architectural thinking. *Systems of formation* is defined by Foucault as 'not only mean the juxtaposition, coexistence, or interaction of heterogeneous elements (institutions, techniques, social groups, perceptual organizations, relations between various discourses), but also the relation that is established between them – and in well determined form – by discursive practice' (Foucault 1972 [1969]: 72). The obvious analogy to this is the construction-configuration of the AbR research situation. A *discursive formation*, says Foucault, 'presents the principle of articulation between a series of discursive events and other series of events, transformations, mutations and processes' (Foucault 1972 [1969]: 74). Parallels can be drawn here to critical modelling. *Points of diffraction* are 'points of incompatibility' where two incompatible parts are formed by the same set of rules and 'instead of constituting a mere defect of coherence, they form an alternative' (Foucault 1972 [1969]: 65). These are similar to key points in the spatial construct, or may also be identified as elements (actors) with strategically interesting agencies. Such connections between discourse theory and architectural thinking could be explored further, not the least through modelling or other non-verbal modes of communication.

Seeing the research situation and problem, or the modelling set-up, as a landscape where key points of different character (points of diffraction or convergence) create configurations of tensions and generate power relations, one may investigate them in terms of the spatial analogy to discursive formations, bringing the discursive, critical analysis in direct parallel with a spatial, even bodily, experience of tensions, relationships, positions, etc. Thus modelling has an analytical-innovative-critical potential to stage discourse theory, and performance is a powerful way to make statements. Again, this means that the hierarchy between theory and practice are levelled; and conceptual frameworks are generated not only by philosophers of science, but through artistic activity as well.

The recognition of heterogeneity and the performative, staging and modelling interplays with a situation, brings about possibilities for AbR to take on a stronger critical position, compared to 'ordinary' discursive, analytical or argumentative research approaches. The combination of critical positioning and invention, inherent in AbR, with the ability to communicate in multimodal ways, can develop a new integrity of academic research. The search for general evidence is being eclipsed by good examples, convincing analyses (design-based or otherwise scientific) and critically reflective arguments (artistic and/or rhetorical) to form both the goals and the processes for AbR. Setting architectural or other research situations into relevant scenarios and research configurations then becomes fundamental to qualified problem definitions in heterogeneity. Modelling builds a basis for research methodology, and heterogeneity is not merely a point of departure and precondition for research, but also the driving force in the searching and exchange of knowledge.

Theme 6: constructing the assemblage

With an analogy to 'systems of formation' the construct of the research topic can be understood as a way to gradually form a relevant open system, an *assemblage* made up from three main kinds of components: *key points*, *links* and *relationships*. Key points can act as knowledge nodes, points of diffraction, 'trigger points' of special interest or strategic agents for different actions to be taken. Although they often evolve over time, architectural-spatial thinking is helpful for identifying important key points. Between key points, or from key points to various aspects related to them, links can be explored and established, temporarily or with permanence. Relationships can be defined as specific qualities of these links, qualities that can be investigated and, in turn, this may affect the identification of key points and links. Reference material from various relevant and reliable sources can be directly connected to different key points or links, and the research process can be understood as an active, investigative choreography in a 'landscape', where the hegemony of verbal language is replaced by multi-modal communicative actions. Thus, the assemblage is a kind of constructed and successively updated mindmap for navigation. It is both a *composition of relevance* (identifying important questions as aspects) and a *relevant composition* (it provides a useful instrument for the research process). Again, the research abstract as a rhetorical tool can be of assistance in the construction of assemblages, and the basic research questions – *what, where, when, for whom* and *how* – reappear in a new role, to redefine positions or trigger changes within the assemblage.

There are several advantages of constructing assemblages for the research situation instead of speaking of problem context. First, while context is inclusive and covers an area in which the problem is inscribed, the assemblage is a composition. Thinking in terms of context may lead to extensive, unspecific areas being connected to the research situation, making it extremely difficult to handle. In contrast, as the assemblage is a continuous composition-mapping-recomposition; it is a tool more in accordance with the criss-crossing processes of invention-intervention-analysis-construction. Second, assemblages relate to system thinking, which is part of architectural thinking. But where system thinking tends to present schemes that neutralize the qualities of relationships between components, assemblages underscore the particular character of links and relationships, and connect them to critical perspectives and standpoints. Third, assemblages support change as the research process develops. They are non-static configurations, mapped at certain stages of the process, and thus the sequence of assemblages provides an itinerary of the research process, making it possible to go back and locate changes, decisions and special discoveries. Fourth, while context can easily be seen as a passive surround to the problem, the assemblage is deeply involved in modelling activity. It can set the game rules for performance and explorative experiments; it can provide a score for simulation, or in itself be an object for simulation; that is, it can be tried out in different forms of representation, and key points, links and relationships can be challenged. Finally, as assemblages stress the compositional act of the research process they promote the gradual invention-setting-emergence of research issues.

In heterotopic conditions 'place' and 'site' are constantly competing, forming diverse and multiple interactions. *Place*, as (traditionally) a location saturated with a specific set of qualities that produce 'identity', is confronted with *site* as a location in space connected to other sites and spaces. In this sense, key points are sites in an assemblage. Identities become relational, equally tied to the qualities of relationships as to the roles of defined key points. In this complexity of constant change we are compelled to make choices and to construct meaning, and therefore, in academic knowledge production, we also need to train construction and composition. As architectural thinking modulates heterotopic conditions, it constructs assemblages as configurations of relevant components in the research situation, at the same time producing tools for mapping the research set-up and representations for navigation. The researcher gradually develops skills in setting up relevant and interesting assemblages for navigation.

This brings us back to the research process as a compositional activity where we can recognize four basic types of performative actions: *mapping*; *solution-oriented*; *exploratory*; and *discursive* or *critical action*. Mappings *bring in*, or gather, reliable facts, relevant reference material and site conditions that need to be considered in the research situation. Solution-oriented actions can *bring about*, or produce, temporary or stable statements generated during the research process. Exploratory actions *bring out*, or reveal, the unknown and open up for the unexpected. Discursive/critical actions *bring up*, or discuss, alternative perspectives that may invert or question the constructed assemblage and its components.

To sum up, these four categories take the investigation through a selective oscillation between convergence (focusing, stabilizing) and disruption (opening up or rethinking) in the research process, and create loops between identification (analysis) and scenario/staging (explorative action and innovation). The process will generate a heterogeneous, transient, composed set of assemblages that serve as a double strategic tool. On the one hand the assemblage provides a mindmap that gives an overview of the present state of the configuration – its components of key points, links and relationships. On the other hand the successive sequence of assemblages generates a flexible itinerary, a route map where decisions and reconfigurations can be traced as a list of actions or a graph of the chosen trail through the mindmaps as the research develops.

Conclusions

It has been my intention to show how art-based research can use architectural, time contingent, multi-dimensional thinking to develop research, with construction and composition set in the foreground, in symbiosis with perception and conceptualization. There is an urgent need to develop strategies that can deal with heterogeneity and non-linear investigative processes, where the re-thinking and re-configuration of problems are as important as answers. The research process is seen as a continuous, collective act with the product (the journal article, the exhibition, or the PhD thesis in different forms) as an intermediate statement. The body in 'embodied realism' is emphasized as a reference point for exploring the world, but at the same time the interaction between bodies (things, persons, the relative other, etc.) and other artefacts (representations, images, etc.) is stressed, as this interference produces the dynamics with which the research configurations are established.

Apart from *architectural thinking* as a multidimensional mode to construct, perceive and conceptualize complex situations, five other themes were discussed. In their making and communication of 'fuzzy' research problems, *performance* and *performativity* subvert traditional hierarchies between theory, method and action, as well as between answer and question, argument and example. They also help to combine different modes of representation in research.

Staging explorative experiments use invention, intervention and discovery as the main driving forces when setting up and actively examining specific situations. This may reveal the unexpected, repressed or hidden, and it trains the researcher in rapidly switching between associative and systematic thinking, to develop an intuitive precision and different types of logic.

Modelling and *simulation* as interactive tools of enquiry in heterogeneity stress questions of what a model can do, rather than what it represents. It helps the researcher to consciously operate with fiction, linger actively in uncertain states of the process, and take a question or a material into extreme conditions or liminal, intermediate states. Modelling often moves between disruptive and converging mechanisms and may serve as a contrapuntal tool to interfere with, and compose, research material that generates new meaning.

Critical construction and reflection, including remodelling, is necessary as a strategy to maintain research integrity and to navigate in heterogenic knowledge production, not only for ethical reasons but also to confront and re-examine the research situation with subversive or alternative interrogation in order not to jump to conclusions but to deepen and develop a material. It may also be a conscious position from which the researcher starts an investigation. Drawing from Michel Foucault, critical remodelling can make fruitful analogies to discourse theory.

At the end, *assemblages* were presented as a gradual creation of configurations for research situations. The theme could just as well have been a starting point for this chapter, as assemblages can act as layout, mindmap and instrument for navigation in heterogeneity for the other approaches discussed. Through key points, links, and qualities/character of relationships the assemblage structures 'context' and helps to compose the research situation and its specific connections to other research and relevant material, examples, etc.

These six themes constitute different approaches to the interaction between thinking-doing/acting-composing. In each of them, traditional research questions can appear as tools for creative, analytical, associative and critical confrontation with other operations – to help open up the situation when it threatens to become stagnant, and to generate precision as the research problem is constructed, when hidden aspects are revealed, knowledge produced and new meaning (through argumentation, in whatever medium) is composed.

One may ask, then: how does this affect – and attract – other research practices? Today's heterogenic, often transdisciplinary conditions of enquiry, I would argue, need a non-linear approach that provides system thinking that is flexible and open enough to replace context with assemblages of relevance. The mode of architectural thinking, as a fundamental cognitive practice, is essential here. Research strategies cannot be simplified into a prescription for action, but combinatory approaches can be suggested that open up new formations of generating knowledge, or as John Ziman concludes: 'In the long run, moreover, the post-academic drive to "rationalize" the research process may damp down its creativity' (Ziman 2000: 330). A large part of the research community recognizes knowledge as being socially and culturally constructed in a collective practice. Therefore, we equally need to accept the element of fiction and artistic creativity, not merely as an exception to 'truth' and 'proof' but as a necessary part of innovative practice inherent in research.

But what about the playful and the uncontrollable? Most scientists claim that playing and creativity form an important part of scientific work. Systematic, operative models and controlled experiments belong to the scientific game rules and, I would argue, they have an inherent beauty, a stringency that could well be included as elements in AbR, but only if not converted to dogma. As for the uncontrollable, this is a necessary part of innovation and cross-disciplinary contact and therefore not only acceptable, but also needed as an ingredient in most research processes today – to find out new things, one has to let go of some old conventions.

And what about this other kind of precision that has to do with intuitive accuracy in relation to complexity, to do with artistic skills and insight, with the competences of the art-based researcher? Artistic practice is often accused by scientists of being imprecise and overly relativistic in the handling of data and controllable experiments, while scholars from the humanities may claim that a constant doing-making leads to theoretical eclecticism and a lack of stringency in argumentation. But, I would argue, with an increased awareness of the fact that contexts must be constructed, and therefore composed, to function in relevant ways, all research is challenged to develop intuitive accuracy. This accuracy can best be trained by combining several intelligences, by using diverse modes of representation and modelling as well as critical reflection, and by becoming ever more familiar with the triangle of thinking-performing-composing.

Most people today, including researchers, realize the challenge, or the complement, to the written text offered by other modes of communication. Technical scientists are often familiar with simulation, practical laboratory work and construction, while this may sometimes still be strange to people from the humanities tradition. Will advanced techniques for producing images and sounds challenge or even threaten the hegemony of philosophy to construct concepts, theories of science, or models of thought? Or will they offer new combinations of conceptualization and artefacts, experimentation and theory? Most people have the senso-motoric ability to make spatial analogies and experiences of models and maps; landscapes that can be imagined and constructed. Therein lies the opportunity for a more extensive use of new tools for modelling and imagery, and of making-action-performance.

Of course there are performative power struggles ahead: forming new disciplines, fighting for academic positions and funding, defining the most urgent problems. The academic fashion industry is fit for institutional fights. But in essence, the nineteenth-century, 'stable' classification system of disciplines has outlived its function. Learning traditions develop along much more combinatory lines. Interesting topics of research are found inbetween established investigative results. To 'build on existing knowledge' does not mean to range within existing categories but to collectively and continually place each project in relation to other projects, and reconnect to other researchers' strategies and methods.

While, ten years ago, artistic investigative practices were still often looked upon with suspicion by other research paradigms, today I meet curiosity when lecturing in different research environments. Many scholars see the possibilities of trans- or cross-disciplinary collaboration where different types of precision and modelling, performance and experiments can be combined, confronted and exchanged. As the fine arts demystify AbR, it will gain its full potential.

It is my hope that it is not only art-based researchers within the making disciplines who can recognize themselves in the descriptions of these spatially founded making-composing-actions, critical reflections and setting of assemblages; but that this multiple, modelling, non-linear way of working with constructions of knowledge will reach to other scholars and bridge gaps between different traditions of inquiry. To be scholarly, conscientious and creative always includes the use of relevant material, systematized data and critical consideration of conditions linked to the research problem. But, in addition, it is through the conscious operations with fiction, innovation and composition that knowledge is produced, and new meaning emerges.

Notes

1 For practical reasons, the term art-based research (AbR) is used here as a general approach including practice-based or design-based research or research by design.
2 http://www.usit.nu (accessed 22 January 2010).
3 'Zones of convergence' are described by neurologist Antonio Damasio as part of the thinking-acting-creating in 'sensomotory maps' (Damasio 2006).
4 Urban Sound Institute, http://www.urbansound.org/eng/index.php (accessed 12 February 2010).

14
INSIGHT AND RIGOUR: A FREUDO-LACANIAN APPROACH

Malcolm Quinn

Introduction

The term 'creative practitioner' facilitates a certain kind of research, one that unites the notion of a level playing field for art and design production, with an analysis of creative lifeworlds from within. However, the universally applicable notion of the creative practitioner, which seems so distinct from the elites and coteries of genius, nonetheless continues to introduce ideas of creative exceptionalism, even at the highest levels of analysis. In 2007 in the UK, for example, an AHRC Research Review on 'Practice-led Research in Art, Design and Architecture' asserted that 'The argument that professionals and teachers in ADA [Art Design and Architecture] need an approach to research that does not undermine their identity as creative practitioners is hard to refute' (Rust *et al.* 2007: 48). A crucial argument that I will advance in this chapter, is that a psychoanalytic orientation shows that this 'irrefutable' assertion can indeed be refuted. The AHRC Research Review shows that a challenge still needs to be offered to the special or protected status accorded to the self-identity of the creative practitioner as a 'given' of arts-based research, despite the claim of Macleod and Holdridge in this volume, that current thinking has moved beyond theory as against practice (Chapter 20). I am however in agreement with MacLeod and Holdridge's thesis that 'arts research relates to the experience of the researcher whose world is drawn into the research project and within which, the formulation of the research is relative to the subject positioning of the researcher'. Psychoanalysis offers a specific investigative orientation, in which the act of making an address to unconscious thought as an analyst, researcher or investigator affects the construction of self-identity. A psychoanalytic approach emphasizes how the act of becoming an investigator places the researcher in a particular relationship to knowledge. Assuming the mandate of an artist-researcher within a psychoanalytic aegis would mean that one was inviting the possibility of a new understanding of the artist and a new conception of the art object. This is why most 'applied psychoanalysis' in art and design is not psychoanalysis at all, since it leaves existing relations of subject, object and practice intact. The position that I advance in this chapter, is that the only properly psychoanalytic view in research is not the view from a theory or a practice, but the view from a subject position that has initiated the investigation. In the final section of this chapter, I show how this subject position that constitutes the rigour of the researcher, could arise as the response to a challenge to the identity of the creative practitioner. In this instance, the challenge arises not from an authoritative interpretation of art and design objects, but as a request for the articulation of the 'function' of the artist in a scrawled note at the 2008 Turner Prize.

In order to demonstrate why a psychoanalytic framework is useful to arts-based research, it is first necessary to understand why the transition from creative genius to creative practitioner, has preserved the primacy of identity while raising the tantalizing possibility of research. This possibility or potential for research is constrained by the bounds of a lifeworld or life nexus that establishes the domain of practice within which the creative practitioner is said to operate. Here, the researcher cannot refute the identity of the creative practitioner without simultaneously eliminating the field of research activity. Nor can the artist-researcher effectively bracket their own identity in order to conduct research; their research must in some way prove its self-reflexive or self-conscious character. In this respect, this chapter differs from the analysis of the self in arts-based research offered by Morwenna Griffiths in this volume. While I would concur with the way that Griffiths raises the issue of hiding behind identity (Chapter 10), her analysis employs the model of a reflexive self 'embodied and embedded' in physical and socio-political contexts. In this chapter, I am more concerned with a Freudian 'determinism of mental life', in other words how the relation of psyche and self produced by an unconscious, affects the relation of self and world. The inherent constraints that the self-identity of the creative practitioner can produce, are also expressed by Kozel in this volume, that 'practices point to different models of knowledge and the models offer up refinements of the practice' (Chapter 12). The crucial distinction she introduces here between 'different models' of knowledge and 'refinements' of practice, is an indication of the limitations that may be placed on research activity by the identity of the creative practitioner. These foreclose the possibility that research might lead to the more radical outcome of *different models of practice*, as well as the potential for change that Kozel herself attributes to 'the virtual'.

It is at this point of impasse, where the identity of the creative practitioner becomes an irrefutable element of the research equation controlling the parameters of the research outcome, that psychoanalysis can make a contribution to art and design research. However, it is first important to identify the epistemological basis of that contribution. Psychoanalysis, which offers a means to disregard creativity at the level of identity while examining it at the level of an unconscious utterance, thereby establishes a distinction between its own way of operating, and models of research in the humanities and social sciences and in the natural sciences. Psychoanalysis is not part of social science or humanities research because it does not begin with the idea of social actors in the context of practice or life nexus. It is not part of natural science research because it asserts that the statement or utterance itself is what matters, rather than the content of the utterance, such as a scientific formula or equation. This chapter begins with an elucidation of this epistemological difference, with particular focus on the distinction between Sigmund Freud and Wilhelm Dilthey's approach to genius. While Dilthey offers a model for psychological and social scientific research in which artistic identity is at once 'made ordinary' and yet preserved by being contextualized within a life-nexus, Freud discusses the genius of Dostoyevsky and Leonardo da Vinci, while explicitly showing how his investigation places identity in question. In the Leonardo essay there are two versions of the subject of the investigation and two practices, Leonardo the artist and Leonardo the researcher.

The possibilities and problems of research that Freud discusses in the Leonardo essay, are taken forward in this chapter in relation to Salvador Dalí's essay 'L'Âne Pourri' (The Rotten Donkey) which was published in the first issue of *Surréalisme au service de la Révolution* (Dalí 1930). Dalí's essay is significant because it isolates a possibility for arts-based research that uses a psychoanalytic framework, while simultaneously showing how research agency is hampered by the problem of identity and the artistic personality. This divide is most clearly shown in the manner in which Dalí's account of paranoiac-critical method helped the psychoanalyst Jacques Lacan to accomplish his 'return to Freud' on the basis of a distinction between identity and utterance, while Dalí himself became increasingly obsessed with the public spectacle of his own artistic celebrity. The significance of this is not that there was a plagiarism of Dalí by Lacan, but rather that there was an effective demonstration of the limits of knowledge within Dalí's project. Dalí's paranoiac-critical method had offered the potential for the agency of the researcher to emerge within the process of making art, through a specific shift in the status of the creative practitioner. Yet the potential for research agency developed in Surrealism was assumed by Jacques Lacan rather than by Dalí himself, and as the example of the AHRC report quoted above shows, nearly eighty years later, creativity as such is still identified with the creative practitioner in a way that limits the possibility of arts-based research.

The contrasting position introduced by a Freudo-Lacanian approach to arts-based research, is that before research in art and design can assume a particular content (i.e. what the research is 'about') it must first of all be seen as something that has the potential to change the subjective structure and position of the designer or the artist, and consequently the meaning of art and design activity and its patterns of social recognition. The shift from the uniqueness of genius to the generality of the creative practitioner, does not accomplish the kind of structural change that inaugurates a new kind of subject that can rightly be called an 'artist-researcher'. In the latter part of this chapter, I offer a model of how the problematic inauguration of the artist-researcher can be addressed using a psychoanalytic framework. I cite the work of the 2008 Turner Prize winner Mark Leckey as a demonstration of the vicissitudes of the artist researcher, insofar as Leckey adopts the practices and formats of pedagogy and research such as the public lecture, while avowing an autodidactic position and a disavowal of knowledge. The adoption of the position of the researcher or the position of knowledge would require a shift in Leckey's subject position that he does not take up. While one can simply attribute that refusal to his status as an artist rather than an arts-based researcher, Leckey's oscillation between what Jonathan Jones (2008), refers to as Leckey's PhD-style 'subjective anthropology' on the one hand, and a disavowal of knowledge on the other, illustrates some of the problems involved in assuming a research mandate from within the terms of a practice. Furthermore, the conclusions of the AHRC Research Review show that this overt or covert refusal of the position of knowledge and research is a common problem for arts-based research in art schools and universities. I shall show that the manner in which psychoanalysis offers a model of creativity conducted at the level of utterance, is useful in addressing this problem.

In conclusion, I will show how this distinction between utterance and identity allows for a separation of the function of psychoanalysis within arts-based research on the one hand, and within art school-based 'theory' on the other. This also allows for a reconsideration of the championing of theory in art schools undertaken by Terry Atkinson in his essay 'Phantoms of the Studio', and his assertion that 'Nowhere has the idea of the unconscious been more symptomatically half-digested, and nowhere is it a more entrenched agency of meaning-fixing ... than in art school teaching' (Atkinson 1990: 51).

Psychoanalysis and the creative practitioner

In his 'Ideas Concerning a Descriptive and Analytical Psychology', Wilhelm Dilthey expressed an ambition to 'make accessible to conceptual analysis what the great poets, Shakespeare especially, have expressed in images' (Dilthey 1977 [1894]: 68). In this way, Dilthey expressed a recurrent theme of research in the creative arts, namely, how does one capture the essence of the 'lifeworld' in which an artist and his works are embedded, within the rigour of a conceptual analysis? As Dilthey framed it, this problem in the matching of a creative practice with an appropriate method of analysis, would be the same for an artist or a designer analysing their own practice, as it would be for a sociologist or an art historian conducting research within art and design fields. Here, within an acknowledgement of the genius of Shakespeare, we have a discernible shift from the uniqueness of genius to the generality of practice. As Kurt Müller-Vollmer has put it, Dilthey asserted that 'the mental constitution of the poet did not differ fundamentally from that of other human beings ... The man of action, the philosopher, and the poet have to rely on the same constitutive elements of experienced reality' (Müller-Vollmer 1963: 97). Dilthey's model of the self, used the idea of a preconscious, if not a properly unconscious, notion of psychic life:

> I have no need to bring to awareness the system of my professional obligations in order to subordinate an action to it according to the prevailing situation, and the intention contained in this system of duties continues to be effective without my being conscious of it. In effect, diverse purposive systems[1] intersect in every consciousness sustained by cultural relations.
>
> (Dilthey 1977 [1894]: 71)

For Dilthey, the analysis of creative practice must take place with reference to this preconscious and pre-conceptual level, in which 'enduring relationships that go from individual to individual ... give the practical world its stability' (Dilthey 1977 [1894]: 72). Creative works are a symbolic response to immersion within a field of life experience, and the analysis of life experience must trace and reprise this connection between the individual and the human world. Dilthey's model of a psychic life nexus is at the root of standard definitions of how the term practice is commonly deployed in the human sciences, a usage that has also filtered into art and design.

One thing of which Dilthey was certain, was that the problem of placing Shakespeare within a conceptual framework could be approached only by the human sciences (*Geisteswissenschaften*) which analyse relations of parts to wholes, and contribute to understanding (*Verstehen*) within human lifeworlds, as opposed to the natural sciences (*Naturwissenschaften*) which examine cause and effect and which favour explanations (*Erklärung*) that abstractly theorize, rather than contextualize, phenomena. Psychology, in Dilthey's view, was one of those human sciences. This placed the self within a model of psychic continuity, a whole nexus of lived experience within which a set of inner experiences were contained. This establishes a distinction between psychology seen as a social science, and a natural scientific approach, since Dilthey believed that while we can *explain* the natural world, we could only *understand* the situation of the self in a lifeworld. For Dilthey, description is the preferred analytical tool in psychological understanding, because it relates parts (inner experiences) to wholes (life experience). This is set against the model in which a description of the natural world operates as a synthesis of discontinuous observed objects within a unified explanatory framework. In Dilthey's view, a 'Descriptive and Analytical Psychology', could be used to mark the difference between the continuity of a lifeworld and the discontinuous external world. This raises an immediate problem for research in the creative arts, which is that as soon as one passes from experience itself to the conceptual analysis of experience, no matter how self-reflexive that analysis is, the forbidden spectre of a totalizing and inappropriate explanatory framework arises. This explanatory framework threatens the very division between the continuity of selfhood within practice and the life nexus on the one hand, and a discontinuous, alienated, non-human world on the other. This may also account for some of the superstitions still surrounding the relationship of practice and research, and the perceived need for guarantees that practice and life experience constitutes an inviolable whole that research activity cannot fundamentally challenge. The term 'practice' thus becomes a guarantee of psychic liberty, and describes a field of operations in which the artist and designer can work undisturbed.

This returns us to the problem of where and how to situate the self within a model of research while preserving analytical rigour. At this juncture, a psychoanalytic approach to the question of practice, and practice-led research, becomes useful. While the relation of the analyst and the analysand must be seen as a social bond of a particular type, this bond is an experimental and deliberately artificial one, in which specific elements of the self are staged or deployed. Furthermore, while psychoanalysis is primarily concerned with an analysis of the subject at the level of the utterance, it offers no guarantees on the preservation of self-identity within a continuous framework of experience. In fact, the introduction of the notion of a thinking unconscious immediately places this in doubt. The crucial move that Freud accomplished from preconscious thought to a thinking unconscious, precludes Dilthey's opposition of a continuous life nexus and a discontinuous external world, and instead introduces a fundamental discontinuity within psychic constitution, a splitting or division of thought. The primary division within thought that psychoanalysis introduces, is the basis for Freud's 'first topography' that distinguishes between consciousness, the preconscious and the unconscious, and also underpins his 'second topography', of Id, Ego and Superego (Freud 1961 [1923]). What needs careful elucidation is how the positing of a thinking unconscious in psychoanalysis, affects not just the status and security of subjective identity, but the relation of the subject to knowledge and truth. In his *Introductory Lectures on Psychoanalysis* (Freud 1963 [1915]) he offers a positive view of the problem of interpretation I have identified in Dilthey's psychology, in which research and analysis disturb the continuity of practice. For Freud, the problem with which the analyst is presented is that he knows nothing, and that the analysand knows something but does not know that he knows. This unconscious knowledge is 'the elephant in the room' with the analyst and the analysand. What differentiates the analyst from the analysand is an entirely negative set of attributes – the analyst does not know something (about the analysand's unconscious knowledge), and crucially he also does not believe in something, namely the condition of psychic freedom:

> But in general if the dreamer asserts that nothing occurs to him we contradict him; we bring urgent pressure to bear on him – and we turn out to be right ... Once before, I ventured to tell you that you nourish a deeply rooted faith in undetermined psychical events and in free will, but that this is quite unscientific and must yield to the demand of a determinism whose rule extends over mental life.
>
> (Freud 1963 [1915]: 105f.)

This 'determinism of mental life' affects the analyst and the analysand equally, but the key difference is that the analyst has already taken a crucial step towards the acceptance of that determinism, which is what enables them to conduct the analysis. The analyst operates at the level of the utterance, while the analysand operates at the level of a narration of self-identity. It is this same narration of self-identity that prevents the analysand from gaining access to unconscious knowledge. For the analyst, the determinism of mental life must be conceived of in a materialist fashion, in the same way that the maximum height of a building is determined by its mode of construction and by the materials from which it is made. The analysis consists of observing moments where the materiality or facticity of an unconscious utterance emerges from within the continuous poetic flow or narrative of self-identity that the analysand produces. In a Freudian model, the unconscious is a set of anomalous facts that interrupt the fiction of self-identity. Sometimes these unconscious facts might be literal facts as well. For example, how does knowledge about the price of a particular artwork, or the number of schoolchildren who are obliged to visit it each year as part of their school curriculum, affect a fiction of being in control of objects that is possessed by a museum curator? The stupid and irritating facticity of unconscious thought, on which the free play of conscious thought snags at every turn, shows that in psychoanalysis, stupidity is not the opposite of cleverness. Instead, the stupidity of unconscious thought is what reveals the impossibility of 'being clever'.

This also gives a clue as to how the subjective mandate of the analyst places them in a particular relationship to knowledge, in which truth is not conceived teleologically but causally. In the example I have just given, the truth of cleverness is found in something that causes its fall, and not in its accomplishment. It is this that led Jacques Lacan to assert that in psychoanalysis, 'truth is only a fall of knowledge'[2] (Lacan 1991 [1970]: 216). Lacan was keen to situate psychoanalysis as sharing some of the qualities of the Cartesian *cogito*, which places certainty within the domain of observation rather than accumulated knowledge. Descartes had maintained that 'the things we conceive very clearly and very distinctly are all true' (Descartes 1985 [1637]: 127). However, Lacan's assertion that truth is only a fall of knowledge places this observation, and the certainty established by the facts of unconscious thought, within the domain of knowledge itself. This is very different from the Cartesian idea of a knowledge gleaned from close observation, whose truth is ultimately guaranteed by a benevolent God. The change in the position of the subject that inaugurates the analyst/investigator can therefore be said to be composed of two elements – an initial embrace of the *cogito* with its emphasis on a truth produced by observation, accompanied by a decisive relocation of that truth within knowledge itself, in the form of a division between conscious and unconscious knowledge. The unconscious cannot be observed in its totality as a body of knowledge, but the division between conscious and unconscious thought can be observed as a fall of knowledge. This is the point of view that the analyst adopts as a consequence of his renunciation of a belief in psychic freedom. In contrast, modern science has moved away from Descartes' wager on a divine guarantor for an 'I am', and placed its trust instead in the rigour of scientific method as the guarantee of truth. Psychoanalysis, however, has conceived of investigative rigour differently again. It does this as an orientation or shift in the position of the subject that allows for the location of a rigorous unconscious truth, rather than through the adoption of a particular method by which truth is assured. For Lacan, this subject position of the analyst can itself take the form of a statement, for example in his use of the phrase 'I always speak the truth' (Lacan 2007 [1965]: 3), which, far from being hubristic, is another way of accepting the Freudian idea of a determinism that governs mental life. A phrase such as 'I always speak the truth' also affirms that it is the utterance itself that is the matter of investigation and the locus of truth, rather than either the meta-truths of existence, life experience or praxis beyond the utterance, or a scientific formula or equation that attempts to demonstrate that truth inheres in the rigour of method.

The question of interpretation in arts-based research

Lacan's statement affirming the subject position of the analyst, dispenses with both existential freedom and the freedom of interpretation, since the task of the analyst is to locate a knowledge that the analysand already knows, rather than add an intellectual construction of the analyst's own. Consequently, if an artist-researcher were to adopt a psychoanalytic paradigm, they would be required to note how the adoption of the subject position of a researcher alters their previous view of the determinations of their practice. This might begin with a radical gesture of positively rejecting the thesis that the truths of the artist, the designer and the researcher alike are to be found in the lifeworld of a practice. They would then be required to map the difference that the agency of the researcher introduces within the established patterns of artistic self-identity, noting any particular determinations or facts that arise to disturb the construction of this identity, such as those previously mentioned statistics that might impact the museum curator's belief in his control of the world of objects. It would also be essential for the artist-researcher or designer-researcher[3] who adopts a psychoanalytic paradigm, to avoid becoming the theorist of his or her own objects or adding a new layer of meaning or interpretation. Whether this extra layer of interpretation is derived from psychoanalytic theory, philosophical aesthetics or some other discourse is immaterial. In this regard, I would take issue with Joan Mullin's affirmation in this volume, of the value of 'a rhetor/artist's toolkit that contribute[s] to their own professional productions – critiques, analyses, interpretations' (Chapter 9). Mullin claims that such an auto-critical stance, can accompany the aim to 'create an edginess, dissonance or cohesion in an artefact', whereas from a Freudian perspective, these two aims are incompatible.

At the beginning of this chapter, I made the claim that the only properly psychoanalytic view in research is not the view from a theory, but the view from a subject position that has inaugurated the investigation. This may enable us to understand why some proponents of applied psychoanalysis in art and design can nonetheless see psychoanalysis as offering only potential, rather than actual, rigour:

> I have to admit that I find it [psychoanalysis] less active as my work goes on. Perhaps I'm affected by the insistent abuse of psychoanalysis in the culture at large. I think there is a real difference between the situation in the States, and the situation here and in mainland Europe. In the States, psychoanalysis fled to the academy and died there! But for all its abuses, intellectual and cultural, as with Marxism, it's a rich set of tools if they are used effectively, properly ... I tend to think about 'the right tool for the job' – there is a pragmatics of theory ... I'm not a member of a sect.
>
> (Foster in Grant 2008: 105)

Hal Foster's assertion that he is 'not a member of a sect' may be a way of asserting that he is more interested in the freedom to use psychoanalysis as a tool for interpretation in the context of other possible tools, rather than as something that acts as the origin and limit of an investigation. Nonetheless, the tangible but elusive rigour of psychoanalytic research that he describes, is only available as the rigour of the researcher, and not as the rigour of method, which can hardly be said to exist in psychoanalysis. Freud's scattered commentaries on technique are far less precise than his definition of the subject position and investigative orientation of the analyst. As Hal Foster's insistence on a 'take it or leave it' attitude to psychoanalysis may indicate, the application of psychoanalytic ideas to art and design objects often arises from the assumption that the interpreter and the object of interpretation both inhabit a domain of life experience that guarantees psychic freedom. One way to approach this assumption is through the paradox of 'free association'. 'Free association' in psychoanalysis is not equivalent to psychic freedom, rather it is a specific technique designed to help the analyst to identify facts of utterance, which do not depend on what either the analyst or the analysand believes the correct interpretation of the utterance to be:

> I beg you to respect it as a fact that that is what occurred to the man when he was questioned and nothing else. But I am not opposing one faith with another. It can be proved that the idea produced by the man was not arbitrary nor indeterminable nor unconnected with what we are looking for.
>
> (Freud 1963 [1915]: 106)

This emphasis on the facts of the unconscious might seem to push Freudianism towards the notion of description appropriate to natural science, in which the utterances of the analysand are treated as if they were a set of distinct natural objects that are made sense of within an explanatory scheme. This is not the case, however. Psychoanalysis is not a stand-alone theory, it is a specific orientation towards the materiality of the utterance, accompanied by a renunciation of belief in psychic freedom. This enables a particular form of analysis or investigation to be conducted, based on the close observation of deviations from the path of self-identity:

> there has been a general refusal to recognize that psycho-analytic research could not, like a philosophical system, produce a complete and ready-made theoretical structure, but had to find its way step by step along the path towards understanding the intricacies of the mind by making an analytic dissection of both normal and abnormal phenomena.
>
> (Freud 1961 [1923]: 35f.)

It is crucial to stress, as I have done thus far, that a psychoanalytic reading depends not on the adoption of a particular model of research, but rather on the emergence of an analytic position as a specific orientation of the subject. This orientation moves away from a belief in the psychic freedom embodied in self-identity, and towards the absence of this identity at the level of unconscious knowledge. This is the subject of Freud's exhortations to the Vienna Psychiatric Clinic in his *Introductory Lectures in Psychoanalysis*. Here the possibility of analysis, research and investigation depends upon a shift of position (towards not knowing, and the renunciation of belief in psychic freedom) that produces an agent of research. Dilthey's psychology, on the other hand, offers a model of research that conceals the presence of an intrusive agent of research, and which leaves the structure of life experience intact; hence his advocacy of passive description rather than active interpretation. Freud rejects both description and interpretation for the abductive observation of anomalies in the efficient production of self-identity. Thus the emergence of the researcher in the life nexus that presents a problem for Dilthey, becomes the pre-condition of psychoanalytic observation for Freud. This establishes an important distinction between psychological and psychoanalytic approaches to the creative subject.

A shift in the position of the subject produces a shift in the position of the object

The rigour of the researcher that I have identified as proper to a psychoanalytic approach to arts-based research, also produces a new orientation towards the object of investigation. One way to approach this issue is by looking at how Freud dissects and separates aspects of the creative subject, not in a strictly scientific sense, but as a consequence of his adoption of a psychoanalytic viewpoint. Here it is useful to contrast Dilthey's account of Shakespeare, with Freud's essay on 'Dostoyevsky and Parricide':

> Four facets may be distinguished in the rich personality of Dostoyevsky: the creative artist, the neurotic, the moralist and the sinner. How is one to

find one's way in this bewildering complexity? The creative artist is the least doubtful: Dostoyevsky's place is not far behind Shakespeare. The Brothers Karamazov is the most magnificent novel ever written; the episode of the Grand Inquisitor, one of the peaks in the literature of the world, can hardly be valued too highly. Before the problem of the creative artist analysis must, alas, lay down its arms.

(Freud 1961 [1928]: 177)

This is an odd piece of text, not least because it offers a deft literary analysis of Dostoyevsky, only to foreclose immediately on that interpretative route as an option for psychoanalytic inquiry. Psychoanalysis, Freud claims, can offer a reading of Dostoyevsky as a neurotic, a moralist and a sinner, but not as an artist. This leaves the integrity of Dostoyevsky's 'practice' somewhat challenged. What is significant here, is how Freud's approach to Dostoyevsky begins with a declaration that his position as a psychoanalytic investigator actually alters the status of Dostoyevsky as an object of investigation. The famous author is deliberately not treated as a unified creative subject and a literary genius, but as a fairly shapeless screed of unconscious knowledge. The all-consuming focus on the interplay of conscious and unconscious thought in psychoanalysis, means that where in the Dostoyevsky essay, the analysis is a speculative reconstruction of the architecture of one man's neurosis, on other occasions, such as the introduction of the painter Signorelli in the essay on 'The Forgetting of Proper Names' in *The Psychopathology of Everyday Life*, the artist becomes a mere motif or fleeting instance of Freud's repression of a more crucial and unpleasant event, namely the suicide of an analysand (Freud 1960 [1901]). In this case, of course, Freud's own thought process is also put on display as a shapeless screed of unconscious knowledge, in order to offer a subtle analysis of the difference between forgetting something and the fall of knowledge produced by unconscious thought. The early and notorious essay on Leonardo da Vinci, is the most interesting example of Freud's engagement with the creative artist, not least because its central theme is the manner in which the agency of the researcher intervenes within the activity of the artist:

The investigator in him never in the course of his development left the artist entirely free, but often made severe encroachments on him and perhaps in the end suppressed him.

(Freud 1957 [1910]: 64)

In the Leonardo essay, there is no mediation of the uniqueness of genius by the generality of creative practice, as Freud shifts register quickly from the base level of 'infantile sexual researches' to the reappearance of this obsessive research process within canonical works of art. A key point to note here is that the artistic activity is directed to an audience that confirms Leonardo's genius, while the infantile sexual researches are not directed at anyone, but instead follow the circular path of the Freudian drive (*Trieb*). This inevitably produces a conflict within the production of the art object:

Then, when he made the attempt to return from investigation to his starting point, the exercise of his art, he found himself disturbed by the new direction of his interests and the changed nature of his mental activity. What interested him in a picture was above all a problem; and behind the first one he saw countless other problems arising ... After the most exhausting efforts to bring to expression in it everything which was connected with it in his thoughts, he was forced to abandon it in an unfinished state or to declare that it was incomplete.

(Freud 1957 [1910]: 77)

Here Freud presents two distinct models of creativity, one in which artistic activity and identity can be communicated to an audience through the object of art, and another in which an object is constantly being destroyed and reassembled as part of the operations of unconscious knowledge. What remains at issue for arts-based research is whether the level of the utterance, of the 'speaking truth' that is disclosed by psychoanalysis, can accommodate the making of art and the objects of art. To put this another way, does assuming the rigour of the researcher within a psychoanalytic framework preclude the production of artistic objects? In Lacan's *Ethics of Psychoanalysis*, (1992 [1960]) he suggests a way forward with this issue, and proposes a model of sublimation as the cultural frame of unconscious knowledge, which can indicate a 'tipping point' between the artistic subject and the subject of the unconscious. This depends upon the notion of an actual object that is 'raised to the dignity of the Thing' (*Das Ding*, the fundamental or archaic object posited by the notion of sublimation). A real object thus becomes the indicator of a decisive shift in the position of the subject that inaugurates the possibility of a psychoanalytic investigation. The key example Lacan provides here is the assemblage of matchboxes made by the sometime-Surrealist Jacques Prévert in the straitened circumstances of the Vichy regime in France during World War Two. In an anecdote that concludes his seminar on 'The Object and the Thing' of 20 January 1960, Lacan tells of his delight on seeing a set of matchboxes, linked together by their extruded inner drawers, in Prévert's living room: 'I don't say that it went on to infinity, but it was extremely satisfying from an ornamental point of view' (Lacan 1992 [1960]: 114). Lacan is ambiguous on the question of whether Prévert's slight, unfinishable and unstable work carried sufficient charge as a cultural object:

Perhaps you can even see something emerge in it that, goodness knows, society is able to find satisfaction in. If it is a satisfaction, it is in this case one that doesn't ask anything of anyone.

(Lacan 1992 [1960]: 114)

An object that doesn't ask anything of anyone may or may not qualify as an art object, but it may also qualify as an object that marks the transition from the subject position of the artist to that of the artist-researcher. It could thus be seen as part of the ensemble or 'thesis' that constitutes the rigour of the researcher within arts-based research. It is significant that in the Leonardo essay, Freud aligns the incompatibility of Leonardo the artist and Leonardo the researcher with an assumption that da Vinci's thirst for research and knowledge did not extend to the study of the mind. This is contrasted with the double vision of the conscious and unconscious levels of da Vinci's creativity that is afforded by Freud's adoption of the subject position of the analyst and the assumption of the determinism of mental life by unconscious knowledge. For this reason, Freud saw Leonardo's paintings as the repository of the unconscious knowledge that the artist himself did not know that he possessed. A paradox of psychoanalysis is that while the analyst cannot supplement this unconscious knowledge with his own interpretations, as soon as the analysand begins to articulate this unconscious knowledge, he potentially puts himself in the position of the analyst, that is, a person who fully accepts the determinism of mental life. In the account of Leonardo da Vinci given by Freud, this would be equivalent to a recognition on Leonardo's behalf, that the tension between finishing a painting and not finishing it was related to the distinction between conscious and unconscious knowledge, rather than being a question of existential doubt, creative angst or contingent circumstances. In this admittedly speculative scenario, Leonardo would then have fully shifted his subject position from the artist to an artist-researcher, and would have been enabled to use this rigour of the researcher to produce works that dealt with the cultural aspects of sublimation. This would require a leap of the imagination in which Leonardo da Vinci was deemed capable of making Jacques Prévert's matchboxes, a work in which the existential dilemma of finishing or not finishing a work of art, is transformed by Prévert into the logic and the thesis of the work of art itself. Of course, Leonardo da Vinci did not, and could not, have proceeded in this direction. Nor would we be inclined to hail the genius of a hybrid version of da Vinci and Prévert. Leonardo's agency as a researcher is still understood as a narrative of complexity, ingenuity and genius within the framework of a life experience that can comfortably accommodate Leonardo the artist and Leonardo the researcher. In drawing attention to an incommensurability of these two versions of Leonardo, however, Freud was unintentionally pointing the way to the possibility of properly formulated psychoanalytic research within the creative arts. This is a research paradigm that demands a shift in the subject position of the artist, rather than a notion of practice in which the position of the professional artist and that of the self-reflexive researcher can co-exist. In the next section, I will show why this shift to the position of the researcher presented difficulties even for an artist with a theoretical interest in psychoanalysis and a wish to alter the relations of the artistic subject and the objects of art.

The rotten donkey

The manifold connections between Sigmund Freud, Salvador Dalí and Jacques Lacan are well documented, and include correspondence, the writing of essays and doctoral theses, the construction of paintings and the analysis of madness (Chadwick 1980; Greely 2001). These connections are established around key texts and images. Dalí employed readings of Freud's Leonardo and Gradiva essays in his approach to his version of Millet's *Angelus*. In turn, Jacques Lacan interviewed a man who had attacked Millet's *Angelus*, who had hesitated between this, Watteau's *Embarkation for Cythera* and the *Mona Lisa*. Dalí's engagement with Freud was directed towards the establishment of a method of painting that would consciously reproduce the delirium of the dream. Dalí's self-authored 'paranoiac-critical method' worked against the passivity of Surrealist automatism, based on the individual free associations of the analysand, towards an active automatism that staked a claim to the possibility of collective delirium. The paranoiac-critical method was described in Dalí's essay 'L'Âne Pourri' ('The Rotten Donkey') (Dalí 1930). The method was founded on the idea that any given visual image was open to a 'delirium of interpretation'. Dalí proposed to systematize these multiple possible accounts within an analysis of social reality:

> I think the moment is near when, by a process of paranoid and active thought, it will be possible (simultaneously with automatism and other passive states) to systematise confusion and to contribute to the total discrediting of the world of reality ... it suffices that the delirium of interpretation binds together the meaning of heterogeneous pictures that cover a surface, to ensure that no-one could deny the real existence of this bond. Paranoia uses the exterior world to make the obsessional idea valid, with the disconcerting idea of making this idea valid for others. The reality of the exterior world serves as illustration and evidence and is placed in the service of the reality of our psyche.[4]
>
> (Dalí 1930: 276, my translation)

Dalí's paintings such as *Apparition of Face and a Fruit Dish on a Beach* (1928) and *The Slave Market With a Disappearing Bust of Voltaire* (1940) function as illustrations of this principle of a reality that is both utterly certain and collectively verifiable (a face and a fruit dish) but also completely arbitrary (one minute a face, the next minute a fruit dish). Rather than a paranoid interpretation of reality, Dalí was advocating a 'paranoid reality', or reality as a vehicle for paranoid certainty. A constantly shuffled pack of visual simulations opposes a single and coherent appearance. The young psychiatrist Jacques Lacan visited Dalí in 1930 to discuss 'The Rotten Donkey'. Subsequently, the psychoanalyst and the painter carried on a dialogue of sorts through articles published in the Surrealist press on the subject of paranoia, culminating in the 1932 publication of Lacan's doctoral thesis, *De la Psychose paranoïaque dans ses rapports avec la personalité*. Dalí later approvingly cited Lacan's thesis in the Surrealist journal *Minotaure*, and Lacan published work in the *Minotaure* in May 1933. According to Elizabeth Roudinesco, 'The Rotten Donkey' essay

> made it possible for Lacan to break with the theory of constitutionalism and move on to a new understanding of language as it related to psychosis ... At the time when Lacan was reading Freud, Dalí's point of view provided him with just the element he needed to turn his own clinical experience on paranoia into a theory.
>
> (Roudinesco 1999: 31)

Dalí's notion of the image integrated within the logical chain of simulations, bears a relation to Lacan's elucidation of the external constitution of self-identity, as set out in his canonical essay on 'The Mirror Stage' of 1936, in which the subject appears within an already constituted 'symbolic order' of language. In his later text on *The Psychoses*, Lacan (1993 [1956]) re-visits his Dalían inspiration in his claim that while the neurotic subject 'speaks to himself with his ego' or in other words carries on a dialogue with an external self-image that is somewhat ambiguous and revocable, the paranoiac is exposed to the full force of self-externalization, because for the paranoiac

'It's he [the ego] who speaks of him' in a fundamental dissociation of conscious from unconscious thought. However, it is also worth noting that in *The Psychoses*, Lacan refers to the dangers of an 'authentication of the imaginary' in analysis that begins to address the question of why Dalí's invention of a paranoiac-critical method, despite its shift from personal and passive automatism to collective and active automatism, may not fully confer the mandate of 'artist-researcher' on Dalí. The most obvious reason is that the supposedly collective interpretations of the paranoiac-critical method all belonged to Dalí himself. Rather than accepting the Freudian wager of the researcher who knows nothing confronting the subject who does not know that he knows, Dalí decided to use a method that allowed him to know everything himself. Although some members of the Surrealist group enthusiastically embraced Dalí's ideas when Dalí joined the movement in 1929, the method was used by Dalí alone. The outcome of this was an emphasis on the authentication of the Dalían image as a focus for public spectatorship. As has been previously discussed, in psychoanalysis, unlike science, it is not the adoption of a particular method that confers truth, but a focus on the material truth of the utterance. In *The Psychoses*, Lacan claims that Freud's key innovation consisted of substituting recognition on the symbolic level, the level of the utterance, for recognition on the imaginary level. This recognition depends on a shift away from the study of life experience towards the investigative position of the analyst:

> I'm not going to fall into the myth of immediate experience that forms the basis of what people call existential psychology or even existential psychoanalysis … Freudian experience is in no way pre-conceptual. It's not a pure experience, but one that is well and truly structured by something artificial, the analytic relation.
>
> (Lacan 1993 [1956]: 8)

How would someone who was interested in adopting a psychoanalytic paradigm within arts-based research avoid the pitfalls of Dalí's paranoiac-critical method? The most important focus would be on the difference between Dalí's 'active' automatism and the act of becoming a researcher. While Dalí's method was self-consciously active and socially directed, none of this activity amounted to a decisive act that would place Dalí beyond his 'comfort zone' as an artist, as his insistence on using his own interpretations within the paranoiac-critical method demonstrates. An act or artwork undertaken in the name of research, that puts an artist or a designer outside this comfort zone, points away from an affirmation of the imaginary or a dialogue with the ego, and towards the juncture of self and utterance, or conscious and unconscious. This is the locus of the psychoanalytic investigation. The following section offers a particular genealogy for this form of investigation in arts-based research.

Practice, theory and psychoanalysis

In an article entitled 'Phantoms of the Studio' published in the *Oxford Art Journal* in 1990, the artist Terry Atkinson asserted that 'Nowhere has the idea of the unconscious been more symptomatically half-digested, and nowhere is it a more entrenched agency of meaning-fixing … than in art school teaching' (Atkinson 1990: 51). Atkinson's psychoanalytically-informed critique of art school romanticism, was based on the principle that 'there is no practice without theory':

> No matter how much theory is disguised or repressed, there is no practice without theory. The theory that practice has nothing to do with theory is a theory, a disingenuous or naïve one, but nonetheless a theory.
>
> (Atkinson 1990: 49)

For Atkinson, theory was primarily an activity of reading and reflection, rather than one of making art. 'It would be worth any art student interested in matters of aesthetic ideology carefully studying [Paul] de Man's text'. (Atkinson 1990: 54)

As I have shown with reference to the more recent and world-weary reaction to psychoanalytic theory by the critic Hal Foster, an embrace of theory does not thereby eliminate the intellectual framework of notions of practice, in which the position of the professional artist and that of critic can comfortably co-exist. As well as claiming that there is no practice without theory, it can be added that there is no theory without practice, what Lacan called 'the myth of immediate experience that forms the basis of what people call existential psychology or even existential psychoanalysis' (Lacan 1993 [1956]: 8). What Atkinson states as an art school problem is in fact a general problem for the humanities, where psychoanalytic interpretation services interdisciplinary adventures, offering an alternative interpretive option where others have failed. In art schools, this general humanities attitude to psychoanalysis has become institutionalized within art and design pedagogy in the UK since the so-called Coldstream Report (National Advisory Council on Art Education 1960), which supported and reinforced a distinction between a wide-ranging and interdisciplinary 'complementary studies' and core studio disciplines. Rather than offering an alternative interpretation where others have failed, the proper task of psychoanalysis is to indicate a certain deadlock or failure of interpretation at the very point where critical ambition 'cannot fail' to generate a new interpretation of an artwork using a psychoanalytic toolkit. The deadlock is around the difference between interpretation, grounded in life experience and practice, and psychoanalysis, grounded in nothing except the rigour of an analytical position that can make unconscious knowledge manifest.

If the vicissitudes of Atkinson's UK-based 'artist-theorist' are linked to the integration of art schools within the degree-awarding sector after 1965, where do we locate the historical precedents for an inaugural moment for the artist-researcher? The possibility of the arts-based researcher is predicated on a potential change in the subject position of the artist, partly due to a new significance placed on the designer, which allows for the construction of a unified field of art and design activity populated by creative practitioners. In Britain, this potential shift is to be found in the early development of the publicly funded art school and an associated model of public pedagogy linking art schools, government and museums, following the Reform Bill of 1832 (Quinn 2008). This initiative linked the fate of the artist and designer to mass culture and industrial capital. This historical moment is important to a psychoanalytic orientation, because it emphasized an approach to culture as a signifying system. The kind of mass cultural epistemology that could have emerged from an early nineteenth century model of cultural administration pioneered in Britain, and for which the art school could have been the vanguard institution, remains latent but largely foreclosed to this day, in the current education programmes of museums, art-based research and government policy units.

In this chapter, I have shown that establishing the rigour of the researcher within a psychoanalytic framework, requires an address to the difference between interpretation and analysis, and the status of the object in research. All of these elements are themselves predicated on the crucial shift in subject position that was exemplified in the difference between, on the one hand, the quasi-research 'actions' of Salvador Dalí's paranoiac-critical method, and on the other, and the research 'act' of Jacques Lacan, who used Dalí's thought to step outside the circle of existential psychology and establish his 'return to Freud'. The lure of what I have called 'quasi-research actions' is still very much at work in contemporary art practice. One example of this was provided in the work of Mark Leckey, winner of last year's Turner Prize. Leckey has been accounted for as part of a group of artists labelled 'subjective anthropologists', who 'amass information almost as a PhD researcher might, and yet they are not cool observers, they are eccentric participants' (Jones 2008). Leckey himself has said:

> I like the idea that you let culture use you as its instrument. What gets in the way is being too clever, or worrying about how something is going to function … I am an autodidact – that's why I use bigger words than I should. It's a classic sign.
>
> (Higgins 2008)

One response to such a statement is simply to say that claiming the position of the cultural automaton or autodidact, while using the methods of the researcher and scholar, is simply a contingent ruse. However, it has to be recognized as a position of speech that artists and designers now assume as a matter of course. This position of speech was described by Claire Bishop, in a response to Thomas Hirschorn's autodidact festival, '24 Hour Foucault' at the Palais de Tokyo in 2004, an event in which Hirschorn was careful to declare his position as that of a Foucault fan, not a Foucault scholar. Bishop said:

> Both Hirschorn and Pask represent an approach that differs distinctly from typical contemporary university pedagogy. Professional teaching is steered towards the production and measurement of successful results … Whatever we think of the success of Pask's and Hirschorn's projects as art, their freedom of operation represents an unthinkable autonomy and an unencumbered passion for knowledge.
>
> (Bishop 2007: 88)

Rather than demonstrating an 'unencumbered passion for knowledge', I would claim that Leckey and Hirschorn's lectures and symposia contribute to a situation in which the mere appearance of arts-based research is deemed sufficient, and a collusion between theoretical interpretation and quasi-research actions is now encouraged. A question that remains is how, outside the structures of theoretical interpretation offered by Claire Bishop, could a psychoanalytic orientation chart a progress from pseudo-research actions to the research act? While I have provided a paradigmatic instance of this progress in the relationship of Lacan and Dalí, this does not necessarily provide the means to build a specifically psychoanalytic address to the problem of pseudo-research actions. Rather than add another layer of interpretation, a properly psychoanalytic approach to these actions, and thus a progress towards the act, might begin with an observation of the signifying system in which they are comfortably embedded, and look for anomalies in this system indicating the emergence of unconscious knowledge. In an anteroom to Mark Leckey's Turner Prize exhibition at Tate Britain in 2008, reserved for information, education and public comment, were hundreds of scrawled notes pinned to the wall. Among the notes was a scrawled and ungrammatical text, which asked a question and called for a response: 'I have had a question. What is the function of artist in society? I still don't know after this exhibition. Do you and artists know? Do curator know? [sic]'

In this note, the issue of unconscious knowledge is raised in the inarticulate demand for a real act of knowledge and research, rather than a pseudo action. It is important to see that the writer of the note at Tate Modern, this person who, in the terms set by museum education, is also a member of the fictional forms of an audience, a community or a 'public', has named three people who are responsible for providing an answer to this question – the first of these is 'you', that is, any reader of the note, the second is an artist, the third is a curator. In this way, the writer of the note has provided us with a clue as to how 'you' might begin to answer the question, that is by assuming an individual responsibility for knowledge pertaining to a difficult issue, bearing upon the relationship of art and the world in which it is received and comprehended. Yet the knowledge in question is not new knowledge, but a pre-existing knowledge – the artist is assumed have some kind of social function that is not being disclosed by artists and curators themselves. This requires an investigator who will assume responsibility for this undisclosed knowledge.

The note indicates that artists and curators, the acknowledged experts in answering this kind of question, have not provided an adequate or rigorous account of what they already know, and that what is required is a direct address to an entire body of knowledge and a signifying structure. It is at this juncture that an arts-based researcher might feel able to progress to the act, and move beyond what they already know to what artists and curators as a profession do not know that they know. The demand framed in this note has a specific equivalent in the address of the hysteric to the master in Lacanian psychoanalysis. The hysteric addresses the master, and demands that he or she produce something serious by way of knowledge. The hysteric's demand is what makes knowledge go further, and progress from research actions to research acts.

If arts-based research, as it is defined in the AHRC report I quoted at the beginning of this chapter, is used to place limitations on to research activity that do not undermine the identity of the creative practitioner, then it cannot easily progress from the accumulation of research 'actions' in the form of projects, methodologies and texts, to the status of the research act. Psychoanalysis is useful to arts-based research because it offers a thorough and reasoned argument for the primacy of the investigative act that delivers both the rigour of the researcher and a change in the subjects and objects of art and design. Psychoanalysis can also offer lessons for those engaged in attempts to transcend intra- and inter-institutional 'battles of identity' between theorists and practitioners, or artists and academics, and to embrace the idea that issues of identity should be made secondary to collective research actions that have a public dimension and involve public participation. 'Transdisciplinary research starts from tangible, real-world problems. Solutions are devised in collaboration with multiple stakeholders'. (Chapter 4). A psychoanalytic investigative orientation can complement Mode 2 research, by showing how not only the research problem, *but research rigour itself*, can come from society, as the determinate instance, hiccup or snag in the construction of identity that initiates a new investigation through a shift in the position of the subject. There is no opposition between the 'cleverness' of the researcher and the 'ignorance' of the public. The problem that has been raised by Mode 2 knowledge, and which can be addressed in a psychoanalytic orientation, is how the rigorous, determining instance of the public or the collective prevents the researcher from 'being clever' in the ways that she normally expects to be, and which therefore demands real innovation and change. A psychoanalytic viewpoint suggests that we should be wary of celebrating the cleverness of the academic, the artist, the designer or the theorist – and focus instead on the collective determinations that initiate genuine acts of research.

In conclusion, I will address two questions of usage and application that arise from this chapter. If the determining truths of psychoanalysis can arise from anywhere within a collective field of language, how is the notion of 'applied psychoanalysis' to be understood? If psychoanalysis cannot be applied as a distinct and separate body of knowledge to a research problem in the art and design field, what use is it? Dany Nobus has suggested an answer to these questions, with reference to research activity in any discipline:

> Psychoanalysis cannot be employed as a fully finished doctrine, either within or outside the treatment. And if the psychoanalyst needs to learn that 'his knowledge is but a symptom of his own ignorance' ... other disciplines may use their confrontation with psychoanalysis to adopt a similar stance vis-à-vis their own knowledge and methodologies.
>
> (Nobus and Quinn 2005: 209)

The terms of this general statement suggest four tenets of approach for anyone employing a Freudo-Lacanian approach to arts based research:

1   the research problem appears as a gap, break or inconsistency within an existing practice, discipline or body of knowledge, for example in the dilemma of finishing or not finishing a painting.

2   'the problem teaches' and is thus placed in a dominant position in relation to an existing practice, discipline or body of knowledge. This is more crucial than whether the investigation takes place in a clinical situation or elsewhere.

3   the task is to discover how the problem functions. This cannot be encountered using what one already knows about how an art or design practice functions.

4   for the purposes of research, an existing practice, discipline or body of knowledge must be reconstructed using the terms of the problem. This is demonstrated in Jacques Prévert's matchboxes, a work in which the dilemma

of finishing or not finishing a work of art, is transformed by Prévert into the logic of the work of art itself.

Notes

1 'Zweckzusammenhänge'.
2 'l'effet de vérité n'est qu'une chute de savoir'.
3 Although examples of design research employing a psychoanalytic paradigm are rarer than in fine art research, a psychoanalytic approach to design research is offered by Graves (1996; 1999).
4 'Je crois qu'est proche le moment où, par un processus de caractère paranoïaque et actif de la pensée, il sera possible (simultanément à l'automatisme et autres états passifs) de systematiser la confusion et de contribuer au discredit total du monde de la réalité … Il suffit que le délire d'interprétation soit arrivé à relier le sens des images des tableaux hétérogènes qui couvrent un mur, pour que déjà personne ne puis nier l'existence réelle de ce lien. La paranoia se sert du monde extérieur pour faire valoir l'idée obsédante, avec la troublante particularité de rendre valable la réalité de cette idée pour les autres. La réalité du monde extérieur sert comme illustration et prevue, et est mise au service de la réalité de notre esprit.'

15

TRANSFORMATIONAL PRACTICE: ON THE PLACE OF MATERIAL NOVELTY IN ARTISTIC CHANGE

Stephen Scrivener

What is the relationship between research and art? This is the central question in the international, academic debate around the topic of arts-based research. This way of putting the question places the emphasis on the relationship between the one thing and the other, setting them apart from the outset. This is my emphasis, but it is strongly evident within the literature in expressions such 'research into art', 'research through art', 'research for art', 'arts-based research', 'practice-based research', etc.[1] All such constructions separate research and art, framing thought such that it excludes the possibility that the practices of art include practices that merit the label research, or that its products include outcomes that contribute to knowledge and understanding.

In practice, it has proven difficult for academics to view things otherwise when so much of the debate has been set within change in national educational and research policy; increases in undergraduate, postgraduate and doctoral student numbers; reduction in teaching funding; and the availability of new research funding in some countries, e.g. the UK. These changes have made it almost impossible to explore the question of whether or not art already embodies a research function when funding bodies and the like have already predefined the terms of any conclusion. The context of the debate, which might be argued is its cause, has confined us to think that we have to show that research in fine art, say, is *like* research in physics, or sociology, etc. And how have we done this? The answer, for the most part, is by implicitly or explicitly treating the criteria and expectations of the 'other' field as a standard for comparison (Chapter 2). If, as Biggs and Büchler suggest (Chapter 5), different fields have different values, we should not be too surprised to find that the seeming universality and permanence of these criteria and expectations have promoted disturbance in the art academy (Scrivener 2006), whilst at the same time making it difficult to see research in any kind of art practice or outcome. It would appear that even if we take current artistic practices as our starting point, these practices have still to become research.

In this chapter I want to argue against this conclusion. I accept that the practices of science, say, and art are different, as are the purposes of science and art, but this does not mean that one thereby embodies a practice of research and the other does not. Geological science, for example, is concerned with the study of the dynamics of the Earth, its resources, and the use of those resources. Implicit in this description is the idea of knowledge and its application in the enrichment of human experience, and, in the professional organization of intellectual fields such as geological science, this relationship has been reinforced resulting in a dissociation of the production of knowledge from its productive use. Consequently, when we want to ask whether art practice embodies a function whereby knowledge is renewed, our tendency is to compare it to fields where the research function is clearly isolated and to find art practice wanting.

I would like to propose that we look at this question from a different starting point. Observing what happens when normal science goes astray, Kuhn writes:

> when it does – when, that is, the profession can no longer evade anomalies that subvert the existing tradition of scientific practice – then begin the extraordinary investigations that lead the profession at last to a new set of commitments, a new basis for the practice of science.
>
> (Kuhn 1970 [1962]: 6)

In other words, there are times when the knowledge accumulated through the practice of research brings a science to a point of disorder and renewal. So let's pose the question differently; to investigate whether art embodies a research function, let's ask whether art practice undergoes Kuhnian paradigm shifts, since such renewals appear to be contingent on the production of new knowledge. Since art's 'set of commitments' has been rewritten on several occasions during its history and since, on each occasion, this rewriting constituted a fundamental restructuring or revocation of its conceptual foundations, it follows that there is a *prima facie* case for suggesting that art practice embodies a research function.

With the above in mind, the aim of this chapter is to work toward a theoretical understanding of the interpretational and material practices of artistic renewal, of their interrelationship and interdependence. After briefly discussing current conceptions of art and research, Jacques Rancière's theory of art will be drawn on in which art is understood as a bond between image and text, or image and ideas. Under this theory, the critic's contribution to artistic renewal will be examined before considering the more challenging question, in the context of art and research, of how the material innovations of the artist contribute to change in understanding of art. It will be argued that historically, at least, cognitive surprise can be understood as the primary mechanism responsible for the cognition of material innovation and the activation of its consequences. To illustrate this proposition, the art of the late eighteenth-century English landscape painter, John Constable, will be discussed as a model of the research function in art, since it contributed to a new understanding of art and to its renewal. Finally, it will be concluded that, in the contemporary setting, the conjunction of the historically disjointed practices of material and interpretational innovation might be the price of the erosion of widely shared, collective appreciation and expectation of art.

The place of art in research and art that changes art

There are many different definitions of what we here are calling arts-based research (UKCGE 1997; Gray and Malins 2004; Strand 1998; Scrivener 2002; Hannula *et al.* 2005; Borgdorff 2006; Rust *et al.* 2007) which in one way or the other seek to clarify the relation between art and research. However, Frayling (1993) was perhaps the first to examine this relation, describing three kinds of research: research into art and design, research through art and design, and research for art and design. It has been argued that rather than describing three different types of research,[2] these descriptors say something about the relation of art and design to the conditions of research (Scrivener 2009c). Thus *research into* treats art and design as the *subject* of inquiry: art and design practices and objects are the things to be explored and understood. *Research through* relates art and design to the *method* condition as a means of arriving at knowledge and understanding about something, in fact anything, including art and design itself. Frayling cites George Stubbs (1724–1806) and John Constable (1776–1837) as historical examples of artists who might be described as conducting research through art and design: the one contributing to knowledge of equine anatomy,[3] the other to knowledge of meteorological conditions. *Research for* art and design is that which the artist or designer conducts *for the purposes of* art or design. Such research, often described as little 'r', is not required to yield new knowledge and understanding. Characterized in this way, research for art and design does not satisfy the goal condition of academic and professional research.

Hence Frayling's characterization of art and design research excludes the possibility that works of art in themselves contribute new knowledge and understanding, or if they do it is not a kind of knowledge that we would associate with research: typically, that which can be characterized as communicable, true, justified belief. If works of art cannot in themselves contribute in this way, then the labour of art cannot be understood as the activity that we name as research. However, let us consider Stubbs and Constable, cited by Frayling as examples of artists who might be regarded as having contributed, through their practices as artists, to new understanding in fields outside art. Accepting this claim for the moment, we should also note that both are credited with having changed art. The artistic practices of Stubbs and Constable can be described as transformational because they produced works of art that challenged and, in challenging, changed the contemporary and future perception, reception, production and understanding of art (Scrivener 2006). What is suggested here is that some works of art go beyond the particular ambition attributed to art in any historical period, thereby contributing to its reassignment. If both Stubbs and Constable contributed to science, then this was incidental to their primary contribution to art fact and art discourse. This is not to say that Stubbs or Constable sought intentionally to change art, but that their works of art nevertheless contributed to this effect. Implicit in this account is the notion that a work of art, of itself, can challenge its beholder's beliefs about art and that accommodating this challenge can result in a change in belief system. But it also begs the question: how does a work of art promote change in ideas about art?

Painting in the text

However, before addressing the question posed above, Jacques Rancière's essay *Painting in the Text* (2007) will be drawn on as a framework for thinking about how change arises in art's ambition. Acknowledging the oft heard complaint about the torrent of words that accompany painting, Rancière sets out his goal of moving from the 'polemic denunciation' of words, to a 'theoretical understanding of the articulation between words and visual forms that defines a regime of art.'

According to Rancière, the very idea of art is contingent on a 'regime of identification', a regime of disjunction that gives visibility and meaning to linguistic and non-linguistic practices and which determines, for example, what painting is, what it is to paint and how paintings are seen. However, such a decision requires the establishment of a 'regime of equivalence' between a practice and that which it is not. This, according to Rancière, accounts for Horace's proclamation *ut pictura poësis*, (as is painting so is poetry), which is not the subjugation of one art by another, but the assertion of a relationship between, 'the orders of making, seeing, and saying whereby these arts – and possibly others – were arts' (2007: 74). Rancière describes this relationship as a 'bond', in the first instance between painting and the poetic power of words and fables; a bond between practices of doing, saying and thinking; a bond that is made, unmade and remade. 'What can undo this bond …', he argues is the untying of one relationship and retying of another. Hence, the concept of painting, associated with Clement Greenberg, as an art directed toward nothing other than the use of the medium specific to it, namely paint and a support, 'is a different type of relationship between what painting does and what words make visible on its surface' (2007: 75).[4] The making of this relationship does not necessitate the abandonment of resemblance. Rather, resemblances must be detached from the given order of relationships which ties them to the order of subjects and actions, as in poetry. According to Rancière, a medium is:

> a surface of conversion: a surface of equivalence between the different arts' ways of making: a conceptual space of articulation between these ways of making and forms of visibility and intelligibility determining the way in which they can be viewed and conceived.
>
> (Rancière 2007: 75f.)

The representative regime's demise is not the discovery of art's essence. It is the definition of an, 'aesthetic regime in the arts that is a different articulation between practices, forms of visibility and modes of intelligibility'. However, Rancière continues, this was not the result of a revolution in the practices of painters, but instead a new way of seeing painting of the past that, commencing in the eighteenth century, resulted in the re-evaluation of genre painting and the release of pictorial forms from poetry. Yet this was not painting liberated from words, but a new way of bringing them together; not as the model to be satisfied as a norm, but the means by which its expressiveness can appear on its surface; such 'that words amend the surface by causing another subject to appear under the representative subject' (2007: 76).

In summary, Rancière makes the claim that art's existence relies on the weaving of relations between practices of making, seeing, saying and thinking. These relations are not established once and for all. They are constructed, dismantled and reconstructed according to changing ambition, need and interest: painting once was tied to poetry, then to the spirituality of Kandinsky, then to Greenberg's formalism and so on. Rancière does not seek to be exhaustive: his examples are employed to illustrate and justify his argument about the interconnectedness of ways of making and saying, image and text, and to throw light on what it is for something to be art and for there to be change in art. Each feat of untying and retying specifies an artistic project: to tell stories, to express the spiritual, to conquer the medium, and so on. Each aesthetic regime gives birth to a space for production and a community of interest driven by the logic of the regime toward the attainment of a common goal, but as interests change another regime is born, grows and outgrows its elder sibling. Criticism, born according to Rancière at the same time as Hegel's aesthetics, is the new bond between forms and words, but not simply as a discourse that retrospectively adds meaning to forms, but as one that in the first instance works toward a new visibility, a new way of seeing pictorial forms, which is achieved through a critical practice of de-figuration in which the figures of one aesthetic regime are refigured in another space. Accordingly, Greenberg's counter-posing of the idea of the conquest of the surface against Kandinsky's anti-representative programme is seen as a labour of de-figuration that makes the same painting, namely of abstract figures, visible in a different way. To illustrate this claim, Rancière presents and analyses two extracts from critical texts written in the middle to late nineteenth century, the first critiquing the work of Jean Baptiste Siméon Chardin from the Goncourt brothers', *French eighteenth-century painters*, first published in 1864, and the second, dealing with Paul Gauguin's, *La Lutte de Jacob avec l'ange*, from Albert Aurier's, *Le Symbolisme en peinture*, published in 1891. The first reveals an act of de-figuration that makes visible in a new way the materiality of a work of the past, and the second shows that de-figuration can construct a visibility for painting that goes beyond the material present.

So, in claiming that painting is always an interweaving of practices of making, saying, seeing and thinking, with one hand Rancière erases the idea of the art of painting as the realization of the particularity of its medium and with the other he redraws it as a surface of 'dissociation and de-figuration'. Hence the denial of the representative regime is the assertion of a new correspondence:

> the 'like' that linked painting to poetry, visual figures to the order of discourse. Words no longer prescribe, as story or doctrine, what painting should be. They make themselves images so as to shift the figures of the painting, to construct this surface of conversion, this surface of form-signs which is the real medium of painting [...] a space of conversion where the relationship between words and visual forms anticipates visual de-figurations still to come [...] The surface is not wordless, is not without 'interpretations' that pictorialize it.
> (Rancière 2007: 87–9)

Seen through Rancière's lens, art is always in transition; always transforming itself, even when pushing a given stage of visibility to an end that appears to be the end of all ends; always unfolding a stage of visibility entwined with other stages of visibility, each keeping faith with its own logic. In the context of the debate on art and research, Rancière's ideas are appealing because, first, they demystify art; second, they demand that a bond has to be formed between words and images in order for there to be art; third, they do not demand that interpretational and material novelty are causally or hierarchically connected; and fourth, they provide a ground for thinking about how art rethinks itself and in rethinking itself knows itself anew. Rancière provides a clear and creative potential for the art critic in envisioning the future of the image, but has little to say about the role of material novelty in the change process. Nevertheless, it has been claimed above that painting can change painting, so how might the material creativity of the artist contribute to change in art?

Surprise and cognitive transformation

Kagan writes in the introduction to his book *Surprise, Uncertainty and Mental Structures* (2002: 4) that, 'events that are transformations of an agent's psychological forms are significant incentives for brain activity and its psychological consequences [...] Events that are discrepant from schemata create a state one might call *surprise*.' Surprise occurs when one's expectations do not fit the situation. Meyer, *et al.* (1997) have proposed a staged model of cognitive surprise in which a cognized event is appraised utilizing a mechanism that computes the degree of discrepancy between the cognized event and existing beliefs, and then tests this value against an unexpectedness threshold. Crossing the unexpectedness threshold is accompanied by the experience (emotion) of surprise, followed by the interruption of ongoing information processing and the reallocation of processing resources to the analysis and evaluation of the unexpected event and its resolution, namely the updating and revision of existing schemas or beliefs (Meyer *et al.* 1997; Reisenzein 2001). The surprise mechanism functions to *enable*, by interrupting and refocusing attention and cognitive resources, and to *provide* an initial motivational impetus for immediate adaptation to the surprising event and cognitive change enabling future occurrences of similar events to be handled. Thus surprise generates curiosity by informing the conscious self about the occurrence of a schema discrepancy. Since this information concerns one's belief system it involves a meta-cognitive process: cognition about cognition or knowing about knowing. Surprise, then, provides an impetus for meta-cognition and the exploration and explanation of the unexpected event (Reisenzein *et al.* 1996). Hence, one way that an art work can be instrumental in changing understanding of art is by engendering surprise.

There is nothing new in coupling surprise and art:[5] there are many texts that document encounters with surprising art. One significant example is Louis Leroy's article in *Le Charivari* reporting on the 1874 exhibition of contemporary art held in the salon of the photographer Nadar, in which Leroy, satirizing the artists' work, coined the term 'Impressionism'. This article, written as an encounter at the exhibition between the author and a fictional, academically-trained artist, clearly reveals how Leroy's expectations are so confounded by the exhibited works as to lead him to question their very status as art.[6] However, what we are attending to here is the fact that the coupling of surprise and art is the coupling of cognition and art, and that this coupling can lead to an altered or expanded understanding of art. To illustrate this point, let us consider the passages below, extracted from letters to his wife, dated 1907, of the poet Rainer Maria Rilke in which he recalls his encounters with the art of Paul Cézanne:

All of this happened in the Cézanne room, which makes an immediate claim on one's attention with its powerful pictures. You know how much more remarkable I always find the people walking about in front of paintings than the paintings themselves. It's no different in this Salon d'Automne, except for the Cézanne room. Here all of reality is on his side [...]

I again spent two hours in front of a few [of Cézanne's] pictures today; I sense this is somehow useful for me [...] But it all takes a long, long time. When I remember the puzzlement and insecurity of one's first confrontation with his work, along with his name, which was just as new. And then for a long time nothing, and suddenly one has the right eyes [...]

(Harrison and Wood 2000: 36 and 7)

Four features are prominent in these passages: first, the claim that the paintings made on the writer's attention, interrupting his habitual practice of attending to the audience in preference to the works of art; second, the puzzlement and insecurity they engendered; third, the labour of contemplation required for comprehension; fourth, that this comprehension, although unspoken, has the character of a new visibility, to use Rancière's term.

The above is viewed from the position of viewer and concerns the reception and treatment of surprise, which in Rilke's case is resolved through the construction of a new way of seeing painting. In the following sections we will turn to consider the production and transformational character of the surprising work of art by examining the art of Constable, thereby maintaining a certain thread in the discourse on art-based research. We will begin by articulating Constable's artistic project, as seen through Constable's own account of the development of landscape painting, recorded in Charles Robert Leslie's *Memoirs of the life of John Constable*, first published in 1843 six years after its subject's death. It will be argued that although Constable's paintings substantially realize his artistic ambition, their disjunctive, surprising character resulted in a failure to see them on his terms. It is suggested that, recognizing this fact, toward the end of his life Constable sought to articulate a way of seeing his paintings as conjunctive, rather than disjunctive.

A synthesis of poetry and science

Leslie's biography of Constable (1951) contains the notes to six lectures that the artist gave toward the end of his life, between 1833 and 1836. In the first lecture, Constable opens up six themes that seem fundamental to understanding his attitude to art; past and present. The first is his ambition to, 'separate it [landscape painting] from the mass of historical art in which it originated, and with which it was long connected.' The second is his desire to demonstrate that the former is equal to the latter, such that, 'from being the humble assistant, it became the powerful auxiliary to that art which gave it birth, greatly enriching the dignity of history.' The third is his appreciation of this equivalence, which is for landscape painting to be 'impressive'. The fourth is that this liberation is not revolution, but the resurrection of lost achievement. Referring to, 'the state of landscape painting among the ancients ...', he first criticizes the lack of chiaroscuro in its remnants, such as those found at Herculaneum and the

265

Baths of Diocletian, 'without which it can never be rendered impressive ...', before acknowledging that, according to Pliny and other ancient writers, 'chiaroscuro as well as colour was thoroughly understood and practised by the great historical painters.' Alas, 'All was, however, lost in the general wreck of Europe; and it is hardly to be expected that in the early time of the middle ages anything of so refined a character should reappear.' Constable's diagnosis of a lack of respect for nature as the cause of this malaise constitutes the fifth theme, and the sixth his remedy, adherence to the phenomena of landscape, e.g. 'when historical painting was attempted on a larger scale, and the Passion, the Crucifixion, and the Entombment of our Saviour afforded its most important subjects, landscape, and even some of its phenomena, became indispensible' (Leslie 1951: 290–3). All of these themes can be seen as subsumed in Constable's claim made in the second lecture, that landscape painting, 'is *scientific* as well as *poetic*; that imagination alone never did, and never can, produce works that are to stand by a comparison with *realities*; and to show, by tracing the connecting links in the history of landscape painting, that no great painter was ever self-taught' (Leslie 1951: 303).[7]

At the time of his lectures, landscape painting was already appreciated as a separate branch of art in Britain, and had been viewed as such from the first half of the eighteenth century. The problem for Constable and his contemporaries was that landscape painting still had a lowly status in the hierarchy of painting types, only standing above still life. Hence, Constable's real challenge was to show that it was equal to the highest branch of painting, namely historical painting, in its capacity for elevated poetic expression. This explains why, in his first lecture given at Hampstead, he wants to show that when the landscape component of historical painting was at its peak it was a powerful auxiliary that greatly enriched the dignity of history. This he achieves, in a series of examples that illustrate the contribution that appropriate treatment of landscape makes to the poetic quality of the history paintings under consideration. For example, in talking of Raphael's (1483–1520) treatment of landscape elements, he observes how,

> In his early pictures, generally holy families ... it [landscape] is most beautiful and appropriately introduced; the single leaves of plants, flowers and that religious emblem the trefoil, in his foregrounds are very elegantly detailed; and the soothing solitudes of his middle distances find a corresponding serenity in the features of the benign and lovely subjects of these works'.
>
> (Leslie 1951: 292)

However, for landscape painting to be seen as equal to history painting it was necessary for him to show that it is independently capable of expressing poetically ideas as grand as those embodied in history: in Constable's case, these ideas were to be found in the wonder of nature.

However, poetic excellence in landscape painting is not simply a matter of imagination, nor of mimicking the great masters of the past; instead it relies on truth to nature, and this idea of the union of poetical and scientific interpretation is woven into all of the lectures from the outset, being present in all that he praises and absent in all that he admonishes. Because he uses the term scientific infrequently and because he talks about truth to nature and observation frequently, it is tempting to think that he is merely advocating that painters should closely observe what they see. Of course, he is

266

advocating that they do this, but as a means to a scientific understanding of nature, not in order to record the sensory moment: that is to say, observation is a means of arriving at an understanding of the structure and order of nature that govern the empirical world of events. The importance of scientific understanding is conveyed forcibly in an extended footnote (Leslie 1951: 316f.) that offers a mini-thesis on the reflection and refraction of light, in which he draws on the work of his friend, the scientist George Field.[8] Constable was advocating that if the artist is to *see*, then the artist must *know*: to *know*, the artist should acquire scientific understanding of nature and its effects, and, guided by a scientific method of observation, apply that understanding in poetic interpretation. In summary, Constable was not a realist, his ambitions were not directed toward topographical truth but the poetic expression of the wonder of nature, and the novelty of his project is his commitment to the substantive function of scientific understanding in attaining this goal. To what extent, then, did Constable succeed in his ambition; how was his work received during and after his lifetime?

Conjunctive intent seen as disjunctive presence

In Britain, Constable's art failed to gain significant recognition amongst his contemporaries, notwithstanding his eventual election to the Royal Academy. Wilson (Wilson 1979: 88) notes that his contemporaries, 'were baffled by or disliked' his 'trivial' subject matter, the brightness of his colour and the roughness of his handling. Constable reports a comment made by Henry Fuseli (Leslie 1951: 101) to the artist David Wilkie in which, after first flattering Constable's landscapes as picturesque, of fine colour and correctly lit, observes, 'but he makes me call for my greatcoat and umbrella.' In a similar vein, John Ruskin said of Constable that he was a painter who, 'perceives in a landscape that grass is wet, the meadows flat and the boughs shady; that is to say, about as much as, I suppose, might in general be apprehended, between them, by an intelligent fawn and a skylark' (Mayne in Leslie 1951: xii). Both critics imply that Constable's art offers nothing that elevates the mind; his ambitions to poetry simply passed them by, although they acknowledge his truth to nature. Hence, Constable's synthesis of poetry and science was not visible to most of his British contemporaries. In contrast, when the *Haywain*, was exhibited in France at the Salon of 1824, the response was very different. The painter William Brockedon (1787–1854) wrote to Constable in December 1824 of the division in the school of French landscape painters created by his pictures noting:

> the next exhibition in Paris will teem with your imitators, or the school of nature *versus* the school of Birmingham. I saw one man draw another to your pictures with this expression, 'Look at these landscapes by an Englishman – the ground appears to be covered with dew'.
>
> (Leslie 1951: 132)

The poet Stendhal (1783–1842) wrote of Constable's paintings in the Salon: 'The English this year have submitted magnificent landscapes by Constable. I am not sure there is anything I can say against them. Their truth immediately strikes the viewer and draws him into the work' (Harrison *et al.* 1998: 35).

The contemporary reception of Constable's paintings cannot be easily explained in terms of a conjunction of poetry and science. Instead, what was recognized in both Britain and France was their truth to nature – all that differed was the way these two peoples appreciated that truth. Constable's historical importance is that his paintings, particularly his six-foot paintings, in their immediate reception were disjunctive. They registered a separation between poetic expression and realistic observation that surprised. For those on the side of poetry they failed to satisfy expectation; for others, their naturalism engaged an emergent mode of visibility awaiting conscious articulation and material instantiation. In Rancière's terms, Constable's paintings worked, on the one hand, to loosen an existing bond between practices of making, seeing and saying, namely image and poetry, and, on the other hand, if unintentionally, to begin the ties of a new bond between image and the empirical world. Constable's six-foot paintings were at odds with both existing and emergent modes of visibility; connected to each but neither properly one nor the other. This explains why Brockedon was wrong – post-Constable art history does not teem with imitators. In short, Constable's six-foot landscapes can be understood as transformational in that they mediated the traversal between essentially different modes of visibility and the registration of a new ambition for painting.

France appears to have been more attuned to the artistic potential of realism than its neighbour across the channel[9] and Constable is commonly credited with influencing both the Barbizon school of painters and subsequently the Impressionists.[10] And it is the subsequent trajectory of painting that has shaped much interpretation and appreciation of Constable's art, as can be seen in a preference for his sketches and preparatory works over his six-foot canvases. For example:

> The directness of his large sketch of the *Haywain* [...] was modified in the final picture which now seems dull by comparison but needed 'finish' to be acceptable. Constable's enormous respect for facts – light flickering on foliage, heavy spirals of cumulus cloud – is in his sketches conveyed speedily and essentially.
>
> (Levey 1968: 268)

> The finished picture sometimes established a certain compromise between this vitality [of the larger preparatory studies] and the more static and traditional qualities of finish.
>
> (Gaunt 1964: 136)

In the same vein, Constable is also projected as an innovator who needed to, 'discard the conventions of which landscape had acquired a large store ...' (Gaunt 1964: 132), leading to the production of work that brought about, 'a renewal: his art marks the beginning of a radically new approach to painting which was eventually to lead to modern art' (Wilson 1979: 83).

De-figuration versus disfiguration/pre-figuration

As noted above Rancière emphasizes the creativity of de-figuration: both the Goncourts and Aurier can be understood as constructing a new visibility and populating that visibility with figures, that in Aurier's case await reification. Both cases also admit the possibility that it is in the process of de-figuration itself that the new visibility is constructed or seen in a painting, i.e. the new visibility is not necessarily given *a priori*. Furthermore, no causal connection is assumed between the innovation of painters and the de-figuration of the critic, or between de-figuration and subsequent painterly innovation. Hence, the critic's de-figured conceptual spaces and the artist's innovated material spaces can be understood as unconnected. This being the case, what is it that stimulates the cognition of a new aesthetic regime, a new bond between image and text? For the creative writer, Rancière provides an answer; it is the power of metaphor. The critic, according to Rancière, is privileged in comparison to the painter, because de-figuration demands linguistic tropes that make it possible for images to be transferred into text and text back into images, and it is this that enables us to see not only that we are confronted by the new, but also that which constitutes the new. This is not within the image makers' power because, 'When innovators [the Impressionists] want to make the physical play of light and the hachure of colour directly equivalent, they short-circuit the labour of metaphor' (Rancière 2007: 82). Thus, the painter does not have the means for connecting the old and the new by tools, such as metaphor.

Nevertheless, re-interpretation of Constable's importance suggests one answer to the question posed at the end of the section above entitled *Painting in the Text*, namely it reveals one way by which painting, in its original presence, can mediate between past and future ways of thinking about art. In contrast to de-figuration, works such as Constable's six-foot landscapes might be described as constituting, in the context governing their immediate reception, a mode of figuration not fully commensurate with expectation, and as a consequence unstable, ambiguous and capable of being read as either disfiguration, the marring of what should be present, or pre-figuration, the suggestion of a mode of figuration yet to be, depending upon the outlook of the viewer. Consequently, unlike de-figuration, the instantiation of a new visibility cannot be completed through material innovation and requires a further stage in which a new visibility is resolved in a manner such as that suggested in Rilke's confrontation with Cézanne's paintings or Aurier's engagement with those of Gauguin. In short, the cognitive disruption of expectation in the material present has to be re-described in terms of a new visibility; a connection needs to be made between, 'ways of making, modes of speech, forms of visibility, and protocols of intelligibility' (Rancière 2007: 3).

With this point in mind, let us return to Constable's art in order to show how he actually made this connection for us. The grounds of this demonstration will not need to be sought in his art's effects, as we understand them in retrospect. Instead, it will be argued, it is the material and intellectual achievement of Constable's project that provides the grounds we need; the grounds, that is, that account for its contemporaneous failure, rather than his posthumous success. As demonstrated earlier, Constable was very clear about his aim to elevate landscape painting to the same heights as history painting and he proposed that this could be achieved through the apposite conjunction of poetry and natural science. Furthermore, Constable's belief in this proposition was not without reasons; it was grounded in a careful analysis of the value of the naturalistic tradition in art. Nor did Constable defer to imagination and inspiration as means to the synthesis of art and poetry that he sought. For example, Leslie observes,

> Constable then spoke of the probable manner in which Titian proceeded with the composition of the picture, and whether in every respect he guessed rightly or not, he accomplished his principal object, which was to show that the greatest works of genius are not thrown off as if by inspiration, but on the contrary, are the result of patient labour, and often undergo many changes of plan during their progress.

Instead, as we have seen, Constable advocated and practised a scientifically informed observational rigour, as recorded in his letters, lectures and his notebooks, sketchbooks, drawings and oil sketches, etc. This was coupled with an equally rigorous application of observational understanding to poetic expression. Although Constable was not revolutionary in outlook – he was not opposed to the past – nevertheless, his artistic project was directed toward the collective recognition of a new understanding and appreciation of landscape painting.

As we have seen, Constable's project was not appreciated by his British contemporaries and there are grounds for suggesting that the French, whilst applauding his work, failed to see his work as a synthesis of poetry and science. Furthermore, it is debatable as to whether Constable would have endorsed subsequent realist interpretation of his art or the onward trajectory of modern art. Hence, Constable eventually feels the need to provide his peers (and perhaps even posterity) with the grounds for interpreting his art on his terms. In effect, Constable is forced to become the advocate of his own art and to engage in a process that reveals a new visibility for his art. Thus, his lectures function in the manner of the texts of the Goncourts and Aurier. Through his lectures, Constable provides not an explanation, not a critique, not an assessment of his work, but a conceptual scaffold for its reception and appreciation. In so doing, he makes the connection between its material innovation and a new conception of the poetic potential of painting that makes interpretation possible on his terms. In effect, they work toward defusing surprise by preparing viewers to accommodate both the poetic and the scientific, and by adjusting the appreciative system to demote some evaluative criteria and promote others. In this manner, he prepares his listeners and posterity for a proper appreciation of his art and its ambition, and interpretations of his art can be found that are consistent with the tenor of his lectures and letters. For example, Wilson, acknowledging the two traditions of landscape painting in Britain in the first half of the eighteenth century, namely classical and topographical, credits Constable with, 'finally elevating topographical, purely naturalistic landscape to the very highest realms of art ...' (Wilson 1979: 69), arguing that Constable's fame justly rests on his six-foot canvases as, 'in them he has finally fully assimilated the classical tradition into his own simple vision of nature, discarding the form but retaining the essential qualities: order, harmony, grandeur, monumentality' (Wilson 1979: 86).

In the event, however, the lectures came too late, because Constable's art had already enacted effects, both condemnatory and laudatory, in the latter case stimulating, as argued above, material novelty and de-configured conceptual spaces not entirely consistent with Constable's self-declared project. We can only speculate on the course of art history had Constable used his lectures to prepare his contemporaries for his art. Perhaps Brockedon's prediction would have come about with an art that more closely followed Constable's interests. Or perhaps, given the historical moment, the outcome would have been pretty much the same. Nevertheless, Constable's images and words provide a model for thinking about how the material innovator can perform a function similar to the critical writer's de-figuration, which conjoins text and image so as to construct a visibility appropriate to his or her work's ambition.

Arts-based research as art that changes art

Earlier it was argued that art that changes art should be understood as making a contribution to understanding, since it requires an adjustment to cognitive schemata and semantic networks relevant to the appreciation of art. Although both interpretational and material innovation have been shown to be constitutive of such change, our interest here is focused on material innovation, since this is most closely associated with the creativity of the artist and the mode of innovation that is most difficult for many to see as being consistent with the acquisition of new knowledge and understanding, namely as being understandable as a research function. Notwithstanding the above, it might be argued that neither material disjunction nor critical de-figuration, even when it can be seen in the unfolding of history to have been constitutive of change in understanding of art, should be understood as research, i.e. the acquisition of *new* knowledge, as neither is unambiguously interpretable nor self-justifies its contribution to new understanding.

Let us begin to examine these objections by recalling that Rancière's articulation of artistic change does not demand a causal connection between the innovation of painters and the de-figuration of the critic, even though the Goncourts' critique of Chardin followed the appearance in the Salon des Refusés of 1863 of the paintings that were later to be labelled Impressionist; and even though it is highly likely that the Goncourts, who were prominent figures in the cultural life of Paris at the time, visited the exhibition. Perhaps an affect exerted on the Goncourts by the material presence of the Impressionist paintings was transferred into an appreciation of Chardin's art, but Rancière's point is that the novelty of de-figuration does not depend on prior novelty in painting. Similarly, it is not claimed that Aurier's de-figuring of pictorial visibility caused the re-figurations presented 'by Cubist or Dadaist collages, the appropriations of Pop Art … or the plain writing of Conceptual Art' (Rancière 2007: 87). We are reminded, then, that at the moment of origination the innovative de-configured conceptual space of critic and material space of the artist are free floating – disconnected.

The forward propagation of both modes of invention can be seen as arising in moments of reception between image and observer, or text and reader, in which interests are clarified and activated. For example, after cognizing the surprising work of art, an artist might employ the understanding acquired in the production of new works of art, as was recorded when some artists immediately adopted some of Constable's tenets when his work was shown in Paris. Alternatively, the critical writer might employ the understanding obtained in the engagement with material innovation in the interpretation or reinterpretation of other works of art, and so on. Given that the cognition of each beholder is brought into and modified by artistic or critical invention, productions and interpretations will be manifold and diverse, and to the extent that both forms of outcome are themselves novel, the stimulation of novelty will be intense and uncontained, and its dispersion rapid. Understood in this way, new knowledge is a potential for a certain type of action, or as Johnson advises, 'knowing is a process of intelligent inquiry into and transformation of experience' (Chapter 8). Conceived in this way, neither certainty of interpretation nor the binding of new understanding to that of the past is a necessary precondition for the collective endorsement of new knowledge. In the case of art, these features of new knowledge, which in many other fields are preconditions for the commitment to further investigation, might merely serve to diminish the productive potential of both modes of innovation, since each is an unstable moment in the unmaking and remaking of aesthetics regimes. Novel works of art and criticism are not to be understood as, 'true propositions or statements about how things are and how they work, which can be verified by past, present or future experience' (Chapter 8), that have to be acquired before we can arrive at collective comprehension of a change in understanding of art. Rather they are better understood as unstable, active contributions to the coalescence of collective interest and understanding that make it possible to speak of artistic renewals, such as Impressionism and Cubism, and of artists who changed art.

When the artist remains silent in the presence of the work, the transformational component is experienced by its audiences initially as individual surprise and then as collective surprise, which leads to discourse between those who would reject and those who would accept the work as a work of art. Whilst rejection reinforces the current understanding of art, acceptance requires cognitive adjustment such that surprise can become recognition. This cognitive adjustment amounts to a description of the transformational contribution of the work, historically provided through the criticism and history of art. Art cannot surprise the individual unless that individual possesses art-related cognitive schemas and semantic networks. Collectively surprising art relies on objective-shared traditions, rules, values and expectations. In Constable's day the rules of engagement were clear, public and governed by the Royal Academy, where he himself studied. Such was the common appreciation of this authority that Constable must have thought that it would be obvious to all how his art enhanced its merits. In the end, it was not obvious and he needed to speak of past art in order to clarify the originality of his contribution. Therefore, the artist must be satisfied that his or her work is taken on face value or find ways of influencing its reception. Modernism, the Avant-garde and Postmodernism, if not dismantling all tradition, all expectation, have brought us to a point where collective agreement about art is problematic. We may actually be at a moment when art becomes an arena incapable of cognitive surprise, since the frameworks for reception and interpretation have been eroded. In such an arena, the work of art may not be able to stand on its own without the presence of an 'other' that gives it visibility, to borrow Rancière's articulation of the term. This, perhaps, explains why contemporary artists are increasingly choosing to talk and write, as well as show. In fact, the whole debate around art and research may come to be seen as reflecting this historical turn; the moment when the artist found it necessary to articulate the reflective and projective character of his or her practice.

Conclusion

The question posed at the beginning of this chapter was, 'What is the relationship between the research and art?' The answer given here is that if we are to talk about a relationship, then it is one of inclusion: art subsumes research, if we accept that art that changes art can be understood as contributing to knowledge of what art was, is, or might become. In developing an account of how art changes art, we began by drawing on Rancière's essay, *Painting in the Text*, in which he argues that art depends on a bond between ways of making, seeing, saying and thinking. As emphasized above, for Rancière, 'The surface [of a painting] is not wordless, is not without "interpretations" that pictorialize it.' Each bond between a way of making and seeing, saying and thinking defines an aesthetic regime or regime of art that enables 'another subject to appear under the representative subject' (2007: 76). In the case of painting, up until the Romantic era, the bond was between painting and poetry, thereafter between painting and criticism. The making of a new bond between image and text involves undoing the existing bond and the retying it anew. Rancière (2007: 78–9) assigns to the critical writer the highly creative task, not simply of adding retrospective discourse to the 'nakedness of forms', but of constructing, through de-figuration, the visibility necessary for seeing a new bond between image and text. In short, he offers a way of thinking about art that denies the autonomy of the art from words – the birth of a regime of art is their bonding and its death is their separation. Art that changes art is art that modifies the bond between image and ideas. If we choose to work with his theory, then we cannot talk about the works of art as if they are simply material: we cannot talk about a painting that changed painting and mean that the painting entirely speaks for itself.

Although Rancière provides us with an account of how the critical writer contributes to change in art, namely the act of de-figuration, he has very little to say about the artist's contribution to the making and remaking of a regime of art, notwithstanding that the historical reception of novel works of art is often accompanied by individual and collective uncertainty. It was then argued that cognitive surprise is the primary mechanism underlying the response to material novelty, which arises when the application of existing schemata and semantic networks governing the reception and interpretation of art fail to accommodate the presented forms. Cognitive surprise provides an impetus for meta-cognition and exploration and explanation of the unexpected event, which, as illustrated in Rilke's encounter with the art of Cézanne, resembles de-figuration in that the cognitive process initiated through surprise leads to a new visibility, 'and suddenly one has the right eyes'. To explore the genesis of the surprising work of art we then considered in some depth the art of John Constable. The first exploratory move examined the nature of Constable's artistic project, arguing that it sought to combine poetry and science. It is not claimed that it was Constable's intention to produce art that would change art. In contrast, it is argued that Constable was not at war with the past and, in fact, saw in it the grounds and reasons for his own project. The second move argued that although Constable's art, as epitomized in his six-foot landscapes, can now be appreciated as the attainment of his ambition, in its initial reception it could not be understood as such because his project could satisfy neither the existing, nor the emergent, but as yet invisible new regime of art that would replace the former. The presence of an as yet un-figured new regime of art is implicit in Rilke's engagement with Cézanne and Stendhal's appreciation of Constable, and even more forcefully in the recollection of the French painter, Paul Huet's (1804–1869), 'another veteran of that Salon [of 1824, who], remembered Constable's works coming as the sudden realization of his own dreams' (Fleming-Williams and Parris. 1984: 53).

Nevertheless, it is argued that Constable's art provided a bridge between the bond of his time and what was to become the new bond between image and ideas, functioning as an ambiguous mode of figuration to be read either as disfiguration or pre-figuration depending upon the outlook of the viewer. If it is the case, as has been argued here, that Constable was actually in agreement with art's past and would probably not have been in agreement with its future, then his personal project can be understood as timely rather than prescient. Rather than being based on an interpretation of his art that he would have endorsed, his reputation can be understood as built on its re-reading, in a manner similar to the Goncourts' re-reading of Chardin, through a visibility appropriate to Impressionism, etc.[11] The final move brought us back to the question of arts-based research and art that changes art. Here it is argued that Constable's lectures functioned (if too late to have a major influence on how his art was understood and used) as a response to his critics that was designed to guide his listeners toward the mode of visibility appropriate to his art. As such, it is argued, Constable's lectures, when seen in *conjunction* with his art, function as a counterpart to de-figuration and as a model of art's research function.

The final section above considered the driving motivation of the material innovation of the artist and the conceptual innovation of the critic, arguing that in both cases that novelty can be understood as arising out of a tension between personal and professional interests and expectations. Whilst Rancière's articulation of the de-figuring creativity of the critic is acknowledged, it is suggested that such texts do not govern the rapid and networked transmission of material novelty. Instead, it is postulated that collective recognition and articulation of change arises primarily through the capacity of both novel art work and novel critical texts to engage interest and to stimulate action. Considered in this way, knowledge is better understood as a potential for a certain type of action contributing to an emergent coalescence of collective interest and understanding. Nevertheless, the function of surprise and wonder within this historical system of exchange relies on existing and collectively shared cognitive schemata and semantic networks, namely shared expectations, and Modernism, the Avant-garde and Postmodernism have all contributed to a general dismantling or fragmentation of such certainties. In the contemporary context, the grounds against which novelty can stand out are not pre-given. Whilst for Constable, speaking to his art was forced upon him as a last resort to provide his contemporaries with 'the right eyes' to see his work, we may now be at a moment when it has to be the artist's first resort to establish the ground against which surprise can be registered and its consequences activated, including the coalescing of interests that sustain a cultural bond between image and idea.

Given the artistic transformations drawn upon above, it may seem that this chapter sets out a framework for thinking about research in art that sets too high a standard; one where paradigm shifts are demanded. It may also appear that the artist is required to intentionally produce art that changes our understanding of art. However, as argued above, Constable did not set out to revolutionize art, rather his project was to realize a mode of landscape painting that conjoined poetry and science, both of which already existed as separate traditions within the history of art. In short, he committed himself to an artistic project, but neither he nor his contemporaries could have predicted that the outcomes of his project would have a scope of influence that with the passage of time would establish Constable as a major landscape artist. Constable's artistic programme had a clear ambition, direction, logic and coherence against which its achievements could have been assessed. All that is required of the artist, then, is an artistic project that offers the potential to challenge the understanding of art.

This chapter has outlined a history of art from the moment when the bond between image and text was one in which the conventions and rules of the Academy inscribed the text, enacted in the social practices of the art world. In the demise of schools of art and the Academy, the text was then reconfigured in the interpretations of the art critic, historian and theorist. Today, it is suggested, the artist may need to take personal responsibility for contributing to the renegotiation or reconstruction of the bond between image and text. In Rancière's terms, the research function in art will now require the artist to contribute to the construction of the mode of visibility appropriate to the interpretation of the material innovation of his or her works of art. However, as evidenced by Constable's lectures, this does not amount to a justification of research criteria attainment or adherence to their validity. Furthermore, we have seen three effective, but linguistically different examples, in Constable, the Goncourts and Aurier, of texts that contribute to the visibility of the works of art with which they are conjoined, and it is not difficult to see how de-figuration, disfiguration, and pre-figuration might be productively entwined in the unfolding of an artistic project of transformational potential.

Notes

1 Borgdorff (2006: 12) has used the term 'research in the arts', although his characterization of the term suggests that he accepts that art is a practice that has yet to become research. Macleod and Holdridge (2006: 2) have used the term 'art as research' as an anchor for exploring 'how art can be understood as academic research', again emphasizing that art is at a distance from research.

2 Typically, types of research are defined in relation to a given condition of research, such as subject, e.g. sociological, psychological, etc., or method, e.g. qualitative, quantitative.

3 In 1766, Stubbs published a book entitled The Anatomy of the Horse, which is still in print.

4 In other words, words are necessary for a painted surface to be seen as the conquering of the medium, i.e. for it to be seen as art.

5 There is a philosophical tradition concerning to the notion of surprise. At the one-day conference In Not Knowing, at New Hall College, Cambridge, 29 June 2009, under the title, 'On the value of not knowing: wonder, beginning again, and letting be', Rachel Jones traced part of this tradition from Descartes' proposition that wonder is the first of all the passions, to Irigaray's articulation of wonder as the event of the other.

6 Toward the end of the article, Leroy describes how the fictional M. Joseph Vincent becomes so befuddled as to confuse a municipal guard for a portrait. As far as Leroy is concerned, the boundary between art and reality has disappeared and with it so has art.

7 It might be taken that Constable is suggesting that we should simply learn from other painters and he does indeed cite many painters in his lectures. However, close analysis of his lectures suggests a more complex interpretation. Throughout his lectures, Constable uses examples to evidence a common strength in some artists and weakness in others, i.e. that the great understand nature and the lowly fail to observe nature, relying instead on imagination and imitation of past masters. So artists can learn from great artists, but what they learn is that these masters learnt from

nature. What Constable seeks to demonstrate in the second lecture is how the great landscape artist uses this understanding as the basis of poetic expression and this too is something that artists can learn from the study of great art. Hence, the mannerists are doubly flawed, they don't attend to nature and they slavishly copy past masters.

8 George Field. 1835. Chromatography: or a treatise on colours and pigments. London. A 2007 edition of this text exists, edited by Thomas Salter.

9 Stendhal has been called a romantic realist. Honoré de Balzac (1779–1850) rose to prominence in the early 1840s.

10 In 1854, Eugène Delacroix (1798–1863) claimed Constable as the 'father' of modern French landscape painting, whilst Frédéric Villot (1809–1875) labelled him its 'messiah'.

11 For example, in speaking of pre- and early-Renaissance German, Dutch and Flemish artists, Constable observes that, 'In their hands dignity of subject never excluded meanness, and the wretched material introduced into their historical pictures could have led to nothing', and continues by saying of these schools that, 'The accompaniments even of the Nativity were often, with them, an assemblage of the mean and ridiculous. An owl, seen through a hole in a thatched roof, sitting on a beam just over the head of the Virgin, with a mouse dangling by its tail from his claw; pigs quarrelling at the trough, etc.' (Leslie 1951: 293).

16

TIME AND INTERACTION: RESEARCH THROUGH NON-VISUAL ARTS AND MEDIA

Henrik Frisk and Henrik Karlsson

Introduction

This chapter discusses the challenges related to arts-based research in and through time-based artistic expressions. Even though many of the examples referenced in this chapter belong to the field of musical practice, the issues and challenges they intend to highlight are obviously common to several other real-time scenic and performing art forms. Even art expressions that are not easily associated with the real-time processes of music (e.g. painting, directing, design, etc., as well as hybrid forms converging artistic and technological thinking such as computer-game design and the design of multi-user interactive environments), may in fact prove to have much in common with the time-based art forms.

Although few art forms are unanimously non-real time or real-time, a distinction used below is that between artistic practices that are *embedded in time* (in-time processes) and those that are *contained in time* (over-time processes).[1] For an action to be embedded in time means that the time it takes to perform it matters; that time is a factor whose value is decisive. For example, the difference between reading or writing a book in one day or to do it in one year is not necessarily a difference that changes the meaning or expression of the book, whereas the time it takes to play or listen to a piece of music has everything to do with its expressive qualities: playing the same piece of music in ten minutes or in two hours is likely to make it a very different experience. For this reason it is argued here that there is a difference between a reflection upon the research object as a whole (outside time) and a reflection on the research object as it unfolds in time, and the researcher engaged in arts-based research in the real-time arts should embrace and investigate the in-time properties of the research object. Questions relating to the documentation and dissemination of in-time insights are further discussed and a point is made that the outcome of an arts-based research that investigates the complex feedback loops in the time-based arts may be of interest also outside the art world.

The fact that in music *action* takes place *in* and *through* real time rather than primarily *over* time makes it an interesting, and equally difficult, candidate for artistic research. To gain access to whatever information may be hidden in its in-time properties the researcher needs to resist the temptation of falling back on the investigation of the over-time and out-of-time representations of the art work, such as musical scores, manuscripts, transcriptions, etc. Although most musical expressions offer the same temporal complexity, in the practice of Interactive Music, which is briefly discussed in the first section, the man-machine interactions surface the in-time aspects of music in a particularly useful way. As a hint at the compound nature of time a brief overview of temporal multiplicities is given and further on the artistic practice of Frisk is used to exemplify the research process from within the musical flow, and the feedback between the different aspects of the practice. Finally, turning to Bergson's important writing on memory, it is suggested that even the in-memory (virtual) representation of in-time processes contain and depend on time.

Virtuality and interaction

Both of the two main concepts here, virtuality and interaction, are nested with difficult and sometimes contradictory meanings and connotations. Although they do have significance also outside the field of human-computer interaction this chapter is not the place for an in-depth discussion of all of their readings. In the following we will primarily use them as they are understood and used in the context of human-computer interaction in artistic practice.

Virtual reality

When the technology became usable in the early 1990s, Virtual Reality was seen as a great potential for art production (Moser and MacLeod 1996; Wood 1998; Dixon 2007). Virtual Reality is a game of deception where there is no extension in space (although there appears to be one) and where existence depends entirely on the interactions between the subject and the Virtual Reality technology. The virtual is disembodied and lacks a general visual component: the fact that users are able to mould their own (virtual) visuality is, after all, one of its great qualities.[2] This visuality may be different each time, or it may be identical to any other visuality, since making duplicates is no problem in the digital realm of the virtual. As technology has advanced its positions in Western culture however, the virtual is nearly ubiquitous. To define a Virtual Reality that is distinct from *reality* is almost impossible, because there is a virtual aspect to nearly all activities in the occidental world (Baudrillard 2002: 176–81). Central to the concept of Virtual Reality is the interface through which the user is able to *interact* with the technology and the virtual worlds contained in it, but the aspect of interaction in the field of interactive art and media is problematic as the term *interactive* has to some extent been hijacked by computer interface designers. Though one of its lexicographic meanings is 'reciprocally active', its meaning in the context of computer interface design is more geared towards a methodology of control, than sharing or mutual exchange; aspects that are central to any human-human interaction. In the reduced meaning of computer interaction the actions of one part, the user, are controlling re-actions in the virtual world, often in a one-to-one relation: one action, one re-action. The ethnologist and cultural analyst Robert Willim (2006: 69–86) looks at the simplified user interfaces of much technology as a means to bring lucidity to sometimes extremely complex systems such as the internet or networked computer games. Habit formation and predictability brings order to an incomprehensible virtual world where a mouse click on a given icon on a computer desktop is expected to result in the same machine response, regardless of the user's preceding activities. Interaction in the context of the real-time arts, however, itself a highly complex system in which actions and responses flow back and forth in constantly shifting feedback loops, is rarely about one-to-one mappings, habit formation or predictability, and artistic interaction is not easily transformed to fit the reduced idea of interaction that technology typically offers. Hence, artistic practice is in need of novel approaches to interface design that allow for an extended view on interaction, and this need may fuel both the practice itself as well as the development of computer interface design.

The virtual world offered to one by modern technology is interesting both in the ways that it connects art and art practice to other research disciplines such as computer science and artificial intelligence in the ways described above, but also in the way that it deviates from the real world. Due to their ignorance of conventions and lack of long-term memory, machines are phenomenal individual forgetting devices (Miller 2004) and the absence of an embodied relation between the machine and its operator is consolidating the breach between human cultural heritage and the agnostic nature of the machine. In the virtual world, beneath the predictability of the interface, nothing is hard wired, hence, muscular memory is useless: any one physical movement can have a different meaning each time. Envision the four members of the German pop-group Kraftwerk, standing still and expressionless in front of their keyboards (obviously exploiting their dissociated relation to the machine-instrument). Compare this vision to the physicality of almost any acoustic instrument performer playing live in front of an audience. In an attempt to avoid the temporal and corporeal split between the technology and performer (between body and machine) so particular and well exploited by Kraftwerk, many artists working with computer technology have found ways to circumvent the missing physicality in their virtual tools, either by designing interfaces that allow for more dynamic modes of interaction, or by designing software that models or emulates a sense of embodiment. These efforts derive from the interactive needs of the real-time arts and lead to initiatives and inventions that may inform both the artistic practice as well as our thinking about human-computer interaction; that changes the object of research as well as its context but also impacts a much wider scope. The lack of context particular to the virtuality of electronic art – digital tools may be infinitely updated and revised after which integral aspects of their original version have been altered and any knowledge related to their earlier edition may have become obsolete – is in this sense an asset in the ways that it forces the researcher to constantly rethink his or her practice.[3] At best it enables novel approaches to artistic problems or issues but, it may equally well participate in creating expressions void of inter-musical (or inter-artistic) references. Approaching this field as a researching musician is a difficult task and the scientific as well as the social and cultural aspects of the virtual should be taken into consideration.

Interactive music

Interactive music may be seen as the musical representation of Virtual Reality technology. It is music that involves technology and where the responses from this technology are depicted by real-time stimuli from human and/or virtual performers. The intricacy of the dynamics in the relationship between the man and the machine is of particular interest while working with interactive music, and as a sub-genre of computer music it is interdisciplinary by nature (Moore 1990: 24). In the context of arts based research it is obviously important to draw upon knowledge that emanates from related fields of inquiry but it is equally important to re-evaluate those same sources. Historically there may have been a tendency for computer music to lean towards the natural sciences in a way that has hindered the development of the artistic and humanistic aspects of this genre, and for the researcher engaged in arts-based research it is important to remember that the primary purpose of the research should not be to manifest theories external to the field but to also critically examine and question the related sciences. Though there may be modes of thinking that correspond to and overlap with the practice, owing to the nature of artistic practice, there will surely be aspects that deviate from it. The concept of time, and the idea of music and other time-based art forms as being embedded in time, is one mode of thinking that leads away from the more traditional scientific methods because the interactions between the artist(s) and the object of research are subject to constant change.

Much (but not all) art production, as well as most other abstract operations at least in their early stages, are over-time activities. Painting a picture, conceptualizing an art installation or writing a musical score are (roughly speaking) over-time operations even if the result, or the instantiation of these art works, may be in-time operations. The American art critic Harold Rosenberg, in a discussion of the aesthetics of impermanence, discusses the art work as an 'interval in the life of both artist and spectator' and continues: 'compositions into which found objects are glued or affixed of from which they protrude or are suspended make art subject to time on equal terms with nature and commodities for daily use' (Rosenberg 1966: 92). Further on Rosenberg turns to action painting where the art object is 'abandoned altogether', replaced by a single act of creation: 'composition turns literally to an event' (Rosenberg 1966: 93). In this latter example one could truly speak of visual arts as an in-time process, although this process is nullified as soon as the result of the event, the canvas, is exhibited as an art work independent of its mode of creation.

It is possible in the example above to link the action and the object, to look at the canvas as a carrier of the (in-time) action that gave rise to it, and to argue that research carried out with reference to this canvas may also include the action and the temporalities that were part of its creation. However, when dealing with real-time art forms with or without technology, it is much more difficult to unanimously distinguish the object. The music that is a result of real-time processes such as improvisation, live coding, interpretation, etc., is made up of a volatile substance that is not easily transformed to a researchable entity. While investigating how the virtual sound worlds of computer instruments, created and edited in real-time, may interact with (or fail to interact with) the real world, the questions pertaining to access and documentation will become important. Although the Western tradition has developed powerful musicological methods to represent and document music visually (Bregman 1994), are there methods independent of time that retain the temporal identity of the object rather than do away with it? Video recordings of performances are a practical method commonly used but it is important to remember that, as opposed to the canvas above, a recording is a representation of the object and not the object itself.

Time and multi temporality

As was stated above, performing music, as well as performance in other time-based art forms, takes place *in* time, and we believe it is fair to assume that in these cases there is a difference between investigating 'the object' in-time,[4] while it is unfolding, as opposed to doing it over-time. Hence, the researching artist in these disciplines needs to be able to explore the object in a multifaceted way as a stratum of analytical modes in simultaneous operation, some of which are performed in real-time and some that are performed in non-real-time, accessing the object through documentations of the performance. The question of time is significant as many of these simultaneous processes take place in different time scales or temporal modes. Orchestra conductors are making judgments on the music in the present, based on their knowledge and expectation of what will happen in the future of the music: in the next bar, the next section, the next movement, the end of the concert, the next concert, etc. They are able to simultaneously keep a fish eye view on the piece without losing the details in the process. As is pointed out by Dixon 'theory and criticism in digital arts and performance, as well as artist's own self-reflections, are replete with explanations and analyses of how works "explore", "challenge", "reconfigure", or "disrupt" notions of time' (2007: 522) but the temporalities referred to here are not simply disrupting another temporality (although they do that too), nor do they easily fit into one single 'extra-temporal' category as is suggested by Dixon. They co-exist and operate in parallel with other present temporalities. The ability to simultaneously act in multiple temporalities is not unique to performing artists. It is something one constantly does to various degrees in every day life, but because of the ways in which different temporal and interactive modes unfold in the real-time arts, arts-based research may provide unique insights into this complex area.

To the Greek composer and architect Iannis Xenakis, the question of time was of great importance. His views, most likely influenced by his work as an architect, are used here as a backdrop for the ideas of time, memory and temporality discussed later in this chapter. According to Xenakis (1971), non-synchronicity and discontinuity of events in time is what makes the flux of time perceptible: without it, time would remain hidden, illegible and inapproachable. Xenakis also argued, however, that the same music may exist outside time, as a snapshot, as an abstract representation. This representation, when encoded in our memories, or when described as a musical structure (e.g. a fugue), becomes accessible to us as a whole; a whole which we can navigate, jump back and forth in, and sustain at random access. The whole becomes not a succession, but something non-temporal that 'can be viewed as one *time spectrum* of a fundamental duration' (Roads 2001: 73, my emphasis).[5] This is comparable to the transformation from event to object that was discussed above with regard to action painting and according to this line of thought, even though the activities that lead to the creation of an art work are embedded in time, and entirely dependent on time, another transformation, perhaps an ontological one, forces the art work into its out-of-time representation. That the 'chief attribute of a work of art in our [twentieth] century is not stillness but circulation' (Rosenberg 1966: 93), does not make a decisive difference in this context, as that circulation (in most cases) is an over-time process rather than an in-time process.

That in-time processes such as music are transformed to 'image-representations', or get transformed to their out-of-time representations in the consciousness of performers or audiences, is a common thought that rests on the idea that a performance work may also be seen as an object. In essence, this is also an ontological construct. Xenakis's idea of musical memory as a spatial translation of the musical events contained in it could be traced to his background as an architect, and may have been influenced by his aptitude and sensibility for spatial rendering. If one limits oneself to the realm of the time based arts; is it really possible that our in-memory representation of something such as music, that exists and evolves in time, can be represented *independent* of time? And if it is, what is the coupling between time and space that makes the transformations from one to the other transparent; how is the space/time spectrum calculated? These are examples of questions that may be tackled from within an artistic practice in the context of arts based research. Only from within the flow of time is it possible to fully grasp the time-space transformations and their significance, specifically as well as generally. Xenakis's book *Formalized Music* (1971) is an interesting example of an early practice based research project and a document of a composer's view on questions such as time and temporality in music and they are interesting precisely because of his strong relation to the spatial dimensions.

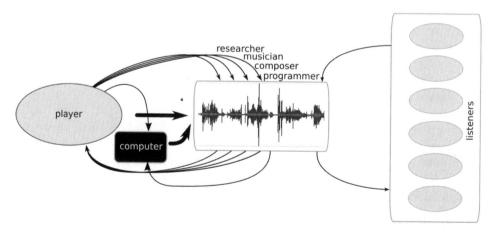

Figure 16.1 A simplified graphic representation of an instant of an improvised performance with an interactive computer. The performer is reflecting upon the output in several different modes of thinking (represented by the arrows leading from the performer to the sound). The feedback of the reflection is represented by the arrows leading from the sound back to the performer.

Performing in practice

Something that is embedded in time will always be difficult – but not impossible – to conceive of as an object (though object is a misleading term here), independent of its temporal context. Despite Xenakis's argument to the contrary, we will argue that this 'object' will not easily transform itself to a spatial representation, mainly because in the real-time arts it is not just the order of the events and the speed at which they are deployed that matters and that gives this object its character. Just as important are the many interactions between the many different agents that play a part in the construction of the in-time event. The performer/researcher working in the field of arts based research should resist the temptation of objectifying the in-time performance and instead embrace the possibilities and the great challenges that lie in investigating the in-the-moment, unfolding, real-time, processes of creative and interactive activities. Their in-time aspects, such as their physicality and inter-subjectivity, are primarily accessible from the inside, from within the creative activity and they risk losing their identity if they are instead looked upon as over-time processes, resolved of their 'in-timeness'.

Performing research in-time is a difficult task, but for arts-based research in time based arts to be different from, e.g. standard musicological research, the practitioner and researcher has to face these difficulties and attempt to access the object from the inside. The means both doing it, and the methods by which it can be done, will inevitably have to differ depending on the nature of the practice. Investigating and acknowledging the differences between divergent temporal domains and temporalities is a prerequisite, regardless of the discipline. In other words, to engage in arts-based research, accessing the object of research as an in-time process constitutes an activity that may offer an interesting alternative to the otherwise dominant visual modes of research expression. To visualize a flow of time, i.e. to perform the kind of time/space transformation as was suggested by Xenakis, is admittedly a powerful and pedagogical trick, but it is a transformation of an

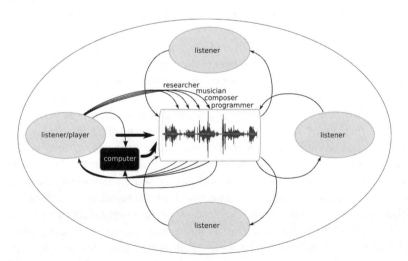

Figure 16.2 A modified version of Figure 16.1, in which the linear conception of a producer and a group of consumers is replaced with a distributed 'sphere' of listening.

in-time process to an over-time process, and in the shift, temporal, interactive, as well as other kinds of information is bound to get lost.

Performing reflections: Henrik Frisk

As a performer engaged in an actual performance with an interactive computer system, and simultaneously a researcher, I combine several different roles and disseminating processes at once. As can be seen from Figure 16.1, I at once access and evaluate the object in different modes of thinking relating to the different tasks I carry out, or have carried out in preparation for the performance (as a programmer, a musician, a composer, etc.). The object in this case is simplified to constitute the bare audible trace left by what I and the computer produce together. In the same way as the conductor, the evaluation is simultaneously done at different rates and against different inner 'templates', expectations or value judgments (of which some may be downright banal). Is this note in tune? Is this good music? Does this work against the pre-conceived form? Is this computer programme functioning the way it should? Will this work in the next concert?

In addition to the performance specific reflections, in arts-based research there is also the research activity. In my own experience the point of intersection, the convergence, between the in-time music and the research upon that process, is an area that is laborious to navigate wisely and honestly. It is easy to get lost and it is easy to get drawn outside the temporal flux so particular to musical practice. It is always tempting to detach the research from the in-time process and let it operate in its own temporal mode, more closely related to how musicological activities are carried out. Intimidating questions relating to the validity of research performed from within *bad* art (i.e. bad art but good research) makes the task even more difficult for the researcher (if at all possible, no artist researcher will ever be proud to have performed excellent research but bad art). However, many of these distracting questions relate to the (false) idea that the researcher could somehow be distinct from the performer, as if a Cartesian split between the rational investigator and the unpredictable creator was possible and desirable.

In Figure 16.2, representing a slice of time of a performance, the trajectories of reflection create a feedback loop between the object of research and the musician. A corresponding loop may also be found in between the listeners and the music, representing the listener's reflections upon that same music as it takes place in real time. Although they are unlikely to be entirely synchronous with those of the performer, provided the performer and the listeners share some musical references or have a common cultural ground it is conceivable that some of the reflections made by the listeners will overlap with some of the performer's. It is as a listener I (as a performer) am able to reflect on that which I play and in that sense the audible trace, although produced by me, is a shared object of reflection for both myself and the listeners.

In this view of our interactions, the producer-consumer conception of performer-listener is resolved in favour of a relation more geared towards an inter-subjectivity. Marcel Cobussen, in his book *Thresholds: Rethinking Spirituality in Music*, discusses listening and suggests an understanding of 'listening to music' that really means 'listening *to and fro* music' (Cobussen 2008: 135, emphasis in the original). When experienced, this oscillating movement of coming and going moves beyond the idea of the listening subject and the sounding object. According to Cobussen, 'to listen to and fro de-centres them, wipes them out'. Through the shared act of listening the subject-object divide between the listener and the sounding object is erased, and the producer-consumer distinction between the performer and the listener is blurred. If the performer is a listener among other listeners, the traditional view on a flow of communication from a creator to a listening subject indeed becomes difficult to maintain. Instead we may consider the image of a group of listeners in which some members are *also* performers and creators (Figure 16.2).

Interaction and feedback

According to improviser Vijay Iyer, the sense of 'shared time' is an important property of music listening and is a crucial aspect of musical improvisation. Listening to a performance of improvised music is to experience the improviser's real-time struggles, their in-time processes. Also to non-dance oriented music, listening to music is a co-performance, a 'participatory act of marking musical time with rhythmic bodily activity [which] physicalizes the sense of shared time, and could be viewed as embodied listening' (Iyer 2008: 276). According to both Cobussen and Iyer, the interactions between the agents at play (listeners, performers, creators, etc.) are central, not only at each end of the flights of communication between the agents involved, but also in the continuum *between* them. Applied to the context of arts-based research this would mean to complement introspective reflections and reflections on the object with an investigation of what goes on in the interactions with the listeners/viewers, the technology in use, the other performers, or with any other zones that influence the artistic practice.[6] Before looking at the aspect of multi-temporality within these interactions, however, we will briefly return to the nature of the in-time reflections in the imagined performance sketched in Figure 16.1.

In the interactions and feedback loops between the performer and the audible trace in Figures 16.1 and 16.2, it is difficult to separate artistic evaluations and reflections from those that are research oriented. Or, perhaps more accurately described, a research oriented reflection may also very well result in an alteration of the object, an alteration that changes the output. The in-time research oriented reflection resists the theory versus practice divide in that it operates in parallel to the practice, and as such it undoubtedly also has an impact on that upon which it reflects.[7] Not all art practice is arts-based research but all arts based research performed in-time in the ways described here will alter the artistic expression in some respect. Furthermore, the research activity may constitute meta-reflection, reflections upon purely musical reflections (e.g. why is it important that this note is in tune?) forming compound reflections of both an artistic and research oriented nature, further influencing the present and future expressive qualities of the creative work. In other words, although the trajectories of reflection may be distinct from one another, their responses are not.

The different temporalities of the elements involved in an interactive performance are important to understand and acknowledge for the arts-based researcher. A computer, as a concept and before engaged in an interactive performance, may be seen as the ultimate representation of an over-time process: its operations are almost entirely independent of time. The need to understand and evaluate the reasons for the changes in the computer output as well as the changes themselves in an interactive computer performance, is without a doubt one of the more challenging aspects of being an artist engaged in real-time digital art forms. It involves having to evaluate the abstract and largely outside-time functionality of a computer programme in performance, while simultaneously engaging in the temporal flux of the in-time progress of the output. Using and writing computer programmes to be used in interactive performances are difficult tasks. To hold different temporal representations active at the same time may be second nature for a musician, but the added aspect of the interactive computer makes it both more complex to understand and more difficult to perform. However, the computer may also help the performer-researcher to understand and acknowledge these different temporalities, not least through the range of documentation possibilities it offers and which may be explored by the researching performer.

Interacting with the virtual

The almost mystical sensation of simultaneously being able to be in time, 'now' and in memory – in the recollection of a previous now – is an important and powerful aspect of time-based arts in general and music in particular. Imagine listening to a well known melody being played. As the melody is unfolding there is a perpetual interaction between its in-memory representation and its real-time representation. Sometimes, if the memory of a particular piece of music is really strong, it may overshadow the real life version of it and conversely, if the performance is powerful and expressive it may overwhelm the original memory, overwriting it with the new version. As was discussed above, it is tempting, and practical, to gather musical events into larger structures (e.g. notes into melodies, movements into symphonies, songs into song-cycles, etc.) and regard them as singularities, as image representations of what they represent. As such they would have no reference to time. Their temporality would get transformed into a kind of spatiality, and conceptually they would approach a representation of infinite time (Roads 2001), or as Xenakis put it, time is abolished in such structures: 'one could say that every temporal schema, pre-conceived or post-conceived, is a representation outside time of the temporal flux in which the phenomena, the entities, are inscribed' (Xenakis 1971: 264). They become virtual translations of the original in-time representations, similar to how the resultant canvas of action painting may be seen as an outside-of-time representation of an in-time action. But if time really is abolished, how is it that we can keep track of such time specific data as duration, and silence, in our memory of representations of music, plays, movies, etc.? This question is not merely of theoretical or philosophical import; it has great impact on the way one understands and executes practice-based research in the real-time arts. To examine an artistic practice from within – as opposed to examining it from the outside – one needs to be able to access the object in real-time. And to gain access to it in real-time it is necessary to understand what real-time is relative to non real-time, i.e. in-memory representations.

In the survey of memory and imagination in Paul Ricœur's seminal book *Memory, History, Forgetting* (2004), in the first chapter he critically discusses Husserl's concept of memory in general and the ideas of retention in particular.[8] The duration of a musical

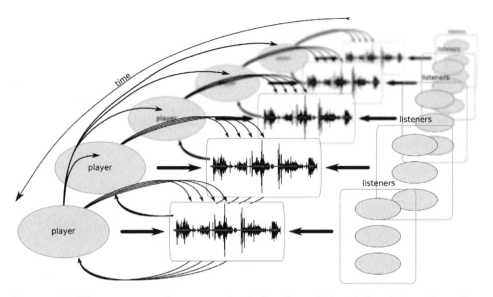

Figure 16.3 The imaginary performance as sketched in Figure 16.1 with the addition of time. Past events are fading out but held on to by the in-time performer as is represented by the arrows pointing back into previous nows. It should be noted that this is an extremely simplified graphic representation of phenomena that are infinitely more complex.

note is used to address the question of what it means for something that endures to remain (but any other event unfolding in time may equally well symbolize the phenomenon). And this is indeed at the heart of the matter for the present discussion: when in music, or any other real-time art form, one performs, there is a complex interplay between creation and duration and the elements that make up the art work has both a virtual, in memory, and a real representation. These entities endure and as they develop in time they create duration.

How is this possible? How can the present 'now' and the memory of the past 'nows' coexist? How can the memory of the preceding now co-exist with the memory of a 'now' six months ago? Husserl, using the sounding note as an example, states that the note, as it is played, makes the now perceptible, and, as it continues to sound it 'has an ever new now, and the now that immediately precedes it changes into a past'. The 'ever new now' is what constitutes the modification in the perception that constructs the duration. The 'now' that is pushed back by the 'new' now however is not disappearing but is held on to, and it is this 'holding on to' that Husserl labels *retention* (Ricœur 2004: 32). Hence retention is, in a manner of speaking, a way to hold on to the note while it is sounding; as a modified perception of it. The new now, that can never become the 'real' but one which can trail the present, and can be experienced almost as if it took place in the real domain as a virtual (re-)presentation moving alongside of, or being pulled by, the real in a continuous flow in time. The real and the virtual as sketched above may further be seen as modes of perception: outwards, listening to one's own or others' sounds as they disclose in time, and inwards, listening to past experiences and memory representations. Both of these modes continuously co-exist and interact with one another.[9]

The double reflection; reflection upon that which is present in a 'now' and a reflection upon past experiences and memories, is by no means particular to the field of musical practice and it should be of interest to the arts-based researcher to explore the difference between these two modes of reflection, although it may raise some methodological concerns. As mentioned above, video documentation has proven to be useful, but even with a video and audio recording of a performance, unwrapping the different processes and their influence on the events may be difficult.[10]

Memory

According to Henri Bergson, we can look at the present-past axis as an inverted cone (like an ice-cream cone) where the tip is the present and the other end represents the oldest unconscious memories. Each segment of this cone represents a virtual plane, a region in the past (Bergson 1991: 170–232). In Gilles Deleuze's reading of Bergson each such region contains the totality of the past in different levels of contraction or relaxation, and at any time one can make a leap to any segment of the cone, to any past memory, bringing it back into consciousness (Deleuze 1988: 60). The cone is not to be understood as a storage device in which memories are put, slice by slice in succession, but rather it is an abstract visualization of the human capacity to place oneself in the past, while still having access to everything prior to that particular point in time, as well as everything past it. 'It is in this sense that one can speak of the regions of Being itself, the ontological regions of the past "in general", all coexisting, all repeating one another' (Deleuze 1988: 61). The cone symbolizes a dynamic process, more dynamic than the image can represent, because there are several motions in simultaneous operation. While the base of the cone remains still, the tip of the cone, which at all times represents the present, moves perpetually along the plane of existence 'of my actual representation of the universe' (Bergson 1991: 152). If this is the horizontal movement there are corresponding vertical movements where pure memories are descending down to the tip, to where action takes place, and images from the present are ascending up into memory (Lawlor 2003: 47–8). In other words, one has (at least) two contrasting movements, one of the cone moving on the plane of existence and one inside the cone affecting the level of contraction at any virtual plane within the cone. Hence the virtual plane of memory is not a static *image* of a time in the past, but a constantly changing one. Following this conceptualization of the relation between the present and the past, the idea of a temporal schema outside time that Xenakis brought forth should perhaps be questioned. Does not the memory of a musical event vividly hold on to the temporal aspect of its origin? Is it not so that the temporal relations between the events contained in a memory matters to its representation?

The virtual planes of memory discussed above are likely to be linked to the virtuality present in all artistic creation. Common to both the virtual planes of memory and to the virtuality of art practice, with or without technology is that, although they generate visual elements and images, they do not depend on them. While the mental leaps back and forth between the present and the past is a natural component to all performing art practices the jump to a virtual plane of the past in the spur of the moment of the performance may also create an unsurpassable breach: an ontological difference that, in the best case, fuels the performance and takes it to new heights, but at its worst, detaches it from the logic of the present. Under such circumstances the virtual plane fails to actualize itself and remains trapped in the memory of the performer(s).

In Figure 16.3 the slice of time discussed earlier is now put into the context of a *flow* of time. Past events are slowly sinking into retention while the reflective listener-performer is able to make leaps back in time. Although only the activities of the performer are plotted, similar leaps back in time are obviously also performed by any given listener. Furthermore, it should be pointed out that the figure is a very rough image of *some* of the processes going on. That time is of great importance to the real-time arts is perhaps self-evident, but the argument that has been pursued throughout this chapter is that the ways in which time operates in performance is of importance to the way arts-based research may be carried out in these art forms, and that research in this field may further our understanding of time and temporalities in more general terms. Many of the central issues that, for example, improvising performers (in any art form) learn and conquer, such as sensitivity to the other, synchronicity, timing, dialogue, interaction, embodiment, entrainment, etc., are concepts that are of great interest to both the natural and social sciences.[11] If arts-based research is able to unpack and communicate some of the aspects concerning the in-time properties of their practices, many other research disciplines may benefit from and seek to further explore this knowledge.

Summary

The distinction is obviously not clear cut between in-time and over-time processes in art. Most art practices, as has already been pointed out, begin with some kind of over-time process in its preparation stage. Even improvisatory practices, which depend extensively on in-time activities, commonly involve stages of preparation in which constraints and limitations are set up. By introducing the interactive computer in this context the over-time articulations (artistic structures, constraints, form, etc.) may be brought into real-time performance, hence a layer of complexity is added for both the performer and the researcher. In the words of Susanne Kozel (Chapter 12) the computer may provide a structure that, in the interactions with a performer, constructs 'a topology of meaning'; in itself a valid metaphor for the holistic nature of the interactions between in-time and over-time processes that have been discussed in this chapter.

Over the last three or four decades a number of successful interactive art works have been produced, surpassing the limitations and quirks of digital systems. The 'ideal' interactive performance system may hide its abstract functionality or may display its full power; it may be the invisible, virtual performer or it may be the dominating force in the interplay with human performers. Considering the great range of expressions that have emanated from interactive technology over the last decades, from a purely artistic point of view there is no need to worry about the computer as a tool or vehicle for artistic production. Although there are a number of ways in which digital technology may be useful in artistic work of all kinds, of particular interest to the present discussion are the ways in which real-time art practices may have needs and place expectations on the technology that will impact on its development. That the corporate world and the applied sciences have looked towards the arts for many years is no news. In 1970 the photocopying and computer company Rank Xerox started Xerox PARC, an entire laboratory dedicated to experimental and artistic work based on the products they developed. The telephone company AT&T's research department Bell Labs, where the foundation for present day information technology was set out, similarly let composers and early sound artists such as James Tenney and Jean-Claude Risset work in their laboratories. And still today it is not difficult to find calls from the applied, natural and social sciences to the world of artistic practice for expertise on various matters. In particular, the field of human-computer interaction seems to ask for input from artists. In a study on perception and performance in both human-technology interaction and music, authors Kirlik and Maruyama (2004) comment on the fact that 'design and training in many socio-technical systems proceed all to often as if "doing it by the book" or working "like a machine" were admirable qualities'. Their hypothesis is that by turning to musical practice, in particular musical improvisation, the design and understanding of the social aspects of human-computer interaction systems can be greatly improved. Designer and scholar Aukje Thomassen similarly mentions music as a means 'to fully research the applicability' of the flow heuristic explored in her thesis and concludes that interdisciplinary work is needed and 'the major disciplines are the field of social sciences such as psychology and cultural studies, but also the field of the arts in particular music and fine arts' (Thomassen 2003: 239). Furthermore, according to authors Engeström and Escalante, there is a tendency to limit the thinking about human-computer interaction to 'microlevel interactions between programmers or users and computers. The broader social forces and structures that constrain such interactions and are themselves reproduced and moulded by microlevel events are often left unexamined.' Arts-based research in the real-time arts has much to contribute here and may provide a useful alternative to the 'naive image of human-computer interaction as narrowly technical and as a problem of cognitive optimization' (Engeström and Escalante 1996: 325).

These are examples of areas in which arts-based research in the real-time arts may interface with other research communities, and although there has been a general tendency on the part of the natural sciences to employ an overly romantic view of artistic practice, requests like the ones cited here should not be neglected. That the results of arts-based research may not harmonize with (scientific) expectations is beside the point: there is an expectation that knowledge specific to the field of artistic practice may be useful in other, related fields of research. More specifically, because of the high demands they impose on technology and due to their largely non-traditional methods, the real-time arts involving computers have great potential to inform the more general field of human-computer interaction research in ways that other research disciplines may not be able to do; not least, in the ways that time and memory is dealt with, and in the ways that the abstract, non-temporality of the computer has to be tackled.

It will always be tempting to approach the object of research as a whole rather than as a distributed agglomeration of interactions but throughout this chapter we have argued that understanding the mutual influence of the in-time and over-time aspects of artistic practice is of great significance for the researcher engaged in arts-based research. Furthermore, we have stressed that the use of interactive computer technology is of interest to the topic of arts-based research in that it foregrounds issues pertaining to time and temporality in the context of real-time arts, but also in the ways that it offers connections to cognate research disciplines.

Coda

Considering the important role perception, reflection and sensibility to visual and auditory stimuli plays for artists in general and for the researching practitioner in particular, it should be of interest and value for the researching artists to further the study of phenomena relating to time and interaction. Regardless of whether the practice involves technology or not, both the constructive and receptive phases of artistic processes are of interest here, particularly if the research is performed in an interdisciplinary environment in interaction with, for example, the behavioural or computer sciences or, for that matter, in collaboration with other artistic disciplines. The scholarly study of computer games, an emerging field of inquiry that Dixon called 'game performance theory' (2007: 621), may be a discipline of interest to the artistic researcher. Both the programming, and the practice of playing them, are interesting arenas for exploring ideas relating to time. The way that computer games create the illusion of immersion, and the way that they often participate in disrupting the time-space relations, makes them appear as contemporary and virtual incarnations of the *Gesamtkunstverk*, and for Richard Wagner questions connected to time and space were foregrounded, at least towards the end of his vast production. In one of the central scenes in his opera *Parsifal*, the protagonist's mentor Gurnemanz mystically explains to him: 'Du siehst, mein Sohn, zum Raum wird hier die Zeit.' (You see, my son, time here becomes space). In a commentary to this scene, German composer Wolfgang Rihm points out the brilliance in the way Wagner stages the time to space transformation. It is not made by a sudden move but rather as a seamless transition, like a walk through a long series of infinitesimal transformations. (In a common staging, along with the music in this passage, Gurnemanz and Parsifal are slowly walking towards a changing landscape, backs turned to the audience.) When portraying the time to space transition, Wagner resists the non-temporal aspect of space to which Xenakis alludes, and focuses on the movement for, as Rihm states, the perception of space requires movement (Rihm 2001).

To Rihm, time is movement. In a constant motion, events are sinking into time (similar to the way the concept of retention was described above), and, according to Rihm, in the process that which one labels musical material is constructed. If musicological research has been focused on describing that material, arts-based research should, among other things, be focused on the motion that precedes it. Furthermore, that knowledge will not only be of interest to the practice itself and to the general field of art practice, but is also likely to be of interest to related fields of inquiry such as human-computer interaction and social practices. In an interesting commentary on Heidegger's essay *The Question Concerning Technology*, Aden Evens concludes that 'art provides the best forum in which to pose and re-pose the question concerning the digital. [...] Art pursues invention and so explores the limits of its media to forge new possibilities and discover unexpected directions' (Evens 2005: 82). It is the responsibility of arts-based research to make these possibilities, discoveries, and directions available to the researching community.

Notes

1. We are indebted for the in-time versus over-time terminology to Vijay Iyer (2008) who refers to it in a discussion on embodiment in improvisation. For the original source along with a few additional on the topic of robotics and cognitive science, see Smithers (1996; 1998), Gelder (1998).
2. Compare William Gibson's famous definition of Cyberspace as a 'consensual hallucination' (Gibson 1984).
3. That this may equally be a frustration is described in Ostertag (2002).
4. Let the object, for the moment, encompass all and any aspects of the artistic practice.
5. See also Stockhausen (1957).
6. Cf. Chapter 10, in which the project Bodies in Flight describes the contemporary human as interstices inbetween various discursive fields and their related technologies.
7. Also compare to how Susanne Kozel (Chapter 12) writes that 'innate to performance is the ability to reflect on what we are doing while we are doing it. I practice, and I reflect upon practice in infinitesimal loops.'
8. The full meaning of this concept, and the significance of Ricœur's thinking upon it, is far beyond the scope of this chapter. We use these sources as inspiration and we do not intend to unpack a full philosophical discussion on time.
9. Henk Borgdorff similarly speaks of a reality of the art work that 'precedes any re-presentation in the space of the conceptual' (Chapter 3).
10. Evidence of this may be found in a study performed by the author Frisk in collaboration with Stefan Östersjö and described in Frisk and Östersjö (2006a; 2006b). Despite numerous analyses of the video material it took us over six months working on the study to realize we had continually misinterpreted what had really been going on in the documented session.
11. For an example in which research in organization theory turns to improvisation as a method, see Lindahl (2003).

17
THINKING ABOUT ART AFTER THE MEDIA: RESEARCH AS PRACTISED CULTURE OF EXPERIMENT

Siegfried Zielinski

Translated by Gloria Custance

Points of departure

In the relations between the arts, sciences, and technologies there have been just as many hot phases as ice-cold ones. According to my observations, the temperature of these relations describes a wave-form that propagates approximately every 200 years. In the early modern era, for example, there was a period of high tension in these relations, from 1600 to 1800, in which the modern-day separations and division of labour developed. After this period, one of the most severe cold phases in recent European history was, to my knowledge, at the end of the eighteenth century. A poet, whom we admire but do not necessarily associate with the technological arts, Friedrich von Hardenberg known as Novalis, wrote his poem *Hymns to the Night* in 1799, which is located at the very centre of the theme that I shall elaborate in this chapter. I shall quote only a few lines of this inimitable poem, which is at the same time a discourse; it is a mixture of poetry and analytical reflections: a depiction of research.

> The old world was in decline. The pleasure garden of the young race withered away – and up towards freer, desolate space the unchild-like, growing humans aspired. The gods vanished with their retinue. Alone and lifeless stood Nature. It was bound with an iron chain by dry Number and rigid Measure. Like dust and air the immeasurable flowering of life crumbled into words obscure.[1]

After the period of violent separations in the Age of Enlightenment, in which lightning was tamed and artificial electricity developed as the soul of the newer media, Novalis attempted to put the unity of the world on the agenda again which the poetizing natural philosophers among the Pre-Socratics had conceptualized so elegantly. Novalis never tires of emphasizing that the sciences must be *poeticized*, and that he himself practises poetry exclusively and in conformity with this propagated unity of art and science, of aesthetic and epistemological research.

This position, which I formulate here at the outset, is programmatic and runs implicitly and consistently through my text. When I speak of art, I am referring to a theory and praxis that as a matter of principle is affected by science and technology. And when I speak of the sciences and their special ability to experiment, I envisage a concept that is porous and exhibits a marked curiosity about the arts. If these prerequisites are not given, there is no point at all in reflecting on the importance of research for the arts (and sciences). If our focus is on the arts, then we do not need just any kind of science. We need science that is poetic and with the capacity to think poetically; we need science that is capable of imagining art, science that can even take on experimental forms itself which might be characterized as poetic.

Within such a system of coordinates research can assume the status of a third party, and in the true sense of the word be a *medium*, the process that mediates between the arts and sciences. The experiment is the practical expression of such research. The culture of experiment and experimental art are mutually dependent. In a society that understands itself as a *test department*, however, this reciprocity does not work.

For the past twenty years I have been exploring and elaborating with my students, and theses and dissertations the epistemological power of artistic images, machine programmes, sounds, and texts. The Romantic idea of unity touches this approach just slightly, but at the same time it tries to avoid the trap of a compulsion to think universally, into which the historical movement has fallen. We decide on a case-by-case basis which form we choose, and not on the foreground of generalizable ideological opinions.

And yet the renewed attempt is always worthwhile, for 'to the person who cannot truly conceive anything as a unity', wrote Adorno in his essay on 'Punctuation Marks' in connection with semicolons and dashes, 'anything that suggests disintegration or discontinuity is unbearable; only a person who can grasp totality can understand caesuras' (Adorno 1991 [1958]: 93).

An operational anthropology of the arts (of knowledge)

In *Hymns to the Night* Novalis was communicating indirectly with a man of his generation for whom he entertained great affection and admiration, and with whom he knew he had a great affinity. The young man in question was Johann Wilhelm Ritter (1776–1810) from Zadamovice, which today again is part of Poland. In 1796 Ritter went to Jena, which at the time was an east German hot spot for encounters between the arts and the sciences, and for several years Ritter was a cult figure for the Romantic poets, scientists, and philosophers. I am focusing on this exceptional intellectual, this genius of scientific experimentation, because he embodies the idea of research as a living microcosm, as an art which is realized through technical media.

Ritter dedicated his short life to a single idea. He wanted to demonstrate that the world we know does not contain anything that is dead, that everything around us is alive. He wanted to prove that everything that exists is in a state of perpetual oscillation. He did not allow himself much time. He died when he was just thirty-four, after making his own body his laboratory. Without a care for the effects on his health,

Ritter constantly exercised the universal importance of galvanism and electricity on himself. In infinitely more radical self-experiments than those of the Italian physicist Alessandro Volta, time and again Ritter connected his hands, lips, temples, eyes, and other highly sensitive body parts to the positive and negative electrodes of electrical apparatus that generated strong and weak current, and meticulously wrote up the effects on the oscillograph that was his body. In his final years Ritter believed he could only endure this torture by recourse to artificial paradises, like opium and alcohol, which hastened the process of physical decay. Shortly after Novalis published his *Hymns to the Night*, the Bavarian Academy of Sciences in Munich appointed Ritter professor, although he had neither a doctoral nor a post-doctoral degree. His last larger book project was *The Theory of Glowing*. It would have been a theory of the frequencies, the oscillations by which means the physical, living world could be described, if he had been able to write it.

For the arts and their interaction with advanced science and technology Ritter's experiments, observations, and conclusions on sound in conjunction with electricity, are of exceptional importance. Through radically changing the position from which he made his observations of so-called Chladni figures, Ritter took the first step toward proving that the graphic patterns on the oscillating hardware were the result of different static charges and not – as was first assumed – of two different states, at rest and in motion. 'The body is only hard ... because of its rigidity. Where there are different values of rigidity, there is also a value of electrical difference between bodies, an electrical charge' (Ritter 1805).

On the basis of such observations, and proceeding from his deep conviction of the unity of physics, life, and art, in 1805 Ritter developed his anthropology of the arts – one of his last publications – the contents of which are quite remarkable. Taking human activity as the most important point of reference, Ritter divided the previous history of the arts into four qualitative stages:

- architecture and urban construction;
- sculpture;
- painting;
- sound and music.

According to Ritter the first three are arts of memory. In urban architecture human deeds are preserved in monumental form; in sculpture they are objectivized; and in painting (which Ritter refers to as *halben Raum* [half-space] or *Schattenkörper* [shadow bodies]) activity reappears because the observer is compelled to supplement the visual information of two-dimensional images. It is only in the time-based form of sound that art truly becomes itself; for Ritter, that means alive.

The critique of what belongs to the past is only of marginal interest to Ritter. His 'beloved' is first and foremost living nature, which he emphasizes should be the study object of the physics of the future. In sound, as a special phenomenon with electrical and electromagnetic properties, he sensed the vibrations of an art of the future, which for him could only be the unity of life and physics (which for Ritter was *the* 'life science') and which would be driven by bipolarity, the principle of life.

A new field is emerging – *time*. Time is also organised and, only from the fusion of *both* organisms, of time and space, does the highest meaning of all life and existence originate. Change is everywhere; nowhere is there stasis. All things have their own time and this does not consist in peaceful succession, which never exists anywhere anyhow.

(Ritter 1803: 213f.)

For Ritter, physics – particularly experimental physics – was a praxis whereby the inner states and processes of the motion of matter, which were imperceptible, could be rendered visible, audible, and felt in his own body: to render what is intangible, yet nevertheless present, perceptible to the senses, to translate it into data, which could then be calculated and materialized in technical artefacts. In Ritter's *Heterodoxies*, as he referred to his essays, sound and light are ultimately one: 'hearing is seeing from within, the very innermost consciousness' (Ritter 1984 [1810]: item 358). They are simply different forms of expression of the one central phenomenon of electricity and its various states of charge and oscillation. For the experimental researcher of nature this was above all a question of the distribution of quantities on an infinite scale: '...when bodies oscillate *extremely fast*, they *glow*'. The dynamic 'light figure' or 'fire-writing', which he enthuses over time and again, are for Ritter extremely high frequency oscillations where sound passes over into light, a phenomenon that is only visible, and which represents for him 'the highest degree of reality' (Rehm 1973).[2]

When Ritter describes the opposite pole – the transitions to the low-frequency sounds that humans can barely hear or not at all – he chooses a curious comparison:

> the rotation of the Earth on its axis, for example, may make a significant sound; this is the oscillation of its internal conditions, which is caused by this; the orbit around the sun may make a second [sound], the orbit of the moon around the Earth a third, and so on. Here one gets the idea of a colossal music, of which our own poor [music] is but a significant allegory ... As a harmony this music can only be heard on the sun. For the sun, the entire system of planets is *one* musical instrument. To the *inhabitants* of the sun its notes may simply appear as the zest for *life*, however, to the sun's *mind itself* it is the ultimate and truest sound.
>
> (Ritter 1984 [1810]: item 360)

Apart from Novalis and his friends from the Jena circle of Romantics, two hundred years ago neither scientists nor artists listened to Ritter. Not least due to his eccentric life style, the passionate experimenter was discriminated against, and for nearly a century he was ignored by the scientific establishment. Even today Ritter is regarded as a refractory and awkward figure whom one only rediscovers arduously and against the resistance of conservative historians of science.

A notable exception was the contemporary modern artist Joseph Beuys. Not only his view that life and art are identical, but many of his drawings, installations, and ready-mades can be read as illustrations of Ritter's work. Beuys' ideas about energy, electricity, specific materials such as felt, fats, and metals like iron and copper, seem as though they have passed through the culture of experiment of the former apothecary's apprentice from Zadamowice. And Ritter's lecture on 'Physics as Art' was a prominent item in Beuys' personal library.

An anthropological intermediate step: Vilém Flusser

Ritter's anthropology of the arts was positive, constructive, and open. It is constituted by a specific attitude toward research, which I think is important for the future. For Ritter the new era, which he associated with the discovery of electricity, was an opportunity to forge ahead, to create something new that the world had not yet experienced or conceived of in quite the same manner. We should not fall back behind the state of knowledge of c.1800 when we discuss how artistic research can be generated today.

For this we shall need the ideas of another exceptional mind from Eastern Europe: Vilém Flusser, a philosopher of culture from Prague, who the Nazis drove out initially to England, and then to São Paulo in Brazil, and who died in 1991 in such a crazy unnecessary way. On the way back from Prague to the south of France, where he had lived since 1974, Flusser died in a car accident, just after he had attended a symposium that had been organized in his birthplace in his honour.

Vilém Flusser was a most lively and energetic thinker, who concurred with Nietzsche that philosophy ought to be danced more than written. He developed an anthropology, which has much in common with Ritter's. I shall abbreviate his argumentation because it is in part a repetition of Ritter's universe. The cultural philosopher from Prague speaks in his earliest work phase of the lifeworld, the temporal-spatial orientation of humans in four dimensions from which it proceeds via the three-dimensional experience with an object, a house, to the two-dimensional image. Everything which takes place in these qualities of history and civilization implies for Flusser classical activity of the imagination with regard to communication. The decisive break for Flusser happened genealogically, when the (one-dimensional) text became dominant culturally, also with regard to the critical interrogation of images, objects, and lifeworld experience.

This is Critical Theory, which we are very familiar with from the history of ideas. Script is its classical medium. Afterwards, for Flusser, there was again a qualitative turn, which proceeded via the zero dimension of numbers, of algorithms. Things, including images, become technical, and tend toward the general. This development from the one-dimensionality of the text to the zero dimensionality of numbers Flusser calls the development from the abstract to the concrete. This operational anthropology of Flusser's, whose universe of thought I can but sketch here, is particularly remarkable because it is an anthropology that is open to the future. Like Ritter's, it seeks to open up new possibilities for action.

Flusser, who hailed from the city of Rudolf II, and many alchemists, did not tend toward the apocalyptic view. The passage through zero dimensions, numbers, and machines that treat and generate images like concepts, Flusser did not regard as a disaster, as the end of experience, but as a space of opportunities through which one could rethink the world anew, re-engage with it. Here a man speaks of a future that can be shaped, whose own experience of the physical lifeworld had been truly terrible. Most of his family was murdered by the Nazis in the death camps, and many of his friends as well. Flusser experienced what the monsters who are also accounted members of humankind were capable of. He also formulated this provocatively: machines cannot be as bad as what humans have been capable of. Let us at least try it out (that was his most important message); let's start again one more time with the new resources we have at our disposal. Flusser was not at all sure whether it would end well. However, he wanted to keep the option open for the challenge of where we might go with the new technologies of abstraction.

Of course Flusser summarized best what he was aiming at with regard to the history of civilization: 'humankind went from images to script, which became dominant, entered a state of crisis, broke out of it, and now we are beyond the script in a new type of imagination which we will have to practise first' (Flusser 1988). We shall have to learn to imagine anew. We have to develop from being a subject to being a project, from a state of being subjected to being something that one creates, what one introduces to others, what lies ahead of one as the beginning of a new work.

This is an apt description of one of my principal motivations for engaging with media over the past decades, with the scholarly study of and reflections on media, and also with the relations of tension between the arts and media. If there were no hope that developing from subject to project is possible, that through the new technological resources we can change the world to its advantage, then the entire effort would be meaningless. To project also means to devise something in the mind that did not exist in the world beforehand and thus has utopian connotations. People entirely lacking in notions of utopia should not practise science, technology, or art.

Media arts

The fields of action and thinking of the arts, sciences, and technology constitute a relationship of tension which is currently summarized in a simplified way in the coupling of art and media. Internationally it has been fostered for the last twenty years under the label *MedienKunst* (media art). Historically, it only refers to this short period of time. Those who are more free-handed point to the period after World War II and begin their short history with the Fluxus pioneers John Cage, Nam June Paik, Wolf Vostell, and other early video artists. Others draw a somewhat longer timeline, taking in approximately the last 150 years – since the art of technical images became established with photography. By describing Ritter's experimental praxis above, I have indicated that such short-sighted historicizations are untenable, and have discussed this subject at length elsewhere (cf. Zielinski 2006); in our present context there are other important concerns.

Media art is a curious *mixtum compositum*. On the one hand the term joins two things that lie close together; the practice of any art needs media so that others may experience it. Media art, however, has been developed as a specific conception of cultural praxis since the early 1990s. From this perspective the *mixtum compositum* contains things that lie far apart. The term seeks to bind together two different worlds in a common perspective and praxis. From its inception this coupling exhibited strategy and tactics, above all at the beginning of the 1990s when a series of art academies were founded in Europe and Asia to investigate the new technological possibilities, such as the new institutions in Karlsruhe and Cologne in Germany, Les Fresnoy in France, and Ogaki-Shi in Japan, and the established academies began to set up special departments.

In the *mixtum compositum* the world of the media stands for a number of paradigms that are traditionally not associated with art. This includes the concept of what is *limitlessly* – in the direct sense of the word – popular. The technical media of the late nineteenth and twentieth centuries no longer addressed the restricted circles of social elites, which Pop Art, with its appetite for reproductions, also targeted. They operated with the possibility of reaching audiences that were socially, regionally, and nationally non-specific. Photography, cinema, telephone, telegraph, radio, television, video recorder, and CDs and DVDs were invented as cultural techniques that would function world-wide, in techno-aesthetic Esperanto. The propensity to cross boundaries is intrinsic to these media. Those who know these media and use them – this applies particularly to telematic media – are no longer simply viewers and listeners, but rather participants in a global event, co-players in a complex context of actions for which administratively the obscene term 'communication' is still used. At the currently most advanced level we are dealing with technical systems that centre on computers and networks with their nodes and servers.

Both the individual machine for processing, saving, and transferring data, as well as the networks for worldwide distribution and dialogue, are high-grade systems for performing calculations. Basically, they are mechanical systems, although they operate with high performance electronics and microelectronics. Mechanical systems are distinguished by the fact that the processes that run on them can be formalized; it is immaterial whether these processes are analogue or digital.

Artistic praxis, too, has different forms of formalizable dimensions. It can be expressed in language and in other sign systems, which operate with the highly ordering and defining properties of sets of rules or grammars. Such rules can be learnt and, therefore, taught. They can be developed strategically. This is the reason why we can speak of artistic experiments and this is why a studio or atelier with predominantly technical equipment can be referred to as a laboratory.

Work in a laboratory consists of developing, investigating, testing, discarding, and achieving results. These activities involve a particularity of artistic praxis that art shares with science and even industry. However, this particularity is of far greater import in art; indeed, for many people it is the distinguishing characteristic of art: intuition/inspiration. It is closely tied to the most important energy source of artistic praxis – the power of the imagination. Intuition/imagination on the one side, and formalizability and calculability/planning capability on the other form the two poles of the *mixtum compositum* between which media art moves. To view these two poles as end points of a scale, as in music, which can be played from both ends, is a meaningful alternative to simple dualism, which is a lazy and disastrous thinking habit. The kind of praxis that develops in the tension zone between the two poles we can call advanced artistic research.

Investigative praxis of this kind has need of places where the activities of taking apart and reassembling, which we also know from structuralism, are not regarded as sabotage but as especially creative. In pre-modern times in Europe such places were called alchemists' laboratories. Only wealthy princes, queens, or emperors could afford them, for example, in Prague, Stockholm, and London. Patrons invited the most exceptional minds, irrespective of birth and background, to work in them so that they could observe at close quarters their protégés labouring on the impossible. For the long process – from separation of the *prima materia* through the various stages of mixing to the projection, the final stage of the alchemical process in which the transmutation of base matter into gold is supposed to take place – was nothing other than incessant labour on the attempt to make the impossible a little more possible.

Obviously, such places were not enduring. They did not exude the same permanence as the columned halls of the classical academies. They were temporary places, places of passage, of taking time, surprises, of starting and breaking off, of being harried, and sometimes of flight. If the patrons ran out of money, or the sorcerer's apprentices turned out to be charlatans and good-for-nothing swindlers, they were consigned to the dungeons or, if lucky, thrown out onto the dangerous highways where they set off for the next place that would serve them as a laboratory for a while.

Particularly in the 1990s there was busy traffic between the various laboratories, primarily among the privileged modern sorcerer's apprentices. The hope that things digital would prove analogous to the alchemical formula for gold created artist-in-residence programmes, grants, and many other forms of sponsorship. The Dutch experimental group Institute for the Unstable Media, V2, moved from provincial Hertogenbosch to the metropolis of Rotterdam, the capital of media creativity in the Netherlands, where it still resides today. The annual festival Ars Electronica in Linz gradually expanded its activities to take in the entire year and now has the dimensions of a medium-sized enterprise. The IRCAM (Institut de Recherche et Coordination Acoustique/Musique) in Paris and STEIM (Studio for Electro-Instrumental Music) in Amsterdam specialized with differing emphases on investigating the worlds of sound produced by technical means, the Centre International de la Création Video (CICV) in Montbéliard-Belfort focused on the electronic processing of images. The C³ (Center for Communication and Culture) in Budapest, in cooperation with the Hungarian Academy of Arts, became a unique eastern European institution which promoted the new processes in research and exhibitions.

That the arts which are based on, or work extensively with, advanced electronic technology have arrived in the European mainstream is demonstrated definitively by the project LABoral (Centro de Arte y Creación Industrial) in the northern Spanish town of Gijón. With grand gestures and after huge investments it was launched in March 2007 with the ambition of becoming – at least in Europe – the most important project for technologically-based design, a kind of Hispanic Bauhaus, including the occasional artistic aspect. Thousands of people attended the private view of the first exhibition. The cost of the buffet alone would have financed several years of art projects.

Art after the media

In this period after the recent *fin de siècle* we are again heading for an ice age in the relations between the arts, sciences, and technologies. At the beginning of the twenty-first century the mechanical, electrical, and electronic media through and with which art is produced, distributed, and received are now taken for granted. They are just as much a part of everyday life as turning a water tap on or off as needed and without thinking much about where the content comes from, what it is made of, and how it will be disposed of after use.[3] In the industrialized parts of the world the infrastructure is oriented on technical media systems and dependent on them. In 2008 commercial firms and public institutions in the USA alone spent an incredible $1,750 billion on information technology and software development. Through our bodies run technical strands that help us to prolong our lives. Networks are no longer merely the hope of an egalitarian reorganization of societies; they have become in themselves effectively structured figures in developed power relations. The generations of scientists, artists, and engineers that are now learning, studying, testing, researching, organizing, and leading have been schooled by their experience with technical media to a greater or lesser extent. The media do not hold any particular attraction for them, but have become self-evident areas of activity in everyday life. When technically everything is now more or less possible, the issue is increasingly to make the possible more impossible.

Motivated by the anthropological deliberations of Ritter and Flusser, some years ago I began to work with an anthropology in the art context, which is also to be understood as operational. Its objective is to keep open the possibilities of being active, of progressive action, for the time to come, both for scientists and artists who are deeply committed to experiment.

In principle this operational anthropology functions by reducing the complexity of the relations between the autonomous fields of knowledge and work of arts, sciences, and technologies, and conceiving them as different historical qualities in the relationship between art and media, as outlined earlier in connection with the strategic and tactical term 'media art'. Art in this context means art that is affected by media, in the sense of an experimental aesthetic praxis which engages with science and technology. Otherwise the qualities of the relations, which are the issue here, would make no sense.

I differentiate between four relational qualities: art *before* media, art *with* media, art *through* media, and art *after* the media. This list should not be understood as a chronological sequence of qualities, but as differently weighted priorities in the deep time structure that interests me. Historically, the qualities overlap and in part run parallel. The second and third relational qualities are the simplest to understand, not only because they reach into the present day.

Art *with* media reflects on the artistic utilization of insights achieved by mathematics, arithmetic, and geometry, their application in mechanics and optics, and the pressure that results from this utilization in the direction of artefacts and technical systems for communicating, learning, illusionizing, shocking, entertaining, and persuasion/ conversion. Art *with* media implies an *instrumental* relationship. In this relational quality flat or curved mirrors, pipes, funnels, rollers, magnetic telex machines, and mechanical combinatory systems serve as prostheses for art, but are not an essential precondition for art to exist. These media expand artistic praxis, can potentially make it more effective, but they do not renew it, and do not necessarily change it. This relational quality is similar to what Raymond Williams, one of the founders of cultural studies, once called an 'accidental' relationship (Williams 1974).

In a narrower historical perspective this quality evolved in Europe since the geometrization of seeing and the mathematization of the image in the second Renaissance; it developed further with the innumerable models for ciphers and elaborately staged spaces for technical images in the sixteenth century, and resulted in first highlights with concepts for the automation of music compositions, the sequencing of harmonious melodies, and the invention of a great number of visual special effects in the seventeenth century. Essentially all mechanical, optical, and acoustic innovations and inventions that followed in the Age of Enlightenment and in the nineteenth century – the founding years of the new media – use this instrumental relational quality. Technical rationality breaks into the world of the imaginary, into artistic production. Artists are obliged to acquire investigative approaches because, confronted by the new demands, they would otherwise sink into oblivion.

Art *through* media means that the artistic process, or the artistic work, is essentially realized by *going through* a technical medium or array of technical media. This became possible with the advent of the artificial generation of electricity. In the Enlightenment the forces of nature like electrical storms were tamed by technology. With the discovery of the physical and chemical principles of electricity, from the 1730s to the 1790s a very rich culture of experimentation developed between London, Paris, and St. Petersburg. Scientific discoveries were demonstrated at spectacular performances in which weak electric current was sent through the bodies of heavy monks or lightweight boys and girls floating in the air. Salon experiments, like the 'Kiss of Venus' in which visitors at soirées touched the lips of an electrified beauty, were the early sensations of bourgeois techno-culture. With the various models of *tableaux magiques*, upon which electrical sparks described awe-inspiring figures, devices were created for instruction and entertainment that generated images in a new modus; namely, in the modus of time.[4] The figures only became visible, or could be felt when touched, when the current was on. Georg Christoph Lichtenberg (1742–1799) froze such contemporary images; Ritter thought them through to the dramatic climax of 'fire-writing', which over 120 years later became legible as an electroencephalogram on the monitor of an oscillograph. Since that time we can watch when people think.

Art *after* the media does not refer to experimental praxis that dispenses entirely with technical media; this is no longer feasible in science, cultural studies, or the arts. Rather, this relational quality draws attention to the fact that we seek an art of experimenting which no longer requires the application of media as a legitimation or as sensationalism, but at the same time does not close its eyes, ears, and mind to the media. Just how art *after* the media will develop is, at the beginning of the third millennium, already foreseeable in certain concrete cases, but is not yet a foregone conclusion. My anthropology, too, represents a modest attempt 'to think the trend of art through from its history', as Ritter formulated it for physics.

Before the ideas, concepts, and notions existed which pushed forward to become the generalization *media* that denoted a special area of theory and praxis (which only happened over the last sixty to seventy years), art did not do without media. In the two and a half thousand years between 1000 before and 1500 after the Common Era, a multitude of optical, acoustic, magnetic, and combinatorial sensations were developed, which can only be subsumed under the umbrella term of media through the coercion exerted by the context of our contemporary perspective. In their own time they did not press forward in the direction of any generalization; indeed they had no need of it. The modular grids and strings with which the ancient Egyptians calculated and constructed the ideal body proportions for their sculptures of the gods (Presas i Puig 2004), from which the Pythagoreans probably derived their geometry-based concept of harmony, the shadow optics of the Chinese Mohists of over 2,300 years ago, the theatre of automata of Heron of Alexandria (20–62 ce), which corresponds wonderfully with the mechanical and hydraulic treasures of Arabian engineers from the ninth to the thirteenth centuries, the optical experiments of the Chinese astronomer Shen Kua with their projections of flying birds and racing clouds in dark chambers in the eleventh century: such singular and isolated sensations from the deep strata of history I term phenomena of art *before* the media. For an an-archaeology that is interested in the creations and developments of technical seeing, hearing, and combining, its iridescent diversity is among the most fascinating of the historical relational qualities.

The conceptual generalization *media* is a twentieth-century invention. The various techniques for communicating, envisioning, and generating knowledge and entertainments are far older. In order to avoid the trap of historicization, for the interim they should not be unified under the umbrella term media. Both as constructed artefacts and as blueprints they are singular, and as such can be regarded as resistant to universalization. To study them requires approaches other than those of mainstream historiography of the media.

Research as an exceptional encounter between art and (natural) science

Before he was murdered by an SS man in the streets of Drohobycz in 1942, the magical realist Bruno Schulz wrote down what he understood by culture as poetic praxis:

> if art is only supposed to confirm what has been determined for as long as anyone can remember, then one doesn't need it. Its role is to be a probe that is let down into the unknown. The artist is a device that registers the processes taking place in the depths where values are created.
>
> (Bruno Schulz in a letter to Stanislaw-Ignacy Witkiewicz,
> in: Schulz 1967: Vol.2, 92)

This way of understanding enquiring artistic work that is informed by curiosity, which the Polish writer and artist expressed, interlaces both aesthetic and ethical aspects as well as indicates what the special meaning of artistic research might comprise. It is fuelled by the porosity of the specific sensibility of an artist's existence with respect to and in the world. Art has always gone beyond the mere portrayal of what is well known. Its most noble task is to make and keep us sensible to the other, for what is strange to us, for what is not identical to us, and to this end it uses its very own resources: painting, sculpture, music, the moving photographic or electronic image, photography or the staged performance. This identity, which has a great deal to do with a particular attitude towards the world and a view of subjectivity as experience at the limits, as Ludwig Wittgenstein understood it, is to a certain extent the opposite pole to the identity and the attitude of the scientist. Between the two poles there are innumerable identities and attitudes with various nuances. True and fruitful collaboration between the arts and sciences can only develop, however, if both sides respect each other's different areas of competence and different talents and skills and make them productive.

Based on the liberal connections that I see between art *before* the media and art *after* the media, in the final section of this chapter I shall describe some research practices and their processes like results. To take them seriously as particularities means that in describing them they must be developed in concrete terms. Here I undertake a historical balancing act on a bridge spanning twelve centuries, and deliberately link the period of art *before* the media and the period of art *after* the media.

A programmable mechanical heart

The geographical and political hot spot of learning and knowledge during the Golden Age of Arabic-Islamic science was the House of Wisdom in ninth-century Baghdad. Its founder Caliph Al-Ma'mun (786–833), who reigned for twenty years, provided for the translation of Classical Greek texts on (natural) philosophy into Arabic, thus also ensuring the survival of these core texts for the European Renaissance, and encouraged young men with enquiring and creative minds to think independently and to approach the world through experiment (Farmer 1931; Zielinski and Fürlus. 2010).

In addition to many others, this profited the three brothers Muhammad, Ahmad, and al-Hasan, sons of Musa bin Shakir, whose smallest possible cooperative encompassed an entire universe of scientific qualifications: mathematics and geometry, astronomy, natural philosophy and medicine, music, and the art of engineering. The brothers have gone down in the history of science and technology as the Banu Musa. They employed multitudes of translators who translated the texts of the great constructor of automata, Heron of Alexandria, amongst others, from Greek into Arabic. Ahmad is considered to be the greatest engineer of the three princes. He is thought to be the main author of their brilliant work *Kitab al-Hiyal* (Book of Ingenious Devices) from the mid-ninth century.[5] The book is a compendium filled with sketches and exact instructions for building around one hundred models (*shakl*); a variety of artefacts, devices and their components, kinetic sculptures and automata, the latter in the direct sense of devices that move of their own accord: filling devices and drinking devices operated hydraulically and mechanically, animals driven by pneumatics that make noises, oil lamps that not only fill up automatically, but also have self-adjusting draught shields so that the flame remained protected and burnt eternally.[6]

That things can be perpetually in motion, incessantly, was evidently very important to the Banu Musa. One of their masterpieces exhibits this characteristic; it is not included in the surviving copies of the *Book of Ingenious Devices*, but experts in the history of the Arabic-Islamic sciences attribute the device to Prince Ahmad. A manuscript containing a description of this device was discovered by Henry George Farmer in the library of the 'Three Moons College' of the Greek Orthodox Church in Beirut, Syria. The manuscript is singular. It describes a continuously playing flautist. 'The instrument, which plays by itself (*Al-alat illati tuzammir binafsiha*)' is the name the Banu Musa gave their device, thus underlining its character as an automaton. The title evidences that they ascribed universal meaning to their technology; apparently, they wanted their invention to be understood independently of any specific form of its realization, such as the flute player.

An essential criterion for whether research has actually been accomplished is if the protagonists succeed in making some new fact or aspect of the world accessible for others. Birds and flute-players, powered by water and moved by pneumatics, are known in ancient Chinese literature as well as in classical Greek authors such as Archimedes, Apollonius the geometer and carpenter, and the Alexandrian Heron. With regard to the mechanisms, the technologically most advanced solutions are attributed to Apollonius.

He had already developed a hydraulic-pneumatic mechanism of such complexity that his anthropomorphic figure could play the flute endlessly – as long as it was provided with a constant flow of water. Owing to a type of circular construction, whereby a second water container filled up while the first was emptying and pressing out air for the flautist, the automaton had a constant inflow of energy in the most direct sense (Wiedemann 1915).

The three princes from the House of Wisdom in Baghdad not only improved and developed the hydraulic and pneumatic mechanisms, but they also described and constructed a complete music automaton, which could vary the rhythm of the music and it was even possible to feed it with different melodies. In his English translation of parts of the manuscript Farmer quotes the intention of the Banu Musa:

> We wish to explain how an instrument ... is made which plays by itself continuously in whatever melody ... we wish, sometimes in a slow rhythm ... and sometimes in a quick rhythm, and also that we may change from melody to melody when we so desire.
>
> (Farmer 1931: 88)

The mechanical heart of the automaton is a hydraulically driven cylinder. On the surface of the cylinder are bands made of wood or metal, which carry small protruding pins of different lengths. Depending on how these pins are positioned on the bands and how the bands are arranged in relation to one another, a mechanical link opens or closes the valve of the flute, a single pipe of an organ, or moves another sound-producing element. *Prographein* means to prescribe. The way the pins are arranged on the cylinder formulate the musical prescriptions or instructions, the *programme* of the instrument; the pins and bands are notation translated into hard material. The hardware is virtually identical to the revolving cylinders with pins that were used 500 years later in the European glockenspiel of the late Middle Ages, and again even later in the mechanical organs of the Renaissance, as well as for writing automata and automatic music instruments in the Age of Enlightenment.

The three sons of Musa bin Shakir from ninth-century Baghdad represented a creative collective, from concept to construction, that today would be called a research group. They carried out research in various disciplines – mathematics, geometry, astronomy, natural philosophy, medicine, music, applied engineering – each on their own according to their individual priorities, and at the same time they worked together very closely on certain projects. They shared with each other all the new knowledge about the world, which in Giovanni Battista Della Porta's *Secret Academy* in pre-modern Naples was the prerequisite for anyone wishing to work in it.[7] The Banu Musa built on the knowledge of the Ancient Greek tradition, which they held in high esteem, and at decisive points they ventured beyond it and created something else, something new. The idea of a universal, programmable control unit for playing musical instruments was one such bold impetus that even many centuries later would have been classed as modern.

A black square

Robert Fludd, who kept up a lively correspondence with Johannes Kepler for several years on the relationship between the exact sciences and the imagination, published the first volume of his magnificent design of the history of the macrocosm and the microcosm in 1617. On page 26 of Book 1, there is a pitch-black, almost square rectangle. On all four sides of the figure is the same text, 'Et sic in infinitum'. For the brilliant English polymath of the seventeenth century this image symbolized the infinity of matter and at the same time that, ultimately, it was impenetrable.

Much later this image would acquire tremendous importance for the entire art history of the modern age. Adapted, modified, and referenced many times, 300 years later in the famous painting by Kasimir Malevich this image became the icon of the dawning of a new worldview. Science was characterized by dynamic, non-Euclidean geometry, discoveries concerning the fourth dimension of time and electronics, the practical and theoretical consequences of Albert Einstein's relativity theory, and the early experiments in quantum mechanics. The arts saw the rise of the cubism, futurism, and constructivism movements and their variants. With abstract forms and kinetic studies artists, as well as musicians, attempted to respond structurally to the increasing complexity of the world using the resources at their disposal. The world as apparatus or automaton, which had been envisaged by René Descartes amongst others, became a pre-eminent theme. Mechanical ballets danced on the stage and on canvas, animated spirals moving into the depths of the image space irritated people's perception, which had become lethargic. Nudes were sent up and down staircases. Surrealists attempted to liberate bodies from the physical laws of gravity and the linear arrow of time – at least in the moving image. Composers experimented with arranging notes in series that fundamentally upset familiar notions of the simple and clear harmony of all elements of the world. At the precise moment in time when the media began to be established as a special area of theory and praxis, when the first models of empirical research on the mass media were developed, and Marshall McLuhan was becoming the first pop star of media theory, John Cage performed his most famous piece, which effectively constituted a radical break with reproducibility and infinite simulations. Cage sat down at the piano for the first performance of this work in 1952 and played for four minutes and thirty-three seconds – nothing. The radical experiment 4'33" was also a particular form of investigating the audible world around us.

Artists and scientists may live on different planets and their aspirations may be fixed on different stars. However, in the *terra incognita* of their hardware and the dissimilar oceans of their consciousness strong affinities are at work and energies are restive that conjoin time and again, especially when they are excellent, exceptional, and powerful. Then, occasionally, they encounter each other at intersections where something wondrous happens.

The operation of *zgodlocator* by Herwig Weiser

Like the beginning of the twentieth century, physics and the life sciences hold a powerful fascination for young artists of today. They engage with genetic algorithms, system transformations, solar-powered frequency modulators, bio-feedback, the pulverization of metals, the breakdown of liquids, dynamic geometry, the analysis of eye movements, morphogenesis, robotics, brain research, particle accelerators, and the design of interfaces between machines and their users. They each do this in their own individual way, in close alliance and with frictions to their exuberant imagination, their

Figure 17.1 The workroom of the Austrian artist Herwig Weiser during the creation of *zgodlocator*: it is more an electrical workshop and laboratory than a classical artist's studio.

impatience, and their strong drive to realize what they are seeking to realize. Artistic research is not work on a concept, but working and concentrating on individual things.

Interface design has emerged as a focus where contrasting concepts of creative work with and on computer-centred media confront each other. This boundary, which I think is more aptly named in German *Schnittstelle* (cut-off line), at once both separates and joins two different spheres: on the one side the world of those who utilize the machines, and on the other the world of active machines and programmes. Technological developments, as well as the dominant media concepts of the 1990s, aimed at making the boundary between the two imperceptible. The idea was that one should learn to use a computer without noticing that one is dealing with an algorithmically constructed machine for calculations and simulations. One should be able to immerse oneself in a so-called virtual reality without feeling and, even more, without knowing that one is dealing with a construction of surfaces and time responses that are precisely pre-structured and calculated. For the user the computer was presented like a *camera obscura*; one can take pleasure in its effects and one can work with it, but one does not need access to the way it functions.

Against the dominant trend of smooth-functioning technological and semiological ergonomics various artists continued to experiment in collaboration with programmers, physicists, and engineers on how it would be possible to enable and develop dramaturgies of difference, also with advanced technologies. Following the classic film and video avant-gardes they insisted that the technical worlds remain accessible as artificially constructed worlds: to construct the interface in such a way that there would be a tension with the world beyond the machine that would enhance the pleasure in these media-worlds and not reduce it.

It is in such a tradition that *zgodlocator* operates, a work created in the late 1990s by the Austrian artist Herwig Weiser in collaboration with the electrical engineer Albert Bleckmann and the techno musician RandomX. The object of the work's operative access to the computer is not the software, but the body within which the programmes run, the hardware. Weiser turns discarded computers into granulate and extracts their most valuable components: gold, silver, platinum, and especially ferrite, which is contained in the magnetic deflecting coils of monitors, amongst other things, as well as ferrofluid, a heavy oil which is present in small quantities in every computer. Under a shimmering sand landscape and the oil, Weiser installs sets of batteries which can be activated in various combinations via a control unit. Visitors hook up to the techno drama as players using simple manual controls and unleash dynamic turbulence in the materials. The drama has its own sound. Sensors register the noise of the computer scrap when it moves, which is fed into a special programme that amplifies the sounds and can be played by the intervention of the participants. In this way the apparatus also becomes a musical instrument.

In *zgodlocator* dead hardware material is given new technical life, reanimated. Expanded cinema of a special kind emerges: in four dimensions, in close interconnection of image and sound, ever-new micro-industrial landscapes of strange beauty are generated by the participants. The prototype of the installation in 2000 took up almost the entire foyer of Cologne's Trinitatis Church where it was first shown. The goal of Weiser and his collaborators was always a mobile *zgodlocator*, which could be packed in a suitcase and set up anywhere. In the meantime several models exist. Collectors, who can afford it, enjoy experiencing this microcosm of the control of physical material.

Marcello Mercado: *Das Kapital* [Capital] (1999–2009)

Marcello Mercado's *Das Kapital* is not a finished product or an art commodity; rather, it is a work in progress, intensive and protracted artistic research. It will only be finished when the artist no longer believes in it or gives up on its spirit. Mercado, a native of the high country of Argentina, has been working on and in this process for ten years. With incredible intensity and utilizing everything that advanced image and sound equipment can provide, he generates objectivized audiovisual time; second by second, minute by minute, and hour by hour. If one were to show the entire material collected so far – over forty hours – the video would run for nearly two days and nights.

Mercado calls his work in progress an 'oratorio', and the work by Karl Marx which provided the inspiration for it, a 'tragedy'. When he came to Europe in 1999 from South America, he brought with him thousands of photos and a great deal of film material, which he had found in Buenos Aires and other Argentine cities in rubbish bins near police stations: pictures of murder victims, victims of violent crimes, maltreated, mutilated bodies of the dictatorship's torture victims, heads with staring eyes, hacked-off body parts, bodies with gaping wounds, dead animals; once-living matter degraded to dead meat. This became the starting point of his never-ending working process.

At that time Mercado gave performances, which even hardened young artists in São Paulo, Hong Kong, Berlin, and Cologne found difficult to take. The artist exposed his own

Figure 17.2 Marcello Mercado, *Screenshot*, pencil and ink on paper, Discreet-Logic-Flint software, Silicon-Graphics hardware, 18cm × 14.4cm, 1999.

body to risks, which in his childhood and youth had often been subjected to violence, and presented this body as mishandled and suffering, but also passionate and rebellious. In Germany, Mercado came more into contact with the worlds of concepts, philosophy, natural sciences, and the intellect. In the new European laboratories for the production of immaterial values Mercado met masters of advanced electronic production: David Larcher, who was his mentor for a short time; Anthony Moore, with whom he undertook in-depth sound research; and the Polish video *compositeur* par excellence, Zbigniew Rybczyński. Mercado became acquainted with very expensive advanced digital tools from world-leading Discreet Logic Inc., which in the 1990s launched the special effects toolsets *Flame*, *Flint*, and *Inferno*, a trio of complete effects systems that precipitated an enormous leap in the capabilities of visual effects systems and cost as much at that time as a well-paid white-collar worker earned in a year. Mercado learnt to play with them as if on a keyboard; physically, he became one with them.

Mercado refuses to acknowledge the separation of the physical and the metaphysical. For him the electronic machines have become the interface between the two worlds. In this way he overcomes their much-stressed dualism. In his animations the images of the maltreated bodies of people and animals have dissolved, like in an acid bath. In certain sequences they suddenly appear again, in the original, as reminders.

In various parts of his research process Mercado operates like an experimental biologist. He soaked several pages of Marx's *Das Kapital* in water, gave them to mealworms to eat, and then took samples for DNA testing. The resulting genetic code sequences he used to organize his complex material. Foetuses are implanted in digital landscapes and robbed in these images of their ostensibly inviolable uniqueness. And time and again Mercado takes different editions of Marx's book into real landscapes and attempts to connect the artificial artefact directly with its natural sources. In one such *Kapital* excursion, Mercado visited the graves of Rainer Werner Fassbinder and

Wolf Vostell, took genetic material from small flowers growing there, and then mixed the fluids so that these two great protagonists of artistic resistance unite in the image.

Das Kapital is an endeavour. As the agenda for a work it is condemned to permanent failure. It exists within a process of permanent adaptation, re-writing, and self-interpretation. At this level of excess and duration that is only technologically and economically possible with digital and electronic machines. The amount of material would be colossal if Mercado were to work in analogue media. His factory fits on a table top. In the beginning he needed to use the massive Silicon Graphics machines that only the laboratories of well-endowed institutions could afford. In recent years he can develop and design his economy of bodies as an image economy on his own lap(top). Thus *Das Kapital* also tells the history of digital image processing during the last ten years, and how an artist has handled it. Marx would have said that with his work Mercado expresses perfectly the state of the means of production. In the beginning he archived the strands of his oratorio on Digibeta made by the Japanese Sony Corporation. Today the image material is stored on external hard disks where it can be accessed for each performance. The economy of magnetic tape, which moves between master and slave spools, is played out.

Yunchul Kim's *self_portrait.jpg* (2004)

I highlighted this above: when I deal with *art after the media* I do not mean art that can exist *without* media. Such art is no longer conceivable for me. Rather, I refer to artistic praxis that has passed through the media, but in a specific manner has left them far behind. The effect that the media had when they were still an attraction no longer plays an important role. The technical and media aspects of such artistic praxis are not the essence of its attraction. Media are utilized as a matter of course by artists; they are no longer the actual sensation.

Mercado's research processes have left the media behind them in a variety of ways. When he works in the field, he only uses technical media for documentation purposes. Herwig Weiser re-integrates the effect into the hardware and controls the material directly. He has already forgotten the monitors and video projectors; instead, he lets the users re-assemble the pulverized physical material with physical interfaces.[8]

In this perspective the work of a young Korean artist is even more radical. Initially Yunchul Kim studied electronic music at Chugye University in Seoul. He is a programmer, computer and video artist, has created numerous performances with computer-generated music, and realized many installations that utilize the most advanced technology. *Self_portrait.jpg* is one of Kim's most unusual works in that at first sight it disappoints all expectations that we entertain of the work of an artist working with advanced media. On a large sheet of finest white Japanese paper measuring 83 × 134 cm curious signs have been written, or rather painted, with great precision in black drawing ink. Closer inspection reveals that these are not just any signs, but the character set of the ASCII code. If one were to count the characters, one would arrive at the impressive number 58,806. In a meditation exercise that lasted three and a half months Yunchul Kim painted the characters on the paper. Every time he made a mistake he had to start again from the beginning. The result of this almost Sisyphean task is a work with a high aesthetic appeal and a special bonus: when the characters

Figure 17.3 Yunchul Kim: self_portrait.jpg (detail), ink on paper, 90 × 140 cm; 58,806 single handwritten characters, 2004.

are scanned into a computer that can read them and then sent to a printer, what is printed out is a portrait of the artist. However, this is just a second level on which the work exists and is perceived. The decisive factor in the idea of *art after the media* is that in this case, for example, the artist is a young man who passed through the advanced technical media in the course of his socialization. *Self_portrait.jpg* succeeds as art in any case, irrespective of technology-based art. It does not need electronics to be performed; it simply hangs on the wall. That I know about the work's technological side enriches my reception of it, but is not a precondition for its aesthetic enjoyment.

There have always been people who are combinations of scientist and artist, who one could term hybrid personalities. The French painter and philosopher Pierre Klossowski, brother of the more famous painter Balthus, was one such personality. Around 1970 Klossowski wrote a remarkable economy, which only became available in print form in the 1990s. In his Introduction, Michel Foucault described it as 'the greatest book of our epoch'. Klossowski simply turns around the cultural pessimists' lament about the commercialization, and thus also the mechanization of the body by economics and technology, and declares the human body a 'living currency'.[9] As a radical continuation of the ideas of the Marquis de Sade, the human body could be integrated into social interaction as an object of exchange. Liberated from the direct and purposeful constraints of reproduction, the body conceived of in this way is free to become a superbly confident actor.

To experiment, which he practised as a special culture in his texts, Klossowski assigned pre-eminent importance in his economy. The manufacture of appliances, he wrote, is confronted regularly with its own 'periodic infertility'. This actually

> becomes more apparent because the accelerating tempo of manufacturing perpetually forces it to prevent inefficiency (in the products), and this inevitably drives it in the direction of wastage. The experiment, the precondition of which is efficiency, presupposes the wasteful mistake. Exploring in experiments what might result in profitable production is geared to the elimination of infertility in the product, but at the price of wasting material and human labour (production costs).

(Klossowski 1998: 10f.)

With another exceptional artist from the second half of the twentieth century I shall conclude my argument for the time being, which has travelled like time's arrow through the operational anthropologies of the past into the future. In August 1966 Pier Paolo Pasolini wrote an autobiographical poem during a stay in New York with the title 'Who Is Me?' At the end of the poem, which he referred to as research, the poet confesses that, actually:

> I want to write music
> in the tower of Viterbo, which I cannot buy
> in the most beautiful landscape in the world, where Ariosto
> would have been beside himself with joy to see the resurgent
> innocence of oaks, hills, lakes, and ravines,
> that I want to write music there,
> the only action of the expression
> perhaps, sublime and inexplicable like the actions of reality.

(Pasolini 1995: 33)[10]

And with this we are back with Ritter:

> The yearning to achieve insights into things is simply striving after the art of loving.

(Ritter 1984 [1810]: 626)

Notes

1 Zu Ende neigte die alte Welt sich. Des jungen Geschlechts Lustgarten verwelkte – hinauf in den freyeren, wüsten Raum strebten die unkindlichen, wachsenden Menschen. Die Götter verschwanden mit ihrem Gefolge – Einsam und leblos stand die Natur. Mit eiserner Kette band sie die dürre Zahl und das strenge Maaß. Wie in Staub und Lüfte zerfiel in dunkle Worte die unermeßliche Blüthe des Lebens (Novalis 1908: Vol.1, 23f.). The English translation above is a reworking by G. Custance of the English translation given online at Projekt Gutenberg, Hymn 5.
2 Ritter, letter to Christian Gottlob Voigt, 26 March 1804, cited in Rehm (1973: 206).
3 This comparison was made already in 1956 by Günther Anders (Anders 1980 [1956]: see particularly 97–211).
4 In the early cabinets of physics these magic tablets were used to visualize the effects of electricity in dark rooms at popular demonstrations; cf. the detailed and illustrated account in Figuier (1868: 485f.).
5 Possibly the caliph is the same person as Muristos, who described the mechanical universal organ.
6 In addition to the relevant texts by Wiedemann (1915), the most authoritative source on the work of the Banu Musa is still Hill (1979). It also contains biographical sketches of the three brothers.
7 For further details see the extensive chapter on Porta in Zielinski (2006).
8 In his most recent artistic research Weiser investigates chemical solutions that separate and combine through electrolysis. Each imaginary pixel is a chemical laboratory in which the changes of the mixtures are generated as combinations of bright colours. The work is being created in close collaboration with academic chemistry departments in Korea and Europe.
9 The title of the French original of 1994 is La Monnaie vivante; I used the first German translation (Klossowski 1998).
10 Pier Paolo Pasolini, Who Is Me – Dichter der Asche (Berlin: Hochroth, 1995), p. 33.

Part III
CONTEXTS

The theme in Part III of this book is an examination of what artistic researchers are doing when viewed in and from other contexts. Artistic researchers are identifiable partly by virtue of the non-traditional activities that they undertake. They use artistic methods and media to produce outcomes that are non-traditional within the university, such as musical compositions, performances, paintings, etc. More generally, one can imagine university rectors saying that they know that artistic researchers are doing something different, but they may not know exactly what that something is. 'Something different' seems to be recognizable from both the academic and the arts practice context. Indeed, from outside the arts, one of its most characteristic qualities is its consistent focus on 'the new'. Originality is therefore a core feature of the creative and performing arts.

Notwithstanding, the artistic concept of originality seems to bear some relationship to the academic notion of intellectual property. When an artist produces an artwork, part of its value lies in the fact that it was produced by exactly this particular artist whose name, as well as skill, contributes to the qualities of the artefact. These factors are exploited when the work is bought and sold. In academic research the value of an individual contribution relies not so much on the reputation of the individual researcher as much as on the scholarship and appropriateness of the methods that have been employed. Of course, well-known researchers are very experienced and are perhaps more likely to produce such contributions. However, the academic value lies more in the anonymous properties that enable the original contribution to enter into the web of knowledge. These two different interpretations of originality are given significance by the conceptual and market structure in which they operate.

Within the academy the concept of novelty has a particular meaning and significance. Unlike the arts, the strangeness of a novel phenomenon is not part of its attraction. Indeed, traditional research tends to emphasize the familiar rather than the strange. A large part of academic research – reflected in the training given to researchers – is the thorough mastery of the existing literature in the field of study. The purpose of mastering the literature is two-fold: first, to familiarize oneself with the key terms and concepts and, second, to identify a gap in knowledge that can be exploited. This exploitation is validated in terms of the key concepts from the literature. As a result, the academic research process tends to encourage small incremental steps that are expressed in terms of existing concepts. Revolutionary breakthroughs of the kind that are common in the arts, are correspondingly difficult to validate in such a context.

One of the bridges between the new arts research and the traditional expectations of the academy is the role of writing. It is interesting that, despite calls from some parties to abandon the written text in favour of artefact-only research outcomes, one can also find artists who produce very extensive texts in addition to their artefacts. One might ask, what is the role of these texts in relation to the artefacts, what does each contribute and for whom. In the current context, in which the arts faculty could be perceived as the relative newcomer, one might conclude that the written text is a way of speaking to the academy through a medium that they will understand. But if the context were different and the art school had somehow absorbed the university rather than the other way around, might not the *lingua franca* of research be artefacts instead of words? Thus the present position of the arts and the strategies for justifying or describing its benefits reflect the balance of power between the established university and the entering field of arts research.

All this could seem very separated from the world of professional arts practice. The concerns described have been academic ones; however, the arts researcher has been trained in new skills and enculturated in new values. On the one hand they have been trained as future professional artists with craft and conceptual skills for the production of significant cultural outputs. On the other hand they have been trained to work as academic researchers within the arts. Usually, both of these branches of training have been undertaken in a period of time when an individual would normally train for just one specialist activity. Identifying the benefit of having a single individual with both of these trainings will also contribute to identifying what artistic research brings that was not available before.

Identifying the professional role of artistic researchers will also help to identify the potential they bring to the research context and help in the evaluation of quality: when one knows what artistic research does, one will be able to know when it is being done well. Evaluating quality in terms of the existing activities of academic research and professional arts practice may put artistic research at a disadvantage. Traditional academic research involves meeting criteria of scholarship and argumentation, etc., leading to outcomes that make an identifiable, if small, increment to the totality of academic knowledge. Similarly, professional arts practice has its own, but different, criteria and expectations. Ambiguity about which standards to meet leads to apparently paradoxical questions such as 'can one do good research leading to bad art?'

It has been our strategy in this book to try to approach core issues on research in the arts from a number of different points of view. We have grouped these as foundational, related to voice and related to context, but we recognize that they could also be regarded as multiple strands in a complex web. Owing to the protean nature of artistic research we anticipate that some of these positions will be more resonant with some audiences than with others. In our view all of the issues discussed in this book are essential to the development of research in the arts, and one gets different views on what such research is like according to which issue one places at the centre of the inquiry.

18

CHARACTERISTICS OF VISUAL AND PERFORMING ARTS

Annette Arlander

In the following I am mainly discussing such research undertaken by artists, where artworks or artistic practices are part of the research, and which is conducted as research, not as art practice as such. The notion of what constitutes art (inquiry, skill, expression, originality, critical comment, decoration, entertainment, etc.) has an impact on other questions such as the role of experimentation (originality, novelty, innovation, interpretation), the characteristics of the artwork (unique object, prototype, ongoing practice, event, the artist as the artwork, etc.), the position of the artist (as *auteur*, producer, provider of services, first spectator, performer, etc.) and the amount of collaboration (with co-artists, spectators, participants, etc.) and all these influence research. However, the notion of art is treated by writers in the section focusing on foundations.

Different art forms create different problems for artists starting with research, depending on what dimension of research seems especially alien to ordinary art practice within that field. Is verbal articulation widely used or not? Is documentation part of the practice? Fine art is discussed extensively after the fact, while stage performances often involve discussions during the making. Performance art is often carefully documented while theatre and dance performances are haphazardly recorded, or then developed into separate genres like radio plays or screen dance. Differences between art forms are reflected in the choice of research problems. What kinds of issues are considered relevant to explore, or, depending on the approach of the artist-researcher, what questions are conventionalized and traditionally overlooked within the field, and thus important to focus on? I started my own research on performance space (Arlander 1995) which was considered a rather marginal question within theatre research in Finland at the time. Traditional issues of debate, historical models, conventional modes of discussing work, inherited value systems and, last but not least, differing modes of production within each art field influence research more than the formal characteristics and concerns of the art forms as such.

Ideas of what is the main work and what is a side issue differ greatly between various areas of visual art, music, film, dance, theatre, circus, performance art and Live Art practices. What do you look at or listen to carefully, and what do you let pass unnoticed – these conventional choices are important when we consider what are relevant issues to explore, and what is an innovation or an original research contribution for the field in question. Relevant research questions vary for different disciplines, as do the adequate (or accustomed) ways of going about finding answers to them. Does art practice involve research activities in itself, like location research in film scenography, or text analysis in drama theatre? What are the customary and expected ways of creating, presenting and discussing work? Who takes part in the discussions and at what stage of the process? In questions like these, what is ordinary in one art world is considered extraordinary in another. Sometimes traditional customs are hard to articulate, since most artists and participants take them for granted. The explicit self-understanding of a field does not always include consciousness of its own habits. A private studio is a basic tool for many visual artists, like an instrument for a musician, self-evident. An ideal rehearsal space for dancers is different from that of theatre rehearsals. The amount of discussion needed for creating a new theatre performance is astounding for somebody normally working as a painter. The amount of interpretative talk generated around an artwork seems odd to a performer who prefers the immediate response of an audience or wants to deliver a statement. And so on.

It is useful to remember that most dichotomies presented in the following, such as the juxtaposing of visual arts and performing arts are – if not patently absurd – at least much too broad and loose to be useful as starting points for research. However, the traditions and conventions within various art worlds have a strong impact on the motivation, questions, methods, discourses of and difficulties for research. And one of the first tasks of an artist researcher is to try to become aware of the various preconceptions and presuppositions she has inherited or chosen with her field.

A case combining visual and performing arts, a small video work called *Year of the Dog in Kalvola – Calendar* (4 min.)[1] performed in 2006, exhibited in 2007, can serve as an example of the importance of context. The work was performed and recorded once a month in the same place, a village about 120 kilometres northwest of Helsinki, Finland. The video shows a human figure with a yellowish scarf, hanging from the branch of an old pine tree and then leaning on the trunk, with the seasons changing around them. Performing was used in the creation of the work and the result was presented as visual art, as part of a larger project, not as a research outcome explicitly. If I would place it in context in various art fields (as a quick thought experiment only) I would focus on very different issues. From a visual art perspective the form of the work – a video of the artist performing a simple action – is fairly traditional and could be understood as a form of performative self-imaging (Jones 2006), or could be discussed as commenting on the tradition of *Rückenfiguren* in German romantic painting, especially Caspar David Friedrich (Andrews 1999).

From a performing arts perspective, the work could be looked at differently depending on the art form. As a documentary film the peculiarity of the work could be the use of a static camera, the repeated returning to the same place and the use of the same framing, but some explanation would probably be needed for the lack of voice-over or commentary. Within theatre the work could be discussed in relation to the possibilities of digital scenography or as an example of a dramaturgical device to show the passing of time, but would be peripheral to the problems usually discussed, centred on acting. Working in a dialogue of sorts with a pine tree could perhaps be examined as a more or less successful attempt at focusing on ecological issues (Kershaw 2007). As a dance made for camera, the work could be presented as a documentation of a still-act (Lepecki 2006) or be used as an argument for the independence of screen dance, since it is a work that could not be made live on stage, although it would perhaps not be accepted as dance by the wider dance community because the body displayed is not a dancing body.

Within performance art the 'theatrical' illusion of the passing of a year created by editing (instead of real-time documentation of a prolonged endurance session) could be contrasted to classical one-year works created by Linda Montano or Tehching Hsieh (Heathfield and Hsieh 2009). Within the context of Live Art the work could be hard to defend, since there was no exchange with the public, neither during the working process nor in the presentation, but could be discussed through a specific relationship to place (Hill and Paris 2006). The task of travelling to a childhood site once a month and walking the 5 kilometres there and back could be discussed as a performance practice in terms of autobiographical performance (Heddon 2007). How to contextualize the work within music is harder to imagine – perhaps by looking at the recordings of the changing sound environment (Schafer 1994 [1977]). As this example hopefully shows, there is no shared tradition or context of performing arts in the same way as we can speak of some kind of common legacy within visual art, or at least modern and contemporary art in the West.

Traditional dichotomies

Visual arts and performing arts are a strange pair to start with. Together they cover most art forms, leaving mainly architecture and literature aside. Visual arts could be juxtaposed with audio arts and music. Performing arts have traditionally been juxtaposed with creative arts, and still sometimes are, in fields demanding extreme virtuosity. However, a dichotomy based on creation and performing is rarely used today (with the exception of classical music perhaps). Visual art can be understood as an extension of fine art, whereas the term 'performing arts' is an umbrella concept used to cover various fields. There can sometimes be greater differences between forms of performing arts, like say music and film, than between performance and visual art. After all performance art is a genre of visual art. The relationship between a film and its script is usually different from a musical score and its performance (the script is a plan for a particular film, a composition is supposed to be interpreted and played again and again). There is a difference between a painterly and a musical sensibility beyond vision and sound; the idea that a composition can be played by somebody else differs from the idea that the work is singular and signed like a painting.

Contrasting rather than combining creative and performing arts has had its strongest impact within classical music. The composer is thought to be engaged in creative arts, whereas the musician is engaged in performing arts or 'executing' arts.[2] The same distinction is sometimes made in classical theatre; the playwright is the author, the creative artist, whereas the director and the actors are interpreting and performing the work. Today this distinction is rarely emphasized. In contemporary theatre the director is usually the author, using texts or material produced by the performers in much the same ways as contemporary choreographers work with dancers. And a performance artist creates and performs her own work, with or without a written score. 'Creative industries' probably covers most cultural activities.

Visual art is a shifting category. Sometimes it is used for fine arts only (painting, sculpture, graphic art, etc.) and distinguished from art and design, as in Finland. Sometimes it is used as a broader category including crafts and visual culture. Arts centred on vision can be juxtaposed with arts centred on sound, like music, though many works today are audiovisual. We could also speak of the visual textual as opposed to the sonic oral. To complicate matters, audio art or sound art is a genre within contemporary visual art; and dance, theatre and film are all visual, even though we can speak of visual performance as a genre. The focus on the distant senses of vision and hearing in western art, disregarding smell, touch, taste and proprioception as aesthetic media has been criticized, and some Live Artworks deliberately try to remedy this neglect (Banes and Lepecki 2006).

Other traditional classifications include the division into temporal and spatial arts. Music and literature work with time, as do film, dance and theatre. Time-based works exist within visual art as well, but the procedures of display are founded on spatial, immobile forms with extension in space rather than time. Another dividing line is between fine art and applied arts, which has been strong within visual culture, creating divisions into different academies for painting and sculpture, or architecture, industrial design, photography, ceramics, textiles, etc. In performing arts this dichotomy is not so prominent, although applied forms like drama pedagogy or dance therapy do exist, and a division between social forms of dance and dance art is often maintained. In some sense all performing arts could be called applied arts since they are very audience-oriented. In music a strict dichotomy prevails between classical music and popular music, which reflects the more general division into art or entertainment, which is alive and well despite years of post-modern proclamations to the contrary.

Within visual arts the technique based divisions into painting, sculpture, graphics, etc. have faded in importance together with modernism. This development might seem inevitable in other arts as well. However, the worlds of music, dance, theatre and film – though overlapping in many instances – still retain their cultural institutions, legacies, practices and research traditions, as can be seen in disciplines like musicology, art history, theatre research, film studies, etc. In art universities the legacies of specific art forms are often emphasized; they are the institutional conservers of tradition. According to the research university model developed by Wilhelm von Humboldt, teaching in universities is based on research. This could ideally be the case in art universities as well. Research is important to help articulate the tradition and for developing a discourse within institutions, which have developed from a conservatoire type of vocational approach. This is especially so in performing arts, which are often ephemeral in character, and thus tend to be either overtly conservative in order to maintain a tradition (like ballet) or more or less a-historical, always starting anew (like experimental theatre).

From a visual art perspective performing arts are supposed to be time-based, embodied and 'performing' in the sense of having a live audience. However, installations, community projects, time-based work and 'live' practices are increasingly common in contemporary art. The influence of new genre public art (Lacy 1995), relational aesthetics (Bourriaud 1998) and ideas of participation (Bishop 2006) means that the active engagement of a live audience is often sought. The temporal and embodied quality of most performing arts has stimulated debates around the ephemeral non-reproducible quality of the performance event (Phelan 1993), issues of 'liveness' (Auslander 1999), the importance of the energy exchange between performer and spectator and a demand for the valorization and study of the repertory along with the archive (Taylor 2003). An ambivalent relationship to documentation prevails, although areas like music and film have developed huge industries based on the reproducible documentation of performances.

Traditional differences between visual arts and performing arts concern the division of labour (solitary work or group work), distribution (producing objects for investment, ephemeral events or repeated performances) and impact (creating a canon versus immediate audience response). However, areas of shared interest and the blurring of boundaries are many, like installation art, scenography, lighting design, video art, screen dance, audio art, site-specific practices and so on. Performance art (body art, action art) and Live Art practices form an inbetween zone, which can be looked at from a visual arts perspective or from a performing arts approach.

Any general characteristics of visual and performing arts would be hard to find (and fairly useless as well). Instead of listing conventions and presuppositions about various art forms within visual and performing arts,[3] I will, in what follows, take up only a few aspects for comparison – such as the role of research in artistic practice, the position of the artist and the place of the artwork.

There is one more dichotomy that has relevance for artistic research, however, namely the traditional division between artistic inquiry and history of art (or history of music, dramatic literature) and scholarship in humanities, which is often also institutionalized. Concerning this division (as well as other dichotomies) we can ask whether it is desirable to accentuate differences, or to minimize them by emphasizing continuities. It seems reasonable to emphasize continuities rather than artificial dichotomies, but the idea of one research world encompassing all forms of research (history, philosophy, science, social sciences, practice-based research, etc.) is not truthful. Arts and humanities have many things in common, but sometimes artists come closer to scientists than historians since they engage in experimentation, and sometimes they have more in common with philosophers than social scientists, since they question the nature of reality. The term art-based is apt to underscore continuity – and to create confusion – since all traditional forms of art research could be considered art-based. Is not renaissance art history art-based? The term is perhaps best known from art therapy (McNiff 1998). Another option is to speak of art-as-research (as opposed to science-as-research) and to focus on truth as impact (Bolt 2008). A strict dichotomy between art-based (or artist-based?) research and other forms of research is probably not useful. Combining different forms of research, even different research traditions – could be fruitful. However, if artistic research (or art-based research) would be nothing special, if it had nothing particular to contribute, at least potentially, why engage with it, why propagate it, why write a book about it?

The role of research in artistic practice

Research is a normal part of artistic work in many areas of contemporary art (as exploration, investigation, trial and error) though only rarely developed as formal inquiry. We could even consider artistic research as the latest trend in contemporary art. There is a demand for research 'from the inside' arts practices, but various art forms need time to formulate key issues and develop their own methods. Research methods could preferably be developed from the working methods existing within a field and not imposed from the outside (Chapter 5). And this is true for performing arts as well. Many artists are ambitious and artistic research in performing arts can provide a place for challenging experiments, which are impossible within ordinary show business. For those critically inclined research can offer a site to question some of the assumptions of the art world. For those conservatively minded, research can provide a means to articulate and document the tacit knowledge in the field. For those who want to focus on the reliability and validity of artistic research as knowledge production, on equal terms with other research discourses, one way is to try to fulfil all the various expectations listed by Borgdorff.

> Art practice – both the art object and the creative process – embodies situated, tacit knowledge that can be revealed and articulated by means of experimentation and interpretation. [...] Art practice qualifies as research when its purpose is to broaden our knowledge and understanding through an original investigation. It begins with questions that are pertinent to the research context and the art world, and employs methods that are appropriate to the study. The process and outcomes of the research are appropriately documented and disseminated to the research community and the wider public.
>
> (Borgdorff 2006: 16)

Art as inquiry is more common within fine art, whereas technical and interpretative skills are in focus within classical music and dance. The task of producing an original contribution to knowledge and understanding, sounds probably more familiar to contemporary visual artists, while articulating tacit knowledge from within an existing practice would seem more familiar to practitioners of performing arts (though, these kinds of generalizations are doing injustice to the huge variety of approaches).

The terms practice-based research or performance as research are sometimes preferred in performing arts, rather than art-based or artistic research, as can be seen in the name of the IFTR (International Federation for Theatre Research) working group 'Performance as Research',[4] and in two recent publications *Mapping Landscapes for Performance as Research* (Riley and Hunter 2009) and *Practice-as-research in Performance and Screen* (Allegue *et al.* 2009). This is partly due to a different conception of art. In performing arts (music, theatre, film, etc.) 'art' often describes a sub-genre or is used as a term of quality (like art films), not for the field as a whole. Research involving articulation and theorizing of an ongoing practice of acquired (and thus partly unconscious) skills has an altogether different emphasis than artistic or art-based research that strives to develop and reflect on an original artwork or design product and explicate the route to that result. In fact, artistic research can be practice-based, when artistic practice is more important than a specific artwork, or design-oriented, when a specific object or artwork is produced. But this division is not strict, since many forms of design (stage design, costume design, light design, sound design, etc.) are included in performing arts.

Practice-based and art-based research frequently has a practical, critical or emancipatory knowledge interest, whereas artistic research seems to find contact points with philosophical research, sharing its speculative freedom. Nevertheless, research involving artworks or artistic practice inevitably has an empirical dimension (Nevanlinna 2002). The motivation for artistic research is rarely mere knowledge production as such. Most artists turn to research either because they disapprove of existing artistic practice, they have a vision or dream or they want to experiment and play.[5]

The role of experimentation and innovation in ordinary practice is different in contemporary visual art and various forms of performing arts. The role of experimentation varies on a wide scale, from classical ballet – where innovation has limited importance – through collective improvised forms like jazz music or contact improvisation in dance – to industrial design, where innovation can be the main *raison d'être* of the work. Within contemporary visual arts experimentation and critical questioning are included in the common understanding of art practice itself.

> Art is a creative and intellectual endeavour that involves artists and other arts practitioners in a reflexive process where the nature and function of art is questioned and challenged through the production of new art.
>
> (ELIA 2006a)

Not all performing artists would agree with this. Traditionally performers (actors, dancers, musicians) have concentrated on acquiring mastery in specific conventionalized skills and sensitivity in applying them in live situations. Though innovation and improvisation is valued in contemporary forms, experimentation or questioning would not be included in the general definition of the practice. The playfulness of some performing arts comes close to experimentation, but often seems to suggest untrustworthiness in the eyes of scholars. Seducing and confusing performances, mixing illusion and reality, fiction and fact, are regarded as the very antithesis of a scientific demonstration. This difference in relationship to exploration and inquiry has implications for the status of research within the art community, and for the change in attitude and approach the artist researcher has to undergo when starting a research project.

Research is considered distant to ordinary practice in many forms of theatre, dance and film. Though most choreographers and directors use experimentation extensively, and some form of background research is used by many film directors, the main focus is on expression and on reception. When thinking of research the first impulse for theatre artists is often some kind of reception research, since their main interest is in providing an experience for the spectators. Developing research processes based on artistic practices without including the spectators would be hard. To understand that a large part of the preparation for a production involves activities resembling research

– both archive research and field research – could help practitioners of theatre, dance and film to see that the difference from more formal research procedures is often one of degree only.

Do formal research procedures imply that art-based research simply applies existing methods from social sciences and pedagogical studies? Many artist researchers borrow qualitative methods related to phenomenology, hermeneutics, ethnography, narrative approaches, grounded theory, etc. This is convenient, for instance, in situations where artistic work is created in the beginning of the research process and where the research questions change during the process. Then artworks can be turned into research data, rather than research outcomes and qualitative methods can be applied to analyse the documentation of the creative process, like data from interviews. However, this is not really art-based or artistic research in a strict sense, since it could be done by anybody. A situation where the artist stops being an artist after completing the work, and turns into a researcher looking at the material created by the artist, has been criticized (Hannula *et al.* 2005). This is inevitable to some extent. It is what reflexivity is all about, but other alternatives could also be developed.

One way is to understand art making as a method. Making art can be a kind of method, if it is articulated and systematized as such (McNiff 1998). An example of such a method would be video filming a still act once a week in the same place and then analysing the material while editing a year later, to use my own art practice as an illustration. Another example would be to gather a group of dancers to do contact improvisation and discuss their experiences with them after each session. However, if art making is a method, does it have to produce art or is it enough that one uses the same procedure? Can the result be something other than art? Yes, probably the result can be a demonstration or even a report only, depending on the object and purpose of research.

If research methods are developed out of the working methods used within each field, then the research process will have specific characteristics due to the chosen methods. Could an artistic research project resemble empirical experimentation? The idea of variations resembles an experimental situation. The analogy can be problematic, however, since there are inevitably too many variables in a large production like a stage performance or a film. Alternatively, could an artistic research project criticize some previous theory on the basis of practical experiments? This could be easier, since one can expose weaknesses in a model through experiments, without being able to solve all those weaknesses. In my doctoral work (Arlander 1998) I used the analytical model developed by Peter Eversman (1992) and criticized its limitations using my own performances as examples. This type of critical experimental approach is rather exceptional today. A more common way is to start with a topic or a problem, to create your performances or artworks around it, and choose how to focus your reflection as you go along. This resembles an ethnographer's approach, and inevitably places stronger demands on the written part, the reflection and analysis of experiences.

Today the topic that interests me is landscape, and I work with the following question: how to perform landscape? It is too general a question to be a really useful formulation, but it is a question to start with since I can attempt to answer it by means of artistic practice. What makes my works in and with landscape examples of artistic research instead of ordinary artistic work, which includes development of approaches and methods? What makes these works a means to produce new knowledge and understanding instead of a means to produce experiences and insight for a potential spectator? Not much necessarily. But perhaps something: my wish to relate them to previous research and present them in a research context, my openness to documenting them and discussing choices made during the process, and lastly and perhaps most importantly, my willingness to write about them (Arlander 2008).

However, for a doctoral student or artist researcher starting with a project which is to be examined as a dissertation I would not recommend this way as a model. To make art first and contextualize it as research afterwards, will probably produce more problems than planning a research project which includes experimentation and artworks to begin with. The question of experimentation can be understood more formally – like testing a hypothesis – or more creatively – like exploring the unknown – or as an ongoing process of observation and analysis. In all cases it leads to the point: is there something you really want to find an answer to, or, is there a problem that you want to try to understand or solve or clarify? If not, it might be good to consider what it is that makes your project research. We could of course argue that in the same way as performance documentation is performative, since documentation constitutes a performance as performance art (Auslander 2006), an art project is constituted as research when it is documented as research. And we could even claim that if we can study any activity as (if it were) performance (Schechner 2002), we can look at any art process or performance as (if it were) research.

Based on my experiences with the dilemmas of doctoral students, I would recommend an artist researcher to try to stick to at least one of the following three, in the turbulent twirls of a creative research process – the question, the method or the data. However, by choosing which one of these you try to keep constant, you immediately sign in on a research tradition as well (discussed by other writers in this book, e.g. Chapter 5).[6] To try to formulate and fix all of them in advance in order to keep the research plan constant during the process is often sheer idealism (and sometimes even crippling) in an art-based or artistic research process where all aspects are often in flux and evolving. Most artists are good at exploring the unknown and living with uncertainty in their creation process, and that could be an important asset for research.

The position of the artist

The position of the individual artist is different in visual arts or contemporary art and in performing arts like theatre, dance, film and most forms of music. Generally the artist in performing arts is subordinated to conventions and production demands (even in non-commercial productions). A status as 'auteur' or 'virtuoso' can help, but it is not granted to all practitioners to the same degree. In visual (fine) art the artist is more independent or self-directed, though perhaps tied to demands of creating a 'brand' of herself or her works. The so-called freedom of the artist is most effectively propagated and defended in fine arts. In performing arts and applied arts the individual artist is in principle part of a production team and dependent on the customer or the public and all the specificities of the moment.

Performance art and to some extent Live Art are exceptions, or perhaps illuminating intermediaries. They can be approached from a visual art context and from a dance or theatre context. The position of the artist is taken from fine art with the legacy of important performance artworks, rather than from the entertainment industry. The performance artist is free or 'omnipotent' in the same way as a painter; she plans and pays for the artwork herself and she is responsible for all of her choices, though she can be placeless and marginalized as well. Many active performance artists have no art education and some of them adopt a position as street artists or consider themselves closer to activists. The average venues or festivals are small scale, and a large part of the audiences consist of colleagues, like a subculture, almost an equivalent to a research community. Whether a performance artwork is a small gesture or a provocative endurance test, it is often regarded as a contribution to the debate on current issues or on the nature of performance art and treated with due respect from colleagues, rather than as an entertainment to be discussed in terms of publicity, audience numbers or the enjoyment of the spectators only, as is often the case with other types of performances. Traditionally the position of the beholder is less that of a consumer than in theatre and dance, though some Live Artworks would be hard to distinguish from these. The performance art world can be hostile to 'theatricalization', 'academicization' and art institutions in general, which can be a challenge to artist researchers.

In using her own body the performance artist or Live Artist exemplifies another issue which has implications for research, blurring the ancient theory-practice (mind-body, intellectual-labourer) divide. She is performing herself, using her own body (like dancers, actors, performers and musicians) rather than working with an object, performance or event outside her body, a work that can be looked at and listened to from a distance like painters, sculptors, composers, directors, choreographers, playwrights, sound and light designers, costume designers, scenographers, video artists and so on. The multiple tasks of composing an artwork, performing an artwork, being an artwork and sharing an artwork with an audience (in case of Live Art often creating it together with the public) and then reflecting upon it as research can be quite demanding. However, a performer (actor, dancer, musician) accustomed to or dependent on feedback from a director, choreographer or conductor can find a research situation where she is supposed to work alone even more challenging.

The role, status, independence and agency of the artist within the art world or field in question and within the average creation process in that field, certainly has implications for how easy it is to adopt the role of researcher or to assume responsibility for an extended research project. Looking at the amount of collaboration or joint creation is another way of approaching the same question. To put it roughly: insisting on doing your own thing is a problem in performing arts, whereas it is expected in visual art. Hierarchical ways of working in theatre, music and dance have met much critique and are one of the key issues motivating research. Many artists turn to research in order to empower themselves, to be able to work more independently, to state their personal agenda, or to investigate why they cannot do that in ordinary production circumstances.

In contemporary visual art collaboration is mostly initiated by an individual artist and regardless of the amount of professional and non-professional participants the project evolves to become part of her *œuvre*. In classical music the conductor and the orchestra are interpreting the work of the composer. In jazz and contemporary improvisational forms, musicians perform together. In theatre and dance, works are named after the director or choreographer (in drama theatre, the author), though all the other artists and designers involved share credits (and copyrights) in the creation. I tried to explain to some visual artists interested in using actors in video works that actors are not only there to execute what they are told to do; they are – if they are any good – creative artists to collaborate with and give tasks to solve. Here again Live Art and performance art are something of an exception, since most performance artists prefer to work on their own. However, some Live Artists eagerly collaborate with their audiences.

Performance art and Live Art exemplify another distinction which has relevance for research: is the performance a separate entity (even if it is ephemeral), a defined, planned and more or less fixed sequence of actions? Or is it a loosely structured situation, an ongoing activity, a constantly evolving improvised exchange, created by or together with the spectators or participants, as many Live Artworks are? Collaboration can involve the audience as well, with the beholder not only integral to the work but an active participant in creating it. Needless to say, this has implications for research.

The habituation to collective forms of creation, where a group of artists produces something more than each individual artist could do alone, the use of intensely communicative processes and to a shared knowing, could be useful for research projects. Research collaboration is not yet widely used in artistic research, though various forms of joint creation and performing together are common working methods in performing arts. Most artist researchers work with other artists in the role of artists only. Collaboration among artist researchers is an interesting possibility (Rouhiainen 2008). Co-operation between a scholar and an artist almost inevitably leads to the scholar doing the research and the artists producing art. In projects aiming at technological innovation intensive collaboration between artists, researchers and various experts is more common (Chapter 12). Shared creation can thus be both the subject of inquiry (how to create new, less hierarchical ways of working) and a methodological approach (shared reflexivity). Artistic ways of working together could form interesting models for research procedures as well.

Many artists who engage in artistic or art-based research understand research as a way of developing and improving their art. But some artist researchers try to avoid discussing their own practice in their research, since they do not want to explicate their intentions. Often artists prefer not to interpret their own artwork, feeling that the work has a life beyond its maker, and sensing that their main contribution to knowledge and understanding is elsewhere. Some are influenced by old taboos: 'it is not the job of the artist to explain her works'. The positions of the artist and the scholar (as the curator/producer, critic and historian) have traditionally been separated, as is reflected in the degrees of MA and MFA; the curator or producer creating a context for, the critic evaluating, and the historian canonising, a work. Even though the divide has been eroded from both sides, many unspoken rules still influence the field.

The idea that the researcher is herself involved in producing the objects she studies is especially problematic in visual and performing arts, since traditional divisions have developed between people who make art (painters, composers, theatre directors, performance artists, etc.) and people who study artworks or artists (such as art historians, musicologists, theatre researchers, performance theorists, etc.). To some extent this has served to make artists anti-intellectual. If artists are constructed to be like 'beautiful animals', who do not know what they do, they need somebody else to manage them, and to study and explain what they do. This sounds outdated and degrading, but in some instances it has been useful. Art historians understand other aspects of a work of art than does the artist herself, and can look at the work as part of a historical development. Many artists enjoy being curated, interpreted and given a semi-mythological status or the liberties granted for children. Perhaps they (we) fear losing their (our) power as artists if given full agency as humans. This position resembles the situation regarding women and the vote during the nineteenth century. Will women lose their charming and enticing capacities and their soulfulness if they are given a chance to develop their agency as citizens? It all comes down to this: developing art-based or artistic research has a political dimension.

When artist researchers turn their attention to their colleagues or their field, either because they want to (or are asked to) contextualize their work and look at the broader circumstances of production, or because they try to emulate models of what they think is (or what they are told is) proper research, they easily leave their own work aside out of modesty, or relegate it into some small corner of the research project – a situation which can be counterproductive to the development of artistic research in the long run. What if using your own experiences and your own material were considered slightly equivocal in other forms of research, like ethnography? Here the support and encouragement of supervisors is especially needed.

Artists have the situated and embodied knowledge of the process of making and performing art (though not only that, of course). Basically people who are involved in a field should be able to undertake research in that field. However, one of the mistakes made by early career artist researchers is to try to 'solve the mystery of creation' or to assume that all artists work in the same way. Nevertheless, artistic research should be undertaken by artists, and should try to benefit the field of art in question. This does not mean that art-based or artist-based research would be completely different from other forms of research. However, as an artist being told how and what to do by researchers in other fields, it is important to remember that it is not only the artists' knowledge that is embodied, situated and partial.

The place of the artwork

The idea of what is an artwork is different in contemporary visual art and performing arts. Some performing artists – like improvising dancers and musicians – prefer to understand their art as an ongoing practice rather than as singular artworks. Traditionally the relationship to reproduction has been a significant issue. A painting or sculpture is one signed work. A photograph or print can be multiplied, a film or video can be copied (if digital, endlessly). A choreographed dance performance can be re-staged. A musical score can be reprinted, a musical performance recorded and distributed. A play can be interpreted ever anew. A performed poem can be performed again, even translated. There are more variations than the difference between a musical and a painterly sensibility (a composition to be played by somebody else and a singular and signed painting) mentioned at the beginning.

In performance art – in contrast to performing arts – the ephemeral, intangible and unique performance event has been fetishized, and reproduction and repetition resisted, though the status of individual performance artworks in the canon is often based on striking documentation (Auslander 2006). Contemporary visual art can also be site-specific and ephemeral. Installations are often both unique and temporary, though they too can be re-installed (Bishop 2005). In Live Art, the artwork is a more or less context dependent event.

Some performance forms are also memorising practices (Schneider 2001). Traditionally many performers like to downplay the role of documentation since they 'are' the documentation themselves. Portraits can be made or press photos taken, but the performance itself would not be reproduced, since the interaction with the audience could not be represented properly. Most artists today are accustomed to document everything and are not hostile to cameras, but it is still common to assume that it is impossible to document a theatre performance. A dance performance can be documented much more easily, simply because many choreographers use video as a tool to make notes in rehearsal. In contemporary 'performative' practices, documentation often constitutes the final artwork, since the actual performance takes place for a non-art audience, or unbeknownst to the public. This tendency to value the document over the event has also been criticized by Live Artists. These approaches to reproduction and documentation have an impact on research practices, which mostly require systematic documentation.

The question of ownership, who owns the artwork, or who has the right to use it, is a related issue. Is the artwork something with an independent existence, or is it bound to the repeated action, presence and performance of the artist? Or is the work something created in a shared exchange with the audience, the spectators or participants, something produced as a relationship between those present? Key questions can be: how to combine (commercial) production and research; or how to do artistic research in a meaningful way without creating a full production? A large production is often too complicated to be suitable for research, except in reflection. Unlike performed poetry or drawing, for instance, dance and especially theatre and film need heavy material organization, both for production and for studying them. Many experimental productions are produced in harsh circumstances, far from ideal for research.

The care and concentration devoted to studying an artwork can be different if it is seen as a conceptual statement, a conservable investment object, a consumer product or a celebratory event. Is the ultimate value of the artwork to be deemed by a virtual posterity or in the momentary encounter between performer and spectator? Is the most esteemed artwork the longest possible running show for the largest number of paying spectators seeing a film, or the legendary action art event almost nobody has witnessed but almost everybody has heard about? These traditional (simplified) notions have consequences for research practices. And they are reflected in traditional art research as well. It seems to be more difficult to consider a momentary event to be worthy of an extended research process than a tangible art object that can be returned to repeatedly. Sometimes simple but radical works are studied more eagerly than huge and complex shows, unless they are considered culturally or socially important phenomena.

Besides these (and other) differences in the presumed characteristics of an artwork in various art forms, the place of the artwork in the research process can vary. The artwork or performance itself can function as data for research in various ways. Making the artwork or the performance can function as a method of research. The artwork or performance can be the result or outcome of the research. And of course the artwork or performance can function as a presentation or distribution of research outcomes. This dimension is the one performing artists often feel most comfortable sharing and therefore one on which they focus in research contexts as well, by making presentations of past work. Artists involved in design, on the other hand, are often familiar with sharing unfinished work, and trained to present plans, questions, ideas or sketches before the work is done.

In contemporary art more and more emphasis is put on procedures and on conceptual framing. In performing arts – with the exception of performance art, Live Art or socially engaged practices – this approach is rare. What counts in theatre, dance and film is the end result, what the audience sees and hears, and its impact. The performance is the ultimate goal, and the way to get there is the professional secret of the artist, or something she does not even know herself. Alternatively it is considered the concern of the working group, as in theatre practice, where 'being in process' is common jargon during rehearsals. Focusing on the research process versus research outcomes (artworks or performances) is an interesting question to consider.

New challenges for academic conventions are encountered when artworks or performances are treated as research outcomes and evaluated as such. Then we can ask, with Borgdorff (2006), what makes an artwork a research result, the outcome of an original investigation. Is it the originality or conceptual rigour, or some quality of the artwork as artwork which makes it a research outcome? Or is it rather the research question, the explanation of working procedures, the theorizing commentary or perhaps the contextualization of the work, or all of these together? If I have a research question, albeit a loose one, or even a hunch, I can claim that sitting on a rock once a week for a year is a possible answer to that question. But if I start by sitting on a rock once a week for a year, I probably have to explain in detail why I have chosen that way of performing and how the work is supposed to be understood, if I want to claim it as research.

The question could be formulated as: What is the place of your artwork or your artistic practice within your research project? The artwork is rarely the question directly. But is the artwork the method? Not all artistic practices are easily systematized.

Most commonly the artwork or artistic practice constitutes data for research, for reflecting on experiences afterwards. After creating several artworks or productions the questions you started with have probably changed. So sticking to your data, and changing the questions you ask of it, as well as the methods for analysing it (and thus perhaps even the theoretical framework), is the path most commonly used, and comes close to proceedings in qualitative research. Probably the best way of producing significant results would be to have questions for which you really try to find answers. Producing interpretations, contextualization and articulation of experiences around one's art is more common and can be valuable as well, especially in areas where little explicit knowledge articulated from the artist's side exists.

It is not always easy to determine what the place and role of the artwork in the research project is. Are the artworks or performances evaluated as research results, or are they considered as tools only, a method of research or are they material or data to be treated in the written report? If the artwork is considered to be data, the research resembles any ethnographic or pedagogical research, where the researcher uses her own experiences as material. This is what practice-based research mostly has come to mean, and one wonders what the fuss is about. Only very scholarly oriented researchers working mainly with archival knowledge would probably find problems with that. The same applies when artistic work is used as a method, which can be complemented by other methods, and the research outcomes discussed on the basis of the written report only. New questions and problems arise when artistic work is evaluated as research outcomes, as parts of the dissertation or research report.

One problem in doctoral research is that artworks and performances tend to live a double life, first as public productions in their own right, and then, almost hidden from the audience, as research outcomes to be evaluated and examined as part of a dissertation. Earlier approaches based on the idea of equivalence between art and research emphasized artistic excellence, which is easily read as a need for mainstream credibility. In contemporary art, artworks often include knowledge production, so explanations are not considered an alien practice. The research is often easily incorporated into the artwork. In theatre, dance, music, film and Live Art preliminary information given to the public mostly serves the purpose of marketing, though a terminology of investigating issues is becoming more common. There is a lack of funding for experimental artistic research, especially in performing arts. So many artist researchers have to rely on commercial productions as parts of research. When artistic research becomes more common, it will hopefully not be necessary to hide from the public the fact that something is research and perhaps there will be opportunities for esoteric experiments created explicitly for research purposes.

Another problem in doctoral research is the tendency for the artworks or performances to remain in the background in the final discussion and evaluation. The written report tends to be considered the real research work (an influence from the humanities and social sciences), regardless of the scale of the artworks or productions, and their examination in live situations. This risk is particularly germane in performing arts, when the performance is often long gone at the time of the final dissertation, though today this applies for many forms of contemporary art as well. If the evaluation takes place in the same context, it is unnecessarily exhausting for the performer (dancer, actor, poet, musician or Live Artist) who has to jump directly from the performance to defending the dissertation, especially if the evaluation is a formal public event as in Finland and most other Scandinavian countries.

A third problem in doctoral research is how to present artworks and performances as research outcomes, or as demonstrations of research outcomes, in such a way that the issues and questions central to the investigation are brought to the fore. Sometimes the focus on the written contribution is due to the fact that the artist researcher herself prefers to put emphasis on the theoretical part and considers the artworks as ephemeral, trivial or too personal (or wants to safeguard their integrity as artworks). For an examiner, a vital question is how to avoid the inevitable lure of looking at art as art, or enjoying a performance as a performance. Paradoxically, the examiners sometimes wish to focus on evaluating their experiences of the performances or artworks, rather than on the contribution to knowledge and understanding in the report, a situation the ambitious artist researcher might want to avoid. If artworks are assessed as good or bad with regard to their quality as art, or as interesting or boring in terms of spectator experience, as can be the case in performing arts, it is no wonder that many artist researchers prefer to stress the theoretical part in order to be heard as researchers. However, by being explicit about what is the research focus, and by trying to point that out among other possible aims of the work, the artist researcher can help the examiners to focus on core concerns.

A fourth problem in doctoral research is the fact that most artists begin their research projects by producing artworks or performances. They start with creation and exploration, since that is what they know how to do, and become more aware of methodological and theoretical questions only when they start reflecting upon their work and writing reports. Then the artworks turn into data and the situation resembles qualitative research in which one collects material and then formulates questions prompted by that material, etc. This is a possible method for artistic research, of course, but why then assess the artworks or performances as part of the dissertation? Consequently, if performances or artistic parts are used as data, they should not be examined as research outcomes and if they are evaluated as research outcomes, they should not take place at the start of the research process.

These and similar problems are dealt with in different ways by different artists and institutions, and also depending on the traditions of presentation within various art forms. In my experience it is important to focus on the artworks or artistic practices, and try to keep them and their needs in mind when planning procedures and creating research environments, since they are the ones bringing new challenges to (humanistic) academic customs. If not, artistic work will take place in the margins, off side, almost as 'illegal pleasures' compared to the serious part, the 'real work' in research seminars. And this would be rather absurd, if we really want to develop art-based or artistic research.

Problems and possibilities

So what are the core problems for the further development of artistic research in visual and performing arts?[7] Much depends on what type of research is in question, what the role of the artwork or the artistic practice is within the research project, and what the role of research is in the artistic practice in the field in question. A central concern is to decide for whom the research is for; who is supposed to benefit from the results of the research, and what is the context for the research. Perhaps the core problem of art-based research or artistic research is to understand what art means in various contexts and how art (artworks, artists, the art world) is supposed to transform and change thanks to various forms of research.

Another problem could develop if research is the only form of further education available in arts, since there is a great need among artists to improve their skills, their status, their thinking and their capacities to engage in society. Inevitably artistic research as a means of career development or artistic development will have other aims than artistic research as knowledge production. Combining them is possible, but often complicates matters.

A third problem is almost the opposite, namely, how to incorporate interesting experimental work that is created outside academia into research The traditional recipe for this has been the collaboration between prominent experimental artists and scholars. In that way some level of excellence and expertise is maintained on all levels. However, this can be counter-productive since it keeps the dichotomies intact, and could lead to extremely conservative outlooks, even a kind of apartheid. To put it in another way: it is important that research is developed by artists themselves, otherwise colonization by traditional 'scientific' approaches will continue. And what is more important, the potential for creating (truly) new questions is overlooked. To put it roughly: when artists, who sometimes lack sufficient intellectual education and have survived and thrived due to their special skills or charm, are forced to try to please and satisfy their new audiences of research connoisseurs in the same way as their previous bourgeois audiences, not much is gained.

Further problems for artistic research in both visual and performing arts have been, and sometimes still are a) attempting to claim a parallel status for art, an 'equivalence' in relationship to research instead of actually being research; b)attempting to collaborate mainly as 'birds' with 'ornithologists', that is, as artists with art researchers (people studying artists), instead of working with other researchers on subjects of common interest; c) attempting to do a philosophical investigation. Though philosophy can inspire art making, it is necessarily speculative rather than empirical (besides being a tradition of its own); d) attempting to work in the inbetween as a means of double escape – justifying sloppiness as research by saying 'this is art' and justifying sloppiness as art by saying 'this is research', rather than exploring the inbetween as a challenging area (Sand 2008).

Ways of avoiding some of these problems could be a) to admit that there is art which is a form of research, but that most art in itself is not research; b) to focus on the purpose of the research c) to try to think of producing knowledge and understanding for the field in question d) to be clear about the place and function of the artwork or artistic practice within the research; e) to allow artists to venture into historical, philosophical, sociological, or pedagogical research if they wish, but to really encourage and support those artists who are prepared instead to do artistic research, that is, use their art making to produce knowledge and understanding about art and the making of it.

To summarize some of the specific problems related to artistic research in performing arts, especially theatre and dance and to some extent Live Art, they could be listed as follows: a production format demanding resources is a limitation to experimentation; the playful character is conducive to exploration but creates difficulties in terms of credibility; the tradition of valorizing virtuosity over critical thinking creates problems for some artist researchers; lacking habits of documentation (cherishing the perishable moment) is a challenge for some practitioners; focusing on the audience, and on instant response makes long-term focus difficult for some artists; complaining how impossible it is to verbalize embodied practices can become a self-fulfilling prophecy; the collaborative nature of a performance, both the creation process (with extreme cases like mainstream theatre) and the actual event (with extreme cases like Live Art created by the participants), provides challenges and possibilities for research.

What could artist researchers in contemporary visual art and performing arts learn from each other? In performing arts we could learn to respect the so-called freedom and independence of the artist, to focus on the intention, and to see the artwork as a contribution to an inquiry, something that is supposed to be different from what precedes it, and to work with a long-term view – since all these aspects are related to traditional academic ideals in other forms of research (such as academic freedom, integrity and critical thinking, systematic inquiry, etc.). In contemporary visual art we could learn to respect the skills of collaboration, dialogue, sharing ideas and working as a team, and to respect the tacit knowledge embodied in practices – since these are related to traditional academic ideals in other forms of research (like a self-correcting discourse, research groups of scientists, situated knowledge, etc.).

Other issues to develop in a cross-breeding manner, looking at choices of specific artists or projects rather than the general characteristics and conventions of whole fields, could be the uses and abuses of subjectivity and the dependency on context (on all levels), though, perhaps I find these particularly interesting only because they are relevant to my personal artistic research practice. Probably the main thing to remember for an artist researcher (or a supervisor or even an examiner) is: there is not one general form of research for the artist-researcher to try to approximate, just as there is not one generally approved concept of art upon which to base art-based research.

Notes

1 For a video clip see http://www.av-arkki.fi/web/index.php?id=35&artist=2064 (accessed 15 February 2010)

2 In Swedish there is a special term for it: 'utövande konst', executing art. In Finnish the term 'esittävä taide' can mean both performing art and representational art.

3 The characteristics of such broad cultural industries as music and film cannot be discussed 'from within' by this writer, who has some experience in practising theatre, dance, performance art and contemporary visual art only.

4 For information on the working group see http://www.firt-iftr.org/index.php?option=com_content&view=article&id=26 (accessed 15 February 2010).

5 A comment by Peter Eversman at a seminar organised by the graduate school Elomedia in Helsinki.

6 What do I mean by this? Am I serious about these simplifications? Perhaps they can be used like thought experiments rather than guidelines: if you stick to your question, all means and methods in trying to answer that question are acceptable, that is, you can change your methods, your theoretical framework, let the process unfold, find new data, etc., without losing track of what you are doing. (This is the approach supported by Feyerabend (1993 [1975]), as far as I understand – and comes close to the common sense in my view.) If you stick to your chosen method, and that method is valid or at least approved in the research community in which you work, you will produce some kind of research results, even if you abandon or modify your research questions and all the aims and assumptions you started with (this comes close to the 'normal science' tradition, as far as I understand). And lastly, if you stick to your data, you can change your research questions and your methods of analysing that data, letting your material guide you (as is the tradition of qualitative research, as far as I understand).

7 I discussed some of these issues with professors Eeva Anttila and Esa Kirkkopelto when we were renewing the guidelines for artistic research at the Theatre Academy in Helsinki.

19

DIFFERENTIAL ICONOGRAPHY

Henk Slager

The content of artistic research can be understood as a non-philosophical articulation of how various media – such as photography, public space, and scientific models – present the world visually in the form of perceptual regimes and strategies. Artistic research stands up critically against each mode of visual reduction and cultural disciplining in the form of a dynamic mapping of a series of heterogeneous, open-ended rearticulations, thus showing different forms of knowledge production. In so doing, artistic research deals intrinsically with the crucial question of the artistic image's role and its medium-specific position in current visual cultures.

Prolegomena

Our current artistic decade is filled with an excess of rhetorical moments: crisis, change, but most of all challenge. One of the challenges in today's art world concerns the Bologna process that started ten years ago as a reconstructive trajectory focusing on rethinking and reformulating the paradigm of the art academy. Slowly but surely, it becomes clear that the romantic model of master-pupil education has definitely reached its final stages and now makes room for a variety of course-based programs demanding space for critical and contextual studies, collaborative and interdisciplinary projects, experimental productions, and above all communication and presentation skills. At the same time, it turns out that gratuitous production of artefacts for a neoliberal art market directed towards speculation and financial profit must end with an academy regaining its traditional connotation of giving room for debate and research.

However, when looking at the present situation of European art education, one discovers a dramatic devaluation: the critical autonomous space of art as once put forward by Adorno, has evaporated greatly in the practice of many art academies. No more than a 'Temporary Autonomous Zone' is what has remained, i.e. a fleeting experience of freedom in a world drowning in an iconography of visual culture and the opportunistic rhetoric of the creative industries. One-dimensional strategies of signification seem to directly derive their implicit structure from a formatting awareness of the late-capitalist ideology of a free market system. Ultimately, it seems that the notion of art could be erased in the title of art academies whereupon they subsequently could continue as 'academies for creative industries' dominated by the paradigm of a world characterized by economic and financial dogmas without any commitment to other worlds.

In the context sketched above, there is yet another alarming trend. Remarkably enough, the established practice of curating exhibitions started to expand the notions of academy and education during the last couple of years. Increasingly, exhibitions are emerging characterized by a curatorial paradigm based on notions such as 'the expanded academy' or an 'educational turn in curating'. Obvious examples are the curatorial concepts of *Manifesta 6: notes for an art school* and *Dokumenta 12: what is to be done?* These connotative expansions contributed to a further disintegration of the position of the art academy as such. If the entire domain of the art world can be determined by academic parameters, it clearly seems to be the case that the art academy as such has inevitably lost its unique position. With that, the academy seems to have demonstrated the unmistakable crisis of its institutional redundancy.

The Bologna rules and its challenges mentioned above, i.e. the introduction of a Bachelor-Master (BA-MA) system in art education ultimately seem to have delayed the above mentioned crisis in a positive way. Fortunately, the curriculum to be introduced in the European art educational system as per 2010 will also necessitate a re-evaluation of the specificity of art education (de Greef 2008). Such a reflection will position the debate on the specificity of the academy in the context where it should be conducted, i.e. within the institutional framework of art education. This will not lead to a homogenizing framing, as some conservative criticasters fear; it will rather result in a form of differential thought enabling the rethinking of the somewhat obsolete concept of autonomy while turning it into an autonomy of commitment. Because of that reformulation of the curriculum and its related production of room for thought, the art academy could become the pre-eminent location in the cultural domain to generate innovative processes during the upcoming decade.[1]

Art education should again be aware of its responsibility in the fields dominating our various cultural and intellectual domains. Clearly, those domains have been dominated by an economic-financial paradigm in an almost catastrophic way. Therefore, today's art academy should entirely focus on re-evaluating its original task of creating novel forms of perception and critical awareness from the perspective of committed forms of autonomy while combating prevailing economic models of thought.

Artistic research

Until recently, the curricula of many art education institutes turned out to be dominated largely by an art historical model of reflection. Consequently, one gratuitously employed a clear-cut duality where on the one hand, artists produced artistic work, while on the other hand external professionals (mostly art historians) supplied frameworks for interpreting those works. In the last decades, standard works such as *Art and Illusion* (Gombrich 1977) and *Truth and Method* (Gadamer 1975) have provided a methodological foundation for such a nearly dogmatic art historical hermeneutics (cf. Slager 1995: 133–41).

Today's practice of visual art demonstrates, though, that time has come to abandon monolithic thought framed in binary models of truth (the hermeneutic method) and illusion (the visual creative method) and declare them obsolete. Moreover, art practices show that art and method could link in various constructive ways, since a shift has emerged from art practices focusing on end products to art practices dealing with experimental, laboratory-style environments and researching novel forms of knowledge and experience. In other words, artistic practices have become dynamic points of departure for interdisciplinary experiments governed by reflexive perspectives.

Time and again, the concept of research as such unmistakably evokes certain expectations. Obviously, research implies organized modes of approach, systematic information, and significant contributions to the knowledge and information economy. Furthermore, research points to ethical responsibilities such as a better understanding or improvement of the world. Are those the utmost characteristic elements of research (cf. Chapter 3)? One could also argue that each form of research is focused on developing and formulating a methodology. Research may or may not be inspired by a great cause or an accidental discovery ('serendipity'), yet ultimately lead to novel, methodologically formulated forms of knowledge. The force of the method seems to determine the value of the result. Therefore, continuous control should clarify how methodological conditions have been applied and to what extent. Although research methods obviously differ with regard to field and subject, they still share a fundamental basic principle: methodological research is primarily engaged in formulating questions and providing answers. Thus, research as such could be described most adequately as the methodological interconnection of both questions and answers, and answers and questions.

As mentioned above, a similar interest in research activities has emerged in topical artistic work. In the visual domain, however, the trans- or interdisciplinary research conducted by artists in their artistic practices is not characterized by an objective, empirical approach. Art knows a different form of research strikingly described during one of the first European conferences on artistic research by Sarat Maharaj as 'spasmic, interdisciplinary probes, haphazard cognitive investigations, dissipating interaction, and imaginary archiving' (Maharaj 2004: 50). That form of research cannot be channelled through rigid academic-scientific guidelines dealing with generalization, duplication, and quantification, since it engages in the unique, the qualitative, the particular, and the local.

In that respect, artistic activities still perfectly match Baumgarten's classic definition of the aesthetic domain, where knowledge is described as a knowledge of the singular.[2] Although artistic knowledge as *mathesis singularis* – because of its focus on the singular and the unique – cannot be comprised in any sense in laws, it does deal with a form of knowledge, says Baumgarten. Yet, the aesthetic domain's emphasis on the singular and the unique does not mean that artistic research is impossible as, for example, philosopher of science Karl Popper tried to bring to the fore. After all, artistic research completely satisfies the most fundamental research criteria with its focus on the importance of communication, critical attitude, and autonomy of research.

In contrast to academic-scientific research and its stressing of generating 'expert knowledge', the domain of art deals with a different form of knowledge called experience-based knowledge. Whereas pure scientific research is often characterized by purposeful uselessness, artistic research's focus is on involvement, on social and non-academic goals. Still, artistic research as a form of idiosyncratic research should be able to answer two well-defined questions. First, how could the chosen methodology (as compared with research projects of other artists) be described? Second, how does the domain of visual art necessitate the specific autonomous research?

Methodological mapping

The epistemological perspective of the unique, the qualitative, the particular, and the local, and the methodological questions concerning artistic research, demand a further investigation. As argued above, different from established forms of research, the methodological trajectory of artistic research cannot be defined in a strict and clean-cut manner.

Artist Herman Asselberghs' research project *Where is Cinema* could serve as an example of an artistic research trajectory reverberating a variety of theoretical questions and perspectives. His research project engages in the ubiquitous character of film as a medium and its role in how we perceive and understand the world today. Asselberghs also tackles the issue of the methodological consequences of the cinematographic perceptual regime for artistic research. The core of his project is how the question of 'what is cinema' is replaced by the question of 'where is cinema.' In other words, ontology makes room for cartography and geography. 'Where is Cinema' asks where we are situated and where we are going. Asselberghs claims, 'amidst momentary disorientation and provisional reorientation, a cartography of film might help to brush up worn paths, revisit overlooked locations, and open up new horizons' (Asselberghs 2008: 25). There are quite some things to map out in the proto-form world of film: economic shifts, financial transactions, historical turning points, technological innovations, social transformations, cultural movements, and political swings. How could these topics be mapped? According to Asselberghs, film as a medium is the pre-eminent medium to research these topics at a multi-level.

> Similar to how map readers find their way through a jumble of geographic information (types), meanwhile projecting their presumptions, fantasies and recollections onto those data, the film audience also looks at the moving images on the screen, while implying various memories of other films, their own lives and those of others in both the perceptual and interpretative experience.
>
> (Asselberghs 2008: 29)

Obviously, a terminology filled with maps, and a cartography or geography of film, points to Deleuzian philosophy. In *Negotiations*, Deleuze claims:

> what we call a 'map' or sometimes a 'diagram' is a set of various interacting lines (thus the lines in a hand are a map). There are of course many different kinds of lines, both in art and in a society or a person. Some lines represent something, others are abstract. Some lines have various segments, others do not. Some weave through a space, others go in a certain direction. Some lines, no matter whether or not they are abstract, trace an outline, others do not.

The most beautiful ones do. We think lines are the basic components of things and events. So everything has its geography, its cartography, its diagram. [...] There are various spaces correlated with different lines, and vice versa (here again, one might bring in scientific notions like Mandelbrot's fractals). Different sorts of lines involve different configurations of space and volume.

(Deleuze 1995: 33)

The Deleuzian multiline or multiplicity-based network, produces a specific mode of analysis:

based on two components: a two-line streaming mode of analysis based on the thought of philosopher Henri Bergson and the form of motion produced by quantum mechanics and its emission of particles and exchange of packets of energy producing the concept of non-localizability. [...] Deleuze's multiplicity mode of analysis creates a fascinating visualization of a figure of thought where a correlating, open system of two streams of interacting concepts [...] [are] all based on the interplay of lines, dimensions, strata, planes, spaces, and plateaus.

(Balkema 2006: 13)

Thus, the streaming two-line mode of analysis, and its related multiplicity mode of analysis, yields two continuously interacting domains producing a stream of novel concepts and insights.

Artistic researchers seem to deploy such methodology of a streaming two-line mode of analysis dealing with the two interacting lines or domains of activation of imagination and knowledge production. Different from academic research, the perspective of artistic research cannot be determined beforehand. Therefore, artistic research creates the interaction, intermingling, and traversing of these two lines of analysis in an operational, process-based, and experimental way while producing a variety of unexpected perspectives.

The perspective of the first line, activation of imagination, is clearly underscored by the modernist definition that the artist has the capacity to observe what others keep unnoticed. After all, through mere visual means, the artist succeeds in making visible what ordinary vision fails to see. Because of that, the everyday categories of perception become dislocated in a flash. The artist compels us to see – for one moment – the world in a different way; according to different norms, according to different habits; images ultimately replacing reality are replaced by images as novel visibilities. With that, art determines a variety of polymorphic ways for flexible observation. The artistic image provides an open view while liberating the spectator from a frozen perspective. 'Essence or existence, imaginary or real, visible or invisible, art disrupts all our categories by revealing its dream universe of sensuous essences, of striking similarities and silent meanings' (Merleau-Ponty 1964: 35).

The perspective of the second line is expressed in the postmodern maxim that, in their research of visuality, artists should pose the epistemological question of what art is. Or better put, in their transcendental research, artists should investigate whether the institutional or territorial foundations of the concept of art should be deconstructed or not. With this, questioning the essence of art implies questioning the concept of art. That is, 'a work of art is a kind of proposition presented within the context of art as a comment on art.' If this perspective is implemented too extremely or too one-sidedly, then art risks becoming the equivalent of its definition.

> Art has evolved in such a way that the philosophical question of its status has almost become the very essence of art itself, so that the philosophy of art, instead of standing outside the subject and addressing it from an alien and extended perspective, became instead the articulation of the internal energy of the subject.
>
> (Danto 2005: 37)

However, the creation of a third line, a flashing line of flight constituting a *zone of reflexivity*, seems to be of immense, topical interest in today's visual art (Deleuze and Guattari. 1988 [1980]: 293). After all, artistic research as an operational process is 'an open-ended work-in-pre-growth' (Maharaj 2004: 53). In artistic practices, it is by definition impossible to research the artistic process in a manner different from a form of operational process. Therefore, in artistic research, a self-reflexive movement continuously questions shifting situations and also determines shifting positions in a constant process of interacting, intermingling, and traversing of its lines and domains of analysis. As a consequence, artistic research continually produces novel connections, accelerations and mutations in temporary, flexible, and open systems. These systems run up against problems, but rather than creating solutions, novel methodological lines are created that enable the production of various metamorphoses in the research process.

It is for that reason that it is only possible at the end of an operational artistic research to determine whether the trajectory of the proposed methodological process has indeed produced novel insights. Artistic research could be described as a *methodicē*: a strong belief in a methodology founded by operational strategies which cannot be legitimized beforehand. Artistic research is a form of mapping, it constantly produces novel lines of thought and novel lines of research. Indeed, those are the essential characteristics of artistic research.

Medial matters

In such a dynamic methodological context, several research questions come to the fore: questions only to be posed in the domain of visual art; questions only to be investigated from the domain of visual art; and most of all questions to only be responded to adequately by the artistic strategies and methodologies described above. What are those questions? They are questions such as, 'How is the (experience of) current reality medially constructed?', 'What premises and limitations occur when people interpret their environment artistically?', 'What is the effect of specific technology on temporal conceptions?', 'Is perception medially disciplined? What is the role of remediation and hyper-mediation?', 'How do novel media transform the visual vocabulary?', 'Could artistic media create novel concepts and percepts?[3]

Indeed, a major issue seems to be whether a topical artistic concept can be formulated, a concept suitable to produce a novel artistic visual grammar or language. That issue is intimately linked with how a visual language is constituted in different ways by various media perspectives ultimately considered transmedial or intermedial. To what extent can visual language contribute to diagnosing, criticizing, or deconstructing perceptual regimes related to medialization and cultural disciplining is still a pending research topic? Also the overarching subject of the role and position of the artistic image in our current visual culture invites research from various disciplinary perspectives. It is true, Rosalind Krauss has argued, that the current artistic image and image production is determined by a post-medium condition. However, the question is whether that statement would also imply that, for example, the photographic image could no longer be viewed as a mere aesthetic registration of a situation in the real world. It seems to me that the topical photographic image demands a hyper-mediated investigation of how the photograph as an iconographic medium produces various forms of realities still based on perspectival capacities. Research in the form of a critical re-evaluation – either through other media or through the history of the photographic medium – of the photographic image as such could clarify various theoretical positions as well as the factual input of the photographic paradigm in the field of topical visual art.

Other medium-specific practices evoke similar research questions – whether or not from a visual culture determined by a post-medial condition. Is reflection from the perspective of the painterly paradigm still relevant for understanding a topical artistic production? Does the visual language of cinema or a screen-based reality influence the iconography in current visual art? How could constructive forms of interdisciplinarity with other visual domains be envisioned? In the light of the exploration of the preconditions of the artistic communication process as such, the issue of contextualization of the artistic image should be investigated. What is the optimal context for a specific, artistic image? What communicative preconditions does such an image require? Under what circumstances should it ultimately be presented? Could site-specific data be explained and understood medially?

These research questions will lead the discussion in the next sections. First, the photographic medium will be the core issue. From a historical perspective and articulated for the first time in Walter Benjamin's work, the photographic medium was the medium to give a first impetus to a critical reflection and artistic investigation of the *a priori* perceptual categories of space and time.

Flash cube

Since its acceptance as a form of art around the 1930s, photography has been forced as no other artistic medium to justify its medium-specific qualities. Particularly the Greenbergian heydays of Modernism have produced such pressing urge for justification. At that moment around the end of the 1930s, painting had surpassed by far its interest in the subject of perspectivist illusion. As a consequence, twentieth-century painting entirely concentrated on the qualities of the two-dimensional surface implying a passion for painterly components such as planes, colours, and lines.

From that time onwards, the artistic working field of perspectivist painting would be remediated by photography as an artistic medium and would start to be considered the pre-eminent, transparent medium. Photography could parade to be better, more realistic, and more complete, but how was it possible that the medium of photography could be experienced as more transparent than painting? The answer to that question has been given recently by Bolter and Grusin (1999) in *Remediation*. Remediation implies imaging one medium in another medium. In fact, because of imaging, around the year 1850 people could understand daguerreotypes, since the daguerreotypes mechanically reproduced reality in a painterly mode, i.e. with a central perspective and a flat plane. Indeed, that moment of painting being remediated through photography also produced the possibility of understanding the medium-specific conditions of painting.[4]

Yet, what are the specific characteristics of the medium of photography? Until now, Roland Barthes' impressive essay *Camera Lucida* is still the utmost authoritative study on the medium-specific qualities of photography.[5] In a compelling way, Barthes tells us about the 'ontological desire' he has experienced through the medium of photography, i.e. the overwhelming need to know what photography really is and what its essential difference is compared to other types of images. Barthes argues that there are thousands of photographs for which we could feel a certain interest, some might even touch us, but such sensation is always mediated through the rational inbetween stage of a moral and cultural development. The type of photograph characterized by a tolerant effect and a cultural interest could best be described with the notion of *studium*. Studium refers to embedding a specific cultural order in the sense of a combination of knowledge and civilization enabling the spectator to enter into the perspectives and infra-knowledge that constitute and impassion a particular work. The photographic studium signifies that what Barthes calls unary photography. 'The photograph is unary when it emphatically transforms "reality" without doubling it, without making it vacillate (emphasis is a power of cohesion): no duality, no indirection, no disturbance' (Barthes 1984: 41).

Some photographs, however, do vacillate our perception since they undermine the uniformity of the studium. These photographs dominate perception entirely since they give rise to a mutation of interest. Barthes calls that second photographic effect the punctum. The punctum is a deconstructive detail since it creates a sense of immense consideration in the spectator. No matter how instantaneous the punctum acts, it will always be accompanied by a vast and expansive power that often appears to be metonymic. In Barthes' view, that salient detail cannot be deliberate since it functions as a supplement in the field of the photographed object, both inevitable and informal.

Classic examples of the punctum seem to specifically occur in a topographic approach of photography characterized by a detached, panoramic perception entirely directed towards buildings and how they are situated in their urban or natural environment. Hardly any people can be noticed in the images of this photographic tradition. That effect of dehumanization of the image could already be noticed in early forms of photography where artistic and aesthetic motives had started to generate a vast production of empty or deserted urban images. Some of those images emulate the clarity of architectural drawings. Others draw attention to the abstract play of light and volumes or simply surpass the characteristics of the studium while evoking a sense of sublime terror, disruption, fear or alienation through a subtle intermingling of spatial details.

Yet, the deconstructive detail breaking through an arranged order still does not make us grasp the essence of photography, says Barthes. After all, painting can also simulate the reality of the detail without having been actually observed. That discourse connects a series of signs based on referents, but those referents could eventually turn out to be linked to chasing shadows. Conversely, photography can never deny that something has indeed been there. Therefore, photography is characterized by the double condition of past and present which really signifies the pre-eminent essence touching the heart of photography. Photography does not tell what is no longer there, but emphatically underscores what is there. With that, photography demonstrates its establishing power which is not so much related to the object as to time. Indeed, the issue is a punctum different from the above discussed detail. The novel punctum is the existential given of time, the distressing emphasis of the photographic noeem.

However, the twentieth-century distinction of two clear punctum effects, a punctum of space and a punctum of time, seems to have lost its persuasiveness in the topographic turn that characterizes photography today. Current photographic images show how a hectic street life and a form of density have substituted emptiness and openness where physical closeness has given room to distance and aloofness, and slowness and the decisive moment have been dissolved in speed and repetition. These images seem to unambiguously demand a critical transformation of the concept of punctum.

Indeed, the image no longer needs a punctum fastened to an ontological awareness of space or time. A twenty-first-century image requires a dynamic punctum producing flexible, vibrating, and fluent connections between the categories of time and space. Exactly that necessity of fluidity in temporal and spatial concepts could be signified by the notions of flashing and cubing and their interconnected movement of flash cube as a promise of serial, instantaneous exposures. Therefore, the introduction of a novel punctum indicated as a flash cube punctum might redefine the absolute and functional definitions of time and space while transforming them into operational forms of intensity and potentiality.

The operational flash cube punctum specifically emerges in elastic, reflective images claiming an investigation of how the photograph as an iconographic medium produces various forms of realities and worlds still based on perspectivist capacities. These images are produced by a novel generation of photographers with a researching attitude focused on spatial environments and architectonic constellations. Such artistic research in the photographic realm is connected with interesting, topical forms of photographic criticism on functionalist ways of thought paralleling perspectivist-based photography where a three-dimensional world subdivides into transparent, comprehensible, and instrumental entities. With this, a centralizing perspective has cleared the way for fragmentary entities, where functionality makes room for forms of dysfunctionality.[6]

The work of South-Korean artist Kim Sang-Gil is a fine example of such an artistic approach. What is the artistic strategy the artist adopts for fragmenting the programmed character of our knowledge of the world? Or put more concretely, how does Kim Sang-Gil adequately select artistic images in the context of that desire to demonstrate the logical conditioning of our consciousness? For Kim Sang-Gil only one criterion constitutes each of his artistic decisions and that is the exposure of the functional presence of solidity. His photographic images tell us again and again about the solid way in which the societal order succeeds in displaying its organizing capacities by means of distinct and fixed functions. Kim Sang-Gil emphatically underscores that form of exposure through a visual confrontation with real-size prints.

In his dealing with images, Kim Sang-Gil seems to be inspired by the conceptual and aesthetic-autonomous approach of the Düsseldorf School, i.e. Bernd and Hilla Becher and their students Andreas Gursky, Axel Hutte, and Candida Hofer. Yet, there is an important difference between the photographic images of the Düsseldorf School and the South-Korean artist. The ultramodern images of the Germans are rooted firmly in a historic tradition. Their images clearly demonstrate a historic, or if you will, archaeological consciousness. Such consciousness is characterized by a historic accumulation and a process of signification produced by a continuous series of references. As a starting point for his artistic production, Kim Sang-Gil adopts a form of consciousness focusing on the functionality of the here-and-now while erasing any historic accumulation. More than that, his conception of consciousness does not even permit any form of historic signification. Kim Sang-Gil's view seems to incorporate a Deleuzian process of deterritorialization where notions such as accumulation and forms of resonance are replaced by the mutations and accelerations of the here-and-now while producing a multiplicity of streams of thought. The Deleuzian movement of deterritorialization connects with the exposure of conditional functionality that, as appeared above, is a theme in Kim Sang-Gil's work.

However, in a Deleuzian sense, the movement of deterritorialization implicates the attack of a counter force called reterritorialization. In this combat, the flowing, decoding movement of deterritorialization is resegmented by the power of reterritorialization as a continuous process. Kim Sang-Gil's *Remodel Series* seem to portray such a process. The *Remodel* photographs show the empty interiors of vacant offices and other working spaces. Obviously, we have arrived in the twilight zone of functionality where the traditional, clear-cut situation of functionality has stopped. No longer is the space a lobby, a station

Figure 19.1 Kim Sang-Gil, *University Series*, 2007.

hall, or an office space. Rather, the vacant spaces demonstrate a potentiality of novel forms of functionality and actuality, of novel forms of reterritorialization. Moreover, those temporary vacancies without any function necessitate the investigation of the traditional link of form and function. After all, if it is valid to argue that architectonic form follows function, isn't it also true that these photographs portraying the lack of function demonstrate at the same time a lack of architectonic form, namely a zero degree of both function and architectonic form?

The investigation of the connectivity between function and architectonic form re-emerges in Kim Sang-Gil's most recent work, the *University Series*. The photographs in these series show facades of various university departments such as astronomy, natural science, and the humanities. The buildings are characterized by various forms of architectonic solidity, which, no doubt, correlates with the solidity of the specialized knowledge their inhabitants believe they construct. Strikingly, though, the photographs show the facades of university architecture in a mere two-dimensional fashion. Any three-dimensional perspective on the academic environment has been erased from the photographs. That is a conscious artistic decision Kim Sang-Gil made. The absence of a perspectivist vanishing point produces a mode of representation escaping a centristic model of control and domination. A similar perspective once constituted a classifying reason which, inspired by Cartesian subject-object thought, divided knowledge production into functional departments and faculties accommodating specialized forms of sciences. The need for functional control created a form of thought focused on a transparent system of classification. With that, a fluid and flexible concept of knowledge was doomed to disappear.

The two-dimensional images of the *University Series* create dysfunctionality in yet another way. They erase photographic depth, i.e. the medium specific quality of photography. Whereas the *Remodel Series* dealt with the confrontation of a perspective filled with emptiness, the *University Series* demonstrates the disappearance of any centristic perspective. The two-dimensional images no longer show a perception focused on a controllable way of representation. Parallel to this intrinsic way of criticizing the framing activities of the photographic image, the facade images also question how a classifying reason once divided knowledge into specialized departments. Kim Sang-Gil's images seem to stress that the time has come for a movement of decoding creating a renovation, an extreme make-over of knowledge production. Such a make-over invites systems of knowledge to renounce their frame of functionality and welcome instead fluid, dynamic connections. An extreme make-over could erase familiar fields of knowledge and metamorphose at the same time related forms of knowledge production. Indeed, Kim Sang-Gil's *University Series* seems to foreshadow an academic dysfunctionality which necessitates an extreme make-over as a moment of dislocating any existent form of academic knowledge production.

Context responsive research

In a great number of topical art practices, a clear need can be noticed to work in the realm of public space and create art dealing with urban and social issues. Of course, there is a long tradition of art in public space, but during the last decennium a strikingly different artistic attitude emerged in that respect. Most artists working today in public space no longer view this – as was the case in the 1970s – as a strategic action to oppose the white cube of the institutionalized visual art museum. Today artists engage in researching the medial conditions of public space. Art historian Miwon Kwon was the first theorist to observe the initial signs of this paradigmatic shift. In her now classic study *One Place after Another*, she argues that public art no longer focuses on a physical, spatial, or institutional relationship, but rather is interested in a discursive bond. Subsequently, Kwon concludes that site-specific art has lost its site and because of this, it has in fact been dematerialized. In short, the once inseparable connection with the material surrounding – the surrounding characterized by physical and architectonic elements taking the viewer into the mode of a 'phenomenological vector' as Merleau-Ponty puts it – seems to no longer exist. Partly inspired by the institutionalized critique of the 1970s, the practice of today's public art seems to develop an aesthetics defining the notion of space anew. In this aesthetics, the notion of space is understood as a discursive construct: space as a platform for knowledge, intellectual exchange, and cultural debate. Today, artists engage in societal, social, historical, and political themes as spaces of artistic research. This development meant that recent site-specific art resulted in art approaching the site 'as predominantly an intertextually coordinated, multiple located, discursive field of operations' (Kwon 2002: 33).

Thus, no longer is the literal relationship between the work of art and its immediate surroundings central. At stake is now a reflection on the cultural-political conditions within which public art is presented and produced. Although this artistic strategy also leads to a form of site-specificity, this manifestation of art is ultimately disconnected from its concrete topographical space. An indexical relation between the discursive space and the artistic interventions is no longer relevant. Consequently, a mobile, multi-faceted space comes into being as an ambulant field where aspects such as openness, mobility, and ambiguity express the involvement of today's artistic practice. In line with this, qualities such as consistency, continuity, and certainty are considered obsolete resulting in a public art drowning in a ubiquitous visual culture. Subsequently, the danger is lurking that such public art will become an illustration of late-capitalist levelling out because of its loss of specificity.

Therefore, in *A Voyage on the North Sea*, Rosalind Krauss (1999) claims that public art should also be aware of its medium specificity. Only the medium has a critical potential anchored in its inherent aesthetic domain, Krauss argues. This aesthetic domain is connected with a layer of conventions which, in Krauss' view, is characteristic of artistic mediation. The artistic medium as a complex structure of perceptual and conceptual conventions could not be reduced to a form of communicative one-dimensionality. According to Krauss, medium-specificity exists thanks to a multi-layeredness which could never coincide with the physical conditions of the signifier.

That raises the question whether the site as 'discursive issue' could also be understood as medium; for example, in the form of a public art disconnected from the material parameters of locations, but employing instead the history – photographs, books, historical objects – of a certain place as building blocks for an archive-type of documentation based on artistic research.

These issues are starting points for two research projects: *Shelter 07*, The Freedom of Public Art in the Cover of Urban Space[7] and *Translocalmotion*, the seventh Shanghai Biennale.[8]

The objective of *Shelter 07* was to draw attention to the history of the Dutch city of Harderwijk. To achieve this goal, the genealogical significance of the name Harderwijk, 'an elevated place offering a safe shelter to refugees in troublesome times', serves as the point of departure for this exhibition in public space. The genealogical significance makes notions such as safety and freedom inextricably bound to Harderwijk's history. But how did that connection arise? To investigate that question further, eight artists were invited to produce artistic research projects related to a number of significant locations for the history of Harderwijk. The artists were asked to develop specific proposals, underscoring the above problematics in an artistic form. Interestingly, in their research projects, a number of related issues and topics emerged.

Jeanne van Heeswijk extensively investigated the historical archive of the city of Harderwijk. Based on that investigation, Van Heeswijk developed a series of wallpapers placed on the bricked-up windows of old houses around the church square, retelling last century's lingering tales: about the symbolic poet Rimbaud, who lost his identity as a poet during his stay in Harderwijk and vanished in the grand myth of the foreign legion; about the first big stream of (Belgian) refugees who found temporary shelter during World War I in camp Harderwijk; and about the circulating rumours of missing passports popping up during the transformation of the AZC (Refugee Centre) Jan van Nassaukazerne into luxury condominiums, as proof of the search for shelter in a new, safe identity for its former inhabitants.

In order to understand site specificity as a medium, Lara Almarcegui employed an archaeological method eliciting that which precedes space, i.e. the granting of room. On the *Blokhuisplein*, a historical location renowned for its straightness and power, she created a fallow field presenting a temporary autonomous zone as a dysfunctional,

Figure 19.2 Hito Steyerl, *DeriVeD*, 2008.

undefined, and unfounded space escaping the grid of geography. At the same time, the autonomous zone was able to shelter the experience of a total freedom of interpretation.

Also *Translocalmotion* intended to examine the conditions of human life in dynamic urban environments, including socio-economic conditions, the logics of mobility and its subsequent cultural implications. Could these conditions, related to the current form of human movement and urbanization and the cultural implications as reflected by and from topical visual art, perhaps be described as a 'migratory aesthetics'? An aesthetics which, contrary to the relational aesthetics of the 1990s, no longer concentrates on the actual creation of social environments for intersubjective meetings, but rather adopts the form of a 'documentary aesthetics' revealing all components related to mobility such as arrival, change, combination, departure, deterritorialization, displacement, encounter, interface, location, loss, memory, movement, passage, reconnection, relocation, revisiting, separation, reterritorialization, and transformation. Yet, it is also an aesthetics of mapping other phenomena connected with today's culture of mobility, such as the effect of newcomers on public space; an aesthetics stressing that indeed the artistic reflection of the multifaceted culture of mobility gives way to a more fluid form of perception, i.e. a plurality of sensory experiences that both transform and modify the way we perceive the world.

To research these issues, the curatorial team decided to deploy the immediate surroundings of the Shanghai Art Museum as a starting point for their endeavours. The People's Square actually functions as a microcosm of the complex dynamics affecting the current issue of mobility. If you take a closer look at The People's Square, you will find issues of migration and transition, traces of ultra-modernist urban planning and manifestations of the power of the topical rhetoric of capitalism. In short, The People's Square, as a microcosm, may hold great potential for artistic inquiries and artistic research projects. Thus, the *Seventh Shanghai Biennale* treated The People's Square as a location of knowledge transfer, connection, meeting, and exchange. It is exactly from this perspective of knowledge transfer that the artists invited for the *Seventh Shanghai Biennale* were commissioned.

For example, Tiong Ang's project *Models for the People* employed the historical map of The People's Square, the 1930s map where the building of the Shanghai Art Museum still functions as the clubhouse for the equestrian sporting club. In those days, the building was a specific location where entertainment created a clear awareness of a collective identity. That form of constructed identity, as Tiong Ang's dialogic exploration shows, seems to have been replaced in The People's Square by today's logic of mobility and the more fragmented experience of the collectivity a karaoke bar creates. Such experience is characterized by repetition and difference based on an ongoing confrontation with various stereotypical systems of classification.

The installation *DeriVeD* by Hito Steyerl could be described as an artistic project of re-mapping. The methodology of this work is formed by a psycho-graphical mapping process of The People's Square as an unofficial but comprehensible film archive. On the one hand, The People's Square has been the setting for many films made by classic film directors such as Antonioni; on the other hand, The People's Square has a number of locations where immigrants sell bootleg copies of (these) films. That is a micro-economic activity giving the square an additional connotation as a location for distributing its own imaginary narratives. By mapping these hidden flows of desire and moving images, *DeriVeD* offers – entirely in line with *Translocalmotion*'s documentary aesthetics – a deterritorializing experience characterized by open-endedness, new connections, pluri-form categories of perception, and a contingent understanding of the public domain.

The complex of relationships within these installations or interventions based on research, reinterprets the specific history of a certain location in a dynamic way. The material found during research appears to function indeed as a medium, i.e. as a mediator or vector between specific location and viewer. Both *Shelter 07* and *Translocalmotion* show that themes or subjects such as today's 'migratory aesthetics' appear to be able to be deployed as places of artistic research turning them into the medium of a topical art practice searching for the most adequate spaces, locations, and places, to pose issues such as mobility and migration. In *Translocalmotion*, the curators expected:

> the artistic research projects to provoke a series of redefinitions of topical urban conditions in non-disciplinary modes. In varied ways and different media, the participating artists will explore and document the aesthetic dimension of mobility by means of their own singular artistic strategy. In forms such as mapping the traces of micro-economic activities, documenting the new faces of the urban landscape, and depicting personal narratives, the *Seventh Shanghai Biennale* will produce new ways of understanding modern-day mobility. The *Seventh Shanghai Biennale* proposes a chance to review and remap our world from different viewpoints within expanded geographies.
>
> (Slager 2008: 62)

Delta knowledge

In the discussion of various forms of aesthetics Baumgarten, as the art historian coining the concept of aesthetics, should certainly be mentioned. When Baumgarten introduced the concept of aesthetics in the year of 1750, he spoke of a *cognitio sensitiva*, a 'sensuous knowledge.' That characteristic elucidated that not only the sciences, but also the arts could be considered cognitive phenomena. But what then is the specific aspect of artistic knowledge? Knowledge can manifest itself in various ways as Aristotle already claimed. In addition to Plato's *epistēme* of universal, general, not-contextualized forms of knowledge, the *technē* presents practical, production-based knowledge whereas the *phronesis* deals with an experience-based, prudence, practical wisdom, concerning how to act in particular situations. These three domains of knowledge distinguished by Aristotle seem to have been institutionalized 2,500 years later more or less as alpha, beta and gamma sciences.

What is the location contributed to artistic knowledge in that current three-stream landscape? Or better put, how does such understanding of knowledge manifest itself today? Is it perhaps the form of knowledge that today, as Kim Sang-Gil's deconstructive work has suggested, has been marginalized since it is considered mundane, illusive, irrelevant, and useless in the context of academic instrumentality? Unarguably, the academic institutions appear to simply refuse to accept anything of value outside their own self-accredited metrics.

However, the scientific way of representation is also a clear and distinct form of mediation. After all, the scientific metaphors and narratives frame our perception and faculty of imagination to quite a large extent. Precisely that process of scientific mediation is the core of attention for many artistic research projects today. At stake are specifically projects rearticulating the medial processes of the sciences, the visual boundaries of art history, the narrative logic of history, and the iconography of the social sciences in the form of an artistic methodology.

The results of these artistic research processes are by definition mutually inspiring. On the one hand, in these confrontations, artists become necessarily aware of a more transparent contextualizing of the research process; on the other hand, a more fluid form of contextualizing will no doubt make the scientist inevitably reconsider the framework of their own paradigms. Indeed, in these confrontations, proper catalyzing will be possible, since dynamic exchanges between as yet distinct forms of knowledge could occur, whereas existing molecular boundaries could ultimately be shattered and cause novel constellations of knowledge production to be generated. Those are forms of knowledge production coming into being by unexpected connections between the standardized mediation of the scientific knowledge production and the artistic knowledge production aiming for different modes. Therefore, the question is whether this latter form of knowledge production could be defined. Intending to define artistic knowledge also implies to accept implicitly or explicitly – and thus to partake in – the established academic power-knowledge system of accountability checks and evaluative supervision, as Foucault once claimed.

> Though acceptance does not necessarily imply submission or surrender to these parameters, a fundamental acknowledgment of the ideological principles inscribed in them remains a prerequisite for any form of access, even if one copes with them, contests them, negotiates them, and revises them.
>
> (Holert 2009)

Not only defining, but even merely speaking about artistic knowledge production seems to include positioning oneself with respect to academic frames of thought. Does one, in line with James Elkins, choose to present artistic knowledge in such a way that it will be recognized as a position in the debate about knowledge production by a more extended academic conglomerate (Elkins 2005b)? Or does one choose a more deconstructive point of view as Irit Rogoff does in arguing that alternative practices of communality and knowledge generation might provide an empowering capacity (Rogoff 2007)?

Yet, both positions assume that this form of knowledge production can only be the sole outcome of a researching practice characterized at all times by an absolute open, non-disciplinary attitude and an insertion of multiple models of interpretation.[9] In spite of much academic scepticism, today there is indeed a visual research practice satisfying the essential components of widely accepted research. Particularly artistic research projects critically scrutinizing the process of scientific mediation clearly underscore that view. Research conducted by artists – similar to research in the traditional sciences such as the humanities, social sciences, and natural sciences – is also guided by the, since time immemorial, most important maxim of any scientific activity: the awareness

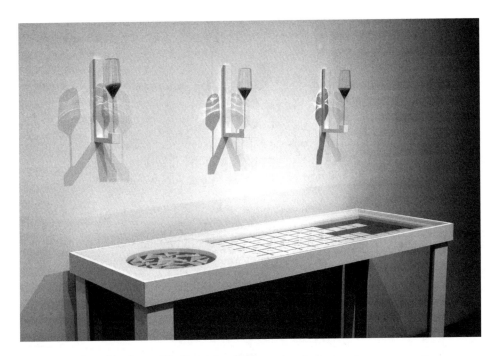

Figure 19.3 Irene Kopelman, *Ubx Expression*, 2008.

of the necessity of a transparent communication. The artist as researcher needs to explain clearly why the domain of visual art necessitates the research questions and, the other way around, why those questions should necessarily be articulated in the visual domain. In addition, the researcher should be able to justify both the process and the chosen operational methodology and trajectory. In that context, one characteristic turns out to be specifically remarkable. A striking methodology in the topical practice of artistic research appears to be the formulation of a certain hypothesis from a specific situation-based artistic process and, furthermore, to interconnect that hypothesis in an open constellation with various knowledge systems and disciplines.

Those artistic research projects seem to thwart the well-defined disciplines. They know the hermeneutic questions of the humanities (the alpha-sciences); they are engaged in empirically scientific methods (the beta-sciences); and they are aware of commitment (the gamma-sciences). Because of that capacity and willingness to continuously engage in novel, unexpected epistemological relations in a methodological process of interconnectivity, artistic research could best be described as a delta-science. A *modus operandum* characterized, on the one hand, by the literalness of the notion of delta, i.e. creating novel, significant connections, but, on the other hand, also characterized as a fourth discipline (next to the alpha, beta, and gamma disciplines) by a research method not *a priori* determined by any established scientific paradigm or model of representation; an undefined discipline as 'nameless science', directed towards generating flexible constructions, multiplicities, and new reflexive zones.[10]

That undefined non-paradigmatic discipline as nameless science was the curatorial departing point for the project *Nameless Science*.[11] All presented artistic research projects dealt with an artistic reinterpretation of representation(al) models, existing disciplines, comprehension strategies, and academic classification systems. Consequently, these research projects did not only produce fluent forms of interconnectivity and methodology accompanied by different forms of knowledge production; they also led to novel artistic strategies and intensities of perception.

In his project *See and Seen* (2006), Matts Leiderstam, for example, investigated the art historical conventions for the ideal landscape developed as techniques of perception in eighteenth-century painting (e.g. artistic seeing instruments like the Claude Lorrain Mirror). A research trajectory consisting of the investigation of historical reports and contexts and a production of various artistic strategies led to the issue and implications of current spectatorship and how to address that subject in artistic work.

> My method for See and Seen was to research the different historical accounts and the contexts of the representation of landscape. I was not so much interested in the accumulation of knowledge but in how I could put it to work in general to reproduce the landscapes through various artistic techniques and strategies. I adopted different roles when I approached the landscapes through mimicry – the copyist, the tourist and the art historian – used in both projects as routines for seeing.
>
> (Leiderstam 2007: 28)

Do natural sciences allow an artistic intervention and reverification of visual representation? That question was the starting point for Irene Kopelman's research project *Space in-between Spaces*. Kopelman investigated how various Natural Science collections used to base their display system on nineteenth-century forms of categorization and logics of identity, a classifying logos excluding differences and singularities.

> During the 19th century, a scientific project needed to force things into categories in order to visualize the rules they followed and which organized the world in a logical system. This was a fundamental process to schematize how we look at things and simplify it to the extreme, thus overlooking any singularities. My research project concentrates on reopening some of these categories, and to look upon differences and singularities. The project uses elements from the history of science as resources and attempts to generate, from both art practice and artistic thought, a type of knowledge extrinsic to the field of philosophy or history of science, but still touching upon issues they all share.
>
> (Kopelman 2007: 40)

In the form of a concentrated series of artistic interventions and deconstructions of device systems, Kopelman develops alternative forms of archiving and display for a number of Natural Science collections.

Differential iconography

The artistic research projects discussed above – the affect of the photographic medium, public space as an artistic medium, the relationship of artistic knowledge production with other forms of knowledge production – clearly demonstrate that artistic research should approach critically at least three perspectives: a reductivist visual culture, retinal consumptive models, and universalist iconographies favouring certain forms of identity and subjectivity through (a localized) hypostatizing and reification. Against these static, one-dimensional visualizations, the practice of artistic research posits open-ended statements characterized by fundamental aspects such as indefinability, heterogeneity, contingency, and relativity. Therefore, artistic research projects explicitly request an open, non-disciplinary attitude, and the insertion of multiple models of interpretation. (This in line with Søren Kjørup's earlier plea for preserving a multiform research concept: Chapter 2.) Such artistic research practices seem to be able to make new connections with existing disciplines or comprehension strategies, while producing novel epistemological models such as knowledge-in-action, nominalist knowledge systems, non-knowledge production, and perceptual systems able to disclose a pluralist experience of the world. All models are forms of a nominalist production of knowledge unable to serve a retinal, one-dimensional worldview characterized by transparent singularity, but rather creating – and if necessary demanding – room for the undefined, the heterogeneous, the plural, the contingent, and the relative.

Furthermore, in the artistic research projects, novel perceptual systems are based on utilizing media in such a way that a topical iconography could be developed, able to open new registers of perception related to novel possibilities of orientation. In other words, a novel, differential iconography emerges – such as a documentary aesthetics – able to bring an experience without precedent – such as ubiquitous mobility – within the reach of experience. But also an iconography demanding novel forms of presentation, since the realm of presentation should also find ways to deal with the various modalities of artistic knowledge production. How can otherness be posed without imposing an epistemic frame? How can known forms that reduce difference to sameness be circumvented?

Through their research projects, artists have created representations and methodologies for intellectual labour on and off-display.[12] They founded migrating and flexible archives aiming at transforming the knowledge spaces of exhibition spaces. Models emerged criticizing the suggestion of perfect communication as imposed on us by diagrams and plans; models demonstrating the shortcomings, the white spots on the map of the information society and the knowledge economy; models starting from the apparent incompatibility of non-knowledge with values and maxims of knowledge-based economies (efficiency, innovation, and transferability) focusing on providing strategies for escaping such dominant regimes; and models inventing dynamic notions of mapping (or counter mapping) able to communicate the experience of a world in the process of becoming fluid, transparent, and open.

Notes

1 In that context, the PhD research trajectories (the so-called third cycle) connected with the Bologna rules are of great importance. Such a form of research does not need the guidance of the formatting models of established scientific domains, nor is it swayed by issues produced by the late-capitalist free market. Rather, it is an authentic form of research emerging from mere artistic necessity while erasing a dependence on any form of rhetoric connected to social-economic relevance. Such programmes offer artists an intellectual sanctuary where they can reflect on their artistic motives and strategies while creating a qualitative impulse with respect to their artistic practices. The participating, mainly mid-career, artists have a chance to focus on issues inherent to their artistic practices. In addition, such a novel, experimental sanctuary for autonomous artistic (PhD) research creates an environment able to function as an example for the art academy at large. After all, it is important for such artistic research to function as the art academy's conscience and, in that sense, govern the continuously pressing issues of the paradigm of art education.

2 In his book *Aesthetica* (2009 [1758]), Baumgarten introduced the concept of aesthetics as a philosophy of the senses. He says, 'Aesthetics should investigate for accuracy analogous to logic, that is at the basis of scientific knowledge, the concepts constituting sensibility.' In 'Camera Lucida', Barthes (1984) describes similar research as a mathesis singularis, 'a science of the person, which can attain a generality which does not belittle nor shatter.'

3 Such questions are the starting point for my exhibition project 'The Intermedial Zone', Boijmans Van Beuningen (2006). See also Slager (2006).

4 Still, the issue of painterly mediality returns again and again. Also, today artists pose questions such as: is there such a thing as a painterly paradigm in current iconography? What is the role of painting within today's media culture? What are the present conditions for a painting to be defined as a painting. How are the boundaries of the painterly domain being established?

5 Barthes' Camera Lucida (1984) could be viewed as a good example of an artistic research project avant la lettre because of its mathesis singularis methodology.

6 Flash Cube, Samsung Museum of Art, Leeum, 2007. http://www.e-flux.com/shows/view/4419 (accessed 22 February 2010).

7 Shelter 07. The Freedom of Public Art in the Cover of Urban Space. Harderwijk, 2 June–31 August 2007.

8 Translocalmotion (Seventh Shanghai Biennale), Shanghai, 9 September–16 November 2008. http://en.shanghaibiennale.org/content.php?nid=24 (accessed 22 February 2010).

9 That mode of research has been strikingly described in the 1970s by the philosopher of science Feyerabend in a then utopian fashion as 'anarchist methodology' and 'Dadaist epistemology' (Feyerabend 1993 [1975]).

10 Cf. Agamben and Heller-Roazen (2000). Here Aby Warburg's research is sketched as 'unnamed discipline': a mode of being freed from a formalizing, academic disciplining.

11 Nameless Science, Apexart, New York, 10 December–31 January 2009 (Slager 2009b).

12 Such artistic research should be viewed as a potential for opening up reflexive spaces that surpass a simple investigation in visual cultures.

20

WRITING AND THE PhD IN FINE ART

Katy Macleod and Lin Holdridge

This chapter will address the role of writing in the formulation of a PhD in Fine Art. It will view writing as part of a negotiation between setting out the thesis as research proof and critical engagement with it through conceiving and making art. Through brief but detailed analyses of five submitted PhDs and an insight into two current studies, it will adumbrate how the role of the researcher is embedded in the enquiry; that this is essential to the 'unfinished business' of the research (Chapter 3). The chapter will demonstrate how an artist who is in pursuit of further art research will not have produced an argument and drawn conclusions so much as provided a provocation to produce more art, contingent to the changed conditions s/he has effected through the PhD (Chapter 14). We will provide details of this process. We will also claim it demonstrates a critical reflexivity which is touched upon by a number of chapters in this book, notably by Morwenna Griffiths (Chapter 10). However, where Griffiths is concerned to clarify research distinctions between, say, critical reflection and critical reflexivity, we deploy the latter as an encompassing term which registers the way in which the PhDs cited here turn back to engage critically both with their own purposes and institutional contexts. This is partly due to those purposes of art research which refuse the convention of a written thesis, also the shifting of the central focus of research from sources external to it, to the art, which then becomes the enquiry, itself. It is not our intention to provide a theoretical exegesis to identify such art research, nor will this chapter present an argument which draws clear conclusions in that sense. However, we will provide insight into the value of critically reflexive PhDs whose formulation of questions outweighs the more conventional demonstration of an argument, proving that satisfactory research has been produced and that training has been completed; hence, the case studies have been selected to demonstrate certain critically reflexive qualities, which are enhanced by an appropriate deployment of writing.

The chapter will be in three parts: the first will offer a brief overview of sources and ideas; the second and key part, will present examples of doctoral practice and submissions and the third will address the requirements for building appropriate research cultures. In our view there is a particular imperative attached to research 'for' art because the processes involved are central to the discipline of Fine Art and its essential transformative aspirations (Chapter 15). These have been duly noted by the sources we deem to be important to art practice and doctoral study research development.

Sources appropriate to doctoral study and art practice research

One of the reasons for the ongoing contentious nature of doctorates in Fine Art is quite simply the politics of institutional powers which dictate what is valued *as* research and thus what a PhD in the Arts might be. This line of argument is taken up by Henk Borgdorff (2006), when he points out that debate still rages around institutional issues such as parity, benchmarking and the effective delivery of universal rules and procedures for the conduct of doctoral study and submissions. We will offer evidence in support of a plurality of approaches to research because there is too much at stake in our emerging cultures, most particularly in the UK and Australia, as well as in the more robustly independent cultures of Sweden and Finland, to enforce homogeneity. We view this as important to the individual achievements of research artists who have delivered thinking through their PhDs which could not easily have been predicted and might well not have emerged had particular rules and procedures been in place. This unanticipated and unpredictable research has been noted by very few scholars internationally, partly because it is difficult to produce anything like a comprehensive understanding of what these new PhDs might propose. One of the sources in this context which refuses the often distracting debate about the required demonstration of 'new knowledge', is *Research, Relativism, and Truth in Art'* by Dena Shottenkirk (2007).

Shottenkirk spells out very simply that we must take for granted that a PhD in Fine Art produces new knowledge, as does any other doctoral study, and that the context within which the broader research arenas must recognize this is one where relativism is prevalent and most appropriate to understanding how PhDs in Fine Art function. This is very much the context for our selection of PhDs where relativism and the ensuing uncertainty of any fixed positioning, most particularly of theory, are axiomatic. Methodologies, for instance, are not subject to theory but have to be found within the research art practice: publications by Hannula (Kiljunen *et al.* 2002; Hannula *et al.* 2005; Hannula 2008), demonstrate a tenacious understanding of the fundamentals of doctorates, where methodologies are produced in this way. These texts illuminate how arts research relates to the experience of the researcher whose world is being drawn into the research project, and within which the formulation of the research is relative to the subject positioning of that researcher. In other words, there is a highly reflexive tension between author and context. The demands that this makes on artist researchers has not been fully recognized within the literatures, either within the UK, the EU or what is being developed in the US. One of our central sources in this area has been an issue of the Swedish journal Geist[1] on 'method', in which, like Hannula's publications, there is a clear understanding that art does make such demands. One of the most important findings within 'method' is the understanding of an 'aesthetics' of arts methodologies which arises from an artist being 'inside' the processes of research. A compelling argument by Malcolm Quinn in this book has lent insight to this process through psychoanalytic theory (Chapter 14). It might be useful to add a proviso, however, that while such theory adds to an understanding of artists' experience of research processes, it is also appropriate in our view to be cautious about the deployment of a theory to explain processes devised to unsettle it. This does not prevent us from underlining, like Quinn that the processes of art research are emphatically against standardization and involve what Roy Ascott (2008) calls the 'unmaking of the subject', that is, both the subject of enquiry and the researcher him/herself. Within both *Geist* and *Practice as Research: Approaches to Creative Arts Enquiry* by Barrett and Bolt (2007), there is a proposition that methods appropriate to the research practice of the arts are 'immanent', that is, not fixed, not predictive, but arising through and from the research itself. In other words, research 'for' art is particular to its author, its contexts and the capacity to reflexively unsettle.

Appropriately, in this context John Wood provides a generic understanding of the limitations of scholastic rigour in 'The Culture of Academic Rigour: does design research really need it?' (Wood 2000). He also provides an understanding of more empathetic models of writing. In Wood's view, in the context of design, this relates to designing for a specified client and 'thinking as, thinking for and thinking into their nominated reader'. This is useful to understanding artist researchers' thinking in relation to interpretation. It is not generally a question in Fine Art of the nominated reader, but it is very definitely a question concerning authorship, subjectivity and accountability to interpretation. It underlines what our research has revealed about the many ways in which artists' doctoral research touches on, refers to and critically engages with the contexts within which the research is conducted. Again, this is an aspect of the argument put forward by Wood in his analysis of how to develop more entrepreneurial, reflexive and more socially responsible researchers and to avoid what he sees as the diminishing incursions of bureaucracy and the developing schism between the academic library and the design studio. Ultimately what Wood and we will propose, and what we will substantiate, is writing which is empathetic to art(s) research, whose context is in production and the result of embodied learning which has the potential to be 'critically reflective and broadly relational and is above all dependent on human judgment' (Wood 2000: 56), that is, how the work might function and be of value.

The development of independent criticality is fostered by new journals such as *The Journal of Writing and Creative Practice* in the UK. This journal's mission is to explore and demonstrate 'the deep purpose of the writing task for Art and Design research students and to provide a forum for debate' (Lockheart and Wood 2008: 113). It is a journal which has a substantially relevant history, based in the Writing-Pad research project[2] and the subsequent conferences, symposia and development of its network. This is an example of the importance of careful networking and publication which we are now beginning to see in the UK. Another timely journal is *Art and Research: A Journal of Ideas, Contexts and Methods* which aims to engage in 'the dynamic and unresolved relationship between image and text, vision and language and writing and research' and determine the 'constitutive function of text in articulating the research process'.[3] Issues to date have been exemplary in their approaches to defining what might be research 'through' art.[4] Schottenkirk's research article on relativism and truth in art is simply one of many appropriate papers. The strength of this journal is its ongoing interviewing of artist researchers and descriptions of research projects, which demonstrate the many ways in which artists have approached the business of research. For instance, in the interview with Joanne Tathum, we can pick up precisely how Tathum began to use words 'to find, manipulate or establish a particular meaning or direction' for her work. She says:

> the writing that I initially wrote as an artist was about trying to forget about logic in a way and trying to move forward in a way which meant writing was more skilful or crafted. So there was an interim period where I was trying to use words in a way which I felt was useful or appropriate.
>
> (Thompson 2006)

The long process of Tatham beginning to understand how words work is set out in this interview and becomes part of her analysis of an artwork's 'ability to occur simultaneously in many different spaces at the same time, to be many things equally and exactly'. This is also part of her conscious understanding that there are structures for the interpretation of her work and that the use of written language was a key element of entering into a 'performative space of interpretation', that is a space which is socially responsive and reflexively exacting. Susan Melrose has also written several papers on performativity, and in 'Entertaining Other Options: restating theory in the age of practice as research', she outlines the 'multi-planed and multi-faceted schematics of writing and performance' (Melrose 2002). She also endorses the particularity of what she calls 'insider knowledges' which lead to 'performance theory-and-practice'. In other words, this is a conjoining of what we might call tacit knowledge and intellectual achievement. Notable in this essay is its analysis of a 'crisis' in writing which arises from the 'diverse sites of semiotic engagement of the performer, choreographer and spectator, etc.' This has been very little recognized in the literature on research in the arts and it arises out of paying attention to the event of theatrical performance. Melrose makes clear that we need 'a professional, writing-productive context and economy'. In the next section of this chapter, we will indicate why individual doctoral studies might make a contribution to the cultures of both postgraduate academic study and of professional productivity.

Case studies: doctorates in fine art

In this second part of the chapter we will present individual PhDs with a view to providing insight into the research process, final submission and what Melrose has called 'professional productivity'. It will be useful to say right from the start that our research is drawn from either supportive research cultures and/or knowledgeable, or appropriate and supportive research supervision, that is supervision which is fully conversant both with the student's area of art practice and with the cultures of postgraduate research. In our view it is important that PhD research is conducted within a substantial environment where a range of different research activities are undertaken and supported; it is not appropriate for the PhD researcher to enjoy an isolated position divorced from lively research cultures sufficiently robust to function alongside and in relation to other disciplines. This is the case with our first example drawn from the broad area of technical and technological innovation. However, like all our examples, it cannot be confined to the well researched area of research 'through' the arts and indicates how researchers themselves have moved the debate forward.

In the first PhD, the thesis/antithesis produces software art to induce social agency (Cox 2006). In other words, the artist has produced a software program to be activated by whoever encounters the PhD on completing reading of the written submission: thus, within the context of the five written chapters, setting out the definitions, the history, technology and ideological and political basis for the thinking behind the program, the reader is invited to operate another anti-thesis program using Perl. The latter will provide an internal contradiction and set up a provocative dialectic which puts into question what the written text has apparently proposed; it can be seen as a demonstration of critical reflexivity in action. While the results of the proposed action on the part of the reader/activist is difficult to describe, the action itself is not. That is the point. There are, after all, some actions and resulting experiences which are not fully accommodated by language.

The written part of the study is comprehensive and provides an overview of its field. It explores Marxist and Benjaminian ideas, alongside current theorists such as Friedrich Kittler, Kevin Kelly, Roy Bashkar, Inke Arns and Roy Ascott. It also presents a broad understanding of Chomsky's ideas about how language functions politically and socially. Overall, it conveys a clear understanding of how software *as* art can be proposed as something that can be both read, understood and executed to at least allow for the possibility of social change. It proposes its essential thesis within its own form by leaving the written component unfinished, that is without a full stop, so that it can express and induce a particular kind of labour and new knowledge when the reader activates the Perl program; the program will then induce a scrambling and a destabilizing within what has been presented. Through the careful proposal of what software art is and how it might function and how an emergent history might be described in relation to a complex technology and technological development, this thesis proposes ideas about the complexity of labour within current culture and opens itself to becoming a software praxis; through its formulated identity as artwork, action and coda it presents an inventive dynamic. This is complex. However, its simple, lucidly described purpose is carefully contextualized. It owes a great deal to what Walter Benjamin calls 'putting on display', that is, not describing or reducing the thesis to a completed contextualization, but actually presenting the PhD as a full, open and responsive art work (Cox 2006: 65). It becomes a kind of open source knowledge which entices the reader to become a new writer of programs. It is a without-end product. It is performative in the public realm, but also reflects its own structure and offers a critical site against the status quo of theory, which as Hannah Arendt posited, 'cannot alone transform society' (Cox 2006: 179). In other words, this PhD functions critically in the world, it is professionally didactic in that sense.

This is a dramatic point to start our examples and it will be useful to say straight away that the author of the PhD is a well-established artist/academic whose work has already been substantially published through exhibitions, conferences, books and curating. However, this is not the reason for its inclusion here. We propose it because it is aimed at a readership and a particular kind of social usefulness, and contains within it the distinctive tensions employed by many of the PhDs which we have studied. It suitably mirrors 'thinking as, thinking for and thinking into' a potential and active readership (Wood 2000). It also has the capacity to 'draw us beyond ourselves and throw us back upon our own subjectivity and agency', which remains a central theme in our research (Melville and Readings 1995). This is a theme pursued by Hannula *et al.* (2005) and is bedrock to a proper understanding of what the cultures of research in the arts stand to lose if they curtail the ambition of these individual studies in the name of increased homogeneity, parity and bureaucratic ordering. While we do not anticipate that art research will necessarily offer conventional reasoning or even ideas that appear useful, our evidence is of its distinctive and critical independence, most particularly from institutional norms of accountability, such as predictive forms of writing for the comprehensive literature review and subsequent argumentation.

Our second PhD example concerns the locus of decision which the author proposes at 'the limits of subjectivity' (Bowden 2006), that is at the limits of what an individual can do. This study demonstrates a sophistication concerning issues of authorship and the subject of enquiry in its relation to the author of it. We will not explore this here, but in describing the study, we hope that it will add to the insightful understanding of Susan Kozel in this book (Chapter 12), concerning consciously embodied research. It provides a set of chapters setting out Kierkegaard's ideas concerning the particularities of a singular decision in its urgent relation to the development of what we could call individual conscience and humanness. In the two central parts of the written component, Kierkegaard's theory is clearly presented. However, the particular nature of the PhD is exposed by the accompanying DVDs, the first after Chapter 2, and the second after Chapter 4, of part one. Both DVDs explore ideas concerning the subjectivity of the author and its centrality to any theoretical exegesis. In the first DVD she presents a fictional encounter between two philosophers each of whom is in fact an actor and both read scripts of her own devising concerning philosophical exchange about the nature of the decision. In the second, we see her describing the process of reading Michel Henry whose work is central to her analysis of radical subjectivity, still drawing on Kierkegaard as her main theoretical source. In this DVD, she talks of her life's interruptions to this singularly intellectual endeavour and playfully inscribes her own daily experience against the seamlessness of the written research. In this way, the researcher both provides substantive literary and theoretical contextualisation and playfully inventive discursions: the latter create a tension with the intellectual construction and provoke the reader/viewer to understand the anxiety and crisis involved in any profound decision-making process. It also inscribes the 'radical' subjectivity proposed by the researcher. It leads her to propound that 'subjectivity is not something that can be designated as a fixed category as such. It is rather like the point at which all external (and often contradictory) categories of life coincide: the biological, social, political, legal and so on' (Bowden 2006: 31). She also offers the compelling idea from Derrida that 'we know less than ever where to cut'; that is, we know less than ever about the relationship between experiencing and what is experienced, what we do and what we make of it; what it is to take any decision at all given that we know so little about how to make sense.

This PhD actively and inventively deploys philosophical writings in the enactment and presentation of the decision as a locus of subjectivity and *vice versa*. It clearly indicates crucial differences between philosophic discourse and art's work, that is how art functions in the world. The actual form of the thesis plays out the character of the decision as a locus of argument, self-identity, fiction, surmise or speculation. Like the first example, it is the result of sustained and exacting thoughtfulness about how to formulate a PhD in Fine Art, what and how it might be. It also provides a kind of 'synergy between the philosophical concerns and the form of their explication' (Bowden 2006: 1) and refuses any separation of theory and practice because it pursues a theorizing principle, that is theory put into action as it were, within the art work (cf. 'material ontology', Chapter 12).

The theorizing principle was proposed early in our researches into PhDs in Fine Art through the work of an artist whose PhD proposed an ethical praxis of reconsidering and re-envisioning relationships across racial and cultural difference within a sexualized and gendered subject identity (Mooney 1999). This study had the potential to provoke an exacting response from its readership who is called to understand the limits we impose on how we acknowledge and communicate with the 'other' – that is, with those who do not share the same racial, sexual and/or national identity and attendant value systems. In other words, it was a call to ethical action. Hannula has raised the question of ethics insistently (Kiljunen *et al.* 2002; Hannula *et al.* 2005; Hannula 2008). In our view there is both a strength and weakness in this approach in relation to arts research because while there is the need to justify what artists produce *as* research within the broader research and bureaucratic arenas, we must remember that there is an ethics in intellectual and artistic integrity itself.

One of the seminal PhDs which Macleod has studied at length, proposes its central thesis as both a 'terse economy', that is, the appropriate functioning of an art work as intellectual and political aspiration *and* hoax, for instance (Price 2000). Although this thesis should not readily be subsumed within its related histories of Duchamp-ism and Surrealist playfulness, what it does do is to assert the disinterestedness of art when it comes to its own purposes. We do not intend to dwell on the well-documented flirtations of key artists and movements with the current political climates of the day, but if we think briefly of Surrealists' endless provocations to new thought, we must recognize that much of this achievement was precisely because they ensured that their work was never overtaken by ideological or political niceties. It was always in pursuit of the new. Again, this is an idea which has been very little understood in the literatures on research in the arts. One useful source, however, is *Outside "The True": Research and Complexity in Contemporary Art Practice* by Peter Dallow (2005). In his essay, Dallow carefully proposes that if artists wish to continue challenging practices they are dependent on the anticipation that what they produce will be 'new' in the cultural environments within which they work, that there is indeed some continuum between what is produced as art research and the arenas of both contemporary arts and sociality. Price's PhD was submitted and awarded in 2000, and yet is still in progress. Within this period of time it has been transformed through the deployment of different media and presentation in group shows. This is important to note because there is so little understanding of the necessity of artist researchers being able to go on producing and presenting art subsequent to the production of the PhD. Indeed, we would say it is absolutely vital that research cultures provide support for this requirement. If PhDs are to substantiate claims for the production of more challenging art, then they will need arenas in which to be shown and some of them will be outside the existing gallery system because the most exacting PhDs do change the contexts within which they are produced. If we want to see interesting developments within our emerging research cultures, in other words, we must foster what artists are and have already produced *as* research.

The idea of an artists' professional continuum is established perhaps more easily within the more conventional area of research 'into' art (Frayling 1993). There are many examples internationally of Fine Art and Art History supervisory teams helping an artist to situate their practice through providing an appropriate history and theoretical context for their work. This has a relatively long history, particularly in the UK. An appropriate example, among many, is a study which explores the 'changing perceptual and material conditions of space, place and viewer in contemporary European abstract painting' (Khatir 2008). The structure is well-organized and cogent in relation to its intentions. Broadly there are three chapters on historical concepts and three on contemporary painting practice, with a final section on the artist's own work. The whole study is introduced through the visual presentation of the artist's current painting. It proposes what the author calls 'painting surface/painting and that which is not painting'. This is a difficult proposition, but through a careful presentation of the art historical, relevant art criticism, literary and critical theory, a substantive context is provided within which to understand and extend the debate about flatness and literalness. It also provides an understanding of new ideas concerning spatiality and the theatrical in relation to paintings which deal with the aesthetic of their precise location. The thesis provides an oscillation and exchange between the exhibition of art works and the written chapters, and it does not fall into the trap of providing sub-standard art history to substantiate its research (Elkins 2005a). Its careful organization owes much to appropriate supervision and the developed confidence of the painter, who at the end of the study, has demonstrated painting which is 'uncontained by its physical limits … responds not only to its immediate surroundings, but also to other artists' places, times and events'. It also presents ontological, topological and culturally conscious painting and opens up to 'new material, spatial, theoretical and philosophical possibilities' (Khatir 2008: 1). One can see from this example that such a PhD would convince of the probity of doctorates in Fine Art.

Relatively new indices to PhD theses in the UK, such as the Art and Design Index to Theses (ADIT), hosted by Nottingham Trent University, include many examples of similar research which is appropriately contextualized, both historically and theoretically. This is heartening and important, because there has been an established history in this area, most particularly because of the institutional relationship between Fine Art and Art and Design History. However, this is not where we have concentrated our research. The examples which have compelled our interest are more in tune with Fine Art, and have provoked formulations where the writing becomes a complementary element to the research intentions rather than providing a justification of them; they have also engendered a critical reflexivity which is not confined to a scrutiny of context but rather concentrates on a broader consideration of purpose and value.

The fifth example of doctorates which should compel our mutual interests is a study whose central concern was to rethink the concept of absence in relation both to art practice and the critical metaphysics of Jacques Derrida and Jacques Lacan (Roulstone 2006). On one level, like the first example, the written text provides a cogent set of exegeses on Derrida's thinking about absence and related ideas formulated by Lacan concerning what one might take to be real. The written text is deliberate, careful and intellectual in a conventional manner. However, the introduction prepares for what is a lack of engagement with the concept of absence within current art criticism and this is taken up at the end of section two within what the author/artist has called 'a first motion of absence' (Roulstone 2006: 38-41). One could describe this 'motion of absence' as an active kind of art criticism where the author apparently responds intuitively to a still from the video work of Douglas Gordon. However, it is also an enactment of the presence of an author who has turned critic and reflects back on contemporary art practice which presents and embodies concepts of absence. What this does is to propose another level of theorizing which might take for granted the phenomenological imperative of so many PhDs in Fine Art. However, within this context, it quite simply sets up a tension between theoretical exegesis and the research practice of the artist, whose paintings in the final part of the PhD provide what she describes as 'a faulty vehicle for absence'. This is not at all to offer an understanding of the limits of painting within the theoretical domain because the study has already proposed intimate critiques of the metaphysics of both Derrida and Lacan. It is simply to conjoin both theoretical positioning and the outcomes of artistic practice as unable to resolve the philosophical enquiry into what absence might be, also their equivalence in its non-predication upon a negative. In other words, art practice and theory view absence as also presence.

Overall this PhD posits the tensions and elisions and also the gaps between theories and art practices, both through criticism and intellectual exegesis and in relation to art works. It demonstrates the versatility of the concept of absence and its relevance to its core subject, which is the research paintings and what is proposed. The PhD deftly cuts into the space between the visual and theoretical, both in its form, through its three 'motions of absence' and its layered content. Its major generic findings can be said to be the deployment of paintings as equivalent to and in excess of theories. It is again a formulation of its subject, which is absence. It does not add to the available literature in a conventional sense but nudges towards a distinctive research formulation where existing theory is a substantial component of that which eludes its reach. It can be considered to be both a satisfactory PhD submission and one which like all our examples, proposes what a PhD might be within a field of research which is under construction and predicated on the uncertain. It is also a field which responds to current culture where no matter how dense and theoretically charged the cited sources, the artist is always subject to her own embodied, critical scrutiny and her actual and intellectual position in a given space and time. Indeed, one of the distinctive qualities of this and other PhDs studied is that the conventions for the systematic process of research programme and full delivery is extended so that the doctorate ceases to be contained within its submitted form, but takes on the subject of its enquiry. In the case of this PhD, a critical metaphysics is expounded and experienced through theoretical exegeses and the final submission of paintings: the painted surface of fleeting gesture and barely discernible mark becomes a palimpsest for the thesis. In other words, the whole thesis proposes absence: that is the four sections of the written text, its introductory explanations concerning absence in the visual arts, the exegeses on the metaphysics of Derrida and Lacan and the five 'motions of absence', the last of which presents the twenty research paintings themselves, altogether provides the thesis. Together they provoke ideas and 'new' thinking about how to present absence in relation to theory and practice and to refuse value distinctions.

Hitherto, there has been a paucity of current literature on research in the arts which sufficiently reveals the nature of art research and addresses its contemporary contexts, whatever these might be. One of the main reasons for this is the peculiar complexity of understanding how this works. However, the issue of *Geist* on method sets out how a broadly based approach through semiotics and hermeneutics lends considerable insight into the qualitatively distinctive methods of art research. One of the findings is a declaration of an 'aesthetics' of methodologies in the arts (Bärtås 2008). This is a formulation of research which is judged appropriate to its intentions 'inside' the research process and practice, and relates strongly to our last PhD example. Authors in *Geist* on method, point out clearly that art as research is also art as art, that there is a particular rhetoric which does not mean that art is subject to the rules of linguistic formulation, but that it is a kind of 'rhetoric in action' (Weckman 2008). This clearly mirrors all the key examples we have briefly explored and points up a field where translation, interconnection and the rhetorics of dissemination are important (Chapter 9). It is also worth mentioning that it highlights connections through individual doctoral studies and research projects. In this context, in Ascott (2008) we can see how the idea of the research subject being 'unmade' through the process of research relates directly both to our first example, who was supervised by Ascott, and to others. The relation of the individual researcher to permeable fields of influence has yet to be traced. It is surely a question, as it is with any research field of both conventional interconnections and consolidating of research areas and new discoveries. In this chapter we do not propose any new theorizing, but rather introduce the idea that individual doctoral research practices might prove to be key sources for the development of our various research fields. As a passing observation, in the editorial of *Geist* on method, insistence on the orientation and re-orientation involved in artistic research, the 'dynamic relationship where practice recurrently restructures its own conditions' adds to current conversations on arts research. The idea of a recurrent restructuring of the research project's conditions is central to a clear understanding of what it is to research as a consciously embodied subject.

We can pursue the theme of the embodied subject/researcher through numerous examples in the UK, some of which successfully negotiate the pitfalls of the autobiographic. We will pick out one doctorate from a feminist context, where much of this work stems, to highlight. This is a study which looks at and produces 'creative passages into the self' (Zia 2001). Its thesis is formulated through excerpts from the artist's journal, her diary, exegeses specifically on current feminist theory, play scripts, albums and paintings. Together they provide what the author calls a genealogy of the feminine. It is highly literary, poetic and almost constructs its own set of enacted literary and artistic myths. It deploys both writing and art works as generative sources to realize the self as 'a complex becoming between the numinous and the ordinary' (Zia 2001: 3). The artist proposes a poetic zone where the numinous is said to enter into the ordinary as a particular space, place and moment of becoming more truly 'a self'. Again, it would be relatively easy within the UK to find a range of examples of PhDs which posit an autobiographical narrative as central to research findings. However, within the processes of research, we have found that there are many examples of research formulation which posit complex questions of subjectivity within their research without recourse to literal autobiography: some of the most ambitious new work, which is still in progress, posits writing as a kind of unravelling of the subject in question and any authorial certainty within that process. If we take two examples of work by current artist researchers, we hope to demonstrate how each of them provides thinking which does 'force us back on our own agency and take us beyond ourselves'. In this endeavour, writing becomes instrumental to what cannot be fully grasped through a satisfactory conclusion or watertight hypothesis. What we are given is a possibility for new thought, new speculation and new and provocative insights into what it might be to think as a creative practitioner.

In the first study, the intention is to throw light on the philosophical problem of what art might be and to show the limits of the philosophical issues drawn on to sustain any creative practice in visual art (Chapman, University of Reading). It is a highly abstract analysis of the contemporary moment which sees 'rigorous thought on creativity undermined by institutions, modelled and remodelled by market capitalism'. Its base line is a politics of engagement with the institution, but only with the intention of understanding the unresolved relationship between art making and research, and the requirement for the singular and unpredictable configuration of these terms. The research employs a key theoretical source in Deleuze (also Bergson through Deleuze), in the construction of its own distinctive self-referencing method. Like key published sources we have already mentioned, notably Barrett and Bolt (2007), we propose the method is in the research and changes as new ideas are encountered. Like our first PhD example, there is an elision of the research, its sources and its presence as art work; it is proposed as a 'writing-artefact'. Writing, of course, is central to the production of its developing thesis, the positing of art as creative method. In the development of its findings, fictional characters and aliases' discourses are set beside Deleuzian theory in such a way that there is no status differentiation and no boundary construction between unstable self-identification and theory. Each is conjoined in what Deleuze proposes as a self differing, that is, at the limits of its own identification. In simpler words, artist researcher, fictional characters and theories are formulated within writings which set them in tension, so that no one intellectual and/or embodied positioning can be fully grasped. In this way, the philosophical problem of research through art is thrown into relief. We freely acknowledge that such ambition can only flourish in substantial and supportive research cultures. The culture within which this PhD has been undertaken is a cross-disciplinary Philosophy and Fine Art culture at University of Reading, UK, headed up by an artist who also writes as a theorist (Alun Rowlands) and a philosopher who writes on art and is art trained (Jonathon Dronsfield). The culture is reinforced through symposia where researchers from both these disciplines are invited to enter into prolonged conversations about what it is they do. This must sound unalterably commonplace, but it is not. In our experience, for many researchers in the UK, the EU and Australia, to say nothing of what is proposed in the US, research takes place in stilted research environments, sometimes dominated by researchers from a related discipline and those for whom the literary and the written thesis is of paramount importance. In this chapter, through the selected case studies, we have proposed simply that writing is one component of the PhD. In our view it is fundamentally important, but its identity can also be challenging. As our examples show, it is not easy to predict how writing should be approached; it is part of what we would hope, is a precise formulation of a research project which might take many different forms and employ many different methods in pursuit of its ideas. That is its essential and critical strength.

It is perhaps appropriate that our last PhD example will again approach the question of decision, this time from the point of view of the performance writer (Greenwood, Kingston University). In this last example, a performance artist is considering ideas of mediation, re-reading, re-contextualization and notions of self-surveillance in pursuit of what a decision might be within performance and through performative writings. Research methods involve the construction of poetic texts, manifestos, both textual and performance work and sustained 'endurance' demonstrations of *la durée*, that is both a compression and extension of time within a performance (cf. Bergson). It involves an ontology of performance which is recorded, documented and participates in a circulation of representations. It is not intended to present labour as distinct from any other, but proposes and examines the nature and economy of labour itself, that is, the labour of the performer, who might play out scenarios of gambling, for instance. It is again a question of the artist attempting to resist ideas where capitalist modes of thought are always and already embodied within the systems within which he operates. In relation to this, the individual artist's performative texts enter into a series of mediations and reproductions of art as performed in time and those spaces where it happens to be, also in response to what is common to social relationships. The study is socially responsive and active in that sense.

We might suggest that even through this brief insight into two PhDs which are still in progress, the self-critiquing, the 'unmaking' or critiquing of the subject of enquiry, runs through each study like the lettering through seaside rock. It is a reflexive gaze which is at the heart of the profession and practices of art and although it might owe much to the enquiries of sources such as Donald Schön and its various proponents, it is not a question of professionalization so much as a working at its limits, because this is what PhDs in Fine Art can offer the profession. They also take the discipline of Fine Art to its furthest limits and begin to form a gap between researching artists, what they produce, and the cultures of contemporary art. Of course, they will draw on their contemporary cultures, but just as a scientist, a mathematician or an anthropologist will hope to inhabit a framed space in order to conduct their disinterested research enquiries, it is also necessary for artists to feel confident that they can take their practices to spaces which may not exist because they are not already predicted within the art world. Barrett and Bolt (2007) has made the case very forcibly to see art research as a resistant and creative force for change. Future possibilities are legion but only with the proviso that we take seriously the question of research environments, the development of cultures and appropriate research training. This is primarily because the reflexive critiquing involved in these PhDs is endlessly demanding and in ways which are difficult to predict and thus to manage.

Building research cultures

Central to an appropriate development of substantial research cultures is the active presentation and dissemination of PhDs. Our research has found that where this is the case, research groups have together developed the requisite confidence to build up a defined culture with at least a core of shared ambitions. While this may not be completely identifiable with a specific field, such as performative writing or new technologies, or indeed schools of thought such as continental aesthetics, it is at the moment underestimated how important it is to see group cohesion, shared understandings and mutual support as instrumental to the furtherance of research cultures. In the UK we are fortunate that in the area of performance in particular, the practice of networking is well established by appropriate websites such as PARIP[5] It hosts challenging papers, extensive bibliographies, summaries of research symposia, conference and projects as well as well-maintained descriptions of current PhDs and research fellowships, etc. PARIP is of course well funded, and has worked within the terms of the Arts and Humanities Research Council (UK), which is often difficult when the discipline is outside Humanities departments. With appropriate funding, PARIP has been able to give guidance on the development of research cultures and publish reports, such as that by Nelson and Andrews (2003). This report gives substantive advice on admissions, research development, the balance between the written and practical outcomes; standards and expectations, research methodologies and the role of the written. It also offers advice on examination and examiners, as well as supervision and supervisory issues and although its description of the role of writing is too prescriptive in our view, it is the kind of report that could prove indispensable to the development of appropriate research cultures in the arts.

It might be useful in this context, to take a side look at a very different report. In this report, James Elkins (2005a) posits the idea of five kinds of written dissertation: first, the dissertation is art history; second, the dissertation is philosophy or art theory; third, it is art criticism; fourth, it is natural history or economics or any of the fields outside the humanities; or fifth, it is a technical report. Whilst we do not have space to give a fuller account of these types, there is ample evidence that the PhDs cited in our chapter do not simply fall into one type. Indeed, in this text, Elkins proposes that the technical report is an appropriate description for the PhD cited earlier which provides the 'terse economy' of writing and making an individual piece of work, which might also constitute 'a hoax' (Price 2000). It cannot therefore be placed within the context of a technical report; that would be to repress its complex provocations. We should at this point be cautious about categorization. We propose that considerable work still needs to be done to present PhDs more fully and to attend to them more carefully. Publications by Mika Hannula, have begun this process. The results of such attention to the detail of submissions have lent insight into what writing is, for instance:

> Writing is simultaneously thinking and doing, both observing the world and creating it … writing itself is one of the forms in which reality is created.
>
> Writing as a way of thinking, doing research and reporting it has to find a way of treating language in the pluralist manner so that the uniqueness of artistic experience is not lost when our thinking about it is communicated!
>
> (Hannula *et al.* 2005: 4, 37)

It is easy in this context to begin to identify how writing might be developed within research communities. Some of the most useful resources to build up such an understanding are the journals briefly mentioned in the first part of the chapter.

In addition to *Art and Research* we must place the *Journal of Visual Art Practice,* and *Working Papers in Art and* Design[6] hosted by the University of Hertfordshire (UK). It is here that debates about, for instance, art works *as* research are proposed. If a potential or existing supervisor were to deploy the papers published in the latter by Scrivener, Reilly, Smith and Harrison, they would be able to approach the question of how, if and in what circumstances, art work counts as research from a number of different perspectives and discipline bases. This is useful because it takes the supervisor and those he or she supervises or intends to supervise, outside the intimacies of an actual or potential relationship and draws her/him into an arena of scholarly exchanges, carefully managed and appropriately presented, also accessible for international engagement. Active networking and cross-disciplinary exchanges almost inevitably enhance ambition as well as tempering an eccentric research frame. Earlier we looked briefly at some aspects of literature in the field, where one of the key sources was Borgdorff's understanding of both the urgency and scope of current debates in 2006. These resources are appropriately complemented by websites and journals such as *Art and Research* which draws to itself artists who have undertaken PhDs, artists scholars of international reputation, as well as offside contributions which have caught the eye of an editor. Editors ensure that the journal is a suitable vehicle and forum for debate and that its various contributions attest to 'the deep purpose of their writing task' (Lockheart and Wood 2008: 113). In the case of the *Journal of Writing and Creative Practice*, the editors also attest to: 'The style and beauty of a dialogue' conducted by artists and designers (Lockheart and Wood 2008: 115). We would hope that the PhDs that we have briefly outlined in the second part of this chapter will attest to the same.

Concluding comment

In this chapter, we have touched on some of what we take to be the key issues for an appropriate recognition and development of PhD research cultures in Fine Art. We have addressed the role of writing, described the role of the researcher and his or her embodied and active relationship to and within the research, and touched on the implications of this. We have described the submissions themselves. On one level, we have placed ourselves, just like our key research sources, in a paradoxical position of wanting to refuse any imagined rules, guidelines and protocols for the presentation of PhD research studies in Fine Art and to produce convincing evidence of research. It has been our intention to enter into a reflexive space of enquiry to give credence to the nature of these critically reflexive and complicated PhDs cited here.

In relation to the literature in the field, there are guide books which cover some areas of our research, for instance, Barrett and Bolt (2007), Graeme Sullivan (2005) and Gray and Malins (2004). However, in our view, there is still so much that such guides have been unable to identify in their drive towards giving practical assistance and historical or theoretical substantiation within these developing research fields. This is not our intention. We hope that whoever reads this chapter will be inspired as we have been to attend to PhDs in Fine Art, to their methodological form, to their provocations and their risky and uncertain outcomes; we hope that the complex role of writing within these studies can be more fully understood and that writing can be more readily explored and developed within the PhD. We hope too that the insistent conventions of argument and the preceding comprehensive literature review, as well as the assumption of objectivity, might at least be jostled; in this way PhDs in Fine Art could prove useful to the broader arenas of research. For instance, as proposed by Haseman (2006b), research in the creative arts will add to existing methods and definitions of *qualitative research*. This is partly due to the constant testing out and re-planning involved in the processes of critical reflexivity, such as an insistent questioning of purpose and value. This distinctive internal critiquing, whose exacting qualities predict questions about authorship, subjectivity and an ethics of engagement, has become a central theme to this chapter almost against our will. It can be identified with what Barrett has called an 'emergent method'. The concept of an emergent method strongly relates to the status of Fine Art as a permeable discipline which does not so much promote inter-disciplinarity, but simply rejects boundaried discipline-ness. Fine Art is of its essence an open and speculative discipline within which artists apply multi-sourced methods and *bricolage*-like approaches to their research enquiries. It might be useful finally, to remind ourselves that this is in no way new or radical, in that this is precisely what artists have always done.

In an essay by White (2008), we are reminded of Robert Smithson's work which, if we are to be engaged in it, invites us to be involved in an understanding that the project itself carries within it 'the seeds of its own destruction'; that it is 'an openly contingent value system or cultural context'. It is also something of 'an architecture of fiction'. What Smithson produced are narrative fragments from an uncertain authorial point of view. His work remains of enduring interest to contemporary artists. It also reflects certain aspects of what art does: it disrupts narrative; it re-enacts; it makes direct address; it employs fiction: art employs its strategies to provoke what an artist believes at the moment of conceiving or making to be new (Leighton 2006). Whether we conceive it as new in the context of the PhD remains firmly in artists' hands. Or, does it?

We hope that we have shown that writing is integral to the PhD research process: that through the documenting, charting, formulating or even fictionalizing of the research enquiry, writing can convince us that we have gained new insights and understandings and the potential to be critically active in our own contexts. As Shottenkirk (2007) proposes, we need not worry overly about the concept of new knowledge; by taking artist researchers on, we have done so on the understanding that they will provide new knowledge, however, whether we accept that they have given us new knowledge or insight into our worlds (institutional or otherwise), remains subject to the politics of our environments and possibly whether we have been able to retain open minds.

Notes

1 http://geist.se/ (accessed 2 February 2010).
2 http://www.writing-pad.ac.uk/ (accessed 31 January 2010).
3 http://www.artandresearch.org.uk/v1n1/v1n1editorial.html (accessed 15 February 2010).
4 We follow Borgdorff's (2006) adoption of research 'through', rather than Frayling's (1993) research 'for' arts practice.
5 http://www.bris.ac.uk/parip (accessed 2 February 2010).
6 http://sitem.herts.ac.uk/artdes_research/papers/wpades/index.html (accessed 15 February 2010).

21

RESEARCH TRAINING IN THE CREATIVE ARTS AND DESIGN

Darren Newbury

Introduction

Since the 1990s considerable work has gone into developing resources and programmes to support arts and design-based doctoral students, who are now an established, if still relatively small, feature of the international academic landscape. To be provocative, I might argue that whilst the epistemological debate around artistic research has developed its own dynamic, the more significant work has taken place at the coalface, dealing with the needs of students as they attempt to shape projects which answer the twin demands of academic rigour and significance to the field. However, rather than recount the early history of this 'emerging' field, I want to take the opportunity provided by this chapter to try and discern a sense of what good practice in research training looks like and to consider some of the challenges we face as we look to the future. This is not to argue that history is not important; of course the particular historical development of arts and design education has contributed significantly to the contexts within which the discussion of arts-based research has come into being. But others in this volume have had the opportunity to tackle this topic more fully and in this chapter I want to place my emphasis on the present and the future.[1]

The chapter is organized into four main sections. First, I want to start by setting out a number of assumptions on which the discussion is based. There have been long, and often heated, debates about the nature of research in the creative arts and design, and its relationship to other fields in which doctoral study has a much longer history. It is not my intention here to dwell on these debates, but it is important for readers to know the position from which I am writing, because the conclusions I reach are grounded in specific ideas about what constitutes research in general and doctoral research in particular.

Second, I want to consider what it means to be a trained researcher in our field. After all, if a doctorate is a training in research, then those of us who organize such programmes should be able to specify what it means to offer training for doctoral students in the creative arts and design, and articulate the outcomes of such training.

What are the skills and the areas of knowledge that define competence as a researcher in the creative arts and design? I propose a number of headings under which we might group core research skills and consider the implications for arts research. There has also been much effort on the part of national and international bodies (for example, organizations such as Research Councils UK) to define the complement of generic research skills expected at doctoral level. I consider the challenge these represent to the sufficiency of project focused research training.

Third, moving from content to delivery, the chapter reflects on the organization of research training. How can research training programmes be implemented to meet the specific needs of doctoral students in the creative arts and design? What are the practical issues those setting up doctoral research training programmes need to consider? My intention here, as elsewhere in this chapter, is to consider the practical and pedagogical issues involved, as well as the philosophical principles which underpin specific provision.

Finally, I want to consider the challenges for the future. What work needs to be undertaken to further develop the curriculum for doctoral studies? Here I look specifically at three areas: interdisciplinarity; the relationship between arts practice and writing; and research ethics. It is important that the emphasis on generic research skills does not work against the development of more specialist methodological training. Whilst there is a need for a common discourse around research and research training, greater confidence and maturity in the field should lead to more, not fewer, institutional specialisms, each with their own unique flavour.

Creative arts and design research and the PhD[2]

The discussion below regarding the content and shape of doctoral research training flows from an underlying set of ideas about what it means to conduct research. It is necessary therefore for me to state how I define research in general and doctoral research in particular. A paper I wrote previously on this topic prompted the criticism that it sought to impose a form of logical empiricism on research in the visual arts and design (Bell 2006).[3] As this was at the time, and remains, a long way from my intention, and indeed my own research practice, I would like to try and avoid such confusion here. As I understand it, the confusion resulted from my attempt to offer a working definition of research that might be useful for students to think with and around (and whilst I did not say as much, I would not have a problem with efforts to think against it). The purpose was to prompt students to step back from the investigative practices they were engaged in and to see how similar, or not, they might be to practices of research in other disciplines. And, importantly, to begin to develop a language with which to speak about research. If I was attempting to do the same now, I would suggest that research requires the presence of two key components – namely ideas and evidence – and their articulation through argument. At the most general level, these represent the necessary and sufficient conditions that qualify an activity as research. Ideas are necessary because they give shape and meaning to the research material. Evidence without ideas is simply information or meaningless data (to some extent the very term 'evidence' already implies that the shaping through ideas has begun). Evidence is necessary because without it ideas are mere speculation; in a sense ideas require the material of evidence on which to feed otherwise they simply slip away. Research is the work of assembling ideas and evidence and bringing them into a productive relationship. To avoid misunderstanding, I want to be clear this is not to suggest a linear relationship between ideas and evidence. It is, rather, dialogical; in creative arts research (though not only here) one may literally manufacture or bring the evidence into being, and reshape it as one brings it into a meaningful relationship with evolving ideas (though of course as any practitioner knows the material world is not infinitely malleable; there is both objectivity and rigour in the process). Nor am I seeking to prescribe the shape ideas or evidence might take. Evidence could be experiential, visual or numerical amongst other forms, and primary or secondary; ideas could be written down, or embodied in artefacts or performances. My argument is not dissimilar to that offered by Mark Johnson (Chapter 8) who, following John Dewey, puts forward a definition of research as: 'ongoing inquiry aimed at the transformation of a problematic situation into one that is more harmonious, fluid, expansive, and rich in meaning'. The 'problematic situation' here might be reconceived as troubling evidence in search of ideas; the work of research is the struggle to bring ideas to bear on the situation and to derive meaning from it; the process should be conceived as proactive, it is one of making the situation meaningful, rather than simply discovering meaning that is latent in the situation. It is important to recognize the interdependence between ideas and evidence. I am not sure I would name something as research in which I could not perceive both of these components.

It may be argued that there is a need for explicit research questions. To a large extent I would not disagree. Research ideas and arguments often start life as questions: questions that emerge from reading, questions that emerge from experience or observation, questions that are given by a supervisor or funding body. Sometimes these questions are poorly articulated, but without some sense of questioning there cannot really be research. However, explicit questions or at least the right questions are not always clear at the outset of a research project. Initial questions often change shape during the project, indeed sometimes one gets very near the end of the project before realizing that the questions one started with are wrong-headed; and as I always tell students, the work of formulating a research question is part of the process of researching, not something which takes place prior to research. This is particularly true of qualitative forms of inquiry.

High quality and original research of course requires good/original ideas (or questions) and good/original evidence, by the standards and in the forms that are meaningful to a particular research community; something which I think applies across the arts and humanities as well as the sciences, whether or not we use a different language to talk about them. To be a researcher one needs not only a solid grasp of the ideas current in a particular field, but an understanding of the evidence that supports those ideas, the techniques by which it has been gathered and so on. Research training, therefore, provides a critical insight into the process of knowledge production.

At this level, in my view, research in the arts does not depart significantly from research in any other field of enquiry. The differences lie in the kinds of ideas and questions being explored and the nature of the evidence that is brought to bear upon them. That, indeed, is why I see no harm in comparative thinking, and reject the special pleading that has on occasion accompanied discussions of arts-based research.

370

For example, artists, filmmakers and musicians who are exploring the possibilities their particular medium affords for the creation of new forms of expression or communication are therefore, by this definition, engaged in a research process. The originality of the end result and its contribution to the field are not established through rhetorical claims, but with reference to the evidence provided before one's eyes and ears. It goes without saying that not all claims to originality are well evidenced.

However, before we go further it is important to acknowledge that just because something is research it does not make it worth a doctorate. A doctorate is a particular form of research, one which requires a kind of methodological self-consciousness and reflexivity that is more pronounced than in most of one's subsequent research. (This is one of the reasons why most PhDs, even many very good ones, require significant work to become equally good books; and maybe the same applies to PhD arts practice). Why is this the case? I would suggest there are two distinctions here that need to be appreciated: the first, between academic and non-academic forms of research; and the second, between academic research in general and the PhD.

Academic research, of which the PhD is a particular subset, brings with it a particular set of values, at the heart of which are commitments to methodological transparency and communicability. Academic researchers are required not just to present their findings, but to account for the research journey; in some cases as a well documented set of experiments or exercises in data collection, in others as a series of intellectual engagements with ideas, theories and practices. It is at this point, rather than in the act of research itself, that the culture of arts and design practice often has difficulty accommodating to the culture of the academy. The commitment to opening up and accounting for the research process and, related to it, the collective project of building the knowledge base and scholarly discourse of the subject, whilst an explicit commitment for the academy, is not of equal importance for professional practice. Of course the relationship between the creative professions and the academy is not set once and for all, indeed arguably it is in a period of profound change, an issue I will return to below; and, to be fair, many areas of professional practice in the creative arts already overlap with the academy, so the extent to which there is a clash of values varies considerably (see Chapter 5 for an extended discussion of this issue). However, this distinction is important to understanding the imperatives of academic research.

The second distinction – between the PhD and academic research in general – occurs quite simply because the PhD has a pedagogical imperative: it is about learning to do research. Most, if not all, researchers and practitioners reflect on and review what they do (more or less explicitly, depending on the context), but they do not always offer this reflection up for inspection in a way that the form of the PhD demands. Just think of that classic examination question 'how would you do things differently if you were starting this project again' – reflection is not optional. This is quite different from forms of criticism which take the object as immutable. To my mind both within doctoral research, and more broadly, we need (following Raymond Williams) to develop a critical approach that, 'instead of reducing works to finished products and activities to fixed positions, is capable of discerning in good faith, the finite but significant openness of many actual initiatives and contributions' (Williams 1977: 114).[4]

Putting these elements together, a creative arts PhD, therefore, is a training in research through which the student develops *a reflexive competence in the procedures for handling and generating ideas and evidence* appropriate to the specific field of study and demonstrates *the capacity for making an original contribution* to that field of study. The stress is most often on the first word of the phrase 'original contribution', but the latter is no less important, indicating that the knowledge produced through research has a value for a community beyond the individual researcher. Now this does not sound very different, if at all, to the definition of the PhD in any other subject, but then that is precisely the point. I want to emphasize that this is not to impose a kind of methodological uniformity on arts-based research. Nothing could be further from my intention. It is simply to establish a robust definition of doctoral research.[5]

At this point I think I should try to articulate what I believe to be the central value of research in the creative arts and design. This is a somewhat tricky thing to do, perhaps even unwise, especially given my dislike of general theories. Creative arts and design research does not exist as a single coherent programme, and inevitably the specific value of each research project has to be argued on its own terms. I subscribe to a school of thought that argues against the promotion of a single research approach or paradigm to fit all research in the creative arts and design. The pursuit of some abstract notion of pure art or design research methods often seems to me misguided; beg, borrow and steal seems a more productive strategy. The field is by its very nature methodologically diverse, even at times promiscuous. This is a position that finds support in the available record of completed PhDs over the past fifty years. In short, there are many and diverse questions in our fields that justify research and it would seem counter-productive to seek to limit the tools available to respond to them. But I think at a broad level one can argue that a significant contribution of creative arts research is to articulate knowledge from a practitioner perspective, often within arenas of interdisciplinary or multidisciplinary enquiry. By this I do not mean that all researchers need to be practitioners, or vice versa, though many do occupy this position productively, but rather that research has a close proximity to practice.[6] If I take my own area of research – photography – whilst I do not consider myself a photographic practitioner (or at least not any longer), nevertheless, in my research I have sought to develop a methodology that, as I might put it, 'does not forget that photographs are made by photographers', and that therefore attends closely to photographers' accounts. More broadly, any arts-based research should seek 'an attentive understanding of what artists [or designers] actually do when they make work' (Bell 2006). However, if this definition gives a central position to practice and the practitioner, I think we have to remember that this cuts both ways. Its central value depends on its articulation; whilst this might not necessarily be a key value for practice, as I have indicated above it absolutely is for research in the academy. Practitioner-researchers, and anyone who considers themselves to be doing research that is practice-led or practice-based, have to make a commitment to articulating the knowledge they have in forms with which others can engage. And where this research is contributing to debates within a broader public sphere and/or seeking public funds they also have to be prepared to articulate this knowledge for non-specialist audiences. Here again we return to the question of what it means to be a researcher and to the importance of research training.

Defining the trained researcher

At doctoral level, even in well established research fields, the emphasis on the research degree as a process of training is relatively recent. This is more pronounced in the United Kingdom, where the PhD places the emphasis on the doctoral project, in comparison with its US counterpart, where doctoral programmes typically have coursework requirements. Nevertheless, the focus on research skills and their delivery is an aspect of doctoral training that has attracted international interest. Estelle Phillips, one of the authors of the well known book *How to Get a PhD* (Phillips and Pugh 1987), whose own doctoral project examined the PhD as a learning process, was one of the pioneers of this way of thinking about PhD study. She recalled the degree of scepticism that greeted her initial proposal that one might examine the PhD as a generic process of learning. History was on the side of Phillips' argument and subsequent research on the quality and completion rates of the British PhD has by stages led to an increasing degree of specification of the research skills expected of the doctoral graduate.

On the basis of the argument I have put forward thus far, I want, therefore, to propose four headings under which to group the skills and competencies central to a definition of the trained researcher: literature, critical evaluation and synthesis; research conceptualization; research methodology; and communication. I shall look at each of these in turn, and in doing so consider some of the issues they raise for research training in the creative arts and design.

Literature, critical evaluation and synthesis refers to the ability to handle existing research material. It includes knowledge of the sources of literature and contextual research that comprise the research field within which the student is working. In the creative arts and design, this can be far from straightforward. There is no single literature database for research students to consult, indeed the information architecture is complex, and in some cases downright messy. For example, the importance of practice outputs in particular areas presents problems of retrieval. Students therefore need to show both creativity and tenacity in mapping out the research terrain within which they are seeking to establish their own project. But information is not knowledge and therefore the ability to process existing material is also of central importance. Material needs to be reviewed critically and competing theories, approaches and accounts need to be set in relation to each other in order to develop a critical understanding of the research context. Finally, the trained researcher needs the ability to identify and select material from appropriate sources synthesizing them to inform and support the research enquiry. This goes beyond reconstructing the history of investigation into particular ideas and towards developing a position in relation to existing research, thereby establishing a rationale for a research proposal.

Research conceptualization refers to the ability to identify specific research questions, problems or opportunities that are worthy of enquiry. This includes a degree of original thinking and the ability to initiate ideas and lines of investigation. At its highest level one might speak of a research imagination. Creativity in this context is not about beginning with a blank sheet of paper, but rather envisaging the opportunities for reconfigured or expanded understanding in the light of what has gone before. Research conceptualization also includes the skills and discipline that go beyond the initial moment of conception, and which enable the researcher to formulate and develop an idea into something researchable. For example, a researcher needs to have the ability to refine the question and draw appropriate parameters. There is clearly a high degree of interdependence between the skills involved in conceptualizing one's own research project and those involved in critically evaluating prior research. Whilst it is common to think of research building incrementally on what has gone before, for students in the arts and humanities the less linear metaphor of a conversation may be more useful. A research field can be thought of as an ongoing conversation about particular topics or ideas; a researcher needs to listen attentively to what is being said if they are to make a worthwhile intervention in the debate.

Research methodology refers to the knowledge and skills required to select and apply appropriate methods to carry through the research project. In creative arts research this is an area of some controversy: just what are the appropriate methods for our field? Arguments around methodology have tended to present a dichotomy, with, on the one hand, the art and design researcher adopting methodologies from other disciplines in order to satisfy the requirements of a generic notion of research, and on the other the development of art and design specific methods. We need to get beyond this rather limiting dichotomy to develop a more fruitful and less defensive way of thinking about methodology. Doctoral research training should develop students' awareness of methodology,[7] as the working out in practice of the relationship between theory and method in their own research, as well as an appreciation of alternative methods. This certainly involves an introduction to different research approaches and some comparative thinking, but I am not suggesting a universal methods curriculum. Those who argue for methodology training as the comparative study of method need to reveal their own methodological position and specify what they mean by 'comprehensive research methods training', what they see as central and where they draw the boundaries, if they are not to run students ragged trying to cover too much ground. The quality of the engagement with methodological argument is in my view more important than the number of methods. As I have indicated above, research in the creative arts and design is methodologically diverse and I do not believe it is possible to design a single research methods curriculum that works across its full breadth. Rather it would be preferable for individual programmes to develop in specific methodological directions, including making particular interdisciplinary or cross-disciplinary engagements, an issue I want to return to below.

I would also place under this heading the need for research students to develop an awareness of research ethics. There are certainly areas of overlap between ethics and methodology, and ethical awareness contributes to a general methodological understanding.

Communication may appear the most straightforward of the four areas of research skills outlined here, though it too presents a number of issues for creative arts research. The ability to communicate one's findings to one's peers is undeniably central to academic research. This includes not just the ability to structure a coherent argument, linking ideas and evidence through the written word, but also, importantly for arts-based researchers, the ability to make skilled use of visual material to express ideas. This includes competence in various forms of research presentation, such as the delivery of conference presentations and the writing of journal articles, to the creation of exhibitions. However, what is perceived as the tyranny of the written word in the academy (more perceived than actual one might argue) has led, unproductively, to arguments against writing generally, and the PhD thesis specifically, as suitable forms for the communication of arts-based research. I want to return to the question of writing below, so I will limit my comments here, but given the importance of communication and methodological transparency to the definition of academic research it is important to acknowledge that notwithstanding the significance of visual, spatial and sensory forms of communication to research in the creative arts and design, communication through language remains an important element. Practice can without question form a significant element within a PhD submission, but I am sceptical of claims that it is possible to dispense with words entirely and still meet the requirements of the PhD form. It is worth noting that this is one area where students in the creative arts and design often need more support and encouragement. This can be partly a result of lack of familiarity with, and facility in, certain forms of academic communication. It can also be a lack of willingness born out of a conflict between the value research places on transparency and clarity of argument, and the autonomy practitioners wish to grant the object. Similarly, in her contribution to this volume, Annette Arlander notes the lack of 'habits of documentation' in the performing arts and attributes this, in part at least, to 'cherishing the perishable moment' (Chapter 18). Whilst there is a genuine debate to be had about the forms of communication and documentation, this can sometimes simply be a result of confusion over the purpose of writing within some kinds of arts-based PhD, which should not reduce a creative work to mere illustration.

Having begun to define the skills that are required to define the trained researcher, and considered some of the issues these raise for arts-based research training, it is important to acknowledge one way in which this framework could be problematized. So far I have worked from a definition of research outwards, but over recent years there has been an attempt to conceptualize the doctorate from the opposite direction, working back from what might be required of an individual trained at the highest academic level to a more appropriate doctoral experience. This approach is based on the argument that, whatever the output of the doctorate in terms of a research contribution, it has in some way been failing to equip graduates with the skills required for the complex modern world outside the academy, in which many of them will find themselves working. As a result, an increasingly wide range of generic and transferable skills are now considered part of a comprehensive doctoral training programme. The UK Research Councils Joint Skills Statement is an outcome of this approach. It contains seven skills areas: research skills and techniques; research environment; research management; personal effectiveness; communication skills; networking and teamworking; and career management. Of these seven categories, three at least are only implicit within the framework I have set out, and many could not be derived from a definition of research alone, for example: 'understand one's behaviours and impact on others when working in and contributing to the success of formal and informal teams' (RCUK 2001).

Although it does not appear to have explicitly informed the RCUK Joint Skills Statement, there is another more subtle argument, developed by others in this volume (e.g. Chapter 4) that supports a broader skills agenda. The particular appeal for researchers in the creative arts and design of what is referred to as 'Mode 2' or transdisciplinary or practice-based research, that is research which takes place in the context of application rather than within a narrow disciplinary framework, also implies the need for broader skills, including the ability to communicate to non-specialists and collaborate with non-academic partners. Along with Borgdorff (2009a), I do not believe that there is any necessary or straightforward alignment between research in the creative arts and design and 'Mode 2' (I also do not see a sharp divide between the two modes, hence my placing of them in quotation marks), but it does nevertheless further contextualize the research skills debate.

What are the implications of these arguments for the framework I have set out above, and for creative arts research more generally? The key issue to consider is to what extent these skills are embedded in the programmes of research being followed by doctoral students. Clearly, this will vary according to which skills are being discussed, but I think it is useful to distinguish three levels: first, those skills which are central to research and which all students would be expected to develop as part of the conduct of their doctoral research, for example 'the ability to recognize and validate problems'. Second, generic skills which are important to the student's development as an effective researcher, for example the ability to 'develop and maintain co-operative networks and working relationships with supervisors, colleagues and peers, within the institution and the wider research community'. Third, those skills which go beyond what might be considered essential for successful research, but which would nevertheless be desirable for a highly qualified individual, for example the ability to 'effectively support the learning of others when involved in teaching, mentoring or demonstrating activities'. If one defines the doctorate as requiring a *reflexive competence*, then at the first and second levels, it is desirable for the skills to be embedded within doctoral programmes. That is not to say there is not further work to be done here of course. Whilst a programme that did not equip students with first order skills would clearly to failing at a very basic level, the development of doctoral students as competent members of an academic research community does require thinking beyond the individual research project and towards a sense of the research career. I would argue that active researchers are best placed to guide students in this area, but this kind of broader skills development does require a deliberate and conscious effort, and does not happen simply by a process of osmosis. The recent emphasis in UK Higher Education on extending personal development planning (PDP) to doctoral students represents an attempt to focus both supervisors and students on this aspect of research training. Skills at the third level, however, need to be treated in a different, if complementary, way. Research supervisors may not be best placed to deliver such skills training, and, furthermore, not all students are likely to benefit equally from such provision. The assumption of a young career-minded academic hovers behind some of these definitions and one should be mindful of the diversity of the research student body in the arts and humanities.

These questions begin to move the discussion away from a definition of the trained researcher and towards the organization and delivery of research training at institutional and subject level.

The organization and delivery of research training

The organization and delivery of research training has been an area of considerable debate and development across all academic fields, and there are a number of different models that have been adopted, varying from approaches in which the doctoral project is seen as the vehicle for virtually all of the skills development expected of students, to those which place considerable emphasis on the delivery of skills through additional workshops and courses. If one thinks of research training as existing along a continuum, at one end one would find the 'traditional' model of research training as a craft apprenticeship, heavily dependent on the interaction between the individual student and his or her research supervisor, an experienced researcher and subject expert; at the other end one would find menu-based approaches, research skills packaged in short courses and workshops and often delivered through institution-wide graduate schools by professional trainers. Neither of these approaches is entirely satisfactory, and indeed they rarely exist in their pure form. Drawing from each I want to propose a model of research training that seeks to embed research skills at subject level, where the student is neither dependent on a single supervisor, nor experiences skills development as an activity entirely divorced from his or her doctoral project, but within which the development of research skills takes place as part of an active research culture.

First, however, it is necessary to say a few words about masters level provision. Whereas in many subjects the master's degree is predominantly viewed as a preparation for research degree study, this is not the case in the creative arts and design. Master's courses in the visual arts and design have traditionally been a terminal degree, seen as the point at which a student has reached a level of competence suitable for independent professional practice. For many students that is still the case. However, there is now a significant minority of students looking to move from masters to doctoral study. It is worth reflecting for a moment on this specific type of research student. In a context where the boundary between those who produce knowledge and those who use it has become increasingly blurred, it is no surprise that the line between professional practice and research no longer holds; this is an issue that resonates much more widely than the creative arts and design. For these students, masters study does not result in a neatly resolved practice, which they expect then to apply in a professional arena, but generates questions that are simultaneously theoretical and practical, and which warrant deeper and more intensive study. A number of such students look to the PhD to provide a framework within which to pursue these questions. For many of these students, however, the start of doctoral studies is experienced as a significant change in ways of working and styles of thinking. For example, one of the biggest problems such students face when working within the PhD is the lack of ability, and sometimes willingness, to commit to a clear articulation of the research journey, and the struggle to find an appropriate form for doing so. As I have noted above, this can be the result of an apparent clash of values between visual arts practice and research, as much as any lack of research skills.

Over the longer term, the answer must be to embed an understanding of research skills and values within professional practice masters programmes. It is beyond the remit of this chapter to make the case, but the skills involved in handling information and knowledge, including synthesizing knowledge from diverse sources in support of problem-solving in specific situations and generating local knowledge in the context of practice, are arguably central to professional practice in the creative arts and design.[8] This convergence means that what is good for professional practice also supports those students who wish to pursue research at doctoral level. Of course many programmes do this very effectively, but it is not universally the case, especially across the broad international spread of postgraduate study in the creative arts and design. In the short term, therefore, doctoral research training programmes need also to inculcate in students the kind of generic understanding of research that I have outlined.

Taking into account the arguments presented above, I now want to turn my attention to the framework through which research skills are delivered. The model of research training I am suggesting has four levels: (i) individual research supervision; (ii) subject-based research training; (iii) participation in an active research culture; (iv) generic training workshops. There may of course be some overlap, but activity at all four levels is consistent with good practice in research training. Disagreements around research training have occurred most often where one level is prioritized over another, or where there are misunderstandings as to what might be achieved at any one level.

Individual supervision

Individual supervision, by which I mean supervision focused on the individual student's research (not, I emphasize, necessarily a single supervisor) remains central to doctoral study. At the detailed project level, the value of an ongoing dialogue with a supervisor or supervisory team is absolutely crucial. Research supervisors certainly provide specialist subject knowledge, but perhaps more important is the ongoing guidance they provide as the research progresses, enabling the student to develop a reflexive working knowledge of research. At the level of individual supervision, support and advice is tailored to the student's particular needs, introducing issues for consideration and prompting reflection at appropriate points. Doctoral students, typically, are embarking on a significantly larger scale piece of research than they have previously, and one role of the supervisor is to see the development of the student's initial ideas within this larger framework. When it works well individual supervision can be extremely rewarding for students and supervisors. Individual supervision has historically been the dominant model, but it is for good reason that it should not be seen as providing the totality of the doctoral training experience. One disadvantage is that the student's engagement with the institution is dependent on just one or two individuals. This can lead to a sense of isolation on the part of the student, one of the most common complaints voiced by doctoral students in the arts and humanities. There are also advantages, I would argue, in fostering an appreciation of the broader research context within which the student's project is situated.

Subject-based research training

The next level is what I am referring to as subject-based research training. This may be department, school or faculty based, and is where the majority of what we generally think of as research training should take place. This can be viewed simply as a way of achieving economies of scale: rather than each student having some common process explained to them individually, this can be done at small group level. However, my intention here is to suggest a deeper rationale. Bringing students together in cognate areas has two benefits. First, it enables research training to address generic processes and skills embedded within a subject context. Whilst all students need proposal writing skills, what counts as good proposal looks very different in different in subject areas. At an abstract level all subjects share a common definition of research and the PhD, but the practice of research at subject or discipline level can differ radically, and it is at subject level that students need to develop competence. Second, it enables students to broaden their own understanding beyond their specific project focus, but still retaining a sense of shared issues and concerns. Although generic research training programmes have in the past been implemented on an institution-wide basis, these have rarely proved popular with students or supervisors. This does not rule out interdisciplinary engagements (an issue I will return to below), but it is important not to mistake an abstract discussion of research from how this works out at subject level. I would also argue that research advances through developments at subject and discipline level and if research skills are not to become reified and research training is to remain dynamic, there has to be engagement at subject level.

Participation in an active research culture

If one learns the craft of research through practice, then the same applies to learning to be a researcher. Although not necessarily defined as formal training, participation in a research community provides some of the best opportunities for doctoral students to develop many of the contextual skills that are essential to developing a successful research career: skills in research presentation and communication; networking and so on. It is also at this level that there are opportunities for peer learning, which are no less important to doctoral students than students of any other qualification. In Sweden, for example, doctoral students participate in a formal series of seminars at which they are expected to present a first draft, a number of chapters and a near complete version of their thesis, before a final seminar (*slutseminarium*). All of these presentations have opponents in the style of the UK *viva*. Such seminars no doubt serve a training purpose and prepare the students for the defence of their thesis; however, there is also a need for less formal presentations, opportunities for students to share work-in-progress in the spirit of open exchange in order to develop rather than test the quality of their thinking. Reading groups may offer one such mechanism.

Institutions should also actively support students' contribution to the wider research culture, for example through supporting students' attendance at conferences and facilitating student-led conferences and publications. This is also an area where the intellectual generosity of supervisors is important, facilitating students' entry into networks, spotting publishing opportunities and so on. Students in the creative arts and design are often keenly aware of the importance of audiences and users of research, and therefore opportunities for participation beyond an academic context may also be relevant here. The relatively small number of doctoral students in the creative arts and design, the fact that many also study part-time and that they often span professional practice and research poses the question of how these students are integrated into a research culture. One response has been to develop collaborative research training events. For example, the 'Millennium Programme', a collaboration pursued over a number of years between institutions in Norway, Denmark, Sweden and Finland, brought together research students to participate in an innovative research training programme (Dunin-Woyseth 2002).

Generic training workshops

As was noted in relation to definitions of the trained researcher, there are a number of skills areas not necessarily related to the specific doctoral research project, but which nevertheless should be available to doctoral students. I think one should bear in mind here the different types of studentship. Some students are more exclusively project focused than others, and not all are necessarily preparing for an academic research career. Teaching and mentoring skills fall in to this category. Many research students are keen to develop these skills as part of a rounded profile, especially those who are seeking to work full-time in higher education. My own institution, for example, offers a short programme for research students who teach. This provides a valuable training opportunity even if it is not directly related to the PhD project. This level also includes specialist training, in areas such as intellectual property for example, where the benefit depends on bringing the knowledge back and applying it at subject level. Many institutions offer a menu of short courses and workshops that students can attend, and some specify a minimum requirement in terms of the number of courses students should attend in their first year (and in some cases subsequent years). These are usually offered on an institution-wide basis and take place away from the students' home department or school. The extent of this type of research training provision varies from institution to institution, with the more research intensive universities, which typically have a large numbers of doctoral students, able to sustain a wider offering.

There is a question, both here and at subject level, of whether research training should be assessed. Whilst a good doctoral education will include the development of skills across the range, the traditional examination focuses almost exclusively on the thesis as the outcome of the research. Institutions vary in this respect; some (including my own) assess students on their initial programme of research training. The purpose here is both to instil a sense of discipline and to diagnose any problematic areas at an early stage. Some institutions monitor attendance only. Others do neither. A minimum requirement, in my view, is the use of an annual monitoring process requiring students and supervisors to reflect on progression and identifying specific areas where further research training may be necessary or desirable.

Whilst there is no inherent priority in the four levels I have outlined, it is my belief that research training should take its lead from the needs of the subject and the student, building from there outwards and not the other way around.

Developing the research training curriculum

In this final section, I want to turn my attention to some of the challenges that I believe currently face those devising the curriculum for research in the creative arts and design. Notwithstanding the issues of definition and organization set out above, I think there is an emerging consensus around the need to provide generic training for doctoral students. This marks a stage in the maturity to doctoral study in the creative arts and design. Creative arts research is therefore at a critical juncture. The debate over its place in the academy is over; it has been won. There is some unevenness of course. There is still an open question concerning what proportion of creative arts and design academics one might expect to hold a PhD. The evolving relationship between the creative professions and creative arts education has multiple dimensions; where some see the potential to dissolve or at least weaken the boundaries between creative practice and academic research, others are wary of an 'academic drift' that may prevent some of the most outstanding practitioners' promotion within the academy (Chapter 1).[9] I think the shape of our field is such that is not desirable for the PhD to become a prerequisite for an academic career; we are not like history or chemistry. But I do not think it is a question any longer of whether there is a place for research and doctoral study in the creative arts and design. However, this graduation if you like, serves only to propel arts-based research into the busy thoroughfare of the research mainstream, where it will (and indeed should) be expected to hold its own. It is here that we, as supervisors and active researchers, now find ourselves and here that we and our students will find challenges and opportunities to which we will need to respond. I want to mention three: interdisciplinarity; the relationship between visual arts and design practice and writing; and research ethics.

Interdisciplinarity

The challenges and the opportunities of interdisciplinary engagements loom large over much of the research going on in our field, and are international in their scope. I am sure that many in the creative arts and design would regard the visual as being squarely within their domain. Yet, if you take a look at what is going on in the world of academic publishing you will find a vast array of books published over the past five to ten years on visual methods, visual research, visual studies and so on. Very few of these have been authored by those in the traditionally practice-based disciplines. The majority issue from new work in anthropology and sociology, which has invested heavily in research concerned with visual and sensory forms of knowledge and experience. Equally interesting I think is the way in which the language of practice-based research has escaped from the studio. The sociology department at Goldsmiths College, London, for example, now offers a practice-based PhD route,[10] which offers students:

> the opportunity to combine written sociological argument with film, sound, or photographic representation. It will offer new researchers the opportunity to re-think both the conduct of social research and the forms social research writing take in the 21st century'.[11]

As an aside, the approach to quantifying visual work is refreshingly pragmatic: a PhD involves a video or sound feature of approximately an hour in length, or a photographic project consisting of no more than 100 images; the figures for MPhil are 30 minutes and 60 photographs respectively. Whilst academics in the creative arts and design expended considerable time and effort debating definitions of research in their disciplines, others less worried about definitions have been busy getting on with it. Now of course one could argue that there are fundamental differences between how sociologists think about images, and what they want to do with them, and how visual arts practitioners think about and use images. But whilst partly true this seems a little dangerous and short sighted. Visual images are not something that can be kept locked up in a laboratory or studio, brought out like some precious store of radium only for the conduct of experiments; they are out there in the world. And whilst it might not always be tidy, I think there is much to be gained from engaging in dialogue with researchers and practitioners in other fields. Sociological and anthropological approaches to visual and material culture have moved on considerably from the sociology of art I once memorably heard described as 'destined to end badly'.[12] Some of the most interesting research to my mind is happening at the interfaces of disciplines and between research and practice.

What are the implications of this for doctoral education? As I have stated above, I think that we have to recognize the methodological openness, or perhaps promiscuity, of research in the creative arts and design. The increasing interest in interdisciplinary, multidisciplinary or even post-disciplinary research must be seen as part of the evolving research landscape, for which doctoral study should prepare students. This is not an argument against disciplinary research, there is no reason that research on, say, painting should not continue to deal with issues of concern primarily to theorists and practitioners of painting, as Borgdorff (2009a: 17) puts it: 'artistic research can sometimes be very well understood as purely disciplinary experimental research into the aesthetic and formal qualities and universal regularities of elements that constitute an artwork or creative process'. Nor should it be seen as an argument against discipline or subject-based research training, as Dunin-Woyseth points out in her discussion of the different modes of research (Chapter 4), the ability to carry out practice-oriented, transdisciplinary research (Mode 2) is dependent on the development of a disciplinary research (Mode 1) identity. But rather it is to acknowledge that there are some significant points of convergence and opportunities for productive engagements between disciplines, and between the academy and professional practice in the creative arts and design. The shift in anthropology from a predominant focus on language to a greater interest in visual, spatial and sensory forms of knowledge has provided one such opportunity. Where anthropologists have an interest in understanding human value, expression and communication in visual and material form, and are concerned with the interpretation of culture and creativity, they clearly share common ground with creative arts and design researchers and practitioners (e.g. Hallam and Ingold. 2007).[13] Convergent technologies similarly present opportunities for dialogue between disciplines as well as collaborative multidisciplinary research. For example, mobile technologies present research problems and opportunities that cannot be addressed by mono-disciplinary approaches. Research and development in this area will necessitate input from experts in human-computer interaction, cultural geographers and software designers, amongst others. There are threats here as well as opportunities of course. 'Social accountability and reflexivity' (Borgdorff 2009a: 18) – the responsibility of researchers to consider the broader impact of their research in contexts beyond the academy – whilst appealing to those in the creative arts and design whose work has always spanned academic, professional and public domains, could be considered a threat to its critical role: 'art often takes an antithetical stance towards the existing world, and it delivers the unsolicited and unexpected. That is its very strength.' (Borgdorff 2009a: 19). In this respect it is important that research training cultivates a sense of the position from which students speak and conduct their research, as well as enabling them to recognize their contribution to projects that go beyond discipline and subject boundaries.

Writing and the PhD

I am going to be provocative and argue that we will know that creative arts and design research has reached maturity when, instead of trying to hide from the writing problem, it turns around and faces it directly, indeed perhaps even embraces the rich methodological questions that it represents. For a period, pointless arguments about numbers of words seemed to dominate debate. Although we are now beyond that, or at least I hope so, we may still have the legacy to deal with. I recently had a discussion with a supervisor who felt that the earlier redrawing of their regulations regarding word length, supposedly to suit practice-based PhDs, now left them with a format that was constraining rather than enabling. And note here, words do not seem to be the problem, merely committing them to paper. I have not yet heard of any proposal to waive the requirement for the viva for practice-led PhDs, or to reduce by half the number of words spoken. The idea seems slightly perverse, but then to me so does the idea that practice-led PhDs necessarily need half as many words; some do, and some do not.

To argue that art and design has a special problem with writing and therefore should be granted some sort of exemption from the struggle to articulate its methods and findings is unhelpful. Very explicitly for the past twenty years and with less fanfare no doubt much longer, anthropologists have struggled with similar issues; we may have something to learn from them. Rather than try and find arguments to avoid the issue, which often depend on simplistically opposing writing to practice, and hence creating a straw man out of the former, I believe we need a more sustained and constructive focus on the forms of writing (and indeed other forms of documentation) appropriate to the PhD in art and design. It is not a question of deciding between writing and practice, but rather asking how the practice of writing can be brought into a productive relationship with visual arts practice. I think this question justifies some empirical research. There is now a substantial body of completed doctorates where students have grappled, more or less successfully no doubt, with precisely this problem.[14] Finding a mode of discourse and a voice appropriate to the task is not straightforward: I recall one of my PhD students referring to writing in relation to his art practice as a special kind of suffering. In my experience, PhD students in fine art often seem on the one hand to turn to the discourse of art criticism, in effect to become their own art critic; or on the other to look to forms of social or (worse) market research, and account for practice in terms of what others have to say about it. Neither approach seems satisfactory to me. An exploration of more descriptive and reflective forms of writing, which I believe is of central methodological importance to the development of doctoral research, remains a task to be undertaken.[15]

I do not have the space here to develop this argument fully, but I think it might be helpful to suggest a framework which allows for some differentiation in the way writing is considered as part of doctoral research. Rather than think of writing in the singular, I am arguing we should consider, and introduce to students, at least three different kinds of writing that they may need to engage in as part of doctoral study: writing as methodology; writing as reflection; writing as output. The last of these – writing as output – tends to be the one which we are generally speaking of when we talk of writing for research: the written thesis, journal articles and so on. This form remains important of course, but an exclusive emphasis on writing for a public audience is rather limiting. It also contributes to the sense that not only is writing a daunting activity, but also that it should be deferred to the end of the project, writing up. Thinking of writing as methodology or reflection suggests a more flexible and organic approach and can situate writing at the heart of the research. This may be especially important where the researcher is themselves a central methodological tool, as in action research, observational research or research involving the researcher's own arts or design practice. Writing can provide a means of objectifying subjective experience and rendering it usable as research material, as evidence. In a similar way, writing as reflection can serve any research project, providing the researcher with a means of documenting and thinking about the progress of the project, alongside visual or other forms of documentation. Doctoral students who use the written word in this way are likely to find the more formal writing needed for the thesis less onerous and daunting. It may be that doctoral students in the creative arts and design are already discovering this for themselves and moving beyond the writing paradigms more familiar to their supervisors. The PhD research blog is now becoming commonplace, with some students using the form as a central repository of research information, others as an ongoing reflective dialogue, and yet others as a methodological tool and means of communication with a global reach.

Ethics

Explicit consideration of research ethics is relatively new to the creative arts and design. By this I do not mean that ethical considerations have been absent from creative arts and design practice; indeed I think one of the issues is how the latter can be used to constructively inform the former, but rather that research ethics has generally been considered the province of disciplines like health and social science. But it would be wrong to think that other disciplines have formulated ethical practices and procedures that the creative arts and design can simply adopt. Ethics is the subject of considerable debate currently across many subject areas. No doubt this is partly driven by concerns about institutional accountability, but the debates are more complex and wide-ranging, and involve issues which should be of interest and concern to arts-based researchers, for example the way in which digital technologies facilitate the storage and dissemination of information, particularly visual information. In this context, rather than claiming some sort of special position, or turning our back on the ethics debates, arts-based researchers should be active participants in the discussion; we have something important to contribute. To take one example, I recently participated in a focus group discussion on visual research ethics.[16] A majority of the participants were social scientists, though the group also included a university retained legal practitioner. Much of the discussion was given over to issues of anonymity and the protection of vulnerable research participants. In cases where research participants had used photography to record aspects of their lives, some researchers had either excluded or 'anonymized' images (i.e. by blocking out faces and other identifiers) for subsequent presentations or publications. Seen from a social science perspective this might appear to be good practice, in line with practice in dealing with textual identifiers. However, clearly such research projects are engaging young people in creative visual projects, of a kind that I am sure many people working in arts education would recognize. Seen from this perspective the protection afforded by blurring or blocking out faces could be seen as a 'violation' of the image, and riding roughshod over the authorship of those participants who created them. Of course there are many more instances where creative arts practice can come into conflict with and challenge conventional approaches to research ethics, for example the role of copying or sampling in the creation of art works, or the public exhibition of works that upset or challenge the expectations of the audience – there is a long pedigree of deliberately provocative acts by artists. The validation of artistic experiments within the academy can be especially problematic where questions of legality are involved, as was the case recently in Sweden where a student from Konstfack (University College of Arts, Crafts and Design, Stockholm) carried out a final project involving graffiti on metro train carriages (Chapter 23). To what extent can or should these practices be sanctioned by the academy, and what are the implications of so doing? By what criteria might these be deemed (or not) ethical research practices? I do not think there are any simple solutions. There are often multiple and complex considerations to be taken into account, but I do believe the perspective of practice is important. If the creative arts and design are to be taken seriously as research disciplines then these are questions that cannot be neglected. And if researchers in the creative arts and design are not to be overrun by the ethical positions worked out in other fields then we need practitioner-researchers who are able to articulate ethical defences of practice-related research. Naturally, one would expect the research supervisor to advise the student on ethical issues, but in a context where the field has yet to clearly articulate ethical codes that cover the range of creative arts research practice this is only a partial answer.[17]

Interdisciplinarity and associated methodological questions, writing and documenting research practice, and research ethics, all fall within the domain of doctoral research education and training. They are, in my view, key areas where there is much still to be thought through and delivered. There are others which I have not mentioned, for example, knowledge transfer and exchange is an area where creative arts research with its inherent closeness to practice has much to contribute.

In bringing this chapter to a conclusion, I hope to have offered a useful framework for thinking about the research training that should be an integral part of any doctoral programme in the creative arts and design. But it is not my intention to have provided too complete a picture. There are areas where there is more to do, and new developments to which creative arts and design researchers need to respond. In this respect I hope my thoughts and reflections are some starting points for further debate.

Conclusion

I want to end this chapter with a way-finding story. A few years ago I was fortunate enough to find myself in India. As it happened, I had travelled there to participate in a week-long event on doctoral education in design, but that is beside the point. On the penultimate day of my trip, after the lectures and workshops had finished, my host arranged for myself and another academic from Stuttgart, to go to Agra to see the Taj Mahal and the Red Fort. We were accompanied on the trip by a driver, who spoke little English, and a guide, who was relatively fluent. The trip was fascinating for a variety of reasons, but the one I want to draw attention to here relates to our return journey to Delhi. It was already dusk as we were leaving Agra and, as is the way in India, the streets were busy with all variety of traffic moving about in what seemed, to me at least, a completely chaotic fashion. I was tired, not feeling especially well, and at this point keen to get back. As we moved through the busy streets it was clear that neither our driver, nor our guide, knew precisely which way we should go, and as far as I could see there were no street signs. At frequent intervals and as we reached junctions, the guide would lean out, often while we were still moving, and simply shout, 'Delhi'. The response from various other road users, some on foot, some not, was inevitably a vague wave of the arm in a particular direction, some more insistent or reassuring than others, but rarely anything amounting to what this particular passenger felt to be a satisfactory set of directions. Again and again this was repeated. This caused me much consternation at the time, why could we not stop and check a map, or perhaps ask for a more detailed set of directions, and then move forward without this constant interruption and the perpetual uncertainty that at any one time we were heading in the right direction? We did of course return safely to our guest house in Delhi. Perhaps it took us much longer than it need have, perhaps not, I will never know. But this experience stuck in my mind for a long time, and I think speaks to different ways of knowing the world, what we might want to call different epistemologies.[18] From my perspective, knowledge would have been represented in an abstract way by a map, or alternatively by an individual who was able to map out in words the entirety of our route. Our guide and driver however seemed to operate on a different principle. Knowledge for them did not reside in a single individual or artefact, but was widely distributed and available on the streets; even better, should some of their respondents provide poor quality advice, it would soon be cancelled out by the collective knowledge of all those they consulted.

Why am I telling this story? Well, I think it may offer a useful metaphor for thinking of the development of doctoral research. First, it is a metaphor which argues against too much abstract theorizing about the special nature of research in the creative arts and design. Second, it suggests we need to engage with others heading in different directions, but nevertheless traversing the same territory. But above all, it points towards the need to engage with the seemingly chaotic real world of research. Proposals can only take one so far. I am sure we all ask our students to work out coherent proposals at the outset of their research, and indeed funding bodies ask the same of us when we ask for their support, rightly so, but there comes a point where one has to leave the drawing board and immerse oneself in the world outside. And it is only by doing so that doctoral students are able to complete their training.

Notes

1 A number of the ideas in this chapter were first presented in a conference paper (Newbury 2009).

2 I tend to use the inclusive term 'creative arts and design' to refer to the research domain covered by this paper; on occasion for the sake of avoiding awkward sentence construction I abbreviate this to arts-based or creative arts research, but no distinction is implied. My experience is mostly in the visual arts and design, though there is a common set of issues also being debated by those in architecture, music and performance. These might broadly be referred to as 'the making

disciplines', a term common in Scandinavian contexts (Chapter 4). For the purposes of this discussion, it seems more useful to maintain rather loose boundaries between these areas, than to try and impose strict definitions.

3 I think Bell reads rather more into my statement about the nature of research than was there. In other respects this paper speaks a lot of good sense about practice-led research, though to conclude on the inevitability of auto-ethnography as *the* method for practice-led research seems rather restricting.

4 Williams was of course talking about a very different context, but the wording I find very useful here.

5 I hope this definition makes it clear why I find attempts to describe the arts-based PhD in terms of percentages of theory and practice unsatisfactory.

6 Of course research and writing are practices too, though I have avoided that formulation here for the sake of simplicity.

7 I have previously defined methodology in the following way: 'the interrelationship between the theoretical and the practical aspects of doing research – the thinking one does about the significant choices and actions that constitute the research act' (Newbury 2003).

8 This is clearly the same argument that underlies the discussion of Mode 2 research (Chapter 4) just seen from the other direction, wherein knowledge and creativity are perceived as crucial to society and the economy.

9 It is beyond the focus of this chapter, but Torsten Kälvemark's discussion of the Norwegian Fellowship, which provides a parallel route to achieving the equivalent of doctoral standing, provides an interesting alternative. My own view is that whilst these schemes do indeed have an important place, they are not a substitute for doctoral research in the creative arts and design, which remains an important development in its own right. Furthermore, as Kälvemark points out later in his chapter, there is a danger in developments such as the professional doctorate of reinforcing the divide between thinkers and doers.

10 Similarly, the anthropology department at Harvard offers a 'practice-based' PhD in social anthropology (with media) for which the submission includes 'original creative work … in an audiovisual medium' See http://www.fas.harvard.edu/~anthro/grad_media.htm (accessed 2 February 2010).

11 See http://www.gold.ac.uk/pg/mphil-phd-visual-sociology/ (accessed 2 February 2010).

12 The person who made this remark was David Campany, though I can no longer remember the specific occasion.

13 The Center for Ethnography at the University of California, Irvine, has a research theme considering the methodological exchange between design and ethnography http://www.socsci.uci.edu/~ethnog/theme4.htm (accessed 2 February 2010).

14 See Chapter 20 for a more extended discussion, with examples, of specific art PhD writing practices.

15 Desmond Bell offers what seems to me one productive line of development in his argument for creative practice research as implying a form of auto-ethnography. He cites David Davies *Art as Performance* on the epistemological question at its centre: 'the relationship between the generative act that brings a work into existence and the receptive act that is a proper appreciation of that work' (Davies 2004: 26).

16 The focus group took place in 2008 at the University of Leeds but was organized as part of a research project at the ESRC-funded National Centre for Research Methods at University of Southampton.

17 I recently led a funded research project to develop resources for research training around ethics; details can be found online at: http://www.biad.bcu.ac.uk/research/rti/ethics/ (accessed 2 February 2010).

18 My comparison here seems to bear some relationship to the distinction Michel de Certeau's describes between the map and the tour (de Certeau 1984).

22
NO COPYRIGHT AND NO CULTURAL CONGLOMERATES: NEW OPPORTUNITIES FOR ARTISTS

Joost Smiers

Let us imagine that the system of copyright no longer existed: the practice of many artists would surely change considerably. It would not only have significant impact on the daily practice of artists and their entrepreneurs, but also, no doubt, on research. Such studies which consider, for example, how to use different sources of inspiration more freely; how to interrelate with audiences and possibly use their inputs; how to make judgements about quality; how to archive works that may change periodically; how to disseminate works in digital environments while maintaining, or not, an overview of their use; how to organize cultural enterprises in a world in which copyright no longer exists; and finally how creative and performing artists can make a decent living from their efforts.

Next, let us imagine the less imaginable. If we can agree that, from a democratic perspective, cultural conglomerates dominate markets, then we might decide that they should be cut up using anti-trust or competition policies for example, which would result in a substantial increase in the number of owners of the means of production and distribution of artistic expression. The field for the production, distribution, promotion and reception of all forms of the arts would change radically and would, in turn, bring far reaching consequences for the kind of research challenges with which artists would be confronted.

Initially I will argue why such drastic measures like the abolition of copyright and the curbing of market domination of cultural conglomerates would be necessary. This then leads to the question of what are the new realities within which artists and their entrepreneurs could manoeuvre. Furthermore, we might also consider what kind of, perhaps unexpected, issues these artists might find for research in and around their canvas, music scores, e-books, digital films, theatre stages and video screens.

No copyright and no cultural market domination

Copyright has increasingly become an instrument for securing huge investment. In the past decade, it has become one of the major driving forces of Western economies, in particular, the US economy. This development, however, has a major downside: companies owning massive amounts of copyrighted works can, at their whim, ban weaker cultural activities not only from the marketplace but also from the general audience's attention. This is happening before our very eyes. It is almost impossible to ignore the blockbuster movies, bestselling books and chart-topping records presented to us by these cultural giants that own almost every imaginable right to these works. As a result, most people are completely unaware of all those other, less commercialized activities taking place in music, literature, cinema, theatre and other arts. This is a tremendous loss to society, because our democratic world can only truly thrive on a wide diversity of cultural expression, freely expressed and discussed.

There are even fewer numbers of increasingly large and powerful entities that own the exclusive rights to ever more works in the fields of literature, cinema, music and graphic arts. For example, Corbis collects vast amounts of images from all over the world. Together with Getty Images, Corbis is developing into an oligopoly in the field of photographs and reproductions of paintings and other images – in other words, an entity that has a large amount of control over the market. The oligopoly has control over which artistic works we may use for which purposes, and under which conditions.

In most cultures around the world this state of affairs was – and in some cases still is – highly undesirable, even unthinkable. Artists have always used and built upon other artists' works to create new works of art. Indeed, it is hard to imagine that the works of Shakespeare, Bach, and countless other cultural heavyweights could have come into existence without this principle of freely building on the work of predecessors. Yet, what do we see happening now? Take, for example, documentary filmmakers who nowadays face almost insurmountable obstacles owing to the fact that their work almost inevitably contains fragments of copyrighted pictorial or musical content, the use of which requires both consent from the copyright owner and payment of a fee. The latter is almost always beyond the documentary maker's means, and the former gives the copyright owner full rights to restrict the use of the artistic content exclusively to ways the owner deems appropriate.

Instrumental questions arise from this situation for the artists. For example, how can one accept that most existing cultural creations may not be used in a new work, or reworked and forged into a new creation? What kind of society do we live in that permits a great number of artistic creations to be frozen, unable to be changed and doomed to remain in the state the 'owner' of those works pleases?

Where in this scheme of things are our human rights? Human rights should guarantee freedom of communication. The free exchange of ideas and cultural expression is what greatly helped build our modern society. This human cultural development will, however, grind to a halt if a mere handful of persons or companies can call themselves 'owners' of the majority of pictures, texts and melodies that our society has brought forth. This puts them in a position where they alone can dictate whether we can make use of a substantial part of our collective human cultural achievement, and on which terms and conditions. The consequences are detrimental: we are being made speechless; our cultural memory is taken from us and locked away; the development and spread of our cultural identity is stunted, and our imagination is placed in chains by the law.

Contrary to what one might expect, the seemingly endless possibilities of copying and sampling using modern digital technologies have so far only aggravated the situation. Publicly offering even a mere second's worth of copyrighted work will almost certainly attract attention from lawyers on behalf of the 'owners' of the material. Sound artists, who used to freely sample work from others to build new musical creations, are now treated as pirates and criminals. Whole copyright enforcement industries have emerged, scouting the digital universe day and night for even the smallest snippet of copyrighted work used by others – and those who are found out often stand to lose everything they have. One may wonder – and this is a relevant question for artists – why do so many artists let this happen while the cultural industries are united in strongly defending their own interests?

Copyright has yet another intrinsic fault which makes it difficult to defend in a democratic society. Copyright nowadays revolves almost exclusively around so-called intellectual 'property'. This is a problem because the traditional notion of property is largely irreconcilable with intangible concepts such as knowledge and creativity, i.e. a tune, an idea or an invention, will not lose any of its value or usefulness when it is shared among any number of people. In contrast, a unique physical object, such as a chair, quickly becomes unusable as more people want access to it. In this latter case, the term 'property' has a clear meaning and purpose. Unfortunately, in the past decades the legal definition of property has been extended way beyond any physical constraints. These days, almost anything can be someone's 'property', such as fragrances and colours; even the makeup of the proteins in our blood and the genes in our body cells are being claimed as the exclusive property of one company or another, which can subsequently bar anyone else from using it.

It is therefore high time to reconsider the current concept of property. There is ample reason to send our current system of copyright to the scrapheap. Artists will of course feel threatened by such a bold move. The common perception is that copyright, first and foremost, protects the well-being and interests of the artists themselves. After all, without copyright, they will lose all means of existence, won't they? Well, not necessarily. Let us first look at some numbers. Economic research shows that only 10 per cent of artists account for 90 per cent of copyright proceeds, and the remaining 90 per cent of artists share only 10 per cent of proceeds. In other words: for the vast majority of artists, copyright has only marginal financial advantages.

What is called for is a way to ensure that artists can make a fair income from their work without the risk of being pushed out of the market and losing the attention of the larger audience as a result of the marketing power of the cultural industry. The interesting thing is that it is quite feasible for artists to thrive without copyright. After all, copyright is simply a protective layer of armour around a work of art and the question is whether the benefits of this protection outweigh its drawbacks. Artists, and their agents and producers, are entrepreneurs. What then justifies the fact that their work receives vastly more protection – i.e. long-term monopolistic control over their work – than the work of other entrepreneurs? Why can't they simply offer their work on the free market, and try to attract buyers?

Now, let us try to predict what would happen if copyright were abolished. One of the first effects would be intriguing: all of a sudden, it would no longer be of interest for large cultural industries to focus so heavily on bestselling books, blockbuster movies and superstars. If, in the absence of copyright and intellectual property, these works can be freely enjoyed and exchanged by anyone, the cultural industry giants lose their exclusive rights to works of art. As a result, they will also lose their dominant market position, which, in turn, keeps so many other artists out of sight.

Still within the idea of the abolition of copyright, we would have to, at the same time, cut market dominating cultural conglomerates into smaller parts. We could no longer tolerate that just a few companies substantially control the production, distribution, marketing, and the conditions for the reception of films, books, music, theatre and design. Abandoning copyright would remove one major pillar from the dominance of our current cultural industries, but this does not necessarily mean that their dominance would end. Established industries would still hold the means to large-scale production, distribution and marketing of cultural goods and services in a firm grip. Indeed, this is one of the reasons for their current success, i.e. keeping total control over artistic works from the source to the end consumer. This distribution model is what largely determines which films, books, theatre productions and image materials we can enjoy.

This concentration of power is undesirable in every branch of industry, but it is particularly detrimental in the cultural field. Competition policy is the tool for cutting up these cultural giants, but it should be done with cultural interests in mind. Any form of market domination should be driven out, so we could therefore imagine the cultural market subjected to competition laws with a strong cultural bias. This would relate among other things to ownership of the means of production and distribution of cultural goods. Also, legislation may be called for to force large cultural enterprises to (re)present all of the actual cultural diversity being created by both local and foreign artists.

The result would be that cultural markets would become normalized, which would enable more artists to show their work, make themselves known and to make a fair income from what they produce. This income would initially result from being the first in the market with a specific work. But there would be another factor contributing to the artists' success. A more normalized cultural marketplace would offer many more artists an opportunity to build a reputation, like a brand name, which could subsequently be exploited to sell more works at a higher price. This would give more artists an opportunity to keep selling their works to a larger audience in an industry-controlled distribution model. From these changes that I propose, completely new cultural markets would emerge. At first glance, it might be difficult to imagine such new market constellations because we live in a world in which copyright and the dominance of huge cultural giants seem self-evident. They are not, however difficult it may be to envision the existence of completely different market relations. Indeed, we have seen, throughout history, that markets change continuously. Why not in the distant future? Market relations can change, radically. I discuss this further in this chapter and have also done so, more extensively, in a co-authored essay with Marieke van Schijndel (Smiers and van Schijndel 2009).

Obviously, research of this kind is not only the responsibility of, and a challenge for, economists, political scientists and strategic thinkers. Artists themselves should do a major part of the work, i.e. by reflecting on how new market conditions can be shaped in favour of the interests of many of them, what it will give them, what such a market relation should look like, and what they already experience. Their daily practice, and the experiences of colleagues, is the original material for the development of coherent thoughts on how markets can and should be fashioned.

Originality?

What are the challenges that many artists and their entrepreneurs will experience if the cultural field were to change as much as I propose? What are the topics that warrant that creators and performers themselves reflect on the changing circumstances in their professional life?

What first comes to mind is the concept of originality. Let us immediately take away any form of potential misunderstanding. One may have enormous respect for the work of a certain artist and even think that it contains some original aspects. However, is this really our main focus when we are reading a book, watching a film, admiring a theatre performance, listening to a concert? We might feel attracted by the beauty of the specific work, or we may abhor it. Of course the audience knows, to some degree, that it is not the same as a work that we have seen, read or heard before. It is therefore arguable whether the public, in the first instance, judges a work on its supposed originality. We must honestly recognize that this is a relatively recent Western concept that is only a few centuries old. A trend developed around the myth of authors' originality. A work was no longer considered the result of a continuing process of interchange and exchange between artists and audiences, commissioners and buyers, from past and present. But rather, the cultural expression began to be seen as a unique event that could, allegedly, only have been created by a genius. And even in the event of the artists' capacities losing their superhuman status, the creation still remained the act of an individual, a person who rose above the crowd. This person surpassed the collective and his, and sometimes her, creations needed to be properly recognized. This legitimized the individual appropriation of knowledge and creativity. Several centuries later, we may now wonder whether this individualization was actually a harmful development because it meant that the notion that knowledge and creativity that depend on collective contributions was denied, or at least undervalued.

Let us analyse why originality is a relative concept that lacks sufficient substance for granting someone the exclusive and monopolistic right of use of a work. The particular someone in question may even be an enterprise that did not create or perform the work itself, but that nevertheless holds the copyright and thus the moral rights. One can greatly respect the work of artists, irrespective of whether they are world-famous and have been elevated to 'star' status, or whether they are known to only a small circle. However, this does not mean that what they produce is completely original, authentic or unique. The language, melodies and images they utilize are largely drawn from the public domain of creativity and knowledge that we have jointly accumulated through the centuries. Is it therefore not strange to allow an author, a composer, a painter, a designer or a performer an exclusive and monopolistic right to something they largely derive from what many before them have brought into being?

The individual and absolute ownership of creations and inventions is a concept that is alien to many cultures. In most cultures it is not justified that an individual exploit a creation or an invention monopolistically for many decades, nor is it the common practice. After all, the artist or inventor continues with the work of predecessors. Of course, we are well aware that copyright in the Western system is granted on the basis of what artists *add* to the knowledge and creativity that they find in the world around them and in previous cultures. However, this cannot justify allowing them exclusive and monopolistic right to the work.

In the system of intellectual property rights the author is elevated to celestial heights, almost as if he or she had performed something that welled up from a source that existed only within themselves. This is a rather romantic view and is not how artistic works are created and performed. Furthermore, it is nearly impossible to trace back and tease out the added element within the work. And in the rare case in which the addition is discernible, the interest of society in its entirety should still prevail over the interest of a single artist. After all, not a single case exists in which the additional element is of such great value that it would justify the prohibition of an endless number of artists building on it.

I always wonder what is going round in the mind of many artists. They may be realistic enough to recognize that originality is a relative concept, which also concerns their own work. Nevertheless, most of them, including artists working in the digital space, adhere to (or in any case do not deny) the basic principles of copyright that are based on assumed originality that gives them the absolute ownership on their work. I find this schizophrenic, to say the least. The only ones that can do research on this contradiction, based on their practices, are the artists themselves.

There is yet another reason why we should rid the integrity of a work (i.e. the moral right to it) from its legally enforceable status. This has less to do with artists and more to do with democracy. The way moral rights have functioned thus far is diametrically opposed to the opportunity we ought to have, from a democratic perspective, to contradict a work. The moral rights of an author forbid, or at least makes it highly contestable for us as citizens to give an artistic work a different turn. It is a feature of democracy that a story can be told in a different way, a melody can take a different course, an imagination or fantasy can tap into a different dimension, and the same material of a film can be regrouped into a completely different narrative structure and story line. It is alien to democracy to allow the 'owner' of an artistic expression to say: 'my view on the world, on sound, on sentiments, on the framing of images, on the choreography of a dance, on the ordering of words should remain as I have created it'.

Now that I have presented several arguments pertaining to why originality is a relative concept and cannot justify the preservation of even the moral rights aspects of copyright, some artists may feel that I give no justice to their work. They may believe that they have created a unified piece of work that should not be allowed to be violated by others, and must certainly not be used outside the context for which it was meant. They want to see the integrity of the work protected. In copyright they see an appropriate legal instrument to safeguard that integrity, if necessary by getting their due in court. I can well imagine the concern of an artist for his or her work.

This, nevertheless, calls for additional observations. First of all, the degree of attachment to one's work varies considerably between individual artists. Some feel close to their work while others do not; some see it as an extension of themselves; some see it as a part of their reputation, etc. There are also others who consider it a strange phenomenon that they are forced to accept absolute mastery over their work. General opinion in many parts of the world does not assume that an author should claim ownership over a work. With the introduction of digitization we find an increasing number of artists who are not in the least concerned about the supposed ownership they could claim over the work and the integrity protection that flows from it. If artists do not have unambiguous relationships with their work, then it is strange that the moral rights, which are cherished by some, have become a legally enforceable instrument.

For artists this observation has huge consequences. If originality is no longer what is decisive for the quality and importance of a work, a burden may fall off their shoulders. It is not unlikely that this form of freedom – i.e. where there is no longer any obligation to create something that smells of the new – will change the attitude that drives artists' work. One would no longer have to hide that there are sources of inspiration, and that one has used elements of works from wherever. It is certainly attractive (and technically simple) in the digital field to sample from what has been created before. Practice-based research by artists may give important insight into how different sources, from the past and the near present, are flowing into what they are creating and performing at this moment in time. Such research might contribute to the complete redefinition of the concept of originality, and of the act of creation as well.

Struggle over meanings

There is another, and even more profound reason why changing the work of other artists is desirable from a social and cultural perspective. An artist must be able to respond to the texts of others in a book or the colours on a canvas. And we, as citizens ought to have free access to what the artist has created with materials from the public domain of creativity and knowledge. That access must not be obstructed by a package of conditions, and these must certainly not dictate the terms and the atmosphere under which we can enjoy artistic work. Why is this important? Because – no matter how you put it – music, images, dance, film and novels contribute to our personal development. They shape our pleasures and provide us with the opportunity to feel good, to stir up our fantasy, our dreams or unspoken desires and, thus, we as citizens should have unrestrained access to those artistic creations and performances.

The fact that artistic works are blessed with such powers of expression makes it important that we are free to chose and follow our preferences. The importance of free access to artistic work not only matters for the development of an individuals' sense of wellbeing but it is also a fundamental precondition for human communication. We have to be able to communicate our preferences.

> Postmodern dialogic practices of parody, pastiche, irony, and social critique come into tension with the monologism of a modern legal discourse that bestows monopolies over meaning under the authority vested in the proper name in the form of property.
>
> (Coombe 1998: 68)

Rosemary Coombe stresses that if

> what is quintessentially human is the capacity to make meaning, challenge meaning, and transform meaning, then we strip ourselves of our humanity through overzealous application and continuous expansion of intellectual property protections. Dialogue involves reciprocity in communication: the ability to respond to a sign with signs. What meaning does dialogue have when we are bombarded with messages to which we cannot respond, signs and images whose significations cannot be challenged and connotations we cannot contest?
>
> (Coombe 1998: 84–5)

The work of Rosemary Coombe is infused with the inspiring thought that

> culture is not embedded in abstract concepts that we internalize, but in the materiality of signs and texts over which we struggle and the imprint of those struggles in consciousness. This ongoing negotiation and struggle over meaning is the essence of dialogic practice. Many interpretations of intellectual property laws quash dialogue by affirming the power of corporate actors to monologically control meaning by appealing to an abstract concept of property. Laws of intellectual property privilege monologic forms against dialogic practice and create significant power differentials between social actors engaged in hegemonic struggle.
>
> (Coombe 1998: 86)

Dialogic practice is a theoretically appealing ideal, but we know that when put into practice, there is a risk of being overrun by armies of lawyers and, owing to our self-made interferences, the judges will duly charge us for our creative impertinence. Nevertheless, in many cultures it was, and still is, an honour if another person takes your work as a point of departure and polishes it further. This is not so in the contemporary Western culture in which the productive creative dialogue is strictly confined by an exacting system of sanctions. We have elevated the judges to the status of arbiters of the progress of our cultural expressions and opinion forming. Their legal hold is that they, exclusively, are the ones who are entitled to grant the production of that progress to the 'owners' of artistic creative material. A society that is subjected to such bizarre rules is being democratically disadvantaged.

Most artists will not give much thought to the fact that during their creative processes and their performances they are, *par excellence*, communicating meanings that deeply influence the feelings of many in their audience and readership. However, this is what happens and, for the most part, this process goes unnoticed. However, what can be said, performed and expressed is the result of social, economic and cultural struggle, which is sometimes vehement but mostly a matter of fact. Some artists may feel the need, through research based on their practice, to reflect on how they and their colleagues are the targets of forces that try to steer their work in this rather than in that direction. What may seem self-evident can be reflected on more clearly – a consideration that might be helpful for artists to understand in which environment and field of pressures they are operating.

Public domain

I claim that any artistic creation or performance belongs to the public domain. It is derived from the commons, based on the works of predecessors and contemporaries and, therefore, from its moment of conception it takes its place in the public domain. Let us consider an example that clearly shows how damaging copyright can be for the freedom of expression. In the early 1990s copyright scholar Siva Vaidyanathan noticed that rap music was changing: the underlying body of samples was thinning out, becoming more predictable, more obvious and less playful.

> I had heard that there had been some copyright conflicts in 1990 and 1991. So I suspected that lawsuits had chilled playful and transgressive sampling. I was right. The courts had stolen the soul. And rap music is poorer for it.
> (Story and Halbert 2006: 19)

Siva Vaidyanathan's observation was based on a 1991 court decision in the United States that ruled against rapper Biz Markie's appropriation of a Gilbert and Sullivan song in the case Grand Upright v. Warner. This decision changed practice dramatically. At first, the Bridgeport Music Inc. v. Dimension Films ruling stipulated that samples which rise 'to a level of legally cognizable appropriation' must be licensed, but that *de minimis* sampling was still considered fair use. However, this decision was reversed in the appeal to this case, where the court ruled that even the three-note sample was unfair use and that musicians should 'get a license or do not sample'. The consequence is that musicians now have to clear the rights with the owner of the sound recording and the publisher and negotiate a licence fee before using the sample. Rapper Chuck D argues that narrowing the infringement exception means that the 'whole collage element is out of the window'. To make things even worse, 'for music, clearance is required for the performance and for the composition …' (Gowers 2006: 67).

The 2006 British *Gowers Report* on intellectual property rights reminds us that hip-hop

> is not the first genre to 'sample' music: composers from Beethoven to Mozart to Bartok to Charles Ives have regularly recycled themes, motifs, and segments of prior works. Under the current copyright regime, these creators would need to clear permission and negotiate licenses to avoid infringement suites. The barriers that new musicians have to overcome are extremely high, and the homogenization of hip hop music is, critics argue, a direct response to the costs of clearance rights.
> (Gowers 2006: 67)

We should be clear that the fact that one should have the right to make from the work of another artist something that is different, is the same right that another artist has on your own work. For many artists this may mean a complete break in how they experience their own work, i.e. as something that should not be touched by others. Emotionally this might be difficult for some artists. The whole concept of moral rights is melting like snow in the Spring sun.

Untouchability of a work no longer in vogue

If the moral rights along with the system of copyright are nullified, then what should artists do who are disgusted to find that their work has been changed by others or has surfaced in political contexts with which they do not wish to be associated? The most simple, but probably least satisfactory answer is that they have to get used to the fact that the untouchability of their work is no longer in vogue. Those who nevertheless wish to draw attention to a work that has been affected to a degree that is unacceptable must seek to mobilize societal discourse on matters like: what degree of respect does a work deserve; what kind of changes are too horrific to even consider; when is a work abused in the political sense of the word? If we must use the legal toolkit to support a claim of blunt mistreatment, then one could look in the direction of concepts such as libel, insult and unlawful act.

One could well imagine that an artist or producer may claim to be harmed by an unlawful act if a political party uses their work to advocate, for instance, its extreme left or right wing message. However, it is up to the judge to discern whether, for instance, the appropriation of a specific work is justifiable as a normal contribution to the public discourse or whether it is an unlawful act. Only those with convincing reasons for why their work should not be used in specific contexts would be able to forbid certain uses of said work.

Despite all my arguments, I can imagine that some authors feel so attached to their work that they only want it to be (re)presented in ways they consider correct and adequate. Should we not respect and honour their wishes? Out of consideration for the artist and as a form of civilized behaviour we certainly should, but not if this means that they can claim a form of ownership. Again, this does not mean that others should not be allowed to use this work. And, obviously the option to change and adapt a work must be available, as I have said before. However, mention should to be made that the new version *is only based* on the work of an earlier writer, composer or painter, if a radical change of interpretation has been made. This procedure would create a clear distinction between the work of a first author and the new, deviating version of another artist.

Making this distinction – between the primary work and the radical adaptation – is culturally helpful as well. It contributes to raising awareness that artistic creations and performances do not just appear out of the blue. If there is a link between a new work and something that has been created or performed before, it is culturally enriching to disclose the source.

Finally, this is also the right place to discuss a possible misunderstanding regarding my not caring about theft. Of course I do not propose that X should attach his or her name to Y's book or film, and thus suggest they are the author of that work. That would be plain misrepresentation or fraud. If this were to be found out – and it would be bound to happen sooner or later – then the lazy fraudster should receive a fair penalty in court. However, we do not need a copyright system to accomplish this.

Meanwhile, it may have become clear that copyright is an intellectual *property* right. It gives the owner an exclusive and monopolistic right over a work of knowledge or artistic creativity. In this sense it has been made comparable to other property rights, like on a house. However, we should remember that house and copyright ownership have in common that both types of ownership are the objects of constant struggle. Societal interests play a role as well, while limiting or expanding owners' rights. In this perspective nothing is self evident (Nuss 2006). 'All forms of property are socially constructed and, like copyright, bear in their lineaments the traces of the struggles in which they are fabricated' (Rose 1993: 8).

Influenced by neoliberal philosophies we have adopted the position that ownership titles should be without conditions. The reality, however, is that copyright steals many cultural and artistic expressions in our societies from the public domain of creativity and knowledge, to be traded amongst private parties. The set that initially contained only material objects such as land, rapidly expanded to include abstractions such as creative expressions. Rosemary Coombe provides a synopsis of these events:

> Laws of intellectual property generally – copyright, trademark, and publicity rights, in particular – constitute a political economy of mimesis in capitalist societies, constructing authors, regulating activities of reproduction, licensing copying, and prohibiting imitation, all in the service of maintaining the exchange value of texts.
>
> (Coombe 1998: 169)

By the end of the twentieth century, films, songs, books, shows and other forms of entertainment had become big business. Under the logic of the individual appropriation of value(s), it seems plausible that these forms of expression will be brought under increasingly rigorous individual property regimes. The presumed difference between material and immaterial matters will by then have become entirely uninteresting and irrelevant – there is value to be created, therefore it follows that the creator of that value is entitled to almost absolute governance over that value. This is how the juggernaut of legislation progresses in the United States and Europe, and the rest of the world is left with no other option but to follow.

Revenues and entrepreneurship

It is of course commendable that society has a large domain of works of creativity and knowledge at its disposal, as I have claimed. But, one may ask, is this not a matter of living largely at the expense of artists and their producers? After all, they are the ones creating all these works, and they can only do so if they can derive an income from their efforts. Of course, many people are involved in producing creative works, even if this rarely provides them with an income. But it is not fair to leave the producers of artistic works, which we as a society so direly need, out in the cold.

I do not speak here of the contents of the artistic works themselves: the struggle to put colours on a canvas; the slow maturing of a melody in a composer's mind; the hustle and bustle at the film set; the words of a story that have to be rewritten time and again; or the dancer's fight against physical discomfort. Rather, I speak of what happens after all these efforts have been made and when an audience must be found that is willing to buy the work, to commission an assignment, attend the performance or become a supporter of the artistic enterprise. It is possible to imagine many types of customers such as audiences, of course, in all shapes and sizes, but also publicity bureaux, design studios, churches, banks, labour unions, hospitals, municipalities, soccer clubs, restaurants, television channels, maecenases, companies that sail the seven seas with their cruise ships, and this by no means exhausts the list of possibilities. The first and most direct customer for the artwork is usually the concert hall or the theatre, which reaches the audiences for a concert or show. This customer subsequently teams up with the initial producer as cultural entrepreneur to seduce these audiences. To stir up an interest amongst potential buyers for a painting or sculpture the usual channel is the art gallery, but many artists are also perfectly capable of selling straight from their workshops.

It is clear here that part of the artistic profession consists of acts of entrepreneurship, in order to find buyers for the created, or yet to be created, work. Indeed, artists are entrepreneurs, or to put it more precisely, cultural entrepreneurs. Entrepreneurship relies, inevitably, on taking chances. I will come back to this. Artists do not often employ many activities to find a market for their artistic works. It might be that the bulk of the work sells itself through commissioners who commercialize it in one way or another or who profit from it, for example through their own commercial activities. The initiative to produce an artistic creation might also be taken by a producer who approaches an artist, or a group of artists, with a proposal and subsequently markets the created work. Besides the artist him or herself, the producer and commissioner are also cultural entrepreneurs.

In and of itself, this is nothing new. Throughout the centuries, and within all cultures, we have seen that the artist, the commissioner or the producer engages in some kind of activity – thereby taking the initiative – not only to show the artistic work the light of day but also to make it profitable (Hauser 1972; Ginsburgh and Throsby 2006). The societal conditions under which this is done obviously differ considerably. The core of the activity, however, always centres on entrepreneurship. In my alternative for copyright it is not the artist who takes centre stage, but the entrepreneur, regardless of whether he or she is an artist, a patron or a producer.

I certainly recognize that many artists, while creating and performing, do not feel themselves to be entrepreneurs. However, it cannot be denied that a part of the reality of their practice is exactly this even when they have an intermediary who is doing business for them. A much-needed topic of research by artists is how, possibly, those two different instances – creating and performing on one side and doing business on the other side – stand in each other's way, and could perhaps be reconciled.

The urgent question at this point is: which basic conditions need to be met to offer an average entrepreneur – in our case cultural entrepreneur – a fair chance to successfully operate in a world in which copyright no longer exists? One then arrives at a level playing field.

A level playing field is a situation in any kind of market in which no single party can manipulate this market of his own accord. This is an important principle which has many advantages. For aspiring members, entry into that market is unhindered. New inventions can find their way to the public. Due to competition, prices are not driven up to ever-higher levels. Products can be mutually compared in terms of quality.

It goes without saying that markets do not, by definition, tend towards a neat level playing field. It is always possible that a certain party in the markets, for whatever reason, will grow so strong that it becomes dominant. For neoliberals this occurrence has not been, and is not, a problem. On the contrary, when market dominant forces appeared, they have let them be.

My purpose is to put a stop to this philosophy, and to re-establish a fair level playing field in which many cultural entrepreneurs – artists, producers and commissioners – can have risk-bearing opportunities. Diversity of content and ownership will then flourish again, and this huge body of cultural entrepreneurs can make a good living from their work.

It is actually a misunderstanding to believe that markets and regulation are a contradiction in terms. The idea that completely free markets exist, or can exist, is not realistic. 'Regulation and markets, in effect, grew up together' (Polanyi 1957: 68). Karl Polanyi accentuates that never in history, or the present, have self-regulating markets existed. We must realize that the philosophy of self-regulating market is a smoke screen to hide the tough fact that markets have been, and are, regulated day after day – mostly under WTO (World Trade Organization) rules – in favour of 'winner takes all', i.e. under neoliberal conditions.

The difficult task we have is to turn this philosophy upside down. Yes, markets have always been regulated, but now, let us regulate not in favour of winner takes all, but towards the development of the diversity of enterprises. Let us regulate towards the growth of markets that are not overwhelmingly dominated by just a few cultural conglomerates. Let us regulate towards giving audiences, buyers and the public the chance to choose from a plethora of different content, without having their attention directed, almost inevitably, towards a few stars.

A level playing field

It is not an exaggeration to say that this is a difficult task. My objective is to completely redesign cultural market relations. This goes far beyond merely critiquing the neoliberal distortion of our cultural landscape. The task is difficult because we have to imagine the conditions under which a level playing field might emerge. The task is difficult because it is not easy to imagine how markets might develop during the implementation of our proposals and the results of our analyses. The task is difficult because we have to convince others that what we propose is feasible. Nevertheless, I will try and give it my all.

If we as citizens of a country want the market to be organized in such a way that it is open to a wide diversity of cultural expression; if we as citizens insist that no party in the market dominates the production, distribution and promotion of cultural expression; and if we as citizens aspire that no one can call him or herself the 'owner' of cultural expression, then we have to force our governments to commit to a cultural policy that establishes these conditions. This also means that the free trade ideas in which the WTO is fully immersed have to be revised. This should be part of our cultural policy. In concrete terms, this calls for two simultaneous actions.

First, we have to do away with the protective shell for cultural monopolists, namely copyright. This will lead to a new situation: markets will be opened in which many cultural entrepreneurs can offer their creations and productions to audiences without being removed from public attention. This new situation will, in turn, offer them much better potential for increased profit on their work and thus the possibility of earning a much better income than is the case in the present situation.

Second, it is necessary to normalize the preconditions for the production, distribution, promotion and reception of artistic creations and performances. There should be no market party that renders the access to the cultural market, and thus to audiences, impassable. This should also prevent the growth of dominant market parties that could, after the abolition of copyright, appropriate the unprotected works of artists, producers and commissioners, i.e. of an array of cultural entrepreneurs, thus making loads of money.

Six major results

I count six major results that arise from my proposed interventions. First, the scale of cultural enterprises will become substantially smaller. Second, the public will no longer be terrorized by marketing and can thus make their own choices more freely. Third, many artists will have a much better chance of making a living from their endeavours. Fourth, the public domain of creativity and knowledge will be restored. Fifth, and maybe somewhat unexpectedly, normalizing the cultural markets will contribute to healthier economic relations in our countries. And sixth, the change in cultural market relations will have a positive effect for artists and cultural entrepreneurs in poor countries. Below, I will briefly indicate what can be expected from the proposed changes. However, it will be clear that much more research should be done by economists, by my fellow political scientists, and also, perhaps more relevantly, by artists who try to imagine, based on their practices, how their profession and their relation to audiences and the public domain might develop if the proposed changes were implemented.

The first effect we might expect from the proposed radical restructuring of cultural markets is that, with these new conditions, the rationale would be lost for cultural conglomerates to make substantial investments in blockbusters, bestsellers and stars (it is actually unlikely that these kinds of cultural giants will still exist after the introduction of the market regulations I have proposed). After all, by making creative adaptation respectable again, and by undoing the present system of copyright, the economic incentives for production on the present scale will diminish. If we were to commit ourselves to the abolition of copyright and the employment of a cultural competition policy that is the true consequence of this, we would bring about an eruption of cultural markets that would result in a diversity of cultural expression.

Corporation would never again reach such an extravagant size and dominance in the market as they do today. Of course, it would not be forbidden, for instance, for a cultural entrepreneur to invest millions of dollars or euros in a film, game, CD or DVD. However, the investment would no longer be able to be made behind an endless protective wall.

The effect would thus be that no single enterprise would be able to decisively manipulate the cultural playing field. At the same time, through the abolition of copyright, cultural conglomerates would lose their grip on the agglomeration of cultural products by which means they determine the outlook of our cultural lives to an ever-increasing extent. They would have to give up their control of huge chunks of the cultural markets.

This has far-reaching consequences for the way the public relates to cultural production. This is the second effect we might expect. Hitherto, the public's choices were overwhelmingly determined by what the marketing of cultural conglomerates offered them, so they could ensure the public did not miss anything. However, in the situation I propose, these conglomerates will not exist, and thus the public's attention will not be steered in only one direction.

This is a cultural gain, much greater than we can imagine. The public would need to develop their curiosity because it is their principal guiding compass once the marketing by cultural giants no longer exists to influence their tastes. Curiosity is a most valuable characteristic of human beings – it makes us into independent-thinking and reflective citizens.

When copyright is abolished and when the present cultural conglomerates are substantially smaller in size, i.e. are normal enterprises, a level playing field will be in place in which many artistic expressions can find their way to the public, buyers, readers, users and audiences. This is the third effect of my proposals. There will once again be room to manoeuvre for a variety of entrepreneurs in cultural markets, who as a consequence are no longer pushed out of the public's attention by blockbuster films, bestseller books and music, visual arts or design stars. All artists will be able to find audiences for their creations and performances in a normal market.

There is no reason not to believe that there is a demand for such an enormous variety of artistic expressions. In a normalized market, with equal opportunities for everyone, this demand can be fulfilled. It is possible to make a very comfortable living off artistic creations – regardless of the genre to which they belong – without being granted a title of ownership. This increases the possibility that a varied group of artists is capable of extracting a decent living from their endeavours.

Chris Anderson claims that in the long tail of the demand curve the market for niche music, for instance, is huge. 'What if the non-hits – from healthy niche product to outright misses – all together added up to a market as big as, if not bigger than the hits themselves' (Anderson 2006: 8). 'Our culture and economy are increasingly shifting away from a focus on a relatively small number of hits (mainstream products and markets) at the head of the demand curve, and moving toward a huge number of niches in the tail' (Anderson 2006: 52). Chris Anderson is quite optimistic: 'As the audience continues to move away from the Top 40 music and blockbusters, the demand is spreading to vast numbers of smaller artists who speak more authentically to their audience' (Anderson 2006: 82).

If copyright were no longer to exist, works would belong to the public domain from the moment of their creation or performance. However, this does not mean that creators, performers and other cultural entrepreneurs would be unable to make a living from their operations or to make them profitable. In order to understand this process, we need to take into consideration that market relations would also fundamentally change.

The substantial gains that are to materialize reside in the fact that the public domain of artistic creativity and knowledge will be restored. This is the fourth effect of the changes I propose for cultural market relations. It will no longer be possible to privately appropriate works that in actuality derive from the public domain. We may highly appreciate a new work, however it should remain accessible for further creations, appropriations and for critique, and also for changes and amendments. Public debate will then determine whether the alterations are respectful and whether the original work commands this respect. If public debate does not materialize it will be a loss for democracy. Independent and well-informed critique must once again come to play an important part. It is only by testing and dissecting works that we can sense value verses mediocrity. Actually, cultural conglomerates will lose the monopolistic exclusivity over broad cultural areas because artistic materials will be available to all and there will be no limitations on the creative adaptation of art.

An extra benefit of my approach is that the absolute character of property, which wreaks havoc upon our societies, will be loosened and, in this case, undone. In general, ownership has been allowed to occupy far too central a position in our neoliberal societies. Nevertheless, society needs to become much more vocal about its interests – for example in the social, ecological and economic sense – and needs to be able to enforce these interests. In our case of cultural entrepreneurship, it is undesirable even from a human rights perspective to be able to impose an exclusive property right on a creation and development in the area of knowledge. Furthermore, this is unnecessary under normal market conditions.

Another effect of my proposals – number five – concerns global economic policies. If I were Minister of Economic Affairs, or Secretary of Commerce, I would be quite nervous. Viacom, the owner of MTV and Paramount, demanded that Google pay one billion dollars for missed copyrights on YouTube, and took the case to court in 2007. Google bought YouTube for 1.65 billion dollars in 2006. Every day we see these kinds of figures pass before our eyes. We see an industry where fabulous amounts of money have been invested and lost because of copyright issues. One must be blind not to observe that copyright is in its decisive days – not only owing to digitization. Even the massive criminalization of users of artistic materials does not work any longer. Somebody should sound the alarm and all Ministers of Economic Affairs should listen: the billions and billions of dollars and euros invested in these huge cultural conglomerates are on the brink of vanishing into thin air. Currently, the cultural industries are risky businesses. Obviously, they do not like to see it this way.

Poor countries

Will the proposed changes in the structures of cultural markets have a positive effect for artists and cultural entrepreneurs in poor countries? I strongly believe so, and this is the sixth, and last, effect of my interventions. There would be no more threat from huge cultural conglomerates (based in rich or relatively rich countries) that try to dominate the cultural landscapes of countries in the Global South.

Nevertheless, it is relevant to investigate how much risk cultural entrepreneurs – including artists – can bear in poor societies, also in the case in which the (global) market is a level playing field. Evidently, the less that artistic creations and performances cost, the greater the chances of success. However, if greater investments are involved, for instance in technology and infrastructures, it will be more difficult to attract the necessary financial and logistic means – even if investments are modest from a Western standpoint. The following arguments are my response to this challenge.

First, it is clear from a cultural perspective that global trade relations have to be fairer to enable poor countries to develop themselves on a sound economic basis. This means a radical reshuffling of the basic principles and practices of WTO. This makes it even more necessary for artists, cultural entrepreneurs and their movements in the Global South to ally themselves with other organizations (such as environmentally focussed non-governmental organizations) that try to radically change the WTO. It is clear that when countries develop themselves economically, more resources will become available for investment in cultural endeavours.

Second, much can be learnt from a country like Nigeria where every year thousands of films are produced and distributed. New technologies, combined with effective forms of production and distribution, may radically change conditions for reaching audiences and the public.

A third, partial answer to the challenges regarding poorer countries can be found in the *Convention on the Protection and Promotion of the Diversity of Cultural Expressions* (UNESCO 2005). In Article 18 the contracting parties of this convention agree to establish a Fund for Cultural Diversity with the purpose of supporting countries in the Global South to build capacity for the development of infrastructures and technologies for cultural production and distribution. Even more important is Article 16, in which developed countries promise to facilitate 'cultural exchanges with developing countries by granting, through the appropriate institutional and legal frameworks, preferential treatment to artists and other cultural professionals and practitioners, as well as cultural goods and services from developing countries.' When countries take this article seriously, cultural enterprises from the Global South will have a much better chance of enlarging their markets and, consequently, their sources of income (Obuljen and Smiers 2006).

How to position yourself in newly constructed cultural markets?

In conclusion, one may note that most artists will find huge challenges in their artistic career. This is unavoidable. How should they position themselves in these newly constructed markets? Old certainties will probably no longer exist. There will be new chances (certainly with the advent of digitization), but how to explore them? What has been proposed here demands much more research about how to construct cultural markets under new conditions, that will be profitable for many artists in a financial and a creative sense. This should not only be researched by full-time academics. Artists themselves should explore their experiences and the opportunities they see, their failures and successes. Their research is most valuable for the development of the artistic profession in the twenty-first century and for the advance of real cultural diversity that we as a society desperately need.

23
EVALUATING QUALITY IN ARTISTIC RESEARCH

Michael Biggs and Henrik Karlsson

Position statement

The purpose of this chapter is to consider the issues arising from the context of evaluation that is current in academic research. Most countries either have introduced, or are introducing, national-level performance evaluations of research in response to pressures for transparency and accountability in the use of public funds, and also in response to the drive to reduce unnecessary expense. We do not see these evaluations as being primarily driven by an interest in quality, although one outcome is increased conformity by the researchers to the norms and criteria used in the assessment, thereby increasing performance scores. Of course, such norm creation also occurs with respect to research council criteria, which become standards rather than targets owing to their instrumental role in determining assessment practices through the act of establishing criteria. The creative arts are potentially at a disadvantage in this context since their main modes of communication are non-traditional, leading to difficulties in the effective communication of their value and outcomes using traditional means. Therefore their value may not be recognized outside subject-specific funding agencies for the arts. Furthermore, the arts may be seen as essentially transgressive, and therefore their potential contribution risks being overlooked or marginalized in a normatized pan-disciplinary culture.

Rather than advocating that the arts cannot be accommodated in such an evaluative regime, we take the view that the arts need to better understand what its value and its potential contribution to the academy is, in order that the evaluative framework can be adapted to suit it. This does not imply that special evaluative methods need to be designed. Instead it implies that clarity about the benefits of any research activity, expressed through whatever medium, will ensure that the criteria for assessment are appropriately attached to the values and aims of research in the field, rather than being ossified in obsolete forms of presentation or preconceptions about where value and significant contributions can be found. Such changes have occurred in the past, as shown by shifting conceptions of the nature and purpose of doctoral study, the subjects that can be studied at this level, and the personal capabilities fostered by this system. In this chapter we aim to provide a conceptual framework for understanding quality in any area, derived from examples in the creative arts, and thereby to show how relevant criteria can be developed that encourage creative knowledge-building in any subject.

Contextual introduction

In 1884, artists whose works had been rejected (*refusés*) by the normative Société des Artistes Française in Paris, formed the Salon des Indépendents as a protest with the motto 'no jury nor awards' (*sans jury ni récompense*). More than one hundred years ago artists were beset by criteria and judgements, even within the professional realm of arts practice. Now that art has been 'academicized', we can find even more situations in which art and artists are judged, against more or less explicit criteria. And much as art might react against, and even define itself, as that which cannot be categorized, judged or otherwise standardized, nonetheless the conventionalization of actions by institutions and even by communities of practitioners themselves, follows hard on the tail of anyone maintaining the view of art as revolutionary, unclassifiable and beyond qualitative judgements. Paradoxically, artistic judgements have become everyday food for the international TV-audience through 'reality shows' on figure skating, diving, gymnastics and other sports, and musical competitions in the format of the 'Idol' franchise. Commenting on 'artistic' achievements, ranking and voting-off have become a global media success.

Into this context comes academicized art. Of course, artists are not judged (or perhaps they are judged?) by panels of celebrities. They are not judged on the basis of who is the most entertaining, the most annoying or the most flamboyant ... but they are entering into an environment in which judgements of performance extend beyond mere competencies into qualitative judgements and a common opinion that performance includes criteria beyond mere skills. One might argue that it had always been thus, although in recent (Modernist) times, artists were expected to also have a touch of genius, a certain *je ne sais quoi*. In our more materialistic Postmodernist times we know exactly the *quoi* that makes us vote-off the unsuccessful reality show competitor. Thus we might see a historical trend in professional arts practice that results in artists no longer having to merely produce the artworks (as was perhaps the case in 1884), but also to have something to say about the work (as is required by winners of the Turner Prize), or to teach both theory and practice (as is common in university art departments), or to add to knowledge by acting as a researcher through the media of creative arts (as is problematized in this book). How these activities should or could be judged has not always been clear. Certainly the artists' knowledge of theory can be judged in both academic and professional contexts, but judgements about artistic quality are still passionately debated. Judgements of research excellence in the arts, and whether the criteria for judging such artistic research can legitimately be copied from other areas or whether it warrants something quite new, are also debated. If artistic research is a kind of hybrid of professional and academic elements (as is argued in Chapter 3), then are all the respective criteria of performance from both worlds still present in this hybrid, or are some criteria to be sacrificed to compensate for the inclusion of others in order to avoid the threat of the so-called 'double doctorate'? We discuss this further below.

The demands of international coordination according to the Bologna Process (2010) require that awards at various levels, broadly determined by how many years of higher education have been completed, are comparable across the participating nations. One consequence of this process, begun in 1999, has therefore been to create so-called 'third-cycle' courses, generically called doctorates, in countries and in subjects that have hitherto not offered them. The creative and performing arts have been greatly impacted by this drive (Chapter 1). Furthermore, the Berlin Communiqué (Berlin 2003) set up a requirement to standardize the way content and competencies are described in higher education, leading to the so-called Dublin Descriptors (JQI 2004). What is significant for our current discussion is that the Dublin Descriptors apply to all subjects at either first, second or third-cycles, therefore implying that a doctorate in the arts must have comparable content to a doctorate in any subject. This is the source of the problem for those who employ 'special pleading' (Chapter 21) and want the arts to have separate criteria and standards: in the EU there is now a politically driven context that precludes it. Nevertheless, the Dublin Descriptors still allow some scope for the idea that the standards and criteria for doctorates might be fulfilled in different subject-specific ways. For example, none of the following demand that a textual thesis be written, nor that non-textual media such as artworks are excluded:

> Qualifications that signify completion of the third-cycle are awarded to students who:
>> have demonstrated a systematic understanding of a field of study and mastery of the skills and methods of research associated with that field;
>> have demonstrated the ability to conceive, design, implement and adapt a substantial process of research with scholarly integrity;
>> have made a contribution through original research that extends the frontier of knowledge by developing a substantial body of work, some of which merits national or international refereed publication;
>> are capable of critical analysis, evaluation and synthesis of new and complex ideas;
>> can communicate with their peers, the larger scholarly community and with society in general about their areas of expertise;
>> can be expected to be able to promote, within academic and professional contexts, technological, social or cultural advancement in a knowledge based society.
>
> (JQI 2004)

Two competing models

We will assume that the majority of well-informed institutions are using a definition of research more or less compatible with Borgdorff's (Chapter 3) that states that artistic research is a merger of the requirements of professional arts practice and the traditional requirements of the academy.

Art practice qualifies as research if its purpose is to expand our knowledge and understanding by conducting an original investigation in and through art objects and creative processes. Art research begins by addressing questions that are pertinent in the research context and in the art world. Researchers employ experimental and hermeneutic methods that reveal and articulate the tacit knowledge that is situated and embodied in specific artworks and artistic processes. Research processes and outcomes are documented and disseminated in an appropriate manner to the research community and the wider public.

(Borgdorff 2006)

This is a rigorous and scholarly account of best practice in institutions, which we describe as a hybrid approach and results in a range of models that see arts practice and academic research merged together to varying degrees. Unfortunately, this approach brings with it certain problems, or perhaps leaves certain issues untouched, in response to which we will later propose an alternative 'new paradigm' approach.

But first, going back to the account of research as offered by Borgdorff, one of the advantages of accounts of this kind (and there are several usable ones on offer including for example OECD 2002; PBRF 2006; RAE 2006; AHRC 2009; ERA 2010; FAPESP 2010) is that they are based on a consideration of the fundamental characteristics of research, leaning primarily on the requirements of the academy. For the term 'research' to have any meaning in the academic world, it must partake to some extent of the values of originality and of making a contribution to knowledge based on systematic processes, etc. that would be recognizable to other academics outside the arts. We contrast this to what we regard as a less satisfactory approach to defining research based on case studies. The problem of this latter approach is that the cases cited are usually completed doctoral studies. Such cases suffer from the disadvantage that they were judged as successful during the time in which robust definitions of research were not available, hence our present inquiry. Therefore the mere fact that these studies were successfully awarded a doctoral degree cannot be used as a defence of them being successful research projects. This would be an example of the problem of 'circular cause and consequence'(Biggs *et al.* 2008a).

One disadvantage of the 'hybrid' approach is mentioned in Chapter 5. There may be, subject to further research, criteria in the academic world that are incompatible with criteria in the professional arts world, e.g. the value of rigour in the former (associated to methodological approaches that avoid bias in Chapter 10) and an emphasis on the singular experience in the latter (associated to Baumgarten's aesthetics in Chapter 2). If it is the case that there are some criteria that cannot be hybridized then one has a requirement, if not a duty, to be explicit about which criteria are to be included and which excluded. We do not think this classification of criteria has yet been undertaken, and perhaps it represents an opportunity for further research by proponents of the hybrid position.

The alternative 'new paradigm' approach that we mentioned above is a reference to so-called 'new paradigm research' in the social sciences. Since the 1980s there has been a well-documented change in the USA regarding the role of data in social sciences. One change has been from a sceptical stance towards qualitative data, to an acceptance of it. However, this fundamental change from a hard-line largely

Positivist understanding of what constitutes meaningful 'scientific' research, to a more contemporary interpretative approach, was a long struggle. It is interesting in the light of the present discussion about research methods in the arts, to read the accounts of this struggle by Guba (1990), Lincoln (1995) and others, and also to see how the academic context was also changing, resulting in the need for new theoretical understandings and text books (Denzin and Lincoln 1994). Guba and Lincoln (1994), for example, saw the emergence of qualitative methods as having a profound impact in all subject areas leading to a 'new paradigm' based on a constructivist view of how data informs us about the world. Rather than data 'proving' our (scientific) hypotheses, data acts to form our interpretations of what is going on, and so certain types of data are meaningful to us because we believe the world to be this way or that way, while other data does not seem relevant to us. Thus we construct our view of the world based on certain fundamental beliefs. This is a much more 'subjective' view of what the world is like which finds a role for auto-ethnocentricity, and hence seems more relevant to the arts.

Our 'new paradigm' approach falls into this category: a shift of perspective that allows certain activities to become meaningful in the context of arts research, even though those activities may not have been meaningful in either the context of academic research *per se* or the context of professional arts practice *per se*.

We can express the problem based on aims and objectives. There seems to be an agreement amongst the authors in this book that academic research has certain aims and objectives, and professional arts practice has other, perhaps overlapping aims and objectives. We could visualize this process of hybridization towards the creation of an 'arts research paradigm' in a representation of two circles coming together and overlapping (Figure 23.1). The problem is that we do not know the extent of this overlap – there is a range of resulting models, from no overlap to complete overlap. At one extreme (not adopted by any authors in this book but nonetheless identifiable in the literature) we have the claim that there is no overlap at all, i.e. that the interests of arts and academic research are distinct and separate. We could summarize this in the

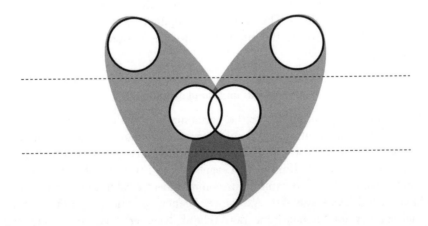

Figure 23. Range of hybrid models that result from the merger of arts practice with academic research, showing three different degrees of overlap.

name 'art or research', shown at the top of Figure 23.1. Such a position would result in a preference for a distinct non-PhD doctoral level award such as the Doctor of Arts. The advantage of a separate award is that there would no longer be a requirement to incorporate any of the criteria of the PhD from other subjects. The disadvantage would be the lack of comparability for pan-disciplinary quality assessments such as the RAE (UK Research Assessment Exercise).

At the other extreme of the hybrid approach (again, not adopted by any authors in this book in our opinion) there is a complete correspondence between the aims and objectives of academia and the professional arts world. This is shown at the bottom of Figure 23.1 where the two circles overlap completely and appear as one. We could summarize this position in the name 'art as research'. Such a position would result in a preference for just the PhD as the doctoral award because neither field would present any additional or problematic demands.

The middle of the range (apparently adopted by nearly all the authors in this book) would defend the position that there is a degree of overlap, but not a complete synonymy, between the aims and objectives of each field. In the centre of Figure 23.1, the two partially overlapping circles represent this position. We could summarize this position in the name 'art and research'. Producing research in this position would result in dissatisfaction with the Doctor of Arts award and also result in concerns over some aspects of the PhD award. There are two basic responses to producing research in this position: either some of the requirements of the PhD are removed, or our understanding of what they require needs to be modified. The former response is the one adopted pragmatically by many institutions, as we claimed above, in which the thesis requirements are made more liberal. The latter response results in the 'new paradigm' approach that we recommend and, in the 1980s in the social sciences interpretative and constructivist methodologies represented such a 'new paradigm'. Conceptual Art and movements such as Art and Language perhaps also represented 'new paradigms' in professional arts practice in the 1960s.

We think it is essential for the art colleges to systematically try out and test methodologies and to develop quality assessment rooted in the needs and horizons of each art genre 'from within', and not to uncritically borrow methods from other research fields and disciplines. This is also, in our opinion, an important foundation for the urgent need of developing the internal meta-level discourse within the arts-based research disciplines.

Standards and standardization

The Bologna Process sets a goal for the harmonization of third-cycle education, i.e. doctorate. This harmonization will require agreement about the basic nature of each qualification. A number of European organizations are already engaged in these questions, including ELIA (European League of the Institutes of Arts).[1] There are also various national-level organizations committed to establishing such norms and benchmarks, e.g. QAA (Quality Assurance Agency)[2] in the UK, and the Swedish National Agency for Higher Education (Högskoleverket).[3] However, inter-subject agreement within their respective national contexts is difficult to achieve owing to the diversity of their methods and outcomes. In particular we highlight that the outcomes of creative and performing arts often include artworks and artefacts in addition to, or instead of, the traditional written thesis.

The enormous diversity of creative production means that identifying a handful of evaluation criteria is difficult, and evaluation systems need to be flexible in order to cater for emerging and novel creative activities. On the other hand, the flexibility of these arts-based criteria and systems should not preclude a strong and explicit connection between evaluation in artistic research and evaluation in other academic subjects. It cannot be advantageous to the arts to have special regulations, and therefore arguably lower or unrelated standards, which are incomparable to other subjects.

In addition to the problem of the form of the outcomes and their communication, we identify a reluctance in some quarters to be explicit about criteria and standards. This may reflect the characteristics of the subject, which include non-verbal rather than verbal communication, and an emphasis on subjective interpretation rather than objective evidence-based assessment. On the latter, we note the emergence of evidence-based assessment in areas such as healthcare as one possible route for the evaluation of quality and performance. The Swedish National Agency for Higher Education criticized the tacit cultures in their evaluation of the curricula at the Fine Arts colleges, having noticed that a great number of staff meetings and talks between lecturers, supervisors and students took place without any written documentation, feedback or evaluations. Neither did the students get any written feedback by the examiner or the external expert at the final exams:

> Legal security for the individual student is highly dubious. This is particularly apparent at […], where the student has only one professor as supervisor and examiner during his or her five-year course of study. Course evaluations are fairly rare, and there is manifest confusion as regards differentiating between evaluating the student's performance and letting the student evaluate a particular course module.[4]

The reluctance to formulate and write down qualitative judgements exists not only in Fine Art colleges but also to a greater or lesser extent in all institutions where the bonds between lecturer and student are strong and personal. This is the traditional master-journeyman relation, which Pierre Bourdieu called 'charismatic pedagogy' (Bourdieu and Passeron 1979; Singerman 1999). Comments, advice and judgements about artistic qualities are of course made all the time but seldom accounted for or written down, and are therefore hard to question or discuss. Regardless of which formal or informal system the lecturers are using, the question is not whether it works or not in practice, but how to transform it into a language that makes it more transparent and communicable.

Forms of third-cycle education

The world of creative and performing arts education now boasts a bewildering array of doctoral (third-cycle) courses and awards. Our purpose in this section is to clarify the similarities and differences between the main types of awards in order to facilitate debate about models for the Bologna Process of harmonization.

The 'gold standard' is the PhD by supervised research. It has this status simply because it is a title that is available under the national education system of most countries around the world, although not necessarily in the creative arts. For example, it is not possible to gain a PhD for creative arts practice in the USA. Indeed, at the moment, one cannot study arts practice at any level at Harvard although a Task Force has recommended that the situation be changed (Harvard 2008). The PhD degree in its modern form originates from the German reformed system of the nineteenth century, pioneered by Wilhelm von Humboldt at Berlin University. The PhD is generally regarded as a training in academic research skills leading to the production and defence of a thesis that makes an original contribution to knowledge in a particular subject. It is the highest award available in most universities, although some countries including Germany, France, Poland, Hungary, etc., have traditionally expected a postdoctoral qualification (*Habilitation*) in order to take up a university teaching post. PhDs 'by supervised research' vary in the proportion of coursework included – from the USA with comparatively high proportion to the UK with often no requirement for coursework at all, i.e. in the UK the candidate typically spends 100 per cent of their time on individual supervised research.

In some countries, experienced researchers who have made a professional career as a researcher without undertaking a PhD can submit publications for a PhD 'by published works'. In general, a selection of publications by the candidate is submitted, together with a critical exegesis of how these individual publications are equivalent to a coherent programme of research of the kind normally developed under supervision. The exegesis is normally a critical assessment of the impact of the published works on the profession. This is a model inherited from traditional universities such as Cambridge that awarded PhDs on this basis.[5] This model is also embodied in the concept of a higher doctorate, such as DLitt or DSc. Higher doctorates are often awarded as honorary degrees for outstanding contribution to a field, or in response to submissions by the candidate following the model of PhD by published work (UKCGE 2008).

The professional impact, rather than the academic impact, of the candidate's research is the focus of the Professional Doctorate (UKCGE 2002), which has been available in the USA since the 1960s. Rather than aiming to make a contribution to knowledge, implicitly understood as academic knowledge or theory, the professional doctorate aims to make a contribution to the professional practice of a subject. Such studies are normally undertaken in partnership between a university and a workplace setting such as a major company. Candidates use their workplace as a source of problem-finding and contextualize the relevance of their solutions in terms of impact on the strategy or performance of the host company through the implementation of the outcomes. Thus the outcomes may be more in terms of modified performance than in terms of a written/theoretical contribution explaining why the interventions were productive.

The Taught Doctorate is based on both coursework as well as on the individual supervised research and is another PhD model. In Brazil, this is the model for a PhD in which the candidate takes certain taught disciplines towards a more detailed understanding of their chosen topic of study. The output of these disciplines is in the form of essays that will compose the chapters of the final thesis. The choice of disciplines and structure of the essays must be justified and defended in the final argument. In the

Taught Doctorate there is a greater integration of the candidate with the research community than in the Supervised Research model for example.

In response to the demands of the arts community for something distinct from the PhD that would facilitate modalities more common in the arts, one can find various non-PhD Doctorates such as DArt, DMus, etc. A Doctor of Music degree will usually require a portfolio of works, with or without accompanying analyses, reflections or comments, but generally does not imply or require a research supervision. Such awards allow institutions to create bespoke structures that reflect professionally-led interests. For example, the DMus degree in piano playing at the Sibelius Academy requires five concerts and a written thesis discussing themes related to the performed repertoire.

One example of a non-PhD doctoral-level course is the Norwegian Research Fellowships in the Arts. This is a unique three-year programme ending with the exam title "First Amanuensis" which is claimed to be equivalent to the PhD and qualifies the holder for an academic post as Senior Lecturer/Associate Professor (Chapter 2). In addition, a new artistic doctorate programme will be launched in Sweden from September 2010 as an alternative to the already existing PhD degree.

The conflict between academic and professional criteria

These different types of doctoral or third-cycle programmes and awards reflect a range of approaches to what is being delivered. Owing to the PhD being an award and a training that is available across disciplines, art departments that seek comparability with other subjects prefer this award. Such comparability has been described as the Situated Position (Biggs and Büchler 2008b). Conversely, departments that adopt the Isolationist Position, in which comparability is neither sought nor deemed possible, prefer awards that are not available in other subjects, such as non-PhD doctorates. The lack of comparability has an impact for the candidate, in some cases putting them in apparently advantageous positions as a subject specialist, but in other cases putting the relative value of the award in question.

Professional criteria can be fully met by programmes that do not aim to also fulfil all the academic criteria inherent in the PhD. Thus the Norwegian Fellowships, for example, can measure the quality of their output against professionally derived criteria such as the ability of the candidate to secure exhibitions, etc. Indeed some systems have a crossover between these criteria, as is the case in Finland. In Finland it is part of the programme of studies leading to the DArt degree that the candidate should have three professional exhibitions. However, the reason why this is a relevant criterion is not explicit, except to

Figure 23.2 The 'new paradigm' approach in which arts research emerges as a distinct and separate field from the existing fields of arts practice and academic research.

the extent that it demonstrates the candidates continuing performance as a professional artist. But if the doctorate is regarded as a training in research, then the relevance of performing as an art professional needs to be demonstrated. If one's research model is the hybrid of all the criteria of a traditional PhD plus all the criteria for professional performance, then having exhibitions would be relevant as part of a PhD programme. In practice, however, what we often hear from Finnish candidates is that they are required to undertake a 'double-doctorate', doing twice as much work as candidates in other subjects owing to a lack of specificity on the part of supervisors to what should be included and what should be excluded from the artistic doctorate.

Professional doctorates could be a solution for which award to give for work under this hybrid model. Such doctorates are awarded for 'an original contribution to professional practice' rather than 'to knowledge'. This would seem fitting in cases where the aim is to contribute to an ongoing professional activity. But even so, a review might be necessary so that the academically-led PhD component had a clear role.

In the 'new paradigm' approach, the communities of professional practice and of academic research have the obligation to define the aims and objectives of research and PhD training. This needs to be considered in the light of what activity the candidate is being trained for. What is the profession of an artistic researcher, what do they do, what makes them and their training particular? We believe it is inappropriate to respond that the candidate must achieve both requirements: for a traditional PhD in, for example, the sociology of art; and also the advancement of professional practice in the current arts circuit. Thus it is likely that in addition to a refinement of the curriculum for an artistic PhD in the new paradigm, clarification will also be needed of the postdoctoral employment context, their skills and activities, and their relationship to the existing worlds of traditional academia and of established professional arts practice.

The problem of describing quality

Various agencies involved with education, both in terms of delivery, e.g. QAA, and in terms of assessment, e.g. RAE, have attempted to establish absolute standards of quality. The QAA uses a system of benchmarking, which sets out key indicators of achievement. As an attempt at establishing minimum skill-sets for students at various levels this approach is quite successful. However, such benchmarks are essentially quantitative rather than qualitative owing to the difficulty of describing the relative quality of the attribute. The UK RAE attempts to overcome this difficulty by setting qualitative impact targets, for example that research should have 'international impact', 'national impact', etc. (RAE 2006). However, when we surveyed the 2008 submission in art and design we found that many items were submitted in the hope of representing internationally significant outcomes merely because they were exhibited or distributed internationally, rather than because they had international impact.[6] Although the additional requirement of a 300-word statement arguing for the significance and impact of each submission was required, it will have fallen on the RAE Panel to discriminate between international as in to be found geographically outside the UK, i.e. overseas, and international as in significant outside the UK, i.e. impactful.

The description of the work being overseas says nothing about quality whereas the description of the work having impact does suggest quality. The concept of quality is therefore an illusive one. We want to make two specific claims about it: that it is both relative and situated. By 'relative' we mean that no absolute standard of quality exists. By 'situated' we mean that the factors that influence our concept of quality derive from the context in which it is being applied, i.e. our understanding of quality varies from one subject to another, and one application to another.

The relativity of any concept, in contrast to the possibility of absolute values, is perhaps a philosophically discretionary point. The situation-dependency of a subject is reflected in statements by quality agencies such as QAA:

> The outcomes of the study and practice of art and design in HE contribute to both the cultural development and the economic well-being of the individual and of society. In both cases, an understanding of the context of the practice is essential.
>
> (QAA 2007: §2.4)

The judgement of quality involves judgements of relative value:

> More divergent forms of thinking, which involve generating alternatives, and in which the notion of being 'correct' gives way to broader issues of value, are characteristic of the creative process.
>
> (QAA 2007: §2.3)

At an apparently more particular level, the QAA discuss subject-specific knowledge and understanding, attributes and skills and determine that these

> will be evidenced in a body of work which demonstrates the graduate's ability to:
> generate ideas, concepts, proposals, solutions or arguments independently and/or collaboratively in response to set briefs and/or as self-initiated activity;
> employ both convergent and divergent thinking in the processes of observation, investigation, speculative enquiry, visualisation and/or making;
> select, test and make appropriate use of materials, processes and environments;
> develop ideas through to outcomes, for example images, artefacts, environments, products, systems and processes, or texts;
> manage and make appropriate use of the interaction between intention, process, outcome, context, and the methods of dissemination;
> be resourceful and entrepreneurial.
>
> (QAA 2007: §4.3)

However, none of these attributes and skills clarifies at what level one might expect this to be achieved. For example, the following is a list of attributes and skills required by 3–12 year olds under the International Baccalaureate programme:[7]

> They acquire the skills necessary to conduct inquiry and research and show independence in learning;

They exercise initiative in applying thinking skills critically and creatively to recognize and approach complex problems, and make reasoned, ethical decisions;

They understand and appreciate their own cultures and personal histories, and are open to the perspectives, values and traditions of other individuals and communities. They are accustomed to seeking and evaluating a range of points of view, and are willing to grow from the experience.

(IBO 2010: 3)

Although these two sets of criteria are not exactly the same, it can be seen that they follow some broadly similar themes, and it would be equally conceivable for us to claim that the International Baccalaureate statement applies to undergraduates as to 3–12 year olds. At either level, these indicators of performance need to be contextualized by experienced professionals who can determine what would constitute average or exceptional performance of these skills at a given level. For this reason we assert that no absolute standard of quality exists.

We also made a second claim above: that quality judgements are 'situated', i.e. subject-specific. One can make a comparison of the QAA benchmarks statements in two very different subjects, e.g. chemical engineering and art.

Chemical engineering:
be able to apply appropriate quantitative science and engineering tools to the analysis of problems;

be able to demonstrate creative and innovative ability in the synthesis of solutions and in formulating designs;

be able to comprehend the broad picture and thus work with an appropriate level of detail.

must have an appreciation of the wider multidisciplinary engineering context and its underlying principles;

must appreciate the social, environmental, ethical, economic and commercial considerations affecting the exercise of their engineering judgement.

must possess practical engineering skills acquired through, for example, work carried out in laboratories and workshops; in industry through supervised work experience; in individual and group project work; in design work; and in the development and use of computer software in design, analysis and control. Evidence of group working and of participation in a major project is expected. However, individual professional bodies may require particular approaches to this requirement.

(QAA 2006: Appendix A)

Art and design:

be able to:
present evidence that demonstrates some ability to generate ideas independently and/or collaboratively in response to set briefs and/or as self-initiated activity;

demonstrate proficiency in observation, investigation, enquiry, visualisation and/or making;

develop ideas through to outcomes that confirm the student's ability to select and use materials, processes and environments;

make connections between intention, process, outcome, context, and methods of dissemination.

At the threshold standard, a student's work will have been informed by aspects of professional practice in their discipline(s). This will be evidenced by some knowledge and understanding of:

the broad critical and contextual dimensions of the student's discipline(s);

the issues which arise from the artist's or designer's relationship with audiences, clients, markets, users, consumers, and/or participants;

major developments in current and emerging media and technologies in their discipline(s);

the significance of the work of other practitioners in their discipline(s).

(QAA 2007: §§6.3, 6.4)

In the QAA statements, in addition to these subject-specific benchmarks, there are also benchmark statements on generic skills (i.e. ones that graduates in any subject would possess) and transferable skills (i.e. ones that might be learnt in one context and transferred to another), in addition to the subject-specific skills (i.e. the ones specific to studying engineering or art, etc.). The skills above are subject-specific. However, they are remarkably similar and show that professional judgement is necessary to interpret what is meant, for example, by problem-solving in engineering as opposed to art.

It can be tempting for a creative artist to be distracted by the apparently radical difference in the form of output from the creative arts compared to traditional research, including video or sound recordings, sketches, diaries and models, etc., accompanying the written thesis or illustrated in appendices. Most UK universities set a word limit for the text whereas other institutions may be more flexible. The arts universities in Helsinki prescribe a scientific text to complement and complete the artefacts and performances – a requirement which often leads to over-ambition and the presentation of a text of more or less the same scope as a full text-only thesis in the humanities, in addition to the stipulated number of concerts, performances or exhibitions. These so-called double doctorates occur because there is no real agreement about the aims and objectives of artistic research, and supervisors believe that the aims of both arts and research have to be satisfied equally. This is a view that we criticized earlier: that the extent of the overlap in the hybrid model of 'art and research' is unclear. Insecurity can sometimes be noticed amongst supervisors that the art is not sufficiently 'weighty' and must be accompanied by a kind of 'academicized practice' (Biggs and Büchler 2010) with the help of citations of authorities such as Heidegger, Deleuze, etc. in order to add 'weight' to the practical work through association.

Experiments with the formats of the theses also reflect ongoing radical structural changes of the art colleges' curricula which will even affect the very groundwork of the art colleges. Some of the challenges are due to the increasing potential of the new digital media and a revaluation of the discipline's and subject's position in the curriculum. Focus might be shifted from the "charismatic pedagogy" mentioned earlier to a student who is supposed to acquire clearly defined knowledge and competences for a future career in a digitalized knowledge society. Therefore many art colleges in Europe are facing demands for changes of the curriculum from crafts-centred training focusing on the material (glass, wood, metal, etc.) to a curriculum which comprises both artistic and reflective competences in order for the students to understand their art work and research in a broader context and participate in the debate both verbally and in writing. This is a challenge to the traditional-romantic role model still prevailing at fine art colleges, above all (Karlsson 2007: 164).

Quality assurance and assessment are not exclusively related to completed results (exams, theses, research reports, etc.) but should be founded on an institution's long-term strategy and involve all stages of the research-training process. This is necessary not only to avoid using doctoral students as guinea pigs without competent back-up from the institution, but also to build up and maintain a creative research environment. The UK Council for Graduate Education reported that almost half of the 82 respondents to their 2001 enquiry had fewer than 11 doctoral students and commented:

> it is clear that collaboration can advance the quality and range of research provision. Despite the often competitive nature of higher education it can be argued that the fields in CPAD [Creative and Performing Arts and Design] will develop more rapidly if there is cross-institutional fertilisation as well as cross-disciplinary co-operation. The intellectual and artistic values are obvious in sharing research ideas, supervision and facilities in order to open up debate, to offer students and staff richer environment, and to generate original work across sub-discipline boundaries.
>
> (UKCGE 2001: 42)

The evaluation of the Swedish Research Council's grants to arts-based research 2001–2005 came to similar conclusions, adding that qualified artists should be involved in assessments on all levels from admissions to final exams, that the development of theoretical knowledge should at all times be linked to practice, and that all art genres need to devote great care in developing the internal 'reflective language' to make it more transparent for cross-disciplinary use (Karlsson 2007: 130–3).

Three cases

In our opinion, art and research have potentially conflicting aims, depending on the model of arts practice one adopts, i.e. this is especially apparent if one adopts the revolutionary and transgressive model of arts practice. Dissatisfaction will occur when researching artists claim their right to provoke, to freedom of expression, to be disrespectful, etc., and at the same time attempt to meet the academic demands of transparency, intelligibility and objectivity. This conflict can be illustrated through three examples of what could be regarded as the supreme 'arts demand' position, that tested or trespassed boundaries in two specific areas, by means of illegal acts and fiction.

Cases 1 and 2: *Unknown Woman* and *Territorial Pissing*

In 2009 two controversial final projects at the University College of Arts, Crafts and Design (Konstfack) in Stockholm were widely discussed at art schools, in newspapers and in numerous blogs. Anna Odell, a student at the Fine Arts institution, staged a fake suicide attempt by standing on a bridge in central Stockholm. Passers-by naturally thought that she was going to jump from the bridge and called the police. She was taken to a mental hospital, kept in restraints and admitted there for the night. Next morning she revealed that she had simulated the event and her acting was part of an art project. The hospital staff reported her to the police for raising a false alarm, fraud and violent resistance, while the general public's indignation centred on her cheating the doctors, nurses and police and occupying a hospital bed without being ill. Her explicit aim was to show the shortcomings of public mental healthcare. The project entitled 'Unknown Woman' (*Okänd kvinna 2009-349701*) was finally presented at the students' annual exhibition in May 2009 and consisted of an installation (a hospital bed), four movies, sound recordings and excerpts from the hospital case books. She was eventually prosecuted and sentenced to pay a symbolic fine of 2,500 Swedish kronor (approximately 250 euros).

A few weeks later another student at the same institution presented a video recording called *Territorial Pissing* as his final project, showing among other things a masked male spraying graffiti on the walls of an underground station and smashing the window of a train. He was reported to the police for the damage. The case was dropped however, since the true identity of the masked vandal could not be determined and the video was the only proof at hand. The Traffic Office, who brought the prosecution, plans to appeal.

It needs to be added that neither of these final projects were labelled 'research', but we suggest that they could be regarded as action projects. The most interesting consequence was not primarily the artistic qualities *per se*, or the artists' intentions, but the debates that followed for the rest of the year, discussing art and ideology, artistic freedom, the legal responsibilities of the college, the supervisors and the individual artists, and who should pay the fines. Blogs and letters to the editor also exposed the latent hatred of modern art amongst the general public. The debate gradually involved the rector, lecturers and students at Konstfack, the cultural minister, all leading art critics as well as the public. Konstfack chose to engage a lawyer to judge if other final projects might be transgressions of the law. The art critic Ingela Lind concluded:

> The old nineteenth-century role of the artist as outsider and rebel has been devoured by the market and the entertainment industry. But at the same time, the function of art as moral and ethical instructor has been soiled by the totalitarian regimes of the twentieth century. Instead, artists often work towards the same aims as journalists and critics: to expose hypocrisy and double standards in society. In doing so, they must stamp on new taboos, and that is exactly what Anna Odell has done.[8]
>
> (Lind 2009)

Case 3: Self Portrait

An explicit research outcome which attracted much attention was a doctoral thesis presented at the University School of Art and Design in Helsinki in 2000. The author Riitta Nelimarkka was a well-known visual artist and author of books for children who trained at the Sibelius Academy. Her thesis consisted of three exhibitions (two real and one virtual on the Internet) and a large book with about 100 charcoal drawings (Nelimarkka 2000). According to the Finnish tradition, separate juries examined artworks and texts. The three prescribed exhibitions were approved. The two opponents recommended that the book be printed but the school's own research council rejected it on the grounds that it was more autobiographical than critical. What followed was a *cause célèbre* that agitated academia in Finland. Nelimarkka took the initiative to appeal and the thesis was finally accepted, but with the lowest grade (*approbatur*). The subsequent public debate did not concern the art works but the content and form of the book, which the artist declared should be regarded as part of her artwork. The thesis had radically advanced the positions and arguments of art-based research. This was accentuated further when Nelimarkka criticized the whole process, the juries and the school's rector in a public press release.

The most offensive elements of the thesis were, according to the critics, the language and the style, for example Nelimarkka's use of three fictitious alter egos (a hare, a ball and the figure Elise) as spokespersons explaining how her artworks originated. From an academic point of view, *Self Portrait* could be regarded as a model of autoethnography, i.e. 'an autobiographical genre of writing and research that displays multiple layers of consciousness, connecting the personal and the cultural' (Ellis and Bochner 2000: 739). These texts can take the form of diaries, essays, poetry, fiction, fragments or multiple layers, often expressed in the first-person. Nelimarkka's alleged academic carelessness about quotes, sources and references could be regarded as a symptom of the post-modern aesthetic, in which fictitious information and fake documents frequently occur. Her thesis would probably have been accepted in ethnology or anthropology if presented there, while the critics regarded it as a parody of doctoral theses and an affront to the academic system.

Some of the most controversial art projects, like 'Unknown Woman', could be regarded as action research methods and should perhaps be documented and assessed as such, in ways comparable to autoethnographic research projects. Critics have observed that today's narrative and aestheticizing journalism is approaching fiction and the arts, through fake and directed documentaries, biographies as novels, etc. Paradoxically, artists who seem to notice more than journalists do, are the only ones with enough time and resources to engage with and disclose reality by means of increasingly politicized installations and projects, while the news media produce fiction.

While journalists do not dare to criticize political and religious fundamentalism, individual artists have stood up with their artwork to defend freedom of speech and the arts' right to deal with, criticize and even blaspheme any values and beliefs. Death-threats have consequently been made against, among others, the Danish artist Kurt Westergaard and the Swedish artist Lars Vilks for their caricatures of Mohammed, which were published in newspapers worldwide.

Some of these clashes between academic and artistic paradigms could have been avoided if the school and its supervisors had been aware beforehand of possible illegal acts and provocations which might impact passers-by or involve people in performances or recordings without their knowledge; that is, transgressing the borders of research ethics. The debate over the thesis *Self Portrait* revealed that at the time there were no agreements about definitions and boundaries between art and research at the institution itself. Fictive elements in a doctoral thesis are not rare but are usually marked as such, for example as a narrative concept or literary style. However, must they always be explicitly declared as pure fiction? It is evident that not just any topic or problem can be admitted for artistic research projects, at least it may not be possible to carry it out without many obstacles and clashes if one aims to be a pioneer in both form and content. On the other hand, cases like the above attracted much public attention, which might ultimately benefit the art world in general, not least by inspiring and raising the level of art criticism.

The changing roles and positions of artists in Western societies – from court painters to bohemians, rebels and society's conscience, to the academic researchers of today – would constitute an interesting multidisciplinary research project. An initial stocktaking of the theme was presented at a series of exhibitions in Berlin in 2008–9 as *Kult des Künstlers* (The Cult of the Artist).[9]

Best practices, canons and paradigms

In our consideration of 'canons' of best practice in arts-based research we find ourselves thinking once again of the Impressionists in nineteenth-century Paris. Working within a narrowly defined genre of art, conventionalized into certain practices that were approved by the Salon, the radicals who were operating outside these 'laws' could be seen as revolutionaries, for better or worse. Since their art is no longer revolutionary in our eyes, it is easy to see this transgressive behaviour as nonetheless lying squarely in the tradition of art production, producing collectable artefacts for connoisseurs. As we look at more recent examples, it is perhaps less easy to see how they fit our expectations of art. And if we hold a revolutionary model of art then the continual requirement of novelty might also present insuperable demands. Likewise in the academic field, revolution can be seen as a mainstay of creativity (perhaps in line with Sullivan's model of creative novelty, Chapter 6). Methodological radicalism has also been somewhat incorporated into the mainstream, through the Popper/Feyerabend debate (Feyerabend 1993 [1975]), and through the emergence of alternative paradigms (Guba 1990). We therefore live in times when canons are under question as unsustainable within a model of continual change, and also under question politically, as a symptom of a dominant hegemony that is also rejected.

If the idea of a 'new paradigm' is to be taken seriously then it must be recognized that few cases are available to be used as models. Similarly, we should be sceptical of early examples, as has been discussed in the case of pioneering PhDs in the arts in the 1990s (Chapter 5). A case-led approach is therefore both impractical and undesirable. Finally, the great diversity of subjects within the creative and performing arts would require an exhaustive list of examples to be useful to trainee researchers seeking models of working within their particular media and scenarios (Chapters 13 and 17). Instead we agree with Newbury (Chapter 21) that frameworks need to be established for the validation of methods in relation to particular problems, contexts and audiences. There can be no off-the-shelf methods to be taught to all doctoral students in the field, because there are no off-the-shelf problems. To make matters worse, creative problems can be characterized as being not only transgressive but also transdisciplinary, in the sense used by Häberli, requiring individual methodological solutions to never-before-seen problems.

> The core idea of transdisciplinarity is different academic disciplines working jointly with practitioners to solve a real-world problem. It can be applied in a great variety of fields.
>
> (Häberli *et al.* 2001: 4)

It could be inspiring to broaden our minds by looking at the strategies for developing a paradigm in other professional disciplines, in this case library and information science. One problem emanates from what Jan Nolin perceives as 'the old model with disciplines monopolising professions' (Nolin 2008: 38), where disciplines that were autonomous and distant from society, establish clear boundaries between each other, for example law and medicine. 'Normal science was based on an atomistic ideal, solving individual problems with individual pieces of knowledge' (Nolin 2008: 39). This does not work any longer, symbolically illustrated by the so-called 'Ch-Ch' syndrome (the Chernobyl nuclear meltdown and the Challenger shuttle crash). These catastrophes made clear the risk of people with restricted knowledge handling the quality control of very advanced technologies. Nolin argues that the focus should be shifted from describing and analysing the role of professions to actively contributing to their improvement, and that a starting point would be to collaborate with the practitioners. He suggests that quality in a profession can be linked to:

> A discipline being open (rather than closed) for several different perspectives that students need to become comfortable with in their schooling to becoming professionals.
>
> A profession and a professional association that is open and interlinked with other related professions. [...]
>
> A profession and professional association that continually strives for high-quality by a never-ending collaboration with Academy.
>
> (Nolin 2008: 47)

As a consequence, Nolin recommends that professions abandon the traditional way of explaining and confirming their identity by generalization from individual case studies. Instead he suggests a 'trilateral concept of truth' as a point of departure for the theory of professions by allowing for truth as understanding (the hermeneutical dimension) and use (the pragmatic dimension) to complete the demand for correspondence between theory and reality, which is too narrow. His conclusions corroborate our opinion that the optimal development of an artistic research paradigm would prosper by collaboration between practitioners and theorists, not by individual art genres or traditional research disciplines trying to define the borders and agenda unilaterally (Nowotny: Preface).

We know that the methodological issues being debated in the arts are also being debated in medicine, law, etc. Thus we find a comparison between 'alternative paradigm research' in social sciences, and its subsequent adoption or interest in nearly all subjects in the academy. We also find the issues of non-traditional methods, visual and non-visual languages, embodied and propositional knowledge, etc., that the arts often raise but which have impact in areas such as philosophy. We believe that the 'new paradigm' of arts research will become a branch of critical theory. Creative and performing arts research has the capability to contribute to the development of a new paradigm precisely because it has had to conduct a rigorous analysis of what it means to do research, especially in an area which does not conform to the current norms of academic research. The mere appearance of individuality in the arts owing to them producing artistic outcomes is, in our view, entirely misleading. The arts, in common with nearly all subjects, would benefit from this critical review and reconstruction of its aims in research, so its actions could be more in line with its values, leading to satisfaction in the communities who undertake this work and consume its outcomes.

We propose that what is valued by the community is a function of its worldview, and some of the problems of intra-national and extra-national harmonization occur as a result of doctoral-level education trying to reflect the worldviews of both academic research and professional practice. Such an enterprise will always be doomed to failure since there is only a partial overlap between the interests of the academic community and the professional arts community. The purpose of training arts researchers should be to prepare them as professionals in arts research. This is not the same as a career in traditional academic research nor is it the same as a career in existing professional arts practice. This is a third professional category that is as yet undefined.

Through a better understanding of what constitutes meaningful actions in the new field of artistic research, the community can identify criteria for determining significant production, i.e. the definition of the doctorate as a significant contribution to a field. This is not a problem that is unique to the arts, but we believe that enduring solutions that are relevant within subject domains must arise from within the subjects themselves. This can be achieved by an analysis of the actions that are regarded as meaningful and productive. Resolving the value system of the community will allow both texts and artefacts to be evaluated, facilitating the development of a system and terminology that considers the specificities of various creative genres. Evaluation should be transparent and intelligible enough to be practised on all levels of artistic research, from auditions to post-doctoral research applications, and replace the present tradition of two separate juries and requirements leading up to the so-called 'double doctorates'.

The potential benefits of the new paradigms are rich, as has been shown with paradigmatic changes in the social sciences in the 1990s. Paradigmatic change, or rather paradigmatic establishment, would directly address what Nowotny (2008: Preface) describes as 'what remains unforeseeable and yet promises to further expand the range of possibilities'.

Notes

1 http://www.elia-artschools.org/ (accessed 20 March 2010).
2 http://www.qaa.ac.uk (accessed 22 February 2010).

3 http://www.hsv.se (accessed 22 February 2010).
4 Rättssäkerheten för den enskilde studenten kan verkligen ifrågasättas. Detta är särskilt tydligt vid [...], där studenten har en enda professor som handledare och examinator under hela sin femåriga studietid. Kursvärderingar är ganska sällsynta, och det finns en uppenbar förvirring när det gäller att skilja mellan att utvärdera studentens prestation eller låta studenten utvärdera ett visst utbildningsmoment (Högskoleverket 2007: 11).
5 The philosopher Wittgenstein was awarded his PhD by the University of Cambridge in 1929 on the basis of his book *Tractatus Logico-Philosophicus* which was published in 1922 [first published in a journal in 1921].
6 http://www.rae.ac.uk (accessed 28 February 2010).
7 http://www.ibo.org/pyp/ (accessed 1 March 2010).
8 Konstnärens gamla 1800-talsroll som outsider och rebell har slukats av marknaden och underhållningsindustrin. Samtidigt har konstens funktion som moralisk och estetisk uppfostrare solkats av 1900-talets totalitära regimer. I stället arbetar konstnärerna ofta med samma målsättning som journalister eller kritiker: att avslöja hyckleri och dubbelmoral i samhället. Då måste de trampa på nya tabun, och det har Anna Odell gjort.
9 http://www.kultdeskuenstlers.de (accessed 13 March 2010).

REFERENCES

aaa (2007) *Urban Act: A handbook for alternative practice*, Paris: PEPRAV.

Adorno, T.W. (1966) *Negative Dialektik*, Frankfurt-am-Main: Suhrkamp.

—— (1991 [1958]) *Notes to Literature*, translated by Shierry Weber Nicholsen, New York: Columbia University Press.

Agamben, G. and D. Heller-Roazen (2000) *Potentialities: collected essays in philosophy*, Palo Alto, CA: Stanford University Press.

AHRC (2009) *Research Funding Guide v1.2*, Bristol: AHRC. Online. <http://www.ahrc.ac.uk/ FundingOpportunities/Documents/Research Funding Guide.pdf> (accessed on 20 February 2009).

Alberti, L.B. (1966 [1435]) *On Painting [De Pictura]*, New Haven, CT: Yale University Press.

Allegue, L., S. Jones, B. Kershaw and A. Piccini (eds) (2009) *Practice-as-Research in Performance and Screen*, Basingstoke: Palgrave Macmillan.

Anders, G. (1980 [1956]) *Über die Seele im Zeitalter der zweiten industriellen Revolution (Vol.1 of Die Antiquiertheit des Menschen)*, Munich: C.H. Beck.

Anderson, C. (2006) *The Long Tail. Why the Future of Business Is Selling Less of More*, New York: Hyperion.

Anderson, S. (2000) 'The Profession and Discipline of Architecture: practice and education', in: Piotrowski, A. and J.W. Robinson, (eds) *The Discipline of Architecture*, London: University of Minnesota Press, 292–305.

Andrews, K. (2009) 'A House Divided: On the future of creative writing', *College English* 71 (2): 242–55.

Andrews, M. (1999) *Landscape and Western Art*, New York: Oxford University Press.

Arendt, H. (1958) *The Human Condition*, Chicago, IL: University of Chicago Press.

—— (1966) *The Origins of Totalitarianism*, New York: Harcourt Brace.

Aristotle (1984) *The Complete Works of Aristotle: revised Oxford translation*, edited by Jonathan Barnes, Oxford: Oxford University Press.

Arlander, A. (1995) 'Some Conversations … in Various Spaces', in: Paavolainen, P. and A. Ala-Korpela, (eds) *Knowledge Is a Matter of Doing* (Acta Scenica 1), Helsinki: Theatre Academy, 118–23.

—— (1998) *Esitys tilana*, (Acta Scenica 2), Helsinki: Theatre Academy.

—— (2008) 'Finding your Way Through the Woods – Experiences of Artistic Research', *Nordic Theatre Studies* 20: 29–41.

Arnheim, R. (1969) *Visual Thinking*, Berkeley, CA: University of California Press.

Ascott, R. (2008) 'Distance Makes the Art Grow Further: distributed authorship and telematic textuality in La Plissure du Texte', *GEIST* 11, 12, 14: §7.

Asselberghs, H. (2008) *Cartographic Strategies: subjective worldviews*, Leuven: ACCO.

Atkinson, T. (1990) 'Phantoms of the Studio', *Oxford Art Journal* 13 (1): 49–62.

Auslander, P. (1999) *Liveness*, London: Routledge.

—— (2006) 'The Performativity of Performance Documentation', *Performing Arts Journal* 28 (3): 1–10.

Bainbridge Cohen, B. (1993) *Sensing, Feeling, and Action: the experiential anatomy of body-mind centering*, Northampton, MA: Contact Press.

Bal, M. (2002) *Travelling Concepts in the Humanities: a rough guide*, Toronto: University of Toronto Press.

Balkema, A.W. (2006) 'Perception and the Lines of Light', *MaHKUzine: Journal of Artistic Research* 1, 13. Online. <http://www.mahku.nl/research/mahkuzine1.html> (accessed on 28 December 2009).

Balkema, A.W. and H. Slager (2007) 'Robbert Dijkgraaf', MaHKUzine: *Journal of Artistic Research* 2, 31–7. Online. <http://www.mahku.nl/research/mahkuzine2.html> (accessed on 29 December 2009).

Banes, S. and A. Lepecki (eds) (2006) *The Senses in Performance*, London: Routledge.

Barrett, E. and B. Bolt (eds) (2007) *Practice as Research: Approaches to creative arts enquiry*, London: I.B. Tauris.

Barry, A.M.S. (1997) *Visual Intelligence: Perception, image, and manipulation in visual communication*, Albany, NY: State University of New York Press.

Bärtås, M. (2008) 'Talk Talk –On Method and the Story of the Work', *GEIST* 11, 12, 14: §2.

Barthes, R. (1977) *Image, Music, Text*, Glasgow: Collins.

—— (1984) *Camera Lucida*, London: Flamingo.

Bate, W.J. (1963) *John Keats*, Cambridge, MA: Harvard University Press.

Battersby, C. (1998) *The Phenomenal Woman: Feminist metaphysics and the patterns of identity*, Cambridge: Polity Press.

Baudrillard, J. (2002) *Screened Out*, London: Verso.

Baumgarten, A.G. (2009 [1758]) *Aesthetica*, Chicago, IL: University of Michigan Library.

Baxandall, M. (1971) *Giotto and the Orators: Humanist observers of painting in Italy and the discovery of pictorial composition 1350–1450*, Oxford: Oxford University Press.

Becher, T. and P.R. Trowler (2001) *Academic Tribes and Territories. Intellectual Enquiry and the Cultures of Disciplines*, Buckingham, UK and Philadelphia: The Society for Research into Higher Education and Open University Press.

Bechtel, W. and A. Abrahamsen (1991) *Connectionism and the Mind: An introduction to parallel processing in networks*, Cambridge, MA: Blackwell.

Bell, D. (2006) 'Creative Film and Media Practice as Research: In pursuit of that obscure object of knowledge', *Journal of Media Practice* 7 (2): 85–100.

Bergson, H. (1991) *Matter and Memory*, Cambridge, MA: MIT Press.

Berlin (2003) *Realising the European Higher Education Area*, Brussels: European Union. Online. <http://www.bologna-berlin2003.de/pdf/Communique1.pdf> (accessed on 8 January 2010).

Beta_space (2009) Beta Space Interactive Art, University of Technology Sydney. Online. <http://www.creativityandcognition.com/betaspace/> (accessed on 18 March 2009).

Biggs, M.A.R. (2002) 'The Rhetoric of Research'. Common Ground – Proceedings of the Design Research Society International Conference, Brunel University: Staffordshire University Press, 111–8.

—— (2003) 'The Role of "The Work" in Research', *PARIP*. Online. <http://www.bris.ac.uk/parip/biggs.htm> (accessed on 12 January 2009). Online. <http://hdl.handle.net/2299/4379> (accessed on 30 June 2010).

—— (2004) 'Learning from Experience: Approaches to the experiential component of practice-based research', in: Karlsson, H., (ed.) *Forskning-Reflektion-Utveckling*, Stockholm, Sweden: Swedish Research Council, 6–21. Online. <http://hdl.handle.net/2299/1775> (accessed on 30 June 2010).

Biggs, M.A.R. and D. Büchler (2007) 'Rigour and Practice-based Research', *Design Issues* 23 (3): 62–9. Online. <http://hdl.handle.net/2299/4414> (accessed on 30 June 2010).

—— (2008a) 'Architectural Practice and Academic Research', *Nordic Journal of Architectural Research* 20 (1): 83–94. Online. <http://hdl.handle.net/2299/4405> (accessed on 30 June 2010).

—— (2008b) 'Eight Criteria for Practice-based Research in the Creative and Cultural Industries', *Art, Design and Communication in Higher Education* 7 (1): 5–18. Online. <http://hdl.handle.net/2299/4412> (accessed on 30 June 2010).

—— (2009) 'Supervision in an Alternative Paradigm', *TEXT: Journal of Writing and Writing Courses* Special Issue 6, 1–14. Online. <http://www.textjournal.com.au/speciss/index.htm> (accessed on 17 February 2010).

—— (2011) 'Transdisciplinarity and New Paradigm Research', in: Doucet, I. and N. Janssens, (eds) *Transdisciplinary Knowledge Production in Architecture and Urbanism. Towards hybrid modes of inquiry*, Dordrecht: Springer Verlag.

Bishop, C. (2005) *Installation Art*, London: Routledge.

—— (ed.) (2006) *Participation*, London: Whitechapel Ventures.

—— (2007) 'The New Masters of Liberal Arts: Artists rewrite the rules of pedagogy', *Modern Painters* 19 (7): 86–9.

Blunt, A. (1940) *Artistic Theory in Italy 1450–1600*, Oxford: Clarendon.

Bode, M. and S. Schmidt (2008) 'Off the Grid', PhD thesis, Valand School of Fine Arts.

Bologna Process (2010) *The Official Bologna Process Website 2007–2010*, Online. <http://www.ond.vlaanderen.be/hogeronderwijs/Bologna/> (accessed on 24 February 2010).

Bolt, B. (2004) *Art Beyond Representation: The performative power of the image*, London, I.B. Tauris.

—— (2006) 'Materializing Pedagogies', *Working Papers in Art & Design* 4. Online. <http://sitem.herts.ac.uk/artdes_research/papers/wpades/vol4/bbfull.html> (accessed on 17 February 2010).

—— (2007) 'The Magic is in Handling', in: Barrett, E. and B. Bolt, (eds) *Practice as Research: Approaches to creative arts enquiry*, London: I.B. Tauris, 27–34.

—— (2008) 'A Performative Paradigm for the Creative Arts?', *Working Papers in Art & Design* 5. Online. <http://sitem.herts.ac.uk/artdes_research/papers/wpades/vol5/bbfull.html> (accessed on 15 February 2010).

Bolter, J.D. and R. Grusin (1999) *Remediation*, Boston, MA: MIT Press.

Borgdorff, H. (1998) 'Holismus, Wahrheit, Realismus. Adornos Musikphilosophie aus amerikanischer Sicht', in: Klein, R. and C.-S. Mahnkopf, (eds) *Mit den Ohren denken. Adornos Philosophie der Musik*, Frankfurt-am-Main: Suhrkamp, 294–320.

—— (2006) *The Debate on Research in the Arts*, (Sensuous Knowledge 2), Bergen: Bergen National Academy of the Arts.

—— (2008) 'Artistic Research and Academia: an uneasy relationship', in: Lind, T., (ed.) *Autonomi och egenart – konstnärlig forskning söker identitet*, Stockholm: Swedish Research Council, 82–97.

—— (2009a) *Artistic Research within the Fields of Science*, (Sensuous Knowledge 6), Bergen: Bergen National Academy of the Arts.

—— (2009b) 'Onderzoek in kunsten bloeit', *Science Guide* 2009. Online. <http://www.scienceguide.nl/200903/onderzoek-in-kunsten-bloeit.aspx> (accessed on 1 March 2010).

Børing, P. and P. Maassen (2003) *Statlige tilknytningsformer i et internasjonalt perspektiv*, Oslo: Norsk institutt for studier av innovasjon, forskning og utdanning. Online. <http://www.nifustep.no/norsk/publikasjoner/statlige_tilknytningsformer_i_et_internasjonalt_perspektiv> (accessed on 25 January 2010).

Bourdieu, P. (1977) *Outline of a Theory of Practice*, Cambridge: Cambridge University Press.

—— (1990) *In Other Words: essays towards a reflexive sociology*, Stanford, CA: Stanford University Press.

—— (1991) *Language and Symbolic Power*, Cambridge: Polity Press.

—— (1992) *The Logic of Practice*, Cambridge: Polity Press.

—— (1998) *Practical Reason: on the theory of action*, Cambridge: Polity Press.

Bourdieu, P. and J.-C. Passeron (1979) *The Inheritors: French students and their relation to culture*, Chicago, IL: Chicago University Press.

Bourriaud, N. (1998) *Relational Aesthetics*, Paris: Les presses du réel.

Bowden, I. (2006) 'The First Cut; the locus of decision at the limits of subjectivity', PhD thesis, University of the Arts London.

Bradley, D., P. Noonan, H. Nugent and B. Scales (2008) *Review of Australian Higher Education*, Canberra: Department of Education, Employment and Workplace Relations. Online. <http://www.deewr.gov.au/highereducation/review/pages/reviewofaustralianhighereducationreport.aspx> (accessed on 8 March 2010).

Brady, M. and D. Pritchard (2006) 'Epistemic Virtues and Virtue Epistemology', *Philosophical Studies* 130: 1–8.

Brady, T. (2000) 'A Question of Genre: De-mystifying the exegesis', *TEXT: Journal of Writing and Writing Courses* 4. Online. <http://www.textjournal.com.au/april00/brady.htm> (accessed on 28 December 2009).

Brand, P.Z. and M. Devereux (2003) 'Feminism and Aesthetics', *Hypatia* 18 (4): ix–xx.

Braziel, J.E. and A. Mannur (eds) (2003) *Theorizing Diaspora*, Cambridge, MA: Blackwell.

Bregman, A.S. (1994) *Auditory Scene Analysis: the perceptual organization of sound*, Cambridge, MA: MIT Press.

Bridges, D. (2003) *Fiction Written under Oath*, Dordrecht: Kluwer.

Brien, D.L. (2009) "Based on a True Story": The problem of the perception of biographical truth in narratives based on real lives', *TEXT: Journal of Writing and Writing Courses* 13. Online. <http://www.textjournal.com.au/oct09/brien.htm> (accessed on 20 February 2010).

Brown, B. (2009) 'Counting', *Critical Inquiry* 35: 1032–53.

Büchler, D., M.A.R. Biggs, G. Sandin and L.-H. Ståhl (2009a) 'Architectural Design and the Problem of Practice-Based Research', *Cadernos de Pós-Graduação em Arquitetura e Urbanismo* 2008. Online. <http://www.mackenzie.br/dhtm/seer/index.php/cpgau/article/view/Biggs.2009.2/311> (accessed on 15 February 2010).

Büchler, D., M.A.R. Biggs and L.-H. Ståhl (2009b) 'Areas of Design Practice as an Alternative Research Paradigm', *Design Principles and Practices: An International Journal* 3 (2): 327–38.

Burns, C. (2000) 'Aligning Education with Practice', in: Piotrowski, A. and J.W. Robinson, (eds) *The Discipline of Architecture*, London: University of Minnesota Press, 260–71.

Burton, G.O. (2009) Silva Rhetoricæ, Online. <http://humanities.byu.edu/rhetoric/silva.htm> (accessed on 3 March 2009).

Butler, J. (2000) *Contingency, Hegemony, Universality: contemporary dialogues on the left*, London: Verso.

Cancienne, M.B. and C.N. Snowber (2003) 'Writing Rhythm: movement as method', *Qualitative Inquiry* 9 (2): 237–53.

Candlin, F. (2000) 'A Proper Anxiety? Practice-based PhDs and academic unease', *Working Papers in Art & Design* 1. Online. <http://sitem.herts.ac.uk/artdes_research/papers/wpades/vol1/candlin2full.html> (accessed on 20 February 2010).

Candy, L. and E.A. Edmonds (1994) 'Artefacts and the Designer's Process: implications for computer support to design', *Journal of Design Sciences and Technology* 3 (1): 11–31.

Carter, P. (2004) *Material Thinking: the theory and practice of creative research*, Carlton, VIC: Melbourne University Publishing.

Castells, M. (1996) *The Rise of the Network Society*, Oxford: Blackwell Publishers.

Cerulo, K.A. (ed.) (2002) *Culture in Mind: towards a sociology of culture and cognition*, New York: Routledge.

Chadwick, W. (1980) *Myth in Surrealist Painting, 1929–39: Dali, Ernst, Masson*, Ann Arbor, MI: UMI Research Press.

Clements, W. and S. Scrivener (2008) 'The Discourses of Practice-based Arts Research and how Contribution is Made', paper presented at Research into Practice 2008, Royal Society of Arts, London.

CNAA (1988) *CNAA Handbook 1988–89*, London: Council for National Academic Awards.

Cobussen, M. (2008) *Thresholds: rethinking spirituality in music*, Aldershot: Ashgate.

Coombe, R.J. (1998) *The Cultural Life of Intellectual Properties. Authorship, Appropriation, and the Law*, Durham, NC: Duke University Press.

Costello, B. (2007) 'A Pleasure Framework', *Leonardo* 40 (4): 370–1.

Costello, B. and E.A. Edmonds (2007) 'A Study in Play, Pleasure and Interaction Design'. Proceedings of Designing Pleasurable Products and Interfaces, New York: ACM Press, 76–91.

Cox, G. (2006) 'Antithesis: the dialectics of software art', PhD thesis, University of Plymouth.

Critchley, S. (2004) *Very Little... Almost Nothing: death, philosophy, literature*, London: Routledge.

Cross, N. (2006) *Designerly Ways of Knowing*, New York: Springer.

Csikszentmihalyi, M. (1996) *Creativity*, New York: Harper Collins.

Dadds, M. (1995) *Passionate Enquiry and School Development: a story about teacher action research*, London: Routledge.

Dalí, S. (1930) 'L'Âne Pourri', *Le Surréalisme au service de la Révolution* 1 (1): 12.

Dallow, P. (2003) 'Representing Creativeness: practice-based approaches to research in creative arts', *Art, Design & Communication in Higher Education* 2 (1–2): 49–66.

—— (2005) 'Outside "The True": research and complexity in contemporary arts practice', in: Miles, M., (ed.) *New Practices, New Pedagogies: a reader*, London: Routledge, 111–9.

Damasio, A. (1999) *The Feeling of What Happens: body and emotion in the making of consciousness*, New York: Harcourt.

—— (2006) *Descartes' Error: emotion, reason and the human brain*, London: Vintage Books.

Danto, A.C. (2005) *The Philosophical Disenfranchisement of Art*, New York: Columbia University Press.

Davies, D. (2004) *Art as Performance*, Oxford: Wiley-Blackwell.

de Certeau, M. (1984) *The Practice of Everyday Life*, Berkeley, CA: University of California Press.

—— (1986) *Heterologies: discourse on the other*, Minneapolis, MN: University of Minnesota Press.

de Greef, W. (2008) 'Opening: a certain MA-ness', *MaHKUzine Journal of Artistic Research* 5, 5–6. Online. <http://www.mahku.nl/research/mahkuzine5.html> (accessed on 21 February 2010).

Delagrange, S. (2009) 'Wunderkammer, Cornell, and the Visual Canon of Arrangement', *Kairos* 13. Online. <http://kairos.technorhetoric.net/13.2/topoi/delagrange/index.html> (accessed on 16 January 2010).

Deleuze, G. (1988) *Bergsonism*, Cambridge, MA: MIT Press.

—— (1995) *Negotiations*, New York: Columbia University Press.

Deleuze, G. and F. Guattari (1988 [1980]) *A Thousand Plateaus: capitalism and schizophrenia*, London: Athlone Press.

DeLuca, K.M. (1999) *Image Politics: the new rhetoric of environmental activism*, New York: Guilford Press.

Denzin, N. and Y. Lincoln (1994) *Handbook of Qualitative Research*, London: Sage Publications.

Derrida, J. (2000) *Demeure: fiction and testimony*, Stanford, CA: Stanford University Press.

Descartes, R. (1985 [1637]) 'Discourse on Method', in: Cottingham, J., R. Stoothoff and D. Murdoch, (eds) *The Philosophical Writings of Descartes*, London: Cambridge University Press, 111–51.

DeSousa, M.A. and M.J. Medhurst (1982) 'The Editorial Cartoon as Visual Rhetoric: rethinking Boss Tweed', *Journal of Visual/Verbal Languaging* 2 (2): 43–5.

Dewey, J. (1972 [1897]) 'The Significance of the Problem of Knowledge', in: Boydston, J., (ed.) *The Early Works: 1882–1898*, Carbondale, IL: Southern Illinois University Press, 4–24.

—— (1973 [1931]) 'The Practical Character of Reality', in: *Philosophy and Civilization*, New York: Capricorn Books, 36–55.

—— (1981 [1925]) 'Experience and Nature', in: Boydston, J., (ed.) *The Later Works. 1925–1953*, Carbondale, IL: Southern Illinois University Press.

—— (1984 [1929]) 'The Quest for Certainty', in: Boydston, J., (ed.) *The Later Works. 1925–1953*, Carbondale, IL: Southern Illinois University Press.

—— (1987 [1934]) 'Art as Experience', in: Boydston, J., (ed.) *The Later Works. 1925–1953*, Carbondale, IL: Southern Illinois University Press.

—— (1988 [1930]) 'Qualitative Thought', in: Boydston, J., (ed.) *The Later Works. 1925–1953,* Carbondale, IL: Southern Illinois University Press.

—— (1991 [1938]) 'The Theory of Inquiry', in: Boydston, J., (ed.) *The Later Works. 1925–1953,* Carbondale, IL: Southern Illinois University Press.

Dilthey, W. (1977 [1894]) *Descriptive Psychology and Historical Understanding,* The Hague: Martinus Nijhoff.

—— (1991 [1883]) *Introduction to the Human Sciences: an attempt to lay a foundation for the study of society and history,* London: Harvester Press.

Diprose, R. (2002) *Corporeal Generosity: on giving with Nietzsche, Merleau-Ponty, and Levinas,* Albany, NY: State University of New York Press.

Dissanayake, E. (1992) *Homo Aestheticus: where art comes from and why,* New York: The Free Press.

Dixon, S. (2007) *A History of New Media in Theater, Dance, Performance Art, and Installation,* Cambridge, MA: MIT Press.

Doloughan, F.J. (2002) 'The Language of Reflective Practice in Art and Design', *Design Issues* 18 (2): 57–64.

Donald, M. (1991) *Origins of the Modern Mind: three stages in the evolution of culture and cognition,* Cambridge, MA: Harvard University Press.

Dreyfus, H.L. (2001) *On the Internet,* London: Routledge.

—— (2005) 'Overcoming the Myth of the Mental: how philosophers can profit from the phenomenology of everyday expertise', *Proceedings and Addresses of the American Philosophical Association* 79 (2): 47–65.

—— (2007a) 'Response to McDowell', *Inquiry* 50 (4): 371–7.

—— (2007b) 'The Return of the Myth of the Mental', *Inquiry* 50 (4): 352–65.

Duggan, J.-A. (2003) 'Beyond the Surface: the contemporary experience of the Italian Renaissance', PhD thesis, University of Technology Sydney.

Dunin-Woyseth, H. (2001) 'Research *on* architecture and spatial planning, *in* architecture and spatial planning and *for* architecture and spatial planning. Complementary perspectives?', in: Linn, B., Enhörning and H. Fog, (eds) *Staden, husen och tiden. Rapport från seminarieserien Staden – allas rum, samt reflektioner om stadens egenart,* Stockholm: Riksbankens Jubileumsfond, Riksantikvarieämbetet, FORMAS, 84–93.

—— (2002) 'The Millennium Programme: looking back, looking forward', *Nordisk Arkitekturforskning: Nordic Journal of Architectural Research* 2: 1–10.

—— (2009) 'On Designed Artefacts. A Case of Diagram Construction in Research Education for Practitioners'. Communicating (by) Design, Sint-Lucas School of Architecture, Brussels: Hogeschool voor Wetenschap & Kunst, Sint-Lucas Architectuur Brussel-Gent and Chalmers Gothenburg, 277–93.

Dunin-Woyseth, H. and J. Michl (eds) (2001) *Towards a Disciplinary Identity of the Making Professions. The Oslo Millenium Reader,* Research Magazine 4, Oslo: Oslo School of Architecture.

Dunin-Woyseth, H. and L.M. Nielsen (eds) (2004) *Discussing Transdisciplinarity: making professions and the new mode of knowledge production. The Nordic Reader 2004,* Research Magazine 6, Oslo: Oslo School of Architecture.

DXARTS (2009) Center for Digital Arts and Experimental Media: PhD Program, degree requirements and timeline, University of Washington D.C. Online. <http://www.washington.edu/dxarts/academics_phd_requirements.php> (accessed on 6 December 2009).

Dyrssen, C. (1995) *Musikens Rum – Metaforer, Ritualer, Institutioner,* Göteborg: Bo Ejeby förlag.

Edmonds, E.A. and L. Candy (2010) 'Relating Theory, Practice and Evaluation in Practitioner Research', *Leonardo* 43 (5): 372–378.

Edmonds, E.A., Z. Bilda and L. Muller (2009) 'Artist, Evaluator and Curator: three viewpoints on interactive art, evaluation and audience experience', *Digital Creativity* 20 (3): 141–51.

Edwards, D. (2008) *Artscience: creativity in the post-Google generation,* Cambridge, MA: Harvard University Press.

Efland, A.D. (2002) *Art and Cognition: integrating the visual arts in the curriculum*, New York: Teachers College Press.

Eisner, E.W. (1981) 'On the Differences between Scientific and Artistic Approaches to Qualitative Research', *Educational Researcher* 10 (4): 5–9.

ELIA (2006a) *Fine Art Tuning Document*, European League of Institutes of the Arts. Online. <http://www.elia-artschools.org/artesnet/_downloads/Tuning_Fine_Art.pdf> (accessed on 15 February 2010).

—— (2006b) 'Re:search In and Through the Arts'. Proceedings of the ELIA conference, Universität der Künste Berlin: European League of Institutes of the Arts.

—— (2008a) *Tapping into the Potential of European Higher Arts Education [inter}artes]*, European League of Institutes of the Arts. Online. <http://www.elia-artschools.org/publications/new#interartes> (accessed on 25 January 2010).

—— (2008b) *The Importance of Artistic Research and its Contribution to 'New Knowledge' in a Creative Europe*, Amsterdam: European League of Institutes of the Arts. Online. <http://www.elia-artschools.org/_downloads/publications/position/research_paper_08.pdf> (accessed on 4 February 2010).

Elkins, J. (2005a) 'The New PhD in Studio Art', *Printed Project* 4. Online. <http://www.docstoc.com/docs/13460127/Printed-Project-4---%E2%80%98The-New-PhD-in-Studio-Art%E2%80%99---James-Elkins> (accessed on 26 January 2010).

—— (2005b) 'The Three Configurations of Practice-Based PhDs', *Printed Project* 4: 7–19.

Ellis, C. and A. Bochner (2000) 'Autoethnography, Personal Narrative, Reflexivity. Researcher as subject', in: Denzin, N. and Y. Lincoln, (eds) *Handbook of Qualitative Research*, London: Sage, 733–68.

Emerson, R.W. (2009 [1876]) *Letters and Social Aims*, Charleston, SC: BiblioBazaar LLC.

Engeström, Y. and V. Escalante (1996) 'Mundane Tool or Object of Affection? The Rise and Fall of the Postal Buddy', in: Nardi, B.A., (ed.) *Context and Consciousness: activity theory and human-computer Interaction*, Cambridge, MA: MIT Press, 325–73.

Engeström, Y., R. Miettinen and R.-L. Punamäki (1999) *Perspectives on Activity Theory*, Cambridge: Cambridge University Press.

Eno, B. and S. Grant (1982) 'Brian Eno Against Interpretation', *Trouser Press*. Online. <http://music.hyperreal.org/artists/brian_eno/interviews/troup82a.html> (accessed on 14 August 2009).

Evens, A. (2005) *Sound Ideas: music, machines, and experience*, Minneapolis, MN: University of Minnesota Press.

Eversman, P. (1992) 'The Experience of Theatrical Space', in: Schoenmakers, H., (ed.) *Performance Theory, Reception and Audience Research*, Amsterdam: Tijdschrift voor Theaterwetenschap & ICRAR, 93–114.

Fanon, F. (1986) *Black Skin, White Masks*, London: Pluto Press.

Farmer, H.G. (1931) *The Organ of the Ancients: from eastern sources (Hebrew, Syriac and Arabic)*, London: William Reeves.

Feldhay, R. (2009) 'Galilei und die Anderen. Hintergründe einer Revolution der Astronomie', in: Renn, J., M. Valleriani and J. Staude, (eds) *Sterne und Weltraum Dossier, 1/2009*, Heidelberg: Spektrum der Wissenschaft Verlag, 84–93.

Feldman, D.H., M. Csikszentmihalyi and H. Gardner (1994) *Changing the World: a framework for the study of creativity*, Westport, CT: Praeger.

Feyerabend, P. (1993 [1975]) *Against Method*, London: Verso Books.

Figuier, L. (1868) *La Machine Électrique, Le Paratonnerre, La Pile de Volta, L'électromagnetisme*, Paris: Furne et Jouvet.

Finnegan, C.A. (2004) 'Doing Rhetorical History of the Visual: the photograph and the archive', in: Hill, C., A. and M. Helmers, (eds) *Defining Visual Rhetorics*, London: Routledge.

Fisher, T.R. (2000) *In the Scheme of Things: alternative thinking on the practice of architecture*, Minneapolis, MN: University of Minnesota Press.

Fleckenstein, K.S. (2007) 'Testifying: seeing and saying on world making', in: Fleckenstein, K.S., S. Hum and L.T. Calendrillo, (eds) *Ways of Seeing, Ways of Speaking: the integration of rhetoric and vision in constructing the real*, West Lafayette IN: Parlor Press, 1–30.

Fleming-Williams, I. and L. Parris (1984) *The Discovery of Constable.*, London: Hamish Hamilton.

Flusser, V. (1988) *Krise der Linearität*, Bern: Benteli.

Fortune, R. (2002) 'Image Word and Future Text: visual and verbal thinking in writing instruction', in: Allen, N., (ed.) *Working with words and images: old steps in a new dance*, Westport, CT: Alblex, 97–116.

Forty, A., N. Albertsen, H. Dunin-Woyseth, R. Lawrence, T.A. Markus and A.W. Spirn (2006) *Evaluation of Swedish Architectural Research 1995–2005*, Stockholm: FORMAS. Online. <http://www.formas.se/upload/arkutv.pdf> (accessed on 10 March 2010).

Foucault, M. (1972 [1969]) *The Archaeology of Knowledge*, London: Tavistock Press.

—— (1999 [1984]) 'Different Spaces', in: Faubion, J.D., (ed.) *Aesthetics, Method, and Epistemology: Essential Works of Michel Foucault 1954–1984*, Harmondsworth: Penguin Books, 175–85.

—— (2002 [1966]) *The Order of Things: an archaeology of the human sciences*, London: Routledge.

Frayling, C. (1993) *Research in Art and Design*, London: Royal College of Art.

Freud, S. (1957 [1910]) 'Leonardo da Vinci and a Memory of his Childhood', in: Strachey, J., (ed.) *The Standard Edition of the Complete Psychological Works of Sigmund Freud*, London: Hogarth Press, 57–137.

—— (1960 [1901]) 'The Forgetting of Proper Names', in: Strachey, J., (ed.) *The Standard Edition of the Complete Psychological Works of Sigmund Freud*, London: Hogarth Press, 1–7.

—— (1961 [1923]) 'The Ego and the Id', in: Strachey, J., (ed.) *The Standard Edition of the Complete Psychological Works of Sigmund Freud*, London: Hogarth Press, 1–66.

—— (1961 [1928]) 'Dostoyevsky and Parricide', in: Strachey, J., (ed.) *The Standard Edition of the Complete Psychological Works of Sigmund Freud*, London: Hogarth Press, 173–94.

—— (1963 [1915]) 'Introductory Lectures on Psychoanalysis, Parts 1 & 2', in: Strachey, J., (ed.) *The Standard Edition of the Complete Psychological Works of Sigmund Freud*, London: Hogarth Press.

Frisk, H. and S. Östersjö (2006a) 'Negotiating the Musical Work: an empirical study'. International Computer Music Conference, San Fransciso, CA: Computer Music Association, 242–9.

—— (2006b) 'Negotiating the Musical Work. An Empirical Study on the Inter-Relation between Composition, Interpretation and Performance'. EMS -06, Beijing. Terminology and Translation: Electroacoustic Music Studies, n.p.

Frith, C. (2007) *Making up the Mind: how the brain creates our mental world*, Cambridge, MA: Blackwell.

Gadamer, H.-G. (1975) *Truth and Method*, London: Sheed and Ward.

Gardner, H. (1973) *The Arts and Human Development*, New York: Wiley.

—— (1983) *Frames of Mind: the theory of multiple intelligences*, New York: Basic Books.

—— (1985) *The Mind's New Science: a history of the cognitive revolution.*, New York: Basic Books.

Gaunt, W. (1964) *A Concise History of English Painting*, London: Thames and Hudson.

Gelder, T.V. (1998) 'The Dynamical Hypothesis in Cognitive Science', *Behavioral and Brain Sciences* 21 (5): 615–65.

Gesche, J. and A. Scheuermann (2007) 'Design as Rhetoric: basic principles for design research', paper presented at Swiss Design Network.

Gibbons, M., C. Limoges, S. Schwartzman, H. Nowotny, M. Trow and P. Scott (1994) *The New Production of Knowledge: the dynamics of science and research in contemporary societies*, London: Sage Publications.

Gibson, W. (1984) *Neuromancer*, New York: Ace.

Giddens, A. (1979) *Central Problems in Social Theory: action, structure and contradiction in social analysis*, Berkeley, CA: University of California Press.

Giddens, S. and S. Jones (2001) *Flesh and Text – a document by bodies in flight*, CD ROM.

—— (2010) 'De-Second-Naturing: word unbecoming flesh in the work of Bodies in Flight', in: Broadhurst, S. and J. Machon, (eds) *Sensualities/Textualities and Technologies: writings of the body in 21st century performance*, Basingstoke: Palgrave Macmillan.

Gillen, S. (2007) 'Synge's The Aran Islands and Irish Creative Nonfiction', *New Hibernia Review* 11 (4): 129–35.

Gillard, J. (2009) Budget 2009–10: New agency to set quality benchmarks in higher education' [media release], (unpublished).

Ginsburgh, V.A. and D. Throsby (eds) (2006) *Handbook of the Economics of Art and Culture*, Amsterdam: North Holland Publishing.

Glinowski, P. and A. Bamford (2009) *Insight and Exchange: an evaluation of the Wellcome Trust Sciart programme*, London: Wellcome Trust. Online. <http://www.wellcome.ac.uk/sciartevaluation> (accessed on 3 January 2010).

Goldhill, S. (1996) 'Refracting Classical Vision: changing cultures of viewing', in: Brennan, T. and M. Jay, (eds) *Vision in Context: historical and contemporary perspectives on sight*, New York: Routledge, 15–28.

Gombrich, E.H. (1977) *Art and Illusion*, London: Phaidon Press.

Goodman, N. (1978) *Ways of Worldmaking*, Indianapolis, IN: Hackett Publishing.

Gowers, A. (2006) *Gowers Review of Intellectual Property*, London: HM Treasury. Online. <http://www.hm-treasury.gov.uk/gowers_review_index.htm> (accessed on 17 February 2010).

Grant, C. (2008) 'Hal Foster in Conversation', *Immediations* 2 (1).

Graves, J. (1996) 'The Object: dead or alive', *Issues in Architecture, Art and Design* 4 (2): 154–64.

—— (1999) 'When Things Go Wrong ... Inside the Inside: a psychoanalytical history of a jug', *Journal of Design History* 12 (4): 357–67.

Gray, C. and J. Malins (2004) *Visualizing Research: a guide to the research process in art and design*, Aldershot: Ashgate.

Greco, J. (2006) The Nature of Ability and the Purpose of Knowledge, Saint Louis University. Online. <http://johngrec.googlepages.com/MexicoTalk10-14-06.pdf> (accessed on 6 February 2010).

Greely, R.A. (2001) 'Dali's Fascism; Lacan's Paranoia', *Art History* 24 (4): 465–92.

Greenbank, P. (2003) 'The Role of Values in Educational Research: the case for reflexivity', *British Educational Research Journal* 29 (6): 791–801.

Grenville, K. (2005a) *The Secret River*, Melbourne: Text Publishing.

—— (2005b) The Secret River: Readers' Notes, Online. <http://kategrenville.com/The_Secret_River_Readers_Notes> (accessed on 10 January 2010).

Griffiths, M. (1995) *Feminisms and the Self: the web of identity*, London: Routledge.

—— (1998) *Educational Research for Social Justice: getting off the fence*, Milton Keynes: Open University Press.

GSA (2007) *Glasgow University Calendar 2007/2008*, Glasgow: Glasgow School of Art. Online. <http://www.gla.ac.uk/services/senateoffice/calendar/calendar2007-08/> (accessed on 10 March 2010).

Guattari, F. (1995) *Chaosmosis*, Sydney: Feral.

Guba, E. (ed.) (1990) *The Paradigm Dialog*, London: Sage Publications.

Guba, E. and Y. Lincoln (1994) 'Competing Paradigms in Qualitative Research', in: Denzin, N. and Y. Lincoln, (eds) *Handbook of Qualitative Research*, London: Sage Publications, 105–17.

Gunther, Y.H. (2003) *Essays on Nonconceptual Content*, Cambridge MA: MIT Press.

Gutkind, L. (1997) *The Art of Creative Nonfiction*, New York: John Wiley.

Häberli, A. Bill, R. W. Scholz and M. Welti (2001) 'Summary', in: Klein, J.T., W. Grossenbacher-Mansuy, R. Häberli, *et al.*, (eds) *Transdisciplinarity: joint problem solving among science, technology, and society*, Basel: Birkhäuser.

Habermas, J. (1972) *Knowledge and Human Interests*, London: Heinemann.

Hales, N.K. (1999) *How we Became Posthuman: virtual bodies in cybernectics, literature, and informatics*, Chicago, IL: University of Chicago Press.

—— (2004) 'Flesh and Metal: reconfiguring the mindbody in virtual environments', in: Mitchell, R. and P. Thurtle, (eds) *Data made Flesh: embodying information*, New York: Routledge, 229–48.

Hallam, E. and T. Ingold (eds) (2007) *Creativity and Cultural Improvisation*, Oxford: Berg.

Halligan, M. (1999a) 'Lapping', in: Craven, P., (ed.) *Best Australian Essays*, Melbourne: Bookman, 208–13.

—— (1999b) 'The Cathedral of Love' *The Age*, Melbourne 27 November 1999: 1.

—— (2001) *The Fog Garden*, Sydney: Allen and Unwin.

Halloran, S.M. and G. Clark (2006) 'National Park Landscapes and the Rhetorical Display of Civic Religion', in: Prelli, L.J., (ed.) *Rhetorics of Display*, Columbia, SC: University of Southern Carolina Press, 141–56.

Hannula, M. (2004) 'River Low, Mountain High. Contextualizing artistic research', in: Balkema, A.W. and H. Slager, (eds) *Artistic Research*, Amsterdam: Rodopi B.V., 70–9.

—— (2008) 'Talkin' Loud & Sayin' Something: four perspectives of artistic research', *Art Monitor* 4.

Hannula, M., J. Suoranta and T. Vadén (2005) *Artistic Research: theories, methods and practices*, Gothenburg, Sweden: Academy of Fine Arts Helsinki, and Gothenburg University.

Haraway, D. (1991) *Simians, Cyborgs and Women*, London: Free Association Books.

Harris, J. (2002) 'The Case for Cross-Disciplinary Approaches in International Development', *World Development* 30 (3): 487–96.

Harrison, C. and P. Wood (2000) *Art in Theory: 1900–2000*, Oxford: Blackwell Publishing.

Harrison, C., P. Wood and J. Gaiger (1998) *Art in Theory: 1815–1900*, Oxford: Blackwell Publishing.

Harvard (2008) *Report of the Task Force on the Arts*, Boston, MA: Harvard University. Online. <http://www.harvard.edu/r/arts_report.pdf> (accessed on 18 January 2010).

Haseman, B. (2006a) 'A Manifesto for Performative Research', *Media International Australia incorporating Culture and Policy* 118: Special issue 'Practice-led Research' 98–106.

—— (2006b) 'Rupture and Recognition: identifying the performative research paradigm', in: Barrett, E. and B. Bolt, (eds) *Practice as Research: Approaches to Creative Arts Enquiry*, London: I.B. Tauris, 147–57.

Hauser, A. (1972) *Sozialgeschichte der Kunst und Literatur*, München: C.H. Beck.

Heathfield, A. and T. Hsieh (2009) *Out of Now – The Lifeworks of Tehching Hsieh*, Cambridge, MA: The Live Art Development Agency and MIT Press.

Heddon, D. (2007) *Autobiography and Performance*, Basingstoke: Palgrave Macmillan.

Herbert, Z. (2007) *The Collected Poems, 1956–1998*, New York: Ecco.

Hicks, M. (1991) *Richard III: the man behind the myth*, London: Collins and Brown.

Higgins, C. (2008) 'I Was Shocked by the Hatred' *The Guardian*, London 3 December 2008.

Hill, C., A. and M. Helmers (eds) (2004) *Defining Visual Rhetorics*, London: Routledge.

Hill, D.R. (1979) *The Book of Ingenious Devices (Kitab al-Hiyal) by the Banu (sons of) Musa bin Shakir*, Dordrecht: Reidel.

Hill, J. (1998) *The Illegal Architect*, London: Black Dog Publishing.

—— (2007) 'Introduction: Criticism by Design', in: Rendell, J., J. Hill, M. Dorrian and M. Fraser, (eds) *Critical Architecture*, London: Routledge, 165–81.

Hill, L. and H. Paris (eds) (2006) *Performance and Place*, Basingstoke: Palgrave Macmillan.

Hirsch, E.D. (1984) 'Meaning and Significance Reinterpreted', *Critical Inquiry* 11 (2): 202–25.

Hockney, D. (1993) *That's the Way I See It*, San Francisco, CA: Chronicle Books.

Hoffman, D.D. (1998) *Visual Intelligence: how we create what we see*, New York: W.W. Norton and Company.

Hofstede, G. (1991) *Cultures and Organizations. Software of the mind. Intercultural Cooperation and its Importance for Survival*, London: Harper Collins Business.

Högskoleverket (2007) *Rapport 2007:25. Utvärdering av grund- och forskarutbildning inom fri konst*, Stockholm: Högskoleverket.

Holert, T. (2009) 'Art in the Knowledge-based Polis', *E-flux Journal* 3. Online. <http://www.e-flux.com/journal/view/40> (accessed on 28 December 2009).

Hughes, I. (2009) *Action Research Electronic Reader*, Lismore, NSW: Southern Cross University. Online. <http://www.scu.edu.au/schools/gcm/ar/arr/arow/default.html> (accessed on 7 December 2009).

Hughes, R. (2007) 'The Drowning Method. On giving account in practice-based research', in: Rendell, J., J. Hill, M. Dorrian and M. Fraser, (eds) *Critical Architecture*, London: Routledge, 92–102.

IBO (2010) *Education for a Better World*, Geneva: International Baccalauriate Organisation. Online. <http://www.ibo.org/communications/publications/ibbrochure.cfm> (accessed on 26 March 2010).

Irigaray, L. (1985) *This Sex Which Is Not One*, Ithaca, NY: Cornell University Press.

IUQB (2005) *Good Practice in the Organisation of PhD Programmes in Irish Universities*, Dublin: Irish Universities Quality Board. Online. <http://www.iuqb.ie/info/good_practice_guides.aspx> (accessed on 8 March 2010).

Iyer, V.S. (2008) 'On Improvisation, Temporality, and Embodied Experience', in: Miller, P.D., (ed.) *Sound Unbound: sampling digital music and culture*, Cambridge, MA: MIT Press, 273–92.

Jackson, T. (ed.) (1993) *New Perspectives on Theatre in Education*, London: Routledge.

Jacob, F. (1983) *Das Spiel der Möglichkeiten. Von der offenen Geschichte des Lebens*, München: Piper Verlag.

Jay, M. (1988) 'Scopic Regimes of Modernity', in: Foster, H., (ed.) *Vision and Visuality*, Seattle: Bay Press, 3–23.

Jeffri, J. (2007) *Above Ground: information about artist III. Special focus New York City aging artists*, New York: Trustees of Teachers College Columbia University/Research Center for Arts and Culture. Online. <http://arts.tc.columbia.edu/rcac/Aging_artists> (accessed on 10 March 2010).

Johnson, M. (2007) *The Meaning of the Body: aesthetics of human understanding.*, Chicago, IL: University of Chicago Press.

Johnson, P.-A. (1994) *The Theory of Architecture. Concepts, Themes & Practice*, New York: Van Nostrand Reinhold.

Johnston, A., L. Candy and E.A. Edmonds (2008) 'Designing and Evaluating Virtual Musical Instruments: facilitating conversational user interaction', *Design Studies* 29 (6): 556–71.

Jones, A. (2006) *Self/Image: technology, representation and the contemporary subject*, London: Routledge.

Jones, J. (2008) 'Perverse and Baffling With an Obvious Winner' *The Guardian*, London, 14 May 2008.

Jorgensen-Earp, C.R. (2006) 'Satisfaction of Metaphorical Expectations through Visual Display: the *Titanic* exhibition', in: Prelli, L.J., (ed.) *Rhetorics of Display*, Columbia, SC: University of Southern Carolina Press, 41–65.

JQI (2004) *Shared 'Dublin' Descriptors for Short Cycle, First Cycle, Second Cycle and Third Cycle Awards*, Netherlands: Joint Quality Initiative. Online. <http://www.jointquality.nl/> (accessed on 2 February 2009).

Jupp, V. (ed.) (2006) *The Sage Dictionary of Social Research Methods*, London: Sage Publications.

Kagan, J. (2002) *Surprise, Uncertainty and Mental Structures*, Cambridge, MA: Harvard University Press.

Kaiser, M. (2000) *Hva er vitenskap?*, Oslo: Universitetsforlaget.

Kälvemark, T. (2000) *Konstnärligt utvecklingsarbete och praxisbaserad forskning: några internationella utvecklingslinjer*, Stockholm: Högskoleverket. Online. <http://www.hsv.se/publikationer/arbetsrapporter> (accessed on 3 January 2010).

Kant, I. (1978 [1790/93]) *The Critique of Judgement*, Oxford: Clarendon Press.

Karatani, K. (1995) *Architecture as Metaphor: language, number, money*, Cambridge, MA: MIT Press.

Karlsson, H. (ed.) (2007) *Kontext – Kvalitet – Kontinuitet. Utvärdering av Vetenskapsrådets anslag till konstnärlig forskning och utveckling 2001–2005*, Stockholm: Vetenskapsrådet.

KEA (2009) *The Impact of Culture on Creativity*, European Commission, Directorate-General for Education and Culture. Online. <http://ec.europa.eu/culture/key-documents/doc2183_en.htm> (accessed on 10 January 2010).

Keats, J. (1817) Letter to his Brothers (21 December), in: Abrams, M.H. and S. Greenblatt (eds) (2000) *The Norton Anthology of English Literature*, 7th edition. New York: W.W. Norton and Co.

Kershaw, B. (2007) *Theatre Ecology: environments and performance events*, London: Cambridge University Press.

Khatir, L. (2008) 'The Vital Space of Painting: changing perceptual and material conditions of space, place and viewer in contemporary European abstract painting', PhD thesis, Bath Spa University.

Kidron, B. (2007) *Anthony Gormley: making space*, DVD.

Kirlik, A. and S. Maruyama (2004) 'Human-technology Interaction and Music Perception and Performance: toward the robust design of sociotechnical systems', *Proceedings of the IEEE* 92 (4): 616–31.

Kiverstein, J. and A. Clark (2009) 'Introduction. Mind Embodied, Embedded, Enacted: one church or many?', *Topoi* 28: 1–7.

Kjørup, S. (1993) 'Forskning i praktisk-æstetiske fag: Nogle overvejelser og idéer'. *Kunstfaglig forskning*, Åsgårdstrand: Norges forskningsråd, avdeling NAVF/RHF, 26–38.

—— (2001) *Humanities, Geisteswissenschaften, Sciences humaines: Eine Einführung*, Stuttgart: J.B. Meltzer.

—— (2006) *Another Way of Knowing*, (Sensuous Knowledge 1), Bergen: Bergen National Academy of the Arts.

Klarqvist, B. (2004) 'Comments on the Fairy Tale', in: Dunin-Woyseth, H. and L.M. Nielsen, (eds) *Discussing Transdisciplinarity: making professions and the new mode of knowledge production. The Nordic Reader 2004*, Oslo: Oslo School of Architecture, 58–9.

Klarqvist, B. and A. Rydberg (2004) 'Securing Housing Safety. A Fairylike Tale on Development in a Public Authority', in: Dunin-Woyseth, H. and L.M. Nielsen, (eds) *Discussing Transdisciplinarity: making professions and the new mode of knowledge production. The Nordic Reader 2004*, Oslo: Oslo School of Architecture, 47–57.

Klein, J.T., W. Grossenbacher-Mansuy, R. Häberli, A. Bill, R.W. Scholtz and M. Welti (2001) *Transdisciplinarity: joint problem solving among science, technology, and society*, Basel: Birkhäuser.

Klossowski, P. (1998) *Die lebende Münze*, translated by M. Burckhardt, Berlin: Kadmos.

KMH (2007) *Grundläggande högskoleutbildning och forskarutbildning*, Stockholm: Kungl. Musikhögskolan i Stockholm. Online. <http://www.kmh.se/internt/pdf/Rektorskollegium_070110.pdf> (accessed on 25 January 2010).

Knowles, J.G. and A.L. Coles (2008) *Handbook of the Arts in Qualitative Research*, London: Sage Publications.

Kopelman, I. (2007) 'UBX Expression', *MaKHUzine: Journal of Artistic Research* 7, 40–3. Online. <http://www.mahku.nl/research/mahkuzine7.html> (accessed on 28 December 2009).

Kozel, S. (1994) 'As Vision Becomes Gesture', PhD thesis, University of Essex.

—— (2007a) *Closer: performance, technologies, phenomenology*, Cambridge, MA: MIT Press.

—— (2007b) 'Virtual/Virtuality', *Performance Research* 11 (3): 136–9.

—— (2008) 'Social Choreographies'. Close Encounters – Artists on Artistic Research, Stockholm: University College of Dance.

Kräftner, B., J. Kröll and I. Warner (2007) 'Walking on a Storyboard, Performing Shared Incompetence: exhibiting "science" in the public realm', in: Macdonald, S. and P. Basu, (eds) *Exhibition Experiments*, Malden, MA: Blackwell Publishers.

Krauss, R. (1999) *A Voyage on the North Sea. Art in the Age of the Post-Medium Condition*, London: Thames and Hudson.

Kress, G. (2007) 'Design and Transformation: new theories of meaning', in: Cope, B. and M. Kalantzis, (eds) *Multiliteracies: literacy learning and the design of social futures*, London: Routledge, 153–61.

Kroeber, A.L. and C. Kluckhohn (1952) *Culture: a critical review of concepts and definitions*, Cambridge, MA: Peabody Museum of American Archæology and Ethnology.

KU (2010) *Ny universitetslov. Historie om LIFE*, Copenhagen: Det Biovitenskapelige Fakultet, Copenhagen University. Online. <http://www.150aar.life.ku.dk/Fortellinger.aspx> (accessed on 25 January 2010).

Kubler, G. (2008 [1962]) *The Shape of Time: remarks on the history of things*, New Haven, CT: Yale University Press.

Kuhn, T. (1970 [1962]) *The Structure of Scientific Revolutions*, Chicago, IL: University of Chicago Press.

Kundera, M. (2006) *The Curtain: an essay in seven parts*, London: Faber and Faber.

Kwon, M. (2002) *One Place After Another. Site Specific Art and Locational Identity*, Cambridge, MA: MIT Press.

Lacan, J. (1991 [1970]) *Le Séminaire, Livre XVII, L'envers de la psychanalyse*, Paris: du Seuil.

—— (1992 [1960]) *The Ethics of Psychoanalysis*, London: Routledge.

—— (1993 [1956]) *The Psychoses*, London: Routledge.

—— (2007 [1965]) 'Science and Truth', in: *Écrits*, London: W.W Norton and Co.

Lacy, S. (ed.) (1995) *Mapping the Terrain: new genre public art*, Seattle, WA: Bay Press.

Lakoff, G. and M. Johnson (1980) *Metaphors We Live By*, Chicago, IL: University of Chicago Press.

—— (1999) *Philosophy in the Flesh: the embodied mind and its challenges to western thought*, New York: Basic Books.

Latour, B. (2005) *Reassembling the Social: an introduction to actor-network theory*, Oxford: Oxford University Press.

Lave, J. and E. Wenger (1991) *Situated Learning: legitimate peripheral participation*, Cambridge: Cambridge University Press.

Lawlor, L. (2003) *The Challenge of Bergsonism*, New York: Continuum.

Lawson, B. (1980) *How Designers Think*, London: Architectural Press.

—— (2002) 'The Subject that won't Go Away. But perhaps we are ahead of the game', *arq: Architectural Research Quarterly* 6 (2): 109–14.

Leibowitz, J. (2003) '"Images" of the Female and the Self: two recent interpretations by women authors', *Hypatia* 18 (4): 283–91.

Leiderstam, M. (2007) 'See and Seen – Seeing Landscape through Artistic Practice', *MaHKUzine: Journal of Artistic Research* 7, 25–9. Online. <http://www.mahku.nl/research/mahkuzine7.html> (accessed on 28 December 2009).

Leighton, T. (2006) *In the Poem About Love You Don't Write the Word Love*, Berlin: Sternberg Press.

Lepecki, A. (2006) *Exhausting Dance: performance and the politics of movement*, London: Routledge.

Leslie, C.R. (1951) *Memoirs of Life of the John Constable*, London: Phaidon Press.

Levey, M. (1968) *From Giotto to Cézanne*, London: Thames and Hudson.

Levi-Strauss, C. (1966 [1962]) *The Savage Mind*, Chicago, IL: University of Chicago Press.

Lincoln, Y. (1995) 'Emerging Criteria for Quality in Qualitative and Interpretive Research', *Qualitative Inquiry* 1 (3): 275–89.

Lind, I. (2009) 'Att spela psyksjuk' [acting psychotic] *Dagens Nyheter*, Stockholm 29 January 2009.

Lindahl, M. (2003) 'Produktion till varje pris: om planering och improvisation i anläggningsprojekt', PhD thesis, Stockholm University.

Linden, D.J. (2007) *The Accidental Mind: how brain evolution has given us love, memory, dreams, and God*, Cambridge, MA: Belknap Press.

Locke, J. (1964 [1690]) *An Essay Concerning Human Understanding*, London: Fontana.

Lockheart, J. and J. Wood (2008) 'Editorial', *The Journal of Writing in Creative Practice* 1 (2): 113–6.

Lossius, T. (2007) *Sound, Space, Body: reflections on artistic practice*, Bergen: National Academy of the Arts. Online. <http://www.trondlossius.no/system/fileattachments/6/original/main_web.pdf> (accessed on 4 March 2010).

Loughran, J.J., M.L. Hamilton, V.K. LaBoskey and T. Russell (eds) (2004) *International Handbook of Self-study of Teaching and Teacher Education Practices*, Dordrecht: Kluwer.

Lubart, T.I. (1999) 'Creativity Across Cultures', in: Sternberg, R.J., (ed.) *Metaphors of the Mind: conceptions of the notion of intelligence*, New York: Cambridge University Press, 339–50.

Luntley, M. (2003) 'Non-conceptual Content and the Sound of Music', *Mind and Language* 18 (4): 402–26.

Lynch, G. (2009) 'Apocryphal Stories in Kate Grenville's *Searching for the Secret River*', *TEXT: Journal of Writing and Writing Courses* 13. Online. <http://www.textjournal.com.au/april09/lynch.htm> (accessed on 28 December 2009).

McArdle, K.L. and P. Reason (2006) 'Action Research and Organization Development', in: Cummings, T., (ed.) *Handbook of Organization Development*, Thousand Oaks, CA: Sage Publications.

Macleod, K. and L. Holdridge (eds) (2006) *Thinking Through Art: reflections on art as research*, Innovations in Art and Design, London: Routledge.

McCloud, S. (1994) *Understanding Comics: the invisible art*, New York: Harper Collins.

McDowell, J. (2007a) 'Response to Dreyfus', *Inquiry* 50 (4): 366–70.

—— (2007b) 'What Myth?', *Inquiry* 50 (4): 338–51.

McNiff, S. (1998) *Art-based Research*, London: Jessica Kingsley Publishers.

Magee, P. (2009) 'Is Poetry Research?', *TEXT: Journal of Writing and Writing Courses* 13. Online. <http://textjournal.com.au/oct09/magee.htm> (accessed on 28 December 2009).

Maharaj, S. (2004) 'Unfinishable Sketch of "An Object in 4D": scenes of artistic research', in: Balkema, A.W. and H. Slager, (eds) *Artistic Research*, Amsterdam: Rodopi B.V., 39–58.

Mahrenholz, S. (2000) *Musik und Erkenntnis. Eine Studie im Ausgang von Nelson Goodmans Symboltheorie*, Stuttgart: Verlag J. B. Metzler.

Maitland, J. (1995) *Spacious Body: explorations in somatic ontology*, Berkeley, CA: North Atlantic Books.

Mäkelä, M. and S. Routarinne (eds) (2006) *The Art of Research: research practices in art and design*, Helsinki: UIAH.

Marcus, G.E. (1994) 'What Comes (just) After "Post"? The case of ethnography', in: Denzin, N. and Y. Lincoln, (eds) *Handbook of Qualitative Research*, London: Sage Publications, 563–74.

Martin, J. (2009) 'Artistic Research in Australia', in: *Konst och forskningspolitik — konstnärlig forskning inför framtiden*, Stockholm: Vetenskapsrådet.

Masterman, M. (1970) 'The Nature of a Paradigm', in: Lakatos, I. and A. Musgrave, (eds) *Criticism and the Growth of Knowledge: Proceedings of the International Colloquium in the Philosophy of Science, London, 1965*, London: Cambridge University Press, 59–89.

Mayer, R.E. (1999) 'Fifty Years of Creativity Research', in: Sternberg, R.J., (ed.) *Metaphors of the Mind: conceptions of the notion of intelligence*, New York: Cambridge University Press, 449–60.

Melrose, S. (2002) Inaugural Lecture: Entertaining Other Options: restaging "theory" in the age of practice as research, Middlesex University. Online. <http://www.sfmelrose.u-net.com/inaugural/> (accessed on 1 February 2010).

Melville, S. and B. Readings (eds) (1995) *Vision and Textuality*, Durham, NC: Duke University Press.

Menger, P.-M. (2006) 'Artistic Labors Markets: contingent work, excess supply and occupational risk management', in: Ginsburgh, V. and D. Throsby, (eds) *Handbook of the Economics of Arts and Culture*, Amsterdam: Elsevier, 765–806.

—— (2009) *Le Travail Créateur. S'accomplir dans l'incertain*, Paris: Seuil/Gallimard.

Merleau-Ponty, M. (1962) *The Phenomenology of Perception*, London: Routledge.

—— (1964) *L'Œil et l'Esprit*, Paris: Gallimard.

—— (1968) *The Visible and the Invisible*, Evanston, IL: Northwestern University Press.

—— (1993) 'Phenomenology and Psychoanalysis: Preface to Hesnard's L'Oeuvre de Freud', in: Hoeller, K., (ed.) *Merleau-Ponty and Psychology*, Atlantic Highlands, NJ: Humanities Press.

Meyer, W.-U., R. Reisenzein and A. Schutzwohl (1997) 'Towards a Process Analysis of Emotions: the case of surprise', *Motion and Emotion* 21: 251–74.

Mill, J.S. (1987 [1843]) *The Logic of the Moral Sciences*, London: Duckworth.

Miller, P., D. (2004) *Rhythm Science*, Cambridge, MA: MIT Press.

Mills, S. (1999) *Discourse*, New York: Routledge.

Miltner, R. (2001) 'Where the Visual meets the Verbal: collaboration as conversation', *Enculturation* 3. Online. <http://enculturation.gmu.edu/3_2/miltner/index.html> (accessed on 17 January 2010).

Mitchell, W.J.T. (1981) 'Diagrammatology', *Critical Inquiry* 7 (3): 622–33.

Mo, L. (2001) *Vitenskapsfilosofi for Arkitekter*, Notat nr. 2001:1, Trondheim: Institutt for by- og regionplanlegging NTNU, Norges teknisk-naturvitenskapelige universitet.

Mooney, J. (1999) 'Praxis-Ethics-Erotics', PhD thesis, Royal College of Art.

Moore, F.R. (1990) *Elements of Computer Music*, New York: Prentice-Hall.

Moran, J. (2002) *Interdisciplinarity*, London: Routledge.

Morley, D. (2007) *The Cambridge Introduction to Creative Writing*, Cambridge: Cambridge University Press.

Moser, M.A. and D. MacLeod (eds) (1996) *Immersed in Technology: art and virtual environments*, Cambridge, MA: MIT Press.

Muller, L. (2008) 'The Experience of Interactive Art: a curatorial study', PhD thesis, University of Technology Sydney.

Muller, L., E.A. Edmonds and M. Connell (2006) 'Living Laboratories for Interactive Art', *Co-Design: International Journal of Co-Creation in Design and the Arts* 2 (4): 195–207.

Müller-Vollmer, K. (1963) *Towards a Phenomenological Theory of Literature: a study of Wilhelm Dilthey's Poetik*, The Hague: Mouton and Co.

Mullican, M. (2008) *A Drawing Translates the Way of Thinking*, (Drawing Papers Number 82), New York: The Drawing Center.

Mullin, J. (1998) 'Alternative Pedagogy: visualizing theories of composition', in: Hobson, E., C. P. and J. Mullin, (eds) *ARTiculating: teaching writing in a visual culture*, Portsmouth, NH: Heinemann/ Boynton-Cook, 57–71.

—— (2009) 'Appropriation, Homage and Pastiche: using artistic tradition to reconsider and redefine plagiarism', in: Haviland, C.P. and M.J., (eds) *Who Owns This Text: plagiarism, authorship and disciplinary cultures*, Logan, UT: Utah State University Press, 105–28.

Murray, L. (1997) 'The Suspect Captivity of the Fisher King', in: *A Working Forest: selected prose*, Sydney: Duffy and Snellgrove, 183–9.

Myatt, A. (2009). Personal communication with Ernest Edmonds.

Nagel, T. (1989) *The View From Nowhere*, Oxford: Oxford University Press.

Nancy, J.L. (2008) *Corpus*, New York: Fordham University Press.

National Advisory Council on Art Education (1960) *First Report of the National Advisory Council on Art Education [known as The Coldstream Report]*, London: HMSO.

Nelimarkka, R. (2000) Self Portrait. Elisen väitöskirja. Variaation variaatio. PhD thesis, University School of Arts and Design. Helsinki: Seneca Oy. CD-ROM in English (Self Portrait. Elise's Dissertation. Variation of a Variation), Seneca 2001. Online. <http://www.nelimarkka.com/files/ nelimarkka_self_portrait_eng.high.pdf> (accessed on 22 June 2010).

Nelson, R. and S. Andrews (2003) *Practice as Research: Regulations, Protocols and Guidelines*, Manchester: Manchester Metropolitan University, and Palatine. Online. <http://www.palatine. ac.uk/files/903.pdf> (accessed on 15 February 2010).

Nevanlinna, T. (2002) 'Is 'Artistic Research' a meaningful concept?', in: Kiljunen, S. and M. Hannula, (eds) *Artistic Research*, Helsinki: Fine Art Academy, 61–71.

Newbury, D. (2003) 'Doctoral Education in Design, The Process of Research Degree Study, and the "Trained Researcher"', *Art, Design & Communication in Higher Education* 1 (3): 149–59.

—— (2009) 'Making the Path as We Walk It: the present and future of doctoral education in art and design', paper presented at Art and Design Education for the 21st Century, University of Brighton.

Nicolescu, B. (2002) *Manifesto of Transdisciplinarity*, New York: State University of New York Press.

Nobus, D. and M. Quinn (2005) *Knowing Nothing, Staying Stupid: elements for a psychoanalytic epistemology*, London: Routledge.

Noffke, S. and B. Somekh (2009) *Handbook of Educational Action Research*, London: Sage.

Nolin, J. (2008) *In Search of a New Theory of Professions*, Borås: University of Borås. Online. <http:// hdl.handle.net/2320/4191> (accessed on 26 March 2010).

NOU (2008) *Sett under ett. Ny struktur i høyere utdanning*, Kunnskapsdepartementet. Online. <http:// www.regjeringen.no/nb/dep/kd/dok/nouer/2008/NOU-2008-3.html?id=497182> (accessed on 25 January 2010).

Novalis (1908) *Novalis' ausgewählte Werke in drei Bänden*, edited by Wilhelm Bölsche, Leipzig: Max Hesse.

Nowotny, H. (2008) *Insatiable Curiosity. Innovation in a Fragile Future*, Cambridge, MA: MIT Press.

Nowotny, H., P. Scott and M. Gibbons (2003) 'Introduction: "Mode 2" Revisited: The New Production of Knowledge', *Minerva* 41 (3): 179–94.

Nuss, S. (2006) *Copyright & Copyriot. Aneignungskonflikte um geistiges Eigentum im informationellen Kapitalismus*, Münster: Westfälisches Dampfboot.

Nyseth, T. (2007) 'Introduksjon', in: Nyseth, T., S. Jentoft, A. Førde and J.O. Bærenholdt, (eds) *I disiplinenes grenseland. Tverfaglighet i teori og praksis*, Bergen: Fagbokforlaget, 15–31.

O'Neill, O. (1996) *Towards Justice and Virtue: a constructive account of practical reasoning*, London: Cambridge University Press.

Obuljen, N. and J. Smiers (2006) *Unesco's Convention on the Protection and Promotion of the Diversity of Cultural Expressions. Making It Work*, Zagreb: Culturelink.

OECD (1998) *University Research in Transition*, Paris: Organisation for Economic Co-operation and Development. Online. <http://books.google.com.br/books?id=-mspVqV201QC> (accessed on 10 January 2010).

—— (2002) *Frascati Manual: proposed standard practice for surveys on research and experimental development*, Paris: Organisation for Economic Co-operation and Development.

—— (2009) Glossary of Statistical Terms: research and development – UNESCO, Organisation for Economic Co-operation and Development. Online. <http://stats.oecd.org/glossary/detail.asp?ID=2312> (accessed on 10 January 2010).

Onega, S. (1996) 'Interview with Peter Ackroyd', *Twentieth Century Literature: A Scholarly and Critical Journal* 42 (2): 208–21.

O'Neill, O. (1996) *Towards Justice and Virtue: a constructive account of practical reasoning*, London: Cambridge University Press.

O'Regan, T. (1994) 'Two or Three Things I Know about Meaning', *Continuum: The Australian Journal of Media and Culture* 7 (2): 327–74.

Orr, S., M. Blythman and J. Mullin (2005) 'Designing your Writing/Writing your Design: art and design students talk about the process of writing and the process of design', *Across the Disciplines: interdisciplinary perspectives on language, learning and academic writing*. Online. <http://wac.colostate.edu/atd/visual/orr_blythman_mullin.cfm> (accessed on 18 January 2010).

Ostertag, B. (2002) 'Human Bodies, Computer Music', *Leonardo Music Journal* 12: 11–4.

Pakes, A. (2003) 'Original Embodied Knowledge: The Epistemology of the New in Dance Practice as Research', *Research in Dance Education* 4 (2): 127–49.

Palasmaa, J. (2005) *The Eyes of the Skin: architecture and the senses*, Chichester: Wiley-Academy.

Parviainen, J. (2002) 'Bodily Knowledge: Epistemological Reflections on Dance', *Dance Research Journal* 34 (1): 11–22.

Pasolini, P.P. (1995) *Who Is Me – Dichter der Asche*, translated by P. Kammerer, Berlin: Hochroth.

Patai, D. (1987) 'Ethical Problems of Personal Narratives, or, Who should eat the last piece of cake', *International Journal of Oral History* 8: 5–27.

PEEK (2009) *Program Document*, Vienna: Austrian Science Fund: Program for Arts-based Research. Online. <http://www.fwf.ac.at/en/projects/peek.html> (accessed on 8 November 2009).

Phelan, P. (1993) *Unmarked*, London: Routledge.

Phillips, E.M. and D. S. Pugh, S. (1987) *How to Get a PhD*, Buckingham: Open University Press.

Pink, S. (2001) *Doing Visual Ethnography*, Thousand Oaks, CA: Sage.

—— (2006) *The Future of Visual Anthropology: engaging the senses*, New York: Routledge.

Piotrowski, A. and J.W. Robinson (eds) (2000) *The Discipline of Architecture*, London: University of Minnesota Press.

Plato (1924) *The Dialogues of Plato, Translated Into English with Analyses and Introductions*, edited by Benjamin Jowett, London: Oxford University Press.

Polanyi, K. (1957) *The Great Transformation. The Political and Economic Origins of Our Time*, Boston, MA: Beacon Press.

Polanyi, M. (1958) *Personal Knowledge: towards a post-critical philosophy*, London: Routledge and Kegan Paul.

Popper, K. (1963) *Conjectures and Refutations*, London: Routledge.

Prelli, L.J. (2006) 'Rhetorics of Display: an introduction', in: Prelli, L.J., (ed.) *Rhetorics of Display*, Columbia, SC: University of Southern Carolina Press, 1–38.

Presas i Puig, A. (2004) *Numbers, Proportions, Harmonies, and Practical Geometry in Ancient Art*, Berlin: Max Planck Institute for the History of Science.

Price, E. (2000) 'Sidekick', PhD thesis, University of Leeds.

QAA (2006) *Subject Benchmark Statement: engineering*, London: Quality Assurance Agency. Online. <http://www.qaa.ac.uk/academicinfrastructure/benchmark/statements/engineering06.asp> (accessed on 26 March 2010).

—— (2007) *Subject Benchmark Statement: art and design*, London: Quality Assurance Agency. Online. <http://www.qaa.ac.uk/academicinfrastructure/benchmark/statements/ADHA08.asp> (accessed on 26 March 2010).

Quinn, M. (2008) 'Critique Conscious and Unconscious: listening to the barbarous language of art and design', *Journal of Visual Arts Practice* 7 (3): 225–40.

RAE (2006) *Panel Criteria and Working Methods: Panel O*, London: RAE. Online. <http://www.rae.ac.uk/pubs/2006/01/> (accessed on 20 February 2010).

Rajchman, J. (1998) *Constructions*, Cambridge, MA: MIT Press.

Rancière, J. (2007) 'Painting in the Text', in: *The Future of the Image*, London: Verso, 69–89.

Rasmussen, H.H. (2008) *Reflections on the Research Project 'Homage to the Hybrid'*, Trondheim: Kunstakademiet i Trondheim, NTNU. Online. <http://www.hanshamid.com/site_additions/text/Reflections_on_the_reseach_project.pdf> (accessed on 10 January 2010).

RCUK (2001) *Joint Statement of the UK Research Councils' Training Requirements for Research Students*, London: Joint Research Councils UK. Online. <http://www.vitae.ac.uk/cms/files/RCUK-Joint-Skills-Statement-2001.pdf> (accessed on 10 February 2010).

Reed-Danahay, D.E. (ed.) (1997) *Auto/Ethnography: rewriting the self and the social*, Oxford: Berg.

Rees-Cheney, T. (2005) *Getting the Words Right: 39 ways to improve your writing*, Cincinnati: Writer's Digest Books.

Rehm, E. (1973) 'Johann Wilhelm Ritter und die Universität Jena', in: *Jahrbuch des freien deutschen Hochstifts*, Tübingen: Niemeyer.

Reisenzein, R. (2001) 'Appraisal Processes Conceptualized from a Schema-theoretic Perspective: contributions to a process analysis of emotions', in: Scherer, K., A. Schorr and T. Johnstone, (eds) *Appraisal Processes in Emotion*, Oxford: Oxford University Press, 187–201.

Reisenzein, R., W.-U. Meyer and A. Schutzwohl (1996) 'Reactions to Surprising Events: a paradigm for emotion research'. 9th Conference of the International Society for Research on Emotions, Toronto: International Society for Research on Emotion, 292–6.

Rheinberger, H.-J. (2007) 'Man weiss nicht genau was man nicht weiss: Über die Kunst, das Unbekannte zu erforschen' *Neue Zürcher Zeitung*, Zurich 5 May 2007: B3.

Ricœur, P. (2004) *Memory, History, Forgetting*, Chicago, IL: University of Chicago Press.

Rietveld, E. (2008) 'Unreflective Action. A Philosophical Contribution to Integrative Neuroscience', PhD thesis, University of Amsterdam.

Rihm, W. (2001) 'Raum, Zeit, hier. Bemerkungen zu einem Axiom Wagners', in: Borris, S., (ed.) *Zum Raum wird hier die Zeit. Parsifal-Zyklus*, Berlin: Berliner Philharmonisches Orchester, 115–24.

Riley, S.R. and L. Hunter (eds) (2009) *Mapping Landscapes for Performance as Research*, Basingstoke: Palgrave Macmillan.

Ritter, J.W. (1803), in: Voigt, J.H., (ed.) *Magazin für den neuesten Stand der Naturkunde*, Berlin: Gesellschaft Naturforschender Freunde, 33f.

—— (1805) 'Johann Wilhelm Ritter, reply to Ørsted', in: Voigt, J.H., (ed.) *Magazin für den neuesten Stand der Naturkunde*, Berlin: Gesellschaft Naturforschender Freunde, 33f.

—— (1984 [1810]) *Fragmente aus dem Nachlasse eines jungen Physikers. Ein Taschenbuch für Freunde der Natur*, edited by Dietzsch, S. and B. Dietzsch, Hanau: Müller & Kiepenheuer.

Roads, C. (2001) *Microsound*, Cambridge, MA: MIT Press.

Roberts-Miller, T. (2009) Understanding Misunderstandings: how to do a rhetorical analysis, Online. <http://www.drw.utexas.edu/roberts-miller/handouts/rhetorical-analysis> (accessed on 18 January 2010).

Rogoff, I. (2000) *Terra Infirma: geography's visual culture*, London: Routledge.

—— (2007) 'Academy as Potentiality', in: Nollert, A., I. Rogoff, B. de Baere and Y. Dziewior., (eds) *A.C.A.D.E.M.Y*, Frankfurt a/M: Revolver Books, 11–8.

Rokeach, M. (1973) *The Nature of Human Values*, New York: The Free Press.

Rolling, J.H. (2004) 'Searching Self-image: identities to be self-evident', *Qualitative Inquiry* 10 (6): 869–84.

Rose, G. (2007) *Visual Methodologies: an introduction to the interpretation of visual materials*, Thousand Oaks, CA: Sage.

Rose, M. (1993) *Authors and Owners. The Invention of Copyright*, Cambridge, MA: Harvard University Press.

Rose, S. (2008) 'Search of the God Neuron' *The Saturday Guardian*, London 27 December 2008: 8.

Rosenberg, H. (1966) *The Anxious Object*, Chicago, IL: University of Chicago Press.

Ross, N. (2004) *Culture and Cognition: implications for theory and method*, Thousand Oaks, CA: Sage.

Roudinesco, E. (1999) *Jacques Lacan*, London: Polity Press.

Rouhiainen, L. (2008) 'Artistic Research and Collaboration', *Nordic Theatre Studies* 20: 51–9.

Roulstone, K. (2006) 'Rethinking Absence: art practice and the critical metaphysics of Jacques Derrida and Jacques Lacan', PhD thesis, University of Plymouth.

Rubidge, S. (2005) 'Artists in the Academy: Reflections on Artistic Practice as Research'. Dance Rebooted, Deakin University.

Rust, C., J. Mottram and J. Till (2007) *AHRC Research Review, Practice-Led Research in Art, Design and Architecture*, Bristol: AHRC. Online. <http:// www.ahrc.ac.uk/About/Policy/Documents/ Practice-Led_Review_Nov07.pdf> (accessed on 2 December 2009).

Rydberg, A. (2001) *Bo tryggt 01: principdiskussioner, råd och förslag till lösningar för en tryggare och säkrare boendemiljö*, Stockholm: Forsknings- och utvecklingsenheten, Polismyndigheten i Stockholms län. Online. <http://www.botryggt.se/> (accessed on 8 January 2010).

Saastad, T. (2007) *Displacements: An Artistic Work Process – There, and Back Again*, Bergen: Bergen National Academy of the Arts. Online. <http://www2.khib.no/futuretextile/wp-content/ uploads/2008/05/tone_saastad_english.pdf> (accessed on 10 March 2010).

Säätelä, S. (2005) 'Aesthetic Experience and 'Non-conceptual' Content', in: Entzenberg, C. and S. Säätelä, (eds) *Aesthetics, Art and Culture. Essays in Honour of Lars-Olof Ahlberg*, Stockholm: Thales, 292–312.

Sand, M. (2008) *Konsten att gunga. Experiment som aktiverar mellanrum*. Stockholm: Axl Books.

Sandahl, C. (2003) 'Queering The Crip or Cripping the Queer? Intersections of queer and crip identities in solo autobiographical performances', *GLQ: A Journal of Lesbian and Gay Studies* 9 (1–2): 25–56.

Schafer, R.M. (1994 [1977]) *The Soundscape: our sonic environment and the tuning of the world*, Rochester, VT: Destiny Books.

Schatzki, T.R., K.K. Cetina and E.v. Savigny (2001) *The Practice Turn in Contemporary Theory*, London: Routledge.

Schechner, R. (2002) *Performance Studies: an introduction*, London: Routledge.

Schein, E.H. (1991) 'What is Culture?', in: Frost, P.J., L.F. Moore, M.R. Louis, C.C. Lundberg and J. Martin, (eds) *Reframing Organizational Culture*, London: Sage, 243–53.

Schiller, G. (2003) 'The Kinesfield: a study of movement-based interactive and choreographic art', PhD thesis, University of Plymouth.

Schlegel, F. (1971) *Lucinde and the Fragments*, Minneapolis, MN: University of Minnesota Press.

Schleifer, R., R.C. Davis and N. Mergler (1992) *Culture and Cognition: the boundaries of literary and scientific inquiry*, Ithaca, NY: Cornell University Press.

Schneider, R. (2001) 'Performance Remains', *Performance Research* 6 (2): 100–8.

Schön, D.A. (1991) *The Reflective Practitioner: how professionals think in action*, London: Arena.

Schulz, B. (1967) *Die Republik der Träume. Fragmente, Aufsätze, Briefe, Grafiken. Herausgegeben von Mikolaj Dutsch*, München: Hanser.

Schwab, M. (forthcoming) 'First, the Second: The Supplemental Function of Research in Art', in: Caduff, C., F. Siegenthaler and T. Wälchli, (eds) *Jahrbuch der Züricher Hochschule der Künste*, Zurich: Züricher Hochschule der Künste.

Scriven, N., P. Rumney and I. Kuksa (2009) The Cosmos Project: exploring how performance languages and active participation influence children's engagement with complex scientific questions, Dragon Breath Theatre. Online. <http://www.dragonbreaththeatre.com/> (accessed on 10 March 2010).

Scrivener, S.A.R. (2002) 'The art object does not embody a form of knowledge', *Working Papers in Art & Design* 2. Online. <http://www.herts.ac.uk/artdes1/research/papers/wpades/vol2/scrivenerfull.html> (accessed on 20 August 2008).

—— (2006) 'Visual Art Practice Reconsidered: Transformational Practice and the Academy', in: Mäkelä, M. and S. Routarinne, (eds) *The Art of Research*, Helsinki: University of Art and Design Helsinki, 156–79.

—— (2009a). Personal communication with Ernest Edmonds.

—— (2009b) *The Norms and Tests of Arts-Based Research*, unpublished: Chelsea College of Art and Design. Online. <http://www.chelsea.arts.ac.uk/docs/NormsandTestsSecondWebDraft.doc> (accessed on 25 February 2010).

—— (2009c) 'The Roles of Art and Design Process and Object in Research', in: Nimkulrat, N. and T. O'Riley, (eds) *Reflections and Connections: on the relationship between creative production and academic research*, Helsinki: University of Art and Design Helsinki, 69–80.

Searle, J.R. (1993) 'Rationality and Realism, What is at Stake?', *Daedalus* 122 (4): 55–83.

Seevinck, J. and E. Edmonds (2008) 'Emergence and The Art System "plus minus now"', *Design Studies* 29 (6): 541–55.

Seggern, H.v., J. Werner and L. Grosse-Bächle (2008) *Creating Knowledge. Innovationsstrategien im Entwerfen urbaner Landschaften*, Berlin: Jovis Verlag.

Sheets-Johnstone, M. (1966) *The Phenomenology of Dance*, London: Dance Books.

Shifreen, F. (2009). Personal communication with Graeme Sullivan (16 February 2009).

Shottenkirk, D. (2007) 'Research, Relativism and Truth in Art', *Art & Research* 1. Online. <http://www.artandresearch.org.uk/v1n1/shottenkirk.html> (accessed on 15 February 2010).

Sidney, S.P. (1922 [c.1583]) 'An Apology for Poetry', in: Jones, E.P., (ed.) *English Critical Essays (Sixteenth, Seventeenth, and Eighteenth Centuries)*, Oxford: Oxford University Press.

Singerman, H. (1999) *Art Subjects: making artists in the American university*, Berkeley, CA: University of California Press.

Skjønsberg, T. (1996) *The Flat Space*, Oslo: Oslo School of Architecture.

Slager, H. (1995) *Archaeology of Art Theory*, Amsterdam: Rodopi B.V.

—— (2006) 'Introduction: is the medium still the message?', *MaHKUzine Journal of Artistic Research* 1, 506. Online. <http://www.mahku.nl/research/mahkuzine1.html> (accessed on 22 February 2010).

—— (2008) 'Research-Based Practices'. Shanghai Biennale Catalogue, Shanghai: Shanghai Biennale, 60–5.

—— (2009a) 'Art and Method', in: Elkins, J., (ed.) *Artists with PhDs*, Washington, D.C.: New Academia Publishing, 49–56.

—— (2009b) 'Editorial: nameless science', *MaHKUzine Journal of Artistic Research* 7, 4–7. Online. <http://www.mahku.nl/research/mahkuzine7.html> (accessed on 22 February 2010).

Smiers, J. and M. van Schijndel (2009) 'Imagine There's No Copyright and No Cultural Conglomerates Too . . .', *Theory on Demand*. Online. <http://networkcultures.org/_uploads/tod/TOD4_nocopyright.pdf> (accessed on 17 February 2010).

Smith, R. (2008) 'Proteus Rising: re-imagining educational research', *Journal of Philosophy of Education* 42 (Supplement 1): 183–98.

Smith, S. and J. Watson (eds) (2002) *Interfaces: women/autobiography/image/performance*, Ann Arbor, MI: Michigan University Press.

Smithers, T. (1996) *On what embodiment might have to do with cognition*, AAAI. Online. <http://www.aaai.org/Papers/Symposia/Fall/1996/FS-96-02/FS96-02-024.pdf> (accessed on 13 February 2010).

—— (1998) 'In Time and Over Time', *Behavioral and Brain Sciences* 21 (5): 651–2.

Snow, C.P. (1959) *The Two Cultures and the Scientific Revolution*, Cambridge: Cambridge University Press.

Solà-Morales Rubió, I.d. (1995) 'Terrain Vague', in: Davidson, C.C., (ed.) *Anyplace*, Cambridge, MA: MIT Press, 118–23.

Solomon, J. (1999) 'Meta-scientific Criticisms, Curriculum Innovation and the Propagation of Scientific Culture', *Journal of Curriculum Studies* 31 (1): 1–15.

Solso, R.L. (2003) *The Psychology of Art and the Evolution of the Conscious Brain*, Cambridge, MA: MIT Press.

Springgay, S., R.L. Irwin, C. Leggo and P. Gouzouasis (eds) (2008) *Being with A/r/tography*, Rotterdam: Sense Publishers.

Stafford, B.M. (1997) *Good Looking: essays on the virtue of images*, Cambridge, MA: MIT Press.

—— (2007) *Echo Objects: the cognitive world of images*, Chicago, IL: Chicago University Press.

Stake, R.E. (1995) *The Art of Case Study Research*, London: Sage.

—— (2006) *Multiple Case Study Analysis*, London: Sage.

Stanczak, G.C. (ed.) (2007) *Visual Research Methods: image, society and representation*, Thousand Oaks, CA: Sage.

Sternberg, R.J. (ed.) (1990) *Metaphors of the Mind: conceptions of the notion of intelligence*, New York: Cambridge University Press.

Stevens, W. (1990) *Opus posthumous*, New York: Vintage Books.

Stjernfelt, F. (2007) *Diagrammatology. An Investigation on the Borderlines of Phenomenology, Ontology, and Semiotics*, Dordrecht: Springer.

Stockhausen, K. (1957) '… wie die zeit vergeht . . .', *Die Reihe* 3: 13–42.

Storr, R. (2007) *Think with the Senses—Feel with the Mind. Art in the Present Tense*, Venice: Fondazione La Biennale di Venezia.

Story, A., C. Darch and D. Halbert (2006) *The Copy/South Dossier*, Copy/South Research Group. Online. <http://www.copysouth.org/en/documents/part-1.pdf> (accessed on 17 February 2010).

Strand, D. (1998) *Research in the Creative Arts*, Canberra: Department of Employment, Education, Training and Youth Affairs. Online. <http://www.detya.gov.au/archive/highered/eippubs/eip98-6/eip98-6.pdf> (accessed on 10 March 2010).

Sullivan, G. (2002) 'Artistic Thinking as a Transcognitive Practice: a reconciliation of the process-product dichotomy', *Visual Arts Research* 27 (1): 2–12.

—— (2005) *Art Practice as Research: inquiry in the visual arts*, London: Sage Publications.

Sutton, S.E. (2000) 'Reinventing Professional Privilege as Inclusivity: a proposal for an enriched mission of architecture', in: Piotrowski, A. and J.W. Robbinson, (eds) *The Discipline of Architecture*, London: University of Minnesota Press, 260–71.

Synapse (2009) Art Science Collaborations, Online. <http://www.synapse.net.au/> (accessed on 3 January 2010).

Taylor, C. (2005) 'Merleau-Ponty and the Epistemological Picture', in: Carman, T. and M.B.N. Hansen, (eds) *The Cambridge Companion to Merleau-Ponty*, London: Cambridge University Press, 26–49.

Taylor, D. (2003) *The Archive and the Repertory*, London: Routledge.

Thomassen, A. (2003) 'In Control: Engendering a continuum of flow of a cyclic process within the context of potentially disruptive GUI interactions', PhD thesis, Hogeschool voor de Kunsten Utrecht.

Thompson, S. (2006) 'The Slapstick Mystics with Sticks and Other Words: Joanne Tatham in conversation with Susannah Thompson', *Art & Research* 1. Online. <http://www.artandresearch.org.uk/v1n1/tatham.html> (accessed on 15 February 2010).

Tidwell, D.L., M.L. Heston and L.M. Fitzgerald (eds) (2009) *Research Methods for the Self-Study of Practice*, New York: Springer.

Tilley, C., W. Keane, S. Kuechler, M. Rowlands and P. Spyer (eds) (2006) *The Handbook of Material Culture*, London: Sage.

Tucker, D. (2007) *Mind from Body: experience from neural structure*, Oxford: Oxford University Press.

Turner, V. (1982) 'Liminality and the Performative Genres', in: MacAloon, J.J., (ed.) *Rite, Drama, Festival, Spectacle: Rehearsals toward a Theory of Cultural Performance*, Philadelphia, PA: Institute for the Study of Human Issues Inc., 19–41.

UiO (2009) *Håndbok om Universitetet i Oslo's historie. Studenter og ansatte*, Oslo: University of Oslo. Online. <http://www.hf.uio.no/forskningsprosjekter/ffu/FaktaUiO/faktadelen/Studenter_og_ansatte.pdf> (accessed on 25 January 2010).

UKCGE (2001) *Research Training in the Creative & Performing Arts & Design*, Lichfield: United Kingdom Council for Graduate Education. Online. <http://www.ukcge.ac.uk/Resources/UKCGE/Documents/PDF/CreativePerfromingArts 2001.pdf> (accessed on 10 March 2010).

—— (2002) *Professional Doctorates*, Lichfield: United Kingdom Council for Graduate Education. Online. <http://www.ukcge.ac.uk/Resources/UKCGE/Documents/PDF/Professional Doctorate Awards 2005.pdf> (accessed on 15 February 2010).

—— (2008) *Higher Doctorate Awards in the UK*, Lichfield: UK Council for Graduate Education.

UNESCO (2005) *Convention on the Protection and Promotion of the Diversity of Cultural Expressions*, Paris: Online. <http://www.unesco.org/culture/en/diversity/convention> (accessed on 17 February 2010).

University of Huddersfield (2009) *University Regulations for Awards*, Huddersfield: University of Huddersfield. Online. <http://www2.hud.ac.uk/registry/awards_regulations.php> (accessed on 6 January 2010).

van Heeswijk, J. (2000) *HNY PS1. Voyage Through a Room – Tales about Art*, Amsterdam: Artimo Foundation.

Varela, F.J. and N. Depraz (2003) 'Imagining, Embodiment, Phenomenology and Transformation', in: Wallace, A., (ed.) *Buddhism and Science: breaking new ground*, New York: Columbia University Press.

Varela, F.J., E. Thompson and E. Rosch (1999) *The Embodied Mind*, Cambridge, MA: MIT Press.

Webb, J. (2004) *Proverbs from Sierra Leone*, Wollongong: Five Islands Press.

Weckman, J.K. (2008) 'Method as a Notion within Artistic Practice and its Research – and Art as Research', *GEIST* 11, 12, 14: §5.

Weisner, T.S. (2000) 'Culture, Childhood, and Progress in Sub-Saharan Africa', in: Harrison, L.E. and S.P. Huntington, (eds) *Culture Matters: how values shape human progress*, New York: Basic Books, 141–57.

Weitz, M. (1956) 'The Role of Theory in Aesthetics', *The Journal of Aesthetics and Art Criticism* 15 (1): 27–35.

Wellcome (2009) SciArt, Wellcome Trust. Online. <http://www.wellcome.ac.uk/Funding/Public-engagement/Past-funding/WTX035067.htm> (accessed on 3 January 2010).

Wenger, E. (1999) *Communities of Practice: learning, meaning, and identity*, London: Cambridge University Press.

White, D. (2008) 'Unnatural Fact: the fictions of Robert Smithson', *Journal of Writing in Creative Practice* 1 (2): 161–75.

Wiedemann, E. (1915) 'Über Musikautomaten', in: Schulz, O., (ed.) *Sitzungsberichte der physikalisch-medizinischen Sozietät in Erlangen*, Erlangen: Universität Erlangen.

Wiest, C. (2001) 'Towards a Rhetoric of Tactile Pictures', *Enculturation: Journal of Rhetoric Writing and Culture*. Online. <http://enculturation.gmu.edu/3_2/wiest/index.html> (accessed on 18 January 20120).

Williams, R. (1974) *Television – Technology or Cultural Form*, London: Fontana.

—— (1977) *Marxism and Literature*, Oxford: Oxford University Press.

Willim, R. (2006) *Virtualiteter*, Lund: Lund University Press.

Wilson, S. (1979) *British Art: from Holbein to the present day*, London: Bodley Head Ltd., and The Tate Gallery Publications Department.

—— (2002) *Information Arts: intersections of art, science and technology*, Cambridge MA: MIT Press/ Leonardo Books.

Windelbrand, W. (1915) 'Geschichte und Naturwissenschaft (1894)', in: *Präludien: Aufsätze und Reden zur Philosophie und ihrer Geschichte*, Tübingen: Mohr.

Wittgenstein, L. (1953) *Philosophical Investigations*, Oxford: Basil Blackwell.

—— (1958) *The Blue and Brown Books*, Oxford: Basil Blackwell.

Wood, J. (1998) *The Virtual Embodied: presence/practice/technology*, London: Routledge.

—— (2000) 'The Culture of Academic Rigour: does design research really need it?', *The Design Journal* 3 (1): 44–57.

Wyss, B. (1997) *Die Welt als T-Shirt: Zur Ästhetik und Geschichte der Medien*, Köln: DuMont Reiseverlag.

Xenakis, I. (1971) *Formalized Music: thought and mathematics in music*, Bloomington, IN: Indiana University Press.

York (2009) Department of Music: MPhil/PhD by Composition, University of York. Online. <http:// music.york.ac.uk/prospective/postgraduate/programmes/mphilphd_comp.php> (accessed on 6 December 2009).

Zeki, S. (1999) *Inner Vision: an exploration of art and the brain*, Oxford: Oxford University Press.

—— (2009) *Splendors and Miseries of the Brain: love, creativity and the quest for human happiness*, Chichester: Wiley-Blackwell.

Zia, P. (2001) 'The Poetic Anatomy of the Numinous: a visual and theoretical search for the other', PhD thesis, University of Plymouth.

Zielinski, S. (2006) *Deep Time of the Media*, translated by G. Custance, Boston, MA: MIT Press.

Zielinski, S. and E. Fürlus (eds) (2010) *Variantology 4. On Deep Time Relations of Arts, Sciences and Technologies in the Arabic-Islamic World and Beyond*, Variantology, Cologne: Walther König.

Ziman, J. (2000) *Real Science. What it is, and what it means*, Cambridge: Cambridge University Press.

Zurbrugg, N. (ed.) (2004) *Art, Performance, Media: 31 interviews*, Minneapolis, MN: University of Minnesota Press.

INDEX